RELIEF AND SOCIAL SECURITY

THE BROOKINGS INSTITUTION

The Brookings Institution—Devoted to Public Service through Research and Training in the Social Sciences—was incorporated on December 8, 1927. Broadly stated, the Institution has two primary purposes: the first is to aid constructively in the development of sound national policies; and the second is to offer training of a super-graduate character to students of the social sciences.

The responsibility for the final determination of the Institution's policies and its program of work for the administration of its endowment is vested in a self-perpetuating board of trustees. It is the function of the trustees to make possible the conduct of scientific research under the most favorable conditions, and to safeguard the independence of the research staff in the pursuit of their studies and in the publication of the results of such studies. It is not a part of their function to determine, control, or influence the conduct of particular investigations or the conclusions reached, but only to approve the principal fields of investigation to which the available funds are to be allocated, and to satisfy themselves with reference to the intellectual competence and scientific integrity of the staff. Major responsibility for "formulating general policies and co-ordinating the activities of the Institution" is vested in the president. The by-laws provide also that "there shall be an advisory council selected by the president from among the scientific staff of the Institution."

———

BOARD OF TRUSTEES

RELIEF

AND

SOCIAL SECURITY

BY

LEWIS MERIAM

WASHINGTON, D.C.

THE BROOKINGS INSTITUTION

1946

Printed in the United States of America
George Banta Publishing Company
Menasha, Wisconsin

PREFACE

The depression of the thirties made provision of relief and social security in the United States a major function of government. Appropriations for relief became an important item of expenditures and a significant cause of the progressive increase in the national debt. The introduction of social insurance for unemployment and for old age brought new factors into the economic and social system. The assumption by the national government of the leading role in policy determination and of a substantial role in financing represented radical changes in the distribution of powers and responsibilities among the several levels of government.

In the late thirties it seemed highly desirable for the Brookings Institution to undertake a comprehensive study of relief and its administration. To further such a study the Institution received special grants-in-aid from Mr. Marshall Field, a member of its Board of Trustees, and later from The Maurice and Laura Falk Foundation of Pittsburgh. Neither Mr. Field nor the Falk Foundation is to be understood as approving or disapproving, by virtue of the grant, any statement or views expressed herein.

Part of the proceeds of these special gifts was immediately used to facilitate independent studies of relief made by co-operating agencies in a number of states. The states were selected in part because of the significance of their experience and in part because of the presence within their borders of a competent agency, members of which had evidenced great interest in the operation of relief programs and had had opportunity to observe and evaluate them.

The agreement of the Institution with these co-operators was that the resulting manuscripts were to remain their property with all rights of publication. The Institution was merely to have the privilege of examining and profiting from them, as it would from other writings by well-informed, competent students.

v

The Institution takes this opportunity to record the names of the leaders of these groups and the agencies with which they were associated and to express its appreciation of the help given by them and their associates. It should, however, be clearly stated that neither the agencies nor any members of them are in any way directly responsible for the conclusions which are arrived at in the present study. The leaders of the co-operating groups were:

H. L. Geisert
University of Alabama

Orren C. Hormell
Bowdoin College, Maine

Edith Abbott
School of Social Service Adminis-
    tration
University of Chicago

A. D. H. Kaplan
University of Denver

Morris B. Lambie
Harvard University

T. Lynn Smith
Louisiana State University

Arthur Dunham
University of Michigan

Paul H. Landis
State College of Washington

William Anderson
University of Minnesota

C. Terence Pihlblad
University of Missouri

Frank Z. Glick
University of Nebraska

Howard W. Odum
Institute for Research in Social
    Science
University of North Carolina

William H. McCullough
University of Oklahoma

William S. Carpenter
Princeton University

Earl Weller
Rochester Bureau of Municipal
    Research

After the outbreak of the war in Europe increasing employment offered an opportunity first to modify the work relief program and ultimately to abandon it. At the same time, a movement was developing for placing primary reliance henceforth on a greatly expanded social insurance program.

Because of this shift in emphasis, it seemed desirable to broaden the scope of the study to cover the whole problem of alleviating or preventing need through payment of benefits from publicly collected funds, or through providing public employment on projects undertaken primarily to relieve distress. To use the terms now current, the present study deals with the problem of providing universal, comprehensive, and co-ordinated protection against want.

When the project was initially undertaken it was assumed that several members of the staff would be available to work on it. The nation in the war emergency had, however, a prior claim on the services of the younger men of the staff. It thus became necessary to place almost the entire burden of the study on one veteran member of the organization. This action necessitated taking more time for completion, but it has probably resulted in closer integration of the several parts than would have been possible in a group project.

When a single member of the staff is responsible for so important and comprehensive a study, it is desirable to present the essential facts regarding the experience that has qualified him for the assignment.

Lewis Meriam specialized in economics and government at Harvard. After graduation in 1905 he entered the United States Bureau of the Census, where he served under the late Joseph A. Hill in the Division of Revision and Results. In that position he had the opportunity to familiarize himself as an editor with the whole broad range of census statistics; but his special interest was in the social field—population, vital statistics, marriage and divorce, child labor, women at work, the employees in the civil service, and the defective, dependent, and delinquent classes.

When in 1912 Miss Julia Lathrop of Hull House became the first Chief of the United States Children's Bureau, she requisitioned him from the Census Bureau for the position of Assistant Chief.

In 1915 Dr. Frederick A. Cleveland, then Director of the New York Bureau of Municipal Research, chose him for membership in a small group gathered to study intensively retirement systems for public employees. As the result of that assignment he wrote his well known *Principles Governing the Retirement of Public Employees*, which was published by the Institute for Government Research in 1918.

Since 1916 he has been a member of the staff of the Institute for Government Research and of the Brookings Institution, of which the Institute became a part. During his connection with the Institution he has rendered extensive service in the development of personnel classification and salary standardization in both federal and state governments. He served as a member of the President's Emergency Committee for Employment; as Director of the Survey of Indian Affairs, made by the Institution at the request of the Secretary of the Interior; and as director of the staff that made the survey of Montgomery County, Maryland, and was personally responsible for the study of the public welfare activities of the County. In the comprehensive investigation of the executive agencies of the federal government, made by the Institution at the request of the congressional committees concerned, he was responsible for the study of all federal activities in the field of public welfare, broadly defined. He has participated in several of the comprehensive state surveys made by the Brookings Institution. His principal assignment on state surveys has generally been on personnel administration, but his work in Oklahoma included in addition all activities in the field of labor, including workmen's compensation. For several years during the depression he was a member of the Montgomery County Maryland Board of Public Welfare. While a member of that Board he directed a Civil Works Administration project, a recreational survey of the county.

On the basis of his research work in the field of social service he was admitted to membership in the American Association of Social Workers. He has also been for years a member of the National Conference of Social Work.

In drawing conclusions and making concrete recommendations in a study such as the present one, it is necessary to proceed on the basis of certain underlying assumptions with respect to which there may be differences of opinion. The assumptions used by the author are, I believe, in accordance with basic tenets of the American system of democracy. They imply the continuation and preservation of the personal freedoms of the individual, the free enterprise system, the federal form of representative democratic government, and constitutional restrictions upon the powers and activities of politically chosen executives and legislative representatives and of appointed officers and employees. The conclusions therefore are evolutionary rather than revolutionary and are designed to give protection against want within the framework of the American system as we conceive it.

The members of the co-operating committee of the Institution on this project were Harold W. Metz and Melvin W. Sneed.

It is a happy circumstance that this comprehensive study of social security should have been conducted by the Brookings Institution—for the first American study of the basic problems of systematic protection for the masses of the people was made by William F. Willoughby, for many years Director of the Institute for Government Research, now a part of the Institution. Dr. Willoughby in the opening paragraph of his *Workingmen's Insurance*, published in 1898, expressed the underlying thesis as follows:

The problem of workingmen's insurance is but one phase of the general labor movement. It is but a part of that great effort now being made by modern society so to modify conditions that the situation of the actual wielders of the tools of production shall be improved. In its complete development it comprehends the care and indemnification of all wage-earning men and women in case they are incapacitated for work, either temporarily or permanently, as the result of an accident or sickness, and the grant to them of a pension after they are no longer able to work on account of physical disability or old age. Under it no one need look forward with apprehension to the privations consequent upon sickness or accident. The ever-constant dread of dependent old age is wiped out at a stroke. It constitutes therefore the latest and most radical measure to grant thorough-going relief in the chief cases of suffering to which the wage-earning classes are now exposed.

HAROLD G. MOULTON,
President.

AUTHOR'S ACKNOWLEDGMENTS AND FOREWORD

President Moulton in his preface has given the history of this project and explained how I happened to fall heir to a large part of the work which it has entailed. Although single authorship may have resulted in better integration of the several parts, I should have preferred carrying the project through more rapidly as a group undertaking with the younger men who were to have been associated with it.

Some of these associates had done a substantial amount of work on the project as originally conceived before they were called to other more pressing activities. I have had the advantage of their work and their counsel. I want to acknowledge this assistance here, because where I have used the results of their labor in preparing the text, the footnote references are necessarily to the sources from which they obtained the data and not to their manuscripts or working papers. In referring to these associates I shall indicate the nature of the activities which in general made further service on the project impracticable.

Lieutenant Melvin W. Sneed of the Navy, whom the Brookings Institution borrowed from the Social Security Commission of Missouri, where he was chief of the Division of Research and Statistics. He was a member of the original directing committee on the project. Because of his wide and intensive knowledge of the field, and particularly of the statistical data, his advice and assistance were invaluable. I shall refer to his contribution again in another connection.

Lieutenant Colonel Charles A. H. Thomson of Military Intelligence. He prepared for the use of those on the initial project an excellent history of the developments in the field, and before he left the Institution had written comprehensive descriptions of the National Youth Administration and the Civilian Conservation Corps.

Lieutenant Charles Stauffacher of the Navy, who was selected for the staff because of his contribution to the co-operative study of Massachusetts made under the direction of Professor Morris B. Lambie of Harvard. Lieutenant Stauffacher made detailed studies of the three public assistance categories of the Social Security Act.

Miss Adah Lee of the Institution staff, who as an assistant to Mr. Charles L. Dearing, had compiled the basic material with respect to the Work Projects Administration. Mr. Dearing was called to the Office of Defense Transportation, before he had been able to do much more than participate in the early discussions of the project. Mr. Dearing's knowledge of public roads, a leading feature of the activities of W.P.A., was such, however, that counsel with him was most helpful.

Mr. Emanuel A. Hacker, who as assistant to Major Daniel T. Selko of the Army Air Forces, had compiled much material on the financing of relief. Major Selko, who was to have been responsible for the chapters on finance, left for England almost immediately on entering the service and before he himself had dug deeply into the details of the program.

To Lieutenant Sneed I am under an additional obligation. His assignment in the Navy brought him back to Washington. Despite his demanding official duties, he found time evenings and Sundays to read the rough drafts of the manuscript. He worked closely with the man who became my other principal adviser, Dr. Harold W. Metz, a former fellow of the Brookings Institution who returned as a member of the staff long after the project had been started. These two men have worked with me closely and constructively. Many improvements, both in form and substance, were made in response to their suggestions.

I am under special obligation to Mr. August W. Nagel, another former fellow now a member of the staff of the Institution, who gave me access to an unfinished thesis which furnished much valuable material on the distribution of surplus commodities and the stamp plan.

Acknowledgment is also due to Lewis Kimmel for reading critically the chapters of Part III that deal with financing relief and social security and for suggesting improvements.

Miss A. Evelyn Breck, the editor of the Institution, Mrs. Medora M. Richardson, who worked with the voluminous manuscript in its many revisions, and Miss L. Esther Breck, whose familiarity with government documents is so helpful, all made contributions that call for grateful recognition.

LEWIS MERIAM

CONTENTS

xv

PART III. MAJOR ISSUES TODAY

A. Social Considerations

B. Cost Problems

C. Administrative Problems

INTRODUCTION

In the field of relief and social security the depression of the 1930's caught the United States almost entirely unprepared. To meet the resulting crisis, the nation had hastily to improvise and experiment. Because of the imperative need for speed, and because of the financial difficulties of many state and local governments, the problem was tackled piecemeal without careful consideration of the duties and responsibilities of the several levels of government as set forth in the Constitution of the United States and the constitutions of the states. Thus the nation now faces the question of how the many programs are to be integrated, expanded, and modified to make a satisfactory whole, which will assure to all minimum protection against want.

The evolution of social security and relief legislation both in the United States and foreign countries suggests, however, that the problem of welding the various programs developed for special classes or categories into an integrated and comprehensive, universal system would have arisen, had we proceeded more slowly without the driving impetus of the depression. Other countries have legislated by individual programs only to discover at the end of many years that co-ordination is essential. Thus in 1942 in reporting on the British programs, Sir William Beveridge said:

... social insurance and the allied services, as they exist today, are conducted by a complex of disconnected administrative organs, proceeding on different principles, doing invaluable service but at a cost in money and trouble and anomalous treatment of identical problems for which there is no justification. In a system of social security better on the whole than can be found in almost any other country there are serious deficiencies which call for remedy.[1]

The British situation which Sir William thus described developed in a nation with an all-powerful central government.

[1] Sir William Beveridge, *Social Insurance and Allied Services* (1942) p. 6. Hereafter cited as *The Beveridge Report.*

Britain faced none of the difficulties present in the United States because of our federal form of government with the division of responsibility between the national and state governments. Even if we had proceeded slowly, the time would have come, possibly some 15 or 20 years from now, when disconnected programs for various classes would have to be reviewed with the objective of dealing justly and fairly with all at a cost that the nation could afford.

The changes in the financial condition of the nation which have resulted from World War II, following immediately upon the difficult years of the depression, make it imperative that this problem be faced immediately as part of the larger problem of determining postwar public policy. Every great commitment of public funds, to be raised through the use of the sovereign power of the state to tax, must be re-examined in the light of the new financial situation which confronts the country.

The large increase in the amount required for interest on the public debt is by no means the only new factor. Expenditures for policing the conquered countries, for the protection of the nation, and for co-operating with other nations in the maintenance of world peace will make heavy demands on the taxpayers of the country. Veterans' benefits will reach new highs. In the interests of advancing the productive capacity of the nation and the welfare of the people, larger expenditures will probably be required for public education and public health. Such demands for additional public funds call for a re-examination of all the expenditures for the several functions of government and a redetermination of relative advantages and relative claims on taxable resources. The demands will be so heavy that the effect on the economy as a whole and upon the American way of life will have to be given careful consideration.

The issue with which the present study is concerned may therefore be broadly stated as: How can the United States develop a universal, comprehensive, and co-ordinated system of social security that will relieve or prevent want at a cost which the nation can afford, without seriously interfering with the American way of life?

In attempting to analyze this question, the first step was to examine the several programs for relief and social security that at present exist in the United States and also several programs, now abolished, that were developed to meet the difficulties of the thirties. The results of this examination are presented in Part I.

Since the major issue is the development of a universal, comprehensive, and co-ordinated system, the material presented in Part I with respect to the several programs is basically descriptive. Special emphasis is placed upon those aspects of the programs which are significant in the study of this over-all problem. As the study progressed, it became increasingly clear that the solution of the over-all problem did not lie along the line of minor modifications or extensions of existing programs but in a fresh approach, going back to fundamentals. In Part I, therefore, no effort is made to suggest how the program being described should be modified or extended to make it better serve its purpose. The view was that sooner or later the question of developing a single comprehensive and co-ordinated system would have to be faced, and it would be in the national interest to face it now, especially in the light of the new financial situation created by World War II and the depression of the 1930's.

Fortunately, within recent years two English-speaking countries which have much in common with the United States, Great Britain and New Zealand, have faced the problem of developing a single universal, comprehensive, and co-ordinated system. In Part II the plans for the reorganization of the British social security system, together with the existing New Zealand system are described.

Examination of the material thus presented disclosed a host of questions that require answers. In Part III these detailed problems are grouped under some 19 major questions. The major questions are in turn grouped under three main headings: social problems, cost problems, and administrative problems. These 19 major questions are not independent. What the nation can do with respect to the social problems obviously depends in part on what the benefits will cost and what the nation can afford. The choice of methods for relieving want will depend in no small measure on whether administrative authority and financial responsibility are vested in the national government or in the state government, or whether a conditional grant-in-aid is made to the states by the national government.

Since the questions are not independent, it is impossible at the end of each chapter in Part III to state categorically the answer which it is believed should be given to the question there treated. Answers can only be given where decisions have been arrived at with respect to fundamental policies. One set of answers would be entirely logical for a totalitarian state with a philosophy of "from each according to his ability and to each according to his need." An entirely different set of answers would be required for a nation that recognizes the rights of the individual and endeavors to preserve for him maximum possible liberty in his own pursuit of happiness.

In the concluding chapter, therefore, a statement is made of the fundamental assumptions which appear to underlie the American way of life and the freedom it has afforded the American citizen. Then answers to the questions are given on the basis of how to prevent want through a relief and social security system with minimum interference with individual liberty. Relief and social security are basically defensive, protective devices. They are not fundamentally positive devices to increase employment and efficiency in the production of desired goods and services. It is upon the maintenance and improvement of productive efficiency that real social security rests, for in the last analysis the productive workers of each generation must supply the goods and services to maintain the dependents of that generation.

PART I

AMERICAN RELIEF AND SOCIAL SECURITY PROGRAMS

CHAPTER I

HISTORICAL EVOLUTION

As was stated in the general introduction, Part I is to be basically descriptive. It will deal first with those programs for relief and social security that are currently in operation in the United States and then with certain other programs, now abolished, that were developed to meet the difficulties of the thirties.

Each chapter dealing with a specific program will not only describe it in some detail but will give briefly its history. It seems desirable, however, to outline the evolution of relief and social security in the United States. In a sense the evolutionary history is part of the history of every specific program. It is given here to furnish a background for consideration of all the programs.[1]

EARLY DEVELOPMENTS

The present programs have evolved over the years. They do not represent the result of a thorough, comprehensive study of all the problems involved in relief and social security but rather an attack on one part at a time. Not infrequently a particular part has received extensive study resulting in the modernization of that part, but often this work has been done with almost no reference to the remainder. If one looks at the structure as a whole, one sees essential parts dating back to Elizabethan England, functioning along side other parts designed by the advanced thinkers of the United States of the 1930's. Conflicting theories of government underlie the different parts, ranging from the local autonomy and responsibility of the early days to the powerful, highly centralized, national government of the current period.

English settlers in the American colonies brought with them the Elizabethan concept that giving public relief to those who could not support themselves, or secure support from relatives,

[1] Footnote references to the statutes and to most other sources will be omitted in this chapter. They will be found in the chapters relating to specific programs.

friends, or private philanthropy, was a proper function of local government. With this concept went the conviction that the poverty of the poor was their own fault, and that they must be severely dealt with to prevent them from living in idleness at the expense of workers who paid taxes. In the early days little consideration was given to the causes of poverty: the morally weak, the physically and mentally ill, the crippled, the aged, and the women and children deprived of the support of the male head of the family by accident, disease, or death were all very largely lumped together. In the United States relatives and friends, even strangers, were quick to provide a home for the children and the women who could at least earn their keep; and in that relatively simple economy with its great demand for man power, even a very young child was worth his keep. Thus the paupers were in a sense the economic and social rejects.

From time to time, as knowledge and social understanding increased, special categories were separated from this social residue and given differentiated care and treatment. Such movements generally had common characteristics that are important for an understanding of the present situation in the United States. The more significant of them were:

1. The administration of the old poor laws was generally so harsh and the public attitude toward the paupers so condemnatory, that an entirely new administrative system was set up for the differentiated category to insure different treatment and if possible to develop a new public attitude.

2. Differentiation necessitated establishing, usually by law, conditions for eligibility to the special category. The eligibility rules were ordinarily fairly sharply defined.

3. To secure what was regarded as reasonably suitable treatment for the new class, standards of treatment or benefits were written into the law or into the regulations made in pursuance of law.

4. Proponents of these reforms frequently either started or ended with state legislatures or in very recent years with the Congress of the United States. Two factors brought them to

the state legislatures: (a) When they wanted new standards applied with some degree of uniformity throughout the state, they had to secure state legislation. (b) In the average state the powers and duties of local governments rest on state laws, and therefore if a local government wanted to do something new for a special class, it had to have state authorization. Thus, frequently the new laws were optional or permissive and were not mandatory throughout the state. Relatively large urban governments might be compelled to adopt them by state law, whereas rural local governments were either omitted from the act or given an option.

5. When a state wished to make the new system mandatory throughout the state and to require administration according to minimum standards, it was generally necessary for the state either to share the tax burden with the local governments or to assume full responsibility for financing the new system. Representatives from the poorer local districts or from districts that did not have the problem would not support the program unless the state contributed toward the costs.

6. Legislation for each special category was customarily worked out as a separate and distinct entity, without reference to basic principles or to what had been done for other classes. The successive measures frequently carried provisions both for financing and administration. Thus in a single state the programs for relief and public welfare were generally complex and uncorrelated.

7. Back of most of the reform measures were organized groups. In the earlier years the leaders generally were not of the class to be benefited, but rather individuals with an understanding of causes and methods of treatment and a compelling social conscience. As economic and social conditions changed, the persons to be directly benefited, their relatives, and friends became active, and in many states they were sufficiently numerous to constitute a pressure group.

These forces led to a mass of agencies and many laws, often with little or no co-ordination either in financing or administration. At the bottom was almost invariably a residue still under old poor laws that had not been overhauled in the light of modern social and economic conditions. Local finance rested almost entirely on the general property tax; which under modern conditions had become in many communities a tax on real property. Many cities and some counties had found this tax inadequate to support modern local government functions, but no other tax suitable for use by local governments had been devised that was a large and effective producer of revenues. Thus the residue left under the old poor laws, or what we now call general public assistance or general relief, was caught between the mill wheels of lack of revenue and old laws and administrative agencies.

SHIFT TO FEDERAL ACTION

When the depression came in 1929, thousands of workers who had previously supported themselves and their dependents, and who had none of the characteristics of the people customarily cared for under general public assistance, required public relief because of mass unemployment. Legally in many states they fell into this category. The general property tax—already overburdened—was a poor producer in bad times. It could not be expanded to yield additional revenue; generally it failed even to produce normal revenue. The existing provisions for relief were totally inadequate to meet the situation caused by the depression. Local governments, state governments, and finally the national government had to improvise, with little or no time to consider theory, principles, or sound administration.

Under American law and practice, at the onset of the depression the primary responsibility rested on the states or their subordinate units, but many of them were entirely unprepared to meet the situation. For the purposes of the present book it is essential to ask: Why? Among the most important reasons were:

1. Many of the states had never modernized their tax systems.[2] They still placed great reliance on the general property tax, which broke down under the strain. Often it was not so much that the states and local governments did not have the

[2] In most states, the state laws prescribe the tax systems to be used by subordinate units.

resources, the capacity to pay, as that they did not have tax devices for tapping their resources. In many states new laws and new administrations were required and in some constitutional amendments.

2. Many states and local governments could not borrow to meet the emergency because: (a) They were already in debt practically up to statutory or constitutional debt limits. (b) Relief was in the main an operating expense of government and not an outlay for capital improvements; and laws restricted borrowing for expenses. (c) Some state constitutions gave the state government no powers with respect to relief and prohibited them from borrowing for an object over which they had no power. (d) The states and local governments had no power over the currency and no real influence over the banking system. They had to go to the banks or other financial institutions to borrow much as a private individual would go. (e) The banks frequently could not safely lend to the state or local government, because they could not collect on a loan unless it complied with all the requirements of the constitution and the laws. The government officer making an illegal loan and not the state or the local government is liable. Repayment of the loan must be made from an excess of revenues—mainly tax revenues —over government payments. In some state and local governments the indications were that the governments would default on the interest if not the principal of outstanding obligations already held by the banks. Many banks were themselves facing failure. Investors would not take the bonds and notes off the bankers' hands.

Under these circumstances the states and the politically powerful municipalities turned to the national government, supported by the mass of voters, not only those who were in need and their dependents, but others who saw the suffering or feared a complete breakdown of our economic, social, and political system. Not only was disorder prevalent in many sections of the country, but it was often apparent that the government officials responsible for maintaining law and order were in sympathy with the objectives of the disturbers if not with their methods. Public sentiment would not sustain the officers who took drastic action. The new political philosophies that had developed in Europe after the first World War added to the fears of many persons.

The first national action was in the form of loans and later grants to the states to enable them to meet the situation. In so far as there was division into categories, it was at the outset primarily the work of the states. The national government first made loans to the states through the Reconstruction Finance Corporation, established under the Hoover administration. Early in the Roosevelt administration it was succeeded by the Federal Emergency Relief Administration. These organizations generally worked with a temporary emergency relief administration, which had been quickly improvised by the states to meet the emergency, for few of them had any permanent co-ordinated public welfare department to assume the heavy responsibility. Experienced welfare workers from state, local, and private agencies often played a large part in organizing and operating the temporary state and local government emergency relief administrations, but these administrations were created almost overnight.

Differentiation was introduced in the early days of the Roosevelt administration, however, apparently primarily on the initiative of the national government. The national government was in the relief business operating on an emergency basis making grants to the states. Thousands of able-bodied, competent citizens were existing on doles or on wages earned on relief projects operated by state or local governments. The administration decided that the national government should get out of the relief business by furnishing employment to the employables on local projects, mainly at the expense of the national government.

The first general national experiment in furnishing relief employment, the Civil Works Administration, under the same direction as F.E.R.A., was almost immediately swamped and was soon abandoned. It offered work on federally financed projects, without any real use of a test of need. A person did not have to be on relief to be eligible. Thousands of workers who were being supported, perhaps more or less unsatisfactorily by primary breadwinners, got C.W.A. jobs, and other workers who had some available resources conserved them by earning C.W.A. wages. Thousands had to be turned away, although the actual need of some of them was far greater than that of persons who were given employment. The impracticability of the program and its political inexpediency were soon obvious, and the government fell back on the Federal Emergency Relief Administration working in co-operation with the states.

THE W.P.A.

The national administration soon returned to the idea of sub-stituting in the case of unemployed employables, work on relief projects mainly at the expense of the national government. Under the new plan which came to be the Works Progress Administration, an evolution from F.E.R.A., two of the major difficulties of the earlier C.W.A. were avoided in that:

1. To be eligible for employment, a person had to be receiving relief or be eligible to receive it. In other words, a means test was used. In most states the means test was administered by the state or local public welfare agency, which certified the applicants found in need to the national W.P.A. agency in the locality.

2. Not more than one member of a family, ordinarily the principal breadwinner, was eligible for employment on W.P.A.

Persons who were not certified as being in need could not get W.P.A. work unless they were hired as regular employees of the organization for administrative and supervisory positions or for required skilled work that could not be done by persons available from the relief rolls.

In the official pronouncements of the period, the position taken was that the national government would assume responsibility for meeting the needs of the unemployed employables through the national work program. The responsibility for persons in need from causes other than unemployment would be returned to the states. The idea was apparently that the states, relieved of responsibility for unemployment relief, would have sufficient funds to meet the need from other causes.

As a matter of fact the program never worked out entirely in accordance with this theory. Whether the unemployed employables secured work on a W.P.A. project depended on many factors, among the most important of which were:

1. The total amount the Congress, acting upon the recommendations of the President, made available for work relief.

2. The amount of the aggregate appropriation allocated to a particular state by the administration, which had wide discretion in making the allocations.

3. Whether there was an approved project with available funds that had openings or positions for the needy unemployed employables in the area.

4. Whether the needy unemployable had qualifications which would permit of his employment in the available positions. Projects were generally selected largely on the basis of furnishing the kind of work that could be done by the type of persons who were available, but in many instances, especially in smaller communities, there were no projects available for workers who did not fit the particular pattern.

In most communities there were unemployed employables on relief or certified as eligible for relief who could not secure positions on W.P.A. The national government did not provide for them but left them to be cared for by the state or the local government. In other words they were generally dependent on the old general public assistance.

Two factors added to the difficulties in some communities:

1. Under the W.P.A. system, the state, the local government, or some other public or quasi-public agency had to put up a sponsor's contribution toward the costs of the W.P.A. project. In communities hard hit by the depression, a sponsor's contribution had a priority over many other demands for public funds. If the community were to get the benefits from W.P.A., it had to have an approved project. Thus in many localities little was appropriated for general public assistance.

2. Although no person could get a work relief job on W.P.A. unless he was certified as being in need, the W.P.A. did not

adjust its wages or earnings to need. Wages and hours of employment were fixed on a basis that resembled in many ways ordinary employment. Skilled workers got more than semi-skilled and semi-skilled more than unskilled. The unskilled worker with a big family of dependents got less for working the standard number of hours than the skilled worker with no dependents. Thus more money went into W.P.A. wages than was necessary for relief.

In several states a conflict developed between the state and local welfare agencies that did the certifying as to need and the W.P.A. officials who were responsible for the success of the projects. Naturally the welfare workers sought employment for heads of families who were in great need, and they certified as employable some persons that an operating officer responsible for results would regard as unemployable. Operating officers, on the other hand, were hard pressed to find competent workers possessed of the skills and personal qualities necessary to do a good job in a reasonable time. Sometimes when they found a good man they sent him to the welfare agency to get him certified as being in need. The welfare agency would not regard him as in need according to the standards it had been applying, and the investigators would be particularly disturbed if the candidate had no dependents. In some localities, particularly in the south, the situation was further complicated by the fact that W.P.A. earnings, working conditions, and methods of payment were more attractive than those in private enterprise. Thus some people were anxious to shift to W.P.A., a process which necessitated being certified as in need. In at least one state an agreement to cease and desist had to be entered between the two agencies, the state and local agency promising to send no more unemployables, the W.P.A. agreeing to send no more persons to get a certificate of need.

When the W.P.A. earnings were insufficient to sustain a big family, the welfare agencies occasionally had to supplement them from general public assistance funds. These agencies could do nothing when W.P.A. earnings paid by the national government carried a worker and his dependents above the standard being used by them to determine need and occasionally even above the prevailing local level. This situation was particularly embarrassing in rural areas where the customary payment for work had been in allowances plus some cash, whereas the W.P.A. paid all cash. The cash went to some persons who had little experience in handling money. From the standpoint of many local people, the national government was paying far more than necessary to those who succeeded in getting on W.P.A., and it was leaving to the locality the responsibility of caring for others whose need was really greater. Some were unemployable, and others were employable but unable to get on a project within a reasonable distance of their homes.

Another element that caused confusion in many communities was the uncertainty with respect to the continuity of W.P.A. employment in the locality. Appropriations and allotments might be curtailed; projects might be completed with no new projects to take their places. The local community might suddenly find itself called upon to provide through general public assistance funds for former W.P.A. workers whom it had regarded as the responsibility of the national government. Neither the local governments nor the state governments knew what the national government was going to do, so that orderly planning, appropriating, and administering were out of the question. The person dropped from W.P.A. who could not find other employment was in many communities in dire need. Often the only relief available for him was surplus commodities distributed at the expense of the national government.

The W.P.A. was ultimately abolished, when the defense and war efforts absorbed most of the unemployed. Under present conditions the unemployed employables who have no benefits coming to them from the unemployment insurance system are now back in the miscellaneous general public assistance category unless they can qualify for some of the other special categories established under the Social Security Act.

SOCIAL SECURITY AND OTHER PROGRAMS

The Social Security Act, passed in 1935, resulted in the differentiation of five additional categories, three in the field of means test relief and two in the field of no-means test social insurance.

By federal grants-in-aid to the states, the national government offered great inducements to the states to set up special relief categories for (1) the needy aged, 65 years of age or over, (2) dependent children living with relatives within the degrees specified by the national law, and (3) the needy blind.

By the exercise of the power to tax, the national government established and operated a system of old-age insurance applicable to persons who were in the status of employee to employer in industries and occupations, but with certain fairly large and important exceptions. By the same power the national government virtually forced the states to adopt systems of unemployment insurance, again applicable to persons in the employee status, but with important exceptions.

This broad outline traces the evolution of the major programs of relief, old-age insurance, and unemployment insurance in the social insurance field and the work program of the thirties, now abolished, for the unemployed employables.

There are other programs that require mention, two in the insurance field and four that stemmed from relief. The two in the insurance field apply to the steam railway industry, one providing for old-age retirement and the other for unemployment compensation. They are both national programs, nationally administered, and came into existence in the thirties. The four in the field of relief and work relief were:

1. The Civilian Conservation Corps, which was originated by the national government in the early days of the Roosevelt administration as a special work program for unemployed boys from families in need. Gradually the requirement that the boys be from needy families and allot most of their money earnings to their respective families was relaxed, and the program became more of a kind of governmental work conducted by the national government in the interest of a special class of youth.

2. The National Youth Administration grew out of the activities of the Federal Emergency Relief Administration. It engaged in two types of activities: (a) work projects in co-

operation with educational institutions to enable needy students to earn money so that they could continue their schooling, and (b) independent N.Y.A. projects to train and educate youth whose formal schooling was completed or interrupted and who did not find normal jobs. Originally conceived as a relief agency, the N.Y.A. gradually shifted its emphasis from relief as such and tended to become an educational agency. It was a national organization, and at least so far as its special work projects were concerned, it was not integrated with the public educational system of the state and its subordinate units.

3. The Farm Security Administration which developed out of the Federal Emergency Relief Administration and the Subsistence Homestead Division of the Department of the Interior, authorized by the National Industrial Recovery Act. The activities of the F.E.R.A. that related to rural relief, rural rehabilitation, and drought relief were merged with those of the Subsistence Homestead Division to form the Resettlement Administration. It, in turn, was transferred to the Department of Agriculture, where with some modifications it became the Farm Security Administration. Still later the F.S.A. was relieved of the nonagricultural projects originally undertaken by its predecessor agencies and became an agricultural agency concerned entirely with farm families who were in need of special assistance.

4. Another program was concerned with the maintenance of the prices of certain commodities—mainly agricultural—through their purchase by the government and free distribution to persons in need. From the outset this program had a dual nature. Part of the funds used came from appropriations for relief administered by F.E.R.A. and part from funds made available to the Department of Agriculture for the removal of surplus agricultural products. The Federal Surplus Relief Corporation was organized to carry on the activities. The corporation was originally controlled by the Secretary of Agriculture, the Federal Emergency Administrator of Public Works, and the Federal Emergency Relief Administrator. Later the name of

the corporation was changed to the Federal Surplus Commodities Corporation and control was vested entirely in the Department of Agriculture. It is important in a study of relief primarily because the surplus commodities were given to persons in need. In some communities, in fact, the surplus commodities thus made available constituted practically the only means of giving relief to persons in need.

DIVISION OF RESPONSIBILITY

Perhaps the most significant fact brought out by this outline of the several programs is the subdivision and the dispersion of responsibility and authority that has taken place. Despite the inherent interrelationships among the several programs, some are administered solely and exclusively by the national government, others by the state governments in cooperation with the national government through conditional grants-in-aid, one—unemployment insurance—by the states under the compulsion of a federal tax law, and one—the residual general public assistance—exclusively by the states or their subdivisions without any national participation.

Uncertainty with respect to the constitutional law of the United States was an important factor in causing subdivision and dispersion of responsibility and authority and the resulting lack of co-ordination and integration. It is clear beyond argument that the Constitution does not specifically include relief and social security among the functions with which the national government may deal, and that powers not granted to the national government are specifically reserved to the states or the people thereof. The national government has therefore been under the constitutional necessity of legislating in these fields by indirection. It did not have the clear and undisputed power to adopt those methods and devices which seemed best suited to achieve the desired objectives; it had always to consider what methods and devices would be sustained as constitutional by the United States Supreme Court. The constitutional law of the country, as made by that court through its interpretation of the Constitution, became moreover a realm of great uncertainty. All concerned with legislation respecting relief and social security had more or less to guess at what the Supreme Court, that would ultimately pass upon the constitutionality of the law, would do, for earlier decisions of the court no longer marked the channel for constitutional legislation.

Although the national government was without expressed power to legislate in this field, five principal indirect avenues were open to it.

1. The national government itself carries on many public works and is responsible for the maintenance of much public property. Without raising any issues of constitutionality, it could expand its public works programs to increase employment and thus diminish the need for relief.

2. The national government makes many contracts for the purchase of supplies, materials and equipment, and for construction. It had constitutional authority to require contractors to comply with such conditions as it might lay down with respect to labor on these federal contracts.

3. It was well settled by constitutional law that the national government could make conditional grants-in-aid to the states to help them carry on functions of government over which the states had exclusive jurisdiction. The establishment of conditions with which the states had to comply to be eligible to receive the grant did not render the national act unconstitutional, since the states theoretically were free to refuse the grant.

4. The national government had expressed power to regulate commerce among the several states.[3] Uncertainties developed with respect to how far the national government could go under this power in regulating the conditions under which goods which enter or might enter interstate commerce should be produced. The extension of the interpretation of this power gave the national government further authority with respect to social insurance.

[3] Constitution, Art. I, sec. 8.

5. Congress has the power "To lay and collect Taxes, Duties, Imposts and Excises, to pay the Debts and provide for the common Defence and general Welfare of the United States . . . ."[4] Uncertainties likewise developed with respect to how far this power to tax might be used as a method of regulation and compulsion in fields in which the direct power of regulation and control remained in the several states or the people thereof. Extension of the interpretation of this power likewise gave the national government further authority with respect to social insurance and relief.

The expansion of the powers of the national government came about, it is significant to note, not by amendments to the Constitution but by the evolutionary process of judicial interpretation, an evolution which results in no small measure from the changing personnel of the court. It seems reasonable to say that several of the methods and devices adopted for relief and social security were selected at the time because of assumptions as to what the Supreme Court would uphold as constitutional. It likewise seems reasonable to assume that if the entire problem of relief and social security should be reconsidered today in the light of changed constitutional law, very different decisions might be reached and a more universal, comprehensive, and integrated system might be developed.

[4] The same.

CHAPTER II

OLD-AGE ASSISTANCE

Old-age assistance is numerically and financially the most important of the purely relief programs in the United States. In 1942 the total expenditures for public assistance by the several levels of government was about 998 million dollars. Of this amount, 63.0 per cent went for old-age assistance as contrasted with 17.2 per cent each for aid to dependent children and general assistance, and 2.6 per cent for aid to the blind.[1] This chapter thus deals with the largest special category in the field of relief.

It will give first a broad statement of the forces that led to the provision of federal grants to the states for old-age assistance in Title I of the Social Security Act passed in 1935. The provisions of that title, as amended in 1939, will then be summarized and briefly discussed. The federal act, it will be seen, did not define need, set up a standard of living below which no elderly person could fall without becoming entitled to old-age assistance, lay down standards to be used in determining the amount of benefit, or force the states to appropriate funds. All these essential matters were left, subject to slight national influence, to the several states. It is necessary, therefore, to summarize briefly what the several states have done with respect to these matters. These subjects will be approached first from the standpoint of state plans, which include both the state laws and the rules, regulations, and procedures developed under the state laws. Then the most significant statistics relating to the program will be presented by states. The chapter will conclude with a consideration of the administrative systems which the states have adopted to carry out this grant-in-aid program. A comparison between benefits under old-age relief with those under old-age insurance will be presented in the chapter on the insurance system.

[1] *Social Security Year Book 1942*, p. 101.

FORCES LEADING TO THE DEVELOPMENT OF THE PRESENT PROGRAM

Economic and social changes in the United States had for many years prior to 1929 brought the subject of the aged up for discussion. Most important among these changes were:

1. In the industrial civilization that had developed, employees in the older age brackets were often, although by no means invariably, less efficient than younger employees even if they escaped disabilities that rendered them actually unemployable. An older employee who lost his job had difficulty finding another satisfactory one.

2. In many households in urban and industrial communities, old people could contribute little to family support, yet housing, food, clothing, and care of the aged cost the family money. Under a money economy in urban communities, the care of the aged was proving very different from what it had been in a rural agricultural economy, with a considerable measure of family self-sufficiency.

3. The absolute number of old persons in the population was increasing, and because of a declining birth rate, an improved mortality rate, and the curtailment of immigration, the percentage which they formed of the total population was also going up. The nation thus had to look forward to having active workers support an increasing number of persons dependent because of advanced years.

Several European industrial nations had adopted programs designed to provide for the aged, and a considerable number of persons were advocating like action in this country. In a few states commissions had been created by the legislatures to study the problems, and occasionally bills were introduced to set up systems, but prior to 1929 they did not arouse great popular interest or support.

Mass unemployment following 1929 completely changed the public interest and attitude. Many elderly persons lost their jobs and were unable to find others. Younger workers who had been supporting elderly dependents found the burden greatly increased as they themselves suffered from unemployment and under-employment. Prophets of gloom found wide acceptance of the philosophy that the United States had a mature economy, that the country was built and never again would have jobs for all willing and able to work. Share the work programs of the early days of the depression had been neither popular nor particularly successful. Thousands of younger workers suffering from unemployment favored the idea of retiring the older workers on pensions, thereby making full-time jobs available for younger workers.

Another idea widely accepted at the time was that the depression and the resulting mass unemployment were due to lack of sufficient purchasing power in the hands of consumers who would use it quickly. Dr. Francis E. Townsend presented a plan the essentials of which were:[2] to levy a national transaction tax which would immediately produce a tremendous revenue, and would produce more and more as transactions increased under improved economic conditions; to distribute the proceeds of this tax among the retired old people in the population without any means test on a per capita basis; to require that the recipients spend the resulting pensions almost immediately for consumption.

We shall not here go into the economic fallacies that were inherent in the plan or the defects in the statistics as to the total amount which would be realized from the tax and distributed on a per capita basis. For present purposes the essential fact is that the plan won thousands of adherents all over the nation, enough to be of political significance. They were organized, loosely perhaps, but on a dues-paying basis, which produced revenues to support a far-flung propaganda campaign. The movement offered great possibilities to any effective political demagogue who would ride it.

TITLE I OF THE SOCIAL SECURITY ACT OF 1935

The old-age assistance payments of the Social Security Act of 1935 were in part designed to deflate the Townsend and allied

[2] The Committee on Old Age Security of the Twentieth Century Fund, Inc., *The Townsend Crusade* (1936).

plans, which had advanced far enough to make it necessary for Congress to hold hearings on bills which had been introduced to embody such a plan in law.[3] The movement clearly demonstrated the power of the pressure groups demanding old-age legislation.

Immediately after the enacting clause of the Social Security Act passed in 1935 comes "Title I—Grants to the States for Old-Age Assistance." Amendments to this title were adopted in 1939, and we shall here discuss the act as amended, with occasional reference to the provisions of the earlier act.

The first point to be noted is that the nation promised a grant to each state that adopted a plan for old-age assistance acceptable to the federal Social Security Board as complying with the requirements of the act. The grant is in two parts. The first provides one half of the amount which the state expended with respect to each needy individual 65 years of age or older who is not an inmate of a public institution, not counting so much of such expenditure with respect to any individual as exceeds $40 in any month.[4] The second part grants the state 5 per cent of the first amount "for paying the costs of administering the State plan or for old-age assistance, or both, and for no other purpose."

The eligibility requirements made mandatory by the national act were: (1) The eligibility age should not be higher than 65 years.[5] (2) The state should not adopt any residence requirement which excludes a resident of the state who has resided therein five years during the nine years immediately preceding the application for old-age assistance and has resided therein continuously for one year immediately preceding the application. (3) The state must not adopt any citizenship requirement which excludes any citizen of the United States.

Under the old poor laws where relief was locally financed and

---

[3] *Economic Security Act*, Hearings before the House Committee on Ways and Means, 74 Cong. 1 sess.; *Economic Security Act*, Hearings before the Senate Committee on Finance, 74 Cong. 1 sess.

[4] The original act put the limit at $30 per month. It was raised to $40 by the 1939 amendment.

[5] Prior to Jan. 1, 1940 the age of 70 was permissible as the lower limit.

locally administered, settlement was frequently required, and to gain settlement required long residence and citizenship. Sometimes receipt of public relief from the local government before acquiring settlement prevented its acquisition. These settlement laws have been very severely criticized. States which had them have been roundly condemned, and other states which never established them have been commended. Statistics, however, indicate fairly clearly that in general the states which had them were those in which the local governments really spent some money for relief, whereas the states which did not have them were those in which little or nothing was commonly spent for this purpose.

New York and the New England states partially overcame the rigors of the settlement requirements by providing for "the state poor," residents of the state who had no settlement in any local government jurisdiction.[6]

The federal act moved in the direction of abating the settlement and citizenship difficulties. It does not provide, however, for an aged person who moves from one state to another and becomes dependent in that state before satisfying the residence requirements permissible under the federal act.

The national act contained several administrative requirements, some of them designed to force the abolition of the old concept that giving and financing relief were exclusively functions of local government. They were that the state plan must:

1. Be in effect in all political subdivisions of the state, and if administered by them be mandatory upon them.[7]

2. Provide for financial participation by the state.

3. Either provide for the establishment or designation of a single state agency to administer the plan or provide for the establishment or designation of a single state agency to supervise the administration of the plan.

4. Provide for granting to any individual, whose claim for old-age assistance is denied, an opportunity for a fair hearing.

[6] Robert C. Lowe, *State Public Welfare Legislation*, Works Progress Administration, Division of Research, Research Monograph XX (1939), p. 29.

[7] The old device of optional or permissive legislation was thus outlawed for the old-age category.

5. Provide such methods of administration as are found by the board to be necessary for the proper and efficient operation, which includes, since the 1939 amendment, methods relating to the establishment and maintenance of personnel standards on a merit basis but specifically does not include authority over selection, tenure of office, and compensation of any individual employed in accordance with such methods.

6. Provide that the state agency will make such reports, in such form and containing such information as the board may from time to time require.

7. Provide safeguards which restrict the use or disclosure of information concerning applicants and recipients to purposes directly connected with the administration of old-age assistance.

There are four related things which the national act does not do that require careful consideration.

1. The act does not define need but with a slight exception that will be mentioned later leaves the definition of need to the individual state.

2. It does not set up any standard of living below which an elderly person may not fall without becoming as of right entitled to old-age assistance.

3. It does not itself lay down any standards which shall be used to determine the amount of benefit to be allowed, although as has been noted the national government will not count "so much of [a state's] expenditures with respect to any individual for any month as exceeds $40."

4. It in no way forces a state to make appropriations for old-age assistance. The national grant is an inducement, not a compulsion.

With such latitude left to the states for the exercise of independent judgment, the natural result is wide variation, which we can here discuss only in a broad way.

THE DEFINITION OF NEED

Chapter XIX of Part III will be devoted to a fairly detailed consideration of the basic question, "What is need?" In the present chapter we shall be concerned almost entirely with the presentation of the facts as to what answers have been given to this question under the old-age assistance programs of the several states.

Need results when available resources are insufficient to meet the essential requirements of an individual or a family. It is a budgetary matter with two sides, income and necessary outgo. Thus attempts to define it legally and administratively have dealt with the two sides of the budget. The income side will be taken up first.

Resources classified. There are some persons who have no resources whatsoever and are totally dependent on public or private relief. In such instances no questions arise on the income side of the budget, all are concerned with how much outgo is essential. The major issues with which we are at the moment concerned arise with respect to those cases where some resources are available. The following outline of the significant resources will furnish a background for the presentation of the facts.

1. Earnings
   a. Of the individual whose need is in question.
   b. Of the person or persons who are responsible according to law or custom for support of the individual.
      (1) Who are living in the same household with him, and who have been contributing to the support of the family of which he is a member.
      (2) Who are not living in the same household with him, and who have not regularly and systematically been contributing to the support of his family.

2. Savings of the individual or of others responsible for his support, including
   a. Cash assets in hand or in banks.
   b. Insurance policies that have a cash surrender value.
   c. Investments in real property.
      (1) Producing a money income.
      (2) Producing no money income but providing shelter for the individual and members of his household.
      (3) Producing no income.
   d. Money paid to an individual, organization, or corporation which puts the recipient under obligation to repay it or to render services or provide whole or partial support in return.

e. Investments in durable personal property.

3. Food, fuel, etc. available to the family substantially without cost through labor of the individual or some other member of the family.

Because of the absence of any controlling national law, a state is free to determine what its policy shall be with respect to each of these classes of resources. Each state, moreover, decides upon its own classifications, the form of its law, and the regulations made in accordance with it, or its "plan," to use the accepted terminology. There is of course no point in a book of this type reproducing state plans or condensed summaries of them.[8] The most that we shall attempt is some general descriptions that seem to us to present the significant issues.

Income. With respect to money income we may divide the states into three broad categories, as follows:

1. States in which the plan establishes as the standard for eligibility a fixed amount of income. If the applicant's income falls below that amount, he is eligible, if above it he is ineligible. This standard may be established in either or both of two ways: (a) the plan under its conditions of eligibility may provide in effect "that income from all sources shall not exceed X dollars per year" or "per month," or (b) in limiting benefits it may say in effect "total income, including aid, shall not exceed X dollars per year" or "per month." Either method or the two combined appear to have substantially the same effect. In 1940 Colorado used as its standard $45 per month ($540 a year), whereas South Carolina used $240 a year. More commonly used figures were $30 or $40 a month.

2. States in which the plan defines need in general terms such, perhaps typically, as "has insufficient means to maintain self on reasonable standard of health and decency." A limit is placed solely upon the maximum benefit that may be paid, such as "not to exceed $30 per month," without any specific reference to income. So far as the plan goes, more discretion is left to administrative officers than is delegated to them in the states of the first group.

[8] See Social Security Board, *Characteristics of State Plans for Old Age Assistance*, Bureau of Public Assistance, Publication No. 16, revised July 1, 1940.

3. States of the third group, small in number, define need in general terms, but place no limitation on the maximum amount of benefit. Massachusetts, which belongs in this group, provided in 1940 that resources, income, and allowances shall be not less than $30 for single persons, $50 for married couples both eligible, and $50 for sisters and brothers both eligible and living together, and $15 additional for each eligible brother and sister. Thus, that state establishes a minimum level of benefits with which its local governments must comply. In 1942 only three states paid average benefits higher than those in Massachusetts. Arkansas, which is among the low-paying states, belongs in this group that had no limitations on benefits in its plan.

In two states, California and Idaho, the plan in 1940 provided for exclusion of earnings or income of certain amounts from certain sources. According to the Social Security Board digest, California provided "Net income from several specified sources up to $15 per month not counted" and Idaho, "Earnings up to $15 per month on odd jobs permitted without deduction from budget."

Several states which fix either a maximum limit for allowances or for allowances plus resources permit payments above the maximum for persons requiring medical care and allow payment of funeral benefits.

Home ownership. Ownership of a house, either free or encumbered, and of household furniture is reasonably common among elderly people. Most state plans have provisions to the effect that an applicant must not have transferred property for the purpose of qualifying. There may or may not be a limit on the time elapsed between the application for assistance and the transfer. The danger that elderly people will transfer property to establish eligibility is real enough so that few states omit this safeguard. This generalization with respect to transfers appears to be the only one that can be made with safety. With respect to other matters of home ownership differences in policy are wide. Some states in their plans ignore the existence of such property.

In a few states the plan specifically permits ownership of real estate occupied as a residence without loss of eligibility. The

1940 digest says: for Colorado, "May own real estate occupied as residence and personal property exempt from execution or attachment"; for California, "Value of use and occupancy of premises owned and occupied by applicant is not counted as income"; and for Florida, "No equity in real property salable at reasonable return above the $5,000 valuation exempt from taxation under the Homestead Exemption Act." The acceptance of assistance does not restrict the property rights under these circumstances.

States which restrict property rights in the home may do so in three ways: (1) The plan may disqualify an applicant who has real property worth more than a specified sum. (2) It may provide that the administering government may or shall take a lien upon the property for the amount of the relief granted, although frequently there are limitations protecting the interests of a dependent spouse or of dependent children by preventing enforcement of the lien while they still need the property for shelter. (3) It may provide that the amount of assistance granted, with or without interest, shall constitute a preferred claim against the estate of a deceased beneficiary. Such provisions, it should be noted, apply to sums obtained as assistance honestly and without fraud, concealment of assets, or failure to report subsequent earnings which made the beneficiary ineligible. Several states, which do not take liens or have a right of recovery on valid payments, permit recovery for assistance secured by improper acts.

The provisions of the Connecticut plan as digested in 1940 may be interesting as an illustration. There was no disqualification for ownership of real property, but the owner might be required to agree to reimburse the state for the total amount of aid plus 4 per cent interest per annum, and the agreement constitutes a lien against the real property and the estate, although enforcement might be suspended during occupancy of the surviving spouse.

Insurance. Insurance was specifically mentioned in the digest of the plans for 13 of the 48 states. In several of them the objective was to permit the applicants to maintain in force a limited

amount of insurance, sometimes provided it had been in force
for a specified number of years before application for assistance.
A face value of not to exceed $1,000 or a cash surrender value of
not over $300 on policies in effect for five years or more would
perhaps typify such provisions. In one or two states insurance
was mentioned only to provide that the policies should be
cashed or turned over to the state. Iowa had a provision whereby an applicant might voluntarily assign a policy to the state
board; in that event the state board was authorized to continue
payment and on the death of the insured reimburse the state
for its advances.

Responsibilities of relatives. Perhaps the most interesting and
socially significant variations are those in the field of the responsibility of relatives. In the northern states where general
public assistance was for a great many years customarily given,
the tendency has been to retain the responsibility of close relatives, provided they have ability to pay. Some progress has been
made in defining capacity to pay. In these states the common
provision appears to be to make the existence of legally responsible relatives able to support a disqualification, but some plans
merely give the state a right of action against legally liable relatives to recover the amount it has paid as assistance. In the
south and the southwest where general public assistance was as
a rule scarcely more than rudimentary and where the old-age
legislation was not greatly affected by traditional practices, the
laws generally do not provide for responsibility of relatives.

A clear-cut issue thus exists as to whether adult children
should be responsible for the support of their parents if these
parents are in need, or whether society as a whole through the
public treasury should support the needy aged. Associated with
this basic issue is a subsidiary one: if children are relieved of
responsibility for the support of their aged parents and if public
funds are used for this purpose, should the children or the state
have first claim on such estate as the parents may leave? This
issue arises mainly in connection with real property used as a
home and household furniture, both of which in some states,
within limits, are exempt from taxation and not subject to

forced sale to satisfy a judgment. With respect to these issues the national Social Security Act takes no stand; it leaves the matter to the several states. Whatever the state may pay as the result of its decisions on these points, the national treasury will match up to one half of the $40 a month limit.

Earnings, home ownership, insurance, and the existence of relatives with capacity to pay are the most essential items on the income side of the budget. We come now to the outgo or the level of living used as a standard.

THE LEVEL OR STANDARD OF RELIEF

The national government permits the states to determine what the standard level of relief shall be. It does not itself attempt to say what items are necessary for the maintenance of a minimum level say of health and decency. Each state is to determine that level for itself. As already noted, some states establish health and decency as a standard without defining it in money terms, whereas others specifically put money limitations in their laws. Thus the national government may pay half the costs of benefits to an aged person or couple in state A, despite the fact that such an individual or couple would not be eligible for relief in state B because they are not in need according to the law of state B. There is no national standard of need to determine whether the national government shall or shall not contribute. Were a national standard to be established, there appears to be no reasonable doubt that individuals not now eligible to receive assistance in some states would be made eligible and that individuals now receiving relief in some states would be made ineligible. Should the national government place the standard where no persons now receiving old-age assistance would be excluded, thousands of persons would become eligible who are now excluded.

The device most commonly used to determine need is the budget deficiency method. Standards are set up by the several states using this method to show, usually in money terms, what the aged individual or couple should have with respect to each of the classified needs. Against these itemized needs are offset the resources available to the applicant. Ownership of a home, for example, may largely cancel the need for shelter, although some allowance may have to be made for fuel, light, and taxes. As a result, a budget deficit is arrived at, and the amount of that deficit is used to determine the amount of the grant. In some states the full amount of the budget deficit is made up; in others where appropriations are insufficient a percentage of the budget deficit is allowed. Adjusting the percentage of the budget deficit allowed may be the device employed for meeting a shortage of available funds.

In some states, which are frequently spoken of as having "the pension philosophy," the practice is to assume that in the absence of resources the elderly person is entitled to the maximum allowance permitted under the state law. From this maximum are deducted such resources as the individual may have that are not allowed by state law. As previously noted, some states specifically exclude certain resources, for example, California which excludes income from several specified sources up to $15 a month; Idaho permitted earnings up to $15 a month without deduction from the budget. This pension practice tends to produce higher average allowances than would be paid under the budget deficiency method strictly applied.

Under either method the investigators in the welfare agency must discover and evaluate the resources. As already noted, a considerable number of states have a provision whereby the state may recover from a beneficiary's estate if it is subsequently discovered that he had resources which were concealed at the time of the application or were subsequently acquired without notice to the welfare agency, and practically all the states declare an individual ineligible if he has disposed of property for the purpose of establishing eligibility. All such provisions are naturally difficult to enforce administratively because of the minutiae of investigation required, the distasteful nature of this part of the job to some investigators, and possibly the climate of public opinion in the locality. The evidence suggests not only wide variations among the several states with respect to such matters but possibly in some states substantial variation among localities.

Appropriations. Fully as important as a cause of variations among the states is the matter of appropriations. Federal payments for old-age assistance and the other assistance payments under the national Social Security Act are made under the grant-in-aid principle and not, as is done under unemployment compensation, through a federal tax with an offset for payments to the state for a like purpose. Within limits, therefore, the individual state determines (1) how much it will appropriate, and as a result (2) how much it will take from the federal treasury. Again, within limits, the more it appropriates, the more applicants to whom it pays benefits, and the higher its benefits the more money it will draw from the federal treasury. The restraining influence is that the state, or the state and the local governments, must pay half.

The federal government through old-age assistance grant-in-aid payments does not serve as a financial equalizing agent. To the state that is generous to its aged, the nation gives relatively more than to the state that is parsimonious. There is no formula by which the federal funds are distributed among the states according to the number of aged in need or according to the financial capacity of the states to support their aged from their own resources. The national government has adopted no device to distinguish between parsimony and lack of capacity to pay. As a result the question of whether an aged person in need receives any money from the national treasury may depend entirely on the action taken by the legislature of the state in which he resides. He may be denied relief because the legislature has not made adequate appropriation, or he may be given a generous benefit because the state legislature has been generous. Failure of the state to provide may in part be due to the fact that the state lacks resources. This subject will be considered further in the third part of the book.

In connection with adequacy of appropriations the fact should be stressed that the individual states under the Social Security Act themselves determine whether any part of the costs of old-age assistance shall be assessed against local governments. The national act specifically requires financial participation by the state, but it does not say how great the participation shall be, nor does it require or limit local contributions. There is wide variation among the states with respect to local participation. Among the 48 states in 1942, 20 reported no contributions from local governments and in 6 the percentage contributed was less than 1 per cent of the cost. At the other extreme are substantial percentages of the aggregate cost, including the federal contribution, coming from local funds; the leaders in this respect in 1942 were: New York 27.1; Kansas 26.6; California 26.1; Nevada 23.8; New Hampshire 23.5; North Carolina 23.4; Alabama 23.1; Virginia 21.4; Indiana 20.8; Wisconsin 20.7; and Wyoming 20.4.[9] A figure above 25 per cent means that local governments pay about as much as the state government if not more. A figure between 20 and 25 per cent represents a heavy contribution by local governments.

It is commonly assumed that a heavy demand on local funds for relief payments creates a local climate of public opinion adverse to liberal determinations. Although on the basis of prior reasoning, we are quite ready to accept the soundness of this assumption, we cannot demonstrate it statistically by interstate comparisons based on the significant statistics regarding old-age assistance programs. Local financing is only one of many variable factors that affect the comparisons. It is, however, significant to present and compare the figures for the several states.

STATISTICS OF OLD-AGE ASSISTANCE BY STATES

The most significant statistics for interstate comparisons are presented by individual states in the table on pages 38–39.

The first section of the table deals with the population 65 years of age or over according to the Census of 1940. It gives first the number of such persons, in thousands; next their number per 1,000 of total population; and third, their number per 1,000 population 21 to 64 years of age. In the main, dependent aged persons must be supported and perhaps cared for by persons of the working ages 21 to 64 years; therefore the ratio of the aged to the persons 21 to 64 seems to us of at least as great significance as their ratio to total population.

[9] *Social Security Year Book 1942*, p. 104.

The second section of the table deals with the number of recipients of old-age assistance. It gives first the number in thousands as of December 1942, second the number per 1,000 aged people in the total population, and third the number per 1,000 persons aged 21 to 64 at the Census of 1940. It may be noted that the numbers per 1,000 aged are taken from a Social Security Board report and are based on its estimate as to the number of aged in 1942. Figures as to the number per 1,000 population 21 to 64 are based on the 1940 population data.

The third section deals with expenditures for old-age assistance in 1942. First it gives the total in thousands, second the expenditures per case, third the percentage of the total obtained from local funds, and fourth the percentage which old-age assistance payments form of all state payments for public assistance of any form.

The final section indicates by a simple "yes" or "no" whether the state plan provides first for relative responsibility and second a lien on property or a right to recover from the individual or estate for assistance properly granted. For relative responsibility "yes" is used for any relative responsibility specifically stated in the plan. Attention should be called to the fact that among states having stated relative responsibility, indicated by "yes," there are variations as to what relatives are liable and their degree of liability. Under liens and recoveries "no" has been used if recovery is only authorized in case of fraud, incorrect answers, failing to report income, and so on, and is not authorized for a grant properly obtained.

The number of aged. So far as population alone is concerned, the number of persons 65 years of age and over per 1,000 persons 21 to 64 years of age seems to us to be the most significant index included in this table. For the United States as a whole this number was 120. States which exceeded the national average by 20 or more were:

New Hampshire	178	Missouri	150
Maine	177	Indiana	148
Vermont	175	Massachusetts	145
Iowa	162	Nebraska	145
Kansas	156	Oregon	142

Division and State	Population 65 Years of Age or Over, 1940[a]			Recipients of Old-Age Assistance		
	Number (In thousands)	Per 1,000		Number in Thousands December 1942[b]	Per 1,000	
		Total Population	Population 21 to 64 Years of Age		Population over 65 Years of Age 1942[c]	Population 21 to 64 Years of Age 1940
UNITED STATES........	9,018	69	120	2,226	238	30
NORTHEAST............	2,880		119	418		17
New England........	715		145	137		28
Maine...........	80	95	177	16	195	35
New Hampshire....	49	99	178	7	143	25
Vermont.........	34	96	175	5	152	26
Massachusetts.....	369	85	145	85	223	33
Rhode Island......	54	75	129	7	130	17
Connecticut.......	129	76	125	17	126	16
Middle Atlantic......	1,875		113	238		14
New York.........	922	68	109	115	119	14
New Jersey.......	279	67	109	29	98	11
Pennsylvania......	677	69	119	94	133	17
Other..............	287		109	43		16
Delaware.........	21	77	134	2	101	13
Maryland.........	124	68	117	15	118	14
West Virginia......	101	53	105	23	210[i]	24
District of Columbia	41	63	92	3	77	7
SOUTHEAST	1,521		105	397		27
Virginia..........	155	58	109	19	119	13
North Carolina.....	157	45	89	39	235[i]	22
South Carolina.....	81	42	89	21	252[i]	23
Georgia...........	159	51	99	71	425[i]	44
Florida...........	131	69	120	43	322	40
Kentucky.........	189	66	131	53	271	37
Tennessee.........	172	59	112	40	227[i]	26
Alabama..........	136	48	96	22	153[i]	15
Mississippi........	115	53	106	26	222[i]	24
Louisiana.........	119	50	95	38	313[i]	30
Arkansas..........	107	55	108	25	227[i]	25
MIDDLE STATES........	2,736		132	732		35
Ohio..............	540	79	134	138	250	34
Indiana...........	288	84	148	69	233	35
Illinois...........	568	72	118	151	254	31
Michigan..........	331	63	109	90	259	30
Wisconsin.........	242	77	136	53	210	30
Minnesota.........	213	77	134	62	282	39
Iowa.............	228	89	162	56	238	40
Missouri..........	326	86	150	113	339	52
NORTHWEST............	510		135	154		41
North Dakota......	39	62	117	9	232	27
South Dakota......	44	68	128	14	313	41
Kansas...........	157	87	156	31	194[i]	31
Nebraska..........	106	79	145	28	259	38
Colorado..........	86	77	137	42	487	67
Utah.............	30	55	108	14	448	50
Montana..........	36	65	112	12	328	38
Wyoming.........	12	50	84	4	260[i]	28
SOUTHWEST	540		103	275		52
Oklahoma.........	145	61	118	78	523	64
Texas............	348	54	99	182	501	52
New Mexico.......	23	44	88	5	210[i]	19
Arizona..........	24	47	91	10	379	38
PACIFIC NORTHWEST.....	269		136	94		47
Idaho............	32	60	114	10	294[i]	36
Oregon...........	93	85	142	21	213	32
Washington........	144	83	137	63	424	60
PACIFIC SOUTHWEST.....	562		128	156		35
California.........	555	80	128	154	267	36
Nevada...........	7	62	103	2	286	29

[a] Compiled from Census of 1940, *Population*, Vol. II, Pt. 1, pp. 56–78.
[b] *Social Security Yearbook 1942*, p. 179.   [c] The same, p. 74.
[d] The same, p. 72.   [e] The same, p. 76.   [f] The same, p 104.   [g] The same, p. 106.

Total in Thousands 1942[d]	Per Case 1942[e]	Per Cent Paid from Local Funds[f]	Per Cent of all Expenditures for Public Assistance[g]	Relatives' Responsibility in Law 1940[h]	Liens Taken on Property or Right to Recover 1940[h]	Division and State
						Expenditures for Old-Age Assistance
$595,952	$23.43	9.4	63.0			UNITED STATES........
						NORTHEAST.............
48,871						New England........
4,046	21.70	—	63.0	Yes	Yes	Maine............
1,995	24.07	23.5	59.1	Yes	Yes	New Hampshire....
1,104	17.97	—	64.2	Yes	Yes	Vermont..........
33,439	34.23	19.0	79.6	Yes	Yes	Massachusetts.....
2,102	24.93	—	47.3	Yes	Yes	Rhode Island.....
6,185	29.88	—	66.9	Yes	Yes	Connecticut.......
74,912						Middle Atlantic......
39,095	28.95	26.7	33.5	Yes	Yes	New York.........
8,152	23.43	17.8	51.8	Yes	Yes	New Jersey........
27,665	25.87	—	40.8	Yes	Yes	Pennsylvania......
10,103						Other..............
355	13.07	—	52.1	Yes	No	Delaware.........
3,768	20.12	16.8	49.6	Yes	Yes	Maryland.........
4,858	17.17	—	43.8	Yes	Yes	West Virginia.....
1,122	27.62	j	51.1	Yes	Yes	District of Columbia
50,441						SOUTHEAST ....
2,452	10.62	21.4	55.8	No	Yes	Virginia..........
4,852	10.40	23.4	63.3	No	No	North Carolina.....
2,654	10.15	0.2	70.4	Yes	No	South Carolina.....
7,036	9.29	5.6	78.6	No	No	Georgia...........
7,228	14.40	—	73.2	Yes	No	Florida...........
6,670	10.20	—	90.8	No	No	Kentucky.........
5,498	12.36	11.8	60.4	No	No	Tennessee........
2,437	9.84	23.1	63.6	Yes	No	Alabama..........
2,923	9.05	0.2	78.3	No	No	Mississippi.......
5,890	14.40	—	47.9	Yes	Yes	Louisiana.........
2,801	14.71	—	64.3	No	No	Arkansas.........
194,030						MIDDLE STATES........
41,263	26.97	—	74.0	Yes	Yes	Ohio..............
16,630	20.90	20.8	67.4	No	Yes	Indiana...........
47,756	27.57	k	58.1	Yes	Yes	Illinois...........
21,664	22.01	k	54.2	Yes	No	Michigan..........
15,308	24.16	20.7	60.0	Yes	Yes	Wisconsin.........
16,935	22.88	18.0	67.0	No	Yes	Minnesota........
14,575	22.06	0.3	79.5	Yes	Yes	Iowa.............
19,899	19.67	0.3	71.6	No	No	Missouri..........
48,262						NORTHWEST........
2,112	19.13	11.1	61.1	Yes	Yes	North Dakota.....
3,403	19.56	0.3	75.1	Yes	Yes	South Dakota.....
8,588	24.27	26.6	63.4	No	No	Kansas...........
6,934	20.85	—	70.4	Yes	Yes	Nebraska..........
18,080	41.06	0.7	80.4	Yes	No	Colorado.........
4,710	27.08	14.9	62.2	No	No	Utah.............
3,363	23.56	17.5	70.0	No	Yes	Montana..........
1,072	26.78	20.4	67.7	Yes	Yes	Wyoming.........
64,997						SOUTHWEST ....
18,765	21.92	—	75.4	No	No	Oklahoma..........
41,221	20.05	—	89.2	No	No	Texas............
1,031	19.08	—	49.6	Yes	Yes	New Mexico.......
3,980	37.22	—	69.7	No	No	Arizona...........
34,726						PACIFIC NORTHWEST.....
2,872	26.80	—	65.7	No	Yes	Idaho.............
6,048	24.71	18.7	72.3	Yes	Yes	Oregon...........
25,806	33.74	—	84.7	Yes	Yes	Washington.......
69,607						PACIFIC SOUTHWEST.....
68,796	36.91	26.1	77.7	Yes	No	California.........
811	31.49	23.8	87.7	No	Yes	Nevada...........

[h] Social Security Board, *Characteristics of State Plans for Old-Age Assistance.*
[i] Rate may be underestimated because of practice with respect to paying benefit to husband and wife.
[j] Not applicable to District of Columbia.   [k] Less than .05 per cent.

States which were below the national average by 20 or more were:[10]

Texas	99	Arizona	91
Georgia	99	South Carolina	89
Alabama	96	North Carolina	89
Louisiana	95	New Mexico	88
District of Columbia	92	Wyoming	84

All the states with low ratios of aged to population 21 to 64 were in the southeast or southwest, excepting Wyoming and the District of Columbia. Of all the southern and southwestern states, Kentucky, with 131, is the only one above the national average of 120, but Florida with 120 and Oklahoma with 118 were close to it. In general, so far as age distribution of the population alone is concerned, the southern and southwestern states occupy a favorable position.

Number of aged recipients of assistance. No consistency among the states is disclosed by the figures with respect to the number of persons 65 years of age and over in the population and the number in receipt of public assistance. For the country as a whole, the number of recipients of old-age assistance per 1,000 persons 65 years of age and over was 238. Although Maine, New Hampshire, and Vermont had higher ratios of aged to total population than any other state, none of them equaled the national average in ratio of recipients to aged population. In fact no northeastern state equaled the national average. States which exceeded the national average by 20 or more are shown in the table on page 41.

Levels of assistance. For the United States as a whole, in 1942 the average old-age assistance payment per case was $23.43 per month. No southeastern state in that year paid as much as $15. The range in the southeast was from $9.05 in Mississippi to $14.71 in Arkansas. Delaware, with $13.07, was the only state outside this group that paid less than $15. States which paid $15 to $20 were West Virginia $17.17, Vermont $17.97, New Mexico $19.08, North Dakota $19.13, South Dakota $19.56, and Missouri $19.67. Of these states which paid less than $20 per month, Vermont with 175 elderly persons per

[10] See table pp. 38–39.

1,000 population 21 to 64, Missouri with 150, and Kentucky with 131 were the only ones in which the relatively heavy numerical load might be a factor in the comparatively low average allowances.

STATES WHICH EXCEEDED BY 20 OR MORE THE NATIONAL AVERAGE
Number of Recipients of Old-Age Assistance
per 1,000 Elderly Population[a]

State	Number of Recipients of Old-Age Assistance per 1,000 Estimated Population 65 Years of Age or Over, 1942	Persons 65 Years of Age or Over per 1,000 Population 21 to 64 Years of Age, 1940
UNITED STATES..............	238	120
Michigan...................	259	109
Nebraska..................	259	145
Wyoming...................	260	84
California.................	267	128
Kentucky..................	271	131
Minnesota.................	282	134
Nevada....................	286	103
Idaho.....................	294	114
South Dakota..............	313	128
Louisiana..................	313	95
Florida....................	322	120
Montana..................	328	112
Missouri..................	339	150
Arizona.	379	91
Washington................	424	137
Georgia	425	99
Utah......................	448	108
Colorado	487	137
Texas.....................	501	99
Oklahoma	523	118

[a] From table pp. 38–39.

States which in 1942 gave average grants of $30 or more are shown in the table on page 42.

Urban versus rural. As one examines these figures, the question arises as to the extent to which differences among the states with respect to size of benefits, load, and so on are related to the degree of urbanization. In 1940 for the country as a whole, 56.5 per cent of the population lived in urban communities. Ten states had 65 per cent or more of their population in urban communities and 14 had less than 35 per cent.[11] In the table on

[11] Census of 1940, *Population*, Vol. 1, p. 19.

STATES WITH AVERAGE GRANTS OF $30 OR MORE, 1942[a]

State	Assistance per Case 1942	Population 65 Years of Age or Over per 1,000 Population 21 to 64 Years 1940	Per Cent of Payment from Local Funds
Nevada	$31.49	103	23.8
Washington	33.74	137	—
Massachusetts	34.23	145	19.0
California	36.91	154	26.1
Arizona	37.22	91	—
Colorado	41.06	137	0.7

[a] From table pp. 38–39.

page 43 we list these states with their percentage urban, their population 65 or over per 1,000 aged 21 to 64, their old-age assistance cases per 1,000 aged 21 to 64, and their average old-age assistance payment.

The first point is that among both the highly urban and the highly rural states there are a few that depart widely from the typical with respect to the size of benefits. Among the urban states with high benefits were California ($36.91) and Massachusetts ($34.23). With these two states eliminated from consideration, the range in the urban states was from $22.01 in Michigan to $29.88 in Connecticut. The two highest paying among the rural states were Arizona ($37.22) and Idaho ($26.80). The remaining rural states fall into two groups, a northern group with payments ranging from $17.17 to $19.56, and a southern group where a range from $9.05 to $10.40 includes all the states except Arkansas ($14.71) and New Mexico ($19.08).

From this review of the statistics as to numbers and levels of assistance it seems reasonably safe to present some conclusions:

1. There were at least six states, Massachusetts, Nevada, Arizona, California, Washington, and Colorado that on a comparative basis were high-paying states. Apparently the level of the benefits results in the main from decisions with respect to policy.

BENEFITS IN STATES WITH SPECIFIED PER CENT URBAN, 1940
I. STATES 65 PER CENT OR MORE URBAN

State	Per Cent Urban[a]	Old-Age Recipients per 1,000 21 to 64	Population 65 or Over per 1,000 21 to 64	Average Benefit
Massachusetts	89.4	33	145	$34.23
Rhode Island	91.6	17	129	24.93
Connecticut	67.8	16	125	29.88
New York	82.8	14	109	28.95
New Jersey	81.6	11	109	23.43
Pennsylvania.	66.5	17	119	25.87
Ohio	66.8	34	134	26.97
Illinois	73.6	31	118	27.57
Michigan	65.7	30	109	22.01
California	71.0	36	128	36.91

II. STATES LESS THAN 35 PER CENT URBAN

State	Per Cent Urban[a]	Old-Age Recipients per 1,000 21 to 64	Population 65 or Over per 1,000 21 to 64	Average Benefit
Vermont	34.3	26	175	$17.97
North Dakota	20.6	27	117	19.13
South Dakota	24.6	41	128	19.56
West Virginia	28.1	24	105	17.17
North Carolina	27.3	22	89	10.40
South Carolina	24.5	23	89	10.15
Georgia	34.4	44	99	9.29
Kentucky	29.8	37	131	10.20
Alabama	30.2	15	96	9.84
Mississippi	19.8	24	106	9.05
Arkansas	22.2	25	108	14.71
Idaho	33.7	36	114	26.80
New Mexico	33.2	19	88	19.08
Arizona	34.8	38	91	37.22

[a] Census of 1940, *Population*, Vol. I, p. 19.

2. There were 12 states with benefits ranging between $9.05 and $14.71, all of which, excepting Delaware, are in the southeastern section. With the exception of Delaware and Florida, they all had more rural than urban population in 1940; and Delaware had only 52.3 per cent urban and Florida 55.1 per cent. The per cent negro in the population of these states in

1940[12] ranged from 7.5 in Kentucky and 13.5 in Delaware to 42.9 in South Carolina and 49.2 in Mississippi. This group of states represents in the main, therefore, the rural south with a high percentage of negroes and a comparatively low cost and level of living.

3. The remaining states can apparently be roughly divided into two groups, the urbanized industrialized states in the north, with payments grouped about the national average of $23.43, and more rural states not in the southeast, with payments per case ranging somewhat lower, say from $17 to $20. The differences between these two groups of states and between states in the same group are not so wide as to suggest radical differences in basic policy and attitudes. Conceivably differences in rents and municipal services as between urban and rural communities where budget deficit methods are used might explain some of the variations between the groups.

4. On the basis of ratio of old people in receipt of assistance to old people in the population or to population 21 to 64 years of age, one would be inclined to question whether Missouri, Oklahoma, Texas, Utah, Montana, and possibly Georgia and Florida should not be grouped with Massachusetts, Nevada, Arizona, California, Washington, and Colorado as states with a possible leaning toward an old-age pension philosophy. The assistance paid per case in these additional states is not high on a comparative basis, but a high proportion of all the old people draw benefits and none of these states has relative responsibility, takes liens on property, or permits recovery of assistance properly given from the estate of a deceased recipient.

Financing. For the nation as a whole in 1942 payments for old-age assistance constituted 63.0 per cent of all payments for public assistance. States which spent less than half their public assistance funds for old age are shown in the table on page 45.

A high percentage of all assistance payments going for old age apparently may result in part from a high level of old-age benefits as in California, Massachusetts, Colorado, Washington, and Nevada or from a concentration on old-age benefits to the exclusion of other forms of public assistance as in Georgia, Mis-

---

[12] Census of 1940, *Population*, Vol. 2, p. 54.

sissippi, and Kentucky. In these three southern states, with average old-age assistance payments of $9.05, $9.29, and $10.20 per case, the percentages of total payments going for old age are 78.3, 78.6, and 90.8. Kentucky, it will be recalled, is the only southeastern state with a ratio of aged to persons 21 to 64 above the figure for the nation.

PROPORTION OF PUBLIC ASSISTANCE FUNDS SPENT FOR OLD-AGE BENEFITS[a]

I. STATES SPENDING LESS THAN 50 PER CENT

State	Per Cent for Old-Age Assistance	Allowance per Case	Number 65 Years or Over per 1,000
New Mexico	49.6	$19.08	88
Maryland	49.6	20.12	117
Louisiana	47.9	14.40	95
Rhode Island	47.3	24.93	129
West Virginia	43.8	17.17	105
Pennsylvania	40.8	25.87	119
New York	33.5	28.95	109

II. STATES SPENDING 75 PER CENT OR MORE

State	Per Cent for Old-Age Assistance	Allowance per Case	Number 65 Years or Over per 1,000
South Dakota	75.1	$19.56	128
Oklahoma	75.4	21.92	118
California	77.7	36.91	128
Mississippi	78.3	9.05	106
Georgia	78.6	9.29	99
Iowa	79.5	22.06	162
Massachusetts	79.6	34.23	145
Colorado	80.4	41.06	137
Washington	84.7	33.74	137
Nevada	87.7	31.49	103
Texas	89.2	20.05	99
Kentucky	90.8	10.20	131

[a] From table pp. 38–39.

METHODS OF FINANCING

The predominant practice among the states was to finance old-age assistance from the general fund. In 1940 all but 18 of the jurisdictions used appropriations from the general fund exclusively, and several of the others depended in part upon them. Several states put some or all of the revenue from liquor, licenses, and amusement taxes into a special welfare fund. Among the states with special provisions worthy of note were:[13]

[13] Social Security Board, *Characteristics of State Plans for Old-Age Assistance*, Bureau of Public Assistance, Publication No. 16, revised July 1, 1940.

ARIZONA—A direct tax levy by the tax commission based on estimate by state board of social security and welfare.

ARKANSAS—Retail sales in addition to liquor, amusements, etc.

COLORADO—Taxes and license fees on retail sales, storage, use, or consumption in addition to liquor.

CONNECTICUT—A poll tax, past payment of which is necessary for eligibility, and general fund.

HAWAII—Tax on compensation and dividends.

IOWA—From revenues of income, corporation, and sales taxes.

KANSAS—Retail sales tax fund.

LOUISIANA—Gasoline tax, sales, and use taxes.

NEBRASKA—Appropriation from motor-fuel taxes, alcoholic-liquor taxes, head taxes, excise taxes, and estate taxes.

NEVADA—Eleven cents ad valorem on all taxable property.

NEW MEXICO—Liquor, corporation franchise, severance taxes, and excise tax on storage, use, and consumption of tangible property.

OKLAHOMA—Consumers' and users' tax.

UTAH—Sales tax.

In those states which require local participation in financing, the more common practice is to appropriate from the general fund. A few states use a special levy earmarked for a welfare fund. Montana used a per capita tax in addition to a real property levy.

ADMINISTRATION

Prior to 1929 in many states the state government itself had little or nothing to do with the administration of public assistance. Such public assistance as was given was administered by local governments. The depression led to the rapid development in many states of State Emergency Relief Administrations which dealt with the national government, first through the Reconstruction Finance Corporation and later the Federal Emergency Relief Administration. The Social Security Act of 1935, with respect to old-age assistance and the two other assistance categories, made it mandatory upon the states to have a state agency responsible either for administering the category or for supervising local agencies administering it. It will be recalled, moreover, that the act also required that the plans be in effect in all political subdivisions of the state, and if administered by them, must be mandatory upon them. Thus the permanent Social Security Act through its grant-in-aid provisions practically made it mandatory that the states which had temporarily entered the relief field during the depression should remain in it.

This action by the national government has great significance with respect to preparedness for any future depression or other emergency which may necessitate granting relief to large numbers. In each state there will be a going organization with at least its headquarters at the state level and with administrative arrangements for covering every political subdivision of the state. There will not be again the confusion, delays, and difficulties that are more or less inevitable in bringing a far-reaching organization into existence almost overnight. State laws and in some instances state constitutions have been amended to make the state practice conform to the requirements of national policy.

The national law left to the states a very considerable leeway for the exercise of legislative discretion with respect to the form of organization which they should adopt. No attempt will here be made to describe the organization in each state. We shall confine our efforts to attempting to indicate some of the administrative issues that arose and the tendencies in solving them.

The Social Security Act provided grants-in-aid, it will be recalled, for three categories of public assistance, the aged, the dependent children, and the needy blind. It made no provision for the ancient residual category, general public assistance. Under the national law the states could, if they would, have a separate state agency for each federally aided category and leave general public assistance entirely to the local governments. Some states set up different organizations for dealing with each federal aid category. In states in which an existing state agency was already working with the blind, there was a tendency to give administration of aid to the blind to it. With this exception, however, the general trend was toward the establishment of a single state department of public welfare with fairly comprehensive jurisdiction.

The national law left each state free to determine whether its welfare department should itself administer directly or whether local agencies should administer under its supervision. American practice with respect to local government of course did not necessitate choice between an extreme form of either alternative. A wide range lay between the two, as is illustrated by the facts for ten states selected and arranged to show gradations, presented in the table on pages 49–51. The headings and descriptions are taken from the Social Security Board's report on *Characteristics of State Plans for Old-Age Assistance*. The percentage of old-age funds supplied by local governments has been added.

An important issue in assistance administration is the form of organization of the state agency, including its relationship to the governor. Some students of public administration believe in what is often termed the strong executive form of organization. Under this form of organization, power and responsibility are centered in the governor, who appoints and removes the one-man head of the administrative agency. In its extreme form the appointee of the governor is not subject to confirmation by the state senate or other legislative body, and if there is any board or council, it is purely advisory and has no legal powers.

In the field of public welfare, few states have adopted this type of organization. As of 1940 only five states had a one-man administration without a board or council and in one of these, Tennessee, a council could with the consent of the governor be appointed by the commissioner. In three of these, Ohio, Kentucky, and Tennessee, appointment was made by the governor alone and in two, Illinois and Minnesota, confirmation by the senate was required. The other states made provision for a board or council.

The extent to which power and responsibility are vested in the legally established council or board and are removed from the governor varies widely. At the one extreme are states in which the legally established board was purely advisory to a director

ADMINISTRATIVE SYSTEMS OF SELECTED STATES

| State | Administration[a] | | | | Percentage Paid from Local Funds[b] |
	Direct Responsibility	Supervisory Responsibility	State Agency	Local Agency	
Delaware....	Old-age welfare commission.	Old-age welfare commission.	Old-age welfare commission (administrative)—4 members appointed by chief justice. Executive director (appointed by commission).		—
Florida........	District welfare board.	State welfare board.	State welfare board (administrative)—7 members appointed by Governor. Commissioner appointed by Governor.		—
Missouri......	State social security commission operating through county offices.	State social security commission.	State social security commission (advisory and administrative)—5 members, qualified voters in the State for 10 years, appointed by Governor with advice and consent of the senate. State administrator appointed by Governor with advice and consent of senate.	County social security commission (advisory)—4 members. Secretary is the executive officer, appointed by State administrator with consent of the commission.	.3
Maryland ...	County welfare board. (Department of Welfare in Baltimore City.)	State department of public welfare.	Board of public welfare—7 members appointed by Governor. Director of public welfare appointed by board.	County welfare board (administrative)—1 county commissioner ex officio, and 6 members appointed by board of county commissioners from list submitted by board of State aid and charities. (Department of Welfare in Baltimore City.) Executive secretary appointed by county welfare board.	16.8

49

[a] Social Security Board, *Characteristics of State Plans for Old-Age Assistance*, Bureau of Public Assistance, Publication No. 16, revised July 1, 1940.
[b] *Social Security Yearbook 1942*, p. 104.

| State | Administration | | | | Percentage Paid from Local Funds[b] |
	Direct Responsibility	Supervisory Responsibility	State Agency[a]	Local Agency	
Minnesota....	County welfare board.	Director of social welfare.	Director of social welfare appointed by Governor with advice and consent of senate.	County welfare board (administrative)—(with few exceptions) 5 members, 3 appointed by county commissioners, 2 by State board from list submitted by county commissioners. Executive secretary appointed by county welfare board in accordance with rules and regulations of State agency.	18.0
New Jersey...	County welfare board.	State department of institutions and agencies; division of old-age assistance.	State board of control of institutions and agencies, 9 unpaid members appointed by Governor and confirmed by senate. Commissioner of institutions and agencies appointed by board.	County welfare board (administrative)—8 members: 5 selected by county board of freeholders, 3 ex officio members, 2 of whom are members of the board of chosen freeholders and the third the county adjuster. Director of welfare appointed by county board.	17.8
New York....	County or city public-welfare district or city old-age assistance district.	State department of social welfare.	State board of social welfare—15 members appointed by Governor with consent of senate. Commissioner of social welfare appointed by board.	City commissioner of public welfare generally appointed by mayor or city council; county commissioner of public welfare sometimes appointed by county board of supervisors but generally elected.	26.7
Washington...	County welfare department.	State department of social welfare.	Social security committee—Governor, director of finance, and third member appointed by Governor. Director of social security appointed by Governor with consent of senate. Welfare survey commission (advisory)—5 members appointed by the Governor.	Boards of county commissioners. Administrator. Advisory committee—5 local citizens appointed by county commissioners in co-operation with the State department.	—

ADMINISTRATIVE SYSTEMS OF SELECTED STATES—*Continued*

State	Administration[a]				Percentage Paid from Local Funds[b]
	Direct Responsibility	Supervisory Responsibility	State Agency	Local Agency	
California....	County board of supervisors—authority delegated to county welfare department or county welfare agent.	State department of social welfare.	Social welfare board (administrative)—7 members appointed by Governor. Director of social welfare, ex officio secretary to the board of social welfare, appointed by State board.	County board of supervisors (administrative)—authority delegated to county welfare department or county welfare agent.	26.1
Massachusetts	Old-age assistance bureaus of the several towns under the local boards of public welfare.	State department of public welfare.	Commissioner of public welfare, appointed by Governor and council. Advisory board—commissioner, ex officio, and 6 members selected in the same manner.	Bureau of old-age assistance, a division of board of public welfare. (Board consists of 3 or 5 elected members.) Selectmen may act as board of public welfare. In cities and towns assisting 100 or more individuals a supervisor of old-age assistance is appointed by bureau. In cities and towns assisting 50 or less, a member of the bureau may be appointed as supervisor.	19.0

appointed and removed by the governor. At the other were North Carolina, where the seven members of the state board were elected by the general assembly upon recommendation of the governor, and the commissioner of public welfare was employed by the state board by and with the approval of the governor, and Delaware, where the four members of the Old Age Welfare Commission were appointed by the chief justice, and they in turn appoint the executive director.

In a few states a small board of paid members actually carries on the detailed administration. For example, as of 1940 Iowa had an administrative board of three members appointed by the governor with approval of two thirds of the Senate for six-year overlapping terms, with the added provision that one member must be a woman.

The more common practice is to have an executive officer responsible for the details of administration with a larger board which meets from time to time. The powers vested in these boards vary widely. As previously noted, some of them are solely advisory to an executive officer appointed by the governor. Some are purely advisory to an executive officer appointed and removed by the board, but this appointing power makes the board responsible for the success of administration. Some, in states where the governor appoints the executive officer, are legally vested with the policy-determining functions so that they are responsible for the quasi-legislative actions but not for the details of administration. Then there are some in which all the legal powers are vested in the board itself, so that it is responsible for both policy and administration; the executive officer appointed by it has no authority beyond that delegated to him by the board.

CHAPTER III

AID TO DEPENDENT CHILDREN

Title IV of the Social Security Act adopted in 1935 provided federal grants to such states as would adopt programs of aid to dependent children that complied with the requirements of the national act. The present chapter will deal primarily with that program. At the outset we shall present in broad outline the evolution in care for dependent children that preceded the passage of the national act. We shall then take up the more essential features of the national act, following that with a generalized description of what the several states have done legislatively with respect to such features as eligibility and amount of grant. We shall then present, for the several states, figures as to the number of children, the number in receipt of assistance, and the amount of grant.

THE EVOLUTION OF AID FOR DEPENDENT CHILDREN

American public opinion has long recognized that dependent children present a distinctive problem. By nature children are dependent. They cannot be expected to be self-supporting or to direct their own affairs. If they are in difficulties, it is generally not their own fault. Childhood and youth are the period of preparation for what may be a long life. The democratic state has an interest in making it a good and useful life. Fairly early in American history came provisions for educating children, for preventing certain forms of cruelty and exploitation, and for caring for orphans.

Private philanthropy and some governments early provided orphan asylums where young children could be sent rather than to almshouses. Frequently, when one parent died, the children were placed in a public or private asylum. Maintaining such an institution was in many instances a function of the church or of a benevolent fraternity, and many a philanthropist in his will left money to these institutions, sometimes even

53

going so far as to establish and endow one. This action represented a great advance over putting the children in a public poor house, giving them to persons who abused or exploited them, or letting them shift for themselves without sufficient care or guidance.

Gradually persons who dealt with dependent children became convinced that institutional care was markedly inferior to home care for the normal child. The children in many institutions were regimented, treated more or less *en masse*, and grew up without family ties. Ties with the institution were commonly broken when the child left, and many of them left as soon as they reached the legal working age. Some of them continued to be problems of social agencies. Helping them to readjust was difficult because of their institutional background and lack of normal connections in the community. The principle became generally accepted that for the normal child a good home was superior to even the best of institutions.

Child placing institutions developed in the communities that accepted this new point of view. They encountered difficulties in finding good foster homes and exercising the necessary supervision over them to see that the children received proper care. It became apparent that many children were being placed in institutions or in foster homes because their widowed mothers were too poor to make a home for them. If the mother went out to earn a living, the children were frequently neglected. Relatives who might have made a home for the family often lacked the means to do so. Then the pertinent question was asked, "If the government pays foster parents unrelated to the children to care for them, why should it not pay a child's own mother or other suitable relatives to care for them?" The argument ran: "The mother who gives a child proper care and supervision is rendering a social and economic service to the state. Ordinarily she is maintained by the earnings of a husband. If something deprives her of this support, why should not the government supply the support and enable her to give the child the advantages of a normal home and normal community associations?"

Early laws adopting this philosophy and providing for payments to mothers for the care of dependent children were called "Mothers' Pension Laws" or sometimes "Widows' Pension Laws." The widowed mother represented the typical case, but children were also rendered dependent by the disability or the desertion of the father and sometimes by the disability, death, or desertion of the mother. Eligibility rules were therefore broadened, and payments could be made to children who were cared for by relatives other than the mother.

State legislation providing for this type of care for dependent children often displayed three common characteristics.

1. Administrative responsibility was frequently vested in a special agency or in an appropriate court, and thus these children were removed from the jurisdiction of the local agencies administering the poor laws.

2. The rules regarding the size of the grants which might be made were more liberal than the prevailing practice with respect to the administration of general public assistance.

3. Frequently the state laws were of the optional or permissive type and were accepted by the larger cities with industrial and commercial economies to a far greater extent than they were by rural districts. States predominantly rural and agricultural frequently did not adopt any laws of this type at all.

In many communities that had a law of this type, the idea prevailed that the new system was to be used only when the mother or other relative who was to care for the child was a superior person, who measured up to community standards of conduct. Grants were frequently denied if the mother or other relative was in the opinion of the granting officer not entirely worthy. Children of mothers not deemed worthy were left to be cared for by the old methods. Many social workers thoroughly disapproved of this distinction. They believed that the grants should be more generally used, and that the families should be carefully supervised in an effort to correct the difficulties, some of which may have resulted from lack of means.

When the Social Security Act was passed in 1935, it provided federal grants to the states for dependent children but required the states to adopt the philosophy of this more advanced method of caring for dependent children.

AID UNDER THE SOCIAL SECURITY ACT

The definition of a dependent child under the act, as amended in 1939, reads:

The term "dependent child" means a *needy* child under the age of sixteen, *or under the age of eighteen if found by the State agency to be regularly attending school,* who has been deprived of parental support or care by reason of the death, continued absence from the home, or physical or mental incapacity of a parent, and who is living with his father, mother, grandfather, grandmother, brother, sister, stepfather, stepmother, stepbrother, stepsister, uncle, or aunt, in a place of residence maintained by one or more of such relatives as his or their own home . . . .[1]

Four points regarding the eligibility requirements of the national act require special emphasis.

1. A dependent child who has no relative within the degrees specified by the act is not eligible for a federal grant. Such a child must be provided for by the state, the local government, or the two combined without federal contribution.

2. If the state or local administrative authorities decide that no relative within the degrees specified by the national government is a suitable custodian of or homemaker for the child, the national government will not share in the cost of relieving the child's need.

3. If existing relatives within the specified degrees decline to assume responsibility for the child, and it is necessary to place him in a foster home, the national government does not pay half the cost of assistance under the Social Security Act.

4. If the physical, mental, or moral limitations of the child make it desirable to place him in an appropriate institution for care and treatment, the national government does not pay under the aid to dependent children title.

The national government thus places great pressure on the state authorities to use that method of provision deemed best

[1] 53 Stat. 1380, sec. 403. The insertions made in the 1939 amendments are printed in italics.

for the normal child who has relatives within the specified degree. The penalty for not using it is no federal participation in the assistance payment.

Four facts must, however, be remembered in this connection:

1. No great political pressure group has ever developed to further adequate provision at public expense for dependent children, in any sense comparable with the pressure group which favors adequate provision for the aged.

2. Despite the inducement of national contributions, many communities still adhere to the view that only morally acceptable relatives should be given the custody of dependent children and indirectly get the benefit of grants to the children.

3. Many states make little provision for needy dependent children who are not eligible under the national act or whose relatives are not deemed suitable guardians by state or local officials.

4. In some states, state and local funds are so largely absorbed in matching federal money for the aged and eligible dependent children that little is left for children who can only be provided for through general public assistance.

The administrative requirements set up by the Social Security Act with respect to dependent children are substantially the same as those already described in connection with old-age assistance.

The residence requirements for aid to dependent children give the states less latitude than do the residence requirements for old-age assistance. No child residing in the state can be denied aid "(1) who has resided in the State for one year immediately preceding the application for such aid, or (2) who was born within the State within one year immediately preceding the application, if its mother has resided in the State for one year immediately preceding the birth."[2]

The maximum grant in which the national government will share is $18 a month for the first child and $12 a month for each additional eligible child. As in old-age assistance the national government under the 1939 amendment shares to the extent of

[2] 49 Stat. 627–28, sec. 402(b).

one half of the grant. It also contributes one half of the expenditures of the state made in administering the state plan approved by the Social Security Board.

As in the case of old-age assistance, the national government does not prescribe standards as to need or the amount of grant nor has it adopted any measures to force the states to make suitable appropriations.

With respect to the maximum grant in which the national government will share, emphasis must be placed on the fact that the grant is made solely with respect to the child. There is no grant with respect to the mother or other relative who is to have the care and custody of the child. Thus for the needy widow 65 years of age or over without any dependent child under 18 the national government will contribute one half of any grant allowed by the state up to $40 a month, whereas for the family consisting of a needy widow with one eligible dependent child, the nation will contribute one half of any grant given by the state up to $18 a month. For the use of the elderly widow the national government will give as much as $20; for the use of the younger widow and child together, as much as $9.00.

WHAT THE STATES HAVE DONE

The national government, as just stated, used the grant-in-aid principle to induce states to adopt a particular and not all-inclusive program for the care of dependent children. It was not unnatural that under such circumstances some states should establish as their maximum child allowances the maximum set by Congress as the limit to what the state would pay. Thus in the state plans for A.D.C. as published by the Social Security Board for 1940, there were eleven states that adopted the national limits as their maximum limits, two that used a somewhat lower maximum, and three that perhaps with an eye to the future used in effect "maximum amount for which federal reimbursement will be made." Two states used the same form of limitation adopted by the national act but raised the maximum to $20 for the first child and increased the maximum for additional children, although not on precisely the same basis. In 20 states the plan provided no limitation, which meant of course that if more than the national maximum were given to any child, the state or the state and the local government had to bear the full cost of the extra allowance.

As in the case of old-age assistance, the national government did not prescribe standards for determining need but left that matter to the several states subject to the approval of their plans by the federal board.[3] Most state plans define need in part by repeating the national definition previously quoted beginning with the words, "deprived of parental support or care." For further definition most of them use general words such as: "Income of legally responsible relatives insufficient to provide adequate care and support of child without public assistance." "Does not have any person and does not live in custody of person who has sufficient income or other resources to provide a reasonable subsistence compatible with decency and health." "Assistance plus income and support to be sufficient to provide a reasonable subsistence compatible with health and decency." "Has no adequate means of support."

In the A.D.C. plans there is a notable absence of attempts specifically to define need in terms of money income as was done by several states with respect to old-age assistance. The 1940 digest of plans however gave: for California, "No child for whose specific support $25 per month is available is eligible for aid. A family may not possess personal property in excess of $500 and no orphan child more than $250 cash"; for Florida, "Liquid assets and income should not usually exceed $360"; for Massachusetts, "Cash on hand not to exceed $300"; for Minnesota, "Mother, father, or child must not own personal property of reasonable market value in excess of $300, exclusive of appropriate and necessary personal belongings"; for Missouri, "May not possess $500 or more in cash or negotiable securities"; for Vermont, "Family with monthly budget deficit of

---

[3] The 1939 amendments added a requirement that the state plan must "provide that the State agency shall, in determining need, take into consideration any other income and resources of any child claiming aid to dependent children." 53 Stat. 1379, sec. 401(b).

less than $5 not eligible. . . . Personal property exceeding $300 will be considered as available for current expenses."[4]

As in old-age assistance, a few states have provisions specifically permitting ownership of specified classes and amounts of property. For example, California permits ownership of real property of not over $3,000 and $500 in personal property for the family or $250 in cash for an orphan child; insurance policies with premiums not exceeding $4.00 per month may be continued; and average earnings under $10 of working children under 18 are not figured in regular income. Delaware permits full or partial equity in a house, income producing property provided such income is not sufficient to meet budgetary needs, and possession of cash not exceeding $1,000. Oklahoma permits the parents or the children to own real property used as a home up to $2,500 in market value and/or in liquid assets, $250 if single, or $400 if married. Rhode Island permits an equity up to $2,500 in a $5,000 home used as a residence provided the carrying charges do not exceed reasonable rental.[5] In some states no family possessed of such resources would be considered in need, but would be required to maintain itself through the use of these resources until they were much more nearly exhausted.

Provisions are not uniform with respect to the maximum age limit for eligibility. It will be recalled that the Social Security Act as passed in 1935 fixed 16 years of age as the upper limit. The 1939 act added the words, "or under the age of eighteen if found by the State Agency to be regularly attending school."[6] Some states have adopted the precise requirements of the national act, others have retained age 16 as the limit, and a few have 18 years without the school attendance requirement.

Use of a precise maximum age limit and failure to make provision for the responsible widow or other relative will result in some cases in a sharp break when the youngest eligible child attains the maximum age limit. We may illustrate this point by a hypothetical case.

[4] Social Security Board, *Characteristics of State Plans for Aid to Dependent Children.* Bureau of Public Assistance, Publication No. 18, revised July 1, 1940.

[5] The same.

[6] Social Security Board, *Compilation of the Social Security Laws . . . .* Jan. 3, 1941, sec. 406(a).

A father died of tuberculosis at the age of 35 leaving a widow aged 30 with three children, aged respectively 10, 8, and 3. For the first eight years following the father's death the family of four would have through A.D.C. a maximum allowance of $42 per month, which incidentally exceeds by only $2.00 the maximum allowance for a needy widow 65 years of age or over under old-age assistance.

Eight years after the death of the father, when his widow would be 38 years old the allowance would be cut to $30 a month, as the oldest child has reached 18. Two years later when the widow would be 40 the allowance would be further cut to $18, since now she would have only one eligible child, aged 13.

Five years later when the widow has attained the age of 45, the allowance would stop, for by then the youngest child would be 18. If she should survive to age 65 and be a resident of a state which pays high benefits to the aged, she might draw from the public treasury almost as much as her family did when it consisted of herself and three dependent children under 18 years of age.

Under the categorical system dictated to the states by the Social Security Act, the state or the state and the local government together are supposed to take care of any needs of the widow and her family, not met through the A.D.C. payment, without any assistance from the national government. There are some states which would do it. Others, as we have noted, devote so much to the federally aided categories that little is available for others in need.

STATISTICS OF THE PROGRAM

As of December 31, 1942 the number of children in receipt of aid to dependent children was about 848,600 and the annual cost of their benefits, exclusive of administrative costs, was about 158.5 million dollars. The average payment per child was a little less than $15 and the average payment per family a little more than $36. Thus the average family in receipt of A.D.C. had two to three children on benefit and had at least one adult member responsible for the children who was not entitled to any direct benefit under this program, but presum-

State	Children Under 18 Years of Age, 1940			Children in Receipt of A.D.C., December 1942		
	Number in Thousands[a]	Number per 1,000 Total Population	Number per 1,000 Population 21 to 64	Number in Thousands[b]	Number per 1,000 Children Under 18[c]	Number per 1,000 Population 21 to 64 1940
UNITED STATES	40,287	306	537	848.6	21	11.3
NORTHEAST	11,314	278	467	251.4		10.4
New England	2,343	278	476	41.4		8.4
Maine	269	318	594	4.9	18	10.8
New Hampshire	141	287	511	2.1	15	7.6
Vermont	112	312	577	1.8	16	9.3
Massachusetts	1,170	271	459	23.9	20	9.4
Rhode Island	198	278	471	3.3	17	7.9
Connecticut	453	265	439	5.4	12	5.2
Middle Atlantic	7,502	272	450	162.8		9.8
New York	3,437	255	408	49.0	14	5.8
New Jersey	1,094	263	428	16.1	15	6.3
Pennsylvania	2,971	300	524	97.7	33	17.2
Other	1,469	316	559	47.2		18.0
Delaware	74	277	471	1.0	13	6.4
Maryland	532	292	501	12.5	23	11.8
West Virginia	718	377	743	30.7	43	31.8
District of Columbia	145	219	327	3.0	21	6.8
SOUTHEAST	10,432	369	717	175.8		12.1
Virginia	933	349	657	13.3	14	9.4
North Carolina	1,403	393	792	21.2	15	12.0
South Carolina	773	407	849	11.2	14	12.3
Georgia	1,150	368	713	11.2	10	6.9
Florida	576	304	529	12.0	21[h]	11.0
Kentucky	1,041	366	719	1.5	1[h]	1.0
Tennessee	1,034	355	673	34.5	33	22.5
Alabama	1,097	387	770	14.9	14	10.5
Mississippi	851	390	787	6.3	7	5.8
Louisiana	846	358	674	34.6	41	27.5
Arkansas	728	374	732	15.1	21	15.2
MIDDLE STATES	10,307	288	496	236.1		11.4
Ohio	1,951	282	482	28.1	14	6.9
Indiana	1,009	294	518	27.1	27	13.9
Illinois	2,104	266	437	57.6	27	12.0
Michigan	1,599	304	525	44.1	28	14.5
Wisconsin	954	304	537	22.7	24	12.8
Minnesota	842	302	532	18.8	22	11.9
Iowa	762	300	540	6.3	8[h]	4.5
Missouri	1,086	287	499	31.4	29	14.4
NORTHWEST	2,205	320	583	60.1		15.9
North Dakota	230	358	689	6.1	26	18.3
South Dakota	217	337	631	4.2	19	12.2
Kansas	541	300	538	13.8	26	13.7
Nebraska	407	309	557	10.3	25[h]	14.1
Colorado	349	311	556	12.3	35	19.6
Utah	208	378	748	6.5	31	23.4
Montana	172	308	538	5.3	31	16.6
Wyoming	81	323	566	1.6	20	11.2
SOUTHWEST	3,404	348	647	80.5		15.3
Oklahoma	828	354	676	41.7	50	34.1
Texas	2,177	339	620	26.6	12	7.6
New Mexico	216	406	828	6.9	32	26.4
Arizona	183	367	693	5.3	29	20.1
PACIFIC NORTHWEST	917	274	462	19.5		9.8
Idaho	181	345	644	6.3	35	22.4
Oregon	285	261	435	3.8	13	5.8
Washington	451	260	430	9.4	21	9.0
PACIFIC SOUTHWEST	1,711	244	389	25.2		5.7
California	1,681	243	388	25.0	15	5.8
Nevada	30	273	441	.2	8[h]	2.9

[a] Compiled from Census of 1940, *Population*, Vol. II, Pt. i, pp. 56–78.
[b] *Social Security Yearbook 1942*, p. 181.
[c] The same, p. 74.
[d] The same, p. 72.
[e] The same, p. 76.

	Payments for Aid to Dependent Children, 1942				State
Total in Thousands[d]	Average Payment per Child	Average Payment per Family Dec. 1942[e]	Per Cent from Local Funds[f]	Per Cent of All Spent[g]	
$158,497	$14.88	$36.25	17.6	17.2	United States........
	19.47				Northeast...........
11,736	23.30				New England.......
898	15.61	43.76	29.1	13.9	Maine...........
475	20.13	50.03	—	13.8	New Hampshire....
279	12.23	32.86	23.9	16.2	Vermont.........
8,154	26.27	64.08	37.7	19.6	Massachusetts....
783	20.58	55.57	11.2	17.6	Rhode Island......
1,147	23.71	61.03	28.0	12.8	Connecticut.......
43,670	20.76				Middle Atlantic......
16,688	26.41	53.42	49.2	14.2	New York........
3,137	13.96	32.11	32.1	19.7	New Jersey........
23,845	19.05	48.21	—	35.5	Pennsylvania......
7,256	11.64				Other..........
189	13.04	35.81	22.7	29.5	Delaware.........
2,079	12.19	34.31	12.7	27.9	Maryland.........
4,501	11.25	30.54	—	40.3	West Virginia......
487	12.82	39.11	—	23.6	District of Columbia
17,763	8.42				Southeast..........
1,205	7.37	20.99	21.6	28.5	Virginia.........
1,998	7.45	17.51	23.2	26.6	North Carolina.....
768	5.52	16.12	.2	20.8	South Carolina.....
1,262	9.57	23.08	5.3	13.5	Georgia..........
1,593	10.48	24.28	11.4	16.2	Florida..........
191	10.73	i	95.9	2.5	Kentucky.........
3,206	7.76	19.61	15.7	35.2	Tennessee........
1,027	5.82	16.53	24.3	28.3	Alabama.........
623	7.89	20.17	.1	16.4	Mississippi........
4,742	11.01	28.26	—	39.5	Louisiana........
1,148	8.47	22.23	—	26.0	Arkansas.........
44,289	15.50				Middle States......
5,308	15.39	40.27	30.2	10.2	Ohio............
5,384	15.01	32.01	22.6	22.2	Indiana..........
8,882	14.35	32.50	.4	11.3	Illinois...........
10,537	19.03	47.55	8.3	26.0	Michigan.........
5,263	17.72	41.95	33.8	20.8	Wisconsin........
3,677	14.76	35.55	34.6	15.1	Minnesota........
720	8.93	19.61	100.0	3.7	Iowa............
4,518	13.30	30.73	.3	16.3	Missouri.........
11,377	14.03				Northwest..........
936	12.06	33.65	25.9	27.4	North Dakota.....
634	12.40	29.01	.4	14.4	South Dakota.....
2,728	15.55	37.85	41.8	20.4	Kansas..........
1,906	13.32	31.63	5.8	20.8	Nebraska........
2,133	12.68	31.68	25.1	10.0	Colorado.........
1,822	17.86	47.40	14.8	24.6	Utah............
929	12.78	31.79	16.3	19.3	Montana.........
289	12.79	34.67	19.1	19.1	Wyoming.........
9,468	10.08				Southwest..........
4,962	9.69	22.60	.1	20.2	Oklahoma........
2,754	9.52	21.33	i	7.1	Texas............
842	12.63	36.59	—	40.2	New Mexico......
910	12.67	34.91	—	16.5	Arizona..........
4.692	18.20				Pacific Northwest.....
1,125	13.41	34.86	—	25.9	Idaho ....
1,083	21.62	50.09	23.8	13.3	Oregon..........
2,484	20.03	49.32	—	8.5	Washington........
8,239	23.36				Pacific Southwest.....
8,207	23.43	57.48	31.0	10.0	California........
32	13.98	25.19	100.0	3.3	Nevada..........

[f] The same, p. 104.
[g] The same, p. 106.
[h] Includes or relates to programs administered under state law without federal participation.
[i] Not computed; data on cases and payments estimated.
[j] Less than .05 per cent.

ably shared in the children's benefits. The children on benefit numbered 21 per 1,000 under 18 years of age as estimated for 1942 by the Social Security Board. There were 11.3 children on A.D.C. on December 31, 1942 for each 1,000 population 21 to 64 at the census of 1940.

Variations among the several states were fairly wide. To show these variations, a summary table is presented on pages 62–63. It shows first the number of children under 18 in the total population, and the ratio of children to total population and to population 21 to 64 years. It then gives the number of A.D.C. and the number per 1,000 children in the population as estimated for 1942 and per 1,000 population 21 to 64 at the census of 1940. The final section deals with finances, showing the aggregate expenditures, the expenditures per child and per family, the percentage of the expenditures which came from local funds and the percentage which expenditures for A.D.C. formed of all expenditures for relief. Some of the more significant facts evident from this table will be briefly considered.

The rural states, it will be noted, generally have a much higher ratio of children under 18 to population 21 to 64 than do the more urban states. This is particularly true in the southeastern states, especially in those with a large percentage of negroes in the total population. In many of the southeastern states the number of children per 1,000 population 21 to 64 years exceeded 700. Outside the southeastern states the only states with 700 or more were New Mexico 828, Utah 748, and West Virginia, which might be classified as southeastern, 743. Arizona fell just short of 700 with 693.

The corresponding table for old-age assistance (pages 38–39), it may be recalled, showed that the southeastern states in general had a relatively light load of persons 65 years of age or over per 1,000 persons 21 to 64. Thus the figures would suggest that in the southeastern states provision for the education and development of the children is relatively of far greater moment than elaborate provision for the aged.

The highly urbanized and industrialized states tend to have a low ratio of children under 18 per 1,000 population 21 to 64 years of age. States with a ratio lower than 475 were:[7]

California	388	Connecticut	439
New York	408	Nevada	441
New Jersey	428	Massachusetts	459
Washington	430	Rhode Island	471
Oregon	435	Delaware	471
Illinois	437		

The entirely urban District of Columbia was lower than any of the states with 327. If the limit be raised to 501 children per 1,000 population 21 to 64, three states would be added, Ohio with 482, Missouri with 499, and Maryland with 501.

The ratio of children in receipt of aid to dependent children per 1,000 adults 21 to 64 for the United States as a whole was 11.3. States which had 20 or more were:[8]

Oklahoma	34.1	Utah	23.4
West Virginia	31.8	Tennessee	22.5
Louisiana	27.5	Idaho	22.4
New Mexico	26.4	Arizona	20.1

States with 8 or less were:[9]

Connecticut	5.2	District of Columbia	6.8
New York	5.8	Georgia	6.9
Mississippi	5.8	Ohio	6.9
Oregon	5.8	New Hampshire	7.6
California	5.8	Texas	7.6
New Jersey	6.3	Massachusetts	7.9
Delaware	6.4	Rhode Island	7.9

The industrialized urban states with a low ratio of children to population 21 to 64 and a low ratio of A.D.C. beneficiaries to that population were in general the ones which gave high benefits per child or per family, for which they have to make substantial contributions from their own funds. The average benefit in 1942 was just under $15 per child. States which paid $19 or more per child are shown in the following table.

---

[7] See table pp. 62–63.

[8] The same.

[9] The same. Kentucky with 1.0, Iowa with 4.5, and Nevada with 2.9 are omitted because the programs there are not comparable.

STATES WITH AVERAGE GRANTS OF $19 OR MORE

State	Average Benefit per Child	Average Benefit per Family[a]	Per Cent of A.D.C. Paid from Federal Funds[b]
New York..............	26.41	53.42	29.9
Massachusetts...........	26.27	64.08	30.2
Connecticut.............	23.71	61.03	31.6
California...............	23.43	57.48	33.3
Oregon.................	21.62	50.09	35.8
Rhode Island...........	20.58	55.57	35.9
New Hampshire.........	20.13	50.03	36.0
Washington.............	20.03	49.32	38.5
Pennsylvania............	19.05	48.21	37.8
Michigan...............	19.03	47.55	36.5

[a] *Social Security Year Book 1942*, p. 76.
[b] The same, p. 104.

The table below gives corresponding figures for states which had a complete program in co-operation with the national government and gave benefits of less than $9.00 per child per month.

STATES WITH AVERAGE GRANTS OF $9.00 OR LESS

State	Average Benefit per Child	Average Benefit per Family	Per Cent of A.D.C. Paid from Federal Funds
South Carolina..........	5.52	16.12	47.0
Alabama...............	5.82	16.53	50.0
Virginia................	7.37	20.99	50.0
North Carolina.........	7.45	17.51	50.0
Tennessee..............	7.76	19.61	50.0
Mississippi.............	7.89	20.17	50.0
Arkansas...............	8.47	22.23	50.0

The extensive use of local funds to support A.D.C. is worthy of note. For the United States as a whole, the percentage of the total expenditures supplied by local funds in 1942 was 17.6 as contrasted with 9.4, the corresponding figure for old-age assistance. According to the Social Security Board, for the children's program there were only 10 states which had no contributions from local governments in 1942 and only 7 where the local contribution was less than 5 per cent. For old-age assistance, on the other hand, there were 20 states with no local contributions and 7 where the local contributions were less than 5 per cent. Thus states with less than 5 per cent from local funds numbered

16 for aid to dependent children and 27 for old-age assistance. Among states which had 5 per cent or more from local funds for both programs, the percentage was generally higher for the children's program.

It would be interesting to know why the percentage of costs borne by local governments was generally higher for the children's program than for old-age assistance. Several different factors may play a part. The old-age program is of course almost everywhere materially more expensive, and the states may pay more because of the costs. For the 50 jurisdictions combined, 63 per cent of all public assistance went for the aged and 17.2 for aid to dependent children. In two states, West Virginia and New Mexico, in 1942 over 40 per cent went for aid to dependent children, almost as much as for the aged. For some of the states with the so-called old-age pension philosophy we find figures such as: Washington, 84.7 for old age, 8.5 for A.D.C.; Colorado, 80.4 for old age, 10 per cent for A.D.C.; Massachusetts, 79.6 for the aged, 19.6 for A.D.C.; Oklahoma, 75.4 for old age, 20.2 for A.D.C.; Arizona, 69.7 for old age, 16.5 for A.D.C.[10]

It is probably true that political pressure is greater for old-age assistance than for aid to dependent children. The mere number of beneficiaries is indicative of the difference; as of December 31, 1942 the numbers on benefit were 2,226,000 for old-age assistance, 848,600 for the children. All the children were below voting age; all the old people were of voting age. Promoters could organize the aged, especially if the bait of universal pensions were used, whereas it would be difficult to organize the dependent children or the mothers of dependent children.

These figures suggest the possibility that in developing programs by separate categories the matter of comparative importance has been at least partially neglected, but that subject will be considered in Part III.

[10] For the figures by states see *Social Security Year Book 1942*, p. 106.

CHAPTER IV

THE NEEDY BLIND

Physical and mental disabilities have always been a cause of need. The disabled one frequently is unable to support himself and those who may have been dependent on him. One of the fairly early groups differentiated from the mass were those suffering from severe mental impairments. Provision for them was made by giving both support and treatment in hospitals for the insane, usually state operated.[1] Much later support and care were frequently provided for the feeble minded, usually in state institutions, and for the tubercular in state or local institutions.

Two other classes of disabled secured special consideration, perhaps mainly as the result of the development of the public educational system. The congenitally deaf—often referred to in earlier days as the deaf and dumb—and the blind from birth or early childhood could not usually be provided for in the public schools operated by local governmental units, and they were not ordinarily sufficiently numerous to warrant the maintenance of special schools by the local governments. State schools for the deaf and state schools for the blind were established by a number of states, furnishing support and special education. These special schools generally had distinctly vocational aspects, because it was obvious that occupational opportunities for these classes were limited. In several states, the state operated workshops for the blind. The state agency responsible for the school for the blind became responsible in some cases for the maintenance of these workshops and for the re-education and occupational rehabilitation of persons who lost their sight after childhood. In many communities the work for the adult blind was little developed, and many who became blind in later life were dependent on general public assistance or private

[1] The care and treatment were not necessarily given without payment by relatives if they had sufficient means to pay at least part of the costs.

68

benevolence. A blind man who begged at crowded centers was not at all unusual.

Groups of able, intelligent persons became greatly concerned for the welfare of the blind, for perhaps two main reasons. First, the plight of the blind naturally enlisted great sympathy and the desire to do something constructive to aid the victims. Second, scientific knowledge had demonstrated that blindness was to a very considerable extent preventable, and that in many instances lost vision could be at least partially restored by remedial action. Hundreds of people were in want because of blindness who, had they the resources, the knowledge of what could be done, and the necessary initiative, could be made self-supporting and independent. These groups were doing effective work for the blind both through public and private agencies.

SOCIAL SECURITY ACT PROVISIONS

When the Social Security Act was proposed, giving among other things federal assistance in provision for the needy aged and for the dependent children, these groups effectively presented the case for the needy blind. Their activity explains the fact that the needy blind were set up as a special category and given aid by the federal government, whereas no provision was made for those disabled from other causes unless they were 65 years of age and over and could thus qualify for old-age assistance. Thus if a state would adopt a plan for the blind acceptable under the national act, the blind were out from under general public assistance where those disabled from other causes had to remain.

The act makes provision for "needy" individuals who are "blind." Both the definition of needy and the definition of blind are left to the states, subject, however, to the approval of the state plan by the Social Security Board. The act specifically excludes from eligibility the blind person who is an inmate of a public institution. It also provides that no aid will be furnished under the plan to an individual covering any period with respect to which he is receiving old-age assistance under the federal-state plan.

State	Recipients of Aid to Blind, December 1942			Expenditures for Assistance to the Blind 1942			
	Number (Actual)[a]	Per 100 000 Estimated Population 1942	Per 100,000 Population 21 to 64 1940	Total[c]	Per Case[d]	Per Cent from Local Funds[e]	Per Cent of All Assistance Payments[f]
UNITED STATES[g]	79,041	60	105	24,674,702			
NORTHEAST	21,915			7,552,989			
New England	2,839			859,377			
Maine	1,027	123	227	291,113	22.95		4.5
New Hampshire	326	69	118	94,301	24.23		2.8
Vermont	156	45	80	42,871	22.60		2.6
Massachusetts	1,035	24	41	328,654	25.46		.8
Rhode Island	96	13	23	26,222	23.11		.6
Connecticut	199	11	19	76,216	31.71		.8
Middle Atlantic	17,233			6,145,148			
New York	2,688	21	32	949,350	30.04	28.7	.9
New Jersey	688	16	27	211,942	25.47	47.5	1.4
Pennsylvania[h]	13,857	143	244	4,983,856	29.78		6.7
Other	1,843			548,464			
Maryland	557	29	52	165,185	23.35	33.6	2.1
West Virginia	996	53	103	271,273	22.02		2.5
District of Columbia	290	35	65	112,006	33.76		5.0
SOUTHEAST	15,583			2,377,009			
Virginia	1,046	37	74	167,287	13.35	20.9	4.1
North Carolina	2,234	64	126	405,834	15.39	25.4	6.0
South Carolina	817	43	90	102,884	10.36	.4	3.0
Georgia	2,187	71	136	284,550	12.20	5.5	3.2
Florida	2,697	138	248	494,308	15.41	.2	5.1
Kentucky	359	13	25	4,475	12.47		.6
Tennessee	1,652	56	108	242,212	12.64	12.0	2.6
Alabama	642	22	45	75,584	10.53	24.2	2.1
Mississippi	1,334	62	123	169,185	10.63	.1	4.5
Louisiana	1,455	60	116	280,449	18.13		2.3
Arkansas	1,160	59	117	150,241	16.20		3.5
MIDDLE STATES	22,562			7,247,301			
Ohio	3,858	55	95	992,442	21.93	34.0	2.0
Indiana	2,348	67	121	678,226	28.25	2.4	2.9
Illinois[h]	7,486	93	156	2,723,869	30.99	50.0[i]	3.2
Michigan	1,373	25	45	434,915	28.16	[j]	1.1
Wisconsin	1,844	60	104	554,616	24.56	20.4	2.2
Minnesota	1,026	38	65	340,449	28.60	4.9	1.4
Iowa	1,527	62	108	502,725	27.93	24.4	2.7
Missouri[h]	3,100	83	142	1,020,054	[k]		3.5
NORTHWEST	3,590			1,110,493			
North Dakota	139	24	42	36,800	20.99	3.1	1.1
South Dakota	255	43	74	46,598	15.59	.5	1.1
Kansas	1,281	74	127	389,932	25.69	36.3	3.0
Nebraska	698	56	95	187,960	22.08	[j]	1.9
Colorado	625	57	100	254,802	33.92	25.2	1.2
Utah	148	27	53	56,221	29.57	14.4	.8
Montana	318	61	99	93,005	25.46	17.5	2.0
Wyoming	126	54	88	45,175	30.17		2.8
SOUTHWEST	6,778			1,691,778			
Oklahoma	2,144	98	175	592,424	23.72		2.4
Texas	3,986	62	113	877,722	23.18		2.0
New Mexico	241	49	92	55,558	22.67		2.7
Arizona	407	88	154	166,074	35.04		2.9
PACIFIC NORTHWEST	1,622			659,432			
Idaho	278	58	99	82,909	27.38		1.9
Oregon	438	41	67	155,649	30.59	19.2	1.9
Washington	906	52	86	420,874	35.97		1.4
PACIFIC SOUTHWEST	6,991			4,035,700			
California[h]	6,964	97	161	4,024,285	46.95	30.2	4.6
Nevada[h]	27	21	40	11,415	35.85	74.5	1.1

[a] *Social Security Yearbook 1942*, p. 182.
[b] The same, p. 74.
[c] The same, p. 186.
[d] The same, p. 76.
[e] The same, p. 104.
[f] The same, p. 106.
[g] Excludes Delaware which has no aid-to-blind program.
[h] Includes or relates to programs administered under state law without federal participation.
[i] Includes expenditures for personnel merit system.
[j] Less than 0.05 per cent.
[k] Not computed; data on cases and payments estimated.

As in old-age assistance, the national government pays one half of the grants to the blind "not counting so much of such expenditure with respect to any individual for any month as exceeds $40." It likewise pays one half of the expenditures for administration, provided the expenditures are found necessary by the national board "for proper and efficient administration of the State plan." The administrative requirements and the residence requirements are substantially like those for the needy aged. There are wide variations among the states, especially with respect to the definition of need.

Nothing in the Social Security Act, as previously noted, requires that the three assistance programs be administered by the same state agency. A few states have one agency administering old-age assistance and another handling aid to dependent children. In a few states aid to the needy blind is independently administered, particularly in states which had work for the blind before the national act was passed. Agencies administering aid for the blind are in a few cases associated with the state department of education rather than as in the great majority of states with the state department of public welfare.

The figures for the several states for 1942 are summarized in the table on page 70 which includes the figures for Illinois, Missouri, Nevada, and Pennsylvania, which were not under the Social Security Act.

From the standpoint of number of recipients and expenditures, the program for the blind was of small moment as compared with old-age assistance or aid to dependent children. For 1942 the totals were:[2]

	Number of Recipients as of December[3]	Benefit Payments for the Year (In thousands)[3]
Old-age assistance	2,229,518	$596,801
Aid to dependent children:		
All special programs	850,921	158,940
Programs approved by Board	842,739	157,968
Aid to the blind:[4]		
All special programs	79,113	24,690
Programs approved by Board	54,643	15,951

[2] *Social Security Yearbook 1942*, pp. 179–86.
[3] Includes figures for Alaska and Hawaii.
[4] In 1942 four states (Illinois, Missouri, Nevada, and Pennsylvania), had programs

QUESTIONS REGARDING OTHER NEEDY CLASSES

Federal participation in assistance to the needy blind raises one issue which should be briefly discussed. Why should the national government extend aid to the needy blind when it does not participate in aid to other classes of disabled under 65 years of age? Persons who before attaining the age of 65 are the victims of crippling accidents or diseases, if in need, must still be cared for by the state and local governments and, as repeatedly noted, some states do relatively little for persons in need who cannot qualify under a federal-aid category.

The attention of the Brookings Institution has on occasion been directed to the alleged fact that in state hospitals for the insane are many persons who (1) are not socially dangerous, (2) cannot be materially benefited by the treatment there given —in fact it is alleged that their conditions would be improved if they were not in such institutions, and (3) are sufficiently numerous greatly to increase the necessary outlays and expenditures for institutional care. It is alleged that they are maintained in these institutions because members of their family are unwilling or unable to provide for them in their own homes, and that the most readily available solution of the family difficulties is to have them committed to the public institutions for the insane and to keep them there. It is asserted that a substantial saving in public funds could be effected and the well being of the individuals enhanced if provision could be made for such individuals in private homes, preferably, although not necessarily, those of relatives. In connection with the aged it has frequently been said that payment of an old-age pension makes it feasible to have the old people cared for in the home of a relative. Would payment of a disability benefit to persons with mental illnesses that do not make them socially dangerous be to their advantage and to the advantage of the state? We do

---

of their own toward which the national government did not contribute. Delaware and Alaska did not have special programs for the blind.

not know the answer to that question. It seems reasonably certain, however, that there are several classes other than the blind who are in need because of physical or mental disability, and who in some states may be neglected because available relief funds are used almost exclusively for the federal categories set up by the Social Security Act.

CHAPTER V

OLD-AGE AND SURVIVORS INSURANCE

The Social Security Act of 1935 established a national system of no-means test old-age insurance for certain classes of salary and wage workers. In 1939 this insurance system was radically amended and its name was changed to old-age and survivors insurance. Because of limitations of space, the present chapter will deal almost entirely with the system adopted under the 1939 amendments, since that is the system the country now has.

At the outset the system will be described in broad outline. The outline will be followed by a more detailed analysis of the following subjects: contributions and finance, the benefit formula, who is actually insured, coverage, the possible beneficiaries and equities, forfeitures and options, including comparisons with private voluntary insurance. At the end of the chapter some comparisons will be made between old-age and survivors insurance and old-age assistance.

By way of general introduction it should perhaps be said that the old-age insurance system adopted in 1935 bore many resemblances to a modern retirement system adopted by public or private employers in the joint interests of themselves and their employees. The 1939 amendments made it far less like a modern retirement system and much more a social welfare system for meeting the needs of covered employees whose average earnings while under coverage are low and for making provisions for dependents and survivors. Despite these changes in the direction of a social welfare system, many of the concepts and practices of private voluntary insurance and individual employer retirement systems were preserved.

Use of the name insurance and preservation of some of the concepts and practices of more orthodox voluntary insurance necessitate examination of the system from a technical standpoint. Does the old-age and survivors insurance system comply with the standards that over the years have been developed

74

to make orthodox insurance meet the needs of the persons covered, with reasonable financial certainty? Does the use of concepts and practices of orthodox insurance further or retard the achievement of the social welfare objectives? Since such issues are involved, it will be necessary in the present chapter to deal with technical matters that are not always simple; but they are of great importance to the insured and those for whose welfare he is responsible, and to the people as a whole who are seeking to protect citizens from want in old age through a system that is sound from the standpoint of public finance.

THE SYSTEM IN BROAD OUTLINE

In the following outline minutiae and qualifications will be omitted. They will be reserved for the more detailed discussion later in the chapter, although in some instances attention will be called to qualifications even in this outline.

Contributions. The old-age and survivors insurance system is to be supported by taxes on salaries or wages, not exceeding $3,000 a year, paid both by the covered employers and the covered employees. If the revenues resulting from these contributions should prove insufficient the deficiency would presumably be made up by appropriations from general revenues. The Social Security Act provided that at the outset the tax on wages should be 1 per cent paid by the employer and 1 per cent paid by the employee. The rate of each tax was to be increased equally and gradually according to a time schedule until for 1949[1] and thereafter it would be 3 per cent each for employers and employees. Congress has, however, thus far postponed the increase from 1 per cent to 2 per cent, which was to have become effective in 1943.

Coverage.[2] The system applies to salary and wage workers with certain important exceptions. The major exceptions among employed workers are agricultural laborers, domestic laborers in private homes, casual laborers, employees of national and state governments and of religious, educational, and eleemosynary

[1] Internal Revenue Code, 1939, Chap. 9, Pts. 1 and 2, pp. 175–76.
[2] Social Security Act, as amended, 53 Stat. 1373, Title 2, sec. 209.

institutions, employees of the steam railway industry, and persons employed by certain relatives. Persons working on their own account are excluded. Most important among them are farmers, business men owning and operating their own establishments, and private practitioners of the professions.

Persons insured. Insurance is not synonymous with coverage: not all persons covered and paying taxes are insured. Before he is actually insured, an individual must have worked in a covered position for a length of time specified in the law. Two types of insured status are provided:

1. Currently insured, which applies only in the event of the death of the worker. A worker is currently insured provided he has been paid wages of not less than $50 for each of not less than six of the twelve quarters immediately preceding the quarter in which he died. A new entrant to the system, if continuously employed at wages amounting to at least $50 a quarter, can attain the status of currently insured in six quarters or one and a half years.[3]

2. Fully insured, which applies to all who remain in the system long enough to meet the legal requirements. For persons who attain the age of 21 years after December 31, 1936, the basic requirement is 40 quarters of coverage. Thus a continuously employed person of this class can permanently attain the fully insured status in 10 years of continuous employment. In the event of death they are insured if they have been covered for a minimum of six quarters and for half of the quarters between the quarter in which they became 21 and the quarter in which they died. After 40 quarters have been served the requirement for serving half the quarters is waived.[4]

For persons who were over 21 years of age on December 31, 1936 the minimum requirement is six quarters and then half the quarters between December 31, 1936 and the quarter in which they attained the age of 65, but this requirement of half the quarters is waived after an employee has been covered for 40 quarters. In event of death an employee in this class is cov-

---

[3] The same, sec. 209 (h).
[4] The same, sec. 209 (g).

ered provided he has served a minimum of six quarters and half the quarters between December 31, 1936 and the quarter in which he died, with the waiver of this rule after 40 quarters.[5]

The benefit formula. The system is so designed that a single benefit formula is used as the basis for determining the amount of each benefit provided under it. It is used for determining the worker's own old-age benefit or his primary insurance benefit to use the terminology of the act. All other benefits are fractions of it, or in the case of a lump-sum death benefit, a multiple of it. The formula reads:

(e) The term "primary insurance benefit" means an amount equal to the sum of the following—

(1) (A) 40 per centum of the amount of an individual's average monthly wage if such average monthly wage does not exceed $50, or (B) if such average monthly wage exceeds $50, 40 per centum of $50, plus 10 per centum of the amount by which such average monthly wage exceeds $50 and does not exceed $250, and

(2) an amount equal to 1 per centum of the amount computed under paragraph (1) multiplied by the number of years in which $200 or more of wages were paid to such individual. Where the primary insurance benefit thus computed is less than $10, such benefit shall be $10.[6]

There are some provisions with respect to minimum benefits that are advantageous to insured individuals where average monthly earnings are small. There are also some maximum limitations on benefits which do not come into operation against the insured himself but limit the additional amount that may be paid dependents and survivors.[7]

The benefits. The benefits included in the system are:

1. The worker's old-age benefit or the primary insurance benefit paid to a fully insured worker who has attained the age of 65.[8] It is provided, however, that if the fully insured person 65 years of age or over renders services for wages of not less than $15 in any month the amount so earned shall be deducted

[5] The same.
[6] The same, sec. 209 (e).
[7] The same, sec. 203.
[8] The same, sec. 202.

from his benefits. Thus if the worker earns more than his old-age benefit in any month he receives no benefit.[9]

2. The wife's old-age benefit or the wife's insurance benefit is payable to the wife of an individual entitled to a primary insurance benefit if and when she has attained the age of 65.[10] Qualifications and limitations are here omitted but will be considered later. The benefit is one half of a primary benefit.

3. The child's benefit is payable to a child under 18 years of age of an individual who is entitled to a primary insurance benefit or of an individual who died fully or currently insured. Qualifications and limitations are again left for later consideration. The child's benefit is one half the primary benefit.[11]

4. The widow's benefit is payable to the widow, 65 years of age or over, of an individual who died fully insured. Again consideration of limitations and qualifications is postponed. The widow's benefit is three fourths of a primary insurance benefit.[12]

5. The widow's current insurance benefit is payable to the widow of an individual who died fully or currently insured, provided she has in her care a child of such deceased individual which child is entitled to receive a child's insurance benefit. Again limitations and qualifications are omitted. The benefit is three quarters of a primary benefit.[13]

6. A parent's benefit may be paid to the parent of a fully insured individual provided (a) the individual left no widow or unmarried child under 18 years of age, (b) the parent has attained the age of 65, and (c) was wholly dependent upon and supported by such individual. Limitations and qualifications are omitted. The benefit is one half the primary insurance benefit.[14]

7. A lump-sum death benefit is payable on the death of a fully or currently insured individual provided he left no surviving widow, child, or parent who would on filing application in

[9] The same, sec. 203 (d).
[10] The same, sec. 202 (b).
[11] The same, sec. 202 (c).
[12] The same, sec. 202 (d).
[13] The same, sec. 202 (e).
[14] The same, sec. 202 (f).

the month in which the individual died be eligible for a benefit for such month. Many details are here omitted. The lump-sum death benefit may not exceed six times the primary benefit.[15]

This generalized description will serve as a background for the more detailed and necessarily more technical consideration which will make up most of the balance of the present chapter.

CONTRIBUTIONS AND FINANCE

In private voluntary insurance, the insured pays a premium which will cover (1) the actuarial cost of the protection the insured is to receive plus (2) the insured's share of the insurance company's costs of doing business, one item of which is taxes levied against the insurance business to support government. In a sound retirement system for public or private employees, the employer and the employees together contribute the money from which the benefits are to be paid. Premiums or contributions plus interest earned by reserves meet the entire cost of the plan, provided it is actuarially sound. The question with which we are now to deal is: To what extent are the taxes levied to support the old-age and survivors insurance system comparable to the premiums in private voluntary insurance or to the contributions of employers and employees under an actuarially sound retirement system in a public or private enterprise?

To help in answering this question a table from the Office of the Actuary of the Social Security Board[16] summarizing the financial position with respect to benefits, taxes, and progress of the reserves is presented on page 80. The most striking fact brought out by this table is that the number of variables in the old-age and survivors insurance system is so great that the actuaries of the system cannot estimate its cost with any degree of precision. They are forced to make two different sets of complicated assumptions, a reasonable low and a reasonable high, and thus to establish a range within which the cost will presumably fall.[17]

---

[15] The same, sec. 202 (g).

[16] Dorrance C. Bronson, *Old-Age and Survivors Insurance 1943–44 Cost Studies*, Actuarial Study No. 19.

[17] For the complicated assumptions, see the same, pp. 11–12.

SUMMARY—BENEFIT, TAXES, AND PROGRESS OF RESERVE[a]

I. LOW

Calendar Year (1)	Covered Pay Roll (In billions) (2)	Tax Income for Year Shown (In millions) (3)	O.A.S.I. Benefit Payments for Year Shown (In millions) (4)	Benefit Cost for Year Shown, as Per Cent of Pay Roll (5)	Level Cost, 1945 to Year Shown, as Per Cent of Pay Roll		Income from Interest (2 per cent) on the Fund (In millions) (8)	Amount of Trust Fund (End of Year) (In billions) (9)
					No Interest (6)	2 Per Cent Interest (7)		
1945	$33.4	$1,336	$ 233	0.70	0.7	0.7	$ 152	$ 8.2
1950	34.6	2,076	587	1.70	1.2	1.2	310	16.5
1955	35.6	2,136	893	2.51	1.7	1.6	486	25.2
1960	35.8	2,148	1,235	3.45[b]	2.1	2.0	650	33.3
1970	35.9	2,154	1,863	5.19	3.0	2.8	932	47.2
1980	36.0	2,160	2,625	7.29	4.0	3.6	1,116	56.2
2000	36.0	2,160	3,232	8.98	5.6	4.7	1,242	62.2[c]

II. HIGH

Calendar Year (1)	Covered Pay Roll (In billions) (2)	Tax Income for Year Shown (In millions) (3)	O.A.S.I. Benefit Payments for Year Shown (In millions) (4)	Benefit Cost for Year Shown, as Per Cent of Pay Roll (5)	No Interest (6)	2 Per Cent Interest (7)	Income from Interest (2 per cent) on the Fund (In millions) (8)	Amount of Trust Fund (End of Year) (In billions) (9)
1945	$51.5	$2,060	$ 325	0.63	0.6	0.6	$ 160	$ 8.9
1950	53.0	3,180	774	1.46	1.1	1.1	402	21.5
1955	54.6	3,276	1,171	2.14	1.4	1.4	682	35.5
1960	55.5	3,330	1,666	3.00[d]	1.8	1.8	950	48.8
1970	57.0	3,420	2,670	4.68	2.7	2.5	1,436	72.9
1980	57.0	3,420	3,958	6.94	3.6	3.2	1,596	90.4
2000	57.0	3,420	6,066	10.64	5.6	4.6	1,854	92.3[e]

[a] Exclusive of administrative expenses.

[b] Benefits reach 4 per cent of pay roll in 1964.

[c] On basis of tax and benefit conditions of year 2000 continuing, fund would keep increasing.

[d] Benefits reach 4 per cent of pay roll in 1967.

[e] Reaches a peak of 97 billion dollars in year 1990; on basis of tax and benefit conditions of year 2000 continuing, fund would decrease thereafter at an accelerating rate reaching zero in 60 years.

For example, according to the low estimate, the costs of benefits will increase from 233 million dollars in 1945 to 3.2 billions in the year 2000, whereas according to the high estimate, they will increase from 325 millions in 1945 to 6.1 billions in the year 2000. The amount required for benefits in the year 2000 is thus more than 13 times the amount required in 1945 by the low estimates and almost 19 times as great by the high estimates. The percentage which benefit payments will form of pay roll (column 5) in the year 2000 is 8.98 according to the low estimate and 10.64 according to the high.

The enormous increase in benefit costs revealed by this table is characteristic of any annuity system that starts, as did O.A.S.I., with all its members on the active roll, paying contributions or causing employers to pay contributions. It starts with no load whatsoever, with contributions pouring in and nothing going out for benefits. Then comes a year when the first class of beneficiaries passes from the active roll of contributors to the pension roll. This first class of beneficiaries receive on the average relatively low benefits because their length of service under the system is short, and thus they get small length of service additions to their benefits. The next year they are joined by a second group who get on the average a little larger length of service increment. Each successive year sees a new group joining the survivors of those who passed to the pension rolls in earlier years, and each successive group has on the average higher length of service increments until the system reaches maturity.

When does such a system reach maturity and achieve a more or less permanent relationship between aggregate contributions and aggregate benefit costs? Roughly, when all the pensioners on the retirement roll entered active service after the system was established and thus had opportunity to earn full additions to benefits for length of service. If it be assumed that the maximum age at death is 100 years[18] and that the minimum age at entrance into the system is 21 years, the difference between the two, or 79 years, is the number of years required for the system

[18] The maximum age at death is now above 100.

to mature. Benefits were first paid under the system in 1937, and hence maturity will be reached about 2016, although the increase between 2000 and 2016 will be slight. The figures for the year 2000 are thus not the peak figures but they may be regarded as approximating the peak.[19]

Columns 6 and 7 show the level cost of the system, up to each calendar year shown, as a percentage of pay roll, column 6 giving the figure without interest on the fund that results from the fact that the system starts without load and column 7 with an allowance of 2 per cent interest on the fund. In the year 2000, the level cost without interest would be 5.6 per cent of pay roll and with interest at 2 per cent 4.7 for the low estimate and 4.6 for the high.

The last column in the table shows the amount of the trust fund. In the year 2000 under the low estimate it would amount to 62.2 billion dollars and according to the official note to the table "On basis of tax and benefit conditions of year 2000 continuing, fund would keep increasing." Under the high estimate the fund would amount in the year 2000 to 92.3 billions, but the note says: "Reaches a peak of $97 billion in year 1990; on basis of tax and benefit conditions of year 2000 continuing, fund would decrease at an accelerating rate reaching zero in 60 years."

In a financially sound going retirement system, the reserve fund tends to grow in amount until maturity is reached, and thereafter it remains fairly stable at the peak level. What is drawn from it to pay pensioners is made up by what is put in as reserves for people on the active roll. In a going system, constantly being replenished with fresh entrants coming into the active service, if the fund turns downward the system is on its way to bankruptcy. The high estimate of the actuaries, it must be emphasized, shows that the fund under those assumptions turns downward after 1990 and that the 97 billion dollars in it on that date will be exhausted in 60 years. According to the

---

[19] There may be some subsequent growth mainly because of increases in the population and improved longevity. Extension of the system to classes not previously covered will, moreover, postpone arrival at the peak.

lower estimates, the fund would still be growing in the year 2000.

These actuarial computations are based on the assumption that the taxes in 1945 will amount to 4 per cent of pay roll and and in 1949 and thereafter to 6 per cent of pay roll. Under the original plan the combined taxes on employers and employees were to be increased from 2 per cent for the years 1939 to 1942, to 4 per cent from 1943 to 1945, to 5 per cent from 1946 to 1948, and to 6 per cent after December 1948.[20] Congress has thus far prevented the increase from 2 per cent to 4 per cent. Thus the figures regarding the fund and its financial position are based on assumptions that are dependent on congressional action which cannot be foretold. It should be reasonably obvious that benefits which give in the year 2000 a level cost from 1945 of 5.6 per cent of pay roll with no allowance for interest or of 4.7 per cent of pay roll with interest at 2 per cent cannot be financed with a 2 per cent tax. If this system were private voluntary insurance or a private retirement system, bankruptcy would be inevitable.

Why has Congress refused to permit the increase in the tax to be made and to keep the system more nearly on a sound actuarial basis? The brief answer is that the Congress does not view the system as one comparable with private voluntary insurance or with the retirement system of an employer. The differences call for brief consideration.

1. In private voluntary insurance and in a private employer's retirement system, the safety of the beneficiaries depends entirely upon the adequacy of the reserves, which in turn depend on the adequacy of the contribution rates. In a compulsory governmental system, the safety of the beneficiaries rests fundamentally upon the sovereign power of the government to tax. Contributions and reserves are devices borrowed from private insurance, but they do not play as essential a role since any deficiencies can be made up through taxation. Considerations of general fiscal policy, or possibly of political expediency, outweigh the niceties of actuarial calculations.

[20] Internal Revenue Code, 1939, Chap. 9, Pts. 1 and 2, pp. 175–76.

2. From the standpoint of national fiscal policy, the practical value of a large social security reserve is questionable. To explain this statement, it is desirable to contrast the management of reserve funds in private voluntary insurance with the management of social insurance reserves.

In private voluntary insurance and in a sound private retirement system, the reserves, which really belong to the insured, are loaned to borrowers who will pay interest for their use and who can practically guarantee to repay the principal when it is due. The borrowers are either private organizations which will invest the money in productive property from which money will be earned to pay principal and interest or governments which pledge their credit for the payment and can use their taxing power to comply with their promises. Through the insurance carrier, one class, the borrowers, promises to pay another class, the insured, the interest on and principal of the sums borrowed from the reserves. There is very little overlapping of these two classes, the debtors and the creditors.

Under the O.A.S.I. system the national government spends the money it receives from the social security tax for the objectives of government that at the moment call for funds. In the fund as security it places the obligations of the national government to pay in the future. As interest becomes due on these obligations, it issues to the fund further obligations to pay in the future. When benefit payments exceed cash income from O.A.S.I. taxes, and a withdrawal has to be made from the reserves to pay benefits, the national government will have to raise the money to cash its promises to pay. It can then tax, borrow, or issue currency if there is no Treasury surplus from which the promises to pay can be redeemed. The reserves therefore are, under this practice, nothing more than promises to pay in the future. It is hard for some members of Congress and students of public finance to see how a promise to pay in the future can be of any assistance to the future generation which is called upon to redeem that promise in order to meet current demands for O.A.S.I. benefit payments. The money collected earlier for O.A.S.I. benefits has been spent for other purposes, and now fresh money must be collected to pay the O.A.S.I. benefits or, if one prefers, to redeem the governmental promises to pay that make up the O.A.S.I. reserve.

To a very considerable extent the persons covered by O.A.S.I. will be the ones who are called upon to pay the taxes necessary to enable the government to redeem its promises to pay that constitute the reserve. There is no such separation of the borrowing class and the beneficiary class as characterizes private voluntary insurance or a private employer's retirement system. The transaction partakes much more of private borrowing by the individual to meet current expenses. The day comes when the obligation is due, and the money to pay it has to be raised.

Thus many question the practical value of national actuarial reserves consisting exclusively of promises to pay in the future, since the future taxpayers must raise the money all over again. From this point of view the amount in the trust fund is nothing but a special part of the public debt, which must be added to the general debt in judging the fiscal position of the government.

Unless, moreover, the amount in the fund is actuarially sufficient to pay the promised benefit, it does not represent the whole of the debt the government has incurred for the system. An inadequate reserve leaves a hidden and unfunded debt that does not appear in the governmental accounts.

History of contribution and reserve legislation. When successive Congresses refuse to permit enactments of an earlier Congress to be put into effect, the legislative history of the sections of the law thus nullified is pertinent to current issues. The history of the tax provisions will therefore be briefly reviewed.

The research and the primary bill drafting for the Social Security Act were not done by Congress itself nor by an agency of Congress. They were done by a Committee on Economic Security, the members of which were designated by the President of the United States. It consisted of the Secretary of Labor, Frances E. Perkins, as the Chairman, the Secretary of the Treasury, Henry Morgenthau, Jr., the Attorney General, Homer Cummings, the Secretary of Agriculture, Henry A. Wallace, and the Federal Emergency Relief Administrator,

Harry L. Hopkins. The Committee selected and employed a small staff of experts. It had the assistance of the "Technical Board on Economic Security," provided for in the President's executive order and composed of twenty people in government service who had special interest and knowledge in some or all aspects of the problem the President directed the Committee to consider. An Advisory Council on Economic Security, appointed by the President and constituted of citizens outside of government service, chosen from employers, employees, and the general public, assisted the Committee in weighing the proposals developed by the staff and the Technical Board and in arriving at a judgment as to their practicability. The Committee also created seven other advisory groups on technical subjects.[21]

The method of selection of this organization naturally meant that all members of the Committee and probably most members of its staff, its Technical Board, its Advisory Council, and its special advisory boards were basically in favor of the fundamental purposes of the act. The record suggests, however, that they were far from agreement with respect to the basic principles regarding financing, which is here under consideration.

The President in his message to Congress transmitting the report of his Committee on Economic Security said:

Three principles should be observed in legislation on this subject. In the first place, the system adopted, except for the money necessary to initiate it, should be self-sustaining in the sense that funds for the payment of insurance benefits should not come from the proceeds of general taxation. Second, excepting in old-age insurance, actual management should be left to the States subject to standards established by the Federal Government. Third, sound financial management of the funds and the reserves, and protection of the credit structure of the Nation should be assured by retaining Federal control over all funds through trustees in the Treasury of the United States.[22]

Secretary of the Treasury Morgenthau before the House Committee recommended:

[21] *Economic Security Act*, Hearings before the House Committee on Ways and Means, 74 Cong. 1 sess., pp. 17–18. (Letter of Submittal to the President.)
[22] The same, p. 14.

. . . The substitution in the contributory old-age annuity system of a scale of contributory taxes and benefit payments that will facilitate the continued operation of the system on an adequate and sound financial basis, without imposing heavy burdens upon future generations; . . .[23]

He proceeded to recommend a scale of contribution rates and of benefits that would in his judgment put the system on a sound financial basis, and he envisioned the gradual absorption of the public debt into the old-age insurance system reserves. He did not, however, recommend the immediate levying of sufficient taxes as actuarial contributions to achieve this objective, but proposed 2 per cent for the first three years, 3 per cent for the next three years, 4 per cent for the third three-year period, 5 per cent for the fourth three-year period, and 6 per cent thereafter.[24]

The record seems to establish beyond question that both the President and the Secretary of the Treasury envisioned practically an actuarial reserve system. A question naturally arises as to why, if an actuarial reserve system were to be established, the full amount of the necessary level premium was not charged at once, instead of providing for the gradual stepping up of the tax rate from the initial 2 per cent to the ultimate 6 per cent. The best answer to that question that has been found is in the formal opening statement presented to the House Committee by Professor J. Douglas Brown of Princeton who worked with the Committee on Economic Security. He gave the three following reasons:

1. The gradual raising of the rates of contribution softens the impact of the new charge on both the employer who has no pension plan at present and the worker and allows time for readjustments.

2. To hold down the income into the fund until disbursements are sufficient to avoid the accumulation of large reserves.

3. A lower initial rate of contribution aids in the enforcement of the tax since coverage is secured and *public support gained while the cost of the tax is small.*[25]

[23] The same, p. 897.
[24] The same, p. 898.
[25] The same, p. 244. Italics supplied.

One of the virtues of a true actuarial reserve system—perhaps its principal virtue in a general social security plan—is that it starts with the full premium necessary to supply the benefits promised and thus puts all interested parties on notice as to the true cost. It sets up a barrier of facts as to cost that has to be hurdled in getting the legislation through. The Committee on Economic Security preferred not to confront employers, employees, and the public immediately with the true full costs.

The truth appears to be that the Committee on Economic Security and their aids and advisers were by no means in agreement with the basic principles of operating the system on an actuarial reserve basis. In the quotation just given from the testimony of Professor Brown, one reason for the gradual stepping up of rates was "To hold down the income into the fund until the disbursements are sufficient to avoid the accumulation of large reserves."

Professor E. E. Witte, Executive Director of the Committee on Economic Security, clearly did not believe in the development of a sacred actuarial reserve. The following extract from his testimony with respect to the old-age assistance payments, which he called pensions, and the purchased old-age annuities is pertinent in this connection:

. . . The old-age pension is a gratuity paid to people that have nothing to live on—that is the essence of it—and whose children will not or cannot support them. That is what the old-age pension is for.

Contributory annuities are something that the man with the matching contributions of his employer builds up for himself. The primary purpose of the tax is to build this annuity up so that when he reaches old age he has this annuity to fall back on. Then he will not need a pension. But this is true, that in the early years of this system, even at the 1-per cent rate with which we start out, there will be enough money brought into the United States Treasury so that the contributions toward the pensions can be borrowed from the annuity fund. We are not amalgamating the two. We want to keep a separate record, because you will need that money later on. But at the beginning you do not have to worry where this $50,000,000 or $125,000,000 the next year is coming from. The earnings tax will give you that money. You are getting more money out of that than you need, and you can borrow that money. You will not have to have an additional tax.[26]

[26] The same, p. 109.

One reason which Dr. Witte advanced in favor of paying unearned annuities to persons who retired in the early days of the
old insurance system was: "If you pay nothing more than the
person himself and his matched contributions will buy, you will
create a reserve, on the 1-to-5 per cent rate of contributions in
the bill which in time—by about 1975 or so—will amount to
$70,000,000,000."[27]

Both these quotations indicate an intention to use the actuarial reserve funds to pay for current expenses, namely, the cost
of old-age assistance benefits and unearned annuities to those
who retire in the early years of the system. Such use of the reserves would operate to increase the obligations of future generations of taxpayers. They were specific illustrations of a general fear that later developed in Congress that the acturial
reserve would be dissipated for current expenses that should be
met from current general revenues and that future generations
would have to make them good from general taxes.

Another fear developed with respect to the huge prospective
reserves; Would there be a sufficient body of public debt to
absorb them? Professor Brown expressed this fear in the following words:

The accumulation of large reserves may necessitate the reduction
of other Federal taxes in order to create new obligations and thus for
a time relieve the rich through taxes on lower incomes.

We certainly do not object to relieving taxes on anybody, but in
this case it would be the accumulation of such a large reserve that the
Government would have to begin to use those funds and reduce other
taxes. In order to find a use for it, and to set up obligations against
that use may require the reduction of other taxes.[28]

The technical experts naturally recognized that the tax on
the employees was an income tax and would be borne by the
employees. With respect to the tax on employers for unemployment insurance, Dr. Witte said:

The costs to the employer, of course, mean costs that are shifted to
the consumer. This is not, however, to be regarded as a sales tax. This
is part of the wage bill. You do not call it a sales tax when the employer pays the wages. You do not call it a sales tax when the employer

27 The same, p. 98.
28 The same, p. 244.

pays workmen's compensation on account of accidents. That is part of the wage costs.[29]

Mr. Murray Latimer, now the Chairman of the Railroad Retirement Board, gave the following testimony:

... Now, my own personal feeling is that the Federal Government should make a contribution; not now, but should make them.

Mr. Vinson. Why not now? That is the point I cannot quite grasp, except for the burden upon the Treasury, and, of course, I realize that.

Mr. Latimer. Not only the burden on the Treasury, but why should we build up extremely large funds which would tend, perhaps, to get us into unwise channels of investment?[30]

Mr. W. R. Williamson, then the assistant actuary of the life department of the Travelers Insurance Company and an actuarial adviser to the Committee, now the actuary of the Social Security Board, presented to the House Committee an excellent statement of the distinction between reserves in private insurance and reserves in social insurance invested in government obligations.

... the reserves are always liabilities as well as assets. As I view it, they are liabilities of the Government just the same as they are assets, and they are misleading in giving the appearance of solvency. The money is spent, and presumably the people as a whole owe the money back to the Government ... .[31]

On the basis of these extracts from the record and other material in them which has not been quoted or specifically referred to, it would seem entirely fair to make several general statements.

1. There was nothing approaching unanimity among the President, his Committee on Economic Security, and the members of its staff with regard to the desirability of a true actuarial reserve.

2. There was no unanimity with respect to the question whether it was or was not desirable to have the national government contribute from general tax funds to the ultimate costs of old-age insurance.

[29] The same, p. 142.
[30] The same, p. 234.
[31] The same, p. 1018.

3. There were members of the group who suggested use of the reserves for meeting current expenses to the relief of current taxpayers, and others who viewed the unwise use of such reserves as one of the outstanding dangers of the entire proposal.

Three points with respect to the work of the Ways and Means Committee should be recorded.

1. The bill before them was one that had been prepared and presented by the administration. It was not one that the Committee had worked out as the result of its own studies or as the result of the study of a congressional committee on which some of the members had served.

2. The subject matter was in many cases in a field new to the Committee members.

3. The Committee had no staff of technical specialists competent to submit the bill or the witnesses appearing in its support to searching, skeptical criticism.

The act was passed in 1935 with provisions for the actuarial reserve and for the rates to be progressively stepped up until ultimately they would reach 6 per cent; but they started at 1 per cent each on the employer and on the employee. A bill thus passed in a heavy fog could not, however, be said really to have settled the issues. A curious phenomenon then took place. The reserve provisions were attacked both from the right and from the left.

From the right the attack was basically on the ground that the huge reserves would be dissipated in unwise public expenditures and that when benefits became payable in the distant future, the money would have to be collected all over again from the taxpayers. The reserves would be merely money to be used in accordance with the prevailing spending philosophy.

From the left the attack was on the ground that the system placed the entire burden on the employees themselves through an income tax and on the employers through a pay-roll tax which would be shifted to the consumers and would have the same general economic effect as a sales tax. If the rate of these two taxes could be held down, a great actuarial deficit would inevitably be created which would necessitate in the years to come raising the necessary funds through general taxes presumably the income tax and the inheritance tax. It was not necessary, however, for those on the left to state the real ground of their objection. They could merely join in the attack on the dangers of a huge actuarial reserve and enlist votes against raising the tax rate on employers and employees. They were not, and it is to be suspected never were, in agreement with President Roosevelt's declaration of principle "that funds for the payment of insurance benefits should not come from the proceeds of general taxation."

The 1939 act amended the provisions with respect to the fund. In the 1935 act the fund was entitled "Old-Age Reserve Account." The law provided:

There is hereby authorized to be appropriated to the Account for each fiscal year, beginning with the fiscal year ending June 30, 1937, an amount sufficient as an annual premium to provide for the payments required under this title, such amount to be determined on a reserve basis in accordance with accepted actuarial principles, and based upon such tables of mortality as the Secretary of the Treasury shall from time to time adopt, and upon an interest rate of 3 per centum per annum compounded annually.[32]

The 1939 act calls the account "Federal Old-Age and Insurance Trust Fund." All reference to accepted actuarial principles and interest has been eliminated. The trustees are to report immediately to Congress whenever in their opinion the trust fund will, during the ensuing five fiscal years, exceed three times the highest annual expenditures anticipated during that period, and whenever the Board of Trustees is of the opinion that the amount of the fund is unduly small.

From the present state of the legislation and the successive actions of the Congress, it may be inferred that the intent is to operate the system practically on a cash basis, in the sense that taxes will be raised only as more money is needed to pay benefits. According to the actuarial report issued by the Social Security Board, by the year 2000 payment of benefits alone,

[32] 49 Stat. 622.

exclusive of administrative costs, will amount to between 8.98 and 10.64 per cent of current pay rolls. In one way or another the taxpayers of the year 2000 will have to pay that sum for the benefits of the present old-age and survivors insurance system.

Conclusions. So far as contributions under O.A.S.I. are concerned, therefore, it is necessary to conclude:

1. That the present contributions of 1 per cent each by employer and employee are insufficient to pay the true cost of the system.

2. That contributions are not like premiums in private voluntary insurance.

3. That since the proceeds of the special taxes are being spent for current expenses, the government will for a large number of years have to raise the full amount required for O.A.S.I. benefits which will in the year 2000 be between 3.2 and 6.1 billion dollars a year and will constitute between 8.98 and 10.64 per cent of the pay roll.

The nature of the contributions is related to the nature of the benefit formula. We shall therefore take up that subject next and follow it with the detailed discussion of who is insured.

THE BENEFIT FORMULA

The benefit formula was quoted on page 77 in the summary description of the system. In this section of the chapter the operation of the formula will be examined and discussed in some detail.

To illustrate the operation of the benefit formula, a table is presented on pages 94–95. It is divided horizontally into six sections, each one devoted to employees who on retirement have the same average monthly wage during their qualifying coverage. For each group having the same average monthly wage, figures are given for five different lengths of qualifying service selected for illustrative purposes. For each length of service the table shows:

1. How much the employee himself would have contributed in cash, (a) if the tax on his wages were to be continued at 1 per cent (column 1); (b) if he should enter after the tax has been increased to 3 per cent (column 3).

Amount of Payment by Employee for O.A.S.I. Old-Age Benefits

I. Average wage $50 a month, $600 a year

Length of Service	Aggregate Contribution by Employee from Tax of:				Annual Annuity under O.A.S.I.		Payment by Employee per $1.00 of Annual Annuity	
	1 Per Cent		3 Per Cent		Man Only	Man and Wife	One Per Cent Tax With Interest	Three Per Cent Tax With Interest
	Without Interest	With 2 Per Cent Compound Interest	Without Interest	With 2 Per Cent Compound Interest				
	1	2	3	4	5	6	7	8
10 years	60	65.70	180	197.09	264	396	.25	.75
20 years	120	145.78	360	437.35	288	432	.51	1.52
30 years	180	243.41	540	730.23	312	468	.78	2.34
40 years	240	362.41	720	3,087.24	336	480[a]	1.08	3.24
44 years	264	417.02	792	1,251.05	346	480[a]	1.21	3.62
II. AVERAGE WAGE $75 A MONTH, $900 A YEAR								
10 years	90	98.55	270	295.64	297	446	.33	1.00
20 years	180	218.68	540	656.03	324	486	.67	2.02
30 years	270	365.11	810	1,095.34	351	527	1.04	3.12
40 years	360	543.62	1,080	1,630.85	378	567	1.44	4.31
44 years	396	625.52	1,188	1,876.57	389	583	1.61	4.83
III. AVERAGE WAGE $100 A MONTH, $1,200 A YEAR								
10 years	120	131.40	360	394.19	330	495	.40	1.19
20 years	240	291.57	720	874.71	360	540	.81	2.43
30 years	360	486.82	1,080	1,460.45	390	585	1.25	3.74
40 years	480	724.82	1,440	2,174.47	420	630	1.73	5.18
44 years	528	834.03	1,584	2,502.10	432	648	1.93	5.79

[a] The wife cannot receive half of her husband's primary benefit because it would make the total exceed 80 per cent of the husband's monthly wage and therefore the combined benefit is cut to $480.

AMOUNT OF PAYMENT BY EMPLOYEE FOR O.A.S.I. OLD-AGE BENEFITS (*Continued*)

IV. AVERAGE WAGE $150 A MONTH, $1,800 A YEAR

Length of Service	Aggregate Contribution by Employee from Tax of:				Annual Annuity under O.A.S.I.		Payment by Employee per $1.00 of Annual Annuity	
	1 Per Cent		3 Per Cent		Man Only	Man and Wife	One Per Cent Tax With Interest	Three Per Cent Tax With Interest
	Without Interest	With 2 Per Cent Compound Interest	Without Interest	With 2 Per Cent Compound Interest				
	1	2	3	4	5	6	7	8
10 years......	180	197.09	540	591.28	396	594	.50	1.49
20 years......	360	437.35	1,080	1,312.06	432	648	1.01	3.04
30 years......	540	730.23	1,620	2,190.68	468	702	1.56	4.68
40 years......	720	1,087.24	2,160	3,261.71	504	756	2.16	6.47
44 years......	792	1,251.05	2,376	3,753.14	518	778	2.41	7.24
V. AVERAGE WAGE $200 A MONTH, $2,400 A YEAR								
10 years......	240	262.79	720	788.38	462	693	.57	1.71
20 years......	480	583.14	1,440	1,749.41	504	756	1.16	3.47
30 years......	720	973.63	2,160	2,920.90	546	819	1.78	5.35
40 years......	960	1,449.65	2,880	4,348.94	588	882	2.47	7.40
44 years......	1,056	1,668.06	3,168	5,004.19	605	907	2.76	8.27
VI. AVERAGE WAGE $250 A MONTH, $3,000 A YEAR								
10 years......	300	328.49	900	985.47	528	792	.62	1.87
20 years......	600	728.92	1,800	2,186.76	576	864	1.27	3.80
30 years......	900	1,217.04	2,700	3,651.13	624	936	1.95	5.85
40 years......	1,200	1,812.06	3,600	5,436.18	672	1,008	2.70	8.09
44 years......	1,320	2,085.08	3,960	6,255.24	691	1,020[b]	3.02	9.05

[b] This amount is the maximum allowed by the law, $85 per month.

2. How much the employee's contributions under each of these taxes would amount to if compound interest at 2 per cent is allowed on his contributions (Columns 2 and 4). Here it is assumed that the average wages were uniformly earned throughout the period.

3. The amount of annual annuity which would be payable under the O.A.S.I. formula with respect to a man with the specified wage and length of service (a) for a single man, and (b) for a man and eligible wife.

4. What the worker would have paid for each dollar of annual annuity for the man (or woman) alone without any other eligible beneficiaries, provided he had bought it with (a) the accumulation from the 1 per cent tax with compound interest at 2 per cent, or (b) the accumulation from the 3 per cent tax with compound interest at 2 per cent.

Attention should be called to the fact that these figures are based exclusively on the contributions or taxes paid by the employees. The employers pay a like tax and therefore the figures regarding contributions and the amount paid per dollar of annuity should be doubled to give the payment by the employer and employee combined.

The employee shown in this table who gets the biggest bargain under the formula is the one who has served 10 years and has an average monthly wage of $50.[33] With a 3 per cent tax and interest he would have paid 75 cents for an annuity of a dollar a year paid to him each year from the date of his retirement to the date of his death. At age 65, according to the United States Life Tables, the average future life time for white males for 1930 to 1939 was 11.9 years. An annuity of a dollar a year for an average of 11.9 years for the payment of 75 cents is a good bargain. The present value of $1.00 a year for 11 years with interest at 2 per cent is $9.79, which indicates roughly what the individual may get for himself for his 75 cents. It will be remembered that he may also get a benefit for his wife and eligible

---

[33] Beneficiaries who retire in the early years of the system with less than 40 quarters of covered service and with the low initial taxes get even better bargains. This table, however, deals only with those who have served 40 quarters or more and are permanently insured for old-age protection.

children, and he provides protection for his eligible survivors.

For the poorest bargain one looks at the last line of the table which gives the figures for the man who has an average wage of $250 a month and has served 44 years. With a 3 per cent tax and interest, his dollar of annuity, for an average of about 11.9 years, has cost him in the neighborhood of $9.05. Per dollar of annuity he has paid a little more than 12 times as much as the employee whose average wage was only $50 and who served only 10 years. By his contributions alone, at the 3 per cent tax and interest he has paid almost the full cost of his own old-age annuity. If he is to get any very substantial amount from his employer's contribution, he must have an eligible wife or eligible children. If he has had during his 44 years of service children under 18 years of age he has had some protection for them and their mother. If, on the other hand, he has had no eligible dependents, he has run the risk of forfeiting his accumulation if he died before attaining the retirement age. Column 4 of the table shows such a man has paid in taxes, plus compound interest at 2 per cent, over $6,000.[34]

The figures in this table also bring out the extent of the discrimination against the workers with long periods of service. With a tax of 3 per cent the man who has served 44 years pays in taxes without interest 4.4 times as much as the man who has served only 10 years. With compound interest at 2 per cent he has contributed 6.3 times as much. The annuity after 44 years of service is, however, only 1.3 times as much as the annuity after 10 years of service. Workers with long service have

---

[34] With a 3 per cent tax and compound interest at 2 per cent the accumulation after 40 years of service ranges from $1,087 for the person with an average monthly wage of $50 a month to $5,436 for the person with an average monthly wage of $250. A man who dies after 40 years of service and before reaching the retirement age cannot leave this accumulation to children who are over 18 years of age regardless of whether they have completed their education and regardless of their mental and physical condition and their degree of need. He cannot leave an annuity to his wife with no child under 18 unless she has attained the age of 65. The physical and mental condition of the wife under 65 and without eligible children and the prospect of her surviving to age 65 are immaterial under the law. The state, in its wisdom, determines that he should forfeit to the social objectives of the fund rather than make provision for those who have been dependent upon him. This subject will be considered further in the discussion of forfeitures later in the chapter.

a comparatively little share in the contributions from the employers and from the extensive use of forfeitures.

In the further consideration of this discrimination in favor of low-income employees and employees with relatively short periods of service, it may be helpful to distinguish between employees who were present in covered employments when the system was introduced and employees who entered covered employment after the system was installed. For brevity the terms present employees and future entrants are frequently used.

An employer in establishing a contributory retirement system is confronted by the fact that contribution rates which will produce a retirement allowance satisfactory for young future entrants and for the younger present employees with long periods of service ahead of them will not yield satisfactory annuities for his older present employees. The employer cannot force the present workers already past middle life to retire at age 65 on the small annuities that would result from contribution rates that yield a satisfactory annuity for younger employees. If the employer is to have the immediate advantage of a retirement system, he must provide some benefits with respect to past services, at least of his older present employees. Since the older employees cannot pay any considerable part of the cost of benefits with respect to past services, the employer must contribute most of this cost from his own funds.

The old-age and survivors insurance system follows this practice, using the employers' taxes to provide satisfactory benefits to present employees who are already near the retirement age. For this purpose, however, the government pools all the employers' taxes. Since all covered employers are compelled to contribute, these pay-roll taxes become a part of the cost of production and in the long run are to a substantial degree passed along to consumers.

Thus under O.A.S.I. present employees who are well along in years get benefits they themselves have not paid for at the expense of employers' taxes, shifted in part to the consumers.

They receive these higher benefits, too, regardless of their means and their need. The elderly present employees get a windfall. There is an issue as to whether the state should tax to provide windfall benefits to present employees who are not in need.

In dealing with future entrants to O.A.S.I., it is necessary to distinguish between those who enter it when they are already beyond middle life and those who enter in their youth. Those who enter when they are beyond middle life are comparable with present employees of like age when the system was installed. The issue with respect to them is whether employers' contributions should be used to pay them relatively high benefits for relatively short service regardless of the provision they have already made for their old age. They may need this help from public funds, or they may not, but the system gives them a great advantage over the employees who are covered for all or the better part of their working lives.

The young new entrant or even the young present employee can have the advantage of the high benefits for relatively short service only if he withdraws from the system. For illustrative purposes we shall confine ourselves to the young man who leaves after 40 quarters of qualifying coverage to enter an uncovered occupation. Whatever degree of success he may attain in his new occupation, he receives on retirement from active work the relatively high O.A.S.I. benefit provided for short service, on attaining age 65, and his survivors have the advantages of the resulting protection.

To show what employees who thus withdraw get after 10 years of service, the figures in the following paragraph are taken from the table on page 100. They relate only to the 3 per cent tax. The windfall is much greater if the 1 per cent tax is retained. In this table the accumulation from the tax alone is used without any interest. The amount of interest will vary depending on the age at which the employee withdraws.

The man who withdraws from O.A.S.I. after 10 years of qualifying service with average wages of $900 a year or less will, on retiring at age 65, draw out in a single year more than he himself paid in taxes without interest. His expectation of life at age 65 is 11.9 years. The man who had an average wage of $3,000 a year will have paid $900 in taxes which will pay his own benefit for 1.7 years. The man who had an average wage of $600 a year who has an eligible wife will in a single year draw out more than twice what he has paid. The taxes paid by the man whose average covered wages were $3,000 a year will pay for the joint benefit for not quite 1.2 years. It is of course true that these fully insured workers may not themselves live to age 65 to draw their benefits but if they leave eligible survivors these survivors can take.

TAXES PAID AND BENEFITS OBTAINED BY PERSONS WHO WITHDRAW FULLY INSURED
AFTER TEN YEARS OF SERVICE

Average Wages for Quarters of Coverage	Employees Withdrawing from O.A.S.I. after Completing 40 Quarters of Qualifying Coverage		
	Taxes Paid (3 Per Cent Tax without Interest)	O.A.S.I. Retirement Benefit per Annum at Age 65	
		Man Only	Man and Wife
50 a month, 600 a year......	$180	$264	$396
75 a month, 900 a year......	270	297	446
100 a month, 1,200 a year......	360	330	495
150 a month, 1,800 a year......	540	396	594
200 a month, 2,400 a year......	720	462	693
250 a month, 3,000 a year......	900	528	792

This feature of the benefit formula presents an issue of social policy. Should younger workers who retire after 40 quarters of qualifying service get the cream of the benefits regardless of their need and their subsequent earnings, whereas those who spend their entire working years under the system get the skimmed milk? If it could be demonstrated that all who withdraw after 10 years or more of qualifying coverage are in fact no longer capable of self support, then something could be said for the social advantages of the system, but in many instances the fact will be otherwise, for some will withdraw because of the greater economic opportunity in uncovered fields.

Under some actuarially sound retirement systems, the able-bodied employable worker on withdrawal before reaching the retirement age is given a paid-up deferred annuity with first payment at age 65, equaling in value his own contributions and those made by his employer in his behalf. He has this old-age protection to show for the working years spent under the system. He can then add to this provision in the remaining working years of his life. Such a system does justice to the ones who withdraw, without penalizing those who spend their entire working life under it.

If the United States unifies and co-ordinates its systems, the special privileges given under O.A.S.I. for persons with short periods of covered service without reference to their need will be eliminated. The tax on employers will not be used to pay these high benefits, and relatively more will be done for persons who can only accumulate for their own old age under the system, since they do not leave it to go into uncovered employments.

MODIFICATIONS OF THE BENEFIT FORMULA

As was noted in the summary of the system, the benefit formula is, under certain conditions, subject to modifications. The law on this subject is contained in Title II, section 203. Three of these limitations will be taken up; they relate to (1) maximum benefits, (2) minimum benefits, and (3) earnings while on benefit.

Maximum limitations. The total amount of benefit which may be paid in respect to the wages earned by any one individual may be as much as $20 a month, without being subject to any maximum limitations. If the total amount of all benefits combined exceeds $20 a month, then maximum limitations may apply. Three such limitations are established: the aggregate of all benefits must not exceed (1) $85 a month, (2) an amount equal to twice a primary insurance benefit of the worker, or (3) an amount equal to 80 per cent of the average monthly wage of the worker. The limitation which gives the lowest aggregate of benefits is applicable. Each will be considered in turn.

The $85 a month limitation ($1,020 a year) constitutes a further discrimination against the employees in the upper-wage brackets who have had long periods of service. To illustrate its operation the following figures are introduced with respect to two upper income classes.

Effect of Maximum Limitation on Aggregate Benefits

I. Average wage $200 a month or $2,400 a year

Years of Service	Aggregate Payment 3 Per Cent Tax No Interest	Annual Annuity under O.A.S.I.				Available for Children per Year if Benefits Are Payable to					
		Man Only	Man and Wife	Widow Only	Child Only	Man Only		Man and Wife		Widow	
						Amount[a]	Number of Children[b]	Amount[a]	Number of Children[b]	Amount[a]	Number of Children[b]
	1	2	3	4	5	6	7	8	9	10	11
10	$720	$462	$693	$346	$231	$558[c]	2.4[c]	$327[c]	1.4[c]	$674[c]	2.9[c]
20	1,440	504	756	378	252	516[c]	2.0[c]	264[c]	1.0[c]	642[c]	2.5[c]
30	2,160	546	819	409	273	474	1.7	201	.7	611	2.2
40	2,880	588	882	441	294	432	1.5	138	.5	579	2.0
44	3,168	605	907	454	302	415	1.4	112	.4	566	1.9

II. Average wage $250 a month or $3,000 a year

Years of Service	1	2	3	4	5	6	7	8	9	10	11
10	900	528	792	396	264	492	1.9	228	.9	624	2.4
20	1,800	576	864	432	288	444	1.5	156	.5	588	2.0
30	2,700	624	936	468	312	396	1.3	84	.3	552	1.8
40	3,600	672	1,008	504	336	348	1.0	12	.04	516	1.54
44	3,960	691	1,020[d]	518	345	329	.95	[d]	[d]	502	1.46

a The amount left from the maximum of $1,020 after other benefits have been paid.
b Number of children who can draw full-scale benefit without deduction.
c This figure would be reduced by the limitation that aggregate benefits may not exceed twice the primary benefit.
d The limitation prevents the wife from drawing full benefit.

The lower section of the table deals with workers who have an average taxed wage of $250 a month. It may be noted first that in the case of the man who has contributed for 44 years the $85 limitation would prevent his wife from drawing the full benefit. If both man and wife in this wage class are on benefit, no child can draw the full benefit, although a child whose father has been in covered service for 10 years will come close to it.

If a man who has had average taxed earnings of $250 a month dies after he has had more than 10 years of service, the $85 and not the formula figure will be the limit for his widow and children if he has two or more eligible children.

The upper section of the table, which deals with men whose average taxed earnings are $200 a month, shows that the $85 limit does not come into operation against a man and wife, but if the man has had more than 20 years of service it would prevent payment of a full formula benefit in respect to one eligible child. In the case of death of the insured leaving a widow, the limitation would have practically no effect unless there should be more than two eligible children. The widow of the man in this class who died after 10 years of service would be affected by the limitation that aggregate benefits cannot exceed two primary benefits.

In examining this table it should be remembered that men past middle life with many years of tax paying under the system may die leaving a relatively young widow and two or more eligible children under 18. The government makes $85 the maximum limit despite the fact that men with long service in the upper wage brackets pay, if interest be allowed for, almost the whole of the cost of their old-age pensions, and if they die before reaching the retirement age, they leave a substantial sum which is available to help pay benefits to the widows and eligible children.[35]

[35] In the table on pages 94–95, it was shown that the man who had served 44 years at an average taxed wage of $250 a month would have contributed with a 3 per cent tax and compound interest at 2 per cent a total of $6,255. If he should die before going on benefit, his widow on attaining age 65 would be entitled to a benefit of $518.40 a year. According to the United States Life Tables, a white woman at age 65–66 has an average future lifetime of 13.1 years. The present value of $1.00 a year for 13 years at 2 per cent is roughly $11.35. His accumulation after 44 years with interest at 2 per cent would thus

The $85 upper limit appears to represent, therefore, a decision on the part of the government as to how employers' contributions and forfeitures to the system shall be distributed. A man who has served in upper-bracket positions for his working life and his dependents or survivors are not to draw from the fund more than $85 a month despite the fact that the man and his employer on his account are the heaviest contributors to the fund.

The limitation that the aggregate of all benefits must not exceed twice a primary benefit does not discriminate among the several average wage classes. In effect it restricts the number of beneficiaries. How it restricts is illustrated schematically below. Since the widow's benefit is three quarters, the illustrations are expressed in quarters of a primary benefit which makes the upper limit eight quarters.

A	The man himself on benefit...	4
	The wife on benefit...	2
	One child on benefit...	2
	Total...	8

If the family has more than one eligible child, the benefits for the dependents must be reduced proportionately to keep the total within the prescribed eight quarters of primary benefit.

B	A widow on benefit...	3
	Two eligible children on benefit...	4
	Total	7

If the widow has a third eligible child, the aggregate family benefit can be raised by one quarter of the primary benefit.

---

pay about $552 a year for 13 years. It would seem that if he retires at 65 he, himself, has accumulated almost the entire cost of his own old-age annuity. If he dies before reaching retirement, leaving an eligible widow, his own contributions will pay for her old-age benefit. If he is to get a substantial amount from funds contributed by employers and from forfeitures to the system, he must live to draw an old-age benefit and have a wife or eligible children who also draw benefits. This statement omits from consideration two factors which operate in opposite directions (1) during the period since he became currently insured he had some protection for his dependents; and (2) if he had no eligible dependents his contributions to the system, minus the amount of the lump-sum death benefit, would have been forfeited to the fund had he died before reaching the retirement age.

Nothing more can be paid the family on account of additional eligible children.

C   A widower on primary benefit........................ 4
    Two children on benefit............................. 4
                                                        ──
        Total.. 8

If the widower has more than two eligible children, no additional payment can be made.

D   Four children of the deceased beneficiary with the mother
    deceased or ineligible because of remarriage.......... 8

This limitation, it will be noted, cannot operate except where children are involved, for the primary beneficiary and his eligible wife use only six of the permissible eight quarter benefits. Since the wife to be eligible to take during the lifetime of her husband must herself be 65 years of age the chances of there being more than one child under 18 are not very great.

The situation with respect to widows is, however, very different. The covered breadwinner may die currently or fully insured leaving more than two children. In that case the legal limitation of twice a primary benefit becomes effective. It should be repeated, moreover, that some men marry women much younger than themselves and may even with long periods of covered service have several children of eligible age. Despite long service and relatively heavy contributions of such workers, they are subject to this same limitation.

The limitation that the aggregate of all benefits must not exceed 80 per cent of the average monthly wage of the insured workers operates mainly against the children of workers whose average monthly wage is $50 or less. For wages of $50 or less the basic part of the formula allows 40 per cent, whereas for wages above $50 and below $250 it allows only 10 per cent. The allowance of only 10 per cent on wages above $50 operates automatically to make this restriction inapplicable in the higher wage brackets.

It may be interesting to see what this 80 per cent of average wage does with respect to widows left with children under 18 years of age by wage earners with average wages of selected amounts of $60 a month or less. Average wages of $30, $40, $50, and $60 a month will be used for purposes of illustration.

THE EFFECT OF LIMITING AGGREGATE BENEFITS TO 80 PER CENT OF AVERAGE WAGES

I. AVERAGE WAGE $30 A MONTH, LIMIT $24 A MONTH

Length of Service	Primary Benefit	Widow's Benefit	Child's Benefit	Available for Children	
				Amount[a]	Possible Number at Full Benefit
10......	$13.20	$ 9.90	$ 6.60	$14.10	2.1
20......	14.40	10.80	7.20	13.20	1.8
30......	15.60	11.70	7.80	12.30	1.6
40......	16.80	12.60	8.40	11.40	1.4

II. AVERAGE WAGE $40 A MONTH, LIMIT $32 A MONTH

10......	17.60	13.20	8.80	18.80	2.1
20......	19.20	14.40	9.60	17.60	1.8
30......	20.80	15.60	10.40	16.40	1.6
40......	22.40	16.80	11.20	15.20	1.4

III. AVERAGE WAGE $50 A MONTH, LIMIT $40 A MONTH

10......	22.00	16.50	11.00	23.50	2.1
20......	24.00	18.00	12.00	22.00	1.8
30......	26.00	19.50	13.00	20.50	1.6
40......	28.00	21.00	14.00	19.00	1.4

IV. AVERAGE WAGE $60 A MONTH, LIMIT $48 A MONTH

10......	23.10	17.33	11.55	30.67	2.7
20......	25.20	18.90	12.60	29.10	2.3
30......	27.30	20.48	13.65	27.52	2.0
40......	29.40	22.05	14.70	25.95	1.8

[a] The remainder after the widow's benefit has been subtracted from 80 per cent of the average monthly wage.

The legal provision that aggregate benefits shall not exceed 80 per cent of the average monthly wage means that 80 per cent of the average monthly wage is practically the total benefit for a widow left with more than one eligible child, if her husband's covered wages averaged $50 a month or less. The figures for the widow and children in cases where the average wage was $60 a month or more illustrate the beginning of the disappearance of the effect of this limitation and the appearance of the limitation that aggregate benefits cannot exceed two primary benefits. The two primary benefits limitation comes into effect, it may be recalled, when a widow has more than two eligible children, since she takes three of the permitted eight quarter benefits and two children take four more, leaving only one quarter additional for the third child. It may be noted, however, that the insured with longer periods of services at $60 a month still falls within the 80 per cent of average wage limitation and will get no additional protection for his widow and dependent children from his long period of tax payment.[36]

This situation reflects the conflict between insurance concepts and welfare concepts. Welfare concepts would dictate that more money raised through the exercise of the sovereign power to tax should go to the widow with six children to rear than to the one with only two. Insurance concepts permit the use of funds so collected to pay substantial benefits to persons who are not in need and yet dictate restricting the amount which may be paid in the event a low-income widow's family has more than two children.

Minimum benefit. With respect to minimum benefits the Social Security Act, as amended, reads:

(b) Whenever the benefit or total of benefits under section 202, payable for a month with respect to an individual's wages, is less than $10, such benefit or total of benefits shall, prior to any deductions under subsections (d), (e), or (h), be increased to $10.[37]

Other restrictions. The two significant sections dealing with deductions for employment and for other reasons read:

(d) Deductions, in such amounts and at such time or times as the Board shall determine, shall be made from any payment or payments under this title to which an individual is entitled, until the total of such deductions equals such individual's benefit or benefits for any month in which such individual:

(1) rendered services for wages of not less than $15; or

(2) if a child under eighteen and over sixteen years of age, failed to

---

[36] For the employee who has had ten years of service at $60, twice the primary benefit is used. It gives $46.20, which is less than $48, the 80 per cent limitation. At 20 years of service twice the primary benefit is $50.40, which is greater than $48 and hence the 80 per cent limitation applies. Service and tax paying beyond about 14.3 years does not add to the protection of the wife with more than two eligible dependent children.

[37] 53 Stat. 1367, Title 2, sec. 203 (b).

attend school regularly and the Board finds that attendance was feasible; or

(3) if a widow entitled to a widow's current insurance benefit, did not have in her care a child of her deceased husband entitled to receive a child's insurance benefit.

(e) Deductions shall be made from any wife's or child's insurance benefit to which a wife or child is entitled, until the total of such deductions equals such wife's or child's insurance benefit or benefits for any month in which the individual, with respect to whose wages such benefit was payable, rendered services for wages of not less than $15.[38]

Administrative costs. Administratively the O.A.S.I. benefit formula is inevitably costly. It necessitates maintaining for each covered worker an exact record of the number of quarters in which he has qualified and the amount he has earned, not in excess of $3,000 a year. These records must be maintained throughout the working life of each covered employee. They must be used in determining the amount of benefit due the retired workers and their survivors. For 1943 the administrative costs for O.A.S.I. were just under 30 million dollars. They will increase as the number of beneficiaries grows. It should be noted that these figures do not include the sums spent by the employers in preparing and submitting the detailed reports required by the Social Security Board. This subject will be further considered in Part III.[39]

PERSONS INSURED

In the summary description of O.A.S.I. given on pages 75 to 79 it was pointed out that mere coverage and payment of taxes to support the system does not insure the worker. To be insured, the worker must have worked in a covered position for the number of quarters prescribed by the law.

The first protection the covered worker gets for his enforced contribution is ordinarily a form of life insurance for the benefit of possible survivors that goes with the status of currently insured. He can attain that status in 6 quarters if he earns not less than $50 a quarter in a covered occupation for 6 consecutive

[38] The same, sec. 203 (d) and (e).
[39] See Chap. 27.

quarters. To retain that status he must have been paid wages of not less than $50 for each of not less than 6 of the 12 calendar quarters immediately preceding the quarter in which he died. Two points in connection with currently insured require emphasis.

1. It is a form of life insurance for the benefit of survivors if the insured has any survivors eligible to take under the law, or to pay a lump-sum benefit for burial expenses. To use an old phrase, the insured has to die to win.

2. It is a form of extended life insurance that once attained expires 6 quarters after the employee has ceased to earn not less than $50 a quarter in a covered occupation. It may expire earlier than that if the employee's work has been irregular and he cannot show 6 quarters with the required earnings in the last 12 quarters. The employee thus attains no permanent protection until he has attained the status of fully insured, and, as will be pointed out in the following discussion, not all fully insured are permanently protected.

Fully insured is the preferred status under O.A.S.I. It can be permanently attained by any individual who earns not less than $50 a quarter for 40 quarters in covered occupations. Thus a person continuously employed under the conditions named can attain in 10 years what may be roughly referred to as "a paid-up policy." After he has 40 quarters to his credit he cannot lose any of his legislative rights, although of course if he remains in covered employment his contributions will continue and his benefits will increase.

The status fully insured may, however, be attained possibly only temporarily by persons after they have had a minimum of 6 quarters of qualifying employment without having the full 40 quarters or 10 years. These persons fall into 2 groups:

1. Those attaining the age of 21 years after December 31, 1936. If they die before attaining the age of 65, they are fully insured if they had qualifying employment for half the quarters between the quarter in which they attained age 21 and the quarter in which they died. It may be noted that this provison

in some cases partakes of the nature of extended life insurance for protection of survivors. For example, a young man beginning at age 21 years works for 4 years or 16 quarters in qualifying employment in a war plant. He then returns to the farm and works in an uncovered occupation. If he should die at any time within the ensuing 4 years he would be fully insured, since he would have been in qualifying employment for half the quarters between his 21st birthday and the date of his death. If he should survive beyond the 4 years, he would lose his fully insured status because he would not have been in qualifying employment for half of the prescribed quarters.

2. Those who were 21 years of age or over on December 31, 1936. They attain a permanent fully insured status or a paid-up policy as soon as they have had qualifying employment for half the quarters between, roughly, December 31, 1936 and the date of their 65th birthday. With credits for half the intervening quarters they cannot lose their protection. For persons who were 45 years of age or over on December 31, 1936, one half the quarters between that date and their 65th birthday is less than 40. If one who was over 45 on the passage of the act died before attaining the retirement age he dies fully insured provided he has qualifying employment for half the quarters between December 31, 1936 and the date of his death.

Here again is encountered a provision in the nature of extended life insurance. A person who leaves qualifying employment after having served 40 counted quarters has a paid-up non-forfeitable policy giving him a legislative right to all benefits. If he was over 45 years of age on December 31, 1936, and has had qualifying employment for at least one half of the quarters between December 31, 1936 and his 65th birthday, he likewise has a paid-up non-forfeitable policy. If he leaves without having attained a non-forfeitable policy, he gets extended life insurance for a limited period for the protection of his eligible dependents or for a lump-sum death benefit, but he loses his own old-age retirement benefit. His extended life insurance lasts only so long as the number of quarters in which he qualified equals or exceeds half the quarters counted in deter-

mining eligibility. When the number of quarters used in determining eligibility is more than twice his qualifying quarters,
his extended insurance that protects his survivors expires unless he returns to covered employment.

The provisions governing currently insured and fully insured are thus so drafted that many covered persons who have
paid the compulsory contributions will forfeit them. Some will
forfeit because they did not remain under the system long
enough to acquire an insured status. Others will forfeit them
because after leaving covered employment they did not die soon
enough to get anything from the extended life insurance feature
of the system. Some who die while still covered by extended insurance will leave no survivors eligible for benefit and their contributions will go for the lump-sum death benefit.

In the preceding discussion it has been noted that a covered
worker can acquire a non-forfeitable legislative right to the
benefits of the O.A.S.I. system in 40 quarters of qualifying employment. One possible result mentioned under the benefit
formula deserves repetition in considering the insured status. A
youth may begin qualifying employment at age 21, serve continuously for 10 years and then withdraw, with his non-forfeitable insurance, to enter an uncovered occupation. He will
reap the advantages of the fact that the benefit formula gives
relatively high benefits for short service in proportion to premium paid. If he happens to be in the lower-wage brackets in
these earlier years of his working life, he will likewise profit from
the relatively high benefits allowed by the formula for low-paid
workers. He would get the cream of the benefits for a relatively
short period of low contributions. He would have a great advantage over a fellow employee who entered covered employment
at the same time and age but left with only 35 quarters of qualifying employment, if both reach the age of 65 years. The one
with 40 quarters of qualifying employment will get a substantial benefit whereas his fellow worker with only 35 quarters will
get nothing.

O.A.S.I. gives a curious preference to protecting eligible
survivors over safeguarding the old age of the contributor.

In many retirement systems an employee who withdraws from active service before reaching the retirement age is given what is in effect a paid-up deferred annuity contract with first payment when he reaches the retirement age. In the more enlightened systems this deferred annuity is based both on the employee's contribution and the employer's contribution. He cannot lose the old-age protection he has earned in the years during which he worked under that system. His survivors come in only in the event the owner of the deferred annuity dies before he reaches the retirement age.

Under O.A.S.I. the worker who withdraws neither fully nor currently insured has earned no old-age protection whatever from his period of coverage, unless later he returns to covered employment and qualifies. If he withdraws currently insured or temporarily fully insured, he gets not a deferred old-age annuity for himself but extended term life insurance for the benefit of possible eligible survivors. So far as providing for his own old age is concerned, unless he has earned a fully paid-up policy, his years under O.A.S.I. are lost years. Because of the nature of annuities, the later he begins the more difficult it will be to make suitable provision.

Persons who have sought to protect the rights of employees under public or private retirement systems have insisted that there should be no forfeiture of the old-age protection that an employee has earned during his service under that system and that he should have the value of both his own and his employer's contributions. If his period of service has been so short that the amount of money involved is inconsequential, immediate payment of a lump-sum settlement to clear the accounts may be advisable, but if the amount is substantial the use of the deferred annuity with first payment at retirement age is preferred. Special provisions are recommended if the withdrawal is due to disability. To many persons it will seem that O.A.S.I. has disregarded the principles which governments should adopt in establishing good retirement systems for public employees and, through exercise of their regulatory powers, make compulsory in private retirement systems.

In the summary outline of O.A.S.I., it was noted that not all employees working for salaries or wages are covered. Certain classes are excluded. Here the reasons for exclusions and the effect of exclusions will be briefly considered.

COVERAGE

Agricultural labor, domestic labor in private homes, casual labor not in the course of the employer's trade or business, and fishermen, with certain exceptions, clearly are not excluded because they are not in need of protection in their old age. Probably more than many other classes of wage workers they are in need of protection. They are presumably excluded, partly because of the difficulty in applying to them the elaborate and intricate O.A.S.I. with its contributions based on pay rolls and its benefits based on average monthly earnings during covered employment. The fact that pay in the excluded occupations is often partly in board and lodging is a further complication. Another factor is that employers might be strongly opposed to payment of the necessary taxes. The situation in agriculture in the thirties was such that employing farmers would have had some difficulties in passing a pay-roll tax along to consumers and of course employers of domestic servants in the private home cannot shift the tax. A tax on them might reduce employment or tend to lower wages.

World War II resulted in a substantial movement from uncovered agricultural labor and domestic service into covered industry so that many persons uncovered originally are at present covered. As has been noted, however, coverage is not synonymous with insurance. If now that the war is over there is a movement back to the farms or to domestic service in private homes, many of the persons making that change will forfeit their payments to O.A.S.I. The general subject of forfeitures will be considered further in a subsequent section of the present chapter.

Service performed in the employ of the United States government or one of its instrumentalities and service which brings the employee under the Railroad Retirement Act are excluded mainly, perhaps, because other provisions are made for the old-age protection of many such employees. In subsequent chapters the federal retirement system and the railroad retirement system will be described in some detail. It will there be noted that such systems are part of the employer's compensation system. The employer's contributions are used to pay benefits to the employees of that employer or industry, and they are not used as the basis for effecting a general redistribution of earnings according to a governmentally determined formula. Under these systems the employer or the industry may pay relatively more per dollar of contribution for the lower-bracket employees than for those in the upper-bracket, but the employer's contributions do not go outside the industry or enterprise. The employees get the full advantage of what their employers are contributing. Abolition of these special systems and inclusion of their members under O.A.S.I. would clearly be against the interests of these workers.

Service performed in the employ of a state or any political division of a state is excluded perhaps primarily because under the Constitution the national government cannot levy a tax against the sovereign states. Several states and local governments have retirement systems for their employees or for classes of their employees that roughly resemble the two retirement systems discussed in the preceding paragraph. Abolition of these systems and substitution of O.A.S.I. would be against the interests of the state and local employees so covered. Moreover, under existing constitutional law, the national government cannot tax the state on its pay roll to raise money to be distributed among all covered employees regardless of their state of residence and their occupation.

Many classes are excluded because the enterprise is religious, charitable, scientific, literary, or educational, and has no net earnings which inure to the benefit of any private shareholder or individual. Such enterprises could not pay the employer's tax out of profits nor pass it along to the consumers. Large, strong organizations of this type often have satisfactory retirement systems. The Teachers Insurance and Annuity Association of America has rendered distinctive service in its field, and certain of the churches have excellent retirement systems, far more advantageous to those covered than the O.A.S.I. would be. On the other hand, there are in the aggregate many employees of agencies of this general type for whom no provision at all is made.

This description of coverage demonstrates that the United States has not yet solved the problem of providing old-age insurance without any interference with the mobility of labor. As the situation stands at present, the country has (1) persons who are under O.A.S.I. and will remain under it long enough to secure protection, (2) persons who are temporarily under O.A.S.I. but will not remain under it long enough to secure protection, (3) persons who are not under any formal system, and (4) persons who are under other systems that are, particularly for upper-bracket employees, far more advantageous than O.A.S.I. A major issue therefore exists as to how the individual is to be free to move from one employment to another, from the status of a wage or salary worker to the status of the self-employed, or from the status of regularly employed to the status of casually employed without forfeiture of what he has contributed toward protection in his old age. This subject will be further touched upon in the present chapter under forfeitures and will be considered at length in Part III.

The O.A.S.I. law does not clearly set forth the distinctions between the benefits provided the male covered worker and those provided the female covered worker. Both men and women pay the same rate of tax on their wage, but the benefits are very different. To further simplify, we shall take up first the benefits for covered men and then the distinctive features with respect to covered women.

BENEFITS EARNED BY MEN

The primary benefit. A fully insured man on attaining the age of 65 and on filing an application is entitled to a primary insurance benefit each month beginning with the month in which he becomes eligible and ending with the month preceding the one in which he dies (section 202 [a]). It should be noted, however, that section 203 (d) provides that deductions shall be made in the grant for any month in which the individual "rendered services for wages of not less than $15." If the applicant is earning wages that equal or exceed the amount of the primary benefit, he will not get any benefit. There is thus no financial reason for applying unless his benefit is greater than his current wages. If the benefit equals or exceeds earnings, there is no financial reason to keep on earning beyond the $15 a month allowed by section 203 (d), except that each additional year of covered work will increase his benefit by 1 per cent of the base amount. For this increase he will have to pay the tax on his current wages.

The wife's benefit. If the male old-age beneficiary has a wife who is the mother of his child or to whom he was married prior to January 1, 1939 or, if later, prior to the date upon which he attained the age of 60, the wife on attaining the age of 65 is entitled to a wife's insurance benefit provided she is living with him at the time of her application.[40] The amount of the wife's benefit is normally one-half of the husband's primary benefit, but adjustments are made if she is otherwise entitled to receive a primary benefit. If the wife is entitled in her own right to receive a primary insurance benefit the amount of that benefit earned by her is deducted from her wife's benefit. Thus, if a wife herself has earned a primary benefit equal to or greater than half of her husband's primary benefit, she takes nothing by virtue of her status as the wife of her husband. The wife's benefit continues until "any of the following occurs: she dies, her husband dies, they are divorced *a vinculo matrimonii*, or she becomes entitled to receive a primary insurance benefit equal to

---

[40] Sec. 209 (n) of the Social Security Act, as amended, reads: "A wife shall be deemed to be living with her husband if they are both members of the same household, or she is receiving regular contributions from him toward her support, or he has been ordered by any court to contribute to her support; and a widow shall be deemed to have been living with her husband at the time of his death if they were both members of the same household on the date of his death, or she was receiving regular contributions from him toward her support on such date, or he had been ordered by any court to contribute to her support."

or exceeding one half of the primary insurance benefit of her husband."[41]

If the wife works for wages after attaining the age of 65, and the wages are $15 a month or more, the amount of the wages are deducted from her wife's benefit and of course cancel it if the wages are equal to the benefit.

If the combined benefit to the man and his wife exceeds $85, the wife's benefit is reduced to bring the total to $85. There are other conditions upon which the wife's benefit may be reduced,[42] but it hardly seems desirable to go into them at this point.

The widow's benefit. If the fully insured man dies, his widow is under certain conditions entitled to a widow's benefit, which is three fourths of the primary insurance benefit of her deceased husband. The conditions are:

1. She must have attained the age of 65.

2. She must have been the mother of his child or been married to him prior to the beginning of the twelfth month before the month in which he died.

3. She must have been living with her husband at the time of his death.[43]

4. She must not have remarried.

5. She must not be entitled to receive a primary insurance benefit equal to or exceeding three fourths of her deceased husband's insurance benefits. If she is entitled to a smaller primary benefit in her own right, the amount of such benefit is deducted from her widow's benefit.

Her right to the widow's benefit terminates if she remarries or later because of her own work becomes entitled to a primary benefit equal to or exceeding three fourths of her deceased husband's primary benefit. Should she work and earn $15 a month or more, her earnings are deducted from her widow's benefit.

The widow's current benefit. If a fully insured man or currently insured man dies leaving a widow, she may, under certain con-

---

[41] Sec. 202 (b) (1).
[42] See sec. 203 of the act.
[43] For definition of living with husband see note 40, p. 116.

ditions, be entitled to a widow's current insurance benefit, which is normally three fourths the primary benefit earned by her deceased husband. The conditions are:

1. That she is the mother of her husband's child or was married to him prior to the beginning of the twelfth month before the month in which he died.

2. That at the time of filing application she must have in her care a child of such deceased individual entitled to receive a child's insurance benefit. The child must be under 18 years of age. The definition of a child and the conditions under which the child can take will be taken up under the child's benefit.

3. That she has not remarried.

4. That she is not entitled to a widow's benefit.

5. That she is not entitled to a primary benefit earned by herself equal to the widow's current benefit. If she has a smaller benefit in her own right, the amount of it is deducted from her widow's current benefit.

6. If she works she must not earn more per month than the amount of the benefit. If she earns less than the benefit but $15 or more per month, her earnings are subtracted from the benefit.

Her benefit ceases (1) if no child of her deceased husband remains entitled to a child's benefit; (2) if she remarries; (3) if she becomes entitled to a widow's insurance benefit, that is, if she reaches age 65; or (4) if she becomes entitled through her own work to a primary benefit equal to or exceeding three fourths of the primary benefit of her deceased husband. Any smaller benefit to which she may become entitled by her own work is deducted from her widow's current insurance benefit.

The child's benefit. The fully insured man on arriving at the age of 65 or on his death and the currently insured man on his death creates a benefit for his children.

"The term 'child' . . . means the child of an individual, and the stepchild of an individual by a marriage contracted prior to the date upon which he attained the age of sixty and prior to the beginning of the twelfth month before the month in which he died, and a child legally adopted . . . "[44] within the same limitations as to time.

[44] Sec. 209 (k).

To be eligible to receive a benefit by virtue of the insurance of its father, stepfather, or adopting father, the child must be: (1) under 18 years of age, (2) unmarried, and (3) must have been dependent upon the father at the time of application or, if the father has died, at the time of death.

With respect to dependency upon the father, the law provides that:

A child shall be deemed dependent on a father or adopting father, . . . unless . . . such . . . [father] was not living with or contributing to the support of such child and—(A) such child is neither the legitimate nor adopted child of such individual, or (B) such child has been adopted by some other individual, or (C) such child, at the time of such individual's death, was living with and supported by such child's stepfather.[45]

The law creates an extremely strong but rebuttable presumption in favor of a child's dependency upon the father. The fact that the child or adopted child was not living with the father or being supported by him does not destroy the child's right to take by virtue of his father's insurance, unless the child has been adopted by someone else or unless on the death of the father or adopting father he was living with and being supported by a stepfather.

The amount of the child's benefit is normally one half the primary benefit of the father. If, however, the aggregate benefits of all who take by virtue of the father's insurance exceed certain limits, section 203 (a) applies.[46]

The child's right to a benefit ceases when (1) he attains the age of 18, (2) he is adopted, (3) he marries, or (4) he dies.

It may be noted that the child's benefit is not canceled by the remarriage of the mother and hence the acquisition of a stepfather. The stepfather is not required by law to assume support of the child. A family which adopts the orphan or half-orphan must, however, forego the assistance which it might secure in the child's support from the child's benefit. If the family merely takes the child in, it can receive the benefit, but if it makes the child legally a member of the family by adoption the benefit ceases.

[45] Sec. 202 (c) (3).
[46] For the discussion of the limitations, see pp. 101–08.

One aspect of the law deserves further special note. Young people sometimes become parents without the formality of marriage. Not infrequently a marriage is arranged to legitimatize the baby. The marriage, however, deprives the child thus married of the right to take by virtue of his father's insurance and makes that child dependent for his own support and the support of the baby upon his own earnings, upon relatives, or upon general public assistance. Thus the child has by the marriage been cut off from a child's benefit. It would seem, however, that if the children involved do not marry until after the age of 18, the fact that they have a baby—illegitimate under the law— does not bar them from a benefit.

Parent's benefit. The fully insured or the currently insured man may, under certain conditions, provide a benefit for his dependent parent or parents. The conditions are:

1. He must not leave a widow or an unmarried surviving child under the age of 18. The existence of either a widow or an eligible child bars a dependent parent.

2. The parent must have attained the age of 65.

3. The parent must have been "wholly dependent upon and supported by such individual at the time of such individual's death and filed proof of such dependency and support within two years of such death."

4. The parent must not have remarried since such individual's death.

5. The parent must not be entitled to receive any other insurance benefit under the law or, if so entitled, does not receive benefits equal to or exceeding one half of the primary benefit of the insured.

Special attention should be called to the words "wholly dependent upon and supported by such individual at the time of such individual's death." Here, obviously, the means test must be used to determine whether the parent is eligible. If several children were supporting the parent at the time of death, the parent apparently would be ineligible. If the parent had income from earnings and savings, and the insured's contribution to the parent was to make the parent's life easier and more comfortable, the parent under the law apparently is not eligible.

The parent's benefit is normally one half the primary benefit of the insured with provisions for adjustment in case he is entitled to other benefits under the act.

Lump-sum death benefit. The fully insured or currently insured man may under certain conditions leave to beneficiaries designated by the law a "lump-sum death payment" which is six times his primary monthly insurance benefit. Since the maximum primary benefit is probably not over $60 the maximum death benefit is $360. The wording of the law, section 202 (g), makes it plain that in the main this benefit is in the nature of a burial allowance. It goes in priority order to the widow, the surviving children, or others in the status of children under the state intestacy laws, the surviving parent or parents or the person or persons who paid the expenses of burial, although if to the last named, only to the extent of their payments for this purpose. Here the words widow, child, or children are used in their ordinary legal sense and not in the special sense in which they are used in the other benefits.

A lump-sum death benefit is paid only if the insured leaves "no surviving widow, child, or parent who would, on filing application in the month in which such individual died, be entitled to" a child's benefit, a widow's benefit, a widow's current benefit, or a parent's benefit. All these benefits take priority over the lump-sum death benefit, and if they are immediately payable extinguish that benefit. The fact that a man leaves a widow who later on attaining the age 65 may become entitled to a widow's benefit does not bar the immediate payment of the lump-sum death benefit. If the widow will a few months later attain the age of 65 she gets the lump-sum death benefit. If a child or widow is immediately eligible but will lose eligibility within a few months after the death of the insured, no lump-sum death benefit is paid, although the fund may not have paid out in the aggregate six times the monthly primary benefit of the insured.

BENEFITS EARNED BY WOMEN

The facts regarding benefits thus far presented relate to the fully insured or the currently insured male worker. We come now to the benefits for the fully insured or currently insured woman worker, who is taxed on her wages at the same rate as the male worker.

No benefits for husbands. Patently a woman worker cannot leave a widow and thus the widow's insurance benefit and the widow's current benefit are not involved in her insurance. No benefits are provided for husbands except that a widower may receive the lump-sum death payment. The law is based on averages or normal conditions, and on the average or under normal conditions, a husband is not dependent upon his wife for support. In some cases, however, a wife works because her husband is unable to make a living; he is physically or mentally disabled or incompetent as a provider. Under these conditions he is not taken care of by his wife's insurance in the event of her death but must depend on their other savings or on relief payments.

The woman worker's insurance provides for her own old age, under certain circumstances for her children under 18 years of age, for her dependent parents, and for the relatives who pay her burial expenses. In discussing these benefits, we shall be mainly concerned with the factors that distinguish them from the benefits for men.

The primary benefit. The old-age benefit, or the primary insurance benefit, for the single woman, or for the married woman where the husband has never worked in a covered employment or who has never worked in such an employment long enough to be permanently fully insured, is virtually the same as that for a single man. On attaining the age of 65 she becomes entitled to a primary insurance benefit provided she had attained the status of a fully insured individual. If she keeps on working and earns wages of $15 a month or more, her wages are deducted from her benefits.

The real distinction between men and women arises when the woman worker is married to a man who works long enough in a covered employment to become permanently a fully insured individual. As has been pointed out in discussing benefits for men, he has been providing not only for his own old age but for the old age of his wife or his widow. If both the husband and wife are working and paying O.A.S.I. taxes, both are providing for their old age. What does the woman worker get for her payments in her old age?

If her primary benefit, acquired through being engaged in covered employment, exceeds one half the primary benefit of her husband, she receives on attaining the age of 65 the primary benefit she has earned herself, but nothing by virtue of her husband's insurance.

If her primary benefit is less than one half the primary benefit of her husband, she receives the benefit she has earned herself plus enough of her share of the primary benefit earned by her husband to bring her total to one half her husband's benefit. More simply stated, she gets no more than she would have received had she never worked in a covered occupation and never paid any pay-roll tax on her wages, except under certain conditions.

If the working wife in a covered employment is older than her husband, she becomes entitled to take before he does, and hence for a few years she may get benefits on her own insurance. If the husband on attaining the age of 65 does not retire and apply for his benefits, the fully insured wife on attaining age 65 may apply for her benefits and draw the full amount. If the husband was over 60 years of age at the time of his marriage to his working wife, she is not his wife within the definition of the act, and she therefore is dependent on her own earned benefit.

If at the time of her husband's death she was not the mother of his son or daughter and had not been married to him for approximately a year, she is not his widow within the definition of the act, and she therefore is dependent on her own earned benefit.

The child's benefit. The covered married woman with children under 18 years of age will find two major differences between what she earns and what a covered father earns. The first difference lies in the assumption as to dependency and the second in the benefits.

The refutable presumption in the case of the father is, as was previously noted, that his children, by nature or by adoption, are dependent on him. The assumption in the case of mothers reads:

A child shall be deemed dependent upon a mother, adopting mother, or stepparent, or to have been dependent upon such individual at the time of the death of such individual, only if, at the time of such death, or, if such individual was living, at the time such child's application for child's insurance benefits was filed, no parent other than such individual was contributing to the support of such child and such child was not living with its father or adopting father.[47]

The language which calls for emphasis is: "A child shall be deemed dependent upon a mother . . . only if . . . no parent other than such individual [the mother] was contributing to the support of such child and such child was not living with its father or adopting father." Thus if the child was living with a father or adopting father, whether he is or is not insured under O.A.S.I., the children cannot take by virtue of the mother's insurance. A strict interpretation of the act would seem to exclude the children who were living with a father or adopting father, even if for one reason or another that father was not actually supporting them and might in fact be dependent on his wife's earnings for his own support. In the normal or typical family the father is the principal source of income and the mother a secondary breadwinner, and the law assumes normal or typical conditions, hard as that may be on the wife and mother who is forced to be the principal source of income for her family.

The provision with respect to the amount of the child's benefit reads:

(2) Such child's insurance benefit for each month shall be equal to one half of the primary insurance benefit of the individual with respect to whose wages the child is entitled to receive such benefit, except that, when there is more than one such individual such benefit shall be equal to one half of whichever primary insurance benefit is greatest.[48]

[47] Sec. 202 (c) (4).
[48] Sec. 202 (c) (2).

This provision read in connection with the one regarding dependency means in general that the child gets one half the father's primary benefit. If the child might under any circumstances take either from the father or the mother, he would take only from the father unless that benefit would be smaller than the one he might get from the mother.

Parent's benefit. The fully insured woman is presumably more of a protection to her dependent parents than a fully insured man because she cannot leave a widow. If she leaves no unmarried child under 18 her dependent parent may take under the conditions previously enumerated. It will be recalled that in order to take the parent must have been wholly dependent upon and supported by the insured individual at the time of such individual's death. The fully insured married woman is thus protecting a parent only if she has no unmarried children under 18 and is the sole support of her parent.

Lump-sum death benefit. The woman is more likely than the man to occasion the payment of a lump-sum death payment of six times a monthly primary benefit, because she is far more likely to die leaving no beneficiaries eligible to take under the other benefit clauses of the law.

EQUITIES, FORFEITURES, AND OPTIONS

Two radically different positions may be taken with respect to the benefit formula, the insured status, and the benefit provisions that have just been reviewed. The first is that the employee's contribution is a tax pure and simple, that the government levies taxes as it sees fit and spends or distributes the proceeds as it sees fit, and that the taxpayer has no moral or legal equity or right in the money thus collected after it has been paid to the government. From this point of view there can be no forfeiture of a tax, because the person who paid it had no right to it.

The second point of view is that the tax paid by the employee under O.A.S.I. is in the nature of an insurance premium by the payment of which an employee becomes possessed of certain contingent legislative rights. O.A.S.I., in accordance with this point of view, is in part at least a substitute for private insurance. Private insurance has taught many of the insured to look into such matters as individual equities, forfeitures, and optional methods of settlement. To one who takes this point of view it seems significant to examine O.A.S.I. with respect to these features, and in a sense to contrast public insurance with private insurance. The more important features of this comparison will be presented below.

Private insurance has in the main been voluntary. An individual often had to be persuaded to buy by a salesman. During the past quarter of a century or so, many public and private enterprises have established retirement systems to provide old-age and other collateral benefits, and many of them have been both contributory and compulsory, but the employers who established them operated in a competitive labor market. They wanted the retirement systems they devised both to hold and to attract good employees, and employees were free to resign or to seek employment elsewhere if the provisions of the retirement system did not appeal to them. In private voluntary insurance, and to a lesser extent in retirement insurance, competition resulted in recognition of individual equities, restriction of forfeitures, and provision of optional methods of settlement.

DEFINITIONS

It is perhaps desirable to define the terms equity, forfeiture, and option and to indicate their significance.

Equity. A private insurance contract is said to be equitable when all members of a class receive the same degree of insurance protection for the same amount of premium paid. It does not mean that all get back the same number of dollars per dollar paid in, for they are buying insurance, but all have the same protection, and all face on taking out the insurance approximately the same hazard. Obviously voluntary insurance in a competitive society must have this attribute or a close approach to it, because few persons would voluntarily purchase insurance when their risks were much lower than the risks of their fellows. Private insurance companies tended, moreover, in one way or another to offer lower rates to those whose hazards were lower.

In retirement systems a tendency developed, at least so far as the employees' contributions were concerned, to relate benefits to contributions or to salaries so that there was a fairly definite relationship between the amount paid in by the employee and the amount of the benefit. In one widely used system the amount of the old-age benefit on retirement depends almost entirely on the amount contributed by the employee and by the employer on his behalf. Such systems were said "entirely to preserve the individual equities."

Forfeiture. A maxim in equity law is "Equity abhors a forfeiture." Clients of life insurance companies rarely want to pay any considerable sums in premiums if in the event of some contingency they will lose all or a considerable part of what they have paid in. Many states have regarded as contrary to public policy clauses in insurance contracts that involve certain forfeitures and have required carriers to provide cash surrender values, extended insurance, and so forth. Although in some instances the forfeitures added to the profits of stockholders in the insurance company, the laws were made applicable to mutual companies where the forfeitures went in the main to the policyholders who continued their insurance in force.

In private voluntary insurance a forfeiture is to be distinguished from the payment made by the insured to cover the costs of administration. Premiums paid for private insurance are "loaded" to cover these costs. In ordinary life insurance the loadings are commonly heavy in the first few years because of the costs of selling the insurance, making the medical and other examinations, and setting up the new policy in the accounts and records. Thereafter the costs are mainly the costs of premium collection. Mail billing costs less than personal collection by an agent. Under mail billing quarterly collections cost roughly four times as much as annual collections, and it costs about as much to collect a small premium as a large one. Weekly or monthly collections by a collector who calls at the house are inevitably administratively costly, and the insured who buys his insurance in this way must pay heavily for administration, even if the company operates with a high degree of efficiency.

The difference between private insurance and O.A.S.I. with respect to taxes is significant in this respect. Both O.A.S.I. funds and the property used in the governmental administration of the system are exempt from national, state, and local taxation. Both private insurance funds and the property used in private insurance are subject to taxation. Thus when the voluntarily insured pays his premium, part of what he pays goes to pay taxes. Both mutual companies and stock companies must cover what they have to pay in taxes in their loadings. Naturally the insured cannot get back the taxes included in his private insurance premiums any more than he can recover any direct tax payments.

Options. As a man goes through life, his reasons for buying or continuing insurance change as his family responsibilities change. Four different stages are especially significant:

1. The period when he has children who need the care and attention of their mother.

2. The period when the children have completed the elementary and secondary schools and are preparing in colleges, universities, or professional schools or in other ways to get established in life in a status the parents regard as appropriate or that lies along the lines of their ambitions for the child or the ambitions of the child for himself. This one may be the period of heaviest financial demands.

3. The period when the children are grown and self-supporting in families of their own, and the father appreciates that the time has come when provision for the children's mother and for his own old age are his major concern. The father perhaps rarely thinks in terms such as "mother is now out of a job as rearer of children and should get out and earn to support herself." He is more likely to dwell on the fact that a mother who has devoted her middle years to the family and has not for years had business experience, if she ever had it, is not ordinarily a

highly employable person, and he suspects she might have a hard time supporting herself at the level to which she has been accustomed.

4. The grandfather and grandmother period when thoughts turn to the future of the grandchildren and especially to that time in the grandchildren's lives when they are preparing for their life work.

Private life insurance companies selling life insurance and annuities to clients, whether the companies are mutual or stock, know how the needs of the client and his family change with the years. They accordingly write life insurance policies and annuity policies with a wide variety of optional methods of settlement. Competition among companies has tended to increase the number of options specifically mentioned in the policy with tabular statements of benefits. It is not unusual to find a clause giving the insured the privilege of any new options that may be later introduced by the company. A common provision often gives the beneficiary the privilege of electing an option if the insured dies without having designated one. If no beneficiary is designated the insurance goes into the insured's estate on his death and is distributed according to his will or in accordance with state law. Thus under voluntary insurance the insured has a wide range of options in the mode of settlement he elects and can adjust his insurance to meet his family needs as he sees them. Voluntary insurance is predominantly an institution for the family.

Against this background of description, equities, forfeitures, and optional methods of settlement, some of the features of O.A.S.I. will be reviewed.

EQUITIES

The old age and survivors insurance system is by no means equitable. The most oustanding inequity results from two facts: (1) half of the contributions come from pay-roll taxes paid by the employers and (2) large numbers of gainful workers and their dependents are excluded from coverage under the act. It is generally agreed that pay-roll taxes levied against employ-

ers become part of the cost of production and in the long run
are largely passed along to consumers. Thus gainfully employed
workers who are not covered are paying indirectly part of the
cost of benefits for covered workers and their dependents. In-
clusions and exclusions are not based on income, need, or the
prospects of need. Agricultural laborers and domestic servants
in private employment are not covered. Marginal workers who
are in and out of covered employment may never derive any
benefit from the system. As it stands today O.A.S.I. is distinctly
class legislation.

The contributions of employers and employees, moreover,
will not necessarily cover the costs of the system. They certainly will not if the Congress continues to hold the rates down
to 1 per cent each. It is entirely possible that a substantial part
of the benefit costs will have to be paid by taxpayers who cannot get any direct benefits from the system for themselves or
their dependents.

Even among the covered workers the individual equities are
not preserved. Certain of the inequities will be briefly summarized:

1. All covered individuals pay exactly the same rate of tax
on $3,000 and under a year regardless of the number and
nature of their eligible dependents. Obviously, women can have
neither wives nor widows and the assumptions in the law run
against their children under 18 being dependent on them. A
single man with no eligible beneficiaries pays the same rate as a
married man with many dependents. Classes in covered employment which have restricted their offspring in order to give
their children better economic and social advantages help pay
the benefits for the classes that do not practice restriction.

2. The benefit formula pays 40 per cent on the first $50 of
wages and only 10 per cent on the balance up to $250 a month.
The employers' tax operates beyond question as a device to redistribute the income according to a governmentally determined
formula. Upper-bracket employees under the system may get
the value of their own contributions, although in view of the
forfeitures inherent in the system one would hesitate to make

a positive statement on this score. Since they spend more than the lower-paid employees, they will pay relatively more through the higher prices necessitated by the pay-roll tax on employers. As the system matures, they may have to pay for high benefits through general taxes.

3. The benefit formula allows only 1 per cent of the base allowance for each year of service. Thus the employees with long service pay far more per dollar of benefits than the covered employees with the minimum length of service necessary to attain the status of currently insured or fully insured. As has previously been pointed out, the man who permanently attains the fully insured status at the earliest possible age and then withdraws to an uncovered occupation may get far more for his money than the man who stays in for his entire working life.

FORFEITURES

The old-age and survivors insurance system as at present designed involves many forfeitures. Among the most important are:

1. The forfeiture on withdrawal before the contributor has attained an insured status. The reason for withdrawal is under the law entirely immaterial. Among the causes may be (a) change in employment from covered to uncovered work, (b) loss of a job in covered employment because the employee is only employable in periods of labor shortage, (c) disability resulting from accident or disease, and (d) for women marriage and domestic responsibilities.

2. The forfeiture resulting from death in the active service before the currently insured status has been attained.

3. The forfeiture of the individual's own old-age protection when he withdraws before he has served long enough to have an established right to it.

4. The forfeiture of survivors' benefits when a currently insured or a temporarily fully insured individual withdraws and lives beyond the term of the extended life insurance to which he was entitled by virtue of his temporary status as a currently insured or fully insured individual.

5. The forfeiture of everything except the lump-sum death benefit when the insured dies leaving no person who ever becomes eligible to receive a benefit under the O.A.S.I. law. This forfeiture may occur despite the fact that the insured at death may have been survived by a widow, children, grandchildren, a nondependent parent, a brother or a sister, a nephew or a niece. The question of whether these relatives are or are not capable of self support, or whether the deceased was or was not actually or morally indebted to them, is under the law generally immaterial. The widow, the children, and the parents can benefit only if they are within the eligibility rules prescribed by the state.

OPTIONAL METHODS OF SETTLEMENT

The old-age and survivors insurance system represents a new concept of the functions of the state and a new restriction of the rights of the individual with respect to liberty and property. Although the taking of private property by the state to relieve want or need has from colonial days been recognized in this country as a function of government, it had not previously been the practice for the state to take property from one citizen to give to another when the recipient was not in need. Under the O.A.S.I. system persons of very modest means may be taxed directly or indirectly to provide benefits for persons who are in fact much more prosperous than the particular taxpayer from whom funds were taken.

Such a system for the redistribution of wealth according to a formula prescribed by the political state can only be made effective by compulsion. A political majority must enforce its will upon the minority. Substantial numbers of persons consulting their own interests and the interest of the members of their family would decline to purchase insurance under the O.A.S.I. system on a voluntary basis. So far as they are concerned, it does not meet their needs.

Under such a system the political state substitutes the judgment of a majority of the legislature for that of the individual with respect to which members of the family may benefit from insurance and upon what conditions. The political state under O.A.S.I. decides against the eligibility of a widow with no child under 18 years of age until that widow attains the age of 65; it renders her ineligible if she remarries; and it rules that until she attains the age of 65 her mental and physical condition, her actual employability, is immaterial. The political state decides that a child is not eligible after he has attained the age of 18, although the insured may have had as a motivating force in his life giving the child the opportunity for higher education and training for professional, scientific, or technical service.

If the people of the United States embrace the philosophy that the political state should go further in the redistribution of wealth than is necessary to prevent want or need, then they must leave to elected legislators the decisions as to what the individual shall do with his earnings and as to what members of his family may share in the fruits of his labor and upon what conditions. Optional methods of settlement are the product of voluntary private insurance and of retirement systems that are part of the compensation system of the employer. They are not consistent with a system designed in no small measure to effect a redistribution of wealth believed by a majority of the legislature to be in the social interest. If the legislators have this power, it is for the majority to determine in what degree it shall be exercised.

O.A.S.I. COMPARED WITH OLD-AGE ASSISTANCE

O.A.S.I. benefits are, as has been noted, paid only with respect to fully insured or currently insured individuals. Persons not covered at all by O.A.S.I. and persons who although at some time included in the system have not attained or retained an insured status are dependent if in need after attaining the age of 65 on old-age assistance. The two programs are thus in a sense complementary, although if the public should develop a preference for one over the other, they might become rivals in the movement to extend social security. For this reason it is significant to attempt some comparison between the benefits under the two programs. Before comparing the benefits, four important distinctions between the two systems should be briefly reviewed.

1. Old-age and survivors benefits are paid to eligibles representing fully insured or currently insured individuals, regardless of their need, although in some cases survivors have to prove dependence on the insured. Old-age assistance benefits are paid only to those determined to be in need according to state laws administered by state agencies.

2. O.A.S.I. is a contributory system; it insures only those who are covered for the specified length of time at earnings of the specified amount; and in the absence of administrative slips, the insured must have paid the specified taxes on their wages through pay-roll deductions for the entire period of coverage. Old-age assistance benefits are non-contributory or, in other words, pure gratuities.

3. O.A.S.I. is a federal system federally administered and supported by federal taxes. The deficits in the O.A.S.I. fund, inevitable unless the higher taxes are enforced, will presumably be made good by general federal taxation. Old-age assistance, broadly speaking, is financed one half by the national government and one half by the state government involved, although the state government in its discretion may pass along part but not all of its portion to subordinate local governments.

4. Benefits under O.A.S.I. can be increased only through congressional action. Within limits—in most states far from reached—old-age assistance benefits can be enormously increased by state action without further national action. This point is so significant that it warrants detailed explanation.

The old-age assistance title of the Social Security Act, it will be recalled, provides that the national government will share with the state the cost of an old-age benefit which the state grants under that law up to $40 per month. In December 1942 the average old-age assistance benefit for all states combined was $23.43[49] or 58.6 per cent of the national maximum. On the average the states could increase benefits by some $16 a month

[49] *Social Security Yearbook 1942*, p. 73.

or some 68 per cent without getting beyond the national maximum. In 1942 old-age assistance payments amounted to 597 million dollars.[50] An increase of 68 per cent would bring that figure to 1,003 millions.

This figure does not, however, represent the upper limits to which the states may go without further congressional action, because administratively the states in this system define needs and the methods of determining need. By amending their definitions and their standards and by increasing their appropriations, they can go materially above this figure of 1,003 millions. By such action they could not only pay greatly increased benefits to those already on the old-age assistance rolls, but they could bring on to these rolls thousands who are not there now. The average benefit for all the states can ultimately resemble closely the average benefits paid by the liberal states, such as in December 1942, Colorado $41.06, Arizona $37.22, and California $36.91. The number of old-age assistance beneficiaries per 1,000 aged population for the country as a whole can increase from the 238 reported by the Social Security Board for December 1942 to figures approaching the 523 for Oklahoma, 501 for Texas, 487 for Colorado, 448 for Utah, and 425 for Georgia.[51]

If all the states had a ratio like that in Oklahoma, the number of beneficiaries in the country as a whole would have been 220 per cent of the actual number in December 1942. Instead of about 2.2 million beneficiaries, the country would have had about 4.8 millions. At an average benefit of $35 per month or $420 a year, the cost for 4.8 million beneficiaries would be about 2 billion dollars a year. In other words, if all the states should liberalize their definitions and their methods and make the necessary appropriations, the costs for old-age assistance payments could increase from around 595 million dollars to around 2 billions, which would represent an increase of about 236 per cent.

Under circumstances such as those just outlined, advocates of free old-age pensions have a wide field open to them through

[50] The same.
[51] The same, p. 74.

advocating a liberalization of state old-age assistance laws and administration and larger state appropriations. Because of these potentialities, it is significant to contrast benefits under old-age assistance with benefits under O.A.S.I.

Under old-age assistance in December 1942, as already noted, the average benefit for all states combined was $23.43. To acquire such a benefit under O.A.S.I., an employee who had worked in covered employment for 40 years would have had to earn on the average $41.80 per month throughout the period. On his monthly earnings he would have had to pay the contribution tax, which under the law started at 1 per cent and is to be, or perhaps was to be increased by steps to 3 per cent after December 31, 1948.

A monthly wage of $41.80 amounts to $501.60 a year. A tax of 1 per cent on this sum would yield $5.016 a year and in 40 years would amount to $200.64

For a person who remains under a system for 40 years, the factor of interest on his own contributions is too significant to be ignored. The fact that the taxes were to have progressed by steps and that Congress has thus far deferred the increase from 1 to 2 per cent makes dealing with compound interest a bit uncertain. To show the significance of interest, we shall give the figures first on the assumption that the tax on the employee remains at 1 per cent and then on the assumption that it was 3 per cent throughout. The latter figures will be applicable to persons who enter after the 3 per cent tax rate is actually imposed. The rate of interest we shall use is 2 per cent.[52]

The O.A.S.I. beneficiary who is to receive an individual benefit of $23.43 a month must earn about $500 a year, and pay $5.00 a year as a 1 per cent tax or $15 a year as a 3 per cent tax.

---

[52] Those who are compelled to insure under O.A.S.I. cannot, as a rule, personally borrow funds at 2 per cent, no matter how wisely or prudently they plan to use the money. They would be charged more than 2 per cent on loans to purchase a house, buy a farm, buy farming equipment, or to conduct a business. If they purchase durable consumers' goods on the installment plan, the borrowed money costs them more. The use of 2 per cent seems to us, therefore, to understate rather than to overstate what the O.A.S.I. member has to pay to get the benefit which the beneficiary of old-age assistance gets as a grant.

Five dollars a year for 40 years at 2 per cent would amount to about $302. Fifteen dollars a year for 40 years would amount to $906. Thus the average old-age assistance beneficiary gets for nothing what would have cost the O.A.S.I. member between $302 and $906, depending on the rate of tax.

In Arizona in December 1942 the average old-age assistance beneficiary drew $37.22 a month. Under O.A.S.I. a man who had been covered for 40 years to be entitled to a benefit of $37.22 must have had average monthly earnings of $115.85, which equals about $1,390 a year. At 1 per cent the tax would be $13.90 a year and at 3 per cent $41.70. With 2 per cent interest in 40 years the 1 per cent tax would amount to about $840, and the 3 per cent tax to about $2,520. Thus the Arizona beneficiary of old-age assistance would get free what has cost the O.A.S.I. beneficiary between $840 and $2,520, with the exact amount depending on what Congress does about the tax rate.

The O.A.S.I. benefit gives the insured a right to a benefit for his wife when she arrives at age 65. It must be remembered, however, that old-age assistance may pay a benefit to both a husband and a wife. In states with an old-age pension philosophy, the benefit for the wife under old-age assistance may be as great or almost as great as the benefit for the husband. If a state with the pension philosophy pays the husband $35 a month and the wife $35 a month, the aged couple thus draws $70 a month.

For a couple to draw $70 a month under O.A.S.I., the husband's primary benefit must be $46.67 a month, which would yield a wife's benefit of $23.33. If the O.A.S.I. beneficiary entitled to $46.67 a month primary benefit dies, his widow would be entitled to three fourths of it or $35 a month if she is over 65 years of age, which is the same amount the wife would receive under the old-age assistance case assumed above.

To be entitled to a primary benefit of $46.67 a month a man who has been under O.A.S.I. for 40 years must have earned covered wages throughout the period averaging approximately $183 a month or $2,196 a year. It may be noted, incidentally, that annual earnings of that magnitude in many communities place the man in a position to support a wife and three children according to a minimum health and decency standard without assistance from secondary breadwinners.

A tax of 1 per cent a year on $2,196 yields $21.96 and one of 3 per cent $65.88. The payment at the end of 40 years at 2 per cent compound interest would amount respectively to $1,326 and $3,979.

These figures show that the old-age assistance beneficiary gets without immediate contributions grants for which the O.A.S.I. beneficiary will have to pay substantial sums if the tax on employees is raised to 3 per cent.

In view of these differences the questions may be asked: What advantages do persons who come under O.A.S.I. have over persons who, if in need, come under old-age assistance? What do they get for their contributions?

From the psychological standpoint the most important fact is that they get their benefits by virtue of a legislative right. They do not have to prove need or submit to a means test. If they should die leaving eligible survivors, these survivors likewise take as a matter of legislative right. Beneficiaries under old-age assistance, aid to dependent children, and general public assistance must prove need and submit to a means test. If survivors have to secure provision under general public assistance, they may in many states have a hard time because of inadequacy of appropriations and rigid, even harsh, administration. O.A.S.I. thus may provide a greater sense of security than old-age assistance.

To answer the question of advantages from the financial point of view, four different groups must be distinguished representing different points on an economic scale.

1. At the bottom of the scale are those elderly people almost entirely without resources in real and desperate need. Under old-age assistance they would qualify for maximum grants. In states with liberal old-age assistance laws liberally administered, people in the low-income brackets covered by O.A.S.I. gain nothing from their O.A.S.I. contributions unless during their

working years they had been in upper-wage brackets during most of the time so that they would get more from O.A.S.I. than from old-age assistance. Most of the people who have very small earnings during their working years would have been financially better off had they not been required to contribute to O.A.S.I.

2. After the persons described in the preceding paragraph come those persons who have some resources of their own but not enough to render them ineligible for old-age assistance. For them the benefits under O.A.S.I. may be greater than the benefits they would receive under old-age assistance. For them the financial results can be expressed by: value of benefit under O.A.S.I. — value of benefit which they would have received under old-age assistance = value received for contributions.

3. Persons who on arriving at age 65 have resources which would render them ineligible for any old-age assistance benefit, but who during their working lives have never earned enough to be subject to substantial federal taxes, particularly income or inheritance taxes. It is this group that profits most from O.A.S.I. for their contributions give them the contingent legislative right to draw benefits paid for in substantial part by taxes on employers and possibly by general taxes. In addition to their contributions, however, they will have paid some indirect taxes resulting from the successful efforts of employers to shift the employers' taxes to consumers. The employers may also pass along to consumers part of the costs of the extensive administrative paper work which O.A.S.I. requires of them.

4. Persons who on arriving at age 65 have entirely adequate resources and who during their lives have paid very substantial federal taxes, particularly income taxes, and who come from families who have paid federal estate and gift taxes. When O.A.S.I. approaches maturity, if the tax is raised to 3 per cent, persons in the upper brackets will have paid through their own contributions most of the cost for the primary benefits they will secure from O.A.S.I. and they will not draw substantially upon employers' contributions or general taxes unless they have eligible wives, children, or survivors. In addition to their contributions they will have paid taxes directly or indirectly to give

benefits to others and meet the administrative costs of the system.

If the tax is left at 1 per cent, persons with capacity to pay will have to contribute heavily to pay the benefits promised under O.A.S.I. If these taxes are added to their pay-roll taxes, they will pay far more than the cost of any benefits they can take under the system.

From the financial standpoint old-age assistance, well organized and well administered, is more favorable than O.A.S.I. to the very low paid and to persons who are in wage brackets that involve payment of substantial taxes. The persons who profit most from O.A.S.I. are those who earn too much to be classified as in need, but who do not earn enough to pay substantial federal taxes.

CHAPTER VI

THE RAILROAD RETIREMENT SYSTEM

In the same period when the national government was adopting and amending the Social Security Act setting up an old-age retirement system for covered workers, it was establishing a retirement system for railway employees. The first Railroad Retirement Act, passed in 1934,[1] was held unconstitutional by the Supreme Court.[2] The present system rests on an act of 1935,[3] radically amended in 1937,[4] with some relatively minor amendments passed later. The two systems have a few points in common, but they present so many differences that it seems necessary to give an independent description of the railroad retirement system.

COVERAGE

The first question that naturally arises with respect to a special system of this type is, "To whom does it apply?" The way the act is drawn places the major answer in the definition of the employers covered by the act. They are:[5]

1. Carriers, which include express companies, sleeping car companies, and carriers by railroad subject to Part I of the Interstate Commerce Act.

2. Any company which is directly owned or controlled by one or more such carriers or under common control therewith and which operates any equipment or facility or performs service (except trucking service, casual service, and the casual operation of equipment or facilities) in connection with the transportation of passengers or property by railroad, or the receipt, delivery, elevation, transfer in transit, refrigeration or icing, storage, or handling of property transported by railroad.

---

[1] 48 Stat. 1283.
[2] *Railroad Retirement Board* v. *Alton R. Co.*, 295 U.S. 330 (1935).
[3] 49 Stat. 967.
[4] 50 Stat. 307.
[5] 50 Stat. 307.

3. Any receiver, trustee, or other individual or body, judicial or otherwise, when in the possession of the property or operating all or any part of the business of any such employer.

4. Railroad associations, traffic associations, tariff bureaus, demurrage bureaus, weighing and inspection bureaus, collection agencies, and other associations, bureaus, agencies, or organizations controlled and maintained wholly or principally by two or more employers as hereinbefore defined and engaged in the performance of services in connection with or incidental to railroad transportation.

5. Railway labor organizations, national in scope, which have been or may be organized in accordance with the provisions of the Railway Labor Act, and their state and national legislative committees, general committees, insurance departments, and local lodges and divisions established pursuant to the constitution and by-laws of such organizations.

The term employees, according to the act, means:[6]

1. Any employee in the service of one or more employers for compensation. This definition covers employees in the ordinary sense.

2. Any individual who is in the employment relation to one or more employers. An individual is in the employment relation if he is on furlough, subject to call for service within or outside the United States and ready and willing to serve or on leave of absence or absent on account of sickness or disability; all in accordance with the established rules and practices in effect on the employer.

3. An employee representative.

To sum up these definitions, one might say the system covers the railroad transportation industry. It does not cover all transportation. The law specifically excludes street, interurban, or suburban electric railways unless operating as a part of a general steam railroad system of transportation.[7] A steam railroad does not lose its character as such if it is operated by any other motive power, such as electricity or oil used in internal com-

[6] 50 Stat. 307, 308.
[7] 50 Stat. 307.

bustion engines. Independent companies transporting passengers or freight by bus or truck and independent air lines are not railroads. Employees in kinds of transportation not within the railroad industry come under O.A.S.I. of the Social Security Act.

CONTRIBUTIONS

To avoid constitutional difficulties, the Railroad Retirement Act was separate and distinct from the original revenue raising Carriers Taxing Act, likewise passed in 1937[8] but now mainly embodied in the Internal Revenue Code.[9] The taxes collected under the revenue act go into the general fund of the Treasury. The Retirement Act authorizes an appropriation from the general fund of the Treasury to a railroad retirement account established by the act in the Treasury.[10] Each of these provisions requires presentation in some detail.

The Carriers Taxing Act levied (1) an income tax on the employees, (2) an excise tax on the employers, and (3) an income tax on employee representatives, based on that part of their compensation not in excess of $300 a month.[11] It will be recalled that in O.A.S.I. the upper limit is $250 a month. The percentage rates of the several taxes are shown in the following table:

TAX SCHEDULE

Years	Percentage Tax on Compensation not in Excess of $300 a Month		
	Employee Income Tax	Employer Excise Tax	Employee Representatives Income Tax
1937–1939	$2\frac{3}{4}$	$2\frac{3}{4}$	$5\frac{1}{2}$
1940–1942	3	3	6
1943–1945	$3\frac{1}{4}$	$3\frac{1}{4}$	$6\frac{1}{2}$
1946–1948	$3\frac{1}{2}$	$3\frac{1}{2}$	7
1949 and thereafter	$3\frac{3}{4}$	$3\frac{3}{4}$	$7\frac{1}{2}$

[8] 50 Stat. 435. The Carriers Taxing Act of 1935 (49 Stat. 974) was declared unconstitutional by the District Court of the United States for the District of Columbia. *Alton R. Co.* v. *Railroad Retirement Board*, 19 Fed. (Supp.) 955 (1926).

[9] 53 Stat. 179.

[10] 50 Stat. 435, 437.

[11] 53 Stat. 179, 180.

If these taxes are regarded as contributions, the employer and the employee share equally, which is characteristic of many modern retirement systems. The employee representative in a union position pays what he would have paid had he not given up his railroad job plus what his employer would have paid on his account.

The railroad retirement tax in the aggregate started at 5 ½ per cent. It progresses by steps, until after the end of 1948 it will become 7½ per cent. Thus far the tax rate has been increased according to schedule. The old-age and survivors tax started at 2 per cent and was to have progressed to a maximum of 6 per cent, but by congressional action it has remained at 2 per cent.

The situation of the employees of the railway industry with respect to the gradual increase in the tax over the years between 1937 to 1949 deserves comment. Probably to a greater degree than in any other large American industry promotions in the railway industry are based on seniority. Introduction of a sound retirement system resulting in the retirement of the older men will, under a seniority system, result in promotions all down the line. Promotions in the railroad industry will largely supply the active employees with the money to meet the higher taxes to be paid by them as the rate goes up. Under a seniority system the younger active workers may not object if some of their contributions go to pay benefits to those already fairly well along when the system is started, since they will get a net increase from advancing more rapidly to higher positions.

The revenues from these taxes under the Carriers Taxing Act flow into the general fund of the Treasury where they become mixed with other general moneys. As taxes they never go into the railroad retirement account. The provision of the Railroad Retirement Act creating that account is sufficiently important to justify quoting it at length:

There is hereby created an account in the Treasury of the United States to be known as the Railroad Retirement Account. There is hereby authorized to be appropriated to the account for each fiscal year, beginning with the fiscal year ending June 30, 1937, as an annual premium an amount sufficient, with a reasonable margin for contingencies, to provide for the payment of all annuities, pensions, and death benefits in accordance with the provisions of sections 228a–228r and former sections 215–228 of this title. Such amount shall be based on such tables of mortality as the Railroad Retirement Board shall from time to time adopt, and on an interest rate of 3 per centum per annum compounded annually. The Railroad Retirement Board shall submit annually to the Bureau of the Budget an estimate of the appropriation to be made to the account.[12]

Under this section of the act, it will be noted, the liability of the national government is not specifically limited by the amount paid in by the special taxpayers. The national government may possibly have assumed a moral obligation to appropriate in each fiscal year enough, on an annual premium basis, to pay the benefits promised by the act. The assumptions upon which the law was based were that the system would be actuarially sound and that a reserve would be accumulated on an actuarial basis; but if a deficit arises through miscalculations of the Railroad Retirement Board, created by the act to administer it or by the Actuarial Advisory Committee likewise created by the act, Congress has in this act the legislative authorization and perhaps the moral obligation to make up the difference. For constitutional reasons, as the Constitution was then being interpreted, the Retirement Act could not provide that if the reserve should prove inadequate, tax rates should be raised or, putting it the other way, if tax returns should prove inadequate to support the benefits, the benefits should be reduced.

The reserve in the railroad retirement account not immediately required for the payment of benefits is, on the request of the Railroad Retirement Board, invested by the Secretary of the Treasury in interest bearing obligations of the United States or in obligations guaranteed as to both principal and interest by the United States. The Treasury is by law authorized to issue special obligations exclusively to the account, which shall bear interest at the rate of 3 per cent. The act continues: "Obligations other than such special obligations may be acquired for the account only on such terms as to provide an in-

[12] 50 Stat. 307, 316.

vestment yield of not less than 3 per centum per annum."[13] When the national government can borrow at less than 3 per cent, payment of 3 per cent on the special obligations constitutes something of a subsidy to the fund.

INADEQUACIES OF THE CONTRIBUTION RATES

Running through the congressional hearings on the railroad retirement bills and the companion tax bills is the clear implication that the cost of benefits was to be met from taxes levied against the employers and employees. It was not the original intention that the national government should contribute from general taxes. One participant in the employer-employee conference which worked out the agreement that was the basis of the 1937 law has thus summarized the position taken by the negotiators on this subject in 1937, in testimony given to the House Committee on Interstate and Foreign Commerce on March 13, 1945.

In the 1937 negotiations, it was agreed that we would hold before us two definite goals, and adhere to them so far as possible. One goal was to set up such a system that its provisions would not cost more in the aggregate than the maximum tax rate which the parties should agree upon. The other goal was that the tax rate to be agreed upon should be sufficient to meet the costs of the retirement system in full.[14]

The technical, statistical, and actuarial data for the conference in 1937 were supplied in the main by the Chairman of the Railroad Retirement Board, Murray W. Latimer, and represented the work of employees of the Board. The President of the United States in asking the employees and employers to confer had proffered to them the technical assistance of the Board.[15] In all subsequent hearings the Board has been represented by Chairman Latimer, who was the public member. It has not been the practice for the other two members of the Board,

---

[13] 50 Stat. 307, 317.

[14] Dr. Julius H. Parmelee, Director of the Bureau of Railway Economics of the Association of American Railroads, was chairman of the employers' representatives at that conference. *Railroad Retirement*, Hearings before the House Committee on Interstate and Foreign Commerce, Pt. 2, 79 Cong. 1 sess., p. 706.

[15] *Retirement System for Interstate Carrier Employees*, Hearings before the House Committee on Interstate and Foreign Commerce, 75 Cong. 1 sess., p. 10.

one representing the employers and the other the employees, to appear, nor have the subordinate actuaries and statistical employees presented direct testimony. The Chairman has commonly been the sole expert witness from the Board.[16]

The tax schedule adopted in the 1937 Carriers Taxing Act was apparently based on the data submitted by Chairman Latimer and prepared by him or under his supervision.[17] It purported to show that the benefits promised could be supported by the proceeds of these taxes.

Our own rather cursory examination of the figures submitted to the several House and Senate committees by Chairman Latimer in 1937 with respect to "essential appropriations to the railroad retirement account 1937–1975" and estimated disbursements from the railroad retirement account 1937–75 seemed to us clearly to indicate that the fund was not on a sound actuarial reserve basis and that an increase in taxes or a reduction of benefits was called for on the basis of the figures submitted by him.[18] Subsequent actuarial valuations made in accordance with the requirements of the 1937 act have justified skepticism.

The second actuarial valuation made as of December 31, 1941 and presented in the *Annual Report of the Railroad Retirement Board* for the fiscal year ended June 30, 1943 indicated that the existing tax schedule is insufficient to support the benefits provided under the act. The report concludes that under the most probable assumptions the pay-roll tax required to support the system would be 10.4 per cent. Expressed in another way removal of the deficit would necessitate adding 3.32 per cent of pay roll to the present tax schedule.

[16] In the House Committee Hearings on Jan. 31, 1945, testifying with respect to H. R. 1362, Mr. Latimer said: "Without having had opportunity to prepare a complete and consecutive statement, I have been unable to submit to the Bureau of the Budget any statement for clearance. What I say here will be in my individual capacity as Chairman of the Railroad Retirement Board and does not represent the views of the Railroad Retirement Board as such." *Railroad Retirement*, Hearings, Pt. 1, pp. 31–32.

[17] Dr. Parmelee testified that the 1937 conferees acted on the basis of the actuarial calculations submitted by Chairman Latimer. The same, Pt. 2, p. 706.

[18] The figures may be found in several places but we shall cite only *Retirement System for Interstate Carriers' Employees*, Hearings before the House Committee on Interstate and Foreign Commerce, 75 Cong. 1 sess., p. 152.

Under assumptions with respect to the future that are highly favorable to the fund, a tax of only 8.1 per cent might restore its solvency but under highly unfavorable circumstances the tax might have to go to 14.5 per cent.[19]

Competent actuaries cannot do more than give a most probable figure and a range between a minimum and a maximum within which the exact figure will probably fall. The width of this range, from 8.1 per cent to 14.5 per cent with 10.4 the most probable figure, results primarily from variations in the assumptions with respect to future railroad pay rolls and pay rates. Taxes are based on total pay roll, exclusive of the amount over $300 a month paid to individual employees. The benefit formula, on the other hand, pays more, per dollar of tax, with respect to low-paid employees than to highly paid employees. Under these circumstances a very large pay roll with relatively few employees in the low-wage brackets would be advantageous to the financial position of the fund. On the other hand a small pay roll with a high percentage of employees in the low brackets would be disadvantageous to the fund.

There are other variables regarding which assumptions as to the future have to be made. Among them are the mortality rate, the retirement rate for the several benefits, and the age at entrance into the service. The number of variables is in fact so great that one is inclined to the conclusion that if the railroad retirement fund is to be kept on a sound actuarial basis, either one of two courses will have to be pursued:[20]

1. The tax rate and the benefits will have to be adjusted frequently in the light of actual developments in the railroad industry. The tax rate, for example, might be adjusted after each triennial actuarial valuation, which unfortunately would mean upward revision in the face of a falling pay roll and lower wage rates.

[19] *Annual Report of the Railroad Retirement Board 1943*, pp. 118–19.
[20] The future of railroad transportation, which is of course only one element of the entire transportation system of the country, is not something about which one would like to be dogmatic. Chairman Latimer may be right in anticipating large pay rolls and large numbers after the war. On the other hand, there is the possibility of a return to something approaching prewar peacetime levels.

2. A complete revision will have to be made in the wage-benefit relationship, with the amount of the benefit in the individual case far more dependent on the amount of taxes paid by or on account of that individual. Under such a plan the rate of tax remains fairly constant, but the amount of benefit which the individual will receive depends on his own earnings.

Another possibility is to have the national government underwrite any deficiency in the railroad retirement fund which results from a wide discrepancy between actual conditions that develop in the future and forecasts of the future developments upon which the financing of the fund rests. This solution, however, raises a very serious problem. As will subsequently appear, the railroad system is far more favorable to the covered employees than is the Social Security System if the tax for O.A.S.I. is raised to 6 per cent. Thus the issue arises as to whether general tax funds should be used to give railroad workers greater benefits than are enjoyed by workers in other occupations. The theory under which the railroad system was planned was that the taxes on the industry would support the benefits. Among the employers and employees, there was apparently no thought originally that the general taxpayers would be called upon directly to support the system.[21] The philosophy

---

[21] Proposals for radical revision of the Railroad Retirement System are being proposed in H.R. 1362, upon which hearings were held before the House Committee on Interstate and Foreign Commerce in January and February 1945. In connection with these proposals, which are sponsored and perhaps suggested by Chairman Latimer, he restates his position. "It is my firm conviction that there should be a Government contribution to all systems of social security. I advocated such a contribution at that time [in connection with the original Social Security Act] and I have advocated it at every point since that time, wherever I had the opportunity." *Railroad Retirement*, Hearings, Pt. 1, p. 232.

As one reads the Chairman's technical actuarial and statistical testimony one gets the impression that he would not be disturbed if deficits in the fund arose which would ultimately necessitate substantial contributions from general public revenues.

For a statement in opposition to the favored treatment of railroad employees, as proposed in H.R. 1362 and advocated by Chairman Latimer, see *Railroad Social Insurance: Favored Treatment versus Uniform Social Insurance* (1945), by Rainard B. Robbins, Vice President of the Teachers Insurance and Annuity Association, a non-profit agency that grew out of the Carnegie Foundation for the Advancement of Teaching.

Upon the assumption that benefits were to be paid exclusively from the fund on actuarial and equitable grounds, the Assistant Grand Chief Engineer and National Legislative Representative of the Brotherhood of Locomotive Engineers presented a

underlying the act would be fundamentally changed by a heavy government contribution.

BENEFITS[22]

The Railroad Retirement Act provides (1) annuities, (2) death benefits, and (3) "pensions to individuals on pension or gratuity rolls of employers" at the time the new act went into effect.

Annuities are granted to individuals of four distinct classes:[23]

1. Individuals who on or after the enactment date shall be 65 years of age and over. The applicant must relinquish such rights as he may have to return to the service of an employer, within the railroad industry, and "of the person by whom he was last employed" (any employer). The law, however, does not prohibit him from getting other employment after he has begun to draw his annuity.

2. Individuals who on or after the enactment date shall be 60 years of age or over and have completed 30 years of service. Their annuities are, however, reduced by one one hundred and eightieth for each calendar month they are under the age of 65 when the annuity begins. Applicants under this section as in (1) above give up the positions they hold at the time of going on annuity, but they are not prohibited from getting new employment.

3. Individuals who on or after the enactment date shall be 60 years of age and over and have become totally and permanently

---

strong case against H.R. 1362, *Railroad Retirement*, Hearings, Pt. 1, pp. 337–424. He said however:

"Again, we have heard the statement that, apparently regardless of whether the present, or proposed, taxes may continue the benefits of the Railroad Retirement Act, the United States Government will never let the employees of the railroads be without their annuities.

"If this committee and the Congress will place itself on record as back of such opinions, or assurances, we shall be most pleased to withdraw any of the present questions of safety that appear proper under our understanding of existing conditions and the provisions of this present bill." p. 349.

Anyone interested in the relationship of Chairman Latimer, the representative of the public on the Board, to H.R. 1362 and the several organizations of railroad employees will find Mr. Corbett's testimony of interest, especially pp. 337–41.

[22] Radical proposals for the revision of the entire benefit structure of the system have been proposed. The discussion here given is based on the existing system.

[23] 50 Stat. 307, 309.

disabled for regular employment for hire. Their annuities are likewise reduced by one one hundred and eightieth for each calendar month they are under the age of 65 when the annuity begins.

4. Individuals, without regard to age, who on or after the enactment date are totally and permanently disabled for regular employment and shall have completed 30 years of service. Annuitants of this class must submit satisfactory proof of the continuing disability from time to time until they reach age 65. If they fail to do so, or if they recover from their disability, the annuity stops. If the recovered person subsequently becomes entitled to an annuity for age alone (65), or for age (60) and length of service (30 years), that annuity is reduced actuarially by the cost of his earlier benefits. Recovered disabled employees can go back to work for a covered employer.

An annuitant cannot be paid in any month in which he renders compensated service for a covered employer or the last person for whom he was employed prior to the date on which the annuity began to accrue.[24]

Certain features regarding these provisions call for special emphasis, partly because they present such amazing contrasts with O.A.S.I.[25]

If any person has been for any length of time after the enactment date an employee of the covered railroad industry, on attaining the age of 65 he is entitled to an annuity provided he gives up the employment he has on attaining that age. The amount of the annuity may be small but by virtue of his coverage even for a short time he has a right. There is no forfeiture here because he has not served long enough to be "fully insured," as under O.A.S.I.

The Railroad Retirement Act does not make attaining the age of 65 an absolute prerequisite for securing an annuity, as does O.A.S.I. An employee can take an annuity at 60 if he has had 30 years of service or if he is disabled. If he is disabled for

[24] 50 Stat. 307, 310.
[25] The proposed changes would eliminate some of these contrasts but would give railroad workers better benefits than are provided under O.A.S.I.

regular employment and has had 30 years of service, he can take an annuity even before he has attained the age of 60. The man who has attained the age of 60 and is disabled takes regardless of his length of service, although the annuity may be small.

The annuity formula for the Railroad Retirement System reads: "The annuity shall be computed by multiplying an individual's 'years of service' by the following percentages of his 'monthly compensation': 2 per centum of the first $50; 1½ per centum of the next $100; and 1 per centum of the next $150."[26]

The length of service includes all services rendered subsequent to December 1, 1936 no matter how long that service may be. If, on retiring, an employee does not have 30 years of such service, he may count railroad service rendered prior to that date. If his prior service and his post service together would exceed 30 years, he can count only that much of his prior service as will bring his total to 30.

The monthly compensation is the average amount earned by an individual in calendar months included in his years of service. In computing the monthly earnings no part of any month's compensation in excess of $300 shall be recognized.[27]

The Railroad Retirement Act has a minimum annuity provision applicable to an employee (1) if he was an employee when he attained age 65, and (2) if he has completed 20 years of service. Special emphasis should be placed on the fact that the man to be benefited by the minimum provisions must have been a railroad employee at the time he reached age 65; he cannot as in O.A.S.I. take advantage of the minimum provisions by virtue of becoming, to use O.A.S.I. terminology, fully insured in the early years of his working life. On the other hand 20 years of railroad service are required for this minimum whereas a lesser time, not exceeding 10 years, is required for attaining the fully insured status under O.A.S.I.

This minimum clause reads:

If the individual was an employee when he attained age sixty-five and has completed twenty years of service, the minimum annuity

[26] 50 Stat. 307, 310.
[27] 50 Stat. 307, 311.

payable to him shall be $40 per month: *Provided, however,* That if the monthly compensation on which his annuity is based is less than $50, his annuity shall be 80 per centum of such monthly compensation, except that if such 80 per centum is less than $20, the annuity shall be $20 or the same amount as the monthly compensation, whichever is less. . . .[28]

In other words, the employee who is working for the railroad industry on attaining the age of 65 and has worked for it in the aggregate 20 years does not get less than $20 a month unless his actual average wages were less than $20, in which case his annuity is the same amount as his wages. If he earned on the average between $25 and $50 his minimum is 80 per cent of his average earnings. If he earned $50 or more his minimum is $40.

Another minimum clause reads: "In no case shall the value of the annuity be less than the value of the additional old-age benefit he would receive under Title II of Chapter 7 of Title 42 if his service as an employee after December 31, 1936, were included in the term 'employment' as defined therein."[29] In other words, if a railroad employee would have received a greater benefit under Title II of the Social Security Act as it was originally passed had he been included therein than he would receive under the Railroad Retirement Act without this special clause, the railroad fund shall pay him what he would have received under the original Title II.

O.A.S.I., it will be recalled, provided a primary insurance benefit for the fully insured covered worker who retires at age 65 or thereafter with additional benefits for the wife and dependent children. The Railroad Retirement Act deals with the question of wife, widow, and children in a different way.[30]

Unlike the O.A.S.I. law, the Railroad Retirement Act affords some optional methods of settlement and permits the worker himself to say, within limits, how his accumulations under the system shall be applied. We shall have occasion to return to this subject in considering death benefits. Here we shall

[28] The same.
[29] The same.
[30] The proposed changes in the railway system would provide benefits for wives, widows, children, and possibly parents as in O.A.S.I. but on more liberal terms.

only note that the railroad worker, within a special time, can on approaching the retirement age elect to take a "joint and survivor annuity" payable to himself and his wife so long as either of them shall live. This annuity is available in three different forms: The surviving wife gets under (1) the same annuity as was paid during her husband's life, under (2) an annuity amounting to 75 per cent of her husband's annuity, or under (3) an annuity amounting to 50 per cent. The actuarial value of whatever annuity is selected is the same as that of the annuity the worker could have had solely on his own life. If, before payment of the joint and survivor annuity begins, either the husband or the wife dies, the marriage is dissolved, or the husband is disabled and takes a disability annuity, the election is canceled. Thus the individual worker has a measure of freedom of choice with respect to old-age annuities and as we shall see in the next section with respect to death benefits.[31]

Death benefits. Because of constitutional difficulties the Railroad Retirement Act does not give the railroad worker a right in any event to recover his taxes, or his contributions, paid under the Carriers Taxing Act of 1937. It accomplishes substantially the same results in a different way. The tax on compensation paid by the employee, it may be recalled, began at 2¾ per cent in 1937 and is to increase to 3¾ per cent in 1949 and thereafter. The basis of all death benefits under the act is 4 per cent of the aggregate compensation earned by the employee in the railroad industry after December 31, 1936, when the taxes on compensation began.[32] This device uses the same base for death benefits as for contributions, and 4 per cent would yield all the employee has paid in as taxes plus some interest on the reserve built up with respect to the individual. In other words, the employee who dies gets back in effect his contributions with some interest, although interest cannot be computed with the simplicity and directness possible in systems that provide for a return of contributions with interest.

[31] 50 Stat. 307, 311.
[32] 50 Stat. 307, 312.

The section of the law dealing with death benefits begins with the statement: "The following benefits shall be paid with respect to the death of individuals who were employees after December 31, 1936."[33] Significant is the fact that this clause does not require that the individual worker shall be a railroad worker at the time of his death or have been one within a given period before his death. Under the existing law there is no such thing as fully insured or currently insured. When a worker dies, a right to a death benefit matures unless in some other way he has exhausted his benefits. Some illustrations are worth while.

A railroad worker, or one who has been a railroad worker, may die before he is entitled to any of the specific annuities previously discussed. In that event the insurance, amounting to 4 per cent of his aggregate railroad compensation since December 1936, becomes payable. If he has designated a beneficiary, it is paid to that beneficiary if surviving. If there is no surviving beneficiary, it is paid to the legal representative of the deceased. If the deceased has left a valid will, the legal representative is bound by the will. The money may thus go to beneficiaries who could not take under the O.A.S.I. Note, however, that this device does not insure protection to his unmarried children under 18 until they attain 18 or marry or to his wife while she is caring for them. If he has such dependents and wishes to provide for them, he must supplement his possible death benefit by private voluntary insurance. This system contains no child's benefits, no widow's benefits as such, and no parent's benefits.

If the individual has already retired on an annuity but has not yet drawn in annuity payments the full "4 per cent of his aggregate compensation since December 31, 1936," a right to the balance as a death benefit matures, unless he has elected a joint and survivor's annuity and the wife survives. If, however, he selected a joint and survivor's annuity and both he

[33] The same.

and his wife die before the 4 per cent of aggregate compensation is consumed, the balance matures as a death benefit.

Thus the man who arrives at the age of 65 can take the annuity which is the product of his own personal contributions with the certainty that if he does not survive to use all his own contributions, the balance will be available for others, and he may designate the beneficiaries in accordance with his own wishes. The law does not designate the beneficiaries for him.

Benefits for women. The railroad industry is largely a man's world, although the relatively few women employees have the same rights and privileges as the men.[34] Section 4 providing for "Joint and Survivor's Annuity" reads as if it might apply solely to men but under Death Benefits in Section 5 occurs the phrase: "If the deceased should not be survived by a widow or a widower who is entitled to an annuity under an election made pursuant to the provisions of section 4." Thus a woman railroad worker can take a joint and survivor's annuity to help protect the old age of her husband or to care for him if he is an invalid. She can make her children her beneficiaries regardless of their age, marital condition, or degree of dependence on her.

Benefits on withdrawal. Special attention should be called to the fact that no cash benefits are provided on withdrawal from the railroad industry by resignation or dismissal. Like many other modern retirement systems, the railroad system is designed basically to provide protection in old age and the employee is not permitted to sacrifice such protection as he has secured by withdrawing his contributions or their equivalent on resignation or dismissal. Exception is made in the event of death in the active service. Provision is also made under certain circumstances for disability benefits.[35]

Under such a law some annuity payments will be very small. The law provides that: "If an annuity is less than $2.50, [a month], it may, in the discretion of the Board, be paid

---

[34] The proposed radical revision of the system would change these provisions and introduce many of the discriminations against women contained in O.A.S.I., but it would reduce the retirement age for women to 60 years. *Railroad Retirement*, Hearings, Pt. 1, sec. 205, p. 6.

[35] 50 Stat. 307, 309.

quarterly or in a lump sum equal to its computed value as determined by the Board."[36] The very small accounts may therefore be settled through a lump-sum payment.

Railroad benefits compared with O.A.S.I. benefits. The preceding discussion of benefits naturally leads to the question, How do the benefits granted under the existing railroad system compare with benefits under O.A.S.I.? No attempt will here be made to attain precise comparisons between systems which are so radically different. Rough comparisons only will be attempted with some qualifying comments.

A table on page 158 compares the retirement benefits under the two systems by the application of the two formulae to selected, illustrative, average, monthly, covered wages for periods of service by ten-year intervals from 10 to 40 years. No allowance is made in the figures for the provision of the railroad system regarding minimum benefits, which will be taken up in the text.

The O.A.S.I. formula, it will be noted, is weighted heavily in favor of persons with relatively short periods of service. At each wage rate shown in the table the O.A.S.I. benefit for the worker alone is higher than the railroad benefit for persons who have served ten years only. If the worker has a wife the advantages of the short-term workers under O.A.S.I. are vastly greater.

With increased length of service, the advantage of the O.A.S.I. worker over the railroad worker tends to disappear rapidly. For any railroad worker who has served 20 years or more and has an average wage of $100 a month or over, the individual benefit is higher than it would be under O.A.S.I. Moreover, an employee who was a railroad worker when he attained the age of 65 and had 20 years of service would come under the minimum provisions which would give him $40 a month had his average wage been $50 or more. After 20 years of service, the O.A.S.I. beneficiary is behind unless he has a wife or eligible children who would receive a benefit.

The O.A.S.I. formula discriminates heavily against the employees in the upper-wage brackets and particularly against

[36] 50 Stat. 307, 311.

those with long covered service. The railroad formula has some discrimination but of nothing like the same degree. For example, the worker who has had 40 years of service at an average wage of $200 would get under the railroad system an annuity

BENEFITS ACCORDING TO FORMULA, RAILROAD SYSTEM AND O.A.S.I. WITHOUT
CORRECTION FOR MINIMUM PROVISIONS

I. $50 AVERAGE MONTHLY COVERED EARNINGS

Length of Service	Monthly Retirement Benefit According to Formula		
	Railroad System	O.A.S.I. System	
		Worker Only	Worker and Wife
10....................	$ 10.00	$22.00	$33.00
20....................	20.00	24.00	36.00
30....................	30.00	26.00	39.00
40....................	40.00	28.00	42.00

II. $100 AVERAGE MONTHLY COVERED EARNINGS

10....................	17.50	27.50	41.25
20....................	35.00	30.00	45.00
30....................	52.50	32.50	48.75
40....................	70.00	35.00	52.50

III. $200 AVERAGE MONTHLY COVERED EARNINGS

10....................	30.00	38.50	57.75
20....................	60.00	42.00	63.00
30....................	90.00	45.50	68.25
40....................	120.00	49.00	73.50

IV. $250 AVERAGE MONTHLY COVERED EARNINGS

10....................	35.00	44.00	66.00
20....................	70.00	48.00	72.00
30....................	105.00	52.00	78.00
40....................	140.00	56.00	84.00

V. $300 AVERAGE MONTHLY COVERED EARNINGS[a]

10....................	40.00	44.00[a]	66.00[a]
20....................	80.00	48.00[a]	72.00[a]
30....................	120.00	52.00[a]	78.00[a]
40....................	160.00	56.00[a]	84.00[a]

[a] The O.A.S.I. pays benefits only with respect to the first $250.

of $120 a month and under O.A.S.I. an annuity for himself of $49. If he had an eligible wife the couple would draw together $73.50.

The railroad system permits the employee to select if he so chooses a joint survivor annuity for himself and his wife according to any one of three types. Thus he does not have to take the large annuity for himself if he has a wife for whom he wishes to make provision.

The fully or currently insured individual under O.A.S.I. who has an unmarried dependent child under 18 has a form of life insurance protection for such child and for his mother also so long as she has the care of such a child. The railroad worker has no such life insurance protecting the family. In event of his death the family would receive only the lump-sum payment of 4 per cent of his total taxed wages. He can leave that sum to his widow or his children whether they would or would not be eligible to an O.A.S.I. benefit. Life insurance to protect dependents is for most people fairly easily procured upon the payment of a premium, and thus most railroad workers could arrange privately for the protection of dependents.

The railroad worker has the great advantage over the O.A.S.I. worker that he has some protection against disability and if disabled does not have to wait until he has attained the age of 65 to be eligible for personal benefits. This disability benefit is of course helpful to his wife and children. O.A.S.I. does nothing for the wife and children in event the breadwinner is disabled before age 65. Unlike life insurance, disability insurance is difficult to procure through private contract. In this respect the railroad employee is far better off than the O.A.S.I. worker.

The railroad system involves no forfeiture of any of the employee's contributions. Upon the contributor's death before retirement, the accumulation goes to the beneficiaries he designates. If after he has retired he has not drawn all his accumulation in benefits, the balance goes to his designated beneficiaries. If he has no beneficiaries who would be eligible to take under O.A.S.I. or who would survive to take under that system, he has a very great advantage over the O.A.S.I. worker under that system.

The greatest advantage possessed by the railroad workers is that all the contributions of the employers remain within the railroad industry and are distributed among railroad workers.

The upper-bracket long-service employees of the railroads get far more advantage from their employers' contributions than do corresponding employees under O.A.S.I.

If it be assumed that O.A.S.I. with its forfeitures can be operated successfully on the basis of a 6 per cent total tax on covered pay roll, and if the actuaries' estimate of 10.4 is accepted for railroad retirement, then there is a basis for comparison of values. What the railroad worker will get is on the average worth more than 1.7 times as much as what the O.A.S.I. worker gets. With workers assessed at 50 per cent of full costs the O.A.S.I. member would pay 3 per cent of taxed pay whereas the railroad worker would pay 5.2 per cent of taxed pay. For the extra payment the railroad worker preserves a good deal of freedom in making his retirement system rights meet his own individual or family requirements as he sees them. He is less subject to governmental dictation and compulsion.

Special attention should be called to the difference between O.A.S.I. and the railroad retirement system with respect to persons with relatively short periods of coverage. Under O.A.S.I. the youth who enters at 21 can withdraw fully and permanently insured at 31 taking the cream of the benefits under the formula. Under the railroad system such an employee would take little cream, because there is comparatively much less discrimination in favor of short service, and moreover the railroad provision with respect to minimum benefits applies only to those who are in the railroad service at 65 and have had 20 years of railroad coverage.

ADMINISTRATION

The guild nature of the railroad retirement system is further exemplified by the Railroad Retirement Board which administers it and by certain other administrative features. The following features of the act with respect to the Board are significant:

1. It is an independent agency in the executive branch of the government. It is not under a department and is not associated with or co-ordinated with the Social Security Board.

2. It consists of three members appointed by the President and confirmed by the Senate for overlapping terms of five years, but:

. . . One member shall be appointed from recommendations made by representatives of the employees and one member shall be appointed from recommendations made by representatives of carriers, in both cases as the President shall direct, so as to provide representation on the Board satisfactory to the largest number, respectively, of employees and carriers concerned. One member, who shall be the chairman of the Board, shall be appointed initially for a term of two years without recommendation by either carriers or employees and shall not be in the employment of or be pecuniarily or otherwise interested in any employer or organization of employees. . . .[37]

3. The Board determines the eligibility of applicants. "Decisions by the Board upon issues of law and fact relating to pensions, annuities, or death benefits shall not be subject to review by any other administrative or accounting officer, agent, or employee of the United States."[38] An employee or other person aggrieved has recourse to the United States district courts.[39]

4. The Board shall establish and promulgate rules and regulations to provide for the adjustment of all controversial matters arising in the administration of the act.[40]

5. The Board in the exercise of its employment powers under the civil service laws and rules "shall give preference over all others to individuals who have had experience in railroad service, if, in the judgment of the Board, they possess the qualifications necessary for the proper discharge of the duties of the positions to which they are to be appointed. . . ."[41]

For constitutional reasons the taxes levied against the carriers and the employees go into the general fund of the Treasury. Congress is then authorized to appropriate to the railroad retirement account each fiscal year:

. . . as an annual premium an amount sufficient, with a reasonable margin for contingencies, to provide for the payment of all annuities, pensions, and death benefits in accordance with the provisions of sections 228a–228r and former sections 215–228 of this title. Such amount shall be based on such tables of mortality as the Railroad Retirement Board shall from time to time adopt, and on an interest rate of 3 per centum per annum compounded annually. The Railroad Retirement

[37] 50 Stat. 307, 314.
[38] The same.
[39] 50 Stat. 307, 315.
[40] The same.
[41] The same.

Board shall submit annually to the Bureau of the Budget an estimate of the appropriation to be made to the account.[42]

From a practical standpoint this provision creates an obligation on Congress to appropriate the sum found necessary by the Board to finance the system even if the carrier taxes prove inadequate. The Board determines this amount with actuarial advice. The provisions for the selection of actuaries are therefore of particular interest. This section of the law reads as follows:

The Board is hereby authorized and directed to select two actuaries, one from recommendations made by representatives of employees and the other from recommendations made by representatives of carriers. These actuaries, along with a third who shall be designated by the Secretary of the Treasury, shall be known as the Actuarial Advisory Committee with respect to the Railroad Retirement Account. The committee shall examine the actuarial reports and estimates made by the Railroad Retirement Board and shall have authority to recommend to the Board such changes in actuarial methods as they may deem necessary. The compensation of the members of the committee of actuaries, exclusive of the member designated by the Secretary shall be fixed by the Board on a per-diem basis.[43]

The guild character of the organization is further evidenced by this quotation. The Board must appoint one actuary from recommendations made by representatives of the carrier and one from recommendations made by representatives of the employees. The actuary designated by the Secretary of the Treasury is the third member and may be regarded as the representative of the general public. It may be noted, however, that the actuaries are advisory only; the Board makes the decisions. Moreover, decisions by the Board upon issues of law and fact relating to pensions, annuities, or death benefits are final.

Real control over the Board rests with the President of the United States. The act contains no restrictions or attempted restrictions on his removal power. If, however, the President removes a board member appointed on the recommendation of representatives of the carriers or of the employees, he must, in accordance with the terms of the act, select a suc-

[42] 50 Stat. 307, 316.
[43] 50 Stat. 307, 317.

cessor recommended in the same manner. An interesting legal question would arise should a president appoint and the Senate confirm a member, other than the chairman, not from recommendations made by the specified class. A president could moreover, remove a member of the Board and abstain from filling the vacancy without stopping the administrative operations, for the law specifically provides: "Vacancies in the Board shall not impair the powers or affect the duties of the Board or of the remaining members of the Board, of whom a majority of those in office shall constitute a quorum, for the transaction of business."[44] Conceivably a president could have the Board operate for a considerable time with only the non-railroad chairman in office.

When all three members of the Board are in office, the law provides: "All rules, regulations, or decisions of the Board shall require the approval of at least two members."[45] If the two representatives of the railroad industry are in agreement they can control the actions of the Board. Under this administrative arrangement, the chairman is without a vetoing vote. If he becomes convinced that the action of his colleagues is objectionable, his only recourse after exhausting argument or persuasion is to refer the matter to the President. The President by virtue of his powers to appoint and remove can, if he sees fit, go a long way in controlling the action of the Board. Either the representative of the carriers or the representative of the employees finding himself in a minority has this same privilege of appealing to the President. The chairman, however, is the one member selected by the President without restrictions other than that the chairman must not be a railroad employee and must not be pecuniarily interested in any employer.

The railroad retirement system is therefore an industrial system administered by the government, with representatives of the employees of the industry and the employers functioning as members of the governing board and with men and women who have had railroad experience preferred for subordinate positions.

[44] 50 Stat. 307, 314.
[45] 50 Stat. 307, 315.

CHAPTER VII

THE NATIONAL CIVIL SERVICE RETIREMENT SYSTEM

The national government, as part of its own system of personnel administration, has several old-age retirement systems. The largest one, and the only one which will be dealt with here, is that applicable to the great body of civilian employees of the national government.

HISTORICAL BACKGROUND

Prior to 1920 the national government made no provision for the retirement of its aged employees. Four reasons for the absence of a retirement system in the early years seem important: (1) the civil service for many years was relatively small; (2) public sentiment was hostile to government pensions for civilian employees; (3) private enterprises generally did not have retirement systems; and (4) for the greater part of the nineteenth century the civil employees of the government were appointed under the spoils system. Rare indeed was the employee who entered the civil service in his youth and spent the balance of his working life in it. The bulk of the employees came in and went out on a change of administration. Under the spoils system civil service jobs were at times given to the politically deserving elderly people in lieu of a pension. The merit system and permanency of tenure did not come until the passage of the Civil Service Act of 1883.[1] That act did not apply at once to all civilian positions. Only slowly by presidential orders and congressional action were positions brought under the act, and there were many backslides, notably when laws were passed specifically excluding whole classes of employees from the operation of the Civil Service Act.

Soon after 1900 it became apparent that permanency of tenure and a career system meant people would grow old in the national civil service. Neither the United States Civil Service

[1] 22 Stat. 403.

Commission nor the law restricted new appointments under the merit system to young people just out of the appropriate schools but admitted applicants for the most part regardless of age. Union veterans of the Civil War had had preference for years, and many of them were covered into the classified civil service as it was extended to new agencies. When the government offices in Washington closed in the afternoon, it was not unusual, particularly if one were near the Pension Bureau or the main office of an old department, to see feeble, elderly persons helped from their desks to a horse-drawn hack waiting at the outside entrance. The general rule was that an employee would be continued on the rolls without reduction of salary so long as he was able to get to the office. Only those were dropped whose disability prevented them from complying with the laws governing attendance, and sometimes those laws were interpreted with great liberality. Few appointing officers—the appointing officers were and still are politically selected—would perform the highly disagreeable task of firing an old person. In the national government there was no profit motive to steel the appointing officer's nerve. On the other hand, it was not unusual for a senator or a congressman to urge the appointing officer, a bureau chief, or a division chief to be considerate of the elderly one. The fact that he might be too disabled to perform any services of real value to the government was generally quite immaterial.

A movement developed, particularly among the elderly employees, for civil pensions to be paid for entirely by the government. The general public, with the history of Civil War military pensions in mind, was cool to such proposals.

About the turn of the century, municipal and state governments which had some years before established contributory retirement systems for public employees, particularly teachers, policemen, and firemen, were witnessing the collapse of these systems through bankruptcy. Contributions which at the outset paid all claims and accumulated a surplus were proving inadequate to meet the rising load. Surpluses vanished and appropriating bodies were unwilling, and perhaps in some cases unable, to meet the growing liabilities which were developing under contributory retirement systems that were financially unsound. The governments were learning that retirement systems, whether contributory or non-contributory, were subject to the same forces that operate in life insurance and life annuities and that retirement systems generally were actuarially far more complicated. It was one thing to promise benefits, and quite a different thing some 20 years later to redeem these promises in cash.

Public-spirited citizens became acutely aware of the weaknesses of local government in the United States, particularly municipal government. Private funds were given for research in municipal government, first for New York City and later for other cities. Soon the movement spread to include the national government and the governments of some of the states.

In all these efforts emphasis was placed on the prime necessity of having a sound system of public personnel administration. Abolition of the spoils system, recruiting qualified employees, permanency of tenure for qualified employees, and a career service were essential in a modern government in an industrial civilization. Permanency of tenure and a career service necessitated a retirement system in the interest of the government as an employer, the employees, and the taxpayers.

Because so many existing retirement systems were already bankrupt or were patently on the verge of bankruptcy, a number of research workers, supported by the new movement, devoted their efforts to an objective, scientific study of pensions. They found that other countries, notably England and some of her colonies, had had much longer experience in this field than had the United States and on several instances had worked out fairly satisfactory solutions. England had for its national service a straight gratuity pension with its mounting costs, but this system had not proved satisfactory to the employees because it failed to provide benefits for those who died or became disabled before reaching the retirement age. For teachers and other employees of local governments the British had established contributory systems on an actuarial reserve basis which were financially sound and tended to meet both the needs of the government for a sound system of personnel administration and the needs of the employees to provide for their old age and for their dependents should the employees die or become disabled before reaching retirement age. These new systems likewise recognized to some extent the rights and interests of the employees who resigned or were dismissed. The British Board of Trade had investigated the unsatisfactory retirement systems of the British railways and had published a comprehensive report on the subject that clearly set forth the new principles. The mass of testimony taken by the British with respect to all this experience was a gold mine to the research workers in the United States. Of especial value was the scientific work of the British actuaries, dating back to William Farr, often referred to as the father of modern vital statistics.

Despite numerous differences of opinion among these research workers with respect to the host of minute details involved in retirement systems, they approached unanimity on several vital points. These were:

1. A retirement system is a necessary part of a sound personnel system for a modern government.

2. A retirement system should be operated on an actuarial reserve basis, at least on a paper reserve basis. The employee on retiring must be sure of receiving the promised benefits. Relatively small benefits actually paid were far better than generous benefits that were paid only to those who retired in the early years and later led to bankruptcy.

3. A contributory system was desirable from the standpoint of the employees if operated on an actuarial reserve basis for two main reasons. (a) It made patent to all the fact that the employee had paid for part of the cost of his benefits by the deductions from his wages. Although he earned a straight pension by his labors, the straight pension had the appearance of a gratuity. Contributions improved public relations which rest on public understanding. (b) It increased the chance that the requirements of the employee for a benefit in the event of death, disability, or withdrawal would be recognized.

4. A contributory actuarial reserve system was desirable from the standpoint of the taxpayers. If the employees had to pay a substantial part of the costs of benefits, they would be obliged to consider costs in connection with their requests for larger benefits.

5. No considerable part of the costs of benefits with respect to past services could be assessed against those employees who were already at or beyond middle age. If they were to secure benefits which would induce them to retire, or would result in their removal if they became incapacitated, the government would have to bear most of the costs of benefits with respect to past services.

6. A contributory retirement system to be effective must, from the standpoint of the government, be compulsory.

The strains of World War I emphasized the fact that the public personnel system of the national government needed complete overhauling. The inequities and injustices of existing conditions stimulated the employees of the government to organize and likewise stimulated the actions of those unions already represented in the national service. The leaders of the new union, the National Federation of Federal Employees, sought a sound system of public personnel administration and the development of a real career service. They were not in disagreement with the research men regarding the broad outlines of a sound retirement system for the national government.

The position of the federal employees in the upper salary brackets deserves comment in this connection, as it explains some of the developments in the national retirement system and has perhaps wide significance. Five features are of particular significance:

1. With a few notable exceptions the upper-bracket employees did not join the new union nor were they members of existing unions.

2. The upper-bracket employees were drawing salaries above the minimum health and decency standard as then worked out for a man, his wife, and three dependent children. Although many of them had been hard hit by the increased cost of living

resulting from the war and the failure of the government to readjust the salaries of those in the old establishments, they did not enlist popular sympathy, nor did they feel that organization was imperative.

3. Some members of Congress—not all by any means—were opposed to increasing in any way the compensation of the upper-bracket employees. These employees had enough, their jobs were secure and involved no business risks. Some members of Congress, however, even at that time, appreciated that the government was not holding its abler upper-bracket employees, that many of them were being lost to other employers, and that a career in the government service was not attractive to a great number of men and women of first-class ability.

4. The general public still retained the attitude toward government employees that had developed under the spoils system. A government employee was considered to be a tax eater with a soft job.

5. A few persons who believed in the economy of paying well the upper administrative, professional, and technical workers in government did not believe in subjecting all their pay to deductions for retirement allowances. They advocated subjecting only a part of it to deductions and basing benefits on that part. They would let the upper-bracket employees provide for more protection in their old age through voluntary insurance.

Such was the general background out of which developed in 1920 the first retirement act: "An Act For the retirement of employees in the classified civil service, and for other purposes."

THE ACT OF 1920[2]

This act originated the retirement system for the great mass of federal employees. It has since, from time to time, been radically revised and amended to make it better adapted to the requirements of the national government and its employees. The details of the present law bear little relationship to the original one. In the main the present law will be the basis for discussion, but a few features of the early law deserve mention.

[2] 41 Stat. 614.

The 1920 act was limited to employees in the classified civil service. It has since been greatly broadened in coverage, so that it includes almost all the federal employees not under some other system.

The 1920 act required all covered employees to contribute 2½ per cent of their base pay regardless of the amount of that pay. Maximum limits were, however, fixed on benefits. For example, an employee who fell in Class A, the highest class, for employees who had served 30 years or more, drew 60 per cent of his average basic pay for the 10 years next preceding his retirement, but not more than $720 or less than $360. The maximum benefit, $720, was 60 per cent of $1,200. Thus the high-bracket employee paid on his full salary but drew benefits only with respect to the first $1,200 of it. Had the law not been amended, the upper-bracket employees who served for 30 or more years under the system would have secured less than he could have bought by putting his contributions into an annuity sold by a private insurance company. Even before the law was amended, some employees found it advantageous to resign just before reaching the retirement age so that they could get possession of their accumulated contributions. The 1920 law was so discriminatory against the upper-bracket employees that it was a factor in leading some of them to withdraw from the federal service.

Eligibility for old-age retirement was based on age and length of service. For the bulk of the employees, the requirement was attaining the age of 70 with at least 15 years of service. For mechanics, city and rural letter carriers, and post-office clerks the minimum age was 65 and for railway mail clerks the age was 62. Retirement on attaining the retirement age was compulsory unless the head of the department, branch, or independent office in which the employee worked requested his retention. Then the employee might be retained for successive two-year periods; but ten years after the passage of the act for not more than two such two-year periods. The rigidity of the age requirements has since been materially modified both in the interests of the employee and the government.

There was no forfeiture of the employee's contributions under the 1920 act. If an employee died in the active service or withdrew from a covered position, the government refunded his contributions with interest at 4 per cent compounded annually. If an annuitant died before having received the amount of his contributions, plus the compound interest, the balance was paid to his legal representative. Note, however, that the employee on death or withdrawal received only his own contributions with interest and nothing from the public treasury. The government contributed only when an employee took an annuity.

After an employee had served 15 years he was entitled to a disability allowance if he became "totally and permanently disabled for useful and efficient service by reason of disease or injury not due to vicious habits, intemperance or willful misconduct." The disability annuity was the same as the old-age annuity for like service and like salary and included the same nonforfeiture provision.

Protection of the wife and the dependent child was provided only through the return of contributions on death or withdrawal and through the nonforfeiture feature of the annuities. Joint and survivor annuities came much later.

The 1920 act was regarded by the students of retirement systems, by many of the employees, and even by some of its leading proponents in Congress as far from ideal. It did, however, establish the principle of retiring employees through a contributory system and permitted the gradual evolution of a better system through amendment without again involving a battle as to the principle of retiring the aged employees.

THE PRESENT LAW

The present law places within the operation of the civil service retirement system all officers and employees in or under the executive, judicial, and legislative branches of the United States government and all officers and employees of the municipal government of the District of Columbia (except elective officers and heads of executive departments) who are not subject to another retirement system for such officers and employees. This coverage is mandatory with the exception of certain officers and employees in the legislative branch, who have the option of acquiring a retirement status. The President has, however, authority in his discretion to exclude from coverage any officer or employee or group of officers and employees whose tenure of office or employment is intermittent or of uncertain duration.

Under the present law consideration has to be given to five different types of benefits: (1) age retirement; (2) optional retirement; (3) disability retirement; (4) separation retirement; (5) refunds. Each of these will be considered in turn.

The old-age benefit. To be eligible for an old-age benefit an employee must have attained the age of 70 and have served at least 15 years. If he has served 15 years, his retirement is compulsory unless the President permits his continuation or his re-employment in the public interest. If he has not completed 15 years of service on attaining the age of 70, the requirement for automatic separation is waived, and the employee may continue to serve until he has the necessary service, unless otherwise separated.

Optional retirement. Optional retirement is available for (1) an employee who has attained the age of 60 and served at least 30 years; (2) an employee who has attained the age of 62 and has served at least 15 years. Either the employee or the head of the department or agency in which he is employed may exercise these options. The administrative officer can exercise them only if the employee is disqualified to perform satisfactorily the duties of his or a similar position and the action of the officer must have the approval of the Civil Service Commission. An employee thus separated by administrative action against his wishes has a right to a hearing before the Civil Service Commission. (3) An employee who has attained the age of 55 and has served 30 years. If an employee exercises this option and selects an annuity payable immediately, the annuity will be of the same value as one an employee would have drawn who retired at 60 with like length of service and salary.

Disability benefits. Disability retirement is now available to anyone who has served five years or more and is disabled for useful and efficient service in the grade or class or position occupied without regard to the attained age. Proof is required that the disability is not the result of vicious habits, intemperance, or willful misconduct on the part of the employee within a period of five years next prior to becoming so disabled. Disability benefits are figured on the same basis as old-age benefits, as will be subsequently described.

Separation benefits. Separation benefits of two types are now available to any person who has served five years or more.

1. For employees who resign voluntarily or who are removed for cause. They receive a deferred annuity with first payment when they attain the age of 62. The amount of the annuity is what their own contributions will purchase plus $30 for each year of service, provided $30 is not more than three fourths of the counted base pay. If the annuity purchased by their contributions exceeds the $30 for each year of service which is given by the government, the government matches the annuity that they purchase.

2. For employees who are involuntarily separated not by removal for cause or charges of misconduct or delinquence. They may take either (a) a deferred annuity beginning at 62 or (b) an annuity of like actuarial value with first payment at 55 or at date of separation if subsequent to that age. These employees can elect which method of determining the annuity shall be used, whereas the employees under (1) above can use only the one plan.

Refunds. An employee on withdrawing from the active service cannot under the present law get a refund of his contributions made after January 24, 1942, unless he has served in the aggregate less than five years. If he has served five years or more he must leave his contributions in the fund and draw them later in the form of an annuity.

Under the earlier law, an officer or employee on withdrawing from the service could receive a refund of his contributions with interest, but possibly with a deduction for the so-called tontine provision on voluntary separation or removal for cause.

If an employee dies without having attained eligibility for retirement or without having established a valid claim for an annuity, the total amount of his deductions with interest thereon is paid to the legal representative of such employee.

If a former employee entitled to the return of the amount credited to his individual account becomes legally incompetent, the total amount due may be paid to a duly appointed guardian or committee of such employee.

The amendments to the law adopted January 24, 1942 eliminate one of the criticisms often levied against the system, namely that the employee who withdrew from the service without having become eligible for a benefit got back all or almost all his own contributions with interest but got nothing whatsoever from the government. Under the 1942 amendment, if he has served five years or more he gets an annuity, generally a deferred annuity, toward which the government contributes.

Under the present law, therefore, the employee has a nonforfeiture right from the outset to his own contributions plus interest, except possibly for the small tontine feature and that after five years of service he has a vested right to a deferred annuity based on what he himself has paid for through his own contributions and what the government gives from the public treasury. His contingent right to a disability allowance also accrues after five years of service. Prior to the 1942 amendment forfeitures of the employers' contributions on withdrawal were more common under the Civil Service Act than under O.A.S.I. Now the situation is reversed. The Civil Service Retirement Act has never provided forfeitures of the employees' contributions, as O.A.S.I. does in the case of employees withdrawing before attaining an insured status.

Benefit formulae. The civil service retirement system, or its predecessor, started in 1920 with a single benefit formula. At present it has three, one of which has subdivisions designed to meet the needs of different employees and to cover different situations. These formulae are generally referred to as "plans."

Under Plan I or the purchasable plan the total accumulation to the credit of the employee, including his contributions and the interest added to the account, is used to purchase an annuity for him of the type which he elects. He gets what his own contributions plus interest will buy. To the annuity which his funds will buy is added the government's part of the annuity, which may be calculated in either one of two ways:

1. A sum equal to $30 for each year of service not exceeding 30, provided this sum shall not exceed three fourths of the average annual base pay received by the employee during any five consecutive years of available service. This means that an employee whose base pay is $1,200 or under gets from the government an annuity of three quarters of his base pay if he has served for 30 years or more. This formula gives the same amount for each year of service and thus is favorable to employees with short service. The maximum allowance under this formula is $900 for 30 years of service or more. Obviously such a formula was unfavorable to young men and women who made a career of the national service, entering it in their youth and advancing to responsible—and according to government standards—well-paid administrative, scientific, and technical positions. This discrimination against the employees in the more responsible positions led to the alternative for the government's share under Plan I.

2. Since January 1, 1940, if the employee's accumulation in his own account will purchase a larger annuity than $30 for each year of service, the government will match the annuity which he has secured from his own contributions.

The employees' contributions started originally at 2½ per cent; they were raised to 3½ per cent beginning July 1, 1926; and to 5 per cent beginning July 1, 1942. Three points deserve emphasis with respect to the 1940 amendment: (1) under it the government matches what the employee has purchased through his own contributions; (2) the government gives the employee nothing with respect to services rendered prior to the establishment of the system; and (3) for employees who entered the service on or after July 1, 1942, the new system provides for the career men and women who spend their working lives in the service such an annuity as will be purchased by a 5 per cent contribution by the government plus a 5 per cent contribution by the employee. This system is one largely used by colleges, universities, and other similar institutions. For many years now there has been a tendency to accept the point of view that the compensation of the upper professional, scientific, and administrative workers in the government should be fairly comparable with that paid by the stronger higher educational institutions of the country. This new formula tends to increase that similarity, although today few private systems can guarantee 4 per cent interest on the accumulations.

Under Plan II or the guaranteed minimum annuity the average annual base pay, not to exceed $1,600 a year, is multiplied by the number of years of service, not to exceed 30, and the resulting product is divided by 40. In other words it gives three quarters pay to a man who has served 30 years and has not earned a base pay above $1,600. The maximum annuity under this plan is $1,200. "This plan," according to the Civil Service Commission, "is generally applicable where the average salary for any five years falls between $1,600 and $2,400," a salary range which includes large numbers of clerical employees of the government.

Plan III or the second form of guaranteed minimum was adopted January 24, 1942. Under this plan the benefit in no case shall be less than an amount equal to the employee's highest average base pay for five consecutive years of service multiplied by the number of years of service, not exceeding 35, and divided by 70. No one who has served 35 years or more is retired at age 70 on less than half pay. This plan is particularly advantageous for people in the higher brackets who have had a considerable number of years of service prior to the adoption of the original retirement plan in 1920. Under it an employee who had by 1942 an aggregate of 35 years of service and had earned an average of $5,600 for his best five consecutive years would receive an annuity of $2,800.

No special benefits for dependents. The Civil Service Retirement Act, like the Railroad Retirement Act provides no specific benefits for dependents. The civil service employee who has such dependents must make provision for them himself either through (1) use of the options and rights afforded by the retirement system, or (2) private voluntary insurance, or (3) a combination of the two.

An employee on reaching the retirement age must take an annuity, but he has his choice among: (1) a forfeiture annuity which will pay him the maximum possible amount but one which will terminate on his death. (2) A nonforfeiture annuity, which will pay him a smaller amount but if he dies before he has received in annuities the amount of his accumulation, will pay the remaining balance to his beneficiary. (3) A joint and survivor's annuity for a still smaller sum payable to him as long as he lives and to his designated beneficiary if he or she survives, either the same amount or half of that annuity as he has elected.

Death benefits. The employee who dies in the active service leaving a wife or a dependent child can leave to them, regardless of their ages, the amount standing to his credit in the fund. This amount depends of course on age and length of service.

A table prepared by the Civil Service Commission[3] gives among other things the approximate accumulations which will stand to the credit of employees who entered the service on July 1, 1930 and earned the stated salaries throughout the length of service specified. In the following table some of these figures are selected for illustrative purposes.

ACCUMULATIONS IN EMPLOYEE'S ACCOUNT AFTER INDICATED YEARS OF SERVICE

Fixed Salary	15	20	25	30	35	40
$1,260	$ 715.83	$1,152.69	$1,684.19	$2,330.83	$3,117.58	$ 4,074.78
1,620	990.37	1,586.15	2,311.00	3,192.89	4,265.85	5,571.27
2,000	1,280.16	2,043.69	2,972.64	4,102.84	5,477.92	7,150.90
2,300	1,508.94	2,404.91	3,494.99	4,821.23	6,434.81	8,397.97
3,200	2,195.28	3,488.56	5,062.02	6,976.37	9,305.48	12,139.20

The accumulated contributions furnish a substantial life insurance benefit for the dependents after the employees have

---

[3] *Synopsis of Retirement Benefits under the Civil Service Retirement Act of May 29, 1930 as amended to March 7, 1942, Inclusive,* May 1942.

been in the service for 20 years or more. If the younger employees have dependents, they have to protect them through voluntary insurance. The system does not require the man without dependents to insure the wives or children of others nor does it require its women workers to insure the wives and children under 18 of the men workers. The woman employee has the same options as a man does. She can select her beneficiary. She pays the same contribution rates that a man pays, and gets either the same benefits or benefits of equal value.

The national government as an employer does not give to each employee the same actuarial value of benefits per dollar of compensation paid. It gives *relatively more*, per dollar of compensation, to the lower-paid workers than to the more highly paid workers, and generally *relatively more* to the employee who has served for a short term than for a long term. *Relatively more* means that the higher-paid workers get more actual dollars than the lower-paid workers, and the employees with long service more dollars than the employees with shorter service. Under the present system, such discrimination as exists is on a relative basis.

Benefits part of compensation. The national system is an individual employer system, although the employer is the government of the United States. Under an individual employer system in a free or competitive economic system, retirement benefits become part of an employee's compensation. British experience demonstrated that even noncontributory straight pensions became part of the compensation. Contributory systems became part of compensation much more quickly and completely. The difference between an individual employer's contribution to the benefits for his own employees and a pay-roll tax paid by an employer to a general social security fund is of such significance that retirement rights as compensation merit some examination.

As soon as the United States government had a retirement system, the Civil Service Commission began to include the essential facts regarding that system in all announcements of examinations to fill positions in the civil service. Possible candidates were told not only what the immediate salary would be, but what percentage would be deducted for retirement benefits and what the benefits would be. The fact that the government had such a system offered an inducement to people to enter its service—especially at first to those in the lower-salary brackets. The compensation offered was not base pay alone but base pay plus retirement benefits.

The benefits under an individual employer's retirement system become an important force in helping an employer retain his employees. Especially as an employee grows older and has a substantial period of service to his credit, he attaches great weight to his accrued retirement rights. Employers hold employees through compensation, and compensation consists both of base pay and retirement system benefits.

Individual employer retirement systems thus become on adoption not only part of the personnel system but an element in the most vital feature of that system, the compensation for services rendered. The national government learned that fact over the years. It discovered that with respect to many of its upper-bracket employees it was in a weak competitive position. If another employer, particularly a private employer, wanted one of its good men, that employer could easily outbid the government on base pay; and the original retirement benefits for the higher-paid workers lacked holding power. It was not difficult for the competing employer to match or exceed the government's retirement offer either under his own retirement system or through a private contract with the employee. An individual annuity contract with a private insurance company for the benefit of the employee was a simple and readily available device, possibly with some life insurance added. The government learned that substantial benefits for its higher-bracket employees were as important when, as under the original law, the upper-bracket employees generally felt—not without cause —that they had a grievance against the government with respect to retirement allowances.

The national civil service system thus represents a gradual adjustment of retirement provisions to employment conditions which the government confronts in running its business. The three plans which it now has—and one of these, as has been noted, offers alternative possibilities—give a wide range of adjustments to different employment situations. The government pays for services partly in current pay and partly in retirement benefits and one of its major personnel problems during the past 20 years has been to develop a system to meet its needs.

An individual employer retirement system in this respect presents a sharp contrast with O.A.S.I. Under O.A.S.I. the employers of covered workers pay a pay-roll tax into the general treasury which goes to help pay O.A.S.I. benefits. The taxes levied against the employer who pays good wages and has a relatively high proportion of his employees in the upper brackets do not go in the main to his own employees except in so far as they may be required for benefits to those who retire in the early years of the system. They go to pay the benefits provided by O.A.S.I. for the low-paid workers in other establishments, possibly to his competitors who operate in lower-cost sections of the country or who have different ideas with respect to wages or the quality of employees it is desirable to use. They are not part of his own compensation plan and are not adjustable to the employment conditions he confronts.

In this connection it may be worth while to refer again to one development in the civil service retirement system that has been previously mentioned. Individual employer retirement systems were often used to tie employees to a particular employer. Often straight pensions were paid only to employees who remained in the system until they reached the retirement age. The United States civil service system never went that far; from the outset it returned the employee's contribution with interest if the employee withdrew before being entitled to an annuity, but it did involve a forfeiture of the government's share. Under O.A.S.I. employers' taxes are never returned to an employer even if the worker who occasioned their payment leaves him or even if the worker leaves O.A.S.I. coverage without acquiring a contingent right to an O.A.S.I. benefit. O.A.S.I. offers no obstacle to the mobility of labor except in so far as it may induce a man to remain in a covered position rather than move to an uncovered one. The civil service system now gives an employee a vested interest in an old-age benefit paid for by the government after he has served five years, and thus it does not offer much of an impediment to the mobility of labor. It is now in some respects superior to O.A.S.I., for, to use O.A.S.I. terminology, the civil service employees become fully insured for an old-age benefit in five years whereas an O.A.S.I. employee does not become fully insured for ten years.

FINANCIAL SECURITY

In the preceding discussion the civil service retirement system has occasionally been referred to as an individual employer system. It has, however, certain features which distinguish it from individual employer systems in private enterprise and to a lesser degree in state and local governments. The more important of these distinctions deserve mention.

Behind the civil service system lies the taxing power of the national government. Although no Congress can bind a subsequent Congress to make the appropriations necessary to fulfill promises made with respect to a retirement system, it is scarcely conceivable that a Congress would fail to make the appropriations to fulfill the obligations of the government under a contributory system that has been developed on the basis of sound actuarial studies and evaluations.

Retirement systems in private enterprise on the other hand have to depend to a far greater degree not only on the application of sound actuarial principles in designing the system but also in accumulating real actuarial reserves. If something goes wrong with their retirement systems, they may not be able to repair the damage from their own funds, and they have no taxes to fall back upon to make up shortages. Private organizations which have done the best work in this field have either selected a sound private insurance company to serve as carrier or have set up special trust funds under competent actuaries to guarantee the payment of the promised benefits. Both the employers' and the employees' contributions are paid either to the insurance carrier or into the special fund as the services are rendered and are invested generally in securities approved for trust or insurance reserve funds.

State and municipal governments have taxing power, but this power has very real practical limitations as the early experience with retirement systems demonstrated. These governments in designing sound retirement systems have generally developed true actuarial reserves to protect the employees and to prevent the development of a deficit so great that it is impracticable to meet it through taxation.

The contributions made by the national civil servants are invested in United States government bonds which have behind them the credit of the national government. So far as payment of principal and interest is concerned no investment could be safer. The actual money paid in is, however, used for governmental expenses and outlays. The interest on the bonds and the principal, when and if it is needed, must come from the taxpayers, a matter which will be considered at length in Part III.

The reserves of well-administered private retirement systems are invested mainly in obligations of persons or agencies other than the employer. The interest and the principal represent for the most part payments flowing into the fund from outside the organization. Reserves of private retirement systems are therefore devices to accumulate capital available for investment. This capital may be loaned either to private, public, or quasi-public agencies. How it shall be invested is determined by private enterprise, often however subject to public regulations, especially if a private insurance company serves as a carrier. A substantial percentage of the reserves may be invested in United States government bonds, but they can be invested in the obligations of other governments or of private enterprises. Private retirement reserves are controlled by private enterprise, whereas the reserves of the civil service retirement system and the railroad retirement system are controlled by the government.

CHAPTER VIII

UNEMPLOYMENT INSURANCE

By the Social Security Act of 1935, the states were forced to adopt and to finance systems of unemployment compensation. Since expert opinion regarding the principles which should control in designing such systems was divided, the national government left to the states wide latitude for the exercise of independent judgment. As a result each state, Alaska, Hawaii, and the District of Columbia has its own unemployment compensation law. No two laws are alike, and in many instances there are great differences with respect to basic principles.

The effort in this chapter will be to describe these systems briefly and to bring out the major differences and issues with respect to policy. The first section will deal with the historical developments prior to the passage of the Social Security Act, and the second with the provisions and requirements of that act. Then the essential elements of unemployment insurance will be taken up as they have developed in the several states and territories. An effort will be made to describe existing provisions and practices and to bring out the variations with respect to both philosophy and practice. Detailed discussion of the issues will come in Part III, where unemployment insurance will be considered as one of the essential parts of a universal, comprehensive, and co-ordinated social security system.

Practically no use of evaluative statistics will be made in this chapter, because unemployment compensation has been in effect for too short a time to produce really significant figures. Almost all the experience with it to date has been under the defense and wartime economy, which has reduced unemployment to lowest terms. Hence evaluations of unemployment compensation systems in the United States must rest more on theory and philosophy than on experience.

HISTORICAL DEVELOPMENT[1]

Prior to the depression unemployment insurance in the United States was in the academic discussion stage. Public opinion in general was at least indifferent if not opposed to it. Neither organized labor nor the great majority of employers favored it. The American Federation of Labor, in fact, actively opposed it.

The depression, however, resulted in a change in public sentiment and a complete reversal of the attitude of organized labor. Proposals for state systems of unemployment insurance began to receive serious consideration from the legislatures of large industrial states, and one state, Wisconsin, actually passed an act early in 1932, although no premiums were collected under that act until July 1934, and no benefits were paid until considerably later. In several other states, bills passed one house of the legislature but were defeated in the other.

Three forces that operated against prompt action by the states at this period deserve brief note.

1. Nothing approaching an accepted pattern for this type of legislation had been developed in the United States. The specialists were sharply divided, the Wisconsin group emphasizing individual employer responsibility and advocating individual or industry reserves, whereas others minimized individual employer responsibility for and influence in preventing unemployment, stressed general economic causes, and urged state-wide pooled funds, more in accordance with European practice. These issues will be discussed in greater detail later in considering the action of the states.

2. A strong feeling existed that in the depths of a depression additional burdens should not be placed on employers. It was feared that, under the business conditions that then existed, taxes levied against employers to support unemployment insurance would lead to further unemployment.

---

[1] In writing this historical summary, large use has been made of the excellent statement of the historical background contained in Part 1 of *Social Security in the United States* (1936) by Paul H. Douglas.

3. Legislatures of states favorable to the principle hesitated to adopt it, lest they subject the employers within the state to interstate competition. In the past, advanced labor legislation in some states had operated to give an advantage to competing states which had less stringent labor laws and smaller expenditures for social and educational services. In the early thirties, moreover, some states in seeking a solution of their own unemployment problems were attempting to entice employers to develop industries within their borders by offering favorable terms with respect to land costs and taxes. If a state should adopt unemployment insurance under these conditions, it would add to the inducement of employers to locate or to expand in other jurisdictions.

The tax method of federal control. The states had recently had a demonstration of interstate competition in the field of taxation which is so important in unemployment insurance that it deserves description. The solution of this tax problem demonstrated the practicability of a new method of control by the national government of what was regarded as unfair competition among the states. Briefly the tax situation was this:

Nature had endowed the State of Florida with a climate that made it a delightful winter playground and haven to which to retire when working years were over. The state had had a phenomenal building boom, characterized by resort hotels, winter homes of the well-to-do, and thousands of year-round homes for retired workers of the middle classes. Additions to property values were so great that it seemed as if Florida could solve its revenue problems by using the property tax, excise taxes that would yield large revenues from tourists, and taxes on parimutuel betting on horse racing and other sports. To encourage persons of substantial means to build in Florida and to become legal residents of the state, a constitutional provision was adopted prohibiting the imposition of an inheritance or estate tax by the state. This law, supplementing the natural advantages of Florida, made it a haven for persons of means who would escape the heavy inheritance and estate taxes that had developed in other states. Moreover, Florida had predominantly a southern rural economy with no large industrial centers, and hence its governmental costs were low as compared, for example, with New York.

The action of Florida constituted a real threat to every urban industrial state of the north and west that had to meet relatively high costs of government and depended in part on income, inheritance, and estate taxes to finance these costs. This threat was met by national action.

The Congress of the United States levied a national tax on inheritances with a provision that the taxpayers could use as an offset to this national tax such sums, within limits, as they had paid as inheritance or estate taxes to the states. That national law meant that residents of Florida had to pay the same national tax as residents of other states, but since Florida had no offsetting tax, all the money flowed into the national treasury, whereas states with their own taxes of this type paid very little into the national treasury. If Florida was to keep the money within the state for state use, it had to impose an inheritance or estate tax, and therefore it amended its constitution and adopted the necessary tax laws.

This experience demonstrated a new method by which the national government could use its power to tax as a device to influence, regulate, or even control the actions of the states. Its possibilities in the unemployment insurance field were quickly appreciated. If the federal government levied a tax on pay rolls but permitted employers to use as an offset against it their payments toward state unemployment systems, three existing difficulties would be overcome:

1. The dangers of serious interstate competition would be almost completely eliminated, for almost every employer in covered establishments would have to pay the pay-roll tax whether his state had an unemployment insurance system or not.

2. The individual states would be practically compelled to establish a system, for without one their payments would flow into the national treasury and be spent for general purposes. If they adopted one, the money would remain in the state to the

advantage of the covered workers if not also of the employers. Naturally the employers would have no desire to have pay-roll taxes used for the general purposes of the national government.

3. The constitutional position was relatively strong. The national government had in the past made two efforts to regulate and control child labor, one based on its power to regulate interstate commerce and the other through a tax imposed on the products of child labor. Both of these acts had been declared unconstitutional by the Supreme Court. Here was a new device that had not been tried in the labor field, and against which there was no unreversed Supreme Court decision. The new device had, in fact, been upheld by a unanimous decision of the Supreme Court in *Florida v. Mellon*.[2]

Early in 1934 a bill that applied the new method and that had been drafted in the United States Department of Labor was introduced in both houses of Congress, but it was not on the administration's "must list." While it was still under consideration the President announced his intention to appoint a Committee on Economic Security to study the whole question and report with a definite program to the new Congress which would meet in January 1935.

The new method was actually adopted in the Social Security Act of 1935. Title III provided "Grants to States for Unemployment Compensation Administration" and Title IX levied the "Tax on Employers of Eight or More." Special emphasis should be placed on the fact that the grants to the states under Title III were exclusively for the costs of administration and that the national government made no grant-in-aid toward the sums required for unemployment insurance benefits. This new system rested almost entirely on the new tax method of federal influence, regulation, or control of the states and not on the old device of grants-in-aid, which was used in the Social Security Act for the public assistance programs for the aged, the blind, and the dependent children.

The unemployment features of the Social Security Act were amended in 1939, and for the purposes of the present book the

[2] 273 U. S. 12 (1927).

description and discussion will relate primarily to the acts as amended.

THE PROVISIONS OF THE NATIONAL LAW

The most vital parts of the national law on unemployment compensation are contained in the tax provisions. They are no longer an integral part of the Social Security Act but constitute Subchapter C of Chapter 9 of the Internal Revenue Code and are entitled "(Federal Unemployment Tax Act) Tax on Employers of Eight or More."

The federal tax on employers. Section 1600 of the revenue act levies an excise tax on employers "with respect to having individuals in his employ," equal to 3 per cent of total wages paid by him during the calendar year for employment, but the terms "employer," "wages," and "employment" are all specifically defined in the law and these definitions are of vital importance.

"The term 'employer,'" the law says,[3] "does not include any person unless on each of some twenty days during the taxable year, each day being in a different calendar week, the total number of individuals who were employed by him in employment for some portion of the day (whether or not at the same moment of time) was eight or more." This provision will occasionally be referred to as "the eight or more rule."

The term wages means all remuneration for employment, including the cash value of all remuneration paid in any medium other than cash, but under the 1939 amendments it does not include:[4] (1) that part of the remuneration in any calendar year that exceeds $3,000; (2) that part of the remuneration made to or on behalf of an employee under a plan or system established by an employer to make provisions for retirement, sickness, or accident disability, medical and hospitalization expenses, and (under certain conditions) death; (3) the payment made by an employer (without deduction from the remuneration of the employee) of the tax imposed on the employee for old-age insurance or of any payment required from an employee under a state

[3] Sec. 1607(a), Supp. 1.
[4] Sec. 1607(b).

unemployment compensation law; (4) dismissal payments which the employer is not legally required to make.

Employments covered. The general defintion of employment is all-inclusive, but it is followed by fifteen specific exceptions, only the more important of which will be briefly noted here.[5]

1. Agricultural labor.

2. Domestic service in a private home, local college club, or local chapter of a college fraternity or sorority.

3. Casual labor not in the course of an employer's trade or business.

4. Service performed by an individual in the employ of his son, daughter, or spouse, and service performed by a child under the age of 21 in the employ of his father or mother.

5. Service performed in the employ of the United States.

6. Service performed in the employ of a state or any political subdivision thereof.

7. Service performed in the employ of a foreign government.

8. Service performed in the employ of a nonprofit agency organized exclusively for religious, charitable, scientific, literary, or educational purposes or for the prevention of cruelty to children.

9. Service performed in the employ of certain agencies exempt from income taxation.

The definitions of wages and employment thus used in the unemployment tax act are since 1939 practically identical with those used in the old-age insurance tax act except that all employers must pay the old-age tax whereas only those with eight or more employees are required to pay the national tax for unemployment compensation. There is a vital distinction between the two systems.

The contrasts with O.A.S.I. O.A.S.I. is a national system nationally administered. Thus an employee in an employment exempted under the national law is excluded from coverage. Unemployment insurance is a state activity state administered. The national tax act forces the states to cover all employees working for covered employers, but it does not prevent the

[5] Sec. 1607(c).

states from adopting laws which give wider coverage. Thus a state may include all employers without reference to the eight or more rule. A state can include agricultural labor, domestic servants, and employees of its own government or the subordinate local governments which it has created. The national act thus prescribes not the maximum but the minimum coverage.

Offsets against the federal tax. Against the national tax, the taxpayer is allowed certain credits with respect to the obligations for unemployment compensation to which he is subjected by state law. The national law on this subject is complicated and will necessitate discussion in some detail.

The first point, however, is simple. "The total credits allowed to a taxpayer . . . shall not exceed 90 per centum of the tax against which such credits are allowable."[6] Thus 10 per cent of the tax goes to the national government. This money is used to pay the "Grants to States for Unemployment Compensation" provided by the Social Security Act. Under temporary law which expires July 1, 1947, any past or current excess of such receipts over the grants and any further sums Congress may appropriate go into a federal unemployment account in the Unemployment Trust Fund. Sums in this account may be loaned without interest to states whose funds fall below a level prescribed by the act.[7]

Types of systems permitted by federal law. The other provisions regarding credits, the complicated ones, are designed (1) to permit the states a choice as to the type of unemployment compensation they will adopt, and (2) to a certain extent to establish minimum standards with which the states must comply in the type which they do elect.

Three broad types are permitted under the national law:

1. The highly socialized type. Under this type every covered employer in the state pays exactly the same rate of tax, and all the proceeds of the tax flow into one common pool. All benefits are paid from this one pooled fund. Employers in highly stable industries pay the same rate of tax as employers in highly unstable industries. Unemployment is regarded as the result of

---

[6] Sec. 1601(c), Supp. 1.
[7] War Mobilization and Reconversion Act of 1944, 58 Stat. 790.

general economic conditions, and the nature of particular industries is immaterial. The unemployment system is a device to compensate for unemployment in the general social interest.

2. The pooled fund with "experience or merit rating." Under this type of system, employers are classified in accordance with their record with respect to employment or unemployment, and the taxes are scaled in accordance with that record. Those with the lowest degree of unemployment pay the lowest tax; those with the highest degree, the highest tax. They are rated and taxed according to their merit or experience. Employers in stable industries pay at a lower rate than employers in unstable industries. An employer who has developed a successful stabilization plan pays at a lower rate than an employer in the same industry who has not been successful in stabilization. All employers' taxes, however, flow into one common pool, and all benefits are paid from that common pool. Thus an insured employee who is entitled to a benefit is protected so long as there are funds in the common pool, regardless of his employer.

3. The individual employer or individual industry type. Under this type there is no common pool into which all the special taxes flow, although there may be a small general pool used as a minor safety device. Individual employers or the employers in an industry build a reserve fund of their own. When this reserve fund has reached the size specified by law, the employers' payments into it may be reduced or eliminated. In a fund established for an entire industry, merit rating may be used. Under systems in this group an employer may reduce his unemployment insurance payments by adopting a guaranteed employment plan which gives his employees assured employment in lieu of unemployment benefits. Under such plans the security of the unemployed worker entitled to a benefit depends basically on the condition of the employers' fund or the industry fund under which he has worked. The particular fund upon which he depends may be bankrupt, while other employer or industry funds are financially flourishing, or his fund may be solvent while other funds are bankrupt. Systems of this type are highly individualistic as compared with the uniform contribution pooled systems described, under (1) above.

We shall not at the moment enter into further discussion of the relative merits of these three types. The point here is that the national act was designed to allow the states a very considerable measure of freedom in deciding which type or what combination of types they would adopt. To give this freedom, under the tax offset method of control, the national tax act had to include elaborate and complicated provisions with respect to tax credits.

Under a system where all employers pay the same rate of tax and the money flows into a single pool, there are no great complications except the ever-present detailed administrative ones of years, pay periods, overpayments, underpayments, and so on. Broadly, under such a system the employer gets a credit against his national tax of the amount he has paid the state up to but not exceeding 90 per cent of the national tax.

To permit of merit rating, the national government must allow the taxpayer to deduct, within the general limitation, what he would have paid the state had he not been entitled to the reduction of the state tax due to his merit rating instead of what he actually paid. The national tax act permits such an "additional credit allowance" only if the Social Security Board finds that under the state law the experience with respect to unemployment or other factors bearing a direct relation to unemployment risk, upon which merit rating is based, relates to not less than the three years immediately preceding the computation date.

The state law may permit the employer to make his payments to a guaranteed employment account[8] and to reduce

---

[8] The following are the provisions of the act with respect to a guaranteed employment account: "The term 'guaranteed employment account' means a separate account, in an unemployment fund, maintained with respect to a person (or group of persons) having individuals in his (or their) employ who, in accordance with the provisions of the State law or of a plan thereunder approved by the State agency,

"(A) guarantees in advance at least thirty hours of work, for which remuneration will be paid at not less than stated rates, for each of forty weeks (or if more, one weekly hour may be deducted for each added week guaranteed) in a year, to all the individuals who are in his (or their) employ in, and who continue to be available for suitable work in, one or more distinct establishments, except that any such individual's guaranty may commence after a probationary period (included within the eleven or less consecutive weeks immediately following the first week in which the individual renders services), and these payments when that account reaches a certain size. To permit deduction from the national tax of more than was actually paid in cash, the Board must find that (1) the guaranty of remuneration was fulfilled in the year preceding the computation date; (2) the balance of such account amounts to not less than 2½ per centum of that part of the pay roll or pay rolls, for the three years preceding the computation date by which contributions to such account were measured; and (3) such contributions were payable to such account with respect to three years preceding the computation date. In other words, to avoid 90 per cent of the federal tax, the employer must for three years pay into the fund 2.7 per cent of covered pay roll and then in subsequent years he can pay less and still get a credit provided the fund amounts to 2½ per cent of the covered pay rolls for the three years, and during the preceding year he actually fulfilled the premises of the guaranteed remuneration.

The provision of the act with respect to employer or industry funds, as amended effective January 1, 1942, reads as follows:

No reduced rate of contributions to a reserve account is permitted to a person (or group of persons) having individuals in his (or their) employ unless (A) compensation has been payable from such account throughout the year preceding the computation date, and (B) the balance of such account amounts to not less than five times the largest amount of compensation paid from such account within any one of the three years preceding such date, and (C) the balance of such account amounts to not less than 2½ per centum of that part of the pay roll or pay rolls for the three years preceding such date by which contributions to such account were measured, and (D) such contributions were payable to such account with respect to the three years preceding the computation date.[9]

The Social Security Board is responsible for passing upon the

---

"(B) gives security or assurance, satisfactory to the State agency, for the fulfillment of such guaranties, from which account, unless such account is exhausted or terminated, is paid all and only compensation, payable on the basis of services performed for such person (or for one or more of the persons comprising the group), to any such individual whose guaranteed remuneration has not been paid (either pursuant to the guaranty or from the security or assurance provided for the fulfillment of the guaranty), or whose guaranty is not renewed and who is otherwise eligible for compensation under the State law." Sec. 1602(c)(4), Supp. 1.

[9] Sec. 1602(a)(4), Supp. 1.

state employment compensation plans to determine whether they comply with the minimum requirements of the national act. It certifies its findings with respect to additional credits to the Secretary of the Treasury and to the state involved. The law includes the necessary provisions to cover cases where the state arrangements are complicated, and some parts and payments with respect to them are in accordance with the national law while others are not.

Substantive requirements of national law. Other national requirements with which the individual state must comply are contained in both the tax act and in Title III of the Social Security Act. With two exceptions these national requirements deal with administration and finance. One exception that relates to broad social and economic policy is Section 1603 (a) (5) of the tax act. It reads:

Compensation shall not be denied in such State to any otherwise eligible individual for refusing to accept new work under any of the following conditions: (A) If the position offered is vacant due directly to a strike, lockout, or other labor dispute; (B) if the wages, hours, or other conditions of the work offered are substantially less favorable to the individual than those prevailing for similar work in the locality; (C) if as a condition of being employed the individual would be required to join a company union or to resign from or refrain from joining any bona fide labor organization.

The other exception is presumably due to Article 1, Section 10 of the Constitution of the United States which reads: "No State shall . . . pass any . . . Law impairing the Obligation of Contracts." In the absence of specific legislation, both employers and employees under state unemployment compensation laws might develop contractual rights which the states could not constitutionally impair by subsequent legislation. The national government therefore requires that state unemployment compensation laws to be acceptable under the tax act must provide: "All the rights, privileges, or immunities conferred by such law or by acts done pursuant thereto shall exist subject to the power of the legislature to amend or repeal such law at any time."

The inclusion of this clause makes it possible for the states from time to time to readjust benefits and conditions governing benefits without depriving employers or employees of contractual rights. The clause amounts to a legislative declaration that unemployment compensation systems are not contractual in nature and that the individual cannot acquire a vested interest in promised benefits of which he cannot be deprived by subsequent legislative action.

National social insurance systems based on national legislation do not have to include such provisions, because the special taxes are paid into the general fund and are not contributions or premiums paid to the insurance fund itself. Hence the arrangement is not one of contract.

Method of handling funds under national law. The financial provisions are three. The first requires that all money received in the unemployment fund of the state shall—with certain exceptions with respect to refunds—immediately upon receipt be paid to the United States Secretary of the Treasury to the credit of the unemployment trust fund. The Social Security Act, section 904, directs the Secretary of the Treasury to invest such portion of this fund as is not required to meet current withdrawals in interest-bearing obligations of the United States or in obligations guaranteed as to both principal and interest by the United States. Such obligations may be acquired (1) on original issue at par or (2) by open market purchase. Obligations specially issued to the fund "shall bear interest at a rate equal to the average rate of interest . . . borne by all interest-bearing obligations of the United States then forming part of the public debt," except that if the average rate is not a multiple of one-eighth of one per cent, the rate shall be the multiple next lower than the average.

The second provision is that all money withdrawn from the unemployment fund shall be used solely for the payment of unemployment compensation, exclusive of expenses of administration, and for refunds of erroneous and certain other payments.

The third was designed to insure the development of an initial reserve. The tax act provides that no compensation shall be payable with respect to any day of unemployment occurring within two years after the first day of the first period with respect to which contributions are required.

As in the case with other social security trust funds, the money which comes into the national treasury for unemployment compensation is spent for the current needs of the national government. Federal government obligations to pay in the future are placed in the trust fund, and as interest becomes due on these obligations additional obligations of appropriate amount are placed in the fund. This practice means that, when the states call upon the national government for the money necessary to meet unemployment compensation claims, the national government will have to take action to raise it. If cash is not available in the treasury, taxes must be raised or bonds sold to the public. Because of the high levels of employment that have prevailed as the result of World War II, the reserves have grown to unexpectedly large proportions. As of August 1945 the trust fund in the treasury amounted to approximately 7 billion dollars.[10]

Administrative requirements under national law. The administrative requirements are contained in the main in Title III of the Social Security Act, although one is repeated in substance in the tax act. This one requires that the state law must provide for payment of unemployment compensation solely through public employment offices or such other agencies as the national Board may approve. Under existing law, in times of peace the employment offices are state offices operated under a national grant-in-aid system. During the present period, they have become agencies of the national government.

In general the state must provide such methods of administration as are found by the Board to be reasonably calculated to insure full payment of unemployment compensation when due. Since the end of 1939, this control over administration includes methods relating to the establishment and maintenance of personnel standards on a merit basis, except that the Board

[10] *Social Security Bulletin*, Vol. 8, No. 10, October 1945, p. 32.

shall exercise no authority with respect to the selection, tenure of office, and compensation of any individual employed in accordance with such methods.

As in several other social security categories, there is the paragraph requiring provision of opportunity for a fair hearing for all individuals where claims are denied and one requiring the state agency to make such reports as the Board may from time to time require.

This summary covers the major requirements and standards prescribed by the unemployment compensation provisions of the Social Security Act and the tax on employers of eight or more. It demonstrates how the states were left completely free to decide many of the broad social and economic issues that are involved in unemployment compensation. To understand the actual program in the United States, one must therefore turn to the laws of the individual states.

THE LAWS OF THE SEVERAL STATES AND TERRITORIES

All 48 states, Alaska, Hawaii, and the District of Columbia —51 jurisdictions—have their own laws. The Social Security Board under the national act has copies of all these laws, and it keeps constantly up-to-date on amendments as part of its supervisory and approving duties. From time to time it publishes digests and comparisons of them. No valuable purpose would be served by reproducing in this book either the full text or a comprehensive digest of these laws as they stood at the time of writing. The compilation would have little reference value, as it would be out-of-date almost as soon as published. Instead we shall here attempt a summary designed primarily to bring out the major issues involved.[11]

A major difficulty in attempting to present issues clearly is that almost invariably they are intimately interrelated—from an expository standpoint one might say hopelessly intertwined.

---

[11] The latest published, minutely detailed analysis is *Comparison of State Unemployment Compensation Laws as of December 31, 1941.* For the more significant elements practically current data are generally available in the *Social Security Bulletin.*

For this reason it seems desirable before dealing with such subjects as the form of the system, the eligibility rules, and the size and duration of the benefits, to review briefly the basic nature of unemployment insurance and the diverse points of view as to the social and economic objectives to be achieved through its use. Against this common background, the differences among the states may perhaps stand out more clearly.

General nature of unemployment insurance. Unemployment insurance, unlike life insurance and old-age annuities, does not deal primarily with natural forces which can be measured with a relatively high degree of precision and change so slowly that forecasts for the future can be made with a reasonable degree of reliability. Almost all the important factors in unemployment insurance are economic and political in nature[12] and are subject to wide and at times sudden change. Attempts at long range economic and political forecasting, and even sometimes at short-range forecasting, have in the past generally been characterized more by failures than by successes. Because the forces in unemployment insurance are so largely unpredictable, practical unemployment insurance has to be designed on a radically different basis. The designing of an unemployment system is far more of an art than a science.

An unemployment insurance system cannot guarantee to cover all unemployment, unless a government places its credit behind the system and agrees to continue payment of promised benefits after all the funds of the system are exhausted. In the absence of such an unlimited governmental guarantee, the designers of the system have (1) to decide and define clearly what part and what nature of unemployment they will cover; (2) how large benefits they will pay and for how long; and (3) what premiums or taxes they must charge to build up the necessary reserves so that the system will weather economic storms of considerable intensity. It is generally recognized that an insurance system based on premiums and designed to weather the severest and most prolonged disturbances would be too costly

---

[12] Political as here used includes war, international relationships, as well as domestic public policy.

to be practicable and that governments must be prepared to step into the breach if the unemployment insurance system breaks down.

When the United States government imposed the 3 per cent tax on covered employers of eight or more, it went a long way toward settling for the designers of state systems, what was to be the maximum or average premium. The problem of the state legislatures then became how to design a system within the revenues which would accrue to the states as the result of this tax method of forcing the states to act.

The national tax of 3 per cent is not a figure based on precise scientific determinations. It represents reasonably well-informed collective judgment as to how far the country should go. Some of course would tax more to give greater protection; others would tax less and leave a larger segment to be covered by disaster relief. The figure represents a legislative compromise of conflicting interests and conflicting points of view.

Unemployment insurance benefits may be regarded as an alternative for public relief, but under the American system they are paid without requiring the beneficiary to prove need. Persons who hold this view would treat the special tax on employers simply as an earmarked special tax and would distribute the proceeds according to formulae, rules, and regulations that give predominant weight to factors that are indicative of probable need. This philosophy leads toward a substantial minimum benefit with few if any allowances above that minimum and under foreign systems to variations in the amount of benefit in accordance with the responsibility of the beneficiary for the care and support of dependents. Unemployment insurance, according to this view, is less part of the wage system of the country than part of its public welfare system.

At the other extreme are persons who take the position that unemployment insurance is a socially and economically necessary part of an employer's compensation system and that the benefits under it are properly regarded as deferred wages. Without unemployment insurance, the employer paid for such of the time of the employee as he used. The employee, his relatives, his friends, or relief agencies paid for such time as the employee awaited re-employment or lost in seeking work under a new employer. According to the wage point of view, the cost of this unemployment was within limits part of the social costs of the goods produced or the services rendered by the employer and should, in fair proportion, be charged against the consumer of these goods or services just as the other necessary costs of production are normally charged against consumers. The practicable method of achieving these results was to require the employer to pay for such unemployment as was reasonably chargeable against his operations.

With respect to employment certain industries are by nature relatively stable, whereas others are relatively unstable. The price of the products of the stable industry under the deferred wage concept would contain little or no charge for unemployment compensation, whereas the price of the products of the unstable industry might contain a substantial sum for unemployment. Competing employers in the same industry may have very different practices with respect to employment. One may have little unemployment, the other a great deal. Consumers buying from the stable producer would pay little for the costs of unemployment, whereas consumers buying from his competitor might have to pay a good deal.

Two concrete examples may help in making this issue clearer:

Thousands of consumers require domestic refrigeration. Competing to supply this demand are (1) the ice industry and (2) the mechanical refrigeration industry with the public utilities furnishing electricity or gas. The production and distribution of ice are highly seasonal and not readily stabilized. The manufacture of mechanical refrigerators and of the power to operate them are naturally more stable and more easily stabilized. If the purchaser of the commodity or service is to pay for the unemployment incidental to his purchase, then the consumer who buys ice would pay for a substantial amount of unemployment, whereas the consumer who selects a mechanical refrigerator would pay comparatively little. The industry which has little unemployment would thus have a competitive advantage.

Two companies are engaged in the manufacture of men's shoes. One determines the number on the pay roll on the basis of the current market situation, employing large numbers and working overtime when demand is heavy and dropping employees and working short hours when demand is slack. Purchasers of shoes manufactured by this company would have to pay for a considerable amount of unemployment. The second company has a highly developed employment stabilization plan designed to reduce unemployment to a minimum. Buyers of its shoes would be paying for little unemployment. Under such circumstances, this company might find that its stabilization plan gave it a real competitive advantage.

If unemployment insurance is regarded as part of the employer's system of paying his workers, the natural tendency of the employer is to attempt to decide questions regarding the amount and duration of benefits with consideration of the needs and interests of his own employees. If he has a fairly stable force with many of the workers earning enough to support their dependents in fair comfort, he may think in terms of relatively high benefits, although he expects rarely to have to pay them, or he may prefer to develop as an alternative guaranteed employment plans. So far as his own workers are concerned, he may see little advantage in very small benefits paid over a relatively long period.

Between this individual employer point of view and the point of view that unemployment insurance is an alternative for public relief made necessary by unemployment, there are almost innumerable gradations. Thus each state in deciding what kind of a system it shall adopt within the framework of the national law has arrived at somewhat different compromises as the result of the legislative process.

In the following parts of this chapter, an attempt will be made to give some generalized description of the 51 unemployment compensation systems established in compliance with the national acts. Such a description is oversimplified. Frequently no attempt is made to point out how individual jurisdictions vary from the broad pattern.

The extent of insurance. Perhaps it may be well to start the discussion of the extent of insurance with the statement that unemployment insurance, as we have it in the United States, resembles fire or automobile liability insurance more than whole life insurance or old-age annuities. The employer on behalf of his employee pays a premium on or before a given date, and that premium at least partially protects the insured against the hazard of unemployment for a specified length of time, but only within limits as to amounts specified in the law. If the period of coverage expires with no loss from included unemployment, the insured takes nothing; he has had protection only in return for the premium. If his loss from unemployment in the period of coverage exceeds the amount of his insurance, he takes only the maximum amount provided by the policy, and he himself has to stand the balance of the loss.

Three implications of this system are of great social and economic significance:

1. Unemployment insurance of this type does little for persons who have long periods of unemployment. They exhaust their benefits paid for while they were employed, and they do no work which results in their being reinsured for a new period. The chief victims of this situation are the elderly, technologically unemployed who have difficulty securing new jobs, persons whose employability has been reduced by physical or mental impairments, and marginal workers who are customarily regularly employed only in periods of high activity.

2. The aggregate duration of an individual's employment without serious unemployment or underemployment has relatively little relationship to the amount or duration of his benefits. As in fire insurance, the fact that the insured has paid premiums for years and has had no losses does not affect current premium rates or coverage.

3. No great reserves comparable with those required for life insurance or old-age annuities are involved because the period of insurance is short, a year or two. Reserves are necessary only to protect against unusually bad years and not to provide, as in old-age annuities, for meeting heavy future drains which will arise at a definitely predictable time in the future.

Attaining an insured status. If a person is to be insured against unemployment, a premium or a tax must be paid on his account. Under the American systems that means he must have worked in a covered employment within a specified time. This specified time in unemployment insurance is generally called the base year or the base period. Some states have the same base year or base period for all employees, fixing it by dates on the calendar, such as April 1 to March 31, in each year. Another common practice is to have a personal base period for each individual worker. It is the year, or other period, preceding the date on which he makes his application for unemployment benefits. For administrative reasons incidental to paper work and records, the end of such a base period is ordinarily a few weeks or months earlier than the date of his application. This lag is introduced for administrative convenience.

In American practice the employee is not actually insured against unemployment the moment he goes to work in a covered occupation. The day he goes to work, his employer becomes liable to the tax or premium with respect to his employment, but it is some time before the employee has worked long enough to make that tax produce any substantial amount. Insurance concepts, therefore, generally lead to requirements that a certain duration of employment is necessary before an employee is actually protected.

Duration in unemployment insurance can be measured in either of two ways: (1) directly by using time measures; or (2) indirectly by using money measures, such as earnings or wages. For numerous reasons, which will not be discussed here, direct time measures are extremely complicated and unsatisfactory. Relatively few enterprises carry elaborate time records through their accounts. Earnings are simple to use and are easily obtained since they are necessary for many purposes. They are with a few exceptions the basis on which duration is actually figured in unemployment insurance. When duration is expressed in time units such as weeks, the figures are frequently derived from wage payments by making certain assumptions.

To be insured against unemployment, the worker must ordinarily have earned in covered employment within the base period, a certain amount specified in the law. An extremely simple device is to name a fixed sum, such as $150. The trouble with this device is that the low-paid worker may have to work several months before he is insured, whereas a well-paid worker may be insured within a few weeks. In many states unemployment benefits are related to wages earned in the base period or some part of it. Benefits of half the normal weekly wage subject to a specified maximum is a rough approximation to many of the provisions. Many states require that to be insured an employee must have earned during his base period a specified number of times the amount his weekly benefit would be were he fully unemployed. Before he has earned that much he is uninsured. After he has earned it he is insured. Even under this system, because of maximum limitations on weekly benefits, the high-bracket employees may become insured more quickly than the low-bracket employees.

This device of giving an employee the insured status when he has earned wages amounting to a certain number of times his prospective weekly benefit presents one anomalous situation. In many states the benefits for the low-bracket employees are proportionately higher than those for the higher-bracket employees. This advantage to the low-bracket employees is frequently provided at least in part by establishing a minimum benefit. The minimum benefit may be highly advantageous to the low-bracket employees if they become unemployed, but when eligibility is determined by use of the multiple of that benefit, the minimum increases the time they must serve to attain the insured status. Thus it may operate against low-paid marginal workers. To avoid such difficulties, some states resort to the use of schedules in the law which classify employees by earnings and fix earnings required for eligibility and benefits resulting from such earnings. This device permits of easy adjustment to meet the opinion of a majority of the legislature.

The benefits. Qualifying wages earned in the base period entitle the insured to benefits should he become unemployed in the benefit period. If the base period is the time between two dates fixed in the law, the benefit period is likewise the time between two fixed dates. If the base period varies among individuals, becoming fixed by an application for, or receipt of benefit, the benefit period is likewise a variable that becomes fixed by the same action. Thus the base period is the premium-paying period, and the benefit period is the time during which the insured is covered. Under the individual system of determining these periods, the insurance for the regular worker is a moving protection. After he has attained an insured status, each week of employment moves the period for which he is insured ahead by a week.

The maximum aggregate amount of benefit which the insured may receive if he is totally unemployed, after a waiting period fixed by law, is ordinarily determined by the legislature on the basis of some fraction of his wages in the base year or part of the base year—usually in the neighborhood of a half—multiplied by a certain number of weeks. The number of weeks varies among the states. As of June 1945 it ranged from 14 weeks in Arizona and Mississippi to 26 in several industrial states[13] for employees who have been employed long enough during their base period to be entitled to the maximum measure of insurance the state affords. Employees who are insured but have not become entitled to the full measure of insurance in most states get benefits for fewer weeks.

Although an approximation to half wages is customarily used, it must again be emphasized that the states apply both maximum and minimum limitations. The maximum limitations on weekly benefits for full unemployment range from $15 to $25 a week,[14] and the minimum from about $3 to $14. As of June 30, 1945, the highest maximum payment in the benefit period in any of the states was $624 in Washington. Figures from $240 to $400 would be more respresentative.[15]

Determination of weekly wages. Determination of weekly wages

[13] *Social Security Bulletin*, Vol. 8, No. 7, July 1945, p. 19.
[14] The same, p. 11. In Michigan and Connecticut a beneficiary with the maximum number of dependents may draw $28. In 1945 these two states and Nevada joined the District of Columbia in providing dependents' allowances. For the details see the same, pp. 16–17.
[15] The same, p. 19.

in unemployment insurance is of course difficult both scientifically and administratively.The distinction between earnings and
rates of pay is familiar. Actual earnings, which can be determined from records, will not serve as a satisfactory basis for
unemployment insurance benefits if employees have been seriously unemployed or underemployed during the base period.
To give actual rates of pay, moreover, actual earnings must be
divided by hours or days actually worked, which represents an
impossibly detailed task. Hourly or daily rates of pay give no
useful results unless multiplied by the hours or the days worked
in a week. Hours or days actually worked are not a satisfactory
multiplier since they are affected by the amount of unemployment and underemployment. Use of "normal" hours per week
or days per week necessitates decisions as to what constitutes
"normal." "Normal" may vary from establishment to establishment and from time to time in the same establishment.
Something determinable on a more nearly factual basis and
without a prohibitive amount of detailed work is necessary.

A device very commonly used is to base unemployment
benefits on the total earnings during the quarter of highest
earnings within the specified base period. Administrators examine all the quarterly reports for the employee during his base
period and take the figure for that quarter in which he earned
the most. If this quarterly figure is divided by 26—the 13 weeks
in a quarter multiplied by 2—it gives one half of the average
amount earned per week in that quarter; and several states use
that method to determine the weekly benefit for full unemployment. Other states take the position that even in the quarter
of highest earnings there is ordinarily some lost time or underemployment, and therefore they do not use the full 26 as a
divisor; they shave it using divisors ranging from 25 to 20.
Other states have different devices, but the most common procedure is the one just outlined, giving as a benefit for full unemployment something in the neighborhood of half the total
earnings within the quarter of highest earnings subject to the
maximum and minimum limitations as to amount of weekly
benefit.

The amount of the weekly benefit the insured may draw, multiplied by the number of weeks he may draw it, gives the total amount he may receive from the insurance fund in the benefit year. That product is the amount for which he is insured. He will draw none of it unless he has compensable unemployment. He may draw upon it, in most states, after the waiting period for either compensable total unemployment or for compensable underemployment. Compensable underemployment will be taken up first.

Benefits for partial unemployment. A disturbing feature of several kinds of insurance is that there are always some people who, having paid a premium or having had one paid in their behalf, feel a compulsion to get a benefit for their money. In unemployment insurance the persons who fall in this category may be either employers or employees.

Under certain circumstances, not to be here elaborated, employers may find it more to their advantage to shut down their entire plant or certain parts of it than to operate on a greatly reduced schedule. Before the advent of unemployment compensation, one reason, often a major one, for continuing operation on a greatly reduced scale was to give some work to the employees. Naturally the employees and the community wanted even part-time operation; it helped keep money in circulation in the neighborhood. After the advent of unemployment compensation, operation at less than half-time gave the lower-bracket employees no more money than they would get from compensation were the plant or a part of it entirely shut down. In some instances it has been charged that some employers tend under unemployment insurance to run at the more profitable percentages of capacity when work is available and then largely to shut down, thus permitting their employees to draw benefits from the fund. Employers may say, "We have paid for the insurance; why should not we and our employees have the advantage of it?"

Employees may ask, "Why should we work less than half-time when if totally unemployed we could draw benefits amounting to about half-pay and have our leisure?" Unless the law contained safeguards, representatives of the employees might call upon management not, as in the old days, to urge continued operation on very short hours but to suggest a fairly complete shut down for a few weeks. "Let everybody take a vacation with pay from the fund until there is work enough to give everybody something materially better than half-pay." At times management would be glad quickly to adopt such a suggestion for the action would be in the immediate financial interest of management as it is in the narrow and immediate self-interest of the employees.

Partially to overcome such forces and partially for social reasons the states generally have introduced into their compensation systems benefits for underemployment or partial unemployment. As has been previously noted, benefits in event of total unemployment are in the neighborhood of half pay subject to a maximum limitation ranging among the states from $15 to $25 a week. In most states when available work falls to a point where the employee cannot earn as much as his benefit would be were he totally unemployed, he becomes eligible for an underemployment benefit. The partial unemployment benefit is generally of an amount which, added to the actual earnings in the reduced hours, will bring the total receipt to the amount of the benefit for full unemployment. Some states offer a little extra inducement to continue work at reduced earnings by providing that partial unemployment benefits shall begin somewhat before earnings have fallen to the level of the benefit for full unemployment and permit the man who continues to work to draw in the aggregate a little more than he would get as a benefit were he totally unemployed.

The extent to which partial unemployment draws on the fund depends, therefore, upon two factors: (1) how much the worker earns through his continued but reduced employment, since the partial employment benefit only makes up the difference, and (2) how long partial unemployment continues. Here again the only practicable measure of the duration of partial unemployment is the amount paid out in benefits.

The practical administrative device is, roughly, to give an

employee a credit for the total amount of benefit he could draw in the benefit period and subtract from this credit such sums as he actually draws whether for partial unemployment or for total unemployment. As a rule if he is partially unemployed within the benefit period he may draw benefits for partial unemployment so long as he still has any credit for the benefit period. Thus a statement as to the maximum number of weeks a worker may draw benefits relates to total unemployment and not to partial unemployment. Benefits for partial unemployment stop only if and when the worker has exhausted all his credit which is figured on the basis of weeks of total unemployment.

In connection with the benefits for both total and partial unemployment, two factors have to be considered: (1) the waiting period, and (2) earnings from other employments.

The waiting period. For three major reasons the states do not compensate for very short periods of unemployment or under-employment. The first is the assumption that the worker can or should be able to take care of himself and those dependent on him for short periods. The loss of earnings may be discommoding, but the employee can adjust to meet the situation. The second is that benefits with respect to short periods of unemployment or underemployment would be very small. The administrative costs of making them might easily equal or exceed the actual amount of the benefit. The employee would be put to all the inconvenience of filing a claim and the administrative office to all the expense of examining it and figuring it for benefits that would be of little real consequence. The third reason is that although each such individual benefit would be extremely small, there would be so many thousands of them that the aggregate amount of them and the aggregate cost of administering them would be very high. The resources of the fund would be materially reduced by paying them, and they are not of great social utility. The social utility of a dollar in the first few days of unemployment is obviously materially less than after several weeks of unemployment.

All the states made use of the waiting period to eliminate the claims for short-term unemployment. The most usual waiting period was originally 2 weeks of unemployment within the benefit year, but by 1945 most states required only one week. According to the laws in effect in 1941 a covered worker had generally to serve only one waiting period in a benefit period; after he served it, all the ensuing unemployment or partial unemployment within the definition was compensable. A few states had more elaborate provisions and required a second waiting period after a period of re-employment amounting to 13 weeks. States with such provisions might recalculate an employee's rights after such a period of re-employment so that in effect he was beginning a new benefit year. Such states might limit the number of waiting periods in any calendar year. Where a state ends the benefit year on a fixed date, an employee on benefit at the end of that year may be permitted to carry over into the new benefit year without serving a new waiting period.

In the majority of states a week of partial unemployment counted as a week of total unemployment in figuring waiting periods. Some states, however, required two weeks of partial unemployment to count as one week of total unemployment. A few states had more elaborate provisions, and some apparently had no waiting period of partial unemployment, although they allowed such a benefit.

Earnings from other sources. A person whether totally unemployed or partially unemployed may have earnings from other activities, partaking of the nature of odd jobs or part-time subsidiary regular work. Neither the odd jobs nor the part-time work are ordinarily covered by the unemployment compensation system. The records and accounts incidental to the operation of that system are already extremely complicated. To add to the records and accounts, figures for minor activities that yield a small and perhaps irregular income would be prohibitively costly. Moreover, since unemployment benefits at best are not much more than half pay and are limited to 14 to 26 weeks, the position may well be taken that employees should be encouraged to have, rather than discouraged from having, a subsidiary way of earning. Through one device or another, a good many of the states permit some earnings—usually limited

in amount—during weeks when the employee is drawing benefits for total unemployment, and these subsidiary earnings are
often likewise disregarded in determining the amount of benefit
for partial unemployment.

Disqualifications in general. Under certain circumstances the
insured worker, although unemployed, is disqualified from receiving the benefits that have just been broadly described. The
major disqualifications will be considered under four headings
(1) voluntary leaving, (2) discharge for misconduct, (3) refusal
of suitable work, (4) labor disputes.

1. Voluntary leaving. Every state in 1941 disqualified an insured worker who left his job without good cause or without a
cause which was recognized as good or acceptable by the state
law. For the great majority of the states, the wording of the law
can be summarized by the words, "leaving voluntarily without
good cause," which means that the administrative agency must
determine in each case of voluntary leaving whether the cause
was good.

Wide variation existed among the states as to the extent of
the disqualification for voluntary leaving or the penalty imposed for it. These variations were so great that it appears to
be quite impossible to cite any particular provisions as typical.
Instead it will be necessary to cite distinctive groups.

Most numerous were the states that disqualified the individual from receiving benefits for a specified period. There were 34
such jurisdictions at the end of 1941, but they fell into two
radically different classes. In the first class, which embraced
19 jurisdictions, the law prescribed a maximum penalty, or a
range of penalties from a minimum to a maximum, and delegated to the administrative authority power to fix the exact
period of disqualification within the limits thus prescribed by
law. Where no minimum is fixed, the administrative agency
would appear to have authority to waive any penalty. But if a
minimum is fixed, at least the penalty is exacted. Upper limits
varied from 5 to 15 weeks. The minima in the 10 states that
used a minimum varied from 1 to 5 weeks, with 8 having 2 weeks
or less. The other class, embracing 15 jurisdictions, fixed the

period of disqualification in the law itself and gave no discretion to the administrative agency. Five disqualified for the entire duration of the unemployment following the voluntary leaving, whereas the others specify the number of weeks varying from 1 to 6.

In the states just discussed, the insured worker who left voluntarily without good cause lost his benefits for the period determined by law or by administrative action, but his benefit account was not charged with any period during which he did not receive benefits. Fifteen states, in sharp contrast, either permitted or required as a penalty for voluntary leaving not only that the employee be denied benefits for a specified period, but that the benefit rights to which he might subsequently be entitled be reduced. In 2 states the penalty charge was discretionary and in 13 it was mandatory, although generally the administrative agency had discretion within the legal range between minimum and maximum.

Students of public administration will note from these facts the extent to which in many of the states the administrative agency is serving in a judicial capacity in passing upon cases of voluntary leaving. In most states they must determine whether the leaving was voluntary and without good cause within the meaning of the law. In many, if they so determine, they must use their discretion within legal limits in determining the penalty. This power makes of especial importance the matters of composition and appeals procedures of the administrative agencies, which will be taken up later in the present chapter.

2. Discharge for misconduct. At the end of 1941 all states except Pennsylvania had provisions to some extent disqualifying an insured employee who was discharged for misconduct connected with his work. As in the case of voluntary leaving, there were wide variations among the states. The commonest provision was to disqualify the insured from receiving benefits for such part of the resulting unemployment as the law prescribed or which the administrative agency might fix within the limits set up by the law. Fourteen states, however, required a reduction of the benefit rights for subsequent unemployment as

an additional penalty subject, however, to a considerable measure of administrative discretion. In general, wide latitude was given the administrative agency in fixing the exact penalty in the individual case.

3. Refusal of suitable work. An insured worker on applying for an unemployment benefit places himself under the jurisdiction of the administrative agency. That agency must not grant him a benefit if suitable work is immediately available. If benefit payments have already begun, they must be discontinued when and if suitable work becomes available. An insured worker cannot refuse suitable work and continue to draw unemployment compensation benefits. What constitutes suitable work is therefore a vital issue in unemployment compensation.

The national government through its Unemployment Tax Act imposed its will upon the individual states with respect to certain aspects of this question. The state cannot deny compensation to the insured if he refuses to accept new work under any of the following conditions: If the position offered is vacant due directly to a strike, lockout, or other labor dispute; if the wages, hours, or other conditions of work are substantially less favorable to the individual than those prevailing for similar work in the locality; if as a condition of being employed the individual would be required to join a company union or to resign from or refrain from joining any bona fide labor organization. Thus of necessity every state must include such provisions in its law or as a penalty subject all covered employers in the state to the 3 per cent national pay-roll tax with no offsets and no benefits.

The states have added other criteria of their own. "The usual criteria are the degree of risk to a worker's health, safety, and morals; his physical fitness, and prior training, experience, and prior earnings; the length of the worker's unemployment and his prospects for securing local work in his customary occupation, and the distance of the available work from his residence."[16]

The wide measure of discretion vested in the administrative

[16] Social Security Board, *Comparison of State Unemployment Compensation Laws as of December 31, 1941*, Employment Security Memorandum No. 8, p. 126.

agency and the extent to which results depend on the integrity, objectivity, judgment, and initiative of the employees of that agency are striking features of this system of insurance. Under the national requirements, the agency, for example, must determine if the wages, hours, or other conditions of work offered are substantially less favorable to the individual than those prevailing for similar work in the locality. Such a provision leaves wide latitude for the exercise of independent judgment in deciding what facts are relevant, what statements are facts, and how the facts are to be interpreted. What difference constitutes a substantial difference? Under the state requirements, What constitutes a risk to a worker's morals? Can an employee without prior experience in a given kind of work learn to perform the duties within a reasonable length of time? Should an employee be allowed to refuse such a job because as a beginner he cannot earn as much as he had earned in his old job now closed to him? Is it suitable work if after a reasonable training period he would be, if successful, earning something substantially like his prior earnings?

Not all the forces in unemployment insurance administration operate in favor of a highly restrictive interpretation of what constitutes suitable work or in favor of paying benefits rather than getting the individual a new job. Two forces operating in the opposite direction deserve mention.

To an active, vigorous, self-respecting person, eager to fulfill his responsibilities to himself and those dependent on him, an unemployment insurance benefit of at best not much more than half-pay and paid, even in a liberal state, for not more than 26 weeks is not a satisfactory substitute for a real job. It is helpful in meeting temporary unemployment, but the beneficiary may grow impatient if repeated visits to the employment office always bring "No suitable opening today" or "Nothing open in your line." These answers may result in "Give me something not suitable" or "Give me an opening and let me acquire a new line."

Responsible administrative officers, moreover, must give consideration to the financial position of the fund. Being rigid and fastidious about what constitutes suitable work increases the drain on the fund. When the demand for labor is excellent, the fund is likely to be in a reasonably good or an improving position, and most beneficiaries can be placed fairly promptly.When employment is slack and the drain on the fund is heavy, the administrators may very properly become anxious and regard almost any opening as suitable under existing conditions in the locality.

In this connection it must be remembered that in the past in private enterprise those personnel practices popularly termed "hiring" and "firing" were selective, often highly selective. Although some modern contracts between management and organized labor have tended to restrict management's freedom of selection, some of that freedom still remains for many positions. Where selection exists as an important factor, a common result is that the average desirability of employed workers of a given occupational class is higher than the average desirability of unemployed workers of the same class. That statement does not mean that no unemployed worker is as good as any of the employed workers, but it does mean that the percentage of good workers is often materially higher among the employed than among the unemployed. Thus the public employment agency administering unemployment compensation does not have an easy placement job for it frequently has to place the less desirable. Moreover, employers, their personnel officers, and their foremen may regard several other sources from which additional employees may be secured as materially superior to the public employment agency.

The public employment office administrator may therefore be in a dilemma. On the one hand he faces the necessity of getting beneficiaries off the fund and into jobs and, on the other hand, if he sends many people who do not measure up to the requirements reasonably well, employers may not use his office in filling vacancies. Among persons seeking employment, the prevailing opinion may become that one does not get a really good job through the public employment service; that other approaches are far more effective. Then to an increasing degree the public agency has to work with less desirable openings and with less well-qualified applicants. Under such circumstances the administrators are not likely to be overly strict with reference to suitable openings nor are the applicants as the end of their benefit period approaches.

As was the case with respect to voluntary leaving and discharge for misconduct, there was wide variation among the states with respect to the extent of the disqualifications for refusal of suitable work. Again some states permitted the administrative agency in its discretion to disqualify for not to exceed a specified number of weeks. Other states required disqualification for a minimum period but allowed the agency to fix a higher penalty within a maximum limit. Still others disqualified for a number of weeks specified in the law but made no charge against the benefits available in case of subsequent compensable unemployment. Then came the states which not only authorized or required disqualification but also either authorized or required a charge against the workers' benefit rights. As the laws stood on December 31, 1941, two states went so far as to cancel all benefit rights based on previous employment if the worker refused suitable employment.

4. Labor disputes. The rule generally is that an insured employee is at least partially disqualified for benefits if his unemployment is due to a stoppage of work existing because of a labor dispute, where the individual was last employed; but this rule is commonly subject to numerous exceptions. Exceptions are in general of two broad types, the first turning on facts relating to the labor dispute itself and the second permitting payment of benefits after the unemployment originating in a labor dispute has continued for a length of time specified in the state law.

A worker may be unemployed as a result of a labor dispute in the outcome of which he has no personal financial interest. He may actually have been opposed to the strike. The principle of collective bargaining, however, involves majority rule; when a majority votes to go on strike, members of the minority who are opposed to the strike are frequently unemployed as the result of it. Occasionally, too, a strike or other labor dispute affecting only one class of workers or one department in an establishment closes down other departments and throws out of work employees whose immediate interests are not advanced by the strike. Although nine states made no exceptions to the general rule, most state laws took some cognizance of these situations, provided an entire grade or class is affected. A minority member of a grade or class that is participating in or directly interested in a dispute is as a rule bound by the action of the majority members and cannot have the disqualifications resulting from majority action waived on the ground that he as an individual was opposed to the strike.

The conditions under which the labor dispute disqualifications do not apply were variously phrased. The most common one permitted the payment of benefits for unemployment due to a strike or other labor dispute if neither the individual nor any of his grade or class was participating in, financing, or directly interested in the dispute. Some states omitted the word financing, since it raises the question of whether payment of union dues constitutes financing. Some included the word financing but specifically provided that payment of union dues is not financing.

A few states waived the disqualification if the labor dispute resulted from what the law regards as improper action by the employer. In some states a lockout by the employer did not prevent the payment of benefits for the resulting unemployment. In some states a strike did not bar the payment of benefits if the strike was called because the employer failed to conform to the provisions of an agreement between employer and employee or to state or national law pertaining to wages, hours, or conditions of work. One state, as of December 1941, did not disqualify if the strike was protesting, or if a lockout was attempting to enforce acceptance of wages or working conditions substantially less favorable than those prevailing in the locality and industry, or where rights to collective bargaining were denied.

Provisions of this type have certain implications to which attention should be called at this point. They are not necessarily interrelated and for the most part bear on subjects discussed more at length in other parts of this chapter. They are:

1. To a greater extent than any other provisions of state unemployment compensation laws, those that permit payments to employees unemployed because of a labor dispute bring out the importance of the quasi-judicial functions vested in the administrative agency enforcing the law. That agency must determine in many of the states whether a labor dispute is or is not a disqualifying dispute, and in certain instances whether no member of a grade or class, unemployed because of a dispute, is participating in, financing, or directly interested in a dispute. A decision in these instances generally affects not one single individual but a whole group of individuals. The decision arrived at, in a period of high tension, may have a profound effect on the financial position of the fund.

2. The history of labor disputes suggests that a sharp distinction must be drawn between those that take place in a period of reasonably full or rapidly rising employment and those that take place in a period of diminishing employment. Often in good times the dispute concerns an increase in wages whereas in bad times it is to protest or prevent a decrease in wages. In good times with rising markets, an employer may be anxious to settle the dispute quickly, and he may have the receipts to justify paying the increase. In bad times the financial results of the labor dispute may not bother him very much, he may be in no hurry to have it settled, and his diminished revenues may not warrant his acceding to the demands of the employees who are out. Labor disputes on a down swing of the economic cycle may therefore make heavy inroads on the insurance fund, impairing the provisions for persons who are unemployed not because of a labor dispute.

3. A sharp distinction must be drawn between states that have individual employer reserves and states that have a pooled fund. Heavy payments resulting from a labor dispute may largely exhaust an individual employer's fund, a fact which both he and his employees must bear in mind; but it does not materially affect the funds of other employers who have suc-

ceeded in maintaining their relationships with their employees without labor disputes. Under a pooled fund, employees who have been involved in no labor disputes may find the reserves upon which they depended for protection impaired by the labor disputes of others.

4. In a pooled fund with no merit rating the employer who maintains good personnel relations has no advantage over the employer who does not, in so far as payments into the fund are concerned. The money he has paid in may go for benefits paid to persons unemployed because of labor disputes.

5. Under an employer's fund or under a merit-rating system small groups or classes of employees occupying key positions may have a powerful bargaining weapon. If they strike, they may make members of other more numerous classes unemployed because of a labor dispute in which they have no financial interest. The numerous class with no interest in the strike will therefore in some states be entitled to unemployment benefits. These benefits will either come out of the employer's fund or under merit rating cause the employer to pay higher taxes. On a dollar and cents basis it may be cheaper to pay the key men more money than to have to pay unemployment benefits to the classes which would be entitled to a benefit by the strike of the key men. With the growth and development of collective bargaining and legal methods for its exercise, there is a possibility that small groups of key men will resort more and more to organization and collective methods and take advantage of the strategic position they occupy because of the limited number of persons possessed of their knowledge, skill, and experience.

A few words are necessary regarding the duration of the disqualification resulting from a labor dispute. The common rule was that the disqualification applies for any week of unemployment so caused. A few states, however, disqualified for a specific number of weeks, and after the expiration of that period the insured employee might go on benefit. If the disqualification does not apply, either because of the nature of the dispute or the relationship of the individual to it, the duration and amount of benefits are not affected. Unemployment is in this respect generally no different from any other qualifying unemployment.

Such disqualification provisions preclude private insurance against unemployment and anything approaching precise actuarial forecasting. To make such a system work, great discretionary power has been vested in administrative agencies. No private insurance company could, for any reasonable or practicable premium, subject its financial position to the discretionary powers that are vested in the governmental administrative agencies. It is even more clear that power to adjudicate claims of this nature, where policy and perhaps even politics and pressure play so great a part, could not be vested in a private company with a financial interest. Providing unemployment compensation is obviously a governmental function.

Receipt of other benefits. In the United States the governmental function of providing unemployment compensation has in general been entrusted to the several states. This brings up another disqualification for benefits of an entirely different nature. Under such a system it sometimes happens that an individual may be entitled to unemployment compensation under two or more state systems. If he worked for a railroad under the railroad unemployment system in the preceding calendar year, he may have unemployment benefits coming to him under that system. If he is 65 years of age or over, he may be entitled to a benefit under the national system of old-age and survivors insurance or the railroad retirement system. As a former member of the armed services, he would be entitled to such unemployment benefits as the nation has granted. Some employers give wages in lieu of notice, dismissal wages, or vacation pay. If an individual could draw all the benefits to which he might be entitled at the same time, he might get far more than was anticipated by any of the legislatures drafting the several systems.

Most of the state laws have a provision to the effect that an individual who receives a benefit with respect to a given week under another state or federal unemployment law is disqualified from receiving a benefit from it with respect to that same week of unemployment. Movement from one jurisdiction to another thus does not give a right to two benefits with respect to a single week of unemployment. If, however, an employee has exhausted his benefits under the one system, or has ceased to draw them, he can secure benefits from the second system, provided he is unemployed and he has not lost his rights because of the expiration of his benefit period. As will be discussed in more detail in the section of this chapter dealing with administration, interstate co-operation and comity have been authorized by law and have been so developed that frequently a worker who has migrated from one state to another files his claim with the agency in the state where he becomes unemployed and draws all the benefits to which he is entitled through that agency.

Similar provisions of law often apply with respect to benefits from other public systems. If an insured worker has a right to a benefit from a trade union or other private association, receipt of such a benefit is generally not a disqualification for a public benefit. In some states receipt of wages in lieu of notice or of vacation pay from a private employer does disqualify for each week in which the insured receives this special benefit.

In the preceding pages an attempt has been made to describe the benefits which the states have provided for total and partial unemployment, and the conditions under which they are granted or withheld. Two important subjects, the way the states finance their systems and the way they administer them, remain for consideration.

FINANCING STATE SYSTEMS INCLUDING EXPERIENCE RATING

In the early part of this chapter, it was pointed out that the national tax law was so drafted that the states could choose the financial arrangements that most appealed to them. The choices were:

1. The highly individualistic employer reserve or industry reserve fund, in practice generally supplemented by a small, pooled emergency reserve.

2. The highly socialized pooled fund into which all pay the same rate of tax, and from which all benefits are paid without any merit or experience rating.

3. The intermediate pooled fund into which different employers pay different rates of tax, with the exact rate depending on their individual experience and the financial position of the pooled fund.

Fifty-one jurisdictions—the 48 states, Alaska, Hawaii, and the District of Columbia—had an opportunity to exercise their choices within the limits permitted by the national law. As of December 31, 1941 the score stood: jurisdictions with individual employer reserves 7; jurisdictions with pooled funds and experience rating 31; jurisdictions with pooled funds with no experience rating 13, but the laws of 11 of these 13 contained provisions for the study of experience rating. By June 30, 1945 experience rating was provided in the laws of 45 states. The number with individual employer reserves fell, however, from 7 to 4. The reason for this latter change was the fear of the heavy drains on individual reserves, and hence the higher taxes which might result due to termination of war contracts.[17] Thus almost all the jurisdictions have adopted an insurance philosophy that the amount of premium an employer should pay should be related to the unemployment experience of his business.

One factor which may have played a part in the heavy preponderance in favor of experience rating was that, so far as the national government went, it placed the entire tax on the employers. It levied no tax on the earnings of covered employees. Although the national law did not prohibit the states from levying a tax on the employees in addition to the tax on employers, few of the states did so. At the end of 1941 only 5 of the 51 jurisdictions levied a tax against the employees. The question may be raised as to whether the results would have been different, had the national law placed part of the tax burden on the employees and thus placed them in a strong position to urge increased benefits, increased duration, or both.

Experience rating is more or less complicated and there are various methods for using it. The one most frequently

17 *Social Security Bulletin*, Vol. 8, July 1945, p. 24.

used—by 21 of the 38 states which had experience rating at the end of 1941—may be briefly described as follows:

1. An individual account is set up for each covered employer.

2. This fund is credited with all the taxes paid by that employer, or all except a small percentage used for other purposes.

3. This fund is charged with all benefits paid to unemployed workers on account of benefit rights to which they become entitled as a result of working for him during the base period or which the law says shall be charged to him.

4. On any date what is termed the employer's reserve may be determined from the employer's account by subtracting the total of the benefits paid to his unemployed workers from the aggregate sum paid by him in taxes and credited to his account.

5. This employer's reserve as figured from his individual account, is an actual number of dollars of either surplus or deficit. Its size depends on two factors: how much unemployment he has had, and how big a pay roll he has had subject to taxation. To get from it an index of unemployment and eliminate the factor of size of pay roll, the dollars of reserve are divided by the dollars of pay roll subject to tax within a specified period. The resulting ratio is the "index of experience" used in determining the rates he will have to pay. There are other ways of arriving at an index of experience used by some states, but it does not seem essential to go into them in detail.

Experience rating would not be anything like as complicated as it is if all covered workers were employed more or less continuously by the same employer; but hundreds of them in the course of the base period work for several different employers. When such a worker applies for a benefit, which of these employers is to be charged with his benefits? Under some systems the employer who had just dropped him and was immediately responsible for his current unemployment may not have had him on his pay roll at all in the base period upon which his right to benefits rests.[18] Thus the state laws or some appropriate

[18] Such a situation may result in states which have a uniform base period for all workers, such as April 1 to March 31 or in states which have an individual base year for each employee but with "a lag" for administrative purposes between the end of the base year and the beginning of the benefit year.

agency must prescribe how the benefits shall be charged to the several employers.

The fairest device appears to be to charge the benefits to each of several employers in the base period in proportion to the beneficiary's earnings in that period. If, for example, the beneficiary earned 35 per cent of his money in the base period from employer A, then employer A is charged with 35 per cent of the benefit payments. All the other employers are charged in the same way. At the end of 1941 of the 29 states that used the charge method 13 distributed the charges in this way. Anyone who has had experience with statistical or accounting work will appreciate the volume of computing involved in communities where there is a good deal of movement from employer to employer.

Some states—9 in 1941—charge the most recent employer, usually in the base period, up to a maximum established by law or regulation, and then charge the next-to-the-latest employer up to the maximum allowed. Thus they work backward, charging each employer in inverse order until the entire amount of the benefit has been charged. Limitations on the amount to be charged against an employer may be expressed as a fraction or a percentage of the employee's earnings in the base period, perhaps with a top limit amount. Here, again, the computing may be bothersome, but it is done for one employer at a time. For benefits of short duration no computing may be necessary, for the most recent employer's account will absorb the whole amount.

A few states simply charge the most recent employer, or the most recent employer in the base period, with all the benefits. This device saves a lot of work, and it may in some states "average out" fairly well, although it tends to place a heavy burden on employers who operate on a job or project basis and run out of work at a time when demand for labor is low. It also may be bad in a community in which there is a large amount of seasonal labor.

In some communities there are groups of workers whose earnings come largely from seasonal employment. During the season they may be reasonably fully employed, but in the off season their employment for wages may be casual. As a matter of fact, some of them may be indifferent as to whether or not they pick up other employment for wages. Four illustrations may be used to support that statement:

Canneries packing fruits and vegetables often operate only seasonally. A large part of their force may consist of women and girls of the neighborhood, who are secondary breadwinners, working during the season to supplement the family income. When the cannery closes they return to their normal domestic tasks. They might not be averse to having other wage-paying jobs in the off season if they can get them in the locality and if the jobs permit living at home and continuing to perform the necessary household tasks. They may be said to be receptive to what is for them suitable work, but they are not seeking employment in the sense that they are prepared to move or radically to change their domestic arrangements for the sake of earning wages.

In the larger urban communities, many retail establishments have found that their business involves peak loads, seasonal, weekly, and even daily. Attractively high wage rates for the part-time workers are a real economy if the employment permits of a reduction in the full-time staff. These people on the roster are often anxious to be employed at the store, but if there is no work at the store they are not actively seeking other employment.

Farmers and agricultural laborers often have dull seasons on the farm and are available for other jobs if there are any available in the locality that do not prevent them from continuing to do the essential chores around the farm. Road construction and maintenance, land reclamation, and the development of water supplies are illustrations of jobs that meet their requirements. Naturally public departments and private contractors responsible for such work must time it so that a supply of local labor will be available, unless they are prepared to import most of the labor they will need. Importing outside labor may not be advisable if the funds being spent come in any considerable amount from local taxes. When projects of this general type are completed, the local workers return to the farm, possibly for more weeks of the dull season and possibly because their own busy season has begun.

A vacation of several weeks duration may be a traditional feature of an occupation. School teachers have a summer vacation. Members of a logging crew or of a construction crew may have winter vacations. Automobile workers may have one when factories are closed for retooling. Persons on such vacations are not necessarily idle. They may get gainful employment, they may be very anxious to get it. Vacation jobs are, however, of secondary importance in their way of life.

Seasonal work of these various types may present a real problem in connection with experience rating, especially if a worker customarily engaged in seasonal work secures other and generally temporary work in his off season. The problem is largely solved if charges for benefits of such worker are prorated among all employers in the base period in proportion to earnings in that period. Short cuts that charge last employers first, even if subject to a maximum, tend to penalize an employer who takes on temporary workers after they have attained substantial benefit rights by virtue of earlier employment. Unless charges for benefits are prorated according to earnings, experience rating may tend to discourage an employer from hiring such a worker at all.

One objection to experience rating is that it may cause employers to seek to attain too high a degree of employment stability. They may hesitate to expand and employ more persons when expansion is possible, for fear they will have to let the new people go when work slackens and either pay them benefits from the individual employer's fund or pay higher contributions into the pooled fund. Stability of employment may not be a virtue if it results in a lessened aggregate of employment over a considerable period. Experience rating and individual employer's funds tend to make the employer's ideal a relatively small force of carefully selected, highly efficient employees continuously employed. Such a system adds further weight to the fact, present in many enterprises, that carefully selected, highly skilled employees give lowest labor costs per unit of output. It also may encourage the introduction of labor-saving machines to facilitate adjustment of output to demand without changing the size of the force. It may likewise lead to meeting peak demands by lengthening the work week rather than by hiring more employees. An employer may prefer to pay overtime, even penalizing overtime, to his highly selected permanent staff— "members of the organization" where the morale is high—than to incur obligations to pay unemployment benefits to temporary workers, especially in enterprises where inexperienced workers give relatively high-wage costs per unit of product and sometimes high spoilage charges.

This argument against experience rating and individual employer's funds thus represents another manifestation of conflicting basic philosophies. One group holds that each individual and each individual enterprise should, within the law, be free to attain maximum efficiency in the production of needed goods and services. The other group believes that limitations should be placed on the output or the activities of the highly efficient, whether owners, managers, or workers, so that there will be work enough to go round and that the less efficient, and perhaps the less privileged, will have an opportunity to work, earn, and purchase goods and services.

The states which use experience rating have different methods of measuring experience and of charging employers where employees have worked for two or more employers during the base period. There are even greater variations with respect to the rates charged to employers with different experience ratings and the methods by which such rates are determined. This subject is extremely detailed and intricate. No attempt will here be made to do more than call attention to some of the broader issues.

In states with the more individualistic point of view, the question of whether an employer is or is not entitled to a lower rate of contribution turns entirely on his own record. He pays such rates as his own record calls for without regard to the condition of a pooled fund or the condition of the individual reserve of other employers. If the pooled fund or the individual reserves of other employers should be in poor condition, the employers who are responsible for that situation, the ones with the poor records, are the ones who will have to pay higher rates and restore the situation.

One can conceive of economic conditions under which establishments with very poor records will be virtually shut down. Although the rates for such establishments are raised to the maximum, the high rates will not produce much revenue because the employer's pay roll has shrunk to almost nothing. His payments will not restore either a pooled fund or his own individual reserve. It must be remembered, however, that since he is virtually shut down almost no new rights to unemployment insurance are accruing with respect to his establishment. A shrinkage of a pooled reserve or of an individual reserve may, therefore, not be as vital as it may appear at first glance, because the shrinkage results from the fact that a heavy body of claims has been paid off and large numbers may have entirely exhausted their benefit rights. The real adequacy of a reserve is to be measured not by its size nor by the amount already paid out in benefits but by the relationship between its present size and the valid claims that may mature against it.

Unfortunately, in this type of insurance it would be difficult to measure with any degree of precision the volume of claims that may mature. Hence one must frankly face the fact that an individual employer's reserve may fail, or that a pooled fund may go bankrupt, even when some employers have excellent records that justify low rates so far as their own experience is concerned. In this connection it is worth noting that the individual employer's reserve maintained by the employer with the fine record survives to protect his employees should they become unemployed. Contributions of an employer with a fine record to a pooled fund may, however, have gone to pay benefits to the unemployed of other employers, and hence should his employees later suffer unemployment they might find the fund exhausted.[19]

The more usual practice among the states is to make the condition of the pooled fund a factor in determining the rates to be charged for a given year or other period. In such states, if the pooled fund is in a weak condition, the rates are raised even for an establishment that has not contributed in any way to that weakness. Here the law departs from the private insurance concept that premiums are based on the degree of hazard and moves toward the concept that contributions are earmarked taxes, levied for the general social welfare.

The employer with the fine record, like other employers, must try to pass his pay-roll taxes on to the consumers of his product. If because of market conditions he cannot pass them along, his alternatives are in the main (1) to pay them out of profits or capital, or (2) to reduce pay-roll expenditures. One way to meet an increase in a pay-roll tax rate is to cut the size of the roll to which that rate applies.

Another rate-fixing device, used by 17 states in 1941, was to vary the rates to make them produce an amount of revenue up to a standard fixed by the law. In three states the revenue required was 2.7 per cent of the taxable pay roll without reference to the condition of the fund or the amount expended in benefits. In the other states using this device, factors such as the size of the reserves or the amount of benefit payments were used in the formula establishing the rates. Use of these factors results in higher rates when the fund is weak or under heavy strain for benefit payments than when things are going well.

A question should be raised at this point as to whether it is a sound procedure to increase rates in the face of falling reserves

---

[19] The same thing may happen with respect to a pooled fund without experience rating. The number of unemployed in the early days of a depression may so far exhaust the fund that the later claimants cannot draw the benefits to which they are entitled. They resemble in a way a man whose insured house burns after the company in which it was insured has gone bankrupt; but with this difference: It may be assumed that in a severe depression a government will come to the relief of a pooled fund that fails to meet its obligations by either giving it or loaning it money.

or even to maintain a fixed rate of pay-roll tax in the face of a serious fall in the amount of employment. A far sounder procedure might be to relate the rate of tax to the index of employment, increasing it as the level of employment rises and diminishing it as the level falls. Then in the face of adverse general business conditions, employers would be relieved of part of the tax and be under less pressure to meet the recession by cutting pay rolls. Such a system might help them to reduce prices in a recession and thus to dispose of a larger volume of goods.

Concepts born of analogies with private insurance would seem to be responsible for the emphasis that has been placed on the size of the reserve. Unemployment compensation is not like private insurance; reserves play a very different part in it than they do in most other kinds of insurance. If unemployment compensation is to serve its purpose, reserves should fluctuate much more widely than do reserves to meet hazards which are, as compared with unemployment, relatively stable. In a period of recession, unemployment reserves should recede and may even vanish. It is this recession against which the system is insuring, and when it comes, the reserves must be used.

The system in the United States is, moreover, not a substitute for public relief for unemployment but only a first line of defense, or as it is often called a cushion to absorb the first shock. Back of it must lie some form of public assistance. This fact should be frankly recognized, and, when a recession is on, pay-roll taxes—taxes on employment—should not be raised to safeguard the reserves. On the other hand, taxes should not be reduced automatically because good times have made the reserves climb. When times are good, pay-roll taxes can largely be absorbed without seriously interfering with employment. A time may come when the reserves have reached levels that are apparently unnecessarily high. Under these circumstances the desirable course would seem to be to have the legislature reconsider the rate structure in the light of experience and make such revisions as may be indicated by the facts then in existence. It would seem, however, that a sound system of unemployment compensation, if it is to be financed through a tax on pay rolls, should charge high rates when employment is high and much lower rates when employment is low.

States which use experience rating differ widely with respect to the degree of differentiation they have introduced between the rates charged establishments with a fine record and those charged establishments with a poor one. Of the 38 states which had experience rating in December 1941, 16 used as their maximum rate the 2.7 of the national law. Twenty-one states provided for higher maximum rates, ranging from 3.25 per cent to 4.1 per cent. Eight used 3.6 per cent and 8 used 4 per cent. Provisions regarding minimum rates were reported by the Social Security Board for 36 states. They varied from zero for four states to 1.7 in one. The most common minima were 1 per cent in 9 states, 0.9 per cent in 7, and 0.5 per cent in 8.

It may be interesting to record the ranges for some of the states. For this purpose we shall take first those states with low minimum rates and show their maximum rates.

	Minimum	Maximum
Missouri..	0	4.1
Wisconsin................	0	4.0
Kentucky.	0	3.7
Hawaii...................	0	2.7
Indiana..................	0.135	3.7
North Carolina............	0.27	2.7
Delaware.................	0.5	4.0
Oklahoma................	0.5	4.0
Texas....................	0.5	4.0
Illinois..................	0.5	3.6
Minnesota................	0.5	3.25
Alabama..................	0.5	2.7
Massachusetts............	0.5	2.7
New Hampshire...........	0.5	2.7

States with relatively high maximum rates not included above are:

	Maximum	Minimum
District of Columbia.......	4.0	1.5
Arkansas.................	4.0	1.0
Michigan.................	4.0	1.0
Oregon..................	4.0	1.0
Wyoming.................	3.6	1.0
Colorado	3.6	0.9
Iowa.....................	3.6	0.9
New Jersey...............	3.6	0.9
New Mexico..............	3.6	0.9
South Carolina...........	3.6	0.9

It would seem as if the difference between paying 4 per cent of covered pay roll as an unemployment tax and paying nothing or as little as 0.5 per cent would, in any establishment where pay roll is a substantial factor in cost of production, offer a considerable inducement to stabilize. If two establishments were competing in an industry where pay roll is an important cost factor, and one had to pay 4 per cent and the other nothing the employer who had stabilized would appear to have a material advantage. If stabilization in an industry was impracticable, and all the competitors in it had to pay 4 per cent, a very considerable tax would be passed along to consumers, and a very considerable advantage would accrue to producers of competing goods if they could produce them under stabilized conditions. Again attention should be called to the fact that taxes on pay rolls running as high as the 2.7 per cent offer a material inducement where it is possible to reduce the importance of pay roll as a factor in the cost of production and to substitute labor-saving machines. The establishment in which labor is an important factor in costs will find such a tax a real handicap in competition with a rival who through mechanization has greatly reduced the proportion of his costs that go to labor.

ADMINISTRATION

From time to time in the earlier sections of this chapter, attention has been called to the importance of administration in unemployment compensation. The systems in use in the various states, which make the actual earnings of an individual so large a factor in determining eligibility and the amount and the duration of benefits, involve an almost overwhelming amount of detailed record keeping, accounting, and disbursing, but such duties are largely routine and ministerial in character. One might say they are fairly typical of governmental statistical and accounting work where modern machine methods are used. They are not, however, what makes unemployment compensation administration so important, nor are they the subject with which we shall be immediately concerned. Of vital importance are those duties which concern policy determination, the sublegislative work incidental to the adoption of rules and regulations, and the administrative adjudication in passing upon individual claims and upon the character of labor disputes that affect rights to compensation.

A few illustrations may be here repeated to indicate the extent to which in many states discretionary power has been vested in the responsible administrative officers.

1. An insured employee on becoming unemployed may be disqualified for benefits, for such things as voluntary leaving, discharge for misconduct, refusal of suitable work, or because under certain conditions his unemployment results from a labor dispute. Even if the legislature has defined the law on these subjects so minutely that no further definition through administrative rules and regulations is necessary, the administrators must determine the facts and apply the law to the facts. In some states the administrative agencies legislate on these subjects.

2. In many states the law makes the penalty for a disqualifying act at least partially and sometimes wholly discretionary. The administrative agency fixes the exact penalty within the minimum and maximum of the law much as a judge fixes a fine in a criminal case when the law directs a fine of not more than so much, or one of not less than a specified minimum nor more than a specified maximum.

3. The decisions arrived at by the administrative agency in cases such as those just described affect the financial position of the fund and hence may affect the degree of protection the fund affords to all insured under it.

4. In some states the rate of tax to be paid by the employer depends on such factors as his reserve, the state of the fund or the amount of benefits paid from a fund. The cumulative result of decisions by the administrators in individual cases may therefore affect the rate of tax and the amount of tax which employers have to pay.

5. In some states using experience rating, the legislatures have delegated to the administrators a large measure of discretionary legislative power extending even in some instances to actual rate making.

6. The degree of efficiency and the attitude of administrators in placing beneficiaries in new jobs may have a significant effect on the soundness of the fund. Inefficiency, indifference, or a policy of hostility toward a given employer or industry or of favoritism toward a particular labor organization may greatly increase the burden.

7. Under unemployment compensation, as under other forms of insurance, the parties in interest may discover ways of taking advantage of the system. Some of them can be stopped by administrative action; some may require new legislation. In either event, primary responsibility rests on the administrators.

In connection with these seven items, it should be recalled that this system extends to a very high percentage of all workers in a state, excepting those in agriculture, domestic service, and the service of governmental agencies and philanthropic and educational units. With this fact in mind, it seems safe to say that in few states is there a state agency whose discretionary powers exceed in importance those vested in the body administering unemployment compensation.

Under such circumstances two factors of administration are of vital concern: (1) the overhead organization that controls the agency, and (2) the rights which a person deeming himself injured by what he regards as an improper action by the agency has for an appeal from that action.

OVERHEAD ORGANIZATION

In the United States when the elected legislature of a state delegates legislative and judicial powers to an administrative agency, the traditional practice has been to create a board consisting of several members. The idea has been that for legislative work several heads are better than one and that in judicial determinations when a citizen's rights are involved an appeal should lie to a superior court consisting of several men, who arrive at their decision by a majority vote. Such arrangements protect the citizens from the possibly arbitrary or narrow action of a single individual.

The major objection to boards is that they are ineffective in getting things done. For this purpose the single executive is likely to be more efficient. To combine the efficiency of the single executive in getting routine work done with the breadth of vision of a board in legislative matters and the fairness of a board in judicial matters, certain other forms of organization have been developed in unemployment compensation. Among them are:

1. The agency has a single executive, but appeals from the action of the executive lie to an entirely independent board of review. Decisions of the board of review are binding on the executive officer, who has no power over it. A decision by the board in an individual case must be followed in all like cases as a binding precedent. If the executive officer prepares a rule or regulation of a legislative nature, an appeal from it lies to the board of review, which has power either to amend it as it sees fit or to send it back to the executive to revise in accordance with the decision of the board. The board thus controls both the judicial and the legislative work, but it does not control or direct the details of routine administration.

2. The board consists of one full-time member who serves as executive officer responsible for day-to-day management. Associated with him are two or more part-time members who participate in legislative and judicial matters and the decisions with respect to broad matters of policy. They may also have authority to review the managerial actions, or sometimes no major managerial action can be taken without their approval.

3. The agency has a single executive director, but it also has an advisory board, sometimes a fairly large board. The law may give this board some real authority over legislative and policy matters or it may make it entirely advisory. If it is purely advisory, it may be almost entirely ineffective, or it may be a real force, depending on its membership, the attitude of the executive officer toward it, and its relationship to the governor or other officer or agency with power to appoint or remove the executive officer.

As of December 31, 1941 the board form of organization prevailed in 32 of the jurisdictions. In these jurisdictions, 17 had full-time board members, 7 had 1 full-time member and the other members on a part-time basis, and 8 had all members on a part-time basis.

Nineteen states had a single executive officer, but as has been noted such a statement is not particularly significant without consideration of the organization for appeals. In 13 of these states a final appeal lay to an independent board of appeals and in only 3 to the administrative agency headed by a single executive. Two states, New Hampshire and Nebraska, had only one appeal to a salaried referee or board. One state, Connecticut, had a unique system: a single appeal lay to a commissioner for the congressional district in which was located the employment office from which the appeal was taken. There was no appeal from his decision; but with the consent of the head of the agency, he could invite two other district commissioners to sit with him. Under such circumstances a decision by a majority of the three was binding even if the resident commissioner was outvoted.

Under the national law the administration of unemployment compensation must, as a rule, be carried on by the state agency which serves as the public employment office. Most states conduct many other activities in the field of labor, some of which are interrelated with employment and unemployment compensation. Thus there is a problem of administrative co-ordination of the various related activities in the field of labor. Nineteen states, at the end of 1941, put the administration of unemployment compensation under a department of labor, an industrial commission, or a board which handled workmen's compensation. Four additional jurisdictions located this function in the state department of labor or its equivalent but gave that department no control over the exercise of the function. Two jurisdictions provided for co-ordination by making the state commissioner of labor ex officio a member of the board administering unemployment compensation. The District of Columbia provided for co-ordination by making the three commissioners who constitute the general government ex officio members of a five-member board. In the remaining 25 jurisdictions, the administrative agency for the employment security program was entirely independent.

The board form of organization permits the introduction, usually by the legislature, of representation of designated groups in the membership. Fourteen jurisdictions, none of which was in the south, required bi-partisan political representation. Twelve states required that employers, employees, and the public should be represented; 2 more required the representation of employers and of employees; and 1 called only for representation of the employees. Of the 14 jurisdictions that called for bi-partisan representation, 6 also provided for employer-employee representation. One state required geographic representation on the board with one member from each of the state supreme court districts.

In connection with the provisions with respect to representation, it is important to note that the typical jurisdiction vests the power to appoint board members—or where there is a single executive officer, that executive—in the hands of the governor. Often the consent of the senate or other advisory board is required. One state, Georgia, had at the head a commissioner of labor elected by the people, and one state, South Carolina, had a three-member commission elected by the General Assembly.

When a governor appoints, even with the consent of the senate or a council, it does not follow that a representative of a political party or of a particular group such as employers, employees, or the public actually represents that group in the sense that the group might have elected him as their representative. A governor may select as a representative of a group a person whose views are opposed to those held by a majority of the group he is supposed to represent.

A not uncommon device is for a chief executive officer to appoint a board or commission which on its face appears to be representative, whereas as a matter of fact every member has been selected because the chief executive officer knows or has assurances that the individual will vote right or act right. Reports emanating from a board or commission thus constituted are not infrequently carefully prepared propaganda documents more or less skillfully designed to advance the policy of the administration. Provisions for representation may partake of the nature of "window dressing" rather than serve as effective devices to make sure that conflicting points of view are considered in policy determination, in legislation, and in arriving at judicial decisions.

At the end of 1941, 36 jurisdictions required the use of state-wide advisory councils and 6 more permitted the use of such councils. Most of the laws providing or permitting advisory councils required equal representation of employers and of employees and some included equal representation of the public. Two states, Missouri and Ohio, gave 2 representatives each to employers and employees and required 3 persons in addition whose training and experience qualified them to deal with unemployment compensation problems, particularly with respect to their legal, accounting, actuarial, and economic aspects.

Seven states at the end of 1941 required the establishment of local advisory councils. Twenty-four permitted the establishment of local councils. In some cases industry councils, or local industry councils, were also authorized.

APPEALS

The national law, it will be recalled, requires that the state law must provide for appeals. The most common arrangement adopted by the state is to provide first for an initial appeal and then for a final appeal.

In most of the states the key man on an initial appeal may be said to be a salaried referee. In 18 states at the end of 1941 the single referee heard the initial appeal sitting by himself. In 2 states he sat with a representative of the employers and a representative of the employees. In 27 states the referee might sit alone or as a member of a board of 3 constituted as just described. Two states that had a board of review, Massachusetts and West Virginia, might have an initial decision made by a referee, or a single member of the board of review. In Massachusetts if the whole board of review or a majority of its members heard the initial appeal, there was no further appeal.

Four of the jurisdictions granted as a right to interested parties only 1 appeal. All the rest under certain circumstances allowed a second or final appeal. In 28 jurisdictions the final appeal lay to the administrative agency itself, and in all but 3 of these the agency was presided over by a board. In 18 jurisdictions the final appeal lay to an independent board of review, in 15 states consisting of 3 members hearing only unemployment compensation cases. Three states had boards of review that heard also appeals under other labor laws.

Provisions regarding the right to a final appeal differed rather widely. In 13 jurisdictions a final appeal could be taken by any party to the initial decision. In 10, a final appeal could be taken only with the permission of the appeals body. Between these extremes were several combinations. Twenty states required permission unless the initial decision was not unanimous. Three jurisdictions gave the right only if the first appeal did not sustain the initial administrative finding. Twenty-four jurisdictions specifically permitted a deputy whose decision had been changed on initial appeal to take the case as of right to the final appeals body.

Particular interest attaches to the procedures in labor dispute cases. The rights of many individuals, as has been noted, may be affected by the decision with respect to the character of a single labor dispute. In 29 jurisdictions in 1941 the legal procedure in a labor dispute issue was to start with the preparation of a finding of fact regarding the dispute. In 13 this finding of fact went immediately to the final appeals body, in 3 to the initial appeals body, and in 7 to the administrative head of the agency. In 6 jurisdictions a special examiner was or might be appointed to pass upon the case.

One state, South Dakota, handled disqualifications in general by having the examiner prepare a finding of fact and then immediately refer it for decision to the final appeals body, in this case the three-member unemployment commission. Such a procedure is undoubtedly practical and even highly advantageous in a state where disqualification cases are not numerous; but it would probably be entirely impracticable in a large industrial state.

Twenty jurisdictions authorized the examiner, in cases for which no special provision had been made, in his discretion to refer original determination to the initial appeals body or in some jurisdictions even to the final appeals body. Such a procedure doubtless saves a great deal of time.

In leaving this matter of appeals, attention should again be called to the fact that in many cases the amounts involved are relatively small. The maximum amount in the state with the highest benefit for the longest period of time would be about $624 and even in such a state the number of cases involving that amount would be small. The bulk of the cases everywhere are in the nature of small claims except where a labor dispute affecting many individuals is concerned. Probably a fair number of appeals cases arise in which administrative costs, from the initial recording of pay and employment data to a decision on the final appeal, constitute a high percentage of the amount of the award.

RECIPROCAL RELATIONS

Since each state has authority to develop its own system of unemployment compensation, it has likewise authority to determine what it will do with respect to persons who move into it from other jurisdictions after they have served under the unemployment compensation laws of the jurisdiction from whence they have moved.

All 51 jurisdictions have adopted laws which permit of developing reciprocal arrangements whereby the employee who has acquired rights in two states can transact all his business with the office of the state to which he has moved. The state of his present residence will pay him the benefits that he has earned in the other state, acting as agent for that state.

The laws of 38 states in 1941 authorized the state to which the employee had moved to give him credit for the wages or services rendered in the other state, provided the state from which he came would reimbruse the present state of residence for such expenditures. As of December 31, 1941, according to the Social Security Board, no reciprocal arrangements had yet been worked out under these laws. It will be noted that such arrangements are of importance mainly in three types of cases: (1) where the employee has not worked long enough in either jurisdiction to be eligible for a benefit but would be eligible for a benefit had all the work been done in one state; (2) where the employee has worked long enough in his present state to be entitled to a benefit, but did not work long enough or recently enough in the other state to be due a benefit from it; or (3) where the employee has a benefit due from the state from which he migrated but has not worked long enough in the present state to have any rights under it. He cannot get credit for such services as he has rendered that have not made him eligible, although had all the service been rendered in one or the other of the two states, he would have been eligible in one or the other or possibly in either.

All but ten of the jurisdictions authorized interstate agreements whereby all the employees of a given establishment may be treated as under the law of the state where the establishment is located, despite the fact that some of them do some or all their work in other jurisdictions. Such an arrangement may be advantageous to both the employers and employees who do some or all their work outside the home state of their employer. The employers may have to pay the federal tax for all employees and yet be subject to a state tax only in the home state. Their employees in other states may not be sufficiently numerous or sufficiently regularly employed there to make their state taxes applicable. Thus it may cost the other states little or nothing to let the home state treat all the employees of an employer in the home state as doing all their work within that state. The traveling employees or the group working regularly in other states thus become eligible for benefits on the same terms as employees at the home office or plant. Mention should also be made of the savings in administrative costs to the employer

who escapes the burden of having to report pay rolls and services to several different states.

Twenty-three states specifically authorized reciprocal arrangements relating to services, facilities, and investigations.
Under such arrangements one state will make investigations and
secure and transmit information for another state in order to
facilitate the operation of the laws of the other state or of the
federal government.

Provisions for reciprocal arrangements would be unnecessary
if there were one national system of unemployment insurance,
nationally administered. To have such a system, however, the
national government would apparently have to apply one uniform system with all the issues of policy determined in one way.
Such a system would have the merit of simplicity. If it provided
a pooled fund without experience rating or with rates under
merit rating adjusted to the condition of the pooled fund, it
might be from the actuarial standpoint fairly strong because
revenues from strong states could be used to help out weak
states. Moreover, national administrators would apply national
policies arrived at in part after consideration of the condition
of the national fund and the pressures brought to bear by pressure groups organized on a nationwide scale.

The country has one nationwide industrial unemployment
fund, that for railroads. It will be the subject of the following
chapter.

CHAPTER IX

THE RAILROAD UNEMPLOYMENT SYSTEM

The railroad unemployment system is a national system operated under acts of Congress and administered by the national Railroad Retirement Board. The present Railroad Retirement Act, it will be recalled, was developed and supported jointly by the employers and the employees with the co-operation of the Railroad Retirement Board. The Unemployment Compensation Act, in contrast, was drafted by the employees' representatives with the co-operation of the Chairman of the Railroad Retirement Board and was opposed by the employers both on its original passage and subsequent amendment. More detail on this difference will be given from time to time in connection with the special features of the act.

COVERAGE

The coverage of the railroad unemployment system is substantially the same as that of the railroad retirement system which was described in some detail in the chapter on that subject. The details will not be repeated here. Broadly, the unemployment compensation system covers the steam railroad industry of the country that comes under the Interstate Commerce Act, including however, the employee representatives of the railroad labor organizations.

FINANCING

Money to support the system comes in general from compulsory contributions of 3 per cent of compensation not in excess of $300 a month, which employers have to pay, and which are collected directly by the Railroad Retirement Board. Under the Railroad Retirement Act, it will be recalled, the revenues were secured from excise taxes levied against the employers and income taxes levied against the employees, and all these taxes were collected by the Bureau of Internal Revenue. The Bureau of Internal Revenue has nothing to do with collections for the railroad unemployment system. The reasons for the difference are constitutional.

The employees of the covered employers make no contributions toward unemployment compensation. In fact the law makes it "unlawful for any employer, or officer or agent of an employer, to make, require, or permit any employee to bear all or any portion of such contribution." The penalty for each violation of this subsection is a fine of not more than $10,000 or imprisonment not exceeding one year, or both.[1]

The only individuals who pay contributions for their own coverage are the officers and representatives of included railway labor organizations. The contribution rate for them is likewise 3 per cent of such of their compensation as is not in excess of $300 per month.

Of every dollar of contribution, 90 cents goes into the railroad unemployment insurance account and is used for the payment of benefits under the system. The remaining 10 cents goes into "The Railroad Unemployment Insurance Administration Fund," which is used for administrative expenditures. The administration fund will be discussed later in connection with the administration of the system. It will be noted that the employers pay 2.7 per cent of covered pay roll for benefits and 0.3 per cent for administrative costs. These rates are the same as those used in the national tax act for general unemployment insurance, but with this important exception. Under many state laws, as was discussed in the preceding chapter, experience rating permits employers with good records actually to pay less than 2.7 per cent toward benefits. Under the railroad act all employers pay 2.7 per cent toward benefits, as there are no provisions for experience rating. The railroad employers with good employment records help the employers with less favorable records. This difference will be taken up later in connection with benefit provisions.

BENEFIT PROVISIONS

The railroad unemployment system has very simple provi-

[1] 45 U.S.C. 359(b).

sions regarding base year, benefit year, benefits, and duration. They can be treated in reasonably brief compass.

Becoming insured. The "benefit year," in the terms of the act,[2] "means the twelve-month period beginning July 1 of any year and ending June 30 of the next year."[3]

The base year means "the completed calendar year immediately preceding the beginning of the benefit year."[4] Since a calendar year begins on January 1 and ends on December 31, this definition provides a six-months lag between the end of the base year and the beginning of the benefit year related to that base year, which gives time to complete the records with respect to the base year.

Benefits in the benefit year are based on the total amount of compensation payable to the individual with respect to covered employment within the base year. The definition of compensation, however, excludes any compensation in excess of $300 in any calendar month.[5]

Administratively this system is simple as contrasted with many state unemployment systems under which each covered individual has his own base year, the dates of which are not fixed until the individual files an application for unemployment compensation. The objection to the simple device, which has led many states to decide against its use, is that it may work a real hardship on new entrants to covered employment unless they begin their service in the early months of the year. It likewise works a hardship on employees whose compensation was materially increased either late in the base year or after the end of it, or who for one reason or another had a bad base year. Because of the relative stability of the operating branches of the railroad industry, the use of this simple device is probably less objectionable than would be its use for heterogeneous occupations.

[2] 45 U.S.C. 351(m).

[3] Except that if a man begins his "registration period" by registering in June and his registration period ends in July, all of the registration period shall be considered to lie within the benefit year ending in June. The meaning of registration period will be given later.

[4] 45 U.S.C. 351(n).

[5] 45 U.S.C. 351(i).

Determining whether a covered worker has attained an insured status is likewise extremely simple under the railroad system. An employee is insured under the law if "there was payable to him compensation of not less than $150 with respect to the base year." Compensation, it will be recalled, is defined to exclude payments in excess of $300 a month. Employees at salary rates of $300 a month or more are therefore insured if they worked half a month in the base year. Employees earning $50 a month will be insured if they work three months in the base year.

The day of the year on which a new entrant begins his service is, however, an important factor in the railroad system. An individual who starts covered railroad work on January 1 does not actually become eligible to receive benefits for 18 months. His first base year will not be completed until December 31 of that year, and his first benefit year will not begin until the following July 1. On the other hand, the employee who enters the service on December 1 at a salary of $150 a month will complete his first base year at the end of that month with qualifying earnings, and he will be eligible to draw benefits after six months should be become unemployed.

The waiting period. The railroad system is rather complicated with respect to waiting periods, as it uses a device termed "the registration period" in connection with the waiting period. The definition of the registration period reads as follows:

The term "registration period" means, with respect to any employee, the period which begins with the first day for which such employee registers at an employment office in accordance with such regulations as the Board may prescribe, and ends with whichever is the earlier of (i) the thirteenth day thereafter, or (ii) the day immediately preceding the day for which he next registers at a different employment office; and thereafter each period which begins with the first day for which he next registers at an employment office after the end of his last preceding registration period and ends with whichever is the earlier of (i) the thirteenth day thereafter, or (ii) the day immediately preceding the day for which he next registers at a different employment office.[6]

[6] 45 U.S.C. 351(h).

The provisions embodying the waiting period read:

Benefits shall be payable to any qualified employee (as defined in section 353 of this chapter) (i) for each day of unemployment in excess of seven during the first registration period, within a benefit year, in which he has seven or more days of unemployment, and (ii) for each day of unemployment in excess of four during any subsequent registration period beginning in the same benefit year.[7]

Perhaps an illustration or two will help toward an understanding of this system.

An employee becomes unemployed and immediately registers with the unemployment office. His unemployment continues uninterrupted, and after he has remained unemployed for seven days—the first waiting period—he becomes eligible for unemployment compensation at the amount per day prescribed by the law. The daily benefit is paid to him each day thereafter that he remains unemployed up to the end of his first registration period. His first registration period ends the thirteenth day after the day on which he registered. If he still remains unemployed he must register again for his second registration period. In his second registration period he has a waiting period of four days and then begins again to draw daily benefits until the end of the second registration period which comes 13 days after the second registration. Should he remain unemployed he would register a third time for a third registration period, again having a four-day waiting period. This procedure would continue so long as he remained unemployed until he had drawn benefits for 100 days, the maximum.

Another employee becomes unemployed and immediately registers with the employment office. He remains unemployed for ten consecutive working days and then returns to work. The first seven of these ten days are the waiting period and are not compensable and therefore he draws compensation for three days. Later he is unemployed again and again registers. He thereupon starts his second registration period within the benefit year and is eligible for compensation for every day of unemployment in that second period after the first four.

[7] 45 U.S.C. 352(a).

If for any reason the unemployed person registers at a second unemployment office before the expiration of the time limit for the current registration period, he thereby terminates that registration period and starts a new one. The new one dates from the day on which he registers at the different employment office. Such a rule presumably operates to discourage an employee from shifting from one employment office to another, except when the registration periods are expiring by virtue of the legal time limits. The four-day waiting time in each registration period after the first gives administrative officers time to act; and the device brings the unemployed person to the employment office or a representative of that office at least once every two weeks during a prolonged period of unemployment.

Duration of benefits. The maximum duration of benefits under the railroad law is 100 compensated days in a benefit year.[8] Waiting periods thus save the fund nothing in those cases in which the employee is unemployed for 100 days in addition to all the waiting days. They do, however, operate materially to reduce the number of employees who will draw benefits for the maximum number of days permitted by the law.

The amount of benefits. The amount of benefits per day of compensable unemployment is set forth in the act in the following manner:

The benefits payable to any such employee for each such day of unemployment shall be the amount appearing in the following table in column II on the line on which, in column I, appears the compensation range containing the total amount of compensation payable to him with respect to employment in his base year:

Column I Total Compensation	Column II Daily Benefit Rate
$ 150 to $ 199.99	$1.75
200 to 474.99	2.00
475 to 749.99	2.25
750 to 999.99	2.50
1,000 to 1,299.99	3.00
1,300 to 1,599.99	3.50
1,600 and over	4.00[9]

[8] 45 U.S.C. 352(c).
[9] 45 U.S.C. 352(a).

This benefit schedule in the law, it will be noted, divides the employees into seven different classes according to their total compensation in the base year. In the lowest class come those with compensation from $150 to $199, and in the highest those who received $1,600 or more. Plans using compensation classes of this type are sometimes called "step plans" because the benefits go up by definite steps and not smoothly as an incline plane. Where benefits are a percentage of earnings there are no definite steps but a gradual smooth rise.

The use of a step plan is regarded by many persons as objectionable, because it results in some unreasonable discrimination among the employees. This fact is illustrated in the table on page 250, which will serve as a basis for a general discussion of the benefit formula. In this table figures are shown for both the upper and the lower limits of each of the seven compensation classes. The terms Class 1, Class 2, and so on, are introduced in this table for expository purposes; they are not taken from the law. For both the lower limit and the upper limit of each class, the table shows in column 1 the total compensation earned during the base year, in column 2 the employer's contribution under the 3 per cent tax, and in column 3 the daily benefit rate. Columns 4, 5, and 6 deal with the maximum benefits in the benefit year, column 4 giving the total, column 5 the benefit per dollar of annual compensation, and column 6 the benefit per dollar of employer's contribution.

Columns 5 and 6 illustrate the reasons for the objection to the step plan. The highest paid man in the lower class gets less per dollar of compensation or of employer's contribution than the lowest paid man in the next higher class. For example, the man in Class 1 who earned $199.99 gets $29.17 per dollar of contribution, whereas the man in Class 2 who earned $200, or one cent more, gets $33.33. There is no reason whatever for a differential of more than $4.00 per dollar of contribution in favor of the man who earned just a cent or a few cents more, except perhaps the appearance of simplicity. To phrase it another way, there is no reason why the man who has earned $200 in his base

RAILROAD UNEMPLOYMENT INSURANCE ACT

Class	Total Compensation 1	Employer's Contribution 3 Per Cent of Compensation 2	Maximum Benefits in Benefit Year		Per Dollar of—	
			Daily Benefit Rate 3	Total 4	Compensation 5	Employer's Contribution 6
Class 1. Lower limit	$ 150.00	$ 4.50	$1.75	$175.00	$1.17	$38.89
Upper limit	199.99	6.00	1.75	175.00	.88	29.17
Class 2. Lower limit	200.00	6.00	2.00	200.00	1.00	33.33
Upper limit	474.99	14.25	2.00	200.00	.42	14.04
Class 3. Lower limit	475.00	14.25	2.25	225.00	.47	15.79
Upper limit	749.99	22.50	2.25	225.00	.30	10.00
Class 4. Lower limit	750.00	22.50	2.50	250.00	.33	11.11
Upper limit	999.99	30.00	2.50	250.00	.25	8.33
Class 5. Lower limit	1,000.00	30.00	3.00	300.00	.30	10.00
Upper limit	1,299.99	39.00	3.00	300.00	.23	7.69
Class 6. Lower limit	1,300.00	39.00	3.50	350.00	.27	8.97
Upper limit	1,599.99	48.00	3.50	350.00	.22	7.29
Class 7. Lower limit	1,600.00	48.00	4.00	400.00	.25	8.33
Upper limit	3,600.00	108.00	4.00	400.00	.11	3.70

year should get 25 cents a day more than the man who earned a cent or even a dollar less in his base year.

Column 6 also brings out the heavy discrimination against the more highly paid workers and in favor of the lower paid workers. For each dollar of contribution paid by the employer the lowest paid worker may draw as a maximum $38.89 whereas the highest paid worker may draw only $3.70. Under the railroad plan, no worker paid $1,600 or over can draw in the aggregate more than $400 in a benefit year. The employer is required to pay $48 a year with respect to the man earning $1,600 and $108 a year with respect to the one earning $3,600, but in event of unemployment each gets $4.00 a day for not to exceed 100 days.

These figures make no allowance for the relative probability of unemployment in the several compensation classes. Railroading is in many respects distinctive industry. For many of the higher-bracket positions, long years of experience are necessary, because the employee must have a thorough, detailed knowledge of the physical plant and its operation, including train schedules and dispatching. As a result, seniority plays a large part in its system of personnel administration, probably a larger part than in any other major industry.

Because of the distinctive nature of the industry, unemployment is less probable among the senior workers in responsible positions than among the juniors or among the unskilled or semi-skilled workers whose jobs do not require a detailed knowledge of plant and operations. Unemployment is most common among the unskilled or semi-skilled workers used seasonally for maintenance of way.[10]

The liberality of the provisions made for the seasonal workers in the railroad system deserves note. To cite the extreme case, a seasonal worker who earns $150 in the base year may, if unemployed, draw $1.75 a day for 100 days, a total of $175 in the

---

[10] During the war the main drain on the fund was for seasonal workers. See *Annual Report of the Railroad Retirement Board, 1942*, p. 94 for a striking diagram showing the importance of seasonal workers.

benefit year. Thus the railroads, which bear all the cost of the compensation system, may have to pay more for the unemployment than they do for the work performed. Such a system naturally makes it disadvantageous for the roads to employ local seasonal workers for maintenance of way—farmers or farm laborers when farm work is slack—and dictates smaller permanent crews for this task with large use of labor-saving machinery. This subject will be considered further in connection with unemployment and other earnings.

The provisions with respect to the upper-bracket employees constitute a discrimination against the railroad industry as compared with competing forms of transportation, which come under the state unemployment compensation laws. This discrimination lies in two points:

1. The railroad industry is required to pay the 3 per cent tax on all compensation not in excess of $300 a month, whereas competing forms of transportation pay only on the compensation not in excess of $250 a month. This provision is not beneficial to the upper-bracket railroad employees, since they can draw no higher benefit than the employee whose average monthly compensation in the base year was $133 a month, nor can they draw it for any longer duration. If after years of continuous service, with few calls upon the fund, they should be the victims of technological unemployment, they can draw only the $400 maximum, despite the fact that the railroad has paid annually $108 with respect to their employment.

2. The railroad industry is required to pay the 3 per cent tax with no reduction because of merit rating, whereas in many states competing carriers can get the advantage of merit rating or employers' funds. As was noted in the preceding chapter, in many of the states employers with fine employment records may after a few years pay very little unemployment tax. Thus the railroads are paying the full tax, whereas their competitors in some states may be paying almost no tax because of the excellence of their record.

Under the railroad system the 3 per cent tax on all compensation not in excess of $300 a month builds a substantial fund and hence encourages a gradual increase in benefits, because the fund obviously can stand it. Under merit rating or individual employer's reserves used in state systems, growth of the fund because of absence of unemployment perhaps generally results less in an increase in the amount or duration of benefits than in a reduction of employers' taxes.

If the railroads had a complete monopoly of all transportation, it might be possible for railway employees permanently to have both a retirement system and an unemployment system that cost the railroads far more than employers in other noncompeting industries are compelled to pay. However, the railroads are in competition with other carriers, and it is generally anticipated that the intensity of this competition will increase rather than diminish after the war. If the railroads suffer from this competition, those railroad employees who survive in the service will perhaps derive some real advantage from the favorable provisions of the railroad systems with respect to unemployment and retirement,[11] but many others will lose their jobs and come under the less favorable general systems or be in classes excluded from social security coverage.

QUALIFICATION AND DISQUALIFICATION

The provisions regarding the attainment of the insured status under the railroad system is, as has been seen, simplicity itself: the employee must have earned $150 in the base year. Unfortunately what constitutes compensable unemployment is in some respects fairly complex and difficult to present simply.

The difficulty arises from the nature of the actual operation of trains. In a typical establishment covered by a state unemployment compensation system, there is a reasonably definite concrete work week. The bulk of the employees work a fixed number of hours on the first five days of the work week and a fixed number of hours on Saturday; they begin at approximately

[11] In Chap. 6 on The Railroad Retirement System the fact was noted that a reduction in the size of the railway pay roll and railway rates of pay will weaken the financial position of the retirement fund. So long as the railroads face real competition, it is questionable whether in the long run the railroads can be forced by the government to provide far better benefits for retirement and unemployment than are offered by their competitors.

the same time and quit at the same time. This work week can be used as a standard by which the hours of the relatively few who work odd hours can be measured. In the actual operation of trains, there is no such uniform work week. Trains are moving on the railroads at all times, day and night, week days, Sundays, and holidays. At almost every minute of the day some men in the operating branch of the railroads are just reporting for work, and others are coming off duty. The railroads therefore have had to adopt their own peculiar and specific definitions as to what constitutes a day's work in the operation of trains.

A run of a specific number of miles on a train of a given class may constitute a day's work. Because of the length of the run, a single trip may constitute more than a day's work for an employee. He may start a run on one calendar day and finish it on another. In another case an employee may take a night local from the terminal, spend the night at the point of destination, and in the morning run the train back to the terminal. Neither hours alone nor miles alone furnish a standard measure, and hence there are many conventions and agreements that have grown up in the railroad industry.

The definition of unemployment in a railroad unemployment compensation system must be adapted to these conventions and agreements. For the purposes of the present chapter, the best procedure appears to be first to set forth as simply and clearly as possible the provisions that relate to the employees who do not actually operate the trains and then take up the special provisions that relate to "train and engine service, yard service, dining-car service, sleeping-car service, parlor-car service, or other Pullman-car or similar service, or express service on trains."[12]

For the nonoperating employees and for operating employees, subject to the limitations to be noted below, "a day of unemployment . . . means a calendar day on which he is able to work and is available for work and with respect to which (i) no remuneration is payable or accrues to him, and (ii) he has, in accordance with such regulations as the Board may prescribe,

[12] 45 U.S.C. 354 (a) vi and vii.

registered at an unemployment office."[13] This definition is simple enough provided remuneration is defined.

Remuneration under the act means pay for service for hire and earned income other than services for hire "if the accrual thereof in whole or in part is ascertainable with respect to a particular day or particular days." It includes pay for time lost— treated as earned on the day lost—and tips, but it does not include any money received pursuant to any nongovernmental plan for unemployment insurance. Thus any labor union benefits for unemployment are not remuneration within the law and may be received in addition to the unemployment benefits under the railroad system.[14]

Annuity payments under the Railroad Retirement Act or other acts of Congress are a disqualification for unemployment benefits, although if the annuity payment is less than the unemployment benefit, the employee may be paid the difference.[15]

Except for employees who have earned less than $150 a year, remuneration does not include subsidiary remuneration. Thus for most of the workers the receipt of subsidiary remuneration does not constitute receipt of remuneration as the word is used in the definition of unemployment.

Subsidiary remuneration means, roughly, pay not in excess of an average of a dollar a day for the period during which it is earned, provided the work for which it is done (1) requires substantially less than full time as determined by generally prevailing standards and (2) is susceptible of performance at such times and under such circumstances as not to be inconsistent with the holding of normal full-time employment in another occupation.[16]

This definition of subsidiary remuneration appears to have a considerable degree of significance with respect to seasonal workers on the railroads. A farmer or farm laborer who earned rights to unemployment benefits during the open months by earning $150 or more might not be disqualified for benefit by

[13] 45 U.S.C. 351 (k).
[14] 45 U.S.C. 351 (j).
[15] 45 U.S.C. 354 (a) (v).
[16] 45 U.S.C. 351 (k).

chores around the farm on the basis of money earnings, the requirement of full time, or interference with normal full-time employment in another occupation provided full-time jobs were available in his locality in the winter months.

The typical nonoperating employee, therefore, who is in receipt of no wages or earnings beyond subsidiary remuneration counts as a day's unemployment each day he is able to work and available to work but has no job. He must, however, satisfy the waiting period requirements. For the first registration period of 14 days, it will be recalled, he must have 7 days of unemployment before he can draw a day's benefit for any additional day of unemployment. In the second or any subsequent registration period of 14 days he must have 4 days of unemployment before he can draw benefit for any additional day of unemployment.

For the nonoperating employee who has served the waiting period, each day of subsequent unemployment in that period is compensable. If he has only one day of unemployment beyond the waiting period before he is called back to work or gets a new job, that day counts for benefit. The system thus operates to give what in a general state system would be called a partial unemployment benefit. The worker is not disqualified because he has had several days of work in the registration period, but only if he has had no days of unemployment beyond the waiting period. In the first waiting period, any day of unemployment after the first seven is compensable whatever work the employee may have had in its remaining days, and in the second period any day beyond the first four whatever the record for the balance of the period.

With respect to the train operating personnel, a limitation is introduced on the basis of earnings (1) within the registration period or (2) within the registration period and the 14 days immediately preceding it. If in the registration period the operating employee has earned 20 times his daily benefit rate he is ineligible for compensation.[17] If in the 28 days before the end of the registration period he has earned 40 times his daily benefit, he is not eligible.[18] The effect of this limitation can be shown

[17] 45 U.S.C. 354 (a) (vi).
[18] 45 U.S.C. 354 (a) (vii).

perhaps most easily by reproducing the benefit scale with the limitations added.

LIMITATION ON BENEFIT SCALE FOR TRAIN OPERATING PERSONNEL

Total Annual Compensation in the Base Year	Daily Benefit Rate	Earnings of Train Service Personnel that Destroy Eligibility	
		Within the 14 Days	Within the 28 Days
$ 150–$ 199.99	$1.75	$35	$ 70
200– 474.99	2.00	40	80
475– 749.99	2.25	45	90
750– 999.99	2.50	50	100
1,000– 1,299.99	3.00	60	120
1,300– 1,599.99	3.50	70	140
1,600 and over	4.00	80	160

These eligibility limitations for the operating personnel constitute another discrimination against the upper-bracket employees in the train service. To illustrate the discrimination, an employee earning $1,600 a year will be contrasted with one earning $3,200 a year. It will be assumed that for each employee the actual working year is equivalent to 275 days. The $3,200 man earning about $11.64 a day would earn the disqualifying $80 in less than 7 days whereas the $1,600 man earning about $5.82 a day would require more than 13 days. To earn the $160 that disqualifies for the 28-day period, the $3,200 man would require less than 14 days, whereas the $1,600 man would require practically the entire 28-day period. In other words, the limitation does not prevent the lower-paid man from drawing compensation for unemployment and underemployment, provided he has been unemployed for the required waiting period. The higher-paid employee to be eligible must have been unemployed for 7 days in the registration period and for 14 days in the 28 days immediately preceding the end of the registration period to be eligible.

These figures further support the conclusion that the taxes paid by the railroads with respect to the wages of its more highly paid workers go largely for the lower-paid, especially the seasonal workers. Again the question previously discussed regarding discrimination against the railroads as compared with their competitors under state systems deserves note.

The other disqualifications provided by the law are as follows:

1. Leaving work voluntarily without good cause.

2. Failing without good cause to accept suitable work, or to comply with instructions from the board to apply for suitable work, or to report, in person or by mail, as the board may require, to an employment office. The employment office referred to is operated by or under the jurisdiction of the board, as will be described later under administration.

3. Being unemployed because of a strike, if the board finds the strike was in violation of the law governing strikes in the railroad industry or of the established rules and practices of a bona fide labor organization of which he was a member.

4. Knowingly making, aiding in making, or causing to be made any fake or fraudulent statement or claim for the purpose of causing benefits to be paid.

5. Receiving benefits for old-age annuities, pensions under the railroad retirement laws or unemployment compensation laws, but with qualifications to be considered later.

Leaving work voluntarily without good cause. The law itself does not specify what constitutes good cause. Thus sublegislative and subjudicial authority to determine good cause are vested in the board, except that leaving work which is unsuitable under the law on that subject is not leaving without good cause.

The penalty for this offense is that none of the thirty days beginning with the day with respect to which the board finds that he left work voluntarily without good cause will be counted as days of compensable unemployment.

Refusing to accept suitable work. The law contains specific provisions regarding what constitutes unsuitable work and the factors which shall be applied in determining what is suitable work. The two sections of the law on this subject read:

(c) Unsuitable work.
No work shall be deemed suitable for the purposes of subsection (a) (ii) of this section, and benefits shall not be denied under this chapter to any otherwise qualified employee for refusing to accept work if—

(i) the position offered is vacant due directly to a strike, lockout, or other labor dispute;

(ii) the remuneration, hours, or other conditions of work offered are substantially less favorable to the employee than those prevailing for similar work in the locality, or the rate of remuneration is less than the union wage rate, if any, for similar work in the locality;

(iii) as a condition of being employed he would be required to join a company union or to resign from or refrain from joining any bona fide labor organization;

(iv) acceptance of the work would require him to engage in activities in violation of law or which, by reason of their being in violation of reasonable requirements of the constitution, bylaws, or similar regulations of a bona fide labor organization of which he is a member, would subject him to expulsion from such labor organization; or

(v) acceptance of the work would subject him to loss of substantial seniority rights under any collective bargaining agreement between a railway labor organization, organized in accordance with the provisions of chapter 8 of this title, and any other employer.

(d) Factors in determination of suitable work.

In determining, within the limitations of subsection (c) of this section, whether or not any work is suitable for an employee for the purposes of subsection (a) (ii) of this section, the Board shall consider in addition to such other factors as it deems relevant, (i) the current practices recognized by management and labor with respect to such work; (ii) the degree of risk involved to such employee's health, safety, and morals; (iii) his physical fitness and prior training; (iv) his experience and prior earnings; (v) his length of unemployment and prospects for securing work in his customary occupation; and (vi) the distance of the available work from his residence and from his most recent work.[19]

Special attention should be called to the fact that under the law a covered employee is entitled to unemployment compensation if he refuses employment or voluntarily leaves employment, where the rate of remuneration is less than the union wage rate for similar work in the locality. Thus in a community where the prevailing wage for a given type of work is less than the union rate, the employee can, if he so elects, draw unemployment compensation.

The penalty for this offense, as in the case of voluntary leaving, is that compensation cannot be drawn for any of the

[19] 45 U.S.C. 354 (c), (d).

thirty days beginning with the day the board determined was the day the offense was committed.

Unemployment due to a strike. A distinctive feature of the railroad industry included under this act is that it is subject to national laws governing employer-employee relations and strikes. Thus the discretion of the board is exercised within the provisions of the national law on the subject. The specific provisions of the unemployment insurance act read:

The disqualification provided in section 4 (a) (iii) of this Act shall not apply if the Board finds that—

(i) the employee is not participating in or financing or directly interested in the strike which causes the stoppage of work: *Provided*, That payment of regular union dues shall not be construed to constitute financing a strike or direct interest in a strike within the meaning of this and the following paragraphs; and

(ii) he does not belong to a grade or class of workers of which, immediately before the commencement of the stoppage, there were members employed in the establishment, premises, or enterprise at which the stoppage occurs, any of whom are participating in or financing or directly interested in the dispute: *Provided*, That if separate types of work are commonly conducted in separate departments of a single enterprise, each such department shall, for the purposes of this subsection, be deemed to be a separate establishment, enterprise, or other premises.[20]

An employee disqualified because of a strike cannot draw a benefit for any day with respect to which the board finds his unemployment was due to that strike.

Making false statements. If the board finds an employee guilty of having made a false statement within the definition given above, the penalty is specifically fixed in the law. He is disqualified for benefits for 75 days beginning with the first day of the registration period in which the board finds that he made the false statement. The board has no authorization to make the penalty fit the crime, but of course it has a wide measure of discretion as to whether the acts actually committed shall result in an application of the penalty.

[20] 45 U.S.C. 354 (b).

Receiving other benefits. The penalty for receiving other benefits is disqualification for an unemployment benefit on any day for which the other benefits were received. If the other benefit for any day is less than the unemployment benefit would have been, the difference is paid from the unemployment account.

ADMINISTRATION

The railroad unemployment insurance system is administered by the Railroad Retirement Board.

Composition and powers of the Board. The composition of this Board has been described in some detail in the chapter on the railroad retirement system. Here it may be briefly repeated that the Board consists of three members appointed by the President by and with the advice and consent of the Senate. One member must be appointed from recommendations made by representatives of the employees and one from recommendations made by representatives of the carriers so as to provide representation on the Board satisfactory to the largest number, respectively, of employees and carriers concerned. The third member, selected without recommendations from either group, must not be in the employment of or be pecuniarily or otherwise interested in any employer or organization of employees. This third member is the chairman of the Board.

This Board was created under the Railroad Retirement Act which had as its legislative companion piece the Carriers Taxing Act of 1937. The Carriers Taxing Act levied an income tax on employees and an excise tax of like amount on employers, so that the burden of the retirement system, with due allowance for the indirectness adopted to circumvent possible constitutional difficulties, was to be shared equally by employers and employees. This financial basis unquestionably was a factor in the decision to have the system administered by a representative board of the type set up by Congress.

Funds for the railroad unemployment insurance system come exclusively from taxes on the employers except for a small amount from the individuals who are employee representatives. All the costs of administration are borne by the employers except for the small amount which comes from the employee union representatives. The funds, both for administration and for benefits, are controlled, however, by this representative Board. When and if the chairman of the Board votes with the representative of the employees, the representative of the employers, who are paying in almost all the money, is practically powerless since a majority vote controls the action of the Board.

The present Railroad Retirement Act was drafted by representatives of employers and employees working together, and both sides united in urging its passage by Congress. The Board was to be representative of the two parties with the government through the chairman acting as the arbiter.

The history of the later unemployment insurance legislation presents a striking contrast. The legislation was supported by the employees' organizations and was effectively championed by the chairman of the Railroad Retirement Board. Because of the composition of the Board, support by its chairman is equivalent under such circumstances to support by a majority of the Board. The employers were in opposition to the original act on the ground that legislation should be deferred until the railroad industry and the country as a whole had had more experience under the federal-state unemployment acts set up by the Social Security Act to which the railroads were then subject. After the original railroad act was passed over their objections, they opposed not all but some of the proposed amendments on three main grounds: that the increases in the benefit provisions were too great, that the act should provide for a reduction of the taxes on the industry when the reserves reached a level deemed adequate for reasonable safety, and that the powers conferred on the Board were excessive. The railroads were represented before the congressional committees not by the railroad member of the board but in the main by representatives of the Association of American Railroads.

As one reads the hearings on the Railroad Unemployment Insurance Act and other hearings on other social insurance acts, one important fact stands out: The executive agency responsible for administering a social insurance system has almost inevitably a virtual monopoly on the factual data necessary to appraise and evaluate the system. The statistics necessary for appraisal and evaluation are a joint product of the administration of the act. In 1942, according to the report of the board,[21] 2.5 million dollars were expended in the administration of the railroad unemployment system. The number of employees on class 1 railroads in June was a little under 1.3 millions. Even with the high employment prevailing in the benefit year 1942, the board received over 90,000 applications and 517,000 claims and made over 448,000 benefit payments, which aggregated over 8.8 million dollars. Almost every transaction in which the board has a relationship with a covered railroad employee produces a fact of statistical significance in appraising and evaluating the act. Not only are hundreds of thousands of dollars expended collecting and tabulating the basic data, but many thousands more must be spent in analyzing them. Moreover, collection, tabulation, and analysis are integral parts of a whole. Employers and private research organizations cannot get independently the necessary data to appraise the workings of the system. They must to a very large degree accept the basic statistics and subsequent analysis of the government agency. Thus the persons who appear in opposition to the chairman of such an agency as the Railroad Retirement Board are almost entirely dependent for much of the fundamental factual material on the figures prepared under the supervision of the board, or a majority of the board, and according to a common governmental practice presented by the chairman of the board.

Because of the virtual monopoly of factual material inherently vested in the board on account of the nature of the work, one naturally examines with a good deal of interest the powers given to the board by Congress and the extent to which its administration is subject to check by the governmental control agencies. The provisions which are of particular significance in this respect relate to (1) control over the payment of benefits and (2)

[21] *Annual Report of the Railroad Retirement Board, 1942*, pp. 2, 87, 91.

control over administrative expenditures. They will be taken up in that order.

Section 355 (f) of the act gives to any claimant and any railroad labor organization of which the claimant is a member, if it is organized in accordance with other federal laws, an appeal to the United States District Court in the district in which the claimant resides or to the United States District Court for the District of Columbia. Such an appeal can be taken only from the final decision of the Board. It will be noted that this section does not give an appeal to the employers, although under this law the employers are compelled to put up all the money. This section has been presented first not because it is the most significant, but because it is referred to in the following paragraph (g) of the law, which is the vital one. It reads:

Findings of fact and conclusions of law of the Board in the determination of any claim for benefits or refund and the determination of the Board that the unexpended funds in the account are available for the payment of any claim for benefits or refund under this chapter, shall be, except as provided in subsection (f) of this section [the one referred to above], binding and conclusive for all purposes and upon all persons, including the Comptroller General and any other administrative or accounting officer, employee, or agent of the United States, and shall not be subject to review in any manner other than that set forth in subsection (f) of this section.[22]

The Board itself collects the contributions from the carriers. It does not have actual custody of the money. The Secretary of the Treasury holds it and disburses it on order of the Board, but the Treasury acts in a ministerial capacity. Under the law no agency or person has authority to review or reverse the findings of the Board with respect to the amount of benefits or refunds or the ability of the fund to stand the strain. Section 360 (b) of the act provides that the Secretary of the Treasury, through the Division of Disbursements, shall make payments directly to the person or company entitled to the benefit or refund "prior to audit or settlement by the General Accounting Office," which eliminates another possible check.

[22] 45 U.S.C. 355 (g).

There is, however, a proviso to this paragraph of the law which reads: "That if the Board shall so request, the Secretary of the Treasury, through the Fiscal Service of the Treasury Department, shall transmit benefit payments to the Board for distribution by it through employment offices or in such other manner as the Board deems proper."

Under the law, therefore, the Board is subject to only two forms of control with respect to benefit payments and refunds: (1) the right of a claimant or his union to appeal a final decision of the Board to a United States district court, (2) the power of the President of the United States to remove a member of the Board.

Funds for administration. The power of the Board with respect to administrative expenditures is almost equally complete. For every dollar paid to a covered worker in the railroad industry not in excess of $300 a month, three tenths of a cent goes into the Railroad Retirement Board's administration fund. For the fiscal year 1941–42, the net receipts from this three tenths of a cent was just under 8.5 million dollars, but during that fiscal year the Board spent for administration only 2.5 millions.[23] Under the law it is directed to turn over to the benefit account at the end of each year so much of the balance for the administration fund as is in excess of 6 million dollars.[24]

If it so elects, the Board has at its disposal for administration in any fiscal year (1) the balance in the administration fund at the end of the preceding fiscal year, not to exceed 6 million dollars, plus (2) the receipts from the three tenths of a cent tax, which in the fiscal year 1942 yielded almost 8.5 millions. In periods of reasonably full employment the Board has within its administrative control a fund to meet administrative costs which is in the neighborhood of 14 million dollars, practically all of which came directly from the railroads and indirectly from consumers. The section of the law that deals with this fund therefore merits close study.[25]

[23] *Annual Report of the Railroad Retirement Board, 1942*, p. 144.
[24] 45 U.S.C. 361 (d).
[25] 45 U.S.C. 361.

The Board itself collects the contribution of the employers and 10 per cent of the contributions go directly into the administration fund. Paragraph (c) of Section 361 begins: "Notwithstanding any other provision of law, all moneys at any time credited to the fund are hereby permanently appropriated to the Board to be continuously available to the Board without further appropriation for any expenses necessary or incidental to administering this chapter. . . ."

This provision exempts the Board from the necessity of going through the customary procedures in getting money to meet its administrative costs for the unemployment insurance act. It does not have to submit its estimates to the Bureau of the Budget or get annual appropriations from Congress. Within the limits of the fund, it draws its own checks. The drafters of the bill, however, included as a resource of the fund "such additional amounts as Congress may appropriate for expenses necessary or incidental to administering this chapter," the type of clause necessary to prevent a further appropriation from being subject to a point of order under the rules of the House.

After the general language of section 361 (c) come specific authorizations for administrative expenditures. They may be divided into two groups: (1) those that specifically exempt the board from some of the controls which Congress has frequently imposed upon other government agencies, and (2) those that give it special powers. The major discussion will be confined to the latter group.[26]

---

[26] The specific authorizations that remove restrictions applicable to governmental agencies under general laws include:

1. Personal services in the District of Columbia and elsewhere.

2. Travel expenses, including expenses of attendance at meetings when authorized by the Board.

3. Reproducing, photographing, and all other equipment, office appliances and labor-saving devices, including devices for internal communication and conveyance.

4. Purchase and exchange, operation, maintenance, and repair of motor-propelled passenger-carrying vehicles to be used only for official purposes in the District of Columbia and in the field.

5. Printing and binding.

6. Periodicals, newspapers, and press clippings in such amounts as the Board deems necessary.

7. Membership fees or dues in organizations which issue publications to members only

Among the distinctive provisions are:

1. Transportation expenses and not to exceed $10 per diem to any person other than an employee of the federal government who may from time to time be invited to the city of Washington or elsewhere for conference or advisory purposes in furthering the work of the Board.

2. Not more than 3 per cent of the annual receipts of the Board for administrative purposes for engaging persons or organizations by contract or otherwise for any special technical or professional services determined necessary by the Board, without regard to the provisions of laws applicable to the employment and compensation of officers and employees of the United States.

With respect to internal financial administration, the Railroad Retirement Board presents one situation that is distinctive. It administers two different systems, each under a different law, but the two systems are intimately related. Not only do the two systems relate to the same industry, but they are identical in coverage and are supported directly or indirectly through taxes on the same pay rolls with the same limitations. Work done on one system is in many cases equally applicable to the other. Many records serve both. Some of the administrative divisions within the Board not only do work on both systems but carry on single activities that are equally required by and equally applicable to each system. Administratively the activities for the two systems are often scrambled. Despite this scrambling, funds for the administration of the retirement system come from regular annual appropriations made by Congress in the customary way whereas, as has just been noted, funds for the administration of the unemployment insurance system come from the board's own administrative fund, without annual appropriations by Congress. The Board has a

---

or to members at a lower price than to others, payment for which may be made in advance.

8. Rentals, including garages, in the District of Columbia or elsewhere.

9. Alterations and repairs.

10. A proviso exempts any purchase or procurement of supplies or services by the board, when the amount involved does not exceed $300, from the general law that requires advertising for proposals for supplies or services for use of the government.

very wide margin in the administrative fund between (1) the aggregate amount in the fund and (2) reasonable or even unreasonable administrative costs.

By virtue of authority contained in the Railroad Unemployment Insurance Act, the Board determines whether the administrative fund for the unemployment insurance act or the appropriation for the administration of the retirement act shall be charged for authorized expenditures, or how the expenses shall be divided between the fund and the appropriation. Such determinations by the Board according to the law "shall be binding and conclusive for all purposes and upon all persons, including the Comptroller General and any other administrative or accounting officer, employee, or agent of the United States, and shall not be subject to review in any manner."[27]

Maintenance of employment offices by Board. The Board in accordance with specific authorizations contained in the law,[28] maintains its own system of free employment offices for the railroad industry. It may use and compensate (1) a railway labor organization duly authorized and designated to represent employees in accordance with other federal laws, (2) one or more employers or organizations of employers, (3) a group of such employers and labor organizations, or (4) a state, territory, foreign government, or the federal government. Under these provisions it has made arrangements whereby employees of the railroads represent the Board at a host of railroad organization units, where the representatives are immediately available to help the men in registering and making out other necessary papers. For such services the Board usually compensates the railroad employees who represent it on a fixed fee basis. This arrangement furthers prompt action, for it means that an employee may make out his papers practically at his place of work, the papers are promptly dispatched to the regional offices where claims are passed upon, and when they get there, they are usually completely and properly filled out and certified.

[27] 45 U.S.C. 361 (c).
[28] 45 U.S.C. 362 (i).

Civil service provisions for Board Employees. The employees of the Board are in general under the classified civil service, but the unemployment act contains the following proviso: "That in the employment of such persons the Board shall give preference, as between applicants attaining the same grades, to persons who have had experience in railroad service, and notwithstanding any other provisions of law, rules, or regulations, no other preference shall be given or recognized."[29] Thus, apparently the act completely wipes out the veterans' preferences applicable to the civil service system in general. With respect to positions with minimum salaries of $4,600 or less, the Civil Service Commission must certify candidates selected upon the basis of such competitive examinations, written, oral, or both, as the Board may request. The Civil Service Commission apparently cannot certify to the board from a general register made up for the use of many departments if the Board requests a special examination. The Board and not the Civil Service Commission determines the type of examination to be used. Under this provision it can give weight to prior railroad experience which would not be possible in a general examination, and it can include questions on railroad work which would be inappropriate to a general examination.[30] The Board has authority to pay the Civil Service Commission for conducting examinations for it if it finds this course necessary to expedite the selections.

These provisions regarding administrative expenses, organization, and personnel make the Board almost unique among federal government agencies. Although within the government, it is also a part of the railroad industry. Subject almost exclusively to the power of the President to appoint and remove

[29] 45 U.S.C. 362 (l).

[30] The act contained the following provision which is of interest in this connection: "A person in the employ of the Board on June 30, 1939, and on June 30, 1940, and who has had experience in railroad service, shall acquire a competitive classified civil-service status if, after recommendation by the Board to the Civil Service Commission, he shall pass such noncompetitive tests of fitness for the position for which the Board recommends him as the Civil Service Commission may prescribe." 45 U.S.C. 362 (l).

Board members, it is controlled by a majority vote of those members. A majority can be made up of either the employer and the employee representatives or of the chairman siding with either representative. Because of the preferences given to persons with prior experience in the railroad industry and the unionization of the railroad industry, the staff is unlike that of an ordinary government agency. It is dominated by employees or former employees of the industry.[31]

[31] In this connection the following section from the unemployment act may be of interest:

"No person shall be excused from attending or testifying in obedience to a subpena issued under this chapter or from complying with any subpena duces tecum issued under this chapter, on the ground that the testimony or evidence, documentary or otherwise, required of him may tend to incriminate him or subject him to a penalty or forfeiture; but no person shall be prosecuted or subjected to any penalty or forfeiture for or on account of any transaction, matter, or thing concerning which he is compelled, after having claimed his privilege against self-incrimination, to testify or produce evidence, documentary or otherwise, but such person so testifying shall not be exempt from prosecution and punishment for perjury committed in so testifying." 45 U.S.C. 362 (c).

This section provides what is sometimes referred to as "the immunity bath." To make constitutional a provision depriving a man of his rights under the Constitution to refuse to incriminate himself, he must be given immunity from subsequent prosecution for "any transaction, matter, or thing" concerning which he is compelled to give testimony. After an "immunity bath" given by a federal agency he cannot subsequently be convicted for the transaction, matter, or thing by the federal courts. Such provisions are found in some of the acts creating the independent regulatory commissions. It is interesting—one might even say disturbing—to find such a power conferred upon a board which in all other respects is an industry agency within the governmental structure and not directly concerned with matters of public policy and law enforcement.

CHAPTER X

PROGRAMS FOR FARMERS AND FARM WORKERS

The major problem with which this book is concerned is the development of a universal, comprehensive, and co-ordinated system of social security for the entire population of the nation, so designed that it will preserve the liberties of the American way of life. One of the principal elements in respect to this problem is, What shall be done regarding the more than 8 million gainful workers on the farms of the country and those dependent upon them? In 1940 the rural farm population numbered over 30 millions and constituted 22.9 per cent of the total population of the country.[1] The occupations of the more than 8 million workers on the farms in 1940 were as follows in thousands:[2]

Farmers and farm managers:		
Farmers (owners and tenants)	5,107	
Farm managers...........................	37	5,144
Farm laborers and foremen:		
Farm laborers (wage workers) and foremen....	1,925	
Farm foremen............ 24		
Farm laborers............ 1,900		
Farm laborers (unpaid family workers)........	1,165	3,090
Total...		8,234

In the preceding chapters it has been noted that farmers and agricultural laborers in general are not covered in the existing social insurance systems. If they or their dependents are in need, they must rely on the public assistance programs, namely the federal-state co-operative plans for old-age assistance, aid to dependent children, and aid to the blind, and the local or state and local plans for general public assistance. In so far as the tax on employers for the support of the existing system of old-age and survivors insurance is passed along to consumers,

[1] Census of 1940, *Population*, Vol. II, Pt. 1, p. 18.
[2] Census of 1940, *The Labor Force*, Vol. III, Pt. 1, pp. 75, 79.

271

the agricultural workers are paying part of the costs, although they themselves and their dependents are ineligible for direct benefits. The basic reason for their exclusion from existing social insurance plans is probably that the distinctive economic organization of agricultural enterprise does not readily permit the use of the devices which have been applied to other industries. Agricultural organization and agricultural problems have led to the development of or experimentation with special programs for rural areas. The present chapter will be concerned primarily with these special programs. Before entering upon a discussion of them, however, it may be well to attempt to set forth briefly those differences between farming and other industries which seem to be significant in considering the more fundamental problems to which Part III will be devoted.

RELEVANT DISTINCTIONS BETWEEN FARMING AND OTHER INDUSTRIES

The distinctions which appear relevant relate to (1) methods of payment for work done, (2) the nature and risks of unemployment, and (3) the importance of capital and management. Each will be considered in turn.

Differences in method of payment. In an urban industrial community the largest group of workers are generally employees working for a wage or salary, usually paid entirely in money at frequent periodic intervals. The number of persons working on their own account is relatively small, and they ordinarily get their fees or profits in money. Thus insurance systems based on money transactions present no great difficulties.

In farming, the bulk of the workers are working on their own account. They get their shelter and frequently a substantial part of their food from their own activities; their net money income generally represents such profit as they have made on their work for the year; and in several branches of farming the bulk of the gross income comes in after harvesting, when crops are marketed. A not uncommon situation is for the farmer during the planting, growing, and harvesting season to invest his own labor and working capital—either owned or borrowed—in the crops he is raising so that for much of the year he has relatively little cash; he gets the bulk of his money reward for his labor and the use of capital in one brief period. Unlike the typical urban worker his net return is not solely for his labor but represents in part interest on both his fixed and working capital. Thus regular periodic deductions from pay roll that characterize unemployment and old-age insurance for employed workers is almost entirely inapplicable to his situation.

As was shown in the figures on page 271, agricultural laborers, as distinguished from farmers and farm managers, are divided by the Bureau of the Census into two classes: (1) "Farm laborers, wage workers, and foremen," and (2) "Farm laborers, unpaid family workers." Obviously the financial devices of unemployment and old-age insurance as used for ordinary industrial workers are entirely inapplicable to the unpaid family agricultural laborer. They may be almost equally inapplicable to many farm laborers who work for wages since in some sections of the country a substantial part of the real wage is paid in kind and consists of quarters and food for the worker and his dependents and in some instances garden space, seed, and feed for such livestock as the farm laborer or his wife may own.

Differences in the risk of unemployment. In comparing the risks of unemployment and underemployment in farming with those in other industries, three types of unemployment, technological, seasonal, and cyclical, must be distinguished.

Technological unemployment has been placed first because since World War I it has been so important a factor in American agriculture. It has resulted from three principal causes: (1) the mechanization of agriculture, (2) the improvement in methods, and (3) the marked decrease in the long-time demand for certain staple crops. The introduction of the tractor and various farm machines has meant a great reduction in the number of man-hours required for the production of a given output and has made unprofitable farms too small to support the capital costs of modern equipment. Farmers who operated small units by technologically outmoded methods have been "tractored out." Their lands to be effectively used had to be consolidated into larger units. These larger units, efficiently operated, did not require enough man power to absorb the displaced farmers and farm workers.

The advances in method have, moreover, tended to make farm labor more and more a skilled trade. The successful worker to an increasing degree must have specialized knowledge, skills, and experience. The forces that have reduced the demand for workers have at the same time raised the level of essential qualifications. An increasing number of farmers and farm laborers have become, so far as farming operations are concerned, marginal or submarginal and cannot expect the security which was theirs when physical strength, willingness to work and a limited amount of knowledge and skill were all that was required.

Failure of the demand for certain commodities to absorb production has been a major factor in the United States. The commodity most affected, cotton, was the staple money crop of many of the southern states. Both the domestic and the foreign markets for American cotton tended to disappear. In the domestic market cotton gave way to competing fibers. Efforts to maintain the price of cotton and sustain the southern agricultural structure enabled other countries to produce it in competition with the United States. World War I made it desirable for some countries for military reasons to have cotton produced under their own flags. The high price of cotton during that war, moreover, got many American growers into financial difficulties from which they could not extricate themselves.

These technological changes resulted in peacetime in surplus man power in American agriculture, particularly in the southern states. Unemployment insurance, as it has thus far been developed in the United States, is not adapted to take care of prolonged technological unemployment and is not a remedy for the conditions that have become chronic in the South.

By nature much farm work is seasonal. Mechanization and large-scale production have tended to intensify the seasonal variation by reducing the man power required for putting in and caring for the crop more than it has reduced the amount required for harvesting. The chances for a fairly long period of work for agricultural labor in a single locality have thus been reduced. Many agricultural laborers if they desire reasonably full employment in agriculture must move with the crops, work for many different employers in the course of a year, and perhaps in several different states. If they remain in a single locality and work only the few months or even weeks their services are in demand, unemployment insurance can scarcely meet their needs.

The kind of unemployment in the event of which our existing insurance system gives protection—temporary or short-run economic dislocations and frictions—plays relatively little part in farming. A farmer must make his decisions and commit himself and his resources at planting time, and once he has committed himself, he must follow through on his plans with only limited opportunity for readjustment. Unless the government will pay him for not producing or for growing on some of his land only soil-improving crops not to be marketed, generally he cannot afford to let his land and equipment lie idle. Almost all the forces dictate that he shall use his resources and his labor in production. Unlike the manufacturer, the miner, or the merchant he cannot adjust promptly to changed circumstances by quickly curtailing production and cutting pay roll. Usually, moreover, the number of hired hands on a farm is small and does not greatly exceed the minimum requirements for caring for the crop until it is ready for harvest.

For some types of farming the major opportunity for adjustment to current conditions comes in connection with what the farmer will pay for extra help for harvesting. In some localities the wage rate for extra harvest hands depends largely on current market price for the commodity being harvested. If the price of the commodity does not appear to the farmer to justify the labor costs of harvesting, the result is unemployment or underemployment for the seasonal workers. It is not, however, the kind of unemployment which results in a factory when workers are discharged because the product will not move at a suitable price. It results from failure of seasonal jobs to open, unemployment against which the present American system gives no direct protection.

Differences with respect to capital and management. Salaried workers, wage earners, and no small number of professional men operating on their own account can increase their earnings without much reference to their ability to accumulate capital and manage successfully their own personal financial affairs. For thousands, work at factory or office and management of personal and family finances are completely unrelated. For farmers there is no such separation. Whether or not a farmer can increase his earnings depends in no small measure on his ability to acquire and manage capital; family finances and farm finances are frequently inseparable. The steps to success often run something like this: work for others long enough to acquire a small working capital and some experience and knowledge of farm management; as a tenant demonstrating capacity for independent management and increasing capital, fixed and working; purchasing a farm of his own perhaps heavily mortgaged and borrowing for machinery, stock, equipment, and working capital; gradually accumulating more and more capital of his own so that he is less dependent on borrowing, or perhaps continuing to use a substantial amount of borrowed capital, materially extending his scale of operations, making effective use of his managerial ability and his knowledge of farming.

Significance of differences. From the standpoint of relief and social insurance four features of these differences require emphasis.

1. The salaried or wage worker and many professional workers may not be materially hampered in their advance, if the government compels them to begin to insure for their old age as soon as they begin to earn. The man who aspires to be a farm owner has a real use for his savings; if he is forced by the government to put some of them into old-age insurance, it will increase his difficulty in acquiring his own capital and the extent to which he must borrow from others. If he is a good manager, he can make considerably more handling his own funds than any interest which can be allowed in an old-age insurance system.

2. The risk of the farmer is not so much that he personally will have no work to do. It is more that the various hazards of farming will overtake him before he has acquired a sufficient equity in his farm, stock, and equipment to weather an economic storm. Insurance to enable him to attain economic security relates more to money and property risks than to employment risks.

3. The farmer, especially in the early years, puts his capital largely into land and productive goods. Unless he has substantial resources he must be sparing in the purchase of consumers' goods, particularly of luxury goods. Whether labor-saving devices for use in the home shall be purchased, turns in no small measure on whether the labor thus saved can be effectively used for some other purpose which will advance economic security. The family may live at a relatively low level in the early years to attain security in the later years.

4. Many salary and wage workers and professional workers in urban communities by contrast advance to a higher level of living just as soon as their earnings permit utilization of credit. Housing may be rented or purchased subject to a mortgage with little money down. Durable consumers' goods may be acquired on the installment plan. If such expenditures are properly related to earnings, the family runs no serious risk of losing its property so long as earnings continue. Absence of thrift in the division of earnings and other income between savings and expenditure for consumption frequently has no such immediate relationship to subsequent earning capacity as it does in farming. Many classes in urban industrial areas will therefore place their emphasis on insuring their money earnings.

Differences in methods of payment, risks of unemployment, and the importance of capital and management mean therefore that relief and social security for farmers and agricultural laborers have followed and perhaps must continue to follow a pattern of their own, which may be in many respects radically different from that adopted for urban workers.

In the ensuing description of relief programs for farmers and agricultural laborers, we shall deal first with some that relate to farmers in general and then to those concerned with individuals who were in need of special aid.

GENERAL AID TO FARMERS

In the preceding discussion it was noted that farmers in general being at the same time capitalists, managers, and workers may suffer severely from a change in the relationship between their financial commitments and the profit they receive from the things they produce. These maladjustments may result in no small measure from factors beyond their immediate personal control, notably crop failures and a drop in the price of the things they raise.

Either a crop failure or a severe decline in price may mean, to the farmer who has borrowed, difficulty in paying the interest on his debt and such principal payments as may be due. Thus when changes in the general economic situation brought serious financial troubles to many farmers, a demand arose that the government should take steps to provide ample credit for them at relatively low rates of interest and on terms adapted to their needs. The government was asked to co-operate with the farmers in supplying the capital necessary for long-term loans on land and buildings, intermediate length loans for equipment and stock, and short-term crop loans. These loans, other than being at relatively low rates of interest on favorable terms, were business loans with no substantial element of gift or relief. The borrower was expected to repay in full at the agreed rate of interest, and the special banks making the loans examined into the credit of the applicant much as a private bank or insurance company would have done. The special banks having been developed in behalf of the farmers were expected to help the farmer out in bad years so far as that could be done with safety to the bank; and progress has been made in developing terms and conditions of loans that permit of substantial adjustment to financial conditions.

Experience after World War I has demonstrated, however, that the cause of the financial difficulties of the farmers was deeper than interest rates and the alleged greed of bankers and Wall Street. The basic cause was that the prices that agricultural products would bring in a free competitive market were not high enough to maintain the financial structure that had developed in American agriculture. If this financial structure were to be maintained, steps would have to be taken to raise agricultural prices. If it were not maintained, hundreds of farmers would have to be financially liquidated with loss of their equities and possibly with substantial loss to institutions which had made loans to them. Steps were therefore taken to raise and maintain agricultural prices.

The natural effect of maintaining relatively high prices by government action was to encourage continued production. High-cost producers who might have been forced out by lower prices were able to continue. To some extent the high prices tended to curtail the effective demand, as was notably the case with cotton. It became evident that to make a program of sustained prices effective, the government would have to take steps to control and in this period to curtail production. The government therefore embarked on its Agricultural Adjustment program which paid farmers, on an acreage basis, for not producing certain crops. Later when the Agricultural Adjustment Act was declared unconstitutional, the program was so modified that the farmers were paid for conserving and developing land which might otherwise have been used for raising the crops the price of which the government was endeavoring to sustain.

Still later when the demand of a second world war if left unchecked would have meant a great increase in the price of agricultural commodities, the government put a ceiling on prices and, to encourage the farmers to produce certain commodities, paid subsidies to them from public funds.

It is unquestionably true that this governmental action permitted many farmers to continue who would otherwise have been forced off their farms and into the labor market at a time when jobs were extremely scarce. The farmers thus saved were as a rule those with high costs of production or with such small equities in their farms that they could not survive a severe fall in prices. Among the reasons for high costs of production were poor land, unfavorable climate, units too small to permit of effective use of labor-saving devices, lack of capital for mechanization, lack of managerial ability, and lack of the knowledge, skill, and initiative to adjust to new conditions. The action of the government prevented many marginal farmers from being made submarginal.

The program was far less favorable to farm laborers and some classes of tenant farmers. Obviously less man power is required to cultivate a small acreage than a larger one. As the acreage that may be planted is reduced, the proportion of the work which the farmer can do himself without hired help tends to increase. With the certainty of income increased and with the necessity for hiring help diminished, there may be a greater tendency to purchase mechanical equipment or to hire certain jobs done by persons who own such equipment. Acreage restrictions on big farms unquestionably result in diminishing opportunities for employment of farm labor. It seems entirely safe to conclude that although the program of price maintenance and crop restriction was immediately and directly beneficial to farmers, large and small, who owned their land or had an equity in it, it resulted in some loss of employment to farm laborers and to tenants who had no equity in the land.

One effect of the program deserves mention in this connection. Under the old agricultural system, when a farmer no longer felt able to do the work involved in keeping his farm in full production, he was likely to retire thus making his land available to someone else, as a tenant or a purchaser, often on mortgage. Pressure to give up ownership or management was reduced when acreage to be worked for profit was restricted and when a substantial amount would be paid by the government for land left idle or worked only for its improvement. The government payments increased the value of the land to its owner and lessened the chance for the potential purchaser to acquire it at all or to acquire it at a price which would permit profitable operation without a continuation of the government subsidy inherent in price maintenance and payment for crop restriction. Thus possibilities for persons who sought opportunity to improve themselves were probably somewhat restricted by the program.

Another effect of the program was to keep up the price that urban families and other nonfarm families had to pay for food and other agricultural commodities. The theory was that price maintenance would sustain and possibly increase the purchasing power of the farmers; they would spend their money for the products of other industries; the resulting demand would increase employment and permit the wage earners in these other industries to earn enough so that they could pay the sustained price of the agricultural commodities. The program would lessen the amount of liquidation which would be entailed in readjusting wages and prices to a new level. Thus the program operated to keep food and some other costs from falling as much as they otherwise would, had it not been for government action.

Purchase of surplus commodities. The methods of price maintenance and crop restriction used for staple agricultural products were not adapted for use in connection with some other crops, and they did not solve the problem of disposing of surpluses of the staples that could not be moved at the prices sustained by the government. To aid the farmers, the government therefore embarked upon a program of purchasing certain surpluses that could not be moved without breaking the price and virtually giving them away to persons who were in need and would not or could not buy them at the sustained price.

This program thus had two sides, first protecting the farmers against a fall in price resulting from a surplus that would prevent them from getting at least cost of production, and second enabling persons in need to have the surplus practically without cost to them. Surplus commodities given free to those in need became an important element in relief administration throughout the nation. This aspect of the program is so important from the standpoint of relief that a subsequent chapter will be devoted to it. In the present chapter the program is cited only as one of the instruments used to give effect to the policy of protecting farmers in general through price maintenance.

The programs just outlined were designed to aid practically all farmers engaged in the production of the commodities affected. No question of the need of the farmer, in the narrow relief sense of the word, was raised at all. Rich farmers and poor farmers, large-scale producers and small-scale producers, shared in such advantages as resulted from them. In general they shared in proportion to the involved acreage they owned, or in case of purchase of surplus commodities to the extent that they were marketing the crop, the price of which was being sustained in their marketing area. The big producer profited more in dollars than the little producer because his stake was larger. The government did not discriminate among the individual farmers, nor did it deal with them as individuals further than was necessary for purely administrative purposes.

SPECIAL PROGRAMS TO MEET INDIVIDUAL NEED

We come now to the programs undertaken for farmers, farm laborers, and their families principally because they were in such difficulties that it was believed they could not be extricated without special assistance from government given to them as individuals on a case basis. From an agricultural standpoint they were in need, although not necessarily in the same degree of need as the industrial worker who had lost his job and used up his resources. Perhaps it would be better to refer to these families as being deemed by the government to be in need of rehabilitation. Four special programs require consideration. They are: (1) the tenant purchase program; (2) the rural rehabilitation program of supervised loans and grants; (3) the resettlement program; (4) the camp program for migratory agricultural laborers. We shall give in some detail the historical material which is more or less common to them all, and then take them up in the above order.

History of the special programs. Agriculture in the United States in general, as already noted, had not been in flourishing health since its boom days of World War I. There were two areas where the situation had been particularly bad: the South, especially the deep South, which had depended so completely on cotton as the major crop; and the more westerly of the middle states which had gone into wheat raising on a large scale during World War I despite the uncertainties of adequate rainfall to mature a crop. Increased mechanization, lack of effective demand, and in the western middle states occasionally lack of rain had forced a substantial number of farmers into the submarginal class. In the South the tenant farmers, the share croppers, and the farm laborers were especially hard hit. Both of these regions were predominantly agricultural so that many of the people had as alternatives staying on the land or moving to other sections of the country where they might find opportunities in industry. Although there was some movement out, many remained where they had their homes.

Early in the depression, public attention was focused primarily on urban industrial communities with their millions of unemployed and secondarily upon the related difficulties for agricultural workers. The governmental program for agriculture at the outset was general in nature and not directed toward assistance for individuals.

When in May 1933 the Federal Emergency Relief Administration was authorized, the act made no specific provision for rural relief and rehabilitation. The ensuing year, however, witnessed widespread droughts and crop failures. In June 1934 the Emergency Appropriation Act[3] appropriated 525 million dollars for relief in stricken agricultural areas, to be allocated by the President "to supplement the appropriations heretofore made for emergency purposes and in addition thereto for (1) making loans to farmers for, and/or (2) the purchase, sale, gift, or other disposition of, seed, feed, freight, summer fallowing and similar purposes. . . ." On April 8, 1935 a joint resolution was passed[4] making further appropriations for relief purposes. In it were the following provisions pertinent to this discussion:

. . . this appropriation shall be available for the following classes of projects, . . . (b) rural rehabilitation and relief in stricken agricultural areas.[5]

[3] 48 Stat. 1021, 1056.
[4] 49 Stat. 115.
[5] The same.

Funds made available by this joint resolution may be used, in the discretion of the President, for the purpose of making loans to finance, in whole or in part, the purchase of farm lands and necessary equipment by farmers, farm tenants, croppers, or farm laborers. Such loans shall be made on such terms as the President shall prescribe and shall be repaid in equal annual installments, or in such other manner as the President may determine.[6]

In carrying out the provisions of this joint resolution the President is authorized (within the limits of the appropriation made in section 1) to acquire, by purchase or by the power of eminent domain, any real property or any interest therein, and improve, develop, grant, sell, lease (with or without the privilege of purchasing), or otherwise dispose of any such property or interest therein.[7]

The language just quoted delegated to the President, within the limitations of the appropriation, practically unlimited discretion. Congress said the loans "should be paid in equal annual installments," but immediately added or "in such other manner as the President may determine." Land or rights in land acquired by the government through the exercise of eminent domain and developed and improved through public funds could not only be sold or leased, they could also be "granted" (in every day language given away), or "otherwise" disposed of. Because of subsequent developments and criticisms, attention should be called to the fact that Congress in this early language authorized "leasing (with or *without* the privilege of purchasing)." The act thus authorized practically uncontrolled experimentation in the field of government activities for individual "farmers, farm tenants, croppers or farm laborers" under the broad terms "rural relief and rehabilitation," which were not specifically defined.

When in June 1934 Congress appropriated the 525 million dollars for relief in stricken agricultural areas, the President allocated to the Federal Emergency Relief Administrator about 56 millions "for making grants to States" and 12.5 millions "for the purpose of increasing employment through the purchase of lands in the stricken areas." Funds for making loans for seed, feed, and the like were allocated to the Farm Credit

[6] The same, p. 117.
[7] The same, p. 118.

Administration and for purchase, sale, gift, or other disposition of seed, feed, and livestock to the Secretary of Agriculture.[8]

The Federal Emergency Relief Administration was at that time operating mainly by making grants to the states for relief, and most states had a state emergency relief administration. This procedure was in full accord with the Relief Act of 1933. Under the F.E.R.A. many state relief administrations established under state laws nonprofit state rural rehabilitation corporations for purchasing, selling, and renting land. To these corporations was given part of the money appropriated by Congress to the President for rural rehabilitation work, under corporation charters that provided that the money could be used for this purpose and no other.[9]

The legality of turning large sums of federal money over to state organized corporations to be used for land purchases with title to the land vesting in that corporation was questionable. The Comptroller General informally held that the procedure was without authority in law. In the meantime, the state rehabilitation corporations had bought land and started some projects, and their charters prohibited use of assets except for rehabilitation purposes within the state. A way out of the resulting legal tangle, approved by the Comptroller General, was to turn the land and other property purchased in the state back to F.E.R.A. to be used for rehabilitation purposes, and to deposit the cash assets in trust funds in the United States Treasury to be used exclusively for rural rehabilitation purposes in the state which had turned the federal money back. This device restored federal control and at the same time permitted the state rehabilitation corporations to comply with their charters and with state laws.[10]

This episode in the history has been mentioned here for three

[8] Executive Order 6747, June 23, 1934.

[9] *Farm Security Administration*, Hearings before the Select Committee of the House Committee on Agriculture, Pt. 3, 78 Cong. 1 sess., p. 961. These hearings will subsequently be referred to as Select Committee Hearings.

[10] See letter of July 31, 1935 from the Comptroller General to the Administrator, Resettlement Administration, reprinted in *Report of Select Committee of the House Committee on Agriculture to Investigate the Activities of the Farm Security Administration*, 78 Cong. 2 sess., H. Rept. 1430, p. 64.

reasons: (1) Some of the projects started by the state corporations were ill-conceived and ill-planned, but when they were turned back to the federal government, federal agencies had to administer them and assume responsibility for them; (2) clearing the land, building or repairing the houses, and building the facilities on some of these projects were done by relatively inefficient relief labor with substandard supervision and direction, and as a result costs were excessive in comparison with what they would have been had the work been done by normal public or private enterprise; and (3) federal reports frequently show things purchased by state corporations or from state corporation funds, but the money came almost entirely from the federal Treasury, and the debt created to secure the money was federal debt.

The Resettlement Administration. In April and May 1935 the President, by a series of executive orders, created an independent agency of government, the Resettlement Administration, and transferred to it the land and related activities of the Federal Emergency Relief Administration and the subsistence homestead work of the Interior Department. The functions and duties of the Resettlement Administration, to be performed by the Administrator, Rexford G. Tugwell, were prescribed by the President in the following language:

(a) To administer approved projects involving resettlement of destitute or low-income families from rural and urban areas, including the establishment, maintenance, and operation, in such connection, of communities in rural and suburban areas.

(b) To initiate and administer a program of approved projects with respect to soil erosion, stream pollution, seacoast erosion, reforestation, forestation, and flood control.

(c) To make loans as authorized under the said Emergency Relief Appropriation Act of 1935 to finance, in whole or in part, the purchase of farm lands and necessary equipment by farmers, farm tenants, croppers, or farm laborers.

. . . .

To the extent necessary to carry out the provisions of this Executive Order the Administrator is authorized to acquire, by purchase or by the power of eminent domain, any real property or any interest therein and improve, develop, grant, sell, lease (with or without the privilege of purchasing), or otherwise dispose of any such property or interest therein.[11]

The Resettlement Administration functioned as an independent agency of the government from April 30, 1935 to December 31, 1936. On that date the President transferred all the powers, functions, and duties of the agency to the Secretary of Agriculture. For some months thereafter the title "Resettlement Administration" was retained, although the Secretary of Agriculture had made some redistribution of functions among the agencies of the department. Later he changed the name to the Farm Security Administration.

The Farm Security Administration. The Department of Agriculture thus fell heir to projects initiated by three predecessor agencies, the Subsistence Homestead Division of the Interior Department, the Federal Emergency Relief Administration, and the Resettlement Administration. It likewise fell heir to an army of employees, many of them veterans of the earlier agencies. With respect to these employees a quotation from the act of May 12, 1933[12] establishing F.E.R.A. is pertinent:

Sec. 3 (b). The Administrator may appoint and fix the compensation of such experts and their appointment may be made and compensation fixed without regard to the civil service laws, or the Classification Act of 1923, as amended, and the Administrator may, in the same manner, appoint and fix the compensation of such other officers and employees as are necessary to carry out the provisions of this Act, ...

The passage of the Bankhead-Jones Act. Prior to July 22, 1937 the Farm Security Administration had no statutory organic act. Its legal authority consisted of sections in various general emergency acts and appropriation acts, broad in terms and made reasonably specific only through executive orders of the President. On July 22, 1937, however, an act of Congress was approved officially cited as "The Bankhead-Jones Farm Tenant Act."[13] Its long title was, "To create the Farmers' Home Corporation, to promote more secure occupancy of farms and

[11] Executive Order 7027, Apr. 30, 1935.
[12] 48 Stat. 56.
[13] 50 Stat. 522.

farm homes, to correct the economic instability resulting from
some present forms of farm tenancy, and for other purposes."

Some persons believed that this substantive act, passed as
permanent legislation, created a new legal framework within
the limitations of which the Farm Security Administration was
henceforth to function. A difference of opinion developed, however, between the administrators on the one hand and members
of Congress and private supporters of the act on the other with
respect to its effect and force. Since the present book is concerned both with substantive law and administration, it seems
desirable to attempt a brief description of this conflict.

The issues arose mainly with respect to rehabilitation loans
and resettlement projects. So far as the farm tenant provisions
were concerned, the two groups were not in substantial disagreement and the Farm Security Administration carried on that
part of its work in accordance with "Title I, Farm Tenant Provisions" of the new Bankhead-Jones Act.

"Title II, Rehabilitation Loans" set forth the new law which
was expected to govern with respect to (1) who was entitled
to a loan and (2) the conditions upon which a loan was to be
made.

"Title IV, General Provisions" included, among other things,
provisions creating the Farmers' Home Corporation and what
was regarded by its supporters as a prohibition of the further
development of resettlement projects. The prohibitive clause,
with the references to executive orders and laws omitted, reads:

Sec. 43. The Secretary is authorized to continue to perform such of
the functions . . . as shall be necessary only for the completion and
administration of these resettlement projects, rural rehabilitation
projects for resettlement purposes, and land development and land
utilization projects, for which funds have been allotted by the President, and the balances of funds available to the Secretary for said
purposes which are unexpended on June 30, 1937, are authorized to
be appropriated to carry out said purposes: . . .[14]

From the point of view of the framers of the act and its supporters, this clause precluded the development of new resettle-

[14] 50 Stat. 530.

ment and allied projects and permitted the Secretary to continue only those for which the President had already allotted funds. By inference it prohibited further activities in this field and restricted the rehabilitation loans.

From the point of view of the Farm Security Administration, Title II of the Farm Security Act was merely an interim act[15] and was not given effect nor was the Farmers' Home Corporation created. The reason was technical. The act had authorized a re-appropriation of existing unexpended balances and further allocation by the President of relief funds appropriated for years prior to July 1, 1939, but it contained no authorization for new direct appropriations by Congress. In the absence of an authorization for new direct appropriations, any attempt by the Appropriations Committee of the House to make direct appropriations would have been subject to a point of order in the House. Curiously, according to the testimony of officers of the Farm Security Administration, the Bureau of the Budget itself in effect made that point of order, when the Administration submitted an estimate for an appropriation to give effect to Title II and no recommendation for one was submitted to Congress.[16]

Thus despite Title II of the Bankhead-Jones Act, further funds for rehabilitation were made available under relief appropriations that passed through the Bureau of the Budget. The money so obtained was spent by the Farm Security Administration under the relief appropriations and the executive orders, without reference to the limitations prescribed in the Bankhead-Jones Act, which had gone through the two houses of Congress as substantive legislation.

The administrative officials of the Department had not sought an advance opinion from the Comptroller General but proceeded on the basis of the ruling by the Solicitor of the Department and later by the Attorney General.[17] When some of the resulting accounts came through for final settlement, the Comptroller General took the position that Title II of the

---

[15] Select Committee Hearings, Pt. 1, p. 19.
[16] Testimony of Administrator C. B. Baldwin, the same.
[17] The same, p. 17.

Bankhead-Jones Act and some other parts of the act governed and restricted the action of the administrative officers.

The Bankhead-Jones Act had been supported by the National Farm Bureau and the Grange, and representatives of these organizations had been highly critical of parts of the program of the Farm Security Administration.[18] The situation naturally resulted in a thorough congressional investigation.

Removal of subsistence homestead projects from F.S.A. One other matter in this summary account of the historical background must be mentioned. The Department of Agriculture, as has been noted, fell heir to some projects that had been designed for persons not engaged in agriculture. By Executive Order 9070, dated February 24, 1942, the President consolidated the housing agencies and functions of the government into the National Housing Agency and took from the Farm Security Administration "all functions, powers, and duties . . . relating to such housing projects as such Administration determines are for families not deriving their principal income from operating or working upon a farm." Thus the Farm Security Administration was relieved of responsibility for projects which represented a capital investment of some 65 millions, produced in 1942 a gross income of $1,552,000, and in that year had an operating obligation of $1,046,000 and a management obligation of $205,000, with no allowance for either interest or depreciation.[19]

This general history was common to the four special programs now to be discussed in some detail. The program to help selected tenants become farm owners will be taken up first. It is placed first not because it was the most important from the standpoint of social security and relief, or because it was the major activity of the Farm Security Administration; but because it is the simplest and the least controversial, and in a sense stands by itself. The tenant purchase program can there-

[18] See the testimony before the Select Committee by Mr. Albert S. Goss, Master of the National Grange, Hearings, Pt. 1, pp. 759–79 and Mr. Edward A. O'Neal, President of the American Farm Bureau Federation, pp. 797–869.

[19] For a list of these projects and a statement of the expenditures connected with them see the Select Committee Hearings, Pt. 3, pp. 1118–19.

fore be presented fairly briefly, clearing the way for the discussion of the other programs which so far as the present book is concerned are the more significant and illuminating.

THE TENANT PURCHASE PROGRAM

The farm tenant purchase program is, as pointed out in the preceding historical section, now conducted under Title I of the Bankhead-Jones Farm Tenant Act. To it one would scarcely apply the term experiment. Its aims and objectives were within the American agricultural tradition, and the methods used were much like those of established agencies lending money for farm purchases. One major issue of policy was involved in its adoption; once that issue of policy was decided, the rest called mainly for good administration in accordance with well-recognized principles and practices. In passing Title I of the Bankhead-Jones Act, Congress laid down the policy and broadly described the practices. It delegated little basic policy-determining power to the administrator.

The major issue of policy was whether the national government should assume the risks involved in lending applicants who desired to become farm owners but lacked the necessary capital a far larger percentage of cost than any ordinary financial institution could do with safety. To make such a policy work, the interest rate would have to be low and contain no charge for the heavy risk element, and the lender might have to forego payments, both interest and curtailment of principal, if a borrower encountered bad times.

In favor of such a policy were three main arguments:

1. The widely accepted view that independent farm owners, operating family size farms, constitute the backbone of a sound democracy in an agricultural economy.

2. The depression in agriculture had set back many farmers who had taken the first steps toward farm ownership and reduced them again to the status of tenants or agricultural laborers.

3. In the absence of governmental action, existing trends would substitute large-scale mechanized agriculture for the family size farm independently owned.

Against the policy were four major arguments:

1. The government would be in competition with the established agencies making loans to farmers; and many of these agencies were co-operative in nature and had been fostered by the government.

2. The recipients of the special loans and the highly favorable terms would have a competitive advantage over others who were never eligible for them or no longer eligible.

3. The plan might tend to increase agricultural production and the numbers engaged in agriculture, whereas in the thirties the difficulties with agriculture appeared to arise largely from overproduction with respect to available markets and from too much man power on farms.

4. The movement toward large-scale mechanized agriculture results from its efficiency in reducing cost of production, which means profits for the growers even when prices to consumers are low.

The decisions on these matters of policy made by Congress are clearly and simply set forth in Title I of the Bankhead-Jones Act. The essential features of Title I may be summarized as follows:

Eligibility. "Only farm tenants, farm laborers, sharecroppers, and other individuals who obtain, or who recently obtained, the major portion of their income from farming operations shall be eligible to receive the benefits of this title. In making available the benefits of this title, the Secretary shall give preference to persons who are married, or who have dependent families, or, wherever practicable, to persons who are able to make an initial down payment, or who are owners of livestock and farm implements necessary successfully to carry on farming operations. No person shall be eligible who is not a citizen of the United States."[20]

Size of farm. "No loan shall be made for the acquisition of any farm unless it is of such size as the Secretary determines to be sufficient to constitute an efficient farm-management unit and to enable a diligent farm family to carry on successful

[20] 50 Stat. 522, Sec. 1(b).

farming of a type which the Secretary deems can be successfully carried on in the locality in which the farm is situated."[21]

Local determinations. The act provides for initial action on applications for loans by a county committee. The committee considers both the eligibility of the applicant and the desirability of the farm to be purchased. The committee also takes account of "character, ability, and experience" of the applicant and must report favorably on the applicant and the farm, and must give its appraisal of the value of the farm.

Amount and terms of the loan. The amount of the loan cannot exceed the value as appraised by the county committee. Within that maximum limit it provides for acquisition and necessary repairs and improvements. The term of the loan must not exceed 40 years. Interest is at 3 per cent on the unpaid balance. Repayment is in accordance with amortization schedules prescribed by the Secretary of Agriculture.

The loan must provide that the borrower shall pay taxes and assessments on the farm to the proper taxing authorities and pay for insurance on farm buildings.

Avoidance of production expansion. "In carrying out this title, the Secretary shall give due consideration to the desirability of avoiding the expansion of production for market of basic commodities where such expansion would defeat the policy of Congress as set forth in Section 7 (a) (5) of the Soil Conservation and Domestic Allotment Act, as amended, and shall, so far as practicable, assist beneficiaries of the program under this title to become established upon lands now in cultivation."[22]

A distinctive feature of the hearings before the Select Committee was the general approval of the tenant purchase program as administered under the congressional act. Whatever the witnesses hostile to F.S.A. said with respect to other programs, they commended this one. The county committees were a feature of the program, the members brought to bear their knowledge of local land and land values, of farming under local conditions, and of individuals and families in the com-

[21] 50 Stat. 523, Sec. 1(c).
[22] 50 Stat. 524, Sec. 5.

munity. In some cases the committee members went at the problems as if they were buying the farms for themselves. One gets the impression that their experience led them to discourage borrowers from overborrowing for equipment and comforts that the farm could not support until the purchaser had made substantial payments on his obligations.

Another feature of the act and its administration was that the borrowers were not as a rule set off in a class by themselves. The method used is sometimes called "infiltration," which means the borrowers' farms are scattered here and there throughout the county as land is available and are not concentrated in big projects. In this connection special attention should be called to section 3 (b) (5) of the law, "the borrower shall pay taxes and assessments on the farm to the proper taxing authorities, and insure and pay for insurance on farm buildings." The borrowers do not become wards of the government, but they are regular members of the local community bearing in full the responsibility to pay taxes and assessments.

The use of amortization schedules that take into consideration the agricultural conditions each year appears to be a valuable feature of the system. In bad years the amount of curtailment of principal required is automatically reduced; in good years it is automatically raised. The long maximum possible life of the loan, 40 years, permits of relatively low annual curtailments, lower than a borrower should ordinarily make in his efforts to get ahead. It is therefore highly desirable that in good years he should make heavy payments of principal as insurance against possible bad years.

On June 30, 1943 the cumulative amount of approved loans was over 191 millions, of which over 14 millions had been repaid, 10.3 millions on matured obligations and 4.62 millions as prepayments.[23]

The statement has been made that the demand for this type of loan exceeds the amount which the national government has made available for the purpose. This situation has led to the

---

[23] The detailed statistics of this program are not included in the present book as they are not of significance in this study.

suggestion that ordinary financial institutions might well carry so much of the loans as are safe investments of private investing agencies, and that the government supply the balance itself or insure private financial institutions in so doing, following the pattern of the Federal Housing Administration.[24]

This review of the tenant purchase program suggests that it is designed primarily to help at least reasonably competent persons to get established as farm owners, rather than to extend relief to those who are submarginal and in great need. We come now to the programs concerned with the more difficult cases.

REHABILITATION LOANS AND GRANTS

The rural rehabilitation program of supervised loans and grants has been the major feature of the work of the Farm Security Administration. In its report to the Select Committee, it presented the following over-all statistics.[25] It placed the number of farm families to which loans have been made at over 950,000 and the number receiving assistance in planning and carrying out their farm and home operations at about 425,000. Over 200,000 had repaid their loans in full. Some 350,000 families to whom loans have been made are not in receipt of supervisory assistance, but the Administration has the duty of collecting from them on behalf of the government if they have income from which the loans and the interest due can be paid. Some have left the farms since the loans were made and are now engaged in other activities.

To give a rough idea of the financial magnitude of this loan program, it may be noted that the aggregate of the loans made in the fiscal years from 1936 to 1943 inclusive was over 778 million dollars and at the end of the fiscal year 1943 the loans outstanding were over 400 millions.[26] The aggregate of non-repayable grants made under the program up to June 30, 1943 is reported as over 152 millions.

The program had its origin, as previously noted, in the relief work financed by the national government beginning in 1933,

[24] Select Committee Hearings, Pt. 2, p. 903.
[25] The same, Pt. 3, p. 982.
[26] The same, p. 985.

but the problem was by no means the result exclusively of the general depression. Part of it was chronic, part of it resulted from the severe drought of 1934 which affected the Great Plains, the Corn Belt, and certain areas of the South. The administrators had in fact to deal with many different kinds of cases which might roughly be grouped in four major categories, although the lines between them cannot be sharply drawn: (1) families which were normally able through their own efforts to make a living on the farms they had, at least up to a reasonable minimum of subsistence, and whose difficulties were mainly attributable to either the general depression, the drought, or the two in combination; (2) families which even in reasonably good times could not make a satisfactory living because of physical or mental deficiencies, habits, character, or managerial ability; (3) families whose difficulties, more or less chronic, resulted basically from a lack of the knowledge, skills, and point of view necessary to enable them to modify or abandon a fixed pattern or activity and adopt a new or modified one that would enable them to get along by their own efforts; and (4) families whose difficulties, again more or less chronic, arose from poor land or poor equipment or a combination of the two.

Outright relief, through grants, in order to prevent want was at least for a time essential for all these families, regardless of the class to which they might be assignable. That fact was fairly obvious. Equally obvious was the fact that relief was not necessary because of unemployment in the urban sense. The necessity for giving relief would not, for thousands of them, be terminated by getting a job. In an urban sense the workers already had work to do; they needed facilities with which to work, and in some cases education, direction, and supervision to make that work effective, and in other cases assistance in correcting or relieving impairments due to physical defects. The program therefore called for:

1. Relief grants made at the outset to carry the family along until it was again on its own feet; and in some cases renewed from time to time thereafter in event of illness or death in the

family, crop failures or human failures where the workers had not succeeded in mastering the new ways or displayed the interest, ingenuity, or "stick-to-itiveness" necessary for even partial success.

2. Loans to obtain necessary equipment, seed, fertilizer.

3. Adjustment of debts due for taxes and prior loans on land, equipment, or crops to prevent foreclosures, evictions, or seizure of necessary equipment and personal property.

4. In some cases, relocation on land that offered an opportunity for a passable measure of success.

5. In many cases a very considerable measure of education, assistance in planning, and at least general direction if not immediate close supervision.

The rural rehabilitation loans and grants were thus made not only to relieve immediate want but to re-establish or establish families in successful agricultural production. This objective raised major issues of two types, which should be briefly presented.

1. Agricultural production in the United States was in excess of effective demand, and the government was spending public funds to curtail it and to dispose of surpluses. Under this new special program, it was spending public funds not only to restore the productivity of farmers who had been temporarily knocked out by the drought but to raise the level of productivity of others, many of whom had never been really successful producers. By these subsidies it was attempting to prevent that liquidation of the less successful which in the absence of government interference comes from improved and cheaper methods of meeting the effective demand.

2. The farm families thus subsidized by the government were competitors or potential competitors of unsubsidized producers. Although attention is frequently directed toward the competition between the large, highly mechanized, and efficient farms and the marginal or submarginal small or family sized farms, it must be remembered that many operators of small or moderate sized farms were not eligible for rehabilitation loans and

grants. This competition will be considered under the headings of eligibility for loans and grants, the necessity for repayment, and interest.

Eligibility. In general a farmer was not eligible for a rehabilitation loan if his position was such that he could secure credit from established financial institutions. As has been previously noted, the government through its farm credit policies had furthered the establishment of a co-operative financial system for making loans to farmers at favorable rates of interest and upon reasonable terms. If the farmer could secure credit in that way he was ineligible for a rehabilitation loan. If a grant to offset his losses as the result of the drought would so far restore his financial position that his credit would be satisfactory, he might be eligible for the grant but not eligible for a rehabilitation loan. As a matter of fact, in the drought areas a substantial number who got temporary relief through grants were not eligible for rehabilitation loans.

The borrower from an established agricultural credit agency operating on a business basis must comply with its requirements. Its officers and directors must preserve its solvency. They cannot make initial loans or renew old ones unless the prospects are that over a reasonable period the borrower will be able to pay principal and interest in full. They are extremely likely, moreover, to refuse to make a loan if they believe the borrower is getting over his depth with respect to either business expenditures and investments or expenditures for consumers' goods that do not enhance capacity to pay.

The administrators of rural rehabilitation loans operated under no such restrictions. In the first place they were lending government money, and the government bore all the risks. Unless they violated the rules under which they were operating, they made no initial loans except to persons whose credit was already too poor to warrant a commercial loan. Under such circumstances they could scarcely be as rigid with respect to repayments, renewals, and supplemental loans as would the officers of financial institutions responsible for preserving solvency. They were spending or investing government money to rehabilitate a family. The evidence suggests that in a substantial number of cases the borrowing permitted for equipment and for consumers' goods that did not materially add to capacity to pay was greater than a thrifty farmer would have approved.[27] Naturally such a business would entail substantial losses to the government.

Interest. The interest rate on rehabilitation loans presents some curious anomalies. The *United States Manual* for the winter of 1943-44 (p. 357) says: "They [the rehabilitation loans] usually are repayable in 5 years at an interest rate of 5 per cent." Had the provisions of the Bankhead-Jones Act with respect to rehabilitation loans been followed, the rate of interest on these loans could not have been at a rate in excess of 3 per cent per annum.[28] Apparently administrative officers vested with discretionary authority did not want it to appear that the interest on rehabilitation loans was lower than the prevailing rates for normal agricultural loans.[29]

The Farm Security Administration, as a matter of fact, never collected anything like 5 per cent on its outstanding loans. According to calculations made by us on the basis of data submitted to the Special Committee of the House,[30] the interest actually collected was less than 1 per cent for each of the years from 1936 to 1939 inclusive. In 1940 it rose to 2.69 and increased annually thereafter to 3.4 in 1943. The average rate for the entire period according to our computations was approximately 2.5.

With respect to interest not paid when due, the F.S.A. did not follow the common commercial practice of adding the unpaid interest to the principal for future calculations of interest. Thus if a borrower failed to pay $20 interest due in 1937, he could satisfy that part of his debt by a payment of $20 at any

---

[27] See Report of Select Committee, p. 9.
[28] 50 Stat. 525.
[29] For testimony with respect to the interest rate see Select Committee Hearings, Pt. 1, pp. 52-54.
[30] The same, Pt. 3, p. 985.

time. Since the average rehabilitation loans were relatively small, $412 for original loans and $202 for supplemental loans,[31] the rule of no interest on interest was not a matter of great financial consequence in this program. It was, however, of great importance in the resettlement program as will be discussed later.

Repayment. The administrators of the rehabilitation loans had authority to make grants, which did not have to be repaid, to persons who were indebted to the government for rehabilitation loans. Such a situation perhaps naturally led to the charge that some borrowers paid part of their debt to the government with money given to them by the government. Administrators denied before the committee that money was granted to enable borrowers to repay, but grants were made for other purposes to borrowers. It is a commonplace in family finance, however, that a gift to meet one pressing family need increases the family resources and thus the amount of money available for other purposes. It is therefore inescapable that the rehabilitation borrowers are on an entirely different basis from that of the independent farmer who receives no personal and individual subsidy.

The status of the rehabilitation loans as of February 28, 1943 is shown in the table on page 301, which distinguishes the loans made from the state corporation trust funds from the generally later loans made from emergency relief and reconstruction finance funds. It also shows separately the loans made to individuals and those made to co-operative associations.[32]

Loans to individuals made from Emergency Relief or Reconstruction Finance Corporation funds have the best record. As of February 28, 1943 the matured principal of these loans was roughly 377 million dollars of which a little less than 325 millions or 86 per cent had been repaid. The delinquent indebtedness for principal was on that date 52.6 millions. Delinquent indebtedness, it will be noted, exceeded the total interest payment of 45.3 millions by some 7.3 millions.

[31] The same, p. 988.
[32] For the figures by states see the same, pp. 995–97.

Rural Rehabilitation Loans as of February 28, 1943
(Figures except percentages, in thousands)

Item	From Emergency Relief and Reconstruction Finance Funds		From State Corporation Trust Funds		
			To Individuals		
	To Individuals	To Associations[a]	All States[b]	States with Complete Data[c]	To Associations[d]
Loan advances............	$684,185	$35,657	$59,598	$55,199	$423
Loans outstanding..........	331,239	34,398	26,882	24,633	299
Matured principal..........	377,264	1,444	—	42,946	163
Repayments on matured principal.................	324,604	1,067	31,756	29,623	124
Prepayments on unmatured principal...............	28,342	191	942	942	1
Interest payments..........	45,270	902	4,557	4,557	23
Ratio of repayments to matured principal:					
Excluding prepayments.....	*86.0*	*73.9*	*—*	*69.0*	*75.8*
Including prepayments......	*93.6*	*87.2*	*—*	*71.2*	*76.5*

[a] No loans to associations in Connecticut, Delaware, Kentucky, Massachusetts, Rhode Island, Vermont, and Hawaii.

[b] No loans to individuals in Connecticut, Delaware, Maryland, Massachusetts, and Rhode Island.

[c] Exclusive of Kentucky, North Carolina, Tennessee, Virginia, and West Virginia, for which figures for maturity and interest payments are not available. See also note (b).

[d] No loans to associations except in Michigan, Minnesota, Mississippi, New Jersey, New Mexico, North Dakota, Ohio, and Wisconsin.

Delinquent indebtedness must be divided into two classes:

1. Where the loan has not been liquidated by foreclosure, and the government still has some security for the loan.

2. Where the security for the loan has been seized and sold, and the proceeds of the sale applied to payment of principal. In rehabilitation loans the sales frequently did not liquidate the debt but left the borrower owing the government an entirely unsecured debt. As of December 31, 1942, F.S.A. showed 26.6 millions due the government from borrowers whose chattels and crops had been sold to satisfy the loan. Proceeds of the sales are of course credited on the books as repayment of matured loans.[33]

With respect to indebtedness remaining after foreclosure the F.S.A. report says:"Even though there is no mortgage security

[33] The same, Pt. 3, p. 994.

behind these liquidated balances, part of the money will be collected."[34] Some thousands of former F.S.A. borrowers thus owed the government in the aggregate about 26.2 millions for a closed chapter. Such debts are a disturbing factor in any benevolent loan program. They represent in the main losses to the government, but more important they may represent failure to individuals and families. Persons who make loans to individuals, particularly individuals with limited financial experience, bear a heavy responsibility. At the time loans are made, it is easy to load the borrower up with a debt he cannot carry unless he is successful and lucky. If independence and self-support are the aim, loans should be kept well within capacity to pay. At times such a rule leads to refusal to make any loan and necessitates meeting the immediate needs of the family through relief in some form until work for wages becomes available.

In the table on page 301 the loans to individuals from state corporation trust funds show the poorest record. If the five states for which data were incomplete are omitted, the matured principal was about 43 million dollars and repayments were about 30 millions, leaving 13 millions or about 31 per cent delinquent. In this connection the following statement from the report of the F.S.A. is pertinent:

When the 43 State rural rehabilitation corporations were transferred in trust to the Resettlement Administration, there was a great variety of commitments which had been made by the corporations, as well as many accounts which were of dubious validity. Many of the corporations had made advances for subsistence, and had established such advances on their records as loans, although it was recognized that cash repayments would not be required of the recipients. In a number of States, funds were advanced with the understanding that repayments could be made in the form of cash, produce, or work. Examination revealed that many clients had not received credit for work performed.

Corrections, therefore, have been necessary in the records of the Corporation trust funds to correctly classify the advances and to give clients credit for work performed. As of June 30, 1942, the total ad-

34 The same, p. 994.

justments effected, including reduction of the book value of the outstanding indebtedness of some accounts, amounted to $10,168,166. This amount, however, is subject to further adjustment since the reduction in book value is restored for those accounts where subsequent collection becomes possible.

The amount of loans, maturities, and collections shown in the accompanying tables are after the adjustments indicated above had been made up to February 28, 1943.[35]

This quotation makes it clear that the books have been "adjusted" to the extent of about 10 millions. Adding 10 millions to the 59.5 million dollar loan advances shown in the table would give nearly 70 millions, which indicates that the sum written off by adjustment was about 14 per cent of the total.

Loans and grants by states. On page 304 we are including a table which shows for individual states geographically arranged the amount of (1) rehabilitation loans and (2) rehabilitation grants cumulative to June 30, 1943, together with the per cent distribution by states and the per capita figures based on total farm population at the census of 1940.

It is apparent that high per capita loans were made in the western states which frequently suffer from inadequate rainfall. The states which had loans of $65 or more per capita of farm population were: Idaho $67.54, South Dakota $79.12, Utah $79.25, Nevada $83.94, Colorado $92.18, Montana $110.43, and Wyoming $213.14. Some of these states likewise stood high in per capita grants although high grants and high loans did not necessarily go together. California and Arizona both had comparatively high payments for grants per capita but not comparatively high ones for loans.

States with per capita loans of $25 but less than $65 were: Mississippi $25.70, Georgia $25.71, Missouri $25.72, Arizona $28.56, Alabama $29.65, New Hampshire $31.37, Texas $31.72, Louisiana $32.21, Arkansas $34.17, Oregon $35.28, Washington $35.78, Kansas $39.27, Florida $40.21, New Mexico $40.56, Oklahoma $41.70, Nebraska $45.12, North Dakota

[35] The same, p. 994.

RURAL REHABILITATION LOANS AND GRANTS BY STATES

State	Farm Population 1940 (In thousands)[a]	Rural Rehabilitation Loans Cumulative as of June 30, 1943			Rural Rehabilitation Grants Cumulative as of June 30, 1943		
		Amount (In thousands)[b]	Per Cent Distributed	Per capita of Farm Population 1940	Amount (In thousands)[c]	Per Cent Distributed	Per capita of Farm Population 1940
UNITED STATES	30,547[d]	$773,851[d]	100.00	$25.33	$151,931[d]	100.00	$4.97
NORTHEAST	3,235	50,707	6.55	15.67	2,489	1.64	.77
New England	622	18,403	2.38	29.59	466	.31	.75
Maine	176	11,116	1.44	63.16	239	.16	1.36
New Hampshire	70	2,196	.28	31.37	66	.04	.94
Vermont	107	2,405	.31	22.48	88	.06	.82
Massachusetts	147	1,329	.17	9.04	37	.02	.25
Rhode Island	17	355	.05	20.88	23	.02	1.35
Connecticut	105	1,002	.13	9.54	13	.01	.12
Middle Atlantic	1,788	21,231	2.74	11.87	1,141	.75	.64
New York	730	10,228	1.32	14.01	533	.35	.73
New Jersey	143	2,680	.35	18.74	136	.09	.95
Pennsylvania	915	8,323	1.07	9.10	472	.31	.52
Other	825	11,073	1.43	13.42	882	.58	1.07
Delaware	46	357	.05	7.76	23	.02	.50
Maryland	246	2,308	.30	9.38	225	.15	.91
West Virginia	533	8,408	1.08	15.77	634	.41	1.19
SOUTHEAST	12,486	262,517	33.92	21.02	26,833	17.66	2.15
Virginia	986	8,660	1.12	8.78	453	.30	.46
North Carolina	1,660	24,894	3.22	15.00	1,675	1.10	1.01
South Carolina	917	18,666	2.41	20.36	2,712	1.79	2.96
Georgia	1,368	35,165	4.54	25.71	3,950	2.60	2.89
Florida	305	12,263	1.58	40.21	1,795	1.18	5.89
Kentucky	1,261	11,215	1.45	8.89	2,414	1.59	1.91
Tennessee	1,276	10,251	1.32	8.03	635	.42	.50
Alabama	1,343	39,819	5.15	29.65	6,267	4.12	4.67
Mississippi	1,403	36,051	4.66	25.70	3,043	2.00	2.17
Louisiana	854	27,504	3.55	32.21	1,409	.93	1.65
Arkansas	1,113	38,029	4.92	34.17	2,480	1.63	2.23
MIDDLE STATES	7,609	140,273	18.13	18.44	18,762	12.35	2.47
Ohio	1,089	14,391	1.86	13.21	988	.65	.91
Indiana	816	13,021	1.68	15.96	375	.25	.46
Illinois	979	15,271	1.98	15.60	1,555	1.02	1.59
Michigan	871	13,515	1.75	15.52	986	.65	1.13
Wisconsin	883	17,200	2.22	19.48	4,381	2.88	4.96
Minnesota	915	20,989	2.71	22.94	3,064	2.02	3.35
Iowa	931	16,947	2.19	18.20	828	.55	.89
Missouri	1,125	28,939	3.74	25.72	6,585	4.33	5.85
NORTHWEST	2,347	152,864	19.75	65.13	71,218	46.87	30.34
North Dakota	328	15,630	2.02	47.65	20,898	13.75	63.71
South Dakota	307	24,291	3.14	79.12	23,175	15.25	75.49
Kansas	607	23,834	3.08	39.27	7,629	5.02	12.57
Nebraska	498	22,472	2.90	45.12	8,509	5.60	17.09
Colorado	253	23,322	3.01	92.18	2,940	1.94	11.62
Utah	105	8,321	1.08	79.25	721	.47	6.87
Montana	176	19,435	2.51	110.43	6,146	4.05	34.92
Wyoming	73	15,559	2.01	213.14	1,200	.79	16.44
SOUTHWEST	3,382	117,777	15.22	34.82	16,393	10.79	4.85
Oklahoma	930	38,783	5.01	41.70	5,926	3.90	6.37
Texas	2,160	68,519	8.86	31.72	5,828	3.84	2.70
New Mexico	178	7,219	.93	40.56	2,114	1.39	11.88
Arizona	114	3,256	.42	28.56	2,525	1.66	22.15
PACIFIC NORTHWEST	802	35,013	4.53	43.66	3,627	2.39	4.52
Idaho	203	13,710	1.77	67.54	929	.61	4.58
Oregon	259	9,138	1.18	35.28	1,156	.76	4.46
Washington	340	12,165	1.58	35.78	1,542	1.02	4.54
PACIFIC SOUTHWEST	686	14,700	1.90	21.43	12,609	8.30	18.38
California	670	13,357	1.73	19.94	12,571	8.27	18.76
Nevada	16	1,343	.17	83.94	38	.03	2.38

[a] Farm Security Administration, *Hearings before the Select Committee of the House Committee on Agriculture*, Pt. 3, 78 Cong. 1 sess., pp. 1020–21.
[b] The same, pp. 986–87.
[c] The same, p. 990.
[d] Obtained by addition of items for individual states.

$47.65, and Maine $63.16. Among these will be recognized some of the western states, not included in the list with very high per capita rates, which have inadequate rainfall in some parts and several of the cotton states. Washington and Oregon are probably in this list because the depression seriously affected the marketing of their fruit crops. Maine and New Hampshire represent states in which many farms have been abandoned in the past because the land is submarginal so far as effective production under modern conditions is concerned.

Farm debt settlements. Incurring debt for making a crop and possibly for family maintenance between one harvest and the next is a common feature in farming. Rural rehabilitation therefore frequently necessitated working out arrangements whereby the farmers could get out from under a heavy burden of accumulated debt. The Farm Security Administration undertook the task of farm debt settlement or adjustment not only for farmers who were applicants for its loans or grants but also for other farmers in the areas where it worked. It rendered a general service of debt settlement.

The usual form of organization for debt settlement was to set up a paid local committee of three members representing creditors and debtors. These local committees were organized, trained, and supervised by regular employees of the F.S.A. The cost for the salaries of the committee members was, however, an insignificant item in total expenditures for farm debt adjustment services. In 1942, for example, expenditures for the committee members were $153,759, as compared with $1,436,487 for salaries paid F.S.A. regular employees for debt adjustment work. Traveling expenses paid for the regular employees were more than twice the amount paid to the local committees.[36] The total cost of the service in 1942 was $1,950,655, which was the highest in the four-year period from 1939 to 1942 inclusive.

The figures for the number of cases handled and the amount of debt adjustment do not show any such tendency to increase in successive years. The highest number of cases involving individuals reported by F.S.A. was 35,303 in 1941. The next high-

[36] The same, p. 999.

est number was 32,871 in 1936. The highest amount of debt involved prior to adjustment was 98.8 million dollars in 1936, reduced to 75 millions, representing a debt reduction of 23.8 millions. In 1937, the next highest year, the debt involved was 95.8 millions adjusted to 70.7 millions, a reduction of 25.1 millions. In 1942, when administrative costs exceeded 1.9 millions, the debt involved was 31.3 millions, adjusted to 26.8 millions, a reduction of 4.5 millions. Thus in 1942 administrative costs were over 40 per cent of the amount saved debtors through the adjustments.

In explanation of the tendency of administrative costs to rise while the amount of debt involved and the debt reduction tended to diminish F.S.A. officials pointed out that the paid committees and the F.S.A. employees paid to instruct and supervise them were devoting their energies to improving the condition of tenancy in the interest of the tenants and to securing increased agricultural production. A question arises as to whether such activities belong in a relief and rural rehabilitation program conducted exclusively by the national government, or whether they should not be in the highly developed federal-state-county co-operative program.

Farm co-operatives. Funds appropriated for rural rehabilitation were used to some extent for the development of co-operatives. Since some of these ventures have been subjected to severe criticism, it seems wise to quote at length from the report of F.S.A. to the House Committee:

The present policies and practices of the Farm Security Administration respecting the financing of cooperatives are quite different from those which prevailed in the Resettlement Administration and during the first year or two of the life of the Farm Security Administration. In those earlier years, cooperatives were viewed chiefly as vehicles for project development, and as agencies through which rather large groups of farmers could be provided with services or facilities of a highly commercial nature. Loans were sometimes made to newly organized associations, whose members had insufficient experience in cooperative activity, and who were lacking in a real understanding of membership responsibilities.

In contrast to these early lending activities the present cooperative program is primarily one of the tools used in increasing the productive capacities and incomes of individual rehabilitation borrowers. It is based on the hard facts of the small farmer's situation and adapted to his needs. Many small farmers cannot afford to own as individuals modern heavy machinery or purebred sires; or are unable to buy high quality seed and similar supplies in small lots at reasonable prices. In many poorer areas, local marketing facilities are either not available or are of a very inadequate nature especially for some of the much needed war crops. It is to meet situations of this general nature that some sort of group activity is necessary on the part of low-income farmers. The Farm Security Administration cooperative program is aimed primarily at financing this type of activity. The earlier loans continue of course to be serviced and the associations aided in improving their financial status. The real emphasis on the cooperative program for the past three or four years, however, has been to bring needed services to rehabilitation borrowers which they cannot economically have as individuals. Borrowers are encouraged and assisted to participate in existing cooperatives which are equipped to give services suited to their needs.[37]

The F.S.A. report then continues with the following statement regarding the loans for simple services:

By far the greatest and most significant part of the Farm Security Administration cooperative program is the making of loans to individual farmers which are used to purchase jointly a piece of heavy machinery, a purebred sire, a farm truck, or some similar piece of capital equipment. The loans are individual loans, but they are pooled by the borrowers for group use; and a plan of group operation of the equipment is worked out.

For instance, if two or more low-income farmers decide that they want to apply to the Farm Security Administration for a group service loan, an application is prepared and loan papers are drawn up for each of them individually. The supervisor helps them work out a sound plan for using the service jointly, and aids in developing a scale of fees for its use. When the loans are approved, the funds are pooled and deposited in a bank account established for the purpose. Checks are written against this account only by the elected secretary-manager of the service, and countersigned by the Farm Security supervisor. These loans bear 3 per cent interest.

After the several borrowers have received their funds and deposited them in the special bank account, the facility is purchased, and an accurate record is kept by the secretary-manager of all services performed, service fees collected, and expenses incurred. The owners,

[37] The same, p. 1000.

as well as other participants, usually pay the customary charge for the use of the equipment or animals. Each borrower mortgages only his fractional ownership interest in the property to the Government and other collateral security as required, and each joint owner is responsible for the repayment of only his share of the total funds borrowed from the Farm Security Administration.

These simple service loans, providing capital resources for small farmers, are the largest single phase of the Farm Security Administration cooperative program. Through December 31, 1942, the Farm Security Administration had aided in the establishment of 21,271 such group services. Of this number, the loans had been completely repaid for 3,670. Only 822 had been failures and were liquidated. The remaining 16,779 were being serviced and supervised, as a regular part of the Farm Security Administration rehabilitation effort. About 185,000 families were participating in these groups. Approximately 9,900 of these groups are providing machinery services. An additional 3,900 are sire services, and the balance represent a wide diversity of capital items commonly used by small farmers.[38]

Leasing and co-operative farming associations. The F.S.A. as part of its rehabilitation program carried on experiments in organizing associations or corporations which carried on collective farming. Three different forms should be distinguished.

1. Land leasing associations. Here the practice was to form an association to lease a large holding from its owner for a period of from five to ten years. F.S.A. would advance the association on a loan enough to pay one year's rent in advance. The association would sublease family-size units to its individual members. The F.S.A. would then lend the individual members enough on rehabilitation loans to operate their units. From their operations they were expected to make enough to pay the rent they owed the association. The rent payments by all the members would supply the money to pay the second year's rent to the owner and make the necessary payments on the government's initial loan for the first year's rent. From the individual farm leased from the association, the operator was also to earn enough to meet the debt charges on his personal loan from F.S.A.[39]

[38] The same.
[39] The same, p. 1001.

2. Co-operative farming associations. Low-income families under F.S.A. leadership would organize a corporation under state co-operative statutes and would rent a large farm, purchased by the F.S.A. for their use and owned by the national government. The members of the association elected a board of directors which appointed a manager, who in turn selected the foremen. Members worked for the association or corporation. They were supplied with quarters, food, and the like and were paid approximately prevailing money wages for hours worked. If the association made a profit, the members shared in the profit in accordance with hours they had worked.[40]

3. Associations operating under long-term leases. The distinctive feature of these associations was that the government leased the land from the owners for long periods, generally 99 years. In some cases the land thus leased by the government was in turn leased to a leasing association which in turn subleased it in family-size units to individuals as in the leasing associations described in (1) above. In other cases the land leased by the government for the long term was operated by a co-operative farming association or corporation as described in (2).[41]

The short-term leasing associations resembled private land holdings where the landlords lease to renters, whereas the collective farms resembled great farms which are managed by a single operator with much hired help. They had three characteristics in common:

1. Since the land was leased or not subdivided into individual units, the person being rehabilitated could not look forward to ownership of the property he was operating. If farm ownership was his ambition, the most he could do as a tenant or a worker for the corporation was to accumulate a reserve toward acquiring an equity in some other property.

2. The government through F.S.A. employees was contributing to the association or the corporation, without cost to it, the direction or supervision which under the private enterprise system would be furnished by the landlord or the owner or manager of the big farm.

[40] The same, p. 1005.
[41] The same, p. 1004.

3. The basic financial risks were borne by the government, whereas the profits went to the members of the association or to the workers for the corporation.

The financial data for the short-term leasing associations presented to the House Committee as of the end of 1942 disclosed, as would be expected, a reasonably satisfactory situation.[42] The associations were not paying for the managerial and supervisory services being supplied by the government. They were reaping the benefits from the strong demand for agricultural products that resulted from the war, while paying rents fixed in prewar years. Except in Louisiana, the associations in each of the seven southern states having them showed a profit on the operations for 1942, and in none of the states was there a default on payments of matured principal. The financial success or failure of such experiments cannot, however, be determined by figures for a few years, especially when several of them have been abnormally good from an agricultural standpoint.

The collective or co-operative farming associations financed from appropriations for rural rehabilitation resemble the resettlement projects established by the F.S.A. and its predecessors. In 1944 the F.S.A. officials reported to the House Committee that the collective farming associations were in process of liquidation. From the hearings one would conclude that there were four major reasons for their liquidation: (1) the use of appropriations for experiments in collective agriculture, especially after the passage of the Bankhead-Jones Act, was of questionable legality; (2) many members of Congress—and it may be contended Congress itself in passing the Bankhead-Jones Act—were opposed to collective farming as were the Grange and the Farm Bureau Association; (3) many of the persons being rehabilitated on collective farms had imbued in them the desire to own and operate their own farms, so that a permanent status that held no prospect of ultimate ownership did not appeal to them; (4) the form of organization and management meant a degree of supervision and direction to which

[42] The same, p. 1002.

they were not accustomed and that seemed to some a benevolent form of slavery.[43]

Health Insurance. The F.S.A. rehabilitation program had one feature of great interest and significance—its provisions for medical care. Although in some countries the provision for medical care for individuals and families has been a first objective of social insurance, such provision is conspicuous by its absence in the national programs in the United States, except for special classes. The rural rehabilitation program is thus described in the F.S.A. report to the committee:

The principle of voluntary health insurance is the foundation of the Farm Security Administration medical care program—voluntary on the part of the families, and voluntary on the part of the local doctors who participate. Each family pays a fee at the beginning of a 1-year period. The money is pooled and divided into 12 equal parts, 1 for each month. The doctors, then, instead of submitting the bills to their patients, submit them to the treasurer of the health association.

Fees range from about $15 in some counties to as much as $40 or more in others, depending on services provided and on the ability of the group to pay for medical services. These fees usually cover physicians' services, including home and office calls and obstetrical care; surgery, limited hospitalization, and ordinary drugs. The doctors are paid on a fee-for-service basis, as they are paid in their private practice. The only difference is that they are paid from a pooled fund made up of annual fees contributed by the families. If the funds are

[43] As persons familiar with lending money to be secured by mortgages know, the lending agency must, as a rule, take some steps to see that the proceeds of the loan are applied in accordance with the purposes for which the loan is made. Such steps are peculiarly necessary in dealing with persons inexperienced in management and the use of money, as a high proportion of the F.S.A. beneficiaries were. The customary device of the F.S.A. was to require the client to have a bank account, to pay the proceeds of the loan by a check so made that it could only be deposited in that account, and by agreement with the banks and the client to have the bank account so controlled that no check drawn by the borrower could be honored unless it was countersigned by the appropriate F.S.A. employee. Since the government had an interest in many other payments made to the client, the device of the controlled account also had to be applied to them. Under the system, in many instances, the clients were, moreover, required to keep detailed accounts and records; the obligation to keep these books was made part of the contract. Viewed from the standpoint of the government administrators, all these procedures were reasonable and necessary, but from the standpoint of many clients, the loss of the privilege of doing as he pleased was too high a price to pay for being rehabilitated by the government. Since the government had not as yet attained a monopoly, the client could still escape, perhaps to less security and to a lower level of living but to a kind of personal freedom which to him was worth the price.

insufficient to cover all bills in full, the participating physicians agree to accept a prorata share for the services they render.

In some cases dental services are covered in medical care plans. In addition, separate dental care plans have been organized in 252 counties. This program is carried on in cooperation with county dental societies. Altogether, more than 242,000 people are members of plans offering dental care on a prepayment basis. . . .

Farm Security Administration health plans are democratically governed. The members select from their own number a committee or board of directors to represent their interests. The doctors select a committee to handle all problems of a medical nature. The Farm Security Administration has little part in the actual operation of the program. It helps to set up a plan, and, where necessary includes in a family's loan the amount needed to pay its membership fee.[44]

F.S.A. in all its activities has given consideration to the improvement of farm sanitation. It is not necessary here to give the details.

THE RESETTLEMENT PROJECTS

The resettlement projects have provoked more criticism of the Farm Security Administration than any other phase of its program.[45] From the report of the F.S.A. to the Select Committee of the House a brief paragraph will be quoted, because it discloses the administrative point of view that prevailed in determining policy.

The resettlement projects were not launched as real-estate investments. They were built with funds appropriated by the Congress to combat unemployment and economic stagnation in a constructive way. The development of these projects added to the value of the Nation's rural communities just as hospitals, post offices, school buildings, sewer systems, and many other types of public works add to the values of cities through billions of dollars of Federal money which the Government does not expect to recover.[46]

If one accepts the point of view thus expressed, the success or failure of these projects is not to be determined by an examination of the financial results. In our judgment, however, the financial results are highly relevant. From time to time experi-

[44] Select Committee Hearings, Pt. 3, pp. 1007–08.
[45] The same, pp. 1030–33.
[46] The same, p. 1031.

ments demonstrate that a certain objective can be obtained in a given way, but the costs of doing it in that way are so high as to make the method impracticable for large-scale use. Especially in dealing with public money in the postwar economy a major problem will be how to distribute the available funds so that they will do the most good. Comparatively costly things which benefit only a relatively small number of persons may have to be abandoned, and the available money applied in ways which affect larger numbers. If choices have to be made among different methods, relative costs deserve careful consideration.

A philosophy that puts resettlement projects in the same class with hospitals, post offices, school buildings, sewer systems, and other general public works is not to be accepted without question. It would seem that in governmental activities a sharp distinction should be drawn between capital outlays that serve all classes of people without discrimination and capital outlays made for the benefit of a specially selected group. The distinction is particularly significant in cases like the resettlement projects where the advantages of the government bounty cannot be extended to all persons who fall in a clearly defined class but only to such members of that class as may be selected for the preferential treatment. Such selection may conceivably be justified in conducting an experiment, but in examining the results it is relevant to consider costs, to ask if it is practicable to extend such a service to all in the class, and if such a program represents the most effective way in which the sums involved could be expended for the general economic and social welfare.

Statistics of cost. From this general point of view we shall examine the summary statistics of the resettlement projects in the rural communities that remained under the F.S.A.

As of June 30, 1942 the total capital invested in these projects was 72 million dollars. Of this sum 55.9 millions had been invested in the development of 9,559 family units. Each unit represented, therefore, an investment of over $5,800. In addition the F.S.A. had made rehabilitation loans to individuals on the projects amounting in the aggregate to over 16.5 millions, of

which a little over 10 millions was outstanding as of February
. 28, 1943.[47]

The recapitulation of the operating costs of these projects as
given by the F.S.A. as of June 30, 1943 is reproduced in the table below.

RECAPITULATION BY PROJECT TYPE[a]

Description	Community Projects	Subsistence Homesteads	Scattered Farms	Total
Operating costs:				
Management.....	$2,466,743.21	$ 96,608.52	$2,477,300.29	$ 5,040,652.02
Operations and main-				
tenance..........	1,012,422.57	34,038.51	970,810.91	2,017,271.99
Taxes.............	844,713.34	12,875.12	1,485,820.16	2,343,408.62
Insurance.........	341,992.83	5,452.37	383,955.11	731,400.31
Other operating costs	431,828.15	38,390.91	230,022.53	700,241.59
Donations.........	25,657.23	62.40	54,452.52	80,172.15
Total operating costs.........	5,123,357.33	187,427.83	5,602,361.52	10,913,146.68
Income to June 30, 1943.............	2,677,171.14	24,921.89	3,385,187.46	6,087,280.49

[a] Select Committee Hearings, Pt. 3, p. 1132.

The first point to be noted is that total operating costs of 10.9
million dollars exceeded income of 6.1 millions by over 4 millions. Management costs alone amounted to 5 millions or
roughly five sixths of income. The reader familiar with operating statements will note the absence of two familiar headings
"Interest" and "Depreciation." The total capital invested in
the projects for which the operating costs are given is about
71.5 million dollars so that interest at 3 per cent would amount
to over 2 millions a year. The developmental costs, excluding
land costs, amounted to 46.2 millions. A depreciation reserve at
3 per cent to write off all the developmental expenses in 40
years would require an annual payment of roughly $600,000
a year.

The omission of interest and depreciation results from the
position taken by F.S.A. administrators that these resettlement
projects are public works in a class with schools, hospitals, and
sewer systems that are designed to serve all classes of the popu-

[47] The same, p. 1117.

lation. With respect to such public works it has been common practice to ignore depreciation and not to charge interest against the project, although interest may have to be paid on the debt incurred to build the project. In some communities, however, water rates include charges to cover in part at least both interest and depreciation. The F.S.A. administrators made no distinction between public works designed for all classes and projects which represent competition with private enterprise. A co-operative farming project publicly financed and managed by employees paid directly or indirectly by the government competes with independent farmers who cannot disregard interest on their debt, and in the long run cannot with impunity ignore depreciation.

In the defense of the F.S.A. resettlement program the administrators included statistics regarding agricultural production on the various projects.[48] Statistics of production, not analyzed with respect to cost of production, are not in our judgment of great significance in the evaluation of the success of an experiment. When the over-all summary figures reveal operating costs of 10 millions, exclusive of interest and depreciation and income of 6 millions, and a capital investment of 71 millions, it is obvious that the cost of production is prohibitively high from a purely economic standpoint.

With respect to many of these resettlement projects and the co-operative farming associations financed from the rural rehabilitation appropriations, it was apparently not the original intention of the responsible administrators that the families should ever become owners of the land, the houses, or the improvements. Such projects were experiments in collective farming or collective enterprise with the national government putting up the money and with salaried employees of F.S.A. giving the over-all direction and doing a vast amount of detailed supervision of the individual workers. It seems fair to say that in the main they were not designed as demonstrations

---

[48] They will be found under the statement of the "Location, Justification, Description and Financial Status" of the several projects, pages 1033 to 1117 of the report of the F.S.A. to the Select Committee.

of the economic practicability of such projects, undertaken to show private farm operators how they could do a better job and provide their tenants and agricultural workers a better level of living under existing agricultural and general economic conditions. Rather the first objective was to give the beneficiaries a better level of living and to extend to them an educational service. In many instances the matter of cost was of minor consideration. Two points of view were frequently encountered in the hearings, (1) it is better to spend the money this way, even for heavy capital outlays than to spend it for relief; and (2) these projects are often in the nature of rural slum clearance and the government should contribute heavily to slum clearance.

Conceivably behind the whole enterprise lay a belief on the part of some concerned with it that the solution of the American agricultural problem lay in the nationalization of land.[49] According to such a point of view, if the agricultural future belongs

[49] Report of the Select Committee, p. 5, says:

"By legal interpretations placed upon certain language contained in the several appropriation acts providing funds for the agency, the officials of the Farm Security Administration continued to operate an ever-expanding land-acquisition program under which it illegally acquired title to and possession of hundreds of thousands of acres of farm land, a very large part of which is not now occupied or in cultivation. Funds which were appropriated by Congress for the purpose of providing loans for needy farm families, to be used in the cultivation and harvesting of crops, were used in the purchase, through corporate devices and schemes, of approximately 2,000,000 acres of farm and ranch lands. At the time this investigation was undertaken by the committee, the Farm Security Administration, through the corporations and cooperatives and other projects which it has been responsible for having created, apparently owned and controlled more acreage of cultivated land than any other public or private agency in the Nation. Moreover, the Farm Security Administration is the Nation's largest landlord and is conducting farming operations on a larger scale than any other individual or corporate farm owner in America.

"The most distressing and disappointing things about this land-acquisition program are the manner in which it has been carried on, the intent with which such lands were acquired, and the use to which such lands have been subjected. Obviously those responsible for having acquired such large tracts of land and such a large number of acres intended that the Government should have the ownership and retain the legal title to such property in perpetuity and, by such program, intended to prevent the return of the title to private ownership under fee simple deeds and conveyances. In this land-acquisition program, the Farm Security Administration, instead of starting low-income farm families on the road to home ownership and financial independence, has operated it in such a manner as to prevent actual home ownership and force tenants to remain tenants. Thousands of those whom the agency has ostensibly undertaken to aid are still tenants, working for the United States Government or an agency thereof, under contracts which in many instances are even more harsh and far more exacting than ordinary contracts between landlords and tenants."

to the big mechanized farms, they should be owned by the nation and operated in the interest of the workers on the farm. No attempt will here be made to debate the pros and cons of that issue. All that immediately concerns us is that no such policy had been decided upon by the Congress of the United States or by the legislature of any state. As a matter of fact it ran counter to American tradition and was vigorously opposed by many farmers and farm organizations.

Farmers operating under a private enterprise system were of course acutely aware of the competition which they had to face from these projects. Although they might pay their workers the same money wage that was paid on the projects, they could not supply the housing and the other facilities which the projects offered. They could not offer a comparable profit-sharing bonus, because their profits could not be figured the same way. They had to pay interest, depreciation, and all taxes and they had to supply or hire management. They had to help pay for roads, schools, and facilities. They had little capital to lend as rehabilitation loans for house furnishings and equipment. Thus the competition seemed to them unfair, especially if energetic F.S.A. officers on the public pay roll actively recruited their tenants and agricultural workers for the government projects.[50] They could not all sell their holdings to the government or lease them for 99 years. Some of them had to compete with the government.

The resettlement and leasing association projects have a characteristic common to most agencies created to rehabilitate families. They are often judged by individual cases. F.S.A.

[50] An important distinction existed between the farm tenant program and the co-operative farms. Under the tenant program a farmer applied for a loan and a case began with his application. A co-operative farm was planned and developed by top management, designed to provide opportunity for a fairly definite number of families or workers. When the houses and other facilities were ready, F.S.A. officers had to get the necessary families. In some cases they had to recruit just as a private farmer may have to do. Occasionally a private farmer lost employees he wanted to keep to the F.S.A. project. On certain of the projects some of the housing units were not occupied because no families wanted them or because the original planning was defective. After the defense and war activities developed, some of them were vacated because families went to defense areas. In a few cases the men went into the armed services or defense industries leaving the women as the occupants of the project houses. Under these circumstances F.S.A. had to compete with private farmers to keep the collective farms running.

naturally cites its most successful cases while embattled farmers naturally cite the bad ones, and unfortunately statistical measurements are not very helpful in arriving at evaluations. One cannot tell from the evidence what the truth is, for obviously the results are not as good as the cases cited by the F.S.A. officers would suggest nor, it may be hoped, as bad as some of the cases by opponents would suggest. For evaluation we shall merely cite the general statement made to the Committee by the Secretary of Agriculture:

Now, much has been said about some of the projects of the Farm Security Administration. You all know that these projects were started for the most part as experiments in trying to find solutions to problems of unemployment and rural poverty. We have carried them as experimental until we could come to some determination as to their value. I believe that we are in agreement now that they have served their purpose and should be liquidated in an orderly manner.[51]

DIFFICULTIES WITH PROGRAMS

In connection with rehabilitation loans and grants and the resettlement programs, three somewhat related matters should be presented: (1) the difficulties of securing competent personnel to direct and supervise the persons whose rehabilitation is being attempted; (2) the reactions of the individuals being supervised to the system; and (3) the political implications of the programs.

Personnel difficulties. It will be recalled that the employees of the emergency relief programs were not subject to either the Civil Service or the Classification Acts. Most of them were not selected through competitive tests of fitness and no legal safeguards were introduced to prevent the appointment of ill-qualified or incompetent persons for purely political reasons. One could hardly expect such extremely difficult experiments to be carried through with reasonable efficiency and economy under such a personnel system. Some of the bungling, waste, and extravagance disclosed through the committee hearings may be attributed to failure to establish and maintain suitable personnel standards.

[51] Select Committee Hearings, Pt. 2, p. 907.

It is not necessarily true, however, that had the best possible personnel practice been followed, the experiments would have been really successful. The task of making rural rehabilitation loans and grants and supervising and directing the families concerned demanded an unusual combination of qualifications. The intimate relationships with the members of the family inherent in the undertaking called for the highest skills of the successful family case worker. Planning and supervising the farm activities called for knowledge and skill in farm management and farm home management. It is perhaps questionable whether the nation had a sufficient number of persons qualified in either of these two fields to have staffed so large an undertaking. It seems unquestionable that it had few individuals who combined the two different types of qualifications that were requisite. Thus even if sound personnel methods had been used, it probably would not have been possible properly to staff so many experiments conducted on so extensive a scale.

From the standpoint of personnel administration one may generalize that success is more probable if radical experiments are started first on a small scale with a competent staff. After that staff has—to use the manufacturer's term—"worked the bugs out of the idea," the experiment if successful can be expanded, using the experienced workers of the initial effort for leaders in the expansion. These leaders can, moreover, not only develop job specifications showing what kind of training is needed, but they can also participate in seeing that the required training is available.

In this connection it may be pointed out that the persons who generate the radical ideas that underlie many experiments are by no means always possessed of the executive and managerial ability essential to demonstrate practicability. When experiments are conducted on a small scale, lack of executive and managerial ability often brings them fairly promptly to financial difficulties. This corrective may be largely absent when experiments are conducted on a grand scale financed from public funds and are not closely followed and checked by skeptical members of appropriating bodies.

The reactions of individuals to supervision and direction. One cannot read the hearings before the House Committee without being conscious of the difficulties that lie in the relationships between the government supervisors and the supervised.

When a financial agency makes a loan to an individual, it is a fairly common practice for it to take such steps as are necessary to assure that the proceeds of the loan are applied for the purposes for which the loan is made. The things done with the loan frequently become in large part the security for the loan. It may be generalized that the less the responsibility of the borrower, from the standpoints of business capacity, experience, character, and financial status, the greater the necessity for strict supervision. F.S.A. was carrying on activities where, it is reasonable to say, a close approach to maximum supervision was in many cases essential.

The device used by F.S.A. was in many instances to have the borrower open a special account in a local bank against which he could draw no check unless it was countersigned by a designated representative of F.S.A. Government checks for loans were so drawn that they could be deposited only in that special account, and some checks for other payments within the control of the government were similarly drawn. Since many of the persons being rehabilitated or resettled had little in the way of other resources, their financial affairs were almost completely controlled by the government.[52] They were, moreover, living in houses controlled by the government and conducting their farming operations according to government approved plans. Such supervision calls for employees whose knowledge and judgment are almost infallible, lest the supervised, like the Klamath Indian, may plead: "We want the chance to make our own mistakes." The employee must also be gifted with extreme tact and skill to know when, and to what extent, to let the supervised exercise his own judgment and initiative, although they may run counter to the judgment of the supervisor.

[52] Persons familiar with Indian administration will recognize the similarity to the "Individual Indian Money Account" where the government held the Indian's money and he could not draw any of it without the consent of the government supervisor.

Administration of such a system calls for minute detailed accounts and records. The sums involved are, however, generally small. Many people with a high degree of literacy and reasonable arithmetical ability abhor the chore of keeping records and accounts. Many of the F.S.A. beneficiaries had had very limited education and found record keeping a continuous source of trouble.

On the collective farms the workers not only were paid approximately the prevailing wage for like work in the community, but they also shared in the profits on the basis of the hours worked. Such a program required a degree of detail and accuracy with respect to hours worked that is not customary on many farms. As one unsympathetic member of the Committee phrased it:

. . . I understand you had a checker that kept the number of hours that each person on that project worked per day. . . .

If he worked in a cornfield for a couple of hours, you gave him credit for 2 hours in the cornfield; and if on that same day he worked in the pigpen for an hour and a half, the checker would give him credit for an hour and a half's work in the pigpen.

The administrative officer replied:

There were two purposes there, one was to determine earnings, and the other was to determine whether the individual enterprises are successful or not.

He went on to explain that the checker was the association bookkeeper. This illustration[53] discloses the expert's passion for precision of measurements and the degree of supervision to which the worker must be subjected if these precise measurements are to be made.

In the case of the leasing associations and the collective farms, the individuals and families subjected to such close supervision and control, it will be recalled, had no chance to become owners of the property they were working. Psychological reactions conceivably might have been different had the individuals been able to look forward to attaining an increasing measure of independence.

[53] Select Committee Hearings, Pt. 2, pp. 518–19.

   These experiments in agricultural collectivism were, moreover, carried on in communities where the conventional pattern
of American agriculture still prevailed. Thus it was relatively
easy for an individual or a family to leave the F.S.A. project and
regain freedom, although perhaps at the cost of a lower level of
living. The experiments were not tried on such a scale that the
national government was a monopolistic employer and the people had to work for it or not work at all. It must be remembered,
too, that the change in general economic conditions that resulted from the war opened many opportunities which permitted escape.

   From what has been said it should not be inferred that the
F.S.A. personnel was necessarily harsh or unfriendly. Although
the congressional committee in its final report says that the government contracts "in many instances are even more harsh and
far more exacting than ordinary contracts between landlords
and tenants,"[54] it does not follow that the employees were harsh
or exacting. On the contrary, the evidence suggests that many
employees went to the other extreme and did more for the beneficiaries than was wise if the objective was to make them at the
earliest possible moment independent. The congressional committee in its final report[55] makes findings to the effect that rehabilitation loans and grants were in some instances made to
raise the living standards of the beneficiaries to somewhere near
the highest prevailing in a community.

   Grants have been made to Farm Security Administration "clients"
who could well have been required to repay a portion of the funds,
instead of reserving this type of assistance for those acutely in want.
. . . The investigation reveals that too many loans in excessive
amounts have been made to individuals who have grown progressively
worse from year to year and seem to be allergic to all thoughts of
rehabilitation. . . . In some instances loans have been urged upon
individuals who were financially able to finance themselves and their
farming operations. Thousands of families who have received financial
assistance from the Farm Security Administration are now more
heavily involved in debt than they were at the time they were taken

[54] Report of Select Committee, p. 5.
[55] The same, p. 9.

on the program. Many came on the program owing nothing and are now involved to the Government to the extent of $7,000 or $8,000 and have no chance whatever of paying the loan now or at any future date.[56]

Political implications. In these programs there were two elements of great political significance.

1. A staff of some 15,000 employees of the national government was widely dispersed through the poorer rural counties of the nation. Most of them had not been selected through open competitive examination. Their salaries were reasonably good. They were administering programs, some of which had aroused serious opposition both among the independent self-supporting farmers in their localities and states and among many members of Congress. Each year their security in their jobs depended on the renewal of the appropriations for the programs.

2. Scattered through these rural counties were in the aggregate hundreds of thousands of families who were indebted to the national government for rural rehabilitation loans, many of them eligible to receive grants. The action the government would take with respect to payment of interest, payment of matured principal, renewal of loans, and supplemental grants was largely dependent on the reports and recommendations of the employees of the national government stationed in the county or in the state. These borrowers could scarcely have been in many instances unaware of the fact that their family financial position depended in part upon the outcome of political primaries and elections. The employees of the national government whether located in the county, in the state, or in Washington thus had in their hands the kind of instrument which can be used effectively by practical politicians in influencing an election. If it be true that the preservation of democracy depends on an uncorrupted electorate, then a major issue with respect to the type of programs we have been discussing is whether devices which are inherently susceptible of being used to corrupt the electorate can be adequately safeguarded.

[56] The same, p. 9.

MIGRATORY LABOR CAMPS

By a joint resolution, approved April 29, 1943 (57 Stat. 70), "Making an appropriation to assist in providing a supply and distribution of farm labor for the calendar year 1943," jurisdiction over the migratory labor camps, which F.S.A. had been operating, was transferred to the Administrator of Food Production and Distribution. This activity was subsequently conducted on the basis of the acute shortage of agricultural labor resulting from the war and in its present form needs no particular discussion here.

The F.S.A. in its report to the Select Committee made the following statements regarding its activities in this field prior to the agricultural shortages.[57]

The first migratory labor camps were constructed and operated by the California Emergency Relief Administration as part of its rural rehabilitation program.

The other phases of the rehabilitation program, as it was then developing, were only available to those who had some stake in the land. However, there was then a large class of migratory labor with no home other than the road and no work other than that which could be picked up by following the crops. These laborers lived under intolerable conditions, frequently camped on ditch banks, in vacant lots, and in scrap heap shacks on the outskirts of small towns and villages. Sanitation was unknown. Not only were these conditions a threat to the health of the laborers, but also the communities which relied upon them for labor. The labor camps were started to ameliorate these conditions.

After the rural aspects of the program of the relief administrations were transferred to the Resettlement Administration, migratory farm workers' camps continued to be constructed, with the approval of the Comptroller General, out of funds appropriated for rural rehabilitation by the Emergency Relief Appropriation Act of 1935 . . . . Similar action was taken under the Emergency Relief Appropriation Acts of 1936, 1937, and 1938. More recently, the Congress has specifically authorized this type of activity. The Emergency Relief Appropriation Act of 1939 (sec. 3 (b) (6)), the Emergency Relief Appropriation Act, fiscal year 1941 (sec. 2 (b) (6) (b)), and the Department of Agriculture Appropriation Act, 1942, in the item entitled "Loans,

---

[57] Pp. 613–28 of the Select Committee Hearings, Pt. 2, contains a description of the camps and the methods of administration.

grants, and rural rehabilitation" all authorize "projects involving the construction and operation of migratory labor camps" while the Department of Agriculture Appropriation Act, 1943, authorizes, under the same item "not exceeding $1,400,000 for the operation and maintenance of existing migratory labor camps."

At the end of 1942, the Farm Security Administration had available 95 migratory labor camps, with accommodations for 19,464 families at one time. Of these camps, 46 were of the permanent, or standard type, and 49 were mobile.[58]

The permanent camps were established in areas where migratory workers are in demand most of the year. The mobile camps, which can be dismantled and moved from place to place by truck or train, are designed for use in areas where workers are only needed for a few weeks or months at a time.

The migratory labor camps offer the barest minimum of sanitary living facilities. In the standard camps, the shelters are one-room structures, built of wood or steel. In the mobile camps, the shelters consist only of tents and tent platforms. All camps, however, stress sanitation. The standard camps contain sanitary buildings provided with toilets, shower baths, and laundry tubs. The mobile camps have tents and in some cases, trailers with shower bath equipment.

The permanent camps generally have clinics, and other community buildings. The mobile camps, where possible, have trailer clinics, and community tents.

Many of the permanent camps contain, in addition, a small number of small cottages known as labor homes for families which have longer employment.

When farm wages were low, rental charges were not collected from the inhabitants. Recently, however, the policy has been changed. During this fiscal year, rental charges have been instituted for shelters at all camps. The charges range from 50 cents to $3.25 a week for each unit, depending upon the type of shelter.

Originally instituted as a relief measure so as to protect the health of the workers and the communities, the camps have more recently developed into a mechanism for assisting in the better utilization of seasonal labor for essential war crops. As labor became more scarce, it became apparent that labor could be more easily attracted into areas which had camp facilities. In addition, the recruiting and placement of labor formerly carried on by the Farm Placement Service of the United States Employment Service was found to be more

[58] Direction of all farm labor supply and camp activities was subsequently transferred to the Office of Labor, War Food Administration, under a joint resolution approved Apr. 29, 1943, 57 Stat. 70.

efficiently carried on at camps. A system was instituted by which the
Service maintained its offices at the camps. This system resulted in a
substantial increase in the utilization of the laborers resident at the
camp.[59]

The findings of the Select Committee with respect to the labor
camps are as follows:

1. For social and economic reasons should the national government attempt to discourage those large-scale mechanized
farms of agriculture that depend on a very considerable body of
migratory labor? Are the resulting advantages of low-cost
production offset by the social and public costs of providing
for the large migratory groups?

2. If a large migratory labor force is necessary, should the
costs of providing for the families be a charge against general
taxpayers, and more particularly national taxpayers, or should
they be assessed against those producers who utilize the services of these workers? Two general lines of procedure are, of
course, open to assess the cost against the growers (a) to require them either individually or through associations to provide facilities or services which comply with reasonable standards established by appropriate labor legislation or (b) to have
public agencies supply the facilities and services and require
the growers to pay for them. Obviously the farmer who operates
a farm with labor from the locality and makes provision for
them in the slack seasons is at a disadvantage if a competitor
uses migratory labor and does not contribute toward the resulting costs.

[59] Select Committee Hearings, Pt. 3, pp. 1164–65.

CHAPTER XI
DISTRIBUTION OF SURPLUS COMMODITIES

In the preceding chapter it was noted briefly that among the programs adopted by the national government to sustain the price of agricultural commodities was the purchase with public funds of so-called surplus commodities. Theoretically the surpluses thus purchased were given away to persons in need, not as a substitute for other forms of relief but as additions to what they were receiving from other sources. Actually, however, the availability of such commodities was taken into account in many localities in determining relief needs. In some states, notably in the South, surplus commodities constituted the only form of general public assistance available.[1]

The present chapter will be concerned primarily with those aspects of the program that relate directly to relief. No attempt will be made to consider the effectiveness of the program in achieving its basic purposes of sustaining the price of the commodities affected, promoting orderly marketing and attempting to give to primary producers and necessary processors a fair return for their labors. These aspects will be touched upon only incidentally.

Since our interest centers in the parts of the program that relate to relief, we shall not go into its history after the economy felt the impact of preparedness and the war. Briefly the activities were transferred in 1942 to the Agricultural Marketing Service, which later became part of the Food Distribution Administration of the War Food Administration.[2] We shall confine ourselves to the period from 1933 to 1940, giving first a brief statement of the legislative history, second, summary statistics to indicate the nature and extent of the activities, and then in greater detail a consideration of the issues presented from the standpoint of relief.

[1] Works Progress Administration, *Average General Relief Benefits, 1933–1938* (1940).
[2] *United States Government Manual, 1945,* First Ed., p. 610.

HISTORY

The surplus removal programs with which we are here concerned had their origins in 1933 in two acts of Congress, the Agricultural Adjustment Act[3] and the Federal Emergency Relief Act.[4]

The Agricultural Adjustment Act levied a processing tax the proceeds of which were appropriated among other purposes "to be available to the Secretary of Agriculture for expansion of markets and removal of surplus agricultural products." It contained, however, no provisions with respect to the disposal of surpluses removed by the Secretary through the use of these funds.[5]

The original Federal Emergency Relief Act provided funds for grants to the states

... to aid in meeting the costs of furnishing relief and work relief and in relieving the hardship and suffering caused by unemployment in the form of money, service, materials, and/or commodities to provide the necessities of life to persons in need as a result of the present emergency, and/or to their dependents, whether resident, transient, or homeless.[6]

Funds for the purchase of surplus commodities thus derived from two sources: (1) part of the revenues of the processing tax and (2) part of the grants to the states for relief which, at the request of state administrators, were used for the purchase of commodities to be distributed by the state agencies to needy persons within those states. It will be noted that the funds from the states were in the main federal funds turned back to be used by a national agency for the purchase of commodities to be distributed by the states among their needy. Since half of the 500 million dollars initially appropriated by the Federal Emergency Relief Act were reserved for distribution in the discretion of the national administrator,[7] there was available to him powerful means of persuading any desired degree of state

[3] 48 Stat. 31.
[4] 48 Stat. 55.
[5] 48 Stat. 38, sec. 12(b).
[6] 48 Stat. 57, sec. 4(a).
[7] 48 Stat. 57.

participation in the surplus removal program as well as ample funds to finance such participation.

To administer the surplus commodities program, a Federal Surplus Relief Corporation was incorporated by the administration under the laws of Delaware. It was a nonprofit corporation with no capital stock and with membership restricted "to the persons holding the offices of Secretary of Agriculture, Federal Emergency Administrator of Public Works, and Federal Emergency Relief Administrator." Its purposes were (1) "to assist in relieving the existing national emergency by the purchase, processing, and distribution for consumption of agricultural and other products as a means to remove surpluses and improve prices; (2) to apply these surplus agricultural and other products in the form of foodstuffs, clothing, fuel, and otherwise to the relief of hardship and suffering caused by unemployment."[8]

On April 7, 1934 an amendment to the Agricultural Adjustment Act was approved which among other things appropriated 50 million dollars "to enable the Secretary of Agriculture to make advances to the Federal Surplus Relief Corporation for the purchase of dairy and beef products for distribution for relief purposes, and to enable the Secretary of Agriculture, . . . to eliminate diseased dairy and beef cattle, . . . and to make payments to owners with respect thereto."[9] This appropriation, it will be noted, left to the Secretary of Agriculture discretion as to how much of the sum he should advance for the purchase of dairy and beef products for distribution for relief purposes.

Further amendments to the Agricultural Adjustment Act were approved August 24, 1935. One of these amendments contained in Section 32 affected surplus commodities.[10] It permanently appropriated an amount equal to 30 per cent of the gross customs revenues collected in each calendar year to constitute a separate fund to be used by the Secretary of Agriculture for three designated purposes. One was to "encourage the

[8] *Monthly Report of the Federal Emergency Relief Administration, December 1, 1933 to December 31, 1933*, p. 39.
[9] 48 Stat. 528, sec. 6.
[10] 49 Stat. 774.

domestic consumption of such [agricultural] commodities or products by diverting them, by the payment of benefits or indemnities or by other means, from the normal channels of trade and commerce." This section gave the Secretary authority to use so much of the special fund thus created as he deemed expedient for the purchase of surplus agricultural commodities.

An act approved June 28, 1937 specifically authorized the Secretary to transfer moneys from this fund to the Federal Surplus Commodities Corporation, which was by the act continued to June 30, 1939. It further provided that purchases could be made "without regard to the provisions of existing law governing the expenditure of public funds" and specifically permitted donation of commodities for relief purposes.[11] By an act of February 16, 1938 the life of the corporation was continued to June 30, 1942.[12]

One other act requires mention in connection with the legal authority of the surplus property distribution. On March 5, 1937 an act was passed authorizing an appropriation of 2 million dollars to enable the Federal Surplus Commodities Corporation "to divert surplus fish (including shellfish) and the products thereof from the normal channels of trade and commerce by acquiring them and providing for their distribution through Federal, State, and private relief agencies."[13]

Although much of the money to finance the purchase of surplus commodities came initially from appropriations for relief, this review of the basic legislation indicates quite clearly that the dominant purpose was to sustain prices by removing surpluses from normal channels of distribution and disposing of them by donations to the needy.

To quote from the annual report of the Corporation,[14]

In 1935 it became apparent that the Corporation's greatest value was not as a relief organization, but rather as an agency to assist the Department of Agriculture in the execution of surplus removal programs conducted by the Agricultural Adjustment Administration.

[11] 50 Stat. 323.
[12] 52 Stat. 38.
[13] 50 Stat. 27.
[14] *Report of Federal Surplus Commodities Corporation for the Calendar Year 1936*, pp. 1–2. The Corporation used the calendar year for the earlier years and for later years the fiscal year.

Consequently, on November 18, 1935, the charter of the Corporation was amended, its present designation—the Federal Surplus Commodities Corporation—was adopted, and its membership changed so that direction of policies and activities was vested in officials of the Department of Agriculture. Through these modifications, the primary emphasis in the activities of the Federal Surplus Commodities Corporation was placed upon the encouragement of domestic consumption by diversion of surplus farm products from normal channels of trade and commerce, rather than upon procurement for supplying direct relief to the needy and unemployed.

SIZE OF THE PROGRAM

To give some idea of the size of the program we shall give a few over-all statistics from official reports.

From October 3, 1933 through June 30, 1940, expenditures for procurement, processing, storage, handling, transportation, and distribution of commodities were in the aggregate a little less than 565 millions.[15] Thus average annual expenditures for this purpose were about 83.7 millions. For the last three fiscal years of the period the figures were 47.4 millions for 1938, 66.6 millions for 1939, and 118 millions for 1940.[16] It seems reasonable to assume that the increase in the expenditures shown by the figures for these later years was due in part to the development of the stamp plan of distribution, which will be considered later, and in part to the increased prices as the economic system felt the impact of war demands.

Administrative costs of the federal government for the surplus commodities program varied widely from year to year. For the period 1933 to 1939, the figures range from $605,000 in the last three months of 1933 and 1934 to a high of $1,578,000 in 1939.[17] Among other major items, expenditures in round numbers for personal services increased from $495,000 in 1937 to $708,000 in 1938, and $1,143,000 in 1939.[18] For 1937 the expenditures for transportation were $62,300; in 1938 expenditures for travel were $179,900 and for transportation of things

[15] *Report of Federal Surplus Commodities Corporation for the Fiscal Year 1940*, p. 7.

[16] Figures from annual reports: 1938, p. 16; 1939, p. 10; and 1940, p. 7.

[17] Figures are taken from the annual reports except for the fiscal year 1939 which was taken from *The Budget of the United States, 1941*, pp. 386–87.

[18] Figures from annual reports: 1937, p. 5; 1938, p. 23. The figures for 1939 are from *The Budget, 1941*, pp. 385–87. The 1939 report omitted the figures on administrative expenses.

$1,500; for 1939 for travel $192,800 and for transportation of things $3,800.[19]

These yearly administrative cost figures are not strictly comparable. Variations in administrative costs from year to year are explained in part by variations in the size of the program in terms of commodities supplied and persons cared for. In part, however, they are attributable to differences in the services required of the Corporation by varying procurement and distribution functions. In 1935, for example, heavy expenses incurred for inspection services rendered in connection with the drought relief program contributed to a high ($1,422,000) administrative cost figure for that year.[20] In 1939 administrative costs were proportionately somewhat higher than in 1938 largely owing to the new administrative burdens involved in the inauguration of the stamp-plan method of distribution.[21]

Figures for the commodities purchased were shown in the 1939 and 1940 reports only by individual commodities alphabetically arranged without any summary by commodity groups.[22] The table on page 333 gives the summary figures by commodity groups shown in the 1938 report (page 17).

Data with respect to the number of persons benefited because of the nature of the program are necessarily unsatisfactory. The 1935 report (page 4) said:

It may be estimated that the agricultural commodities distributed by the Corporation monthly reached from 50 to 90 per cent of the 4,000,000 to 5,000,000 families certified on the relief rolls during 1935, depending upon the perishable nature of the commodity and the efficiency of the local distribution systems.

The 1938 report (page 11) said:

The average number of recipient families per month was 1,930,294, while the average distribution per family per month was 45 pounds.

[19] These figures do not include the cost of transporting commodities, which is included in the expenditures for commodities.

[20] *Report of Federal Surplus Commodities Corporation for the Calendar Year 1935*, p. 9.

[21] Administrative costs of the program to the states, however, were lower under the stamp plan than under the direct commodities distribution method.

[22] For the detail see annual reports: 1940, p. 6 and 1939, p. 10. The 1940 report includes cumulative figures, Oct. 3, 1933 through June 30, 1940.

During the last 6 months of the fiscal year the quantity of surplus commodities available increased materially . . . . The rate per family per month for the later period was 52 pounds.

QUANTITIES PURCHASED AND EXPENDITURES MADE BY THE FEDERAL SURPLUS COM-
MODITIES CORPORATION IN THE FISCAL YEAR ENDED JUNE 30, 1938,
BY COMMODITY GROUPS

Commodity Group	Fiscal Year Ended June 30, 1938	
	Total Quantity Purchased	Total Expenditure
	Pounds	
Fruits and nuts[a]...............	655,300,000	$15,759,000
Cereals, rice, and flour[b]........	646,400,000	13,909,000
Vegetables.....................	442,300,000	8,078,000
Dairy products[c]...............	66,900,000	6,772,000
Eggs..........................	12,100,000	1,724,000
Cottonseed oil (shortening)......	9,800,000	791,000
Fish..........................	3,700,000	263,000
Syrup, cane...................	2,600,000	134,000
Total...................	1,839,100,000	$47,430,000

[a] Fifteen hundred pounds of nuts purchased at a total cost of $180.
[b] Wheat cereal, wheat flour, potato starch, potato flour, and rice.
[c] Butter, cheese, dry skim milk, and fluid milk.

The 1940 report (page 8) placed the number of families served at 3,011,679 and the number of individuals at 11,017,857. In addition, school lunch programs were carried on at 43,369 schools serving 3,025,222 children. It is highly probable that the development of the stamp plan improved both the accuracy and the significance of the statistics, yet one must admit no little skepticism as to the significance of numbers served unaccompanied by a classification as to the nature and quantity of the commodities they received.

As of June 1940 the Corporation reported 83 areas served under the stamp plan. The number of participants was placed at 507,021 cases, which included 1,488,532 individuals. The value of surplus food stamps issued in that month was over 3 million dollars.[23] The report gives the number of families and individuals and pounds distributed by states, but we shall attempt no analysis of them because of the inherent difficulties in interpreting them.

[23] *Report of Federal Surplus Commodities Corporation for the Fiscal Year 1940*, p. 9.

Before leaving the subject of magnitude and going on to a discussion of issues, it may be well to give the figures from the Corporation's balance sheet as of June 30, 1940 showing the value of the commodities listed as "stores."[24]

Dairy products	$ 9,410,534.00
Fruits and vegetables	6,827,667.00
Grain products	15,241,903.00
Pork products	17,636,057.00
Cotton products	7,282,829.00
Timber products	13,065,735.11
Other	22,421.00
Total	$69,487,146.11

PROBLEMS IN THE PROGRAM

A program of giving away surpluses for the purpose of maintaining the price of the balance sold in normal trade presented several important problems from the standpoint of relief and its administration. Among the questions were:

1. How shall the fact of a surplus be determined?

2. How can the products be given away without interfering with the demand for the balance—or for alternative products—at the prices to be sustained?

3. What classes of the population shall be the recipients of the free goods?

4. How shall the free goods be distributed to the beneficiaries? Each of these questions will be considered in turn.

What constitutes a surplus? A surplus of goods, from a practical standpoint, exists chiefly with respect to a price. If the retail price goes low enough, the goods will in general move, although not without losses to producers and perhaps to middlemen and retailers. The price used in determining the existence of a surplus was the price that would protect the farmer, giving him either a reasonable income as reward for his labors or power to purchase, by the return from the crop he had raised, a parity amount of the things he had to buy or would ordinarily have bought. The statistical measures are not precise; their application calls for the exercise of judgment and discretion, and the power to exercise judgment and discretion was vested

[24] The same, p. 10.

ultimately in officials of the United States Department of Agriculture.

Since the objective was to sustain prices to protect the producer or processor, the cause of the surplus was not necessarily a vital factor. Crops may have been too large to move at any price. Temporary local gluts may have occurred through faulty distribution. Consumers may have shown a preference for an alternative commodity either because of taste preferences or because of price differences. Whatever the cause, the government could declare a surplus and provide for removing it by giving it away at government expense.

More important from the standpoint of relief, the commodities to be given away as surpluses were not necessarily selected on the basis of the balanced dietary requirements of persons in need or the most effective use of funds for relief. An oversupply of perishables—goods which must be moved rapidly to prevent spoilage and financial loss to producers and handlers —is of course more likely to break prices than a surplus of goods which can be stored and even carried over from one season to another. Surplus commodities gave the recipients not the best diet that the amount spent by the government would procure, but the things which were not moving in sufficient volume at the sustained price. Some of them were protective foods, some were higher-priced alternative foods which low-income bracket families rarely purchase. Whether the families needed them or not was a matter of secondary consideration, for price maintenance was the major objective.

How can goods be given away without affecting price? If prices are to be maintained by giving away surpluses two principles must be followed:

1. The goods must not be given away to persons who would otherwise buy them at the price to be maintained.

2. The persons to whom they are given must not be permitted to substitute them for alternative articles which they would otherwise buy, the prices of which are likewise to be sustained. Such a gift would diminish a surplus for one commodity by increasing the supply of another and thus defeat the pro-

gram of price maintenance unless the government was prepared to keep pouring money into the program.

The government rules therefore provided that gifts of surplus commodities were not to be substitutes for the food customarily purchased, and that the value of the surplus commodities was not to be considered as a resource of the family in determining whether or not it was in need. The free commodities were to be in addition to relief.[25]

The government, moreover, did not want the families to use the surplus commodities as a means for freeing funds previously used for food for the purchase of non-food products. A family left to its own inclinations might prefer additional clothing or amusements to more food or a greater diversity of food, but such choices would impair the efficiency of the program in attaining its major objective of price maintenance, mainly of agricultural products.

To achieve the objectives, therefore, surplus commodities had to be given only to persons who were in need. Whether a family is or is not in need requires an investigation. In the early days of the surplus distribution, the tendency was to give the articles to any family or individual whose need had been determined by a local public agency as the result of an investigation to determine eligibility for relief. This method had certain defects.

1. In some communities, notably in the South, the only relief programs of any consequence were those supported directly or indirectly by federal funds, W.P.A., N.Y.A., C.C.C., and the three relief categories under the Social Security Act. Few individuals or families not applying for one of these forms of public aid were investigated for eligibility. As a result families had to be investigated for the one purpose of establishing their eligibility to secure surplus commodities. In some cases these commodities were almost all they had to keep them going.

2. The resources of some families, including money received

[25] Doris Carothers, *Chronology of the Federal Emergency Relief Administration, May 12, 1933, to Dec. 31, 1935*, Works Progress Administration, Research Monograph VI, (1937), p. 20.

from other relief programs, carried them above need. Receipt of surplus commodities permitted them to divert money previously spent for food to other purposes. This diversion tended to defeat the main objective of the surplus commodity program. It demonstrated that the demand for food is relatively inelastic, that the desire for other things is often of greater weight than the desire for more food. In some jurisdictions, therefore, persons who were receiving work relief were declared ineligible for surplus commodities. The true index of eligibility for surplus agricultural commodities in a program to maintain prices is not the family budget as a whole but principally the food item in the budget. If that item is reasonably satisfactory, gifts of additional surplus food commodities are likely to result not in additional food consumption but in spending money previously used for food for other things the family wants more, things the farmers buy rather than things they have to sell.

3. The free distribution of surplus commodities resulted in some glaring inequities. They can perhaps best be described by a hypothetical illustration. Two families almost comparable as to size live in the same neighborhood under like general conditions. The standard budget used to determine whether or not these families are in need calls for resources amounting to $40 a month. Family A has resources just above $40 a month and thus is ineligible for relief. Family B has resources of $20 and therefore is given $20 a month in relief. Since Family B is on relief it is eligible to receive surplus commodities over and above the $20 it gets as relief. As the result of governmental action, Family B is now better off than Family A by the amount of the gifts of surplus commodities made by the national government. Family A must pay the governmentally sustained price for the food it gets, and hence its food consumption is curtailed rather than increased by governmental action.

This discrimination was not only inequitable;[26] it operated

---

[26] Certain public relations aspects of these inequities deserve brief note. Mrs. A and Mrs. B in the illustration just cited are shopping in the neighborhood store at the same time. Mrs. A cannot afford any oranges for her children because the sustained price is too high. Mrs. B takes a dozen and pays for them in blue stamps given to her because her family is in need.

against the increased food consumption sought in the program. Thus in several localities low-income families not eligible for relief were declared eligible to receive surplus commodities. The scientific method to make the program effective appeared to lie along the line of (1) classifying families according to size, (2) determining how much families of each size would have to spend for food for a suitable diet, and (3) giving surplus commodities to those families that were below standard in their food expenditures but only to the extent that would bring them to standard, lest larger gifts would result in diversion. Gross income alone, without reference to size of family, was not a satisfactory index because in the case of small families it would result in diversion and inequities.

Thus the question of eligibility for the receipt of surplus commodities in a price maintenance program is substantially different from that of eligibility for public assistance in a relief program since it relates almost entirely to the food item in the budget.

How should free commodities be distributed? The physical distribution of the surplus commodities presented serious problems. In the early thirties when the program began under the auspices of the Federal Emergency Relief Administration, there was considerable confusion. One local relief agency, for example, received notice that a carload of potatoes was being shipped to it for free distribution to eligibles on relief. This agency had had no experience in handling carload shipments of perishable commodities and no facilities for handling them. The immediate solution was to distribute the carload at once to relief clients, but unfortunately many of the families had no facilities for storing the potatoes where they would be protected from freezing. Spoilage rates were high.

A substantial taxpayer far from fishing centers learns that the relief agencies are distributing fine fish to the needy in his community. He is certain that the government has gone mad. He did not know that "purchases of surplus fish were made from 77 vendors having stocks on hand located in 15 States. Wide distribution of this fish to the States for relief use was made, and care was taken to make shipments into areas in which fish had not been used to a great extent in order to encourage future consumption." *Report of Federal Surplus Commodities Corporation for the Fiscal Year 1937,* p. 2.

One solution was to use C.W.A. money and later W.P.A. money to establish central commissariats, where the foods, particularly the perishables, could be properly handled. Relief clients could then go to the commissariat and draw the surplus commodities in quantities related to their immediate needs and their facilities for home storage. In some larger communities neighborhood depots were used to solve the problem of distance and in others door-to-door deliveries were made. Occasionally administrators resorted to parcel post. Under these systems distribution costs were fairly high, but high costs could be defended on the ground that relief labor was used. If the relief workers were not engaged in the distribution of surplus commodities, they would be employed on other relief projects or be in receipt of direct relief, and therefore, from a relief administrator's point of view, the matter of administrative costs was not particularly significant. Indeed, high administrative costs might even be regarded as a virtue under a spending philosophy.

A major trouble with this governmental distribution was that it constituted ruinous competition for grocers with many customers on relief. They had their stores, their refrigerators, and their other special equipment, but they had little or no business in commodities which were surplus at the moment. At times they would find themselves with a stock of perishables they could not sell because their customers could get the commodity or an alternative commodity free from the government. Some of their former customers adjusted to new conditions and depended primarily on surplus commodities. The plight of the retail outlets affected the wholesalers and some of the processors because the government had established a competitive system using relief labor and relief capital.

Some retailers found it to their advantage to co-operate with the relief agencies by carrying stocks of the surplus commodities which they would distribute to their customers in exchange for orders or coupons issued by the relief agencies. Under this system their old customers continued to come to their stores, and the grocers would know more about surplus commodities in stock and expected, and therefore could manage their own businesses more effectively.

The stamp plan. Out of this situation grew the stamp plan, welcomed by the retailers, the wholesalers, the processors, the chains, and many of the relief clients. The stamp plan was introduced experimentally in Rochester, New York and was gradually extended, almost invariably experimentally, in many different communities. There was no uniform pattern for all communities; almost every experiment had its variants from the basic pattern. The basic elements were roughly as follows:

1. The person eligible to receive surplus commodities would buy with his own money, or with relief money given him, orange-colored stamps in denominations of 25 cents. These orange stamps were the equivalent of cash and generally could be used for the purchase of anything which the grocer carried except liquor, although in some experiments there were other restrictions.

2. With the orange stamps the person would be given free blue stamps, likewise in denominations of 25 cents, in the earlier experiments to an amount equivalent to 50 per cent of the value of the orange stamps he had bought. These blue stamps could be used only for the purchase of commodities declared surplus by the Secretary of Agriculture or the Surplus Marketing Administration in the Department of Agriculture, the successor to various earlier organizations stemming back to F.E.R.A.

3. There were usually minimum and maximum limitations on the number of orange stamps that could be purchased and hence on the number of free blue stamps.

4. So far as the grocer was concerned, both the orange and the blue stamps were the equivalent of cash. Orange stamps went through ordinary banking channels until they were cashed by the Treasury out of funds secured from their original sale. Blue stamps went through other channels to be cashed from special appropriations for relief and price maintenance.

5. Grocers purchased their stocks in the normal way through wholesalers or processors, not necessarily knowing what articles would be declared surplus while still on their shelves. From time to time the authorities of the Department of Agriculture

would declare articles surplus, and the grocer could sell them for blue stamps as well as for cash or for orange stamps. Unless a commodity was listed as surplus, he could sell it only for cash or orange stamps and in the case of liquor and in certain localities some other commodities only for cash.

6. The grocer and his suppliers made the same profit on each transaction regardless of whether the customer paid in cash or in orange or blue stamps.

As experience with the system developed, certain defects became obvious. One was that very poor families, especially in communities where funds for general public assistance were low, had no funds with which to buy the orange stamps and therefore they were at first cut off from free surplus commodities. The solution here was for the agency determining eligibility to give them blue stamps without any purchase of orange stamps or to give them a much higher than normal ratio of blue stamps to orange stamps.

Families who had sufficient cash to meet their food needs would use their blue stamps for surplus food and use the orange stamps thus released for non-food products. Two correctives were tried, one to limit the number of orange stamps a family could buy and hence the number of blue stamps they could get, and the other to forbid the grocers to sell non-food articles for orange stamps. As previously noted under eligibility, the trend was toward the use of formulae relating the number of orange stamps that could be purchased to food requirements of the family and determining the number of blue stamps to be given free according to the size and income of the family. The very poor family was given a large number of blue stamps with a small purchase or no purchase of orange stamps. A family with enough money for its food needs could buy only a few orange stamps and would be given a low ratio of blue stamps on this purchase of orange stamps.

Restrictions on the use of orange stamps for nonagricultural products apparently in some cases did not appeal to the beneficiaries. The few blue stamps given them did not compensate for the loss of the freedom of choice that cash confers, yet the restrictions were necessary to effectuate price maintenance and the removal of surpluses.

Some social workers have long believed that under normal circumstances relief should be paid in cash and not in stamps, script, or store orders. There were perhaps two major reasons for this view: (1) the recipient should not be forced to disclose the fact to tradesmen and fellow customers in the stores that the family is on relief, and (2) within broad limits the recipient should have the satisfaction and the responsibility of apportioning available funds according to family needs and desires. Freedom of choice is, according to this point of view, desirable to sustain morale and to train the family in the wise use of money. Obviously the stamp plan is objectionable from this standpoint, but it should be repeated that in several states persons in desperate need would have suffered far more than they did had it not been for the distribution of surplus commodities which ultimately was refined under the stamp plan.

Abuses of the stamp plan. To a cynic the whole program of the free distribution of surplus commodities and especially the stamp system appears to be a fertile field for black market operators and bootleggers. No government could afford to police such a system sufficiently to prevent illegal transactions. It may be worth-while to list some of the more or less obvious methods of "cashing in" on surplus commodites or stamps.

1. The recipient of the free goods can sell or swap them or use them in payment of a debt. The price at which they then change hands will be below the market price the government is seeking to maintain. To prevent this sort of transaction the government would have to police thousands of persons.

2. The recipient of blue stamps can give them away or sell them. If the person who takes them is himself entitled to use blue stamps he may, to avoid difficulties, deal only with a friendly grocer or divide his patronage between several dealers so that the excessive use of blue stamps will not be noted. A purchaser of blue stamps who is not entitled to use them may

find an agent who is or else get the real owner of the blue stamps to purchase the goods and deliver them to him.

3. Since both orange and blue stamps are the equivalent of cash so far as the dealer is concerned, fear of detection is the major force deterring him from illegal transactions. For example, if a customer wants a bottle of whiskey, he can quietly offer $2.00 for it in blue stamps. A clerk can take the blue stamps, give him a dollar in cash to pay for the whiskey at the counter and later convert the blue stamps into cash or use them for the purchase of $2.00 worth of goods for himself. Again, if a customer desires to buy with his blue stamps goods not then considered to be surplus, or he desires to buy non-agricultural commodities with his orange stamps, the sale of such goods can be arranged surreptitiously.

On the introduction of the stamp plan, dealers and their suppliers were eager for it, because it meant an end of government competition and a profit for them on all transactions including the surplus commodities. A strong sentiment existed against irregularities in the store. This sentiment did not prevent customers from trading after they left the store, nor is it likely to survive should such a system become thoroughly entrenched. The fact that the government operates such a system to channel consumers' purchases in the interest of a policy that may not appeal to the buyer adds to the incentives for evasion.

Who pays for the surplus commodities? Ultimately, of course, the general taxpayers must pay for surplus commodities, although during the depression the money used came largely from borrowing by the federal government. Who derives the major benefits from these government expenditures? Producers, processors and, under the stamp plan, handlers and the persons who receive surplus commodities free.

Does the consumer who is not eligible for free surplus commodities have to pay more for what he gets than he would have had to pay had there been no such distribution? In some instances surplus disposal coupled with crop control may result in more orderly marketing so that the consumer gets no distress bargains, but at other times he does not have to pay such high prices on account of shortages. In general, however, the program prevents distress sales to the normal consumer resulting from surpluses but does not prevent the price from rising when there is no surplus. The device is designed for government protection to the farmer. From the standpoint of incidence, it appears to bear most heavily on families whose income is in brackets not greatly above the eligibility level because they spend a relatively high proportion of their incomes for food. On the other hand, while upper-income families with a low proportion of expenditures for food do not contribute much more than other families through higher prices, they will pay the taxes for the money the government uses to buy the surplus commodities or to cash the blue stamps.

Political factors. All members of voting age in a family receiving blue stamps regularly and enjoying the extra food and the diversity of diet made possible through their use should appreciate the bounty of the government. A practical ward worker will want it to appear that he has assisted in securing the privilege of blue stamps for the family even if the family would have secured them without any activity on his part. In the course of a political campaign it is probably inevitable that voters receiving blue stamps will be reminded of the virtues of the party that inaugurated the system, even if it is not suggested that the opposition party would take them away.

Negative incentives. Under the old system an individual might work harder or longer than he had previously worked because he or some member of his family needed or wanted more or better food. Under the stamp plan a worker may appreciate that if he worked a little harder or longer and earned a little more he would lose his eligibility to get free commodities. His extra effort would make him worse off then he was before. He may discover that materially larger earnings are necessary if he is to pay the sustained market price for the goods which formerly were given to him.

CHAPTER XII

THE W.P.A. AND OTHER WORK AGENCIES

The present chapter will be concerned primarily with that major work relief agency, the Work Projects Administration, but it will deal incidentally with other work programs undertaken partially to furnish employment and thus relieve need resulting from the depression. We shall attempt to outline the evolution of W.P.A. and then take up what appear to us to be the major issues that developed.

EVOLUTION OF W.P.A.

Prior to 1929 the national government had no direct responsibility for relief except with respect to its Indian wards and occasionally with respect to victims of disasters. When unemployment resulting from the depression reached disaster magnitudes and caught both local and state governments almost entirely unprepared legally, financially, and administratively, the demand arose for federal action to help meet the emergency. Three things were asked of the national government: (1) that it should adopt legislation that would restore the functioning of the economic system, (2) that it should stimulate the immediate construction of various types of facilities by public or private agencies to create employment, and (3) that it should share with the states and the local governments the costs of relief. These three demands were obviously not separate and distinct but were intimately interrelated. All were devices to attain the same basic objectives, restoration of employment and relief for those in need.

The fact that the objectives were common and the devices interrelated explains why all the devices were used more or less simultaneously. The W.P.A. with which we are immediately concerned, gradually emerged out of the welter of experimentation and assumed its distinctive form. It was not planned, blue printed, and organized in accordance with predetermined prin-

345

ciples. Rather it evolved through a process of improvising without clearly defined basic law or fundamental governing principles arrived at through the customary legislative processes. Its history cannot be given by referring to any organic act or acts and to the hearings and debates that preceded the passage of such acts. It was the product of administrative action, ratified and approved by the legislature rather than a program designed by legislative process and then carried out by the administrative branch of the government.

Emergency Relief and Construction Act, 1932. The earliest action with which we are especially concerned in the present chapter came in the Hoover administration with the approval on July 21, 1932 of the Emergency Relief and Construction Act of 1932.[1] Title I of this act authorized the Reconstruction Finance Corporation, which had been established on January 22 of that year, to loan not to exceed 300 million dollars to the states and territories "to be used in furnishing relief and work relief to needy and distressed people and in relieving the hardship resulting from unemployment." The loans authorized were to bear interest at 3 per cent and were to be repaid "by making annual deductions, beginning with the fiscal year 1935, from regular apportionments made from future Federal authorizations in aid of the States and Territories for the construction of highways and rural post roads" at the rate of one fifth of the grant-in-aid for the roads or one fifth of the relief loan, whichever was the lesser. This requirement was subsequently repealed so that there were no repayments.

Title II of the act authorized the Reconstruction Finance Corporation (1) to make loans or contracts with states, municipalities, and political subdivisions of states, to aid in financing legally authorized projects which are self-liquidating in character, (2) to make loans to corporations formed wholly for the purpose of providing housing for families of low income or for reconstruction of slum areas provided the corporations were duly regulated on specified matters and the loans were self-liquidating, (3) to make self-liquidating loans to private cor-

[1] 47 Stat. 709.

porations for specified works devoted to public use, (4) to make self-liquidating loans to private limited dividend corporations for projects for the protection and development of forests and other renewable natural resources, provided the corporations were regulated by a governmental agency, and (5) to make loans for publicly owned bridges where the loan would be repaid in part by tolls, fees, or rents and in part by taxes already authorized by law.

Title III of the act appropriated about 322 million dollars for the construction of federal public works and for emergency construction on the federal-aid highway system.

Four facts with respect to the policies involved in this initial act require special emphasis: (1) According to the original plan, the national government was to merely loan the money, expecting to get it back, in the case of relief money by deductions from subsequent federal grants for highways and in the case of public works from their self-liquidating character. Self-liquidating was defined in the act. (2) Loans could be made to private corporations for specified purposes provided these corporations were regulated by a state or a political subdivision of a state. (3) The national government served only as a financial agency so far as the states and their subdivisions were concerned. With respect to them it did not become a construction agency. So far as federal construction was concerned, the agencies of the national government would function much as they had in the past. (4) The provision for loans to the states for relief purposes specifically included *furnishing work relief*.

Three facts with respect to the timing connected with this act likewise deserve mention: (1) This act was not on the statute books when the depression developed nor was it passed in the early days of the depression. It did not become law until the depression had been running for many months, and after the 1932 political campaign was already under way. (2) Many of the types of projects authorized could not be started for months either because much time was needed for land acquisition, designing, and the like or laws had to be passed to permit public or private agencies to qualify. (3) By the time the act was passed, a strong movement had developed for outright gifts or grants from the national government.

Soon after the Roosevelt administration came into office in March 1933, new legislation was passed relating to both relief and public works.

Federal Emergency Relief Act, 1933. Two provisions for relief made in the Federal Emergency Relief Act approved May 12, 1933,[2] are important for our immediate purposes: (1) it authorized "grants to the several States to aid in meeting the costs of furnishing relief and work relief and in relieving the hardship and suffering caused by unemployment in the form of money, service, materials, and/or commodities to provide the necessities of life to persons in need as a result of the present emergency, and/or to their dependents, whether resident, transient, or homeless;" (2) it provided for a Federal Emergency Relief Administration, the powers of which were exercised by the Federal Relief Administrator. This administration ultimately evolved into W.P.A.

Funds for the new administration came from the R.F.C. and amounted to 500 million dollars in addition to amounts still available under the earlier act. R.F.C. was prohibited from further relief administration after ten days following the appointment of the new administrator.

Half of the 500 millions was to be distributed among the states on application up to one third of the amount spent by them from public funds. The other half was to be distributed in the discretion of the administrator when he found the money available to any state fell below the need.

Three points with respect to this Emergency Relief Act require emphasis: (1) It made outright gifts of federal funds to the states. (2) It left administration in the hands of the states, although the discretionary power vested in the federal administrator made him highly influential with state officers. (3) Although like the earlier act it made federal money available to the states for work relief, it did not provide for federal work relief or other federal projects to furnish employment.

[2] 48 Stat. 55.

National Industrial Recovery Act. Provision for public works and construction projects were included in Title II of the National Industrial Recovery Act, approved June 16, 1933.[3]
The more essential features of this act were:

1. It provided for both loans and grants to the nonfederal public bodies which should undertake eligible projects approved by the national government in accordance with the act. Grants, however, could not exceed 30 per cent of the cost of labor and materials.

2. The public works eligible were briefly (a) public highways and parkways, public buildings, and publicly owned instrumentalities and facilities, (b) conservation and development of natural resources, (c) projects heretofore constructed or carried on either directly by public authorities or with public aid to serve the interests of the public, (d) low-cost housing and slum-clearance projects under public regulation and control, and (e) any other project that would have been eligible under the Emergency Relief and Construction Act of the Hoover administration.

3. Loans to railroads for maintenance and equipment when approved by the Interstate Commerce Commission were specifically authorized.

4. Administrative authority was vested in a newly created agency, the Federal Emergency Administration of Public Works, "all the powers of which shall be exercised by a Federal Emergency Administrator of Public Works."

5. "With a view to increasing employment quickly (while reasonably securing any loans made by the United States) the President is authorized and empowered, through the Administrator or through such other agencies as he may designate or create, (1) to construct, finance, or aid in the construction or financing of any public-works project included in the program prepared pursuant to section 202" (summarized in paragraph 2 above). The power to make the loans and grants was by this same general language vested in the President.

Two points call for special emphasis: (1) The real power was

[3] 48 Stat. 200, Title II.

vested not in the Federal Administrator of Public Works but in the President. He could delegate authority to the administrator or to any agency he might designate or create. Thus he had authority, if he wished, to give some of the powers to the Federal Emergency Relief Administration. (2) The President had power to determine whether "to construct" or "to finance or aid in the construction of."

The President appointed as Federal Administrator of Public Works, Harold L. Ickes, Secretary of the Interior, who thereafter held both offices during the life of P.W.A. To some extent the work of P.W.A. became integrated with that of the Interior Department, especially with reference to housekeeping functions. As Federal Emergency Relief Administrator the President appointed Harry Hopkins, who became head of an independent agency not tied in with any other department or agency.

The Public Works Administration under Mr. Ickes became in essence a public works financing agency and not in itself a construction agency. It had divisions on engineering, law, and finance which made the necessary studies for approving nonfederal projects and an inspection force to make sure that the loans and grants were applied in accordance with the approved terms. Actual construction was done by agencies selected by the borrowers. P.W.A. could approve federal projects and allot funds to them, subject to presidential approval, but then the actual work was done by other federal agencies and not by P.W.A.

P.W.A. was inevitably handicapped by much the same time factors as have previously been mentioned as holding up action under the Hoover plan. Laws had to be passed in many states and subordinate governments, land had to be acquired, plans had to be drawn and approved, contracts had to be let, and material secured. The projects were as a rule relatively large, and P.W.A. under Mr. Ickes sought to maintain high standards. Experience again demonstrated the long time which must elapse between the inception of a project and the actual employment of men in any considerable numbers.

Civil Works Administration. As the works program under P.W.A. was not furnishing the hoped for employment or doing much toward diminishing the relief load, the President in November 1933 utilized the authority given him under Title II of the National Industrial Recovery Act to establish by executive order[4] the Federal Civil Works Administration, under the direction of the Federal Emergency Relief Administrator. To this agency he allocated the sum of 400 million dollars from the appropriation of 3.3 billions made for the National Industrial Recovery Act. Although C.W.A. was a separate agency, it was identified in the public mind with F.E.R.A. and in the state and local governments commonly functioned through the agencies developed for relief administration.

The objective of C.W.A. was to furnish almost immediately jobs for some 4 million workers, about half of whom were to be taken from the relief rolls. The others were to be employables in need of jobs but not yet on relief. C.W.A. fairly mushroomed. In the month of its creation about 1.5 millions were employed; the next month this figure more than doubled. In January 1934 the goal of the program was more than fulfilled, as over 4 millions received C.W.A. checks.[5] In that month the number of persons benefiting from employment on federal work and relief programs reached an all-time high of about 28 millions, and monthly payments for relief and earnings soared to over 300 millions, a figure not reached again in any month except December 1938.[6]

This program was, however, short-lived. The cost was high; the number of dissatisfied persons not on relief who felt they had a right to a job but could not get one was large; and in the haste to get people at work, numerous projects were undertaken which aroused hostile criticism and ridicule. A wage scale was initially established identical with that used for P.W.A. Under

[4] 6420-B, Nov. 9, 1933.
[5] *Expenditure of Funds Federal Emergency Relief Administration,* S. Doc. 56, 74 Cong. 1 sess., p. 392.
[6] Theodore E. Whiting and T. J. Woofter, Jr., *Summary of Relief and Federal Work Program Statistics, 1933–1940* (1941), pp. 19, 28.

it, hourly rates varied with skill and geographic area, influenced, however, by minimum and prevailing wage principles. Schedules of maximum hours were set up, so a definite weekly wage could be earned by all workers on the programs, irrespective of individual differences in personal or family needs. Average earnings approximated $15 a week when the program was in full swing, but because of costs maximum hours were sharply cut, reducing average earnings to $11.52 for the week of January 27, 1934.[7] By the end of April C.W.A. was discontinued for all practical purposes. In a period of about five months it had cost some 931 million dollars of which the national government had contributed about 90 per cent.[8]

From the standpoint of administrative officers, the C.W.A. was a valuable experiment yielding lessons in how a work program ought to be developed. The President apparently had reached the conclusion that a national work program should be substituted for national contributions for relief for unemployed employables. So far as this class of needy persons was concerned the national government was to get out of the relief business, although at approximately the same time it was planning national grants to the states for the three relief categories of the Social Security Act.

Emergency Relief Appropriation Act, 1935. On April 8, 1935 the Emergency Relief Appropriation Act was approved,[9] which represented the embodiment in law of the policy to substitute a nationally administered program of public works and other projects for grants to the states for the relief of unemployed employables. Rarely if ever in our history have more important determinations of basic fundamental policy been embodied in an appropriation act without any substantive legislation authorizing it and without consideration by any committee of Congress other than the appropriations committees.

Space will not permit us to go at length into the proposals as submitted to the Congress by the administration and the legislative history of the act. Readers interested in this aspect

---

[7] Edward A. Williams, *Federal Aid for Relief* (1939), p. 121.
[8] The same, p. 119.
[9] 49 Stat. 115.

of the subject should read Chapter 2, "The Initial Legislation" in that authoritative work *The Administration of Federal Work Relief* by Arthur W. Macmahon, John D. Millett, and Gladys Ogden.[10] These authors point out that the proposal for the appropriation measure "seemed as vague as it was vast." To quote a little further: "The vagueness . . . was real enough." "The draftsmen had no precise understanding of what the President wished."[11]

The management of the joint resolution after its introduction made the program seem even vaguer than it really was. The defects of the bill's piloting were in part the consequence of the still unresolved questions. Officials of the FERA could have told with considerable accuracy the sorts of projects that would be necessary to provide jobs for relief recipients. But the unsettled question of organization prevented them from claiming the responsibility that such an explanation would have implied. Besides, the strategy of presenting the program as a break with the past forbade emphasis upon the familiar and the humble.

The absence of an authoritative and informed spokesman at the congressional hearings deepened the impression of planlessness.[12]

"To provide relief, work relief and to increase employment by providing for useful projects" the act appropriated "to be used in the discretion and under the direction of the President" the sum of 4 billion dollars plus various unexpended balances from other appropriations which made in the aggregate 4,880 millions available until June 30, 1937.[13]

The President in carrying out the provisions of the act was authorized "to establish and prescribe the duties and functions of necessary agencies within the Government" and "appoint, without regard to the provisions of the civil-service laws, such officers and employees . . . as may be necessary, prescribe their authorities, duties, responsibilities, and tenure, and, without

---

[10] Public Administration Service, Chicago (1941). Under the auspices of the Committee on Public Administration of the Social Science Research Council Professor Macmahon, assisted by Miss Ogden, carried on a "capture and record study," being stationed in Washington and following day-to-day in detail the developments under the 1935 and later acts.

[11] Macmahon, Millett, and Ogden, *The Administration of Federal Work Relief*, pp. 45, 46.

[12] The same, p. 47.

[13] 49 Stat. 115.

regard to the Classification Act of 1923, as amended, fix the compensation of any officers and employees so appointed." But appointments to positions paying $5,000 or more were in general to be made "by and with the advice and consent of the Senate."[14]

Wages for project workers were to be fixed by the President at such a rate "as will in the discretion of the President accomplish the purposes of this joint resolution, and not affect adversely or otherwise tend to decrease the going rates of wages paid for work of a similar nature." He was specifically authorized to "fix different rates of wages for various types of work on any project, which rates need not be uniform throughout the United States."[15]

The law, as finally passed, did not vest in the President entirely unlimited authority to expend the money appropriated for such classes of projects as he saw fit. Limits were established which we shall summarize in millions of dollars:[16]

Highways, roads, streets, and grade-crossing elimination	800
Rural rehabilitation and relief in stricken agricultural areas, and water conservation, trans-mountain water diversion and irrigation and reclamation	500
Rural electrification	100
Housing	450
Assistance for educational, professional, and clerical persons	300
Civilian Conservation Corps	600
Loans or grants, or both, for projects of States, Territories, Possessions, and subdivisions thereof	900
Sanitation, prevention of soil erosion, prevention of stream pollution, sea coast erosion, reforestation, forestation, flood control, rivers and harbors and miscellaneous projects	350

The law went on to provide, however, "That not to exceed 20 per centum of the amount herein appropriated may be used by the President to increase any one or more of the foregoing limitations if he finds it necessary to do so in order to effectuate the purpose of this joint resolution."[17] Twenty per cent of the aggregate appropriation amounted to 976 millions, which gave the President considerable leeway for the exercise of administrative discretion.

[14] 49 Stat. 117, 118.
[15] 49 Stat. 118.
[16] 49 Stat. 115–16.
[17] 49 Stat. 116.

Federal appropriations for highways and roads were by no means new. A complete system of federal-state co-operation for highways had been developed over the years so that there were state highway departments in all the states. The law therefore contained provisions governing the relationships with these departments which we shall attempt to summarize generally because of the importance of the impact of a new federal works program on the established order in an important branch of public works.

1. The sums allocated by the President for highways with certain exceptions were to be apportioned among the states by the Secretary of Agriculture in accordance with certain existing laws "for expenditure by the State highway departments under the provisions of the Federal Highway Act of November 9, 1921, as amended and supplemented" by later laws.

2. The sums for grade-crossing elimination were likewise to be apportioned among the states by the Secretary of Agriculture in accordance with a formula contained in the act itself.

3. "No part of the funds apportioned to any State or Territory under this joint resolution for public highways and grade crossings need be matched."

4. Although the expenditures were to be made under the state highway departments the law provided that expenditures "shall be subject to such rules and regulations as the President may prescribe . . . and preference in the employment of labor shall be given (except in executive, administrative, supervisory, and highly skilled positions) to persons receiving relief, where they are qualified, and the President is hereby authorized to predetermine for each State the hours of work and the rates of wages to be paid to skilled, intermediate, and unskilled labor engaged in such construction."[18]

Expenditures for rivers and harbors, reclamation and public buildings projects were to be carried out under the direction of "the respective permanent Government departments or agencies now having jurisdiction of similar projects."[19]

[18] 49 Stat. 116, 117.
[19] 49 Stat. 117.

In the light of the subsequent war one proviso written into the law in the Senate is highly significant. It reads:

That no part of the appropriation made by this joint resolution shall be expended for munitions, warships, or military or naval matériel; but this proviso shall not be constructed to prevent the use of such appropriation for new buildings, reconstruction of buildings and other improvements in military or naval reservations, posts, forts, camps, cemeteries, or fortified areas . . . .[20]

In concluding this summary of the initial law, attention should be called to one of those persuasive but unenforceable declarations of public policy which are sometimes encountered in legislative enactments. Section 8 of the law reads: "Wherever practicable in the carrying out of the provisions of this joint resolution, full advantage shall be taken of the facilities of private enterprise."[21]

Administration under the 1935 law. This 1935 law, as previously noted, left the question of administrative organization almost entirely in the hands of the President. Although the act was approved April 8, 1935, the executive order[22] setting up the major new organization was not issued until May 6, because real plans and decisions with respect to it had not been made in advance, and many forces had to be reconciled.[23]

Under authority of the act the President established two other agencies: the Resettlement Administration by Executive Order 7027, issued on April 30, 1935, six days before the major order, and the Rural Electrification Administration, by Executive Order 7037, issued on May 11, 1935. The Resettlement Administration has already been discussed in Chapter X.

The organization provided in Executive Order 7034 consisted of three parts:

1. The Division of Applications and Information of the National Emergency Council, which was to receive all applications

---

[20] 49 Stat. 116.
[21] 49 Stat. 118.
[22] 7034.
[23] For an account of the interplay of forces and personalities in the organization period see Macmahon, Millett, and Ogden, *The Administration of Federal Work Relief,* pp. 62 ff.

for projects, cause them to be examined and reviewed, and transmit them to the Advisory Committee on Allotments.

2. The Advisory Committee on Allotments, of which the Secretary of the Interior was designated chairman. The other members fell into two groups: (a) the heads of government departments, bureaus, or offices, which for one reason or another had a special interest in or concern with the program; and (b) representatives of the Business Advisory Council, and of organized labor, farm organizations, the American Bankers' Association, and the United States Conference of Mayors. Its duty was to make recommendations to the President.

3. A Works Progress Administration "which shall be responsible to the President for the honest, efficient, speedy, and co-ordinated execution of the work relief program as a whole, and for the execution of that program in such manner as to move from the relief rolls to work on such projects or in private employment the maximum number of persons in the shortest time possible." The executive order went on to enumerate the specific duties of the Works Progress Administration which can be summarized as (1) to investigate, (2) to secure uniform periodic reports to prevent delay and to serve as a basis for recommending termination of projects not furnishing sufficient employment, (3) with approval of the President to prescribe rules and regulations, (4) to formulate and administer a system of uniform periodic reports of the employment of persons receiving relief, (5) to investigate wages and working conditions and to make reports to the President which would aid him in prescribing working conditions, (6) to provide for the co-ordination of the necessary data and to co-ordinate all requests for opinions and decisions addressed to government offices affecting the program. At the very end came: "Recommend and carry on small useful projects designed to assure a maximum of employment in all localities. The Federal Emergency Relief Administrator shall serve also as Administrator of the Works Progress Administration."

Two features of this order call for special emphasis. (1) Although the President delegated duties to the administrative agencies he created, he delegated no power; the power he kept in his own hands. (2) The order resolved none of the conflicts either between personalities or between concepts or principles that had been responsible for the vagueness of the proposals, the legislation, and the debates.

The major clash of personalities was between Harold Ickes, administrator of public works and Harry Hopkins, made administrator of both the Federal Emergency Relief Administration and the W.P.A. With respect to this conflict two paragraphs from Macmahon, Millett, and Ogden are illuminating.

The implicit rivalry of the FERA and the PWA, personalized in Harry Hopkins and Harold Ickes, was also a particular ground for delaying and for blurring the choice of a form of organization. The two men had, indeed, much in common: they had the same humane sympathies and shared many social values. But as personalities they differed, especially in qualities reflected in their habits of work. In the one man saltiness was linked to an impatience and confidence that were almost imperious; with pungency in the other man went caution and a reluctance to delegate.

The rivalry, of course, was more of institutions than of men. Those who had been associated with the FERA did not think the PWA capable of creating direct employment either quickly or in large volume. The personnel of the Public Works Administration were smarting under the charge of slowness, but they were militantly proud of the reputation of their organization for technical competence and honesty. The projects featured in the early discussions of the works program, moreover, had made it seem an affair that by nature belonged to the PWA.[24]

The conflict in concepts and principles cannot be so simply stated. P.W.A., as we have noted, had developed basically into a financing agency and was not in itself a construction agency. It financed existing and sometimes newly created bodies, mostly public, which operated in the customary manner, although with some modifications with respect to wages, hours, and other conditions of employment. The projects financed through P.W.A. made large use of private contractors who supplied the technical supervision and hired the bulk of the employees. A

[24] The same, pp. 67–68.

fairly high percentage of the money loaned went for materials and equipment. Such purchases unquestionably stimulated what is often referred to as off the site employment, but precise measures of off the site employment can scarcely be made. Estimates have to be used, and estimates are frequently not very convincing, especially when presented by a governmental agency being charged with not producing needed employment. It may perhaps be fairly said that P.W.A. was being used in an attempt to prime the already existing economic pump, although not without some simultaneous effort to redesign the pump.

The W.P.A., on the other hand, put almost all its emphasis on creating jobs of the type which could be filled by persons on relief. It could achieve its purpose more efficiently and more rapidly if it used projects designed to give such employment and operated them with its own directors, supervisors, and foremen. It tended largely to by-pass the existing public works departments of state and local governments and—in so far as these departments had used private contractors—the private contractors and their workers. By proper selection of projects, it could get a relatively high figure for on the site employment.

It has been said that in a public works program designed to increase employment the two forms are complementary, that each has its place. Beyond doubt there are projects of such size and complexity that they can be carried on successfully only by highly organized, skilled, and experienced construction agencies using carefully selected workers. It is likewise true that there are workers for whom in slack periods it is very difficult to find work unless projects are specially created and operated by the government to give them employment. But as one moves down from the big, complicated project at the top utilizing highly organized private construction agencies and up from the sheltered project at the bottom operated by the government itself, one finds increasing and, from the standpoint of the functioning of the economic system, highly significant competition. Decisions resolving this competition between the government and private industry might involve the health of the system of

free enterprise and the extent of freedom of the states from
federal domination. Such a situation called for the drawing of a
boundary line separating the two fields of activity on the basis
of fundamental principles and objectives. The law drew no such
line, although it directed full utilization of the facilities of free
enterprise, and the executive order drew no such line. The
President retained the discretionary power vested in him by the
legislation and made his decisions largely on the individual
case basis.

Gradually as the program developed, it became increasingly
apparent that the decisions were tending in the main toward the
type of projects specially designed to take people off the relief
rolls and give them work they could do on governmentally operated, sheltered projects. Mr. Hopkins' position in the program
became of steadily increasing importance, whereas that of Mr.
Ickes, who had worked through existing state and local construction agencies, diminished. The work program tended to
become the W.P.A. program.

The Emergency Relief Appropriation Act of 1935 was, as the
description of it has shown, the authority for the creation of a
number of different agencies by the President, and the sum of
money it made available was a reservoir from which the President could draw not only to supply the new agencies but also
to make more funds available to existing agencies for additional
works. Over the ensuing years the trend was toward recognizing
certain of the new agencies as separate entities and making
appropriations specifically for them in accordance with the
earlier practices of the government. The trend also was toward making direct appropriations to the old establishments
to enable them to continue the extra work that had been
originally financed by a presidential allotment and that was to
be continued. In some instances, moreover, substantive laws
were adopted covering the new agency and its work. The
W.P.A., however, continued for many years to be financed
through an annual Emergency Relief Appropriation Act, considered in detail only by the appropriations committees of the
two houses.

Numerous changes in the details of the law governing W.P.A. were made in the successive annual appropriation acts that came after the fundamental one of 1935. These changes we shall take up in so far as they seem significant to our problem in the discussion of special issues that is to follow.

THE SELECTION OF PROJECTS

The task of selecting projects for W.P.A. presented new problems, economic, social, and governmental. The simplest way to present and discuss these problems, the solutions arrived at, and the effects is to examine them against a background of the methods which prevailed in the public and the private sectors of the economy prior to the depression of the thirties. Then what was done in W.P.A. can be contrasted with what will be termed "normal."

In the public sector of the economy, the normal procedure was for a representative legislative body to determine, by vote, for what objectives of government public funds should be spent. Legislatures determined the kind and extent of the government services to be rendered and the nature and cost of the public works to be built, although they often acted upon the recommendations of administrative officers. The legislative body was responsible to the electorate. In many local governments this line of responsibility was short and direct. The representatives not only had an ear to the ground; in many localities, particularly the smaller ones, they heard directly from individual citizens and groups of citizens advocating things they wanted and opposing things regarded as unnecessary, wasteful, or extravagant. With respect to certain functions of government the legislators at a lower level might be materially influenced in their decisions by conditional grants-in-aid made available by legislators at a higher level, but even under grants-in-aid a considerable measure of discretion was left to local and state legislators. Both local and state legislatures had to take into consideration the question of revenues and the effect of their action on taxes and tax rates. Thus the elected representatives tended to determine priorities among needs and desires for public services with regard to popular demands and tax revenues and burdens.

For the construction of public works, and in smaller places often for their maintenance, governments commonly employed private contractors. Rarely did governments build substantial public works by force account, or in other words by employing the directing personnel and hiring the necessary labor. Force account was frequently used for routine maintenance and repairs, but when large special projects were involved, the prevailing practice was to employ a contractor who supplied the required equipment for the job, purchased the necessary materials, and hired all the labor with perhaps the exception of inspectors. In a well-administered government the approved practice, frequently the legally required practice, was to let such contracts by competitive bids. Thus in several branches of the construction industry, public bodies constituted an important segment of the market for private enterprise.

In the private sector of the economy priorities in the production of goods and services were normally determined basically by the consumers. For what would individuals spend the purchasing power which they controlled? Groups of consumers with like desires constituted the market for a particular commodity. The state of the market for that commodity, or forecasts as to the future state of that market, influenced producers in making decisions with respect to capital investments in plant, equipment, raw materials, and inventory. Thus priorities in the private sector of the economy were determined by the way in which free individuals spent their money or upon forecasts—which might be incorrect—as to how much money they would have in the future, and how they would spend it.

Decisions of legislative bodies in the public sector and of consumers and producers in the private sector were the basic factors in determining the demand for specific classes of workers or for persons following a particular trade or calling. The more highly specialized a trade or calling, the more the security of the workers in it was dependent upon the maintenance of the market for their product. To a very considerable extent, effective demand over the years determined the occupational distribution of the workers of the country.

In neither sector of the economy was the question of the extent to which a given expenditure would furnish employment normally a major factor in arriving at a decision. Few consumers in purchasing a desired article, or in making a choice between alternative expenditures, give much thought as to what part of the money will go for labor, materials, and a reasonable return to capital. Both public and private consumers ordinarily buy a finished article to meet a particular need or to furnish a particular service.

Selection of projects to be undertaken by W.P.A. was based on very different considerations. It seems entirely fair to say that the dominant consideration in W.P.A. was the extent to which a project would immediately afford additional public employment of a type suitable for the needy unemployed in a given area. Although the utility of a project and the desire of the community for it were factors to be given some weight, they were subordinated to the main purpose—immediate, large, additional, suitable, public employment. Each of these five adjectives is basically significant.

With respect to the requirement for immediacy, a question which naturally comes to mind is, Why was immediacy essential? The answer apparently lies in the realm of political policy. At the time the work program was adopted, the F.E.R.A. was fully organized and was distributing federal grants to the states to relieve the need resulting from unemployment. The states by then had their emergency relief administrations. The system was functioning with improving efficiency. It is obvious that it would have been possible to adopt a program under which a full or a partial transition from an almost purely relief program to a work relief program could have been made far more gradually. The demand for immediacy came from the administration.

Insistence upon immediacy had two effects that deserve comment, the first technological and the second governmental. A major difficulty with a public works program for furnishing employment in an emergency is the amount of time required for planning, the acquisition of land, rights-of-way, and other technical details. In the absence of extensive advanced planning, insistence on immediacy meant a serious curtailment of the time for deliberation and planning or the selection of projects that called for little technical planning or a combination of both. This defect was greatest upon the initiation of the W.P.A. program and tended to disappear as time passed and as competent engineers were introduced into the national organization.

The democratic legislative process is slow as compared with governmental methods which permit a single officer, with such assistance as he may use, to make instantaneous decisions. The assumed need for speed may account in part for the fact that neither the state nor the local legislative bodies had a determining voice in deciding what projects should be carried on in their respective jurisdictions, despite the fact that the projects lay within their legal spheres under the American form of government. It probably also explains why Congress delegated to the President such broad discretionary power in the selection of projects.

The desire for speed in execution may also account in part for the fact that W.P.A. came into the states and the local areas and itself carried on activities which normally would have been administered by established agencies of state or local governments. In this connection, however, it should be remembered that some state or local agencies did not have a high reputation for competence and efficiency, and occasionally they were guilty of or suspected of financial irregularities. National administration may have appeared as one way to avoid local incompetence and perhaps graft; but at the same time it eliminated from controlling positions many state and local agencies which were well-organized, competent, going concerns with a high reputation in their respective fields.

The question is sometimes asked, Why did not the states and the local governments resist this encroachment by the national government upon their jurisdiction and insist upon greater participation both in making decisions and in administration? The facts were that the states and local governments were at the time directly responsible for thousands of unemployed employables, their revenues from taxation were low, they had little power to borrow, and the national government was withdrawing contributions toward direct relief and offering in their stead the W.P.A. program. The states and the local governments had to take what the national government offered, for the national government had effective power to borrow and they did not. In such a situation questions of constitutionality, federalism, and states' rights were academic and inopportune. The government paying the fiddler was in position to call the tune.

Attention should at this time again be called to the vital distinction between P.W.A. and W.P.A. P.W.A., which operated through a fairly close approach to normal procedures, actually gave the states only 30 per cent, later 40 per cent, of the costs of labor and materials; the participating government had to furnish the balance, although they might borrow from P.W.A. Certain requirements of P.W.A. tended toward increased costs and thus part of the national grant went to meet them. W.P.A. gave all but the sponsor's contribution, which was fixed by administrative discretion and ranged roughly from 10 to 25 per cent. In the earlier days of the program, moreover, sponsors' contributions were frequently made up of things or services which the participating governments could supply without new or additional expenditures of cash. Rooms in governmentally owned buildings, use of governmentally owned equipment, services of permanent employees who were already on the pay roll all might figure in the sponsor's contribution. The necessity of assuming liability for 60 to 70 per cent of cost, as under P.W.A., was a very different thing from having to put up a sponsor's contribution of at most 25 per cent, satisfied in part by items that involved no additional expenditures.

The insistence upon immediacy thus led to a wide departure from normal practices and the old distribution of power among the three levels of government.

The objective of the national government was to move large numbers of persons from the relief roll to the W.P.A. rolls. It was, therefore, deemed necessary to choose projects which would have such an effect and to reject those which might have very great economic and social utility but involve relatively small expenditures for on-the-site employment and relatively large expenditures for land, equipment, and material. In normal times the seller of land may put the proceeds of the sale to other uses promptly, and the seller of equipment and material may immediately engage in the production of more. In a depression the seller of land may let the proceeds lie idle in the bank. The seller of materials and equipment may merely convert stock on hand to cash and likewise let the money remain idle. There may be a long lag between the sale of materials and equipment and an actual increase of off-the-site employment resulting from such sale. The labor that actually went into them was often past labor. What the government sought was immediate employment, and it could be sure to get it if only such projects as gave it were selected.

The national government also sought mainly additional employment. It had to take precautions to prevent the state and the local governments from merely shifting customary work to the W.P.A. The rules, therefore, had generally to exclude projects for carrying on the ordinary functions of government or for such maintenance, repair, and construction work as would probably be done almost at once from state and local funds. The objective was to do things which the state and local governments would in all probability not do themselves in the near future and perhaps might never do.

The exclusion of ordinary services and routine operation and maintenance, which may include minor construction, thus substituted the criterion of additional employment for the criterion of relative desirability. Many local governments on becoming possessed of added resources give first priority to the extension and improvement of existing services or to improved operation and maintenance of existing public works. Like individuals, communities are under pressure to put essentials ahead of luxuries. To insure additional employment the W.P.A. had to tend toward projects that were not essential.

Not uncommon in local communities and even in larger jurisdictions is the minority group earnestly advocating what is, for
that community, a new activity of government. If the activity
has to be financed in whole or in part from local funds, this
group frequently has to carry on a long, up-hill, educational
campaign; it has to gain that support of other citizens which
is practically a prerequisite to obtaining an appropriation from
a representative local legislative body. These activities and
projects supported by minority groups frequently met the requirements of W.P.A. for additional employment since the possibilities were remote that the local government would itself
undertake the activity at any time in the near future.

Unemployment is in a sense a selective economic disease. Some
industries and occupations are far more subject to it than others.
Within an industry it may affect the numerous unskilled or semi-
skilled workers relatively more than it affects the skilled, the
foremen, and other key people. Within an occupation, in the
absence of strict seniority rules, its incidence is often related to
the relative efficiency and productivity of individuals. In a free
market the more efficient are the last to go and the first to be
re-employed. Thus the unemployed do not constitute a true
cross-section of the labor force. Because of these conditions, the
W.P.A. had to select projects which would furnish employment
to large numbers of unskilled and semi-skilled workers and
would make minimum demands for skilled workers, specialists,
and experienced foremen and managers. For unemployed skilled
workers whose skills lay in operation and maintenance of highly-
developed machines and equipment, the W.P.A. had to find
other occupations since the requirement of large employment
rules out the extensive use of labor-saving machines.

The fact that in general the projects had to be public further
narrowed the choices. In some communities most of the unemployed employables had worked in an industry which was almost exclusively within the private sector of the economy. If
W.P.A. reopened the privately owned plant and ran it as a
project, it would be in direct competition with other like private
establishments. Its subsidized production would force the com-

peting concerns to curtail production and lay off workers. Thus W.P.A. could not directly enter the private field and produce competing goods or supply competing services, although such goods and services may have had a high priority in ordinary consumer demand.

For obvious reasons, moreover, the W.P.A. could not conduct construction projects for privately owned enterprises. It was true, for example, that in many communities an outstanding need was for improved housing and for the extension of utilities, but if housing construction and the supplying of utilities were privately owned enterprises, W.P.A. was barred. Even public construction occasionally encountered criticism when the result was the indirect enrichment of the owners of the abutting property or when the W.P.A. improvement permitted abutters to escape the betterment taxation to which they would have been subject had the improvements been made by state or local governments.

In the United States the legislative power to determine what shall be public and what private had in the past been vested primarily in the state legislatures. It was not uncommon for a state to permit variation within its boundaries, so that a given utility was publicly owned in one community and privately owned in another. Thus if a major local demand was for the extension and improvement of a utility, W.P.A. could recognize it if the utility was publicly owned but could not if it were privately owned. This obvious difficulty was applicable in all public works programs financed by grants from public funds. It operated to put pressure on both state and local legislative bodies to move in the direction of public ownership.

Supplying suitable public work for such unemployed as musicians, artists, actors, and writers presented especially great difficulty. Neither state nor local governments customarily made any substantial expenditures in these fields. These occupations were largely in a highly competitive part of the private sector of the economy. The product or services of the workers were, moreover, to a considerable degree on the luxury or recreational side, and hence were hard hit as consumers curtailed their expenditures.

National government agencies, often W.P.A. itself, sponsored projects to provide assistance for educational, professional, and clerical people as was authorized by law. In so far as such projects were in the creative field of the fine arts, they frequently had to allow the beneficiary considerable scope for self expression. Under the conditions prevailing prior to W.P.A. the freedom of such workers for self expression was untrammeled, but they were under the necessity of finding someone who would pay for the enjoyment of their creative effort. An almost entirely new situation arose when the government, because of the need of such workers, put them on its pay roll to give them a living wage. In the case of the theatre projects, the government went to relatively heavy expense to supply the necessary theatres, scenery, and light effects.

The creative artists supported by W.P.A. were taken mainly from the relief rolls, which meant that most of them had gone through a painful experience and were far more impressed with the defects of the existing social, economic, and political system than with its merits and accomplishments. They constituted a fertile field for radical ideas and ideals. The result was that many writings, paintings, and plays were strongly opposed to the existing order and were approved only by the more radical element in some of the great eastern cities. Commercially several of the plays, which had been produced at substantial cost to the government, were almost total failures, closing within a few days of their opening, as they were unable to draw an audience even where sympathy for radicalism was strongest.[25]

The 1935 legislation had vested in the President authority to select the projects for such workers. Congress, after investigations by a subcommittee of an appropriations committee of the House, in 1939 curtailed this power. It prohibited the use of

[25] For the details with respect to these projects see *Investigation and Study of the Works Progress Administration*, Hearings before the House Committee on Appropriations, 76 Cong. 1–3 sess.

funds for the operation of any theatre project after June 30, 1939, with certain exceptions for orderly termination, and after August 31, 1939 "for the operation of any project sponsored solely by the Work Projects Administration" which meant in effect that writing, music, and art projects would have to have some other sponsor.[26] The same act prohibited after September 30, 1939 the use of any part of the appropriation to pay any compensation to any person "who advocates, or who is a member of an organization that advocates, the overthrow of the Government of the United States through force or violence" and required all persons employed in administrative or supervisory positions to take the customary oath of office to support and defend the Constitution of the United States against all enemies, foreign and domestic.[27]

It seems entirely fair to conclude that the original requirement for immediate, large, additional, and suitable public employment was in many respects inconsistent with the economic and governmental system which had prevailed prior to the depression. Private contractors frequently employed on public works, owners and managers of privately owned utilities, even owners of rental residential properties, and apparently to some extent officers and employees of some departments in state and municipal governments, experienced what they regarded as unfair and subsidized competition from the national government. A system which might work smoothly and efficiently in a centralized totalitarian state could not without difficulties and inconsistencies be superimposed on a free enterprise system operating under a form of government that gave a large measure of home rule to the states.

As noted above, Congress curtailed administrative discretion with respect to art projects by prohibiting theatre projects and by removing the power of W.P.A. to sponsor projects. Certain other limitations placed on administrative discretion by the 1939 act are worthy of note.

The expenditure authorizations for other than labor costs for all the work projects financed from W.P.A. funds in any state,

26 53 Stat. 936.
27 53 Stat. 935.

territory, possession, or the District of Columbia were not to exceed an average of $6.00 per month per worker, except under certain circumstances the W.P.A. Commissioner could go as high as $7.00.[28] The use of W.P.A. funds to purchase construction equipment or machinery was prohibited "in any case in which such equipment or machinery can be rented at prices determined by the Commissioner to be reasonable."[29]

Payment of more than three fourths of the total cost of nonfederal projects within any state from the appropriated funds was prohibited and the state or its subdivisions was required to pay not less than one fourth.[30] Contributions in kind or in services of the sponsor's own employees were to be valued in accordance with rules and regulations "which shall also allow credit only to the extent that the furnishing of such contributions represents a financial burden which is undertaken by the sponsors on account of Work Projects Administration projects, or other sponsored projects."[31]

Maximum limitations on costs of buildings which might be constructed by W.P.A. were placed at $50,000 total for federal buildings and $52,000 W.P.A. portion of the estimated cost for any nonfederal building, with certain exceptions in the case of commitments already made. Large building construction actually carried on by W.P.A. using relief labor had engendered no little controversy, with many different aspects. P.W.A. had been operating in the building construction field with its loan and grant program that made the state or local government put in 60 or 70 per cent of the cost; W.P.A. gave all the money excepting sponsor's contributions, the actual value of which had in some cases been so open to question that Congress, as noted above, called for the establishment of definite rules and regulations and attempted to lay down a guiding principle to eliminate "water." Frequently the relief rolls could not supply the number of the skilled workers required for large building

[28] 53 Stat. 928.
[29] The same. In some instances sponsors or others had purchased equipment on the installment plan and had then rented it to W.P.A. at what was regarded as an unreasonable rate.
[30] 53 Stat. 928.
[31] 53 Stat. 932.

construction, and hence the W.P.A. had to hire skilled workers not on relief. Such a procedure involved competition with the private construction industry, which in normal times had built most public buildings. The cost of several of the large buildings constructed by W.P.A. was reported by independent investigators acting for the House Committee as materially in excess of the cost of construction by private enterprise. The explanation was that relief labor was not as efficient as normal labor and the extra cost really represented relief. We shall discuss this phase of the subject in a later section of the chapter. Here the major point is that Congress restricted administrative discretion to have W.P.A. construct large buildings.

In the table below we give the amount of W.P.A. and sponsors' funds expended on projects operated by W.P.A. by

EXPENDITURES OF W.P.A. BY TYPES OF PROJECTS AND SOURCE OF FUNDS[a]
(Dollar items in millions)

| Type of Project | Cumulative through June 30, 1940 | | | | |
| | Total | | W.P.A. Funds | Sponsors' Funds | |
	Amount	Per Cent		Amount	Per Cent of Total
TOTAL	$9,578	100.0	$7,785	$1,793	18.7
Highways, roads, and streets	3,727	38.9	2,932	796	21.3
Public buildings	999	10.4	768	231	23.1
Recreational facilities, excluding buildings	855	8.9	743	112	13.1
Sewer systems and other utilities	965	10.1	757	208	21.5
Airports and airways	201	2.1	151	50	24.8
Conservation	379	4.0	326	53	13.9
Sanitation	201	2.1	161	41	20.2
Professional and service	2,060	21.5	1,809	251	12.2
Community service	596	6.2	513	83	14.0
Research and records	413	4.3	356	57	13.9
Sewing	633	6.6	587	46	7.3
Welfare, excluding sewing	312	3.3	255	57	18.3
Other	105	1.1	98	7	6.6
Miscellaneous[b]	192	2.0	138	54	28.0

[a] Work Projects Administration, *Report on Progress of the WPA Program*, June 30, 1940, p. 63.
[b] Includes adjustment of W.P.A. expenditures to total reported by the Treasury Department; sponsors' expenditures for land, land leases, easements, and rights-of-way for which the distribution by type of project is not available; and projects not included under the headings above.

major types of projects and by source of funds cumulative through the year ending June 30, 1940.

The most striking fact brought out by the table is the dominance of construction in the program. Of the aggregate expenditure of just under 9.6 billion dollars, 38.9 per cent went for highways, roads, and streets, 10.4 per cent for public buildings, 10.1 per cent for sewer systems and other utilities, and 2.1 per cent for airports and airways. These items involved expenditures of almost 5.9 billions and made up 61.5 per cent of the total. These dominant projects lay in fields in which departments of state and local governments and private contractors functioned prior to the depression. An issue is thus raised as to whether the entry of W.P.A. into actual construction may not have operated to retard rather than to promote the resuscitation of that sector of the economy which was normally employed in these fields, whether the program did not constitute competition of the national government with state and local governments and with segments of the private construction industry. In this connection the relatively high percentage of sponsors' contributions required for these construction projects will be noted, ranging from 21.3 per cent of the total for highways, roads, and streets to 24.8 per cent for airports and airways.

Projects headed "Professional and service" accounted for a little over 2 billions or 21.5 per cent of the total. Even here there was some performing of functions by the W.P.A. which existing agencies of state and local governments were equipped to handle if they had the expenditure of the funds. Here again is the issue as to whether resuscitation of the existing economy is to be secured by a financial transfusion to the normal agencies or by developing an alternative system dominated and administered by the national government.

A table on page 374 shows for selected periods from March 1936 to June 1939 the distribution of each 1,000 persons employed on W.P.A. operated projects by major types of projects. Here again will be noted the dominant role played by highways, roads, and streets, which at every period accounted for more

DISTRIBUTION OF EACH 1,000 PERSONS EMPLOYED ON W.P.A.-OPERATED PROJECTS, BY MAJOR TYPES OF PROJECTS, SELECTED PERIODS, MARCH 1936 TO JUNE 1939[a]

Type of Project	March 1936[b]	September 1936[b]	March 1937[b]	September 1937[b]	March 30, 1938	September 21, 1938	December 28, 1938	March 22, 1939	June 21, 1939
TOTAL	1,000	1,000	1,000	1,000	1,000	1,000	1,000	1,000	1,000
Highways, roads, and streets	372	388	357	357	430	473	455	442	427
Public buildings	82	89	85	106	76	89	85	81	92
Parks and other recreational facilities	105	100	86	87	86	79	72	70	71
Conservation	67	45	56	39	48	39	42	49	43
Sewer systems and other utilities	90	80	103	93	108	81	88	101	94
Airports and other transportation facilities	19	24	18	18	17	16	15	16	19
White collar	85[c]	110	124	141	106	104	115	119	129
Education	20	17	20	20	14	12	14	14	15
Recreation	12	17	21	18	13	14	14	14	17
Professional, clerical, and service	53	76	83	103	79	78	87	91	97
Sewing	100	104	105	102	76	70	70	68	74
Goods, other than sewing	21	15	16	15	13	12	12	12	13
Sanitation and health	36	28	29	31	31	24	26	24	19
Miscellaneous	23[c]	17	21	11	9	13	20	18	19

[a] Works Projects Administration, Report on Progress of the WPA Program, June 30, 1939, p. 94. Data apply to continental United States only.

[b] Data for March and September 1936 and March 1937 apply to the last half of the month; for September 1937, the entire month.

[c] Not comparable with later periods since miscellaneous group for March 1936 includes certain types of work which have subsequently been included under white collar projects.

than a third of the workers and in September 1938 accounted for 473 in each 1,000.

The objective of the administration in taking the course it did was to furnish, under direct national administration, employment for unemployed employables. We shall therefore proceed to the next subject, the selection of workers.

THE SELECTION OF WORKERS

The brief experiment with the Civil Works Administration, carried on late in 1934 and early in 1935, had quickly shown, it will be recalled, that the cost of offering a job to everyone who wanted a job was stupendous. World War II has demonstrated more clearly than any previous development that the size of the labor force even at a given moment is not something fixed and stable. Rather it is much more elastic than had been appreciated. There are thousands of employable people, mainly secondary wage earners, who do not have to have gainful employment to live, but who come into the labor market when family finances present difficulties, or when extra money earned in a satisfactory job seems more desirable than the alternatives available without employment. C.W.A. brought in thousands of such persons unquestionably willing and able to work, yet not in need in the strict use of that term. Many employed were members of families which contained other breadwinners earning enough to sustain the family, although probably not enough to give the family the level of living it desired.

The new program proposed by the administration and authorized by the act of 1935 was safeguarded against a repetition of the C.W.A. experience. First to be eligible for one of the work relief jobs created by W.P.A. the applicant had to be an unemployed employable in need. As a general rule the fact of need had been established by the state relief agency or its local representative. The applicant was either in receipt of relief or eligible to receive it. Not until need had been established could one get a relief job on W.P.A., although as will be discussed later a person not in need might be hired for an administrative, supervisory, or skilled work job in connection with the operation of W.P.A. or one of its projects.

To prevent the influx of secondary wage earners, the rule was adopted that not more than one member of a family could be employed on W.P.A. Ordinarily the person so employed was the head of the family and normally its principal wage earner. Especially in the later years of the period, however, children of W.P.A. workers and those of low-income families not in need were eligible for work under the Civilian Conservation Corps and the National Youth Administration programs financed mainly from federal relief funds. They will be discussed in subsequent chapters. With these exceptions, the rule was only one member of a family, generally the primary earner, on W.P.A.

A rule of that type offers an incentive to grown sons or daughters of a family to leave home and either to become single workers not living with a family or to marry and start families of their own. A single person not living in a family which already had one W.P.A. worker, if unemployed and in need, was eligible for a W.P.A. relief job. In many communities, however, there were not enough W.P.A. jobs available for all who wanted them, and ordinarily the married applicants had the better chance of assignment.

Application of the requirement that the unemployed person in need should be employable occasioned great difficulty. Whether or not a person is employable under a free enterprise system depends in part upon the condition of the labor market in the locality where he seeks employment. When the supply of labor of the type the person has to offer is ample, he may be unemployable because he is submarginal: he is not possessed of the qualifications that will lead anyone to hire him. When labor of that type is in great demand he is employable, although possibly only for a brief period during peak demand. This description of what constitutes employability, in the sense of the word as used by ordinary employers, both public and private, was however no criterion in administering W.P.A. during the depression, since many of the unemployed were obviously employable at anything approaching normal demand for labor, and the objective was to give work to those who could not secure it under existing conditions.

The initial appraisal as to whether a person was or was not employable was made in practice by the relief agency operated by the state or local government or the two in co-operation. It may be well to review briefly the situation which the employees in the welfare agency confronted after the need of the applicant and those dependent upon him had been established.

1. The applicant must if possible be supplied with at least enough to bring available resources to the point where they will supply a minimum of subsistence.

2. If the applicant is ruled unemployable and hence not eligible for W.P.A., and if neither he nor any of his dependents can qualify under the relief categories of the Social Security Act, he must be provided for through state or local relief funds.

3. In many jurisdictions state and local funds for general public assistance were so inadequate that a decision that the person was unemployable meant unrelieved want for him and any dependent upon him.

4. A W.P.A. job would mean relative comfort at the expense of the national government. The assignment moreover would bring federal money into the community.

The employees of the relief agency were therefore under considerable pressure to declare the best available breadwinner in a family employable.

Now let us look at the problem from the standpoint of the W.P.A. officer responsible for the administration of the project.

1. The successful prosecution of a project ordinarily requires several definite classes of workers. The employees of each class must possess the minimum qualifications necessary for the performance of the duties of that class. From the standpoint of a production manager, a person is not employable on the project unless he possesses the minimum qualifications for a class of work the manager has to have done.

2. If the number certified to the manager as employable and possessed of the qualifications required for a class of work he has to do greatly exceeds the number of jobs available, he as a

producer, or one responsible for production, desires to select the best and to regard the poorer ones as unemployable on the project.

3. If the project manager is skilled and experienced in the kind of work he is directing, he has standards of skill and production by which he judges employability. An employee who falls materially short in skill or production is from his point of view unemployable.

4. If his project requires some relatively high-class persons possessing training, skill, and experience, he is going to be eager to secure them. He will prefer an applicant who has the needed qualifications, though the applicant's own need is slight, to the unskilled, inexperienced applicant whose own needs are serious. The manager may even hunt up the man he requires and then try to get the state or local welfare agency to certify that person as in need of relief.

Thus there was in the W.P.A. program an inherent conflict between the relief or welfare concepts as represented by the social workers in the certifying agency and the efficiency and work standard concepts of the production manager responsible for project results. In one state at least an agreement was entered into that the welfare department would cease its practice of tending to regard need as synonymous with employability and send only persons who were really employable. The project managers on the other hand would cease hunting up competent workers and sending them to the welfare department to get the necessary certificate of need.

A closely related difficulty with employability is that a man may be eminently employable on one job and almost entirely unemployable on another. For example, a man may be adept on a machine job which requires almost no physical strength and of little use on a job which calls for physical strength and endurance. A project manager could hardly say to the skilled or semi-skilled machine operator, "You are unemployable" or "We won't hire you for this job." If no other more suitable work was available under W.P.A. in the locality where the man lived, the project manager was under considerable obligation to make a place for him, for he was obviously employable from the standpoint of the program. We shall discuss this subject in more detail later in considering the preservation and development of skills.

It should again be repeated that eligibility for W.P.A. on the ground of employability and need did not assure a man a W.P.A. job. There had to be a project within a reasonable distance of his home or one to which he could be transported, and it had to have a sufficient allotment of funds to permit of his employment. He might be turned down because of no project in the vicinity or no project with an uncommitted balance. Where available funds would not permit of employment of all eligibles, selection might be made on the basis of qualifications, and then an eligible might be rejected on the ground of no suitable work for him.

As will be more apparent after the ensuing section on wages and hours has been read, W.P.A. constituted a haven of safety after severe storm for no small number of its beneficiaries. Among them were three classes: (1) persons who were rarely employable under a normal competitive system and hence experienced under W.P.A. a continuity of employment new to their experience; (2) persons whose normal employment had been seasonal or sporadic and who found in W.P.A. a preferable regularity and degree of security; (3) persons whose compensation had been at least in part in allowances including quarters, whose hours had been long, and who had little of the freedom that comes from money wages and short regular hours. They preferred the new way of life made possible by W.P.A.

Many such persons tended to stay on W.P.A. and were loath to accept temporary or sporadic employment in private enterprise or normally conducted public enterprise when it developed. W.P.A. was from their point of view a better job. Naturally, too, employers who had customarily employed workers of this type, especially for seasonal jobs, were highly critical when they encountered a labor shortage and a demand for high wages and knew or thought adequate labor at reasonable wages would be available if it were not for W.P.A. Many of them felt that they ultimately would be heavily taxed to pay for a nationally operated work program which was handicapping them in conducting the businesses from which they made the money to pay taxes. The program from their point of view was being made an instrument for economic and social reform.

Gradually Congress began to take action with respect to some of these matters that had evoked criticism. The act for the year 1937 contained the provision:

. . . That no person employed on work projects and certified as in need of relief who refuses a bona-fide offer of private employment under reasonable working conditions which pays as much or more in compensation for the same length of service as such person receives or could receive under this appropriation and who is capable of performing such work, shall be retained in employment under this appropriation for the period such private employment would be available: . . .[32]

It went on to "entitle" an employee who left for private employment "to immediate resumption of his previous employment status under this appropriation if he is still in need of relief and if he has lost the private employment through no fault of his own."[33]

The relative attractiveness of the W.P.A. led to allegations that some beneficiaries continued to occupy positions under it after they or their families were no longer in need. State or local agencies which had certified to their need initially did not keep a continuous check on them. The agencies ordinarily regarded such cases as disposed of when the principal wage earner got a job on the W.P.A. The W.P.A. officers were operating projects and did not do social case work or run a continuous check on the beneficiaries to see that they would still be in need were it not for W.P.A. earnings. In the 1938 act Congress required: "That every relief worker employed on any Federal or non-Federal Works Progress Administration project shall be required, as a condition to his continued employment, to file quarterly a statement as to the amount of his earnings, if any, from outside employment while he was assigned to such a

[32] 50 Stat. 353–54.
[33] 50 Stat. 354.

project," and it was directed that these statements should be taken into consideration in assigning such workers to projects.[34]

The successive appropriation acts providing for W.P.A. were officially entitled "Emergency Relief Appropriation Acts of" the specified year. By 1939 general economic conditions had begun materially to improve and some sentiment was developing that the emergency was over and that W.P.A. should be liquidated. Among W.P.A. officers and protagonists, the economic changes resulted in a change of emphasis; the relief and welfare aspects of the W.P.A. were subordinated to its productive aspects. Throughout its history there had been an element of conflict between relief and productive efficiency. With changes in economic conditions and with changes in the directing officers of W.P.A., more attention was given to relative efficiency. This development was particularly noticeable in the 1939 act, which followed the investigations by the House Committee to which reference has already been made.

The 1939 act provided:

There shall be removed from employment on Work Projects Administration projects all relief workers, excepting veterans, who have been continuously employed on such projects for more than eighteen months, and any relief worker so removed shall be ineligible to be restored to employment on such projects until after (a) the expiration of thirty days after the date of his removal, and (b) recertification of his eligibility for restoration to employment on such projects.[35]

The ensuing section directed all agencies carrying on projects under the act to determine that the beneficiary was possessed of the requisite qualifications and continued "no person shall be employed or retained for employment on any such project whose work habits are such or work record shows that he is incapable of performing satisfactorily the work to which he may be assigned on the project." The requirement for investigation as to need was strengthened, and the W.P.A. Commissioner was directed to cause to be made periodic reinvestigations of need not less frequently than once every six months. Bene-

[34] 52 Stat. 812.
[35] 53 Stat. 933.

ficiaries were again required to accept bona fide offers of private employment, but the language was changed. In the 1937 act, the wages offered privately had to be as much as or more than under the W.P.A. project for a like period. In the 1939 act the beneficiary was required to accept "private employment under reasonable working conditions which pays the prevailing wages for such work in the community where he resides."
The act continued:

> In order to insure the fulfillment of the purposes for which such appropriations are made and to avoid competition between the Work Projects Administration and other Federal or non-Federal agencies in the employment of labor on projects of any nature whatsoever, financed in whole or in part by the Federal Government, no person in need shall be eligible for employment on any work project of the Work Projects Administration who has refused to accept employment on any other Federal or non-Federal project at earnings comparable with or higher than the earnings established for similar work on [W.P.A. projects].

The 1939 act likewise marked the end of a gradual evolution which had been taking place with respect to aliens. The 1939 act required citizenship. The initial 1935 act had no restrictions. The 1936 act introduced restrictions on illegally entered aliens.[36] The 1938 act provided for preferences placing veterans first, citizens second, and aliens who had declared their intention to become citizens prior to the passage of the act and whose declarations were still valid third. Aliens who had not declared prior to the act or whose declaration was invalid were excluded.[37]

Several of the issues of eligibility which we have been presenting had their origin in the extremely difficult problem of wages and hours, which is the next subject for consideration.

WAGES AND HOURS

The idea that persons in need because of unemployment should be given work by which they could "earn" what they required for relief runs far back in history. In some of the early

[36] 49 Stat. 1609.
[37] 52 Stat. 813.

examples under the old poor laws the work really constituted a work test to discourage the needy from attempting to live on relief without work. Often the projects were of the made work variety without any real utility, and thus there could be no relationship between the value of the work performed and the compensation for that work. In some instances the person in need was given what he and his dependents required and in return was expected or allowed to work for a certain number of hours per week on some available simple project at tasks that almost anyone could perform. There might be practically no relationship between hours worked and the amount or value of the relief given. A later development was to have much more elaborate projects, to give the applicant work according to his skill and experience, to calculate the value of his work at something approaching a normal wage, and to allow him to work as many hours in a week as might be necessary to enable him to earn his budget deficit.[38]

Three points with respect to payment of a wage rate related to skill and permitting or requiring the person in need to work a sufficient number of hours to earn his budget deficit deserve emphasis.

1. The person in need gets little if anything more than he would have received through adequate direct relief, since he works no longer than is necessary to earn his budget deficit.

2. Even under such circumstances relief work costs more than direct relief because it involves expenditures for supplies, materials, equipment, and administration, but these costs are partially offset by the value of the resulting product.

3. Administratively the projects are difficult to operate because the length of time an individual works depends on his wage rate and the amount of his budget deficit. Thus the operators cannot get the efficiency that comes from a crew properly balanced with respect to skills working together for substantially the same number of hours. The workers are constantly shifting as men earn their deficiency and leave for the week

[38] See Arthur Edward Burns and Peyton Kerr, "Survey of Work-Relief Wage Policies," *American Economic Review*, Vol. 27 (1937), pp. 711–24.

to be replaced by others. There may not be enough of the higher-priced skilled men who had only short hours to balance the large numbers of unskilled who had to work much longer hours to earn their budget deficits. The skilled man with no dependents may be on the job only a few hours a week, whereas the unskilled worker with a big family might have to work almost all the time the project was operating.

When the national government went into its work program, C.W.A. and later W.P.A., the leaders were not thinking in terms of work to pay for the minimum relief necessary. There was no idea of limiting a man's working hours to those necessary to earn his budget deficit. The government was going to supply jobs for the unemployed employables, provided—after the lessons of C.W.A.—that they were in need. The fact that they were in need made them eligible for a job, but the extent of their need was to have nothing to do with their wage rates nor were hours of labor for individuals to vary according to budget deficits. Projects would operate a definite number of hours a week or a month, and all classes of workers on the project would be expected to work for substantially the number of hours the project was in operation. The concept was that the job would be much like a regular job, the major distinction being that the project was to be undertaken by the national government, and in the main financed by it.

Such a concept meant that the government would determine wage rates, hours of labor, and earnings of workers arbitrarily, if that word be used to indicate freedom from such forces as competition, bargaining, profit, and loss. With millions of persons unemployed and in need and with relief funds radically curtailed, the needy unemployed would have to accept whatever wages and conditions of employment the government offered. The power thus vested in the government would be enormous, and the welfare of large segments of the population would depend on how the administration exercised the arbitrary power delegated to it.

When the proposals were first made in 1935, labor, especially organized labor, and employers in the construction industries and other industries with which the work program might compete were apprehensive. Here was something on a monumental scale that had as possibilities many of the aspects of convict and other institutional labor. The power might be so used that the wages of free labor could not be maintained, and the government would take away from free enterprise many of the projects upon which its existence depended. Both labor leaders and employers wanted safeguards inserted in the legislation which would require the government to pay the prevailing wage for like work in the communities where the projects were undertaken. If the relief workers were to get lower earnings than free workers, that result should be achieved not by reducing hourly rates but by reducing the number of hours the projects were operated per week.

The administration, however, proposed and supported what appeared to be a new concept, foreign to ordinary industrial practice, called the security wage. Relief workers on the projects were to be paid not so much per hour or per day worked but so much per month and the monthly rate was to be enough to give the typical worker security. Emphasis was thus placed on monthly earnings rather than on rates of pay.

The real fight on this issue came in the Senate. Under the compromise provision which finally emerged, the President was to require such rates of pay "as will in the discretion of the President accomplish the purposes of this joint resolution, and not affect adversely or otherwise tend to decrease the going rate of wages paid for work of a similar nature." He was further specifically authorized to fix different rates of wages for various types of work on any project "which rates need not be uniform throughout the United States."[39] Thus the original law did not specifically require payment of the prevailing wage for like work, and it left the administration free to apply the concept of the security wage.

The initial rules and regulations relating to wages, hours of work, and conditions of employment under the 1935 act were

[39] 49 Stat. 118. See Macmahon, Millett, and Ogden, *The Administration of Federal Work Relief*, pp. 52–53.

promulgated by the President on May 20, 1935 in Executive
Order 7046. The schedule of "monthly earnings" from this
order is reproduced below.

SCHEDULE OF MONTHLY EARNINGS
Counties with 1930 Population of Largest Municipality as Indicated

Regionsª	Over 100,000	50,000– 100,000	25,000– 50,000	5,000– 25,000	Under 5,000
Unskilled Work:					
Region I	$55	$52	$48	$44	$40
II	45	42	40	35	32
III	35	33	29	24	21
IV	30	27	25	22	19
Intermediate Work:					
Region I	65	60	55	50	45
II	58	54	50	44	38
III	52	48	43	36	30
IV	49	43	38	32	27
Skilled Work:					
Region I	85	75	70	63	55
II	72	66	60	52	44
III	68	62	56	48	38
IV	68	58	50	42	35
Professional and Technical Work:					
Region I	94	83	77	69	61
II	79	73	66	57	48
III	75	68	62	53	42
IV	75	64	55	46	39

ª Regions include the following states:
I Connecticut, Maine, Massachusetts, New Hampshire, New Jersey, New York,
   Pennsylvania, Rhode Island, Vermont; Illinois, Indiana, Michigan, Minnesota,
   Ohio, Wisconsin; Arizona, California, Colorado, Idaho, Montana, Nevada, New
   Mexico, Oregon, Utah, Washington, Wyoming.
II Iowa, Kansas, Missouri, Nebraska, North Dakota, South Dakota; Delaware,
   District of Columbia, Maryland, West Virginia.
III Arkansas, Kentucky, Louisiana, Oklahoma, Texas, Virginia.
IV Alabama, Florida, Georgia, Mississippi, North Carolina, South Carolina, Ten-
   nessee.

The essential classifications in this executive order, it will be
noted, are: (1) by classes of work with four classes differentiated: unskilled, intermediate, skilled, and professional and technical; (2) by geographic regions; (3) by size of community as
measured by the size of the largest municipality within the
county where the project was located. The order, however, permitted some adjustment to particular conditions. Thus if a

project covered two or more counties with different schedules of earnings, the highest schedule should prevail. The W.P.A. administrator or his representative was given authority to make adjustments varying the schedules by not more than 10 per cent.

Special attention should be called to the fact that the schedule provided for no distinctions within any unit of the classification on the basis of personal efficiency. All unskilled workers on a project in a given sized county in a given region got the same rate of pay regardless of their aptitude, willingness, and work habits. There were no piece work rates, no efficiency steps, and no bonuses.

For persons employed "on a salary basis in accordance with the schedule" as here reproduced, the maximum number of hours was to be fixed by the W.P.A. administrator but "shall not be in excess of 8 hours per day or 40 hours per week."

The concept of salary presented some difficulties with respect to absenteeism on all projects and especially with respect to unavoidable stoppages on construction projects due to inclement weather and other causes common in that industry. Space will not permit tracing the gradual changes which were made in the rules, but we shall quote in full the initial provisions of Executive Order 7046.

The monthly earnings are in the nature of a salary and workers shall be paid for time lost due to weather conditions or temporary interruptions in the project beyond the control of the workers. In order to be credited for such time lost, the worker must report on the job and be officially dismissed for the day unless otherwise notified by the project supervisor. Deductions from monthly earnings shall be made for time lost because of voluntary absence, illness, completion or postponement of a project, or permanent dismissal. In order to assure an adequate income to workers, the Works Progress Administration shall make every effort to provide a continuous flow of suitable projects in each locality.

Since deductions were to be made for voluntary absence, illness, and permanent dismissal—individual matters—it was essential for pay purposes (1) to keep individual records of time worked and (2) to calculate rates of pay per hour, or other suitable unit, so that the required deductions for absenteeism could be made. The distinction between a monthly salary with deductions for absences and the more customary hourly wage rates multiplied by the number of hours worked or counted was thus more a matter of words than of substance, with the advantages of administrative simplicity in favor of the more traditional method. With rates fixed the essential item in determining earnings is obviously the number of hours per month or per year work is available for those willing and able to work.

The compromise provision with respect to the method of fixing the wages that was arrived at in the 1935 legislation survived only that year. The 1936 act read: "The rates of pay for persons engaged upon projects under the foregoing appropriation shall be not less than the prevailing rates of pay for work of a similar nature as determined by the Works Progress Administration with the approval of the President."[40] This provision was repeated in the acts of 1937 and 1938.

The 1939 act, which followed the investigation by the House Committee, represented a radical departure from the previous legislation. It read:

Sec. 15. (a) The Commissioner shall fix a monthly earning schedule for persons engaged upon work projects financed in whole or in part from funds appropriated by section 1 which shall not substantially affect the current national average labor cost per person of the Work Projects Administration. After August 31, 1939, such monthly earning schedule shall not be varied for workers of the same type in different geographical areas to any greater extent than may be justified by differences in the cost of living. The Commissioner shall require that the hours of work for all persons engaged upon work projects financed in whole or in part by funds appropriated by section 1 shall (1) be one hundred and thirty hours per month except that the Commissioner, in his discretion, may require a lesser number of hours of work per month in the case of relief workers with no dependents and the earnings of such workers shall be correspondingly reduced, and (2) not exceed eight hours in any day and shall not exceed forty hours in any week.

(b) The Commissioner may authorize exemptions from the above limitations of monthly earnings and hours of work to protect work al-

[40] 49 Stat. 1609.

ready done on a project; to permit making up lost time; in the case of an emergency involving the public welfare and in the case of supervisory personnel employed on work projects.[41]

Under the 1939 act the current national, average, labor cost per person on the W.P.A. became the standard which was to govern and hours were fixed. In the competitive economy wages were rising with the increased demand for labor. Thus if wages continued to rise, jobs on W.P.A. would become progressively less desirable, and W.P.A. beneficiaries would have greater incentives to leave its sheltered employment. No longer were the W.P.A. wages tied to the prevailing wage as they had been in the acts from 1936 to 1938.

The prevailing wage rule of the earlier laws was in many respects unsatisfactory. As has been noted, the W.P.A. wage schedule provided a single wage rate for all employees of the same class in the same sized community in the same geographic area, with no differentiations on the ground of efficiency, dependability, length of service, personality, and so on. In private enterprise, except where labor unions have achieved a dominant position and have been able to enforce general observance of a uniform wage scale,[42] there are wide variations in the pay rates for individuals doing the same class of work, based at least in part on such personal differences in qualifications as were just cited. As a result, in communities where labor is not generally organized, there is often no such thing as an established prevailing wage that will serve as a governing standard. Sometimes one finds a commonly used hiring rate for the general run of unskilled workers, but data for wages actually being paid show substantial departures from it; good dependable workers get

---

[41] 53 Stat. 933.

[42] In communities where labor was organized the rule apparently was to recognize the union scale as the prevailing wage. The rules promulgated by the F.E.R.A. to govern the civil works program required the establishment of advisory local wage-rate committees consisting of "one representative each from organized labor, and the local relief administration, and a third member from local business or profession selected by the first two." The rules continued: "If there are wage agreements or understandings between local labor organizations and employers in the locality, such rates will be recognized as the prevailing rates." p. 126. F.E.R.A., *Manual of Work Division Procedure*, Nov. 15, 1934, quoted in Williams, *Federal Aid for Relief*.

more and perhaps marginal workers substantially less. Under such circumstances the average wage or the median wage of all employed persons in the class is the prevailing wage, but in many instances data regarding what employers are actually paying from which such an average or median could be calculated are not readily available.

In the absence of a real prevailing wage or adequate data to calculate the average or median wage, administrators have wide discretion in determining what is the prevailing wage, which the Congress directed them to use as the standard. Obviously it is in the immediate interest of the program beneficiaries and of labor in the community to get the highest possible determination of the prevailing wage and incidentally of the cost of living. A high determination of the prevailing rate especially in rural areas had certain disrupting influences:

1. Persons who were regarded by employers in the community as scarcely employable at all got as high a wage rate on W.P.A. as really good workers were paid either on W.P.A. or in private enterprise.

2. W.P.A. in some instances was paying more to its beneficiaries than many private employers were paying. What the private employers were paying was probably in a substantial number of cases more nearly the local prevailing wage. This difficulty came in part from the use of the county as a standard, for not infrequently there are considerable variations among sections of a county, and a tendency apparently existed to use as the standard the higher paying sections of a county.

3. Payment of the prevailing wage, particularly if it has been pitched somewhat higher than the real facts would warrant, made the W.P.A. with its continuity and perhaps its less demanding performance requirements, a strong competitor in many local labor markets where rates were relatively low in private industry. It thus violated an old principle in relief administration that life on relief should be less desirable than independent self support. It also handicapped private employers in making jobs and in hiring workers, for whether an employer can afford to hire a worker depends in part upon the relation-

ship between the wages the worker will require and the value of the services he will render. Wages can be put so high that the employer cannot afford them. Only a government can afford, over substantial periods, to pay workers more than their productive services are worth, and it does so at the expense of the taxpayers.

4. Most communities have some persons who have little desire to work after their immediate and customary needs are satisfied. For them leisure and freedom from the discipline of work are more important than a level of living higher than that to which they have been accustomed. They may have no idea of saving. For such persons work at the prevailing wage for the least number of hours required to supply their wants is preferable to working much longer periods at the same wage rate. With W.P.A. paying prevailing wages for a sufficient number of hours, other jobs paying the same rate but offering better earnings because of longer hours were not attractive, especially since the discipline on the alternative jobs would in all probability be more strict.

One other section of the 1939 law, as quoted above, deserves special emphasis—that which permitted the commissioner in his discretion to require a lesser number of hours per month from relief workers with no dependents with a corresponding reduction in earnings. This provision, it will be noted, represents a return to earlier work-relief concepts where the idea was to let the needy applicant earn only his budget deficit. That concept was practically abandoned by the W.P.A. program at its inception, and workers in the same class on a project got the same wages regardless of the number of their dependents and their budget deficits. Thus one worker might be amply cared for by his W.P.A. wages and his other resources, whereas another with a large family and few resources might have difficulty in getting along or even have to ask aid from relief funds. The wage concepts and the relief concepts were thus frequently in conflict.[43]

---

[43] In one of the field studies prepared in co-operation with the Institution a striking illustration of this situation was given. To meet difficulties in developing projects in each county, a large central project was set up with barracks for the workers who came

FINANCIAL ASPECTS

In discussing the financial aspects of W.P.A., we shall give a summary to show the magnitude of the appropriations during the years from 1935 through June 30, 1942. We shall then take up the allotments or appropriations by individual years for that period and consider the issues involved in determining the size of the national appropriation. How these national funds were distributed among the states will then be considered. At the end of this section data will be presented regarding costs per man-year together with some discussion of the part played by sponsors' contributions.

Presentation of a brief, over-all summary of appropriations is difficult because of the manner in which appropriations were made. In the 1935 act, it may be recalled, the entire appropriation of almost 5 billion dollars was made to the President to be allotted by him to existing agencies or agencies which he might create. The acts for 1936 and 1937 followed the same method, but beginning with the 1938 act Congress tended to return to the traditional method of making specific appropriations to the operating agencies. In the ensuing years specific appropriations for the W.P.A. and for some other agencies were carried in the emergency relief appropriation acts, whereas those for others were either in whole or in part carried in the regular appropriation acts. We have made no attempt to determine to what extent presidential allotments from the earlier relief acts resulted in subsequent additions to the regular appropriations for other agencies. We shall here give the appropriations made in the emergency relief acts and certain related acts for the work program and then proceed to the allotments and appropriations for W.P.A.

The sums appropriated for the relief and work relief programs for fiscal years from 1936 to 1942 were, in millions, as follows:[44]

from a distance. Most of the men in the barracks did the same work and got the same pay. Responsible married men with families dependent upon them lived simply and sent most of their wages home. Some of the men with no dependents and others who were irresponsible lived riotously and intemperately. On the job those who lived simply were at times in much better condition to render productive service, yet all received the same wage regardless of budget deficiencies and personal efficiency.

[44] *Report of the President of the United States to the Congress showing the Status of Funds and Operations under the Emergency Relief Appropriation Acts for the Fiscal*

1936...	$ 4,546
1937...	2,232
1938...	1,806
1939...	2,527
1940...	1,783
1941...	1,433
1942...	916
Total...................................	$15,243

If a work program is to include substantial and fairly costly projects, it is desirable that the appropriations for it shall be available until used, or else that each year a substantial part of the unexpended balances be reappropriated. Such a course is necessary to permit the operating agency to undertake and carry

Sums Obligated and Sums Expended from Emergency Relief Funds, 1935–42[a]
(In millions of dollars)

Fiscal Year	Annual Amounts		Cumulative Total (End of Fiscal Year)	
	Obligated	Expended	Obligated	Expended
1936.....................	$4,250	$3,425	$ 4,250	$ 3,425
1937.....................	2,472	2,861	6,722	6,286
1938.....................	1,832	2,001	8,554	8,287
1939.....................	2,520	2,618	11,074	10,905
1940.....................	1,787	1,835	12,861	12,740
1941.....................	1,431	1,431	14,292	14,171
1942.....................	853	913	15,145	15,084

[a] *Treasury Report on Work Relief*, p. 51.

to completion projects which could not be completed in the fiscal year and possibly could not be completed even in the ensuing year. In many cases construction projects once started must be carried to completion. Left partly built they may be of no value to anyone, an eye sore or even a menace to safety, and the value of such work as was done may be rapidly destroyed unless the partly finished structure can be satisfactorily protected. In a sense, appropriations for a work program must be authorizations for expenditure not necessarily in the fiscal year but over ensuing years. For many purposes, therefore, it is more significant to consider the sums obligated than the sums actually expended by fiscal years. These data are presented in the table above, to which we have added a cumulative section.

Years 1935 to 1942, Inclusive, as of June 30, 1942. Prepared by the U. S. Treasury Department, Fiscal Service, Bureau of Accounts, p. 49. Subsequently referred to as the *Treasury Report on Work Relief.*

The table below gives the expenditures by fiscal years for all agencies and by W.P.A. with a cumulative section. It will be noted that of the 12.7 billions which had been spent on the work program up to June 30, 1940, the W.P.A. had spent almost 8.2 billions, or not quite two thirds of the total.

EXPENDITURES FROM EMERGENCY RELIEF FUNDS BY W.P.A., 1936–42
(In millions of dollars)

Fiscal Year	Annual Amount		Cumulative Total (End of fiscal year)	
	All Agencies[a]	W.P.A.[b]	All Agencies	W.P.A.
1936........................	$3,425⎱	$3,104	$ 3,425⎱	$ 3,104
1937........................	2,861⎰		6,286⎰	
1938........................	2,001	1,428	8,287	4,532
1939........................	2,618	2,157	10,905	6,689
1940........................	1,835	1,462	12,740	8,151
1941........................	1,431	1,285	14,171	9,436
1942........................	913	879	15,084	10,315

[a] *Treasury Report on Work Relief*, p. 51.
[b] The same, p. 52.

Appropriations, obligations, and expenditures all indicate considerable variation from year to year. Such variations give rise to the question how was the amount to be appropriated determined? Estimating and appropriating for the work program presented distinctive features in financial administration, three of which are particularly noteworthy.

1. The national government in the thirties was proceeding on a basis of deficit financing, and hence the question of where the tax revenues to pay for the program were to come from was in no sense an immediate limiting factor. At first the thought appeared to be that the financial position of the nation would be satisfactory if the national budget was balanced over a period of years, instead of annually, and that the restoration of economic activity resulting from the pump priming of a public works spending program would within a reasonable time balance the budget. As the facts failed to demonstrate the soundness of the prediction, this idea gradually gave way to the theory that a balanced budget was unnecessary and that the size of the na-

tional internal debt was a matter of relatively little economic moment. Thus the government could with impunity appropriate as much as it deemed advisable for a work program, although all the money was to come from borrowed funds.

2. No basic law was passed laying down the principles which should govern the expenditures, nor were any standards adopted giving either the states or individuals contingent legislative rights. Because of the absence of principles and rights, the more or less customary estimates as to what would be required to carry out the substantive law were inapplicable. To illustrate the point, since the law itself did not provide that the national government should supply work relief for all needy unemployed employables, it was not the practice to maintain current accurate statistics as to their numbers and to use these statistics as a basis for determining the sums to be appropriated.

3. The costs of the work program were made up of five major elements: (a) the wages paid to needy unemployed employables, (b) wages paid to project supervisors and skilled laborers specially hired, (c) administrative costs, (d) expenses for supplies, material, and equipment, and (e) expenditures for land and the like (usually made by sponsors). Reasonably accurate estimates of costs and hence of sums needed through appropriations thus would have called for a high degree of advanced planning and systematization as contrasted with improvising to meet current conditions. It is also probably true that had Congress been supplied with details regarding projects to be undertaken with their location and nature, difficulties in securing appropriations would have been greatly enhanced.

The practice which developed was therefore not to include estimates for the work program in the regular budget submitted to the Congress at the beginning of each session but to treat the work program as a distinct and separate thing. How much of an appropriation was to be recommended was determined by the President after consideration of the information and advice of his subordinates in immediate contact with the details of administration. Since the appropriations were in general for a future period, economic forecasts were involved, and Congress was largely dependent on the administrative officers for these forecasts.

Macmahon, Millett, and Ogden say on this subject:

The size of appropriation requests for the works program after 1935, however, was never determined in the light of fully worked out estimates and an orderly posing of alternatives. The WPA developed careful records of the man-year cost of giving a person a work relief job at various kinds of tasks and in different states. But no standards of employability were formulated, and at any one time the WPA had no certain information about the number of employables on public relief rolls eligible for federal work relief. Still less did it have exact information about the number of those who, while not at the moment on the relief rolls, might soon be reduced to the necessity of seeking public assistance.

The size of appropriation requests was rather the result of compromise among pressures within the Administration. The principal forces were the Treasury Department and the Bureau of the Budget, on the one hand, and the WPA, on the other. The Treasury Department seemed basically concerned about balancing the budget and looked with disfavor upon the accumulation of federal deficits. There were other potent strategists in the Administration who argued that under the circumstances deficit financing was the one feasible method of channeling excess savings into consumer purchasing power. To this economic argument spokesmen for the WPA could add an urgent sense of the plight of relief and marginal groups throughout the country.

When WPA officials spoke before congressional committees on matters of finance, it was with the consent of the President, who had to balance the various forces. Mr. Hopkins' strategy was never to expose his estimate to a rebuff; the President's caution was anticipated. The President, for his part, almost always got from Congress the amounts that he requested for the works program. But a consideration of congressional attitudes entered into the President's calculus, even as a consciousness of the President's position affected the estimates submitted to him by the WPA.[45]

On pages 398–99 the expenditures of W.P.A. for the fiscal years 1936 to 1940, inclusive, are shown by states, geographically arranged. For each state the average W.P.A. expenditures for the period 1936 to 1940 are also given with a per capita figure based on its population at the Census of 1940, which will serve as a rough indicator of relative expenditures.

[45] *The Administration of Federal Work Relief*, p. 174.

For continental United States the average annual expenditures of the W.P.A. for the fiscal years 1936 to 1940 inclusive were a little more than 1.6 billion dollars or an average annual expenditure of $12.29 for each person enumerated at the Census of 1940. The states which exceeded the national average were:

Montana	19.58	North Dakota	14.28
Ohio	17.82	Washington	14.02
Massachusetts	17.77	Minnesota	13.87
New York	17.07	Wisconsin	13.38
Pennsylvania	16.32	Michigan	13.28
South Dakota	16.19	Utah	13.12
Colorado	15.93	Rhode Island	13.08
Illinois	15.53	Nevada	13.03
New Jersey	15.16	New Mexico	12.90
Indiana	14.32	Missouri	12.85

The first fact which will be noted from this list is that it includes most of the highly urbanized industrial states of the northeast and the great metropolitan centers. It does not contain a single southern state or so-called border state. The more rural states included, Montana, South Dakota, North Dakota, Utah, Nevada, and New Mexico, are all northern or western. The list does not include California, which had an expenditure of $11.75 per capita. It includes all the states, with the exception of California that political writers call "pivotal."

No data of which we have knowledge suggests that states such as Ohio, Massachusetts, New York, Pennsylvania, Illinois, New Jersey, Indiana, Minnesota, Michigan, Rhode Island, and Missouri are so lacking in wealth and capacity to pay their own way that they must depend for relief for their needy unemployed on work projects conducted by the national government and financed by it. The depression caught these states unprepared legislatively and financially; because of their unpreparedness they may temporarily have needed some financial assistance from the national government. It by no means follows that under suitable financial legislation they should not be able to build and pay for highways, public buildings, sewer and water systems, and recreational facilities, with such federal grants-in-aid as the national government may wish to make to stimulate activity at a particular time.

EXPENDITURES OF THE W.P.A. BY STATES, 1936–40[a]
(Per capita figures in dollars, all others in thousands of dollars)

State	Average 1936–40		Fiscal Years				
	Amount	Per Capita[b]	1936	1937	1938	1939	1940
CONTINENTAL UNITED STATES	1,618,354	12.29	1,264,820	1,825,263	1,418,339	2,134,507	1,448,841
NORTHEAST	613,097	15.09	544,586	780,461	563,172	726,934	450,336
New England	*116,613*	*13.82*	*83,637*	*133,338*	*104,124*	*156,591*	*105,378*
Maine	5,135	6.06	4,308	6,182	3,828	6,324	5,033
New Hampshire	5,112	10.39	3,281	6,025	4,443	7,021	4,792
Vermont	2,774	7.73	1,934	2,464	2,268	4,501	2,702
Massachusetts	76,704	17.77	53,925	91,365	68,765	100,810	68,654
Rhode Island	9,328	13.08	6,527	8,473	8,716	13,946	8,980
Connecticut	17,560	10.28	13,662	18,829	16,104	23,989	15,217
Middle Atlantic	*454,761*	*16.51*	*427,443*	*596,804*	*424,885*	*519,840*	*304,833*
New York	230,082	17.07	254,705	314,370	209,963	234,222	137,151
New Jersey	63,069	15.16	45,355	74,032	60,464	80,708	54,786
Pennsylvania	161,610	16.32	127,383	208,402	154,458	204,910	112,896
Other	*41,723*	*8.97*	*33,506*	*50,319*	*34,163*	*50,503*	*40,125*
Delaware	1,760	6.59	1,420	1,686	1,586	2,321	1,789
Maryland	9,426	5.18	8,814	12,188	7,195	10,022	8,909
West Virginia	23,319	12.26	18,549	27,418	19,873	28,662	22,094
District of Columbia[c]	7,218	10.89	4,723	9,027	5,509	9,498	7,333
SOUTHEAST	197,999	7.01	133,818	185,613	148,563	278,218	243,786
Virginia	11,929	4.46	10,160	12,447	9,925	14,381	12,734
North Carolina	16,276	4.56	10,600	13,572	11,261	22,752	23,196
South Carolina	15,104	7.95	8,337	12,654	10,811	21,869	21,849
Georgia	20,972	6.71	14,986	19,163	14,984	30,147	25,580
Florida	19,060	10.05	12,332	16,386	15,270	27,771	23,543
Kentucky	24,686	8.67	13,589	24,436	21,212	37,593	26,597
Tennessee	17,488	6.00	13,194	17,522	11,486	23,326	21,912
Alabama	20,036	7.07	14,043	17,872	13,891	28,269	26,107
Mississippi	15,184	6.95	9,152	14,783	10,993	21,028	19,966
Louisiana	20,153	8.52	16,034	21,279	16,447	26,783	20,220
Arkansas	17,111	8.78	11,391	15,499	12,283	24,299	22,082

[a] From *Treasury Report on Work Relief*, p. 448.
[b] Based on Census of 1940, *Population*.

398

MIDDLE STATES	510,027	14.29	358,221	511,540	446,153	766,671	470,552
Ohio	123,116	17.82	87,910	117,324	106,862	201,223	102,262
Indiana	49,101	14.32	40,758	52,312	44,634	66,263	41,540
Illinois	122,612	15.53	81,884	126,712	107,039	177,837	119,587
Michigan	69,808	13.28	43,917	57,454	59,121	121,341	67,208
Wisconsin	41,997	13.38	31,035	45,262	36,757	59,046	37,885
Minnesota	38,721	13.87	30,306	41,909	35,147	52,228	34,014
Iowa	16,646	6.56	11,427	17,720	15,457	21,737	16,887
Missouri	48,626	12.85	30,984	52,847	41,136	66,996	51,169
NORTHWEST	93,242	13.54	66,520	119,446	86,038	109,554	84,655
North Dakota	9,167	14.28	4,745	15,482	8,369	9,634	7,606
South Dakota	10,411	16.19	5,311	18,329	9,886	10,245	8,284
Kansas	19,395	10.77	15,013	26,279	17,904	21,455	16,325
Nebraska	15,623	11.87	8,916	15,893	15,407	20,349	17,550
Colorado	17,888	15.93	16,637	20,603	15,191	20,960	16,051
Utah	7,221	13.12	6,228	7,365	6,286	8,628	7,597
Montana	10,947	19.58	7,192	12,441	10,824	15,322	8,954
Wyoming	2,590	10.32	2,478	3,054	2,171	2,961	2,288
SOUTHWEST	79,213	8.10	59,824	82,952	61,433	103,458	88,394
Oklahoma	27,107	11.60	21,737	32,290	21,641	35,232	24,634
Texas	39,296	6.13	28,218	36,992	28,690	52,236	50,343
New Mexico	6,861	12.90	5,056	7,155	5,577	8,285	8,250
Arizona	5,949	11.92	4,813	6,515	5,545	7,705	5,167
PACIFIC NORTHWEST	41,577	12.41	29,870	43,020	40,355	55,973	38,667
Idaho	5,718	10.89	4,480	5,357	5,127	7,075	6,549
Oregon	11,520	10.57	8,776	13,307	11,017	13,658	10,841
Washington	24,339	14.02	16,614	24,356	24,211	35,240	21,277
PACIFIC SOUTHWEST	82,597	11.77	71,981	102,231	72,625	93,699	72,451
California	81,164	11.75	70,868	100,633	71,181	91,955	71,183
Nevada	1,433	13.03	1,113	1,598	1,444	1,744	1,268
TERRITORIAL AND INSULAR							
Alaska	4	—	—	2	18	—	—
Hawaii	1,602	—	—	2,524	2,016	2,192	1,277
Puerto Rico	268	—	—	—	—	—	1,338
Virgin Islands	4	—	—	4	—	—	15
Not allocated to specific states	2,910	—	—	1,772[d]	14	12,550	3,756

[d] Credit; indicates collections or repayments in excess of payments, under lapsed appropriations.

Thirteen states had average per capita expenditures for
W.P.A. projects of less than $8.00, or at least one third less than
the average for continental United States. They were:

Virginia	4.46	Delaware	6.59
North Carolina	4.56	Georgia	6.71
Maryland	5.18	Mississippi	6.95
Tennessee	6.00	Alabama	7.07
Maine	6.06	Vermont	7.73
Texas	6.13	South Carolina	7.95
Iowa	6.56		

Of the 13 states with low per capita expenditures, 7 were in
what is sometimes called the solid south and 2, Maryland and
Tennessee, were border states. The other 4 states were Maine,
Vermont, Delaware, and Iowa. The figure for Iowa, $6.56, is
interesting since no other middle central state and no north-
western state had so low a figure. Wyoming with $10.32 and
Kansas with $10.77 were the 2 other low states for these groups.

The figure for Florida, $10.05, is the highest for the south-
eastern states. Arkansas came next in this group with $8.78 and
the average for the group as a whole was $7.01.

The figures presented in the table for individual years call for
some special comment. The first point to be emphasized is that
the figures are for fiscal years and not calendar years. The last
6 months of each calendar year are the first 6 months of each
fiscal year. That means, for example, that national elections
take place in the odd numbered fiscal years, and that the 1937
business recession began in the fiscal year 1938.

In the northern and western states the typical pattern was for
1939 to be the year of highest expenditures with 1937 ranking
second. There were some exceptions, however. In New York
the expenditures were materially higher in the fiscal year 1937
than in the fiscal year 1939, and in Pennsylvania and Maryland
the 1937 expenditures were a little higher. The agricultural
states, North and South Dakota, Kansas, and Wyoming likewise had their high point in 1937.

In the southeastern states the typical pattern is for the
expenditures in the fiscal years 1939 and 1940 to be materially
higher than in any of the three earlier years, generally with 1939
somewhat higher than 1940. Kentucky had a notable increase

in expenditures between 1938 and 1939. For Kentucky they averaged for the entire period about 24.7 million dollars a year; in 1938 they were 21.2 millions; they increased to 37.5 millions in 1939, and then dropped back to 26.6 millions. No other southeastern state shows 1939 the highest year by so large an amount, although for several of them the 1939 expenditures were materially higher than in 1938.[46]

In connection with these figures for expenditures by states, it should be recalled that Congress never laid down standards nor prescribed a formula to control the distribution of funds among the states. Power to distribute was delegated to the executive branch, but the law did not require the executive branch to formulate, publish, and apply either a formula or definite standards. The executive branch was authorized to use its own judgment and discretion, determining for itself both the factors which should be considered and the weights to be attached to the several factors. Macmahon, Millett, and Ogden in discussing this subject say:

The WPA was most reluctant to give out any information about the way in which the state employment quotas were determined. Thus, in 1938 in response to questioning by Senator Lodge of the Special Committee to Investigate Unemployment and Relief Mr. Hopkins replied, "I have a feeling that we can make a good case for the way the 2,600,000 are distributed by States," but he did not attempt to present "the good case." Senator Lodge pointed out that eleven states in the far West, with only 8 per cent of the population, had as large a WPA employment quota as the states of the Southeast with 25 per cent of the population. In a minority report of the committee, signed by Senator Lodge and Senator Davis of Penn-

[46] Kentucky had a spirited conflict in the senatorial primary in the spring and summer of 1938 when Governor A. B. Chandler entered the contest in opposition to Senator Alben W. Barkley. Thomas L. Stokes of the Scripps-Howard organization between June 6 and June 13 published a series of articles charging that the W.P.A. in Kentucky was active in the fight to renominate Senator Barkley. W.P.A. Administrator Harry Hopkins took up the 22 charges made by Mr. Stokes and specifically denied all but 4. In the resulting investigation by the Senate Special Committee to Investigate Campaign Expenditures, the committee's representative reported that Mr. Stokes' charges were substantiated in a majority of the cases cited. This investigation was primarily responsible for the transfer of Mr. Hopkins from the position of W.P.A. administrator to that of Secretary of Commerce. For a detailed account see Macmahon, Millett, and Ogden, *The Administration of Federal Work Relief*, pp. 282-91.

sylvania, reference was made to Mr. Hopkins' statement. The report continued:

"This excerpt contains the admission that the allocation of funds to the states for human relief is not done on a scientific or factual basis, but is merely a 'matter of opinion.' Those who think that executive discretion of this kind is either humane or democratic are at liberty to do so. To us it seems a violation of the principle of giving out relief on the basis of need and a clear invitation by Congress to the Executive to play favorites by giving out relief money where it will help or hurt the friends or enemies of the party in power. No administration should want this discretion. No administration should have it."

In 1940 Colonel Harrington told the House appropriations subcommittee that state employment quotas were determined by giving a weight of 40 per cent to state population and a weight of 40 per cent to the amount of unemployment within the state. The remaining weight of 20 per cent was attached to various factors in the discretion of WPA headquarters, acting upon the advice of its regional representatives. These figures were as much detail as the House or Senate was ever given about the fixing of employment quotas. However much the legislature might be irked by the "unscientific" method of distributing state employment quotas, it was unable to devise any statutory formula upon the fairness of which it could agree.[47]

The average number of persons employed on W.P.A. projects by months from August 1935 through June 1942 are presented in the 1942 report. From these monthly figures of average employment, average annual figures for fiscal years have been compiled. They represent the number of man-years of employment given by W.P.A. in each fiscal year. These man-year figures are included in the table on page 403 and are there used in arriving at expenditures of W.P.A. funds per man-year of employment given. The amount of sponsors' contributions are not included in these figures.

The high year of W.P.A. employment was the fiscal year 1939 when the man-year figure exceeded 3 millions. The second highest year was 1937 with 2.2 millions. Figures substantially below 2 millions did not come until the fiscal years 1941 and 1942 when the economy experienced the upturn resulting from the defense and war program.

[47] The same, p. 223.

W.P.A. Employment and Expenditures[a]

(All expenditure figures in thousands of dollars except "Per person employed" which is in dollars)

Fiscal Year	Average Number Employed[b]	W.P.A. Expenditures				
		Total[a]		Work Projects	Miscellaneous	Administrative Expenses
		Amount	Per Person Employed			
1936......	1,995,423	1,270,267	637	1,013,648	192,056	64,563
1937......	2,230,843	1,830,724	821	1,531,762	232,118	66,844
1938......	1,934,441	1,427,703	738	1,182,358	181,537	63,808
1939......	3,013,614	2,157,202	716	1,834,321	249,480	73,401
1940......	2,054,372	1,461,792	712	1,242,701	165,920	53,171
1941......	1,709,344	1,284,780	752	1,107,448	131,757	45,575
1942......	970,868	879,230	906	756,296	88,217	34,717

[a] Exclusive of rural rehabilitation. Figures from *Treasury Report on Work Relief*, p. 449.
[b] Compiled from *Report on Progress of the W.P.A. Program*, June 30, 1942, pp. 58–61.

The W.P.A. expenditures per man-year of employment given ranged from a low of $637 in the fiscal year 1936 to a high of $906 for the fiscal year 1942. The 1942 figure, however, is not really comparable with those for earlier years, for by then the W.P.A. was becoming more of a work agency to carry on defense and war projects than a work relief agency. Projects were then selected more on the basis of their value for the major task of the nation than on the basis of their suitability for furnishing employment to unemployed on relief rolls. More could be spent for materials and equipment. Selecting projects on the basis of value meant presumably a higher degree of selection on the basis of the qualifications of workers to produce efficiently. The condition of the labor market became such, moreover, that released W.P.A. beneficiaries could find employment in other occupations, since changed economic conditions made them no longer submarginal.

The significant range of costs per man-year was therefore from $637 in the first year of the program, 1936, to $821 in the following year. Thereafter until 1942 the cost ranged from $712 to $752.

A few words of explanation and caution should be given with respect to the figures for administrative expenses that are given in the table on page 403 and included in these costs per man-year. These figures represent the cost of general overhead administration and do not include the immediate cost of project administration and supervision. These costs are charged as project costs and are included as expenditures for work projects.

The W.P.A. could not always get from the relief rolls competent persons to direct projects, to serve as foremen, or to do certain types of skilled work that might be essential to the project. Unless the sponsors could supply them, it had to go into the market and hire them at a wage determined by negotiation, or it may be reasonably presumed at something approaching the prevailing wage. Workers so hired are in W.P.A. statistics commonly included with the beneficiaries of the program taken from the relief rolls. The regularly published data did not show separately either the number of such employees or the amount that went for their wages. The only persons excluded from the number employed on W.P.A. programs as given in the regular official figures are (1) the overhead administrative employees and (2) the workers paid by project sponsors.[48]

The 1940 report on the W.P.A. program states, however, that at no time since the program had been in operation had persons certified from the relief rolls constituted less than 94 per cent of the employment on projects operated by W.P.A.[49] As of the end of June 1940 certified persons formed 96 per cent of the workers paid from W.P.A. funds. For the fiscal year ending June 30, 1940, the wages paid the specially hired noncertified workers formed 7.5 per cent of the W.P.A. expenditures from its own funds and 9.7 per cent of all funds, including sponsors' contributions.[50]

This hiring of persons in the general market for project management and operation and for special jobs requiring skill represented some diversion of appropriated funds from the major objective of taking employables off the relief rolls. Limitations were therefore placed upon the percentage of funds which

48 Work Projects Administration, *Report on Progress of the WPA Program*, June 30, 1942, p. 57.
49 The same, 1940, p. 39.
50 Table obtained from W.P.A.

could be so used, but even so considerable leeway was left, perhaps necessarily, for administrative discretion. If the limitation was applied to the total amount allocated to a state, it was satisfied if the state total was all right, although on some individual projects the percentage was exceeded. If the limitation applied to a project as a whole, it could be satisfied although on some one particular part of the project the percentage was greatly exceeded. For example an extensive park or recreational center project might call, among many other things, for the erection of a small building. Almost all the work on the building itself might be done by skilled labor especially hired for that purpose. The amount of relief labor used on the other parts of the project made the total expenditure for the project as a whole come within the limitation. For this reason, among others, a tendency developed to prefer setting up a single large multiple project consisting of many separable or distinctive parts to having each distinctive part set up as a separate project. The multiple project simplified many administrative problems, such as getting approvals, assigning men, keeping the men employed, and accounting and reporting.[51] The large projects left much more freedom to project managers and made limitations on hiring in the open market less restrictive.

One aspect of this matter of hiring skilled workers and foremen in the open market deserves comment at this point, although it bears also on the question of the efficiency of W.P.A. to be considered later. The W.P.A. made profuse use of illustrations in its expensively printed annual reports and in some of its other publicity. One frequently finds beautifully taken artistic

---

[51] Using large multiple projects in accounting without breakdowns by distinctive parts tends to diminish the value of financial accounts for cost and efficiency analysis. For example, financial accounts for a multiple project show the purchase of several carloads of cement. Some of the cement was used for roads, some for curbs and walks, some for footings and floors for buildings, and the balance for miscellaneous purposes. Under such circumstances unless accurate stores records or cost accounts are kept on the project and unless the time of workers is charged to the various parts of projects, it is impossible to say with any degree of certainty what a particular unit actually cost, and hence comparisons with similar units built by other governmental agencies or by private enterprise are difficult and inconclusive. W.P.A. officials did not view their agency as an engineering and construction organization and did not publish cost analysis. The elaborate central accounts kept by the Treasury do not facilitate them.

pictures, particularly of buildings constructed by W.P.A., which certainly suggest that normally employed skilled labor could not have done better. Other pictures may show W.P.A. workers performing skilled jobs in installing water or sewer systems. A possibility is that practically all the work shown in the photograph was done by men specially hired by W.P.A. because of their skill or supplied by the sponsors, and that persons taken from the relief rolls were employed almost exclusively on other projects or parts of the project. The employment of skilled workers and experienced foremen undoubtedly improves the quality of the product and permits the agency to undertake more difficult and perhaps more permanently useful projects, but it tends to increase the cost per man-year, as the figures for the fiscal year 1942 suggest. There is an inherent conflict between using labor taken from the relief rolls and achieving utility, economy, and quality in production.

The expenditure figures which we have been discussing do not include sponsors' contributions, nor do the man-year figures include workers paid from sponsors' contributions. The table below, reproduced from the 1941 report of W.P.A., shows by fiscal years from 1936 to 1941 inclusive the amount of the sponsors' contributions and the percentage which they formed of all funds spent.

Sponsors' contributions, it should be noted, went in the main

AMOUNT OF W.P.A. AND SPONSORS' FUNDS EXPENDED ON PROJECTS OPERATED BY W.P.A., BY FISCAL YEAR AND BY SOURCE OF FUNDS[a]

(Dollar figures are in thousands)

Year ending June 30	Total Funds	W.P.A. Funds	Sponsors' Funds	
			Amount	Per Cent of Total Funds
TOTAL........	$11,365,407	$9,024,142	$2,341,265	20.6
1936.........	1,326,457	1,193,567	132,890	10.0
1937.........	2,051,890	1,751,286	300,604	14.7
1938.........	1,735,174	1,363,566	371,608	21.4
1939.........	2,561,911	2,067,972	493,939	19.3
1940.........	1,902,929	1,408,572	494,357	26.0
1941.........	1,787,045	1,239,178	547,867	30.7

[a] Report on Progress of the WPA Program, 1941, p. 60.

for purchase of materials, supplies, and equipment, rent of equipment, and other things, not including personal services. Personal services paid from sponsors' funds made up only a small percentage of these funds and of the aggregate expenditures for personal services on W.P.A. projects.[52]

If it be assumed that all the sponsors' contributions, including those for personal services, were essential for operating the projects, then the man-year costs previously given can be adjusted to include sponsors' costs, as follows:

Costs per Man-Year Including Sponsors' Contributions, 1936–45

Fiscal Year	W.P.A. Expenditures per Man-Year	Per Cent W.P.A. Expenditures of all Expenditures	Total Expenditures Including Sponsors' Contributions per Man-Year
1936...............	637	90.0	708
1937...............	821	85.3	962
1938...............	738	78.6	940
1939...............	716	80.7	887
1940...............	712	74.0	963
1941...............	752	69.3	1,085

The per man-year costs adjusted to allow for sponsors' contributions ranged from a low of $708 in the fiscal year 1936 to a high of $1,085 in 1941. Since the persons hired in the market as project managers, foremen, and skilled workers by the W.P.A. and paid from W.P.A. funds are included in divisors used to determine cost per man-year, these figures somewhat understate the cost per man-year of taking unemployed employables off the relief rolls under the W.P.A. program.

There are of course a large number of general overhead costs and indirect costs resulting from a governmental undertaking that do not get charged to or allocated to that program. The costs of approving projects and financial administration, includ-

[52] *Report on Progress of the WPA Program*, 1939, p. 33, gives cumulative figures for sponsors' funds classified by their source through June 30 of that year. The total was 1,303 millions of which only 224 millions or a little more than one sixth was for personal services whereas 601 millions was for purchase of supplies and equipment, 379 millions for rental of equipment, and 99 millions for other purposes. As of that date sponsors' funds had paid 4 per cent of the personal service costs, 57.9 per cent of the materials, supplies, and equipment costs, and 58.7 per cent of the rental of equipment costs.

ing accounting, auditing, budget control, and appropriating may be cited as perhaps the major illustration. For a program such as that of the W.P.A., which involved millions of small transactions, these costs borne by other agencies of government were necessarily relatively high.

It would be desirable to have data to contrast the general overhead expenditures of state and local officials under the purely discretionary system used by W.P.A. with comparable expenditures under a federal grant-in-aid system in which national money is distributed by formula. Where a formula is used, state and local officials are vitally concerned at two points: (1) when the formula is determined or amended and (2) when the appropriations are made which are to be distributed by that formula. At other times they can devote their time mainly to the executions of the plans made in the light of the financing thus provided. Under the W.P.A. discretionary grant system, governors, mayors, and other responsible state and local officials had to turn to Washington as applicants for relief. It seems almost inevitable that the time and money spent for communications, travel, and in some instances maintenance of Washington representatives far exceeded what would have been involved under a system whereby the states, and perhaps also the local governments, received what the federal government contributed by legislative right and not by an exercise of administrative discretion.

ORGANIZATION OF THE W.P.A.

No attempt will be made in the present book either to describe or discuss the organization of the W.P.A. in detail. There are, however, a few points with respect to it that are significant from the standpoint of the present study.

W.P.A., as previously noted, largely evolved from the Federal Emergency Relief Administration. The F.E.R.A. administrator was by the executive order creating the W.P.A. made the W.P.A. administrator. Since the F.E.R.A. was entirely a relief agency making federal grants to the states for relief, naturally key positions in the main were filled if not by social workers at

least by persons with the social point of view, selected by or
under the authority of the national relief administrator. Its
principal administrative relationships were with the several
state emergency relief administrations, which again naturally
were staffed largely by persons with a social point of view.

When the decision was reached that a federal work program
was to replace the federal grants to the states for relief and that
the federal relief administrator was to co-ordinate the new work
program, it was again natural that the administrator should
give many of his key people in the old organization leading
roles in the new and that at the outset the emphasis in W.P.A.
should have been on the welfare aspects of the task rather
than the construction aspects. It would have been nothing
short of amazing had the W.P.A.-F.E.R.A. administrator taken
the position that the new program called for a different kind
of organization with personnel having had construction experience. It must be remembered, moreover, that in the initial
days of the program the national government already had its
Public Works Administration, which was largely staffed by
engineers and others with training and experience in the construction field. The great tactical advantage that W.P.A. had
over the P.W.A. was that persons with the social point of view
operating in the public works field were not hampered by the
standards and inhibitions of trained engineers. If engineers
should be turned loose on a social work job, they would not be
hampered by the standards and inhibitions of the trained, experienced social workers. It was undoubtedly easier for social
workers than for engineers to get large numbers at work on construction projects on short order.

Although W.P.A. from its inception obviously required a
competent chief engineer with a good engineering division behind him, no such arrangements were immediately made. At the
outset no competent engineer occupied a major place in the
W.P.A. hierarchy or had real prestige. The result was some
fumbling and delays. Lieutenant Colonel Francis C. Harrington
of the United States Army Corps of Engineers, who had helped
to set up the Civilian Conservation Corps was asked to make a

survey of W.P.A. Following the survey he became Chief Engineer and an assistant administrator of W.P.A. On Mr. Hopkins' transfer to be Secretary of Commerce, Colonel Harrington succeeded him as head of W.P.A. Commenting on the initial appointment of the Colonel to W.P.A. and the introduction of trained engineers into the organization, Macmahon, Millett, and Ogden say:

> The role of professional army engineers at this stage in the development of the WPA was pronounced. The President was understood to desire their use; the WPA, though jealous for its social service standards, welcomed their prestige, their relative disinterestedness, and their frequent possession of a trained sense of administrative relationships. . . .[53]

The fact that W.P.A. evolved out of F.E.R.A. perhaps explains in part why this national works agency had a field organization for each separate state. In making grants to the states the F.E.R.A. dealt directly with the state emergency relief administrations. When the relief program was changed to a national work program, nationally administered, the W.P.A. developed a national W.P.A. office for each state with a nationally appointed state W.P.A. administrator in charge. There were of course other reasons for the development of state offices.

The W.P.A. was largely engaged in constructing things for state or local governmental bodies. The state or local governments would, as a rule, put up a sponsor's contribution, hold title to the land on which the project was built, and own, operate, and maintain the improvement after it was constructed. It was not in the main a program under which the national government was building things of a type or a size not previously built by state and local governments; the nation was simply, ostensibly temporarily, assuming parts of the functions of state and local governments in the emergency. The issue of states rights and the division of powers might easily have proved embarrassing had the nation used administrative regions that patently lessened the independent authority of the state. The nation, moreover, had to look to the state legislatures for such legal acts

[53] *The Administration of Federal Work Relief*, p. 206.

as were necessary to widen fields for public construction and give more scope for W.P.A. and other projects.

The program, moreover, was designed for unemployed employables in need which meant (1) that need had to be determined and (2) that absence of a suitable job in normally conducted enterprise had to be certified. The first task obviously belonged to the welfare department and the second to the employment service. The W.P.A. had either to utilize the state agencies responsible for these functions or to a large extent duplicate them, and thus lay itself open to the charge of usurping the powers of the states. The N.Y.A. tended to assume such functions, but the W.P.A. throughout co-operated with the state agencies and this co-operation was facilitated by use of the state as the unit for W.P.A. field organization.

Use of the state as a unit also facilitated relationships with Congress, particularly with the Senate. Senatorial confirmation of the higher paid employees of W.P.A. was required. Possibly the use of the state as the unit and the requirement of senatorial confirmation may have increased the use of the W.P.A. for partisan or factional political purposes.

Within the state the W.P.A. set up districts of its own which did not follow the lines of congressional districts. They were smaller in number and were based primarily on administrative factors. The exterior boundaries of districts within the state generally followed county lines so that all of any county was within a single district.

A distinctive feature of W.P.A. was that it brought the mayors or other leading municipal officers in immediate practical contact with federal officers possessed of wide discretionary power. The mayors of the municipalities which had large numbers of unemployed were in an extremely difficult position because their political life depended to no small extent upon their success in getting W.P.A. projects for their communities. In many American states the relationships between the large city and the state government, particularly the state legislature, were far from satisfactory. There was often lack of understanding and sympathy between the highly urbanized and industrialized voters and the voters in the smaller communities and rural areas. Often districting and apportionment gave the smaller communities a greater representation in the legislature per capita of population than was enjoyed by the big cities. Thus many of the mayors of the big cities liked dealing directly with the national government even though the national government had used the state as its administrative unit. They could do business with that national administrative unit without necessarily having to clear with the governor, the heads of state departments, and possibly the state legislature.

Macmahon, Millett, and Ogden report that the mayors of several of the great municipalities sought to have their cities or the metropolitan district of which their cities were a part made independent federal administrative units distinct from the unit set up for the state to which legally they were subordinate. The only instance where a city was made a separate federal administrative unit was in the case of New York. To quote the authors just cited:

The first departure from the state pattern occurred before the WPA actually got under way. New York City sought and obtained special accommodation. It became the "forty-ninth state" administration. Political reasons, apart from the cogent administrative argument of its population, unique in size and compactness, made an exception to strict adherence to state lines for New York City more feasible than for other large municipalities. The city was governed by a fusion, non-partisan administration headed by Fiorello H. LaGuardia, mayor. The mayor's relations to the White House and Congress were such that the separate organization of the city area was readily endorsed. But this precedent was not carried further despite the advocacy of a wide use of cities as main areas by the mayors of metropolitan communities. It failed in part because in states like Pennsylvania and Illinois there was in 1935 little political incentive for treating Philadelphia, Pittsburgh, and Chicago separately.[54]

RESULTS OF THE PROGRAM

The question as to the results of the program will be approached from four standpoints: (1) its efficiency in constructing public works and rendering needed services, (2) its efficiency

[54] The same, p. 200.

as a relief agency, (3) its effect on state and local finance, and (4) its political implications.

Efficiency in construction and service. Over the years experience in American government has led to a widely accepted view that in building substantial public works the people generally get the most for their money if the following steps are taken.

1. The government, either using its own designers and engineers or retaining competent ones from the outside, prepares detailed plans and specifications which fully comply with all essential engineering standards.

2. The government then invites competitive bids from competent contractors who must comply with all terms and conditions set forth by the government, which incidentally may include provisions regarding wages, hours, and other matters affecting conditions of employment.

3. The government lets the contract to the lowest competent bidder, provided his bid is within the sum available for the structure, and requires him to give an adequate completion bond.

4. The government employs its own inspectors of such types as may be necessary to make sure that the contractor builds strictly in accord with the specifications.

Such a procedure honestly administered by competent employees with safeguards against collusive bidding gives the people reasonable assurance that they are paying a fair price for the structure in view of market conditions for labor and materials prevailing at the time of the letting. It does not guarantee that they could not later have built for less, had they delayed construction, or on the other hand had they built some months or even some years before.

If it be assumed that the government is honest and efficient and will demand and enforce full compliance with all specifications and other requirements, the differences in bids will turn on such matters as the amount of profit sought by the contractor, the extent to which his own standards are higher than the minimum standards set by the government, his own appraisal, based on his past experience, on the efficiency of his organization in all aspects of the work, and perhaps on the extent to which he has capital invested in equipment and possibly material required for the project. If the contractor has little other work ahead, has a good organization which he wants to keep together, and has a substantial investment in equipment and material, he may shave the profit item pretty thin to get the job or even forego personal profit and knowingly take a loss.

Three points in this discussion are particularly important for our present purposes.

1. The efficiency of the contractor and his organization is a vital factor in the competition.

2. If wage limits are contained in the requirements, the contractor must use effective equipment and employees well worth the salary or wages paid them.

3. The cost of the structure which he erects depends in no small measure on market conditions at the time the contract was made unless there are provisions in it for increases or decreases upon specified contingencies.

No one should expect W.P.A. to approach the efficiency secured through this competitive bidding system for several reasons, among which the most important are:

1. The W.P.A. was not a going construction organization with skilled and experienced engineers, foremen, and workmen. It was rather a mushroom outfit.

2. W.P.A. did not select personnel on the basis of skill, experience, and other qualifications for the work in hand. It took persons primarily from relief rolls and in many instances assigned them to tasks for the performance of which they had had little prior training and experience.

3. Since private enterprise and regular government establishments tried to retain their most valuable workers, the W.P.A. could not easily secure experienced key men on whom in any enterprise efficiency so largely depends.

4. Since the objective was to furnish employment to persons in need, the use of labor-saving equipment and the investment in it were discouraged rather than encouraged.

5. Since W.P.A. offered no efficiency incentives, the best-equipped workers tended to leave it to return to private employment or normally operated government agencies. Viewed as a construction agency it suffered from "turn over" and adverse selection.

6. Because of its peculiar nature, it could not demand and enforce standards of quantity and quality of output that are essential in private contracting and that prevail in efficient permanent governmental public works agencies.

7. In many instances the objective of giving employment to the needy unemployed employables resulted in assigning more man power to a project than could be effectively used. Some assignments under such conditions approached made work.

The major activities of the W.P.A. were, as has been pointed out, in the field of construction, but it had some service activities and white-collar projects. For efficient administration of service projects, many governments have found it necessary to use the merit system of competition with tests designed to determine the relative capacity of candidates to perform the duties of the positions involved. W.P.A. could not have fulfilled its relief objectives if it had disregarded need and had selected its workers through open competitive examinations. It had to select primarily from those on the relief rolls. Although some from the relief rolls could have more than satisfied reasonable minimum standards, it is unquestionably true that many were employed who would have been rejected as unqualified by civil service commissions or would have had such low ratings that they never would have been reached for appointment. Youths from families not in need and secondary earners from such families would have won the positions in an open competition.

We have found no evidence that would controvert the conclusion that had the money spent through W.P.A. been spent through established agencies of government using efficient practices and where applicable making use of efficient private contractors, the people would have got more products from the expenditures in structures and in services. And, as noted in the discussion of the selection of products, they would have secured things which stood higher on their priority lists. The major justification for W.P.A. must be found in its relief aspects.

Efficiency in relief. If it be assumed that efficiency in relief administration consists in prompt aid to those in want to the extent necessary to bring them to a minimum level of living, then W.P.A. cannot be regarded as having been efficient. The major defects were:

1. The work program never provided jobs for all unemployed employables in need. Whether a member of that class secured a work assignment depended on such factors as (a) the amount appropriated by Congress on the recommendations of the administration, (b) the allocation of appropriated funds by the administration, (c) the development and operation of a project or projects in the locality where the needy were which would provide suitable jobs for all eligibles. Failure at any one of these points left unemployed employables in need without provision from national funds, except for surplus commodities, unless they could qualify under the public assistance categories of the Social Security Act.

2. The W.P.A. program used money to pay wages to certain of the persons in need which more than met their budget deficits. An efficient relief system would have given all persons in need a priority on funds appropriated for relief up to the amount of their budget deficiency. Only after all such need had been met, would funds have been used for wages above budget deficiencies for some workers and for hiring administrators, supervisors, and skilled workers not available from relief rolls to carry on work projects. From the standpoint of relief the more elaborate, more costly program was undertaken before the fundamental objective of actual prevention of want had been attained.

3. The W.P.A. and other work relief programs were not financially or administratively integrated with state relief programs. The state and local governments never knew what part of the load the national government would carry on federal funds, and hence had no knowledge as to what part of it they themselves would have to bear. Even after Congress had passed the

annual Emergency Relief Appropriation Act, they could not tell what part of the appropriation would be allocated to their state or in the case of local governments to their localities. Although the national administration spoke as if it would bear the cost of employing the unemployed employables in need, this principle was not formally adopted or applied, so that the states and local governments could neither legislate nor appropriate on the basis of an established division of costs or on the basis of assured grants-in-aid from the national government.

In view of these facts it is impossible to state that an efficient relief system for needy unemployed employables developed out of the W.P.A. program. On the contrary it seems reasonable to conclude that a more efficient relief system would have been developed under the original 1933 relief legislation which provided grants-in-aid to the states and for which W.P.A. was substituted.

In favor of the work program as a substitute for the grant-in-aid program three major arguments were advanced: (1) it would preserve the skills of the workers, (2) it would preserve their morale, and (3) the public would get some return in public works and services for their relief expenditures. Each of these arguments deserves brief consideration.

On page 418 we reproduce a table taken from the 1936 *Report on the Works Program* which contrasts the distribution by usual occupation of the workers on relief in March 1935 with that of all gainful workers at the Census of 1930.

Among the male workers on relief, 24.6 per cent had been unskilled workers in nonagricultural pursuits, and 11.9 had been unskilled workers in agriculture which gave a total of 36.5 per cent unskilled. Among the women workers on relief, 47.6 per cent had been in domestic and personal service, 5.2 per cent had been unskilled workers in agriculture, and 1.0 per cent unskilled workers in nonagricultural pursuits, a total of 53.8 per cent. Unskilled workers constituted the largest single group with which W.P.A. had to deal.

The second largest group were the semiskilled who consti-

Occupational classification	Workers on Relief (Labor Inventory, March 1935)			Gainful Workers U. S. Census, April 1930		
	Total	Male	Female	Total	Male	Female
TOTAL......................	100.0	100.0	100.0	100.0	100.0	100.0
WHITE-COLLAR WORKERS........	11.2	9.4	19.3	30.2	25.9	45.5
Professional and technical.....	1.7	1.2	3.5	6.3	4.1	14.1
Proprietors, managers, and officials (nonagricultural).......	1.6	1.9	0.5	7.3	8.8	2.2
Office workers...............	4.3	3.2	9.3	9.7	6.2	21.7
Salesmen and kindred workers..	3.6	3.1	6.0	6.9	6.8	7.5
MANUAL WORKERS..............	79.5	79.4	79.9	58.0	59.6	52.4
Skilled workers and foremen...	14.7	18.1	0.4	13.1	16.7	0.8
Semiskilled workers...........	21.6	20.6	25.7	15.3	14.3	18.2
Unskilled laborers:						
(a) Agricultural............	10.7	11.9	5.2	8.2	9.1	5.0
(b) Nonagricultural.........	20.1	24.6	1.0	12.7	16.0	1.4
Domestic and personal service workers...................	12.4	4.2	47.6	8.7	3.5	27.0
FARMERS......................	9.3	11.2	0.8	11.8	14.5	2.1

[a] Works Progress Administration, *Report on the Works Program, March 16, 1936*, p. 21.

tuted 20.6 per cent of the male workers on relief and 25.7 per cent of the female workers. To define semiskilled workers, we shall refer to a detailed occupational table given on page 22 of the 1936 *Report on the Works Program* but not here reproduced.

In this table we find an aggregate of 1,180,975 semiskilled workers on relief. Of this number 310,401, or less than 27 per cent, were from the construction and building industry, whereas 870,574 or over 73 per cent were from manufacturing or other industries. Of the 310,401 semiskilled workers from the construction and building industry 204,994 were truck and tractor drivers, 25,931 firemen (stationary), and 16,031 operators of building and construction equipment. Among the semiskilled in manufacturing and other industries the big items were inside workers, mines, 105,093; iron and steel, machinery, and vehicle industries, 86,579; textile industries, 83,781; clothing industries, 59,914; food and beverage industries, 48,694; laundries and dry cleaning establishments, 34,518; lumber and furniture industries, 32,296; and taxicab drivers, bus drivers, and chauffeurs, 28,203.

With respect to the great majority of these semiskilled workers, the truth is that their semiskill consisted in the capacity to operate a particular machine or piece of equipment or several of them or to perform a particular process or group of processes. With respect to many of those in manufacturing and industries other than building and construction the machines operated or the processes performed were those used in private enterprise. Such semiskills could not be preserved by use unless W.P.A. itself invaded the field of private enterprise. Since it did not enter the fields of manufacturing, mining, and distribution, it could not preserve these semiskills.

The census of workers on relief showed a total of 737,314 skilled workers of whom 492,575 had been employed in building and construction and 244,739 in manufacturing and other industries. Those in manufacturing and other industries were in the main skilled in occupations that are in fields operated by private enterprise. W.P.A. could not supply them with jobs to maintain their skills unless it competed directly with private enterprise. Of the 492,575 in building and construction some 372,000, according to our analysis, belonged clearly in the building trades; included are carpenters, painters, bricklayers and stone masons, electricians, plasterers, roofers, setters of marble, stone, and tile, paper hangers, plumbers, gas and steam fitters, and sheet metal workers. If they were to be given the kind of work in which they could exercise and preserve their skills, W.P.A. would have had to go far more than it did into the field of building construction, where it would in many instances have been in direct competition with private enterprise. Among the remaining 120,000 in building and construction were about 20,000 foremen of whom only 8,307 had been foremen of road and street construction; 32,141 were operators or engineers, stationary and portable construction equipment, and 9,559 structural iron and steel workers.

These statistics strongly suggest that the argument regarding the preservation of skills was more a talking point than an actuality. The unskilled had relatively little in the way of skills to preserve: what they needed to preserve was more good work habits than skills, and it is questionable how far W.P.A. promoted good work habits. The skills of many of the semiskilled and the skilled could only be exercised and preserved by restoring private enterprise to normal levels of employment. Stimulation of the building trades was clearly needed, for which purpose the Public Works Administration and the Federal Housing Administration programs were better suited than W.P.A. and represented less competition with private enterprise.

Preservation of morale seems likewise to have been largely a talking point, although apparently that conclusion cannot be supported statistically. Before an applicant was eligible for a W.P.A. assignment, he had to be certified as in need of relief, generally by the local relief office in his neighborhood. It seems reasonable to assume that by the time it became necessary to apply for a certification of need and a W.P.A. job, the applicant's morale had been seriously impaired. It may be assumed, moreover, that morale is not high among workers who for one reason or another are much of the time submarginal. If W.P.A. had been able to supply a worker with a job where he could exercise such skill as he possessed and make him feel that he was an efficient member of an efficient working organization, morale might have been materially improved, but in many instances that could not be done.

Probably to no little degree morale depends on the prestige of the organization with which the worker is connected. What do the neighbors, associates, former or prospective employers think of the place the worker is employed? Although W.P.A. may not have deserved the bad reputation it gained in many localities— and many of the stories were funny rather than truthful—yet such things prevented the agency from being a real morale restorer. What a worker needs to retain or restore his morale under our existing system is a real job in a private enterprise or in a normally conducted public enterprise. Employment on a sheltered project especially conducted by the national government for the needy unemployed unemployable that segregates the worker from the more fortunate and possibly the more effective did not improve his standing in the community, with his family, or possibly himself. In some communities it was said that private employers regarded experience on W.P.A. as a liability rather than an asset on an application for a job. If such was the fact, or was believed to be the fact, W.P.A. was scarcely a morale restorer.

Unquestionably morale is somewhat restored when need is relieved and when the worker and his family again can have at least the necessaries of life. The question which must be raised is how much difference does it make to morale whether the necessaries are supplied through an unemployment insurance benefit or through a W.P.A. job. A system can of course be so devised that direct relief made necessary by unemployment can take the form of an unemployment insurance benefit. This subject will be more fully considered in the last part of this book.

The people got some useful and valuable public works and services from W.P.A. That is unquestionably true, but it is not the real issue. The real issue is which would have given the people the most for their money: (1) W.P.A. as it was actually conducted, or (2) payments of direct relief to persons in need to the extent of their budget deficiencies, and use of the balance of the money and credit in ways that would stimulate private enterprise and normally conducted public enterprise.

Data are not available to permit an answer to that question. One can say with a good deal of assurance that the system of stimulating private enterprise and normally conducted public enterprise would have led to the selection of projects more in accordance with priority demands. The projects would undoubtedly have been more efficiently and economically conducted. They would have increased employment, but they would not necessarily have taken employees directly from the relief rolls. In some communities local resumption of private construction did almost immediately absorb most of the relief rolls, but the action generally is indirect and involves a lag.

With respect to efficiency in general it can be said, the crisis in the early days of the depression resulted in no small measure from unpreparedness and from failure to legislate on the basis of mutually consistent principles. Four points deserve special emphasis in this connection.

1. Neither the states nor the nation had an effective system of unemployment insurance nor any device whereby persons in need because of unemployment could be assured of prompt, certain relief, at least to the extent of their budget deficit. Absence of such systems created distress, confusion, and a general reaction that experiments must be tried without the delay necessary to give adequate consideration to fundamental principles.

2. In many instances, neither private enterprise nor the established agencies of government had advanced plans for projects which could be put into operation quickly to increase employment. Some of the best projects for the emergency came from more or less permanent, existing agencies, but in general the number was insufficient and the planning not sufficiently far advanced to meet the situation.

3. Neither the states nor the nation had sufficiently debated the issue of the proper division of fields between public enterprise and private enterprise and arrived at guiding lines. Thus conflicts on this issue arose not only between private enterprise and governments but within governments, notably the national government. Private employers with knowledge of the hazards of competing with government enterprises naturally hesitated to make commitments.

4. The revenue systems of the states were in many cases antiquated, and the financial relationships between the national government and the state governments had not been adequately reconsidered in the light of changed economic conditions. As a result the national government with its power to borrow was in a position to assume duties and responsibilities which had hitherto belonged to the states. Decisions as to whether the states or the nation could best perform the functions were not made on consideration of basic principles but rather on the basis of two facts: (a) the urgency of the need and (b) the practically unlimited borrowing power of the national government.

Had an adequate unemployment insurance and relief system

been in effect, had private enterprise and normally conducted public enterprise been prepared with plans and projects, had private enterprise known within what fields and upon what conditions it was free to function, and had the financial relations between the states and the national government been well defined on a sound basis, lags would undoubtedly have been materially reduced, and a degree of certainty and confidence would have prevailed that would have encouraged that resumption of activities necessary for reasonably full employment.

Effects on state and local finance. Special emphasis should here be placed on the effect of the W.P.A. and related programs on state and local government finances. As some of these points have been touched upon previously, we shall deal with the subject summarily.

1. Under the system that prevailed no state or local government knew in advance either: (a) how much money the national government would spend within its boundaries; or (b) what part of the relief load the national government would itself assume.

2. To get national money, the state and local governments had to propose projects which met the requirements of the national government, and these requirements, as we have seen, were especially designed for giving employment to needy unemployed from relief rolls.

3. To get these national projects, the state and local governments had to put up sponsors' contributions. Since a sponsor's contribution of from 10 to 30 per cent would bring into the jurisdiction from the national treasury from 70 to 90 per cent of the cost of projects, the state and local authorities were under great pressure to use available funds for sponsors' contributions and so to legislate that eligible public projects could be presented.

4. The borrowing power of a state or a local government depends basically upon its revenue resources. Its obligations must be contrasted with its resources to determine whether it can meet its debt obligations. In the case of a local government its resources to pay obligations are mainly (a) its own tax receipts,

(b) its share of state taxes turned over to it by the state, (c) grants-in-aid paid to it by the state, which sometimes include federal money, and (d) any money which the local government may receive directly from the national government under a definite law or contract which makes the receipt a certain asset which can be counted upon and does not partake of the nature of an unpredictable windfall. A state must depend on its own taxes and definite grants-in-aid from the national government under definite laws and contracts. National gifts in the nature of windfalls do not materially add to the borrowing capacity of state and local governments, except in so far as they relieve state and local governments of expenses they would otherwise have borne themselves. If the national government levies high taxes within the state, it tends to exhaust the pool of available taxable resources and increases the difficulty of state and local governments to increase their own tax revenues and to borrow on the strength of their prospective future tax revenues.

Programs of the nature of W.P.A. represent therefore an encroachment upon the independence of the state and local governments. Here we should repeat that the major expenditures of the national government through W.P.A. were for (1) highways, roads, and streets, (2) educational, professional, and clerical projects, (3) electric utilities, water sewer systems, and the like, (4) public buildings, (5) public recreational facilities, (6) conservation work, and (7) transportation facilities. In a very large measure W.P.A. carried on through a national agency, mainly at national expense, projects of a type which previously had been almost entirely within the legislative and administrative domain of state and local governments, in some instances of course with grants-in-aid from the national government. Such a program could materially improve the financial position of state and local governments through the device of relieving them of responsibility for activities which they had previously conducted at their own expense.

Political implications. Prior to the depression, the national government had few direct contacts with individual citizens except in the exercise of its sovereign power as a collector of taxes. It provided benefits for veterans and for Indian wards, but in general those functions and activities of government that involved granting benefits to large numbers of individuals were in the hands of state and local governments, predominantly local governments. The legislation of the thirties materially changed past practices in this respect and made millions of people direct beneficiaries of payments from the national treasury. They had a direct and personal interest in the action of the national government with respect to both laws setting forth policy and principles and in many instances also in amounts appropriated. In the case of the three public assistance categories of the Social Security Act the federal payments were grants-in-aid to the states, and the details of administration were in state hands, although subject to federal law and rules and some federal control. The old-age and survivors insurance system of the Social Security Act was federally administered and financed, but all the terms and conditions were set forth in detail in the law and little was left to the discretion of the President or of policy-making officers appointed by him. Pressure groups of beneficiaries could and did develop and probably will continue to develop to make such laws more liberal, but they have to function through the established legislative processes with respect to basic legislation.

W.P.A. and the related programs that had their origins in the Emergency Relief Appropriation Acts were in a class by themselves. The President and the administrative officers appointed by him had unprecedented power to allocate the funds appropriated by Congress. Neither the 1935 act under which W.P.A. was created nor any other subsequent act established a formula to govern the allocation of the federal funds among states or among local governments. No state or local government was given a contingent right to the receipt of federal funds upon meeting the requirements laid down by law. No member of Congress who believed his state or his district unfairly treated could either in the committee or on the floor charge that his state or district, despite compliance with the terms of the act, had been denied what Congress had promised. Congress promised nothing as a contingent right. All the congressman could do was to charge abuse of administrative discretion.

Thus members of Congress, governors, mayors, political leaders without elective office, and individual citizens in seeking W.P.A. projects were petitioning the national administrators vested with wide discretionary powers for an act of grace. As the W.P.A. projects were mainly public, it was inevitable that the petitioners should be principally persons active in political life with a concern for the maintenance of their party organization or, in the one-party South, of their factional organization. The elections of 1932 resulted in giving the Democratic party control in a large number of state and local governments. It will be recalled, moreover, that the original act under which the F.E.R.A. was created and subsequent acts provided for appointment of officers and other employees without reference to the merit system provided for in the Civil Service Act. Later senatorial confirmation of appointments to the higher positions was provided, a device which is usually regarded as increasing rather than diminishing the extent to which partisan or factional forces influence administration. Never before in the history of the United States had such vast sums been available for discretionary distribution with so little control by statutory enactment and without consideration of the political implications of the old proverb, "Self preservation is the first law of nature."

The system meant not only that projects could be secured for the state or local government at relatively little immediate and direct cost to voters of the locality, but also that thousands of voters in need could be given employment. Between January 1936 and June 1941, the number of persons employed out of W.P.A. funds never fell below 1.4 millions (June 1941) and reached a high of 3.3 millions (November 1938). Two points deserve special emphasis with respect to these figures.

1. W.P.A. was not supposed to employ more than one worker per family, and thus these figures represent families. In the Unemployment Census of November 16–20, 1937, only 11.9 per cent of the emergency workers were reported as having no de-

pendents.[55] In February 1939 the percentage of single-person families was 10.7, and the average number of persons per family for W.P.A. workers was 3.76.[56] The number of adults of voting age who benefited from the expenditures made under discretionary power was thus far greater than the mere number of persons employed would indicate.

2. Although a substantial number of persons worked month after month on W.P.A., there was a very considerable turnover, as the variation in employment from month to month demonstrates. Thus the total number of individuals who at one time or another benefited from W.P.A. wage payments is much greater than figures for the number employed in any one month would indicate. For the fiscal year 1938 the average number of workers on W.P.A. financed projects was about 3 millions, but far more than 3 millions were employed on such projects at some time during the year. Thus when allowances are made for family membership and turnover, the number of persons of voting age who have benefited from W.P.A. represents a significant total.

The question of preservation of the independence of the electorate, the prevention of its corruption by "bread and circuses," arises in connection with almost every program which gives individuals personal financial benefits from the public treasury. Even in the contributory social insurance systems that operate under detailed legal provisions, there is a real danger of the development of powerful pressure groups to increase benefits when the increases can only be paid for from the general fund. W.P.A. presented a far more dangerous situation because it did not operate under detailed specific laws creating any contingent legislative rights but vested a tremendous discretionary power in a single, elected official and in subordinates appointed by him whose tenure of office depended upon the success of the party in power at the polls.

[55] *Report on Progress of the WPA Program*, June 30, 1938, p. 44.
[56] The same, June 30, 1939, p. 102.

CHAPTER XIII

THE CIVILIAN CONSERVATION CORPS AND THE NATIONAL YOUTH ADMINISTRATION

The ensuing chapter is to deal with two organizations, the Civilian Conservation Corps and the National Youth Administration, which will be treated together because they both deal with the youth problem. At the outset that problem will be broadly reviewed, and then each of the programs will be briefly considered. Since both programs have now been abandoned, the chapter will be devoted primarily to a presentation of the major issues which should be considered in case any proposals are made to revive them.

THE UNDER-TRAINED YOUTH

In a rural economy in the days prior to machines and mechanization, a youth with strength and willingness to work had little difficulty in finding employment that would provide him at least with room and board. Gradually, in one field after another, power tended to take the place of human strength. The mind assumed increased importance as a factor in determining whether the individual could satisfy the minimum requirements for successful employment in a growing number of positions in both public and private enterprises. Education became more and more essential. The proportion of the youth of the nation who completed high school and the proportion who went on to higher educational institutions enormously increased. Employers, both public and private, tended formally or informally to use education or years of schooling as a factor in selections for employment, partly because the positions they had to fill required knowledge and skills developed in the schools and partly because advancement in school is something of a measure of general all-round capacity. It is not a precise measure, but the youth who has done well in school has a presumption in his favor that is not enjoyed by the youth who for one reason or another was retarded and left school before successfully completing a reasonable number of grades.

Years before the depression dramatized the problem, the difficulties confronting the youth with inadequate educational preparation for success in making a good living were clearly recognized. They were found in the blind alley jobs. Analysis of work certificates in states with child labor laws and other data showed much short-time employment, much moving from job to job. Often the jobs themselves provided little in the way of real training. The successive jobs frequently bore no relationship to each other. The moves were not advancements but chance drifting from one opening to another. Such a supply of labor was naturally drawn upon by persons in need of temporary workers for positions which did not require any substantial amount of training and experience. Unfortunately in some instances the wages offered for temporary blind alley jobs were higher than employers were offering to beginners in jobs which presented some future. A youth who felt that he was really making good money as compared with his fellows who had more regular and routine jobs not infrequently found himself entirely out-distanced in the course of a few years. The experience through which he had passed may have induced him to attempt to live by his wits rather than by continuous, steady, and perhaps routine labor. Having to live by one's wits may lead to an occasional run out of bounds set by the law.

Why did a youth get into this group? Among the reasons are the following major ones:

1. The available school facilities within reach of the youth were inadequate.

2. The things taught at the school or the way they were taught failed to enlist and hold his interest.

3. Personal difficulties arose between the youth or his parents and the teachers and school officials.

4. The parents or guardians lacked the financial resources to keep him in school.

5. They lacked the interest and co-operation necessary to keep him in school.

6. They lacked the interest and ability necessary to keep him from becoming hopelessly retarded at school.

7. The environment in which he lived worked against regular school attendance and a co-operative attitude toward the school personnel and fellow pupils.

8. He was so handicapped by ill health, undernourishment, and so on, that normal progress was impossible.

9. His native intelligence was so far below normal that he could not really profit from schools designed to serve normal or average children.

Probably in few cases is failure to make satisfactory progress in school due exclusively to any one of these factors. In most cases two or more of them are present. Many instances can be cited where youth succeed despite such handicaps because the child or his parents had a spirit that surmounts handicaps. But here we are concerned not with those who escape the group, but those who fall into it.

The Declaration of Independence says that all men are created equal. It sometimes seems as if our public elementary school systems for many years proceeded on the assumption that the political doctrine was biological truth. If the child lacked the capacity to keep up with his fellows, it was undemocratic for the schools to organize something special for him, adapted to his capacities and his interests. He fell by the wayside. For many years, moreover, the schools tended to conform to a pattern academically approved but not put to the test of what happened to the children for whom the pattern was ill designed. The school was to be judged by its graduates and not by those who dropped out. Later in some school systems after attention was focused on those who had in the past never finished, a practice developed of promoting not on the basis of examinations and tests of achievement but on the basis of birthdays. Then on graduation day a certificate might be handed a boy or girl who intellectually had really never progressed much if any beyond the first grade. Such a boy or girl got what he could from a program designed on the basis that all boys and girls are sufficiently equal so that a common pattern can be used for all.

Differentiation of program was many years ago introduced into the high schools, colleges, and universities. With that differentiation we are not greatly concerned because so few of the group we are discussing ever got far enough in the high schools to desire substantial benefits from that differentiation.

An obvious possibility was to provide special training, possibly vocational in nature, for children who could not materially profit from the ordinary elementary school. Such vocational education, however, encountered difficulties that illustrate significant issues.

Domestic science and home making for the girls probably presented no economic or political difficulties. It was quite otherwise with the boys for there the issue arose as to the trade or craft for which they were to be trained.

One can understand the skilled worker in a trade who does not want a public school system turning out hundreds of young persons trained for his trade. He fears a supply in excess of demand and as a consequence lowered rates of pay and diminished employment for the individual workers. He may appreciate that the gap between himself and this group is not wide enough to give him any sense of security. Thus there is opposition not only to training for specific vocations but also to training to develop the special skills that are needed in the trade. Unions that have restricted the number of helpers and apprentices that may be employed in their collective bargaining with employers do not want the public school system turning out at public expense successive classes of potential competitors. Much less do they want vocational training schools entering the field of actual production, substituting school output for the output of normal enterprise.

Many of the youth with whom we are here concerned could be trained efficiently to operate one particular machine or to perform one or more repetitive operations on an assembly line, but such a program does not fit very well into a school program.

The school cannot own all the machines or carry on all the processes. A small group of employers, perhaps only a single employer, in the area may use the machine or the process and thus be the only outlet for the youth trained in the school. If the school trains too many the work is wasted except as it may develop some minor skills and work habits. Not infrequently the employers would rather train their new workers under their own foremen and in accordance with their own rules and procedures, which they may vary from time to time. They may, however, be very glad to have the schools give courses to overcome some of the deficiencies in shop arithmetic, reading, writing, and other subjects.

Vocational training for clerical work and for sales people present no such difficulties for the schools. However, many employers look to the high schools and the colleges for the bulk of the employees in these fields. One can scarcely expect many of those who have dropped out of regular grade schools to go to a special school to become competitors with high school graduates for clerical and sales positions. Some can become expert operators of simple business machines, but the numbers that can be thus absorbed are limited. Here again the school which teaches the operation of such a machine to a retarded person must be reasonably certain that employers in the vicinity use the machines and have employees who do that work exclusively. Unfortunately the use of such a machine is often only one of an employee's duties, and the others involve more head work and more versatility.

Agricultural vocational education of high-school grade had attained really substantial success prior to the depression but note of "high-school grade." Farming, as has been pointed out in an earlier chapter, now requires specialized knowledge, a high degree of skill, and dependability. No small part of the group with which we are here concerned is made up of rural youth who have been "tractored out" and cannot find a place in the new agriculture and are not equipped for successful work in urban communities.

Although, as previously noted, the existence of this large group was well known to students of social and economic conditions prior to the depression, its existence had not been dramatized by striking events. With the depression came thousands of youth, mostly boys but some girls, taking to the road in search of jobs. Many of the Oakies, displaced by the agricultural changes in Oklahoma, were members of the class with which we are here concerned. Naturally the communities upon which they descended, being short of jobs for their own citizens, did not welcome them, for these youth were already in need and even in fair times constitute a serious problem to a community.

One of the first moves in the early days of the depression was through publicity campaigns to attempt to induce this group and others like them to remain in their own communities. Unfortunately, however, many communities were not in the least prepared to handle them, and relief funds were not available to keep them. In some cities the presence of a youth of working age able to work rendered a family ineligible for relief or reduced the amount it would be given. This lack of funds and the resulting administrative practice operated to make more young persons leave home and take to the road.

At this point we should digress to point out that even had our present American system of unemployment insurance been in effect at the time, it would not have done appreciable good to thousands of these youth for the following reasons: (1) many of them had had almost no work experience and hence would have never attained an insured status; (2) many who had work experience had been so irregularly or intermittently employed that they would not have been insured at all or would have been entitled to only nominal benefits; (3) many rural youth who had had work experience had worked in occupations not covered now by unemployment insurance. In a later chapter we shall point out how provision is made for this group in New Zealand. Here the point is that even had there been unemployment insurance of our present type in 1929, it would not have affected substantially the plight of many of this group.

Fortunately for the nation, the government departments unwittingly were fairly well prepared to supply useful work to many of the boys in this group.[1] Particularly in the Departments of Agriculture and Interior there were several agencies which in one way or another were concerned with forests and grazing lands, parks, bird sanctuaries, and so on. During the Coolidge administration an interdepartmental committee under the auspices of the Budget Bureau had made a comprehensive survey of the work needed in such areas for fire protection, roads and bridges, flood control, insect, pest, and plant disease eradication, and the like. Again, unwittingly, execution of most of the projects regarded as necessary by the officers responsible for the conservation of natural resources was deferred because of the magnitude of the expenditures which would have been necessary. Thus worth-while, suitable work was available when the Roosevelt administration embarked on the Civilian Conservation Corps as its first move in supplying work relief for unemployed boys.

THE CIVILIAN CONSERVATION CORPS

From the standpoint of organization and management, the significant fact about C.C.C. was that for the most part the work was done by existing agencies of the national government under the direction of trained and experienced men. The only new administration created was a small, central, overhead coordinating agency under a director. In and of itself it neither operated nor controlled the detailed projects.

Since the projects were in the main in rural and sparsely settled areas, camps were necessary. The responsibility for developing and administering the camps was vested in the War Department. It was of course the one agency of the government with training for and experience in activities of this type. It also had suitable supplies and equipment. The common prac-

---

[1] For a convenient summary of the activities see *Civilian Conservation Corps*, S. Doc. 216, 77 Cong. 2 Sess., pp. 59–84. This report was prepared for Hon. Elbert D. Thomas, Chairman of the Senate Committee on Education and Labor by the Legislative Reference Service of the Library of Congress under the direction of Dr. Ernest H. Griffith.

tice at the outset was for the War Department to obtain a camp director by ordering into the active service a reserve officer with suitable experience and placing him in control of the camp and its operation, including the discipline of the boys.

Technical direction of the projects was vested in the government bureau or agency, usually Agriculture or Interior, which had jurisdiction over the area where the work was being done, or in case of projects on state or local lands, which carried on the type of activities required and often already had co-operative relations with state or local units. The technical agency supplied the project supervisor and the trained foremen necessary to teach the boys the proper procedures and to see that they were carried out with that degree of efficiency essential to attain the objectives. Many of the lesser foremen were locally experienced men ("lems") especially hired for the projects. A good many of the "lems" were unemployed and more or less in need.

As the boys, or the enrollees as they were officially designated, were taken to the work place at 7:30 or 8:00 in the morning and were returned to the camp at 4:00 or 4:30 in the afternoon, there was much leisure time for which provision had to be made by the War Department. A major element in the provision for leisure time was educational. Although the War Department was in administrative control of education, the United States Office of Education served in an advisory capacity. It found suitable teachers for general and vocational education, and it developed or arranged for the development of suitable educational material. It also co-operated in the development of some of the recreational activities with educational aspects. There was, however, no division of authority and responsibility between the War Department and the Office of Education: the authority and the responsibility were in the War Department.

The War Department supplied the chaplains, often with one chaplain serving two or more camps. It was also responsible for providing doctors and medical care, which was often done under contract with the local practitioners and institutions.

The Department of Labor, which in the early thirties had jurisdiction over the Employment Service, was at the outset responsible for recruiting the junior enrollees. Special provisions were, however, made for veterans—older men—who were recruited by the Veterans' Administration. Later the duty of recruiting junior enrollees was transferred to the Civilian Conservation Corps itself. Recruiting had been highly decentralized among state and local agencies. The task of the central national agency was at all times largely directing and controlling and not detailed operating.

The War Department supplied all financial administration as it was well equipped to do because the activities of C.C.C. resembled so closely in this respect those with which that department is concerned.

What has been said thus far relates to the ordinary C.C.C camps operated in continental United States. There were special camps for Indians operated on Indian reservations, entirely administered by the Indian Office. The Indians, not necessarily youths, brought their families with them and camped in their own style near the site of the project. They did their own housekeeping and cooking and did not live in barracks and feed at mess supplied by the government as did the enrollees at ordinary camps. They therefore received in addition to wages an allowance in lieu of subsistence. Special provisions were also made in the outlying possessions, but it is unnecessary to go into detail with respect to them.

SELECTION

As just noted, responsibility for selection was originally vested in the Department of Labor and subsequently transferred to the C.C.C. overhead organization. The Department of Labor formulated and carried out plans according to which state and local public welfare agencies actually selected young men as enrollees and locally experienced men as supervisors. This procedure was not materially changed when the responsibility was transferred to C.C.C.

As required by law and in conformity to the objectives of the program as laid down by the director and the advisory council,[2] eligibility was at first restricted to young men between the ages of 18 and 25 inclusive,[3] members of families on relief, unemployed, in good health, unmarried, without criminal record, citizens, and willing to allot a large proportion of their cash allowance to designated dependents. Special attention should be called to the fact that the young men must be members of families on relief and be willing to allot a large proportion of their cash allowance to designated dependents. Thus at the outset the program was clearly in the nature of relief. By an act of 1937 the requirement that enrollees should be members of families actually on relief was abolished, but it was provided that priority in selection should be accorded to youths who were most needy. Under the act of 1937 orphan youths, or youths not living in families, became eligible. The money which enrollees with families would have allotted to dependents was saved for enrollees without families and paid to them at the end of their service. Thus although need remained a factor, C.C.C. became a distinctive type of temporary government employment.

Under the original requirements the task of the state and local welfare agencies was in many instances to find boys in relief families who met the other requirements, including willingness to allocate a substantial part of their earnings to dependents. Sometimes it was a difficult task. Later when any boy was eligible, with the degree of need the only determining preference, real competition for the jobs developed. C.C.C. jobs were presumably especially attractive to boys whose family responsibilities were such that on completing their service they would receive a substantial sum of earnings saved for them by C.C.C. Before discussing selection in more detail it will doubtless be helpful to insert a statement of wages and costs.

[2] Consisting of representatives of the departments of War, Agriculture, Interior, and Labor. S. Doc. 216, p. 19.

[3] Later set at 17–25, then at 17–28, and by the law of 1937 at 17–23.

WAGES AND COSTS

Under the original authorizing act of March 31, 1933,[4] the level of pay and conditions of payment were set by administrative regulation. The cash pay of a junior enrollee was $30 a month of which $25 had to be allotted to dependents. As the program progressed, some modifications of these pay arrangements were made. Partly as a means of affording recognition for superior work and incentive to better performance and partly to assist in improving camp administration some junior enrollees (about 5 per cent) were, subsequent to 1935, selected as leaders and paid $45 per month. A larger number (about 9 per cent) were chosen as assistant leaders. These leaders and assistant leaders were not required to allot more to dependents than other enrollees; they received the difference each month in cash.

In the act of 1937[5] Congress put the prevailing practice into law with $30 the maximum for ordinary enrollees but allowed $45 for leaders not exceeding 6 per cent of the enrollees and $36 for assistant leaders not exceeding 10 per cent.

Pay in cash was the smaller part of the enrollee's real wage. The total value of all perquisites, including the cash stipend, was estimated officially at $70 per month per enrollee.[6] These perquisites were so complete that it was said the enrollee need use nothing of his own save a tooth brush from the time he enrolled to the time he was deposited back at his place of enrollment at its termination. The total costs per enrollee per year as estimated varied from $1,000 to $1,200 per enrollee. Variations were due mainly to changes in cost of the various perquisites, materials, supplies, and equipment for the work program, and the changing distribution of a relatively stable administrative overhead cost over a fluctuating number of enrollees. Total expenditures, the allotment to members, and the number of enrollees are summarized in the table on page 439.

[4] 48 Stat. 22.

[5] Act of June 28, 1937, 50 Stat. 319.

[6] The actual cost as stated by General Tyner in 1937 was $847.48 per year for each enrollee. *To Establish a Civilian Conservation Corps*, Hearings before the Senate Committee on Education and Labor, 75 Cong. 1 sess., p. 38.

Expenditures and Number of Enrollees—Civilian Conservation Corps, 1933–41[a]

Fiscal Year	Expenditures (In millions of dollars)[b]	Allowance to Members (In millions of dollars)[c]	Enrollees (In thousands)[d]	
			High Month	Low Month
1933........	14.2	e	June 280	April 37
1934........	313.0	e	July 294	Sept. 209
1935........	346.7	e	June 359	March 242
1936........	593.5	150.7	Aug. 520	March 304
1937........	387.6	121.9	Jan. 360	March 252
1938........	325.2	102.4	Oct. 302	Sept. 179
1939........	291.0	105.9	Jan. 294	March 198
1940........	283.7	105.2	Feb. 300	June 243
1941........	256.5	96.6	Aug. 281	June 183

[a] All figures are taken from *Civilian Conservation Corps*, S. Doc. 216, 77 Cong. 2 sess.

[b] P. 138.

[c] Pp. 143–44.

[d] P. 99.

[e] Allowance to members from April 1933 through March 1935 was 202.7 million dollars, p. 142.

TERM OF ENROLLMENT

The initial enrollment was for six months, with the privilege of re-enrollment if the boy had proved himself a satisfactory worker and if he so desired. Restrictions were, however, set up to prevent re-selection under most circumstances, especially within a short period after the termination of enrollment. By the law of June 28, 1937 the maximum period of enrollment was fixed at two years with exceptions in favor of certain classes (leaders, assistant leaders, Indians, veterans, and project assistants). Thus enrollees who worked up to what may be termed the foreman classification were eligible for something approaching a permanent job, which is advantageous from the standpoint of operating efficiency.

Enrollment for a six-months period suggested two enrollment periods a year. Under such a system, however, the number on the roll toward the end of six months was sometimes small. Enrollees were permitted to leave at any time to take up employment or if their presence was urgently needed at home. There were some cases of injury. Desertions, which accounted for losses of 1 or 2 per cent a month, caused more losses than any single factor other than expiration of term. Some enrollees were discharged for disciplinary reasons.[7] To get greater stability the practice therefore developed to take in new classes quarterly.

SIZE

The peak provision for C.C.C. came in the Emergency Relief Act for 1935.[8] It provided for 600,000 enrollees at an average total cost of $1,000 each for the year. This figure along with the peak number of camps necessary to secure it (just short of 3,000) was never reached largely due to the operation of the requirement that all enrollees come from relief families. Actual peak strength was achieved in August 1935 when over 505,000 enrollees were occupying over 2,600 camps.

After 1935, authorized strength was reduced in accordance with rising prosperity indexes. As the number of positions authorized diminished and as requirements for taking enrollees from relief families became less rigid, the process of selection became more discriminating. It is probably fair to say that C.C.C. tended more and more toward becoming a regular agency for carrying on specific governmental projects adaptable to its form of organization. It was ultimately abolished because the man-power shortage made it no longer necessary from the relief standpoint and the boys were needed in other ways.

USEFULNESS

The question arises how valuable was C.C.C. (1) to the government and (2) to the boys. We have made no first-hand investigations to arrive at answers to this question, and hence what we shall say on this subject will be based on reading and in some instances on discussion with government officials.

The first significant point is that as compared with W.P.A. and even N.Y.A. as a whole the C.C.C. was small, which meant it was administratively simple. Most of its activities fell well

---

[7] *Annual Report of the Director of the Civilian Conservation Corps*, 1939, App. 1, p. 117.
[8] 49 Stat. 115.

within the sphere of established government agencies so that the plans were as a rule well considered and well worked out. There was nothing remotely resembling the mad rush to approve projects, costing in the aggregate billions of dollars, that characterized W.P.A.

It can scarcely be questioned that many of the projects undertaken for the conservation of the forests and other natural resources were of really substantial economic value. Forest trails and roads and communication systems were greatly needed to aid in preventing and controlling forest fires. At times C.C.C. boys did yeoman service in fighting these fires. The trails and roads built also facilitated care of the forests and permitted getting out timber that had matured. Projects such as those designed for eradicating white pine blister were of distinct economic value in helping to preserve a highly useful and fast disappearing wood. Although some of the projects may have been less utilitarian, one does not encounter charges of boondoggling and waste that are frequently found in connection with W.P.A.

Use of responsible, trained men from the established agencies of the government and experienced supervisors means ordinarily that reasonable standards of performance characterized most of the activities. The use of reserve officers of the army as camp managers does not suggest lack of discipline. Discipline is actually suggested both by desertions from the camp and dismissals. It is undoubtedly true that, especially in the early days, some boys were selected and sent who did not really have the necessary physique and stamina for that kind of life and work nor interest in it, but nothing suggests they organized militant unions and sought to dominate the army officers and the project foremen. The evidence indicates, on the other hand, that the rules and regulations were progressively improved to make the selective process more discriminating from the standpoint of efficiency in operation. Provisions were included to make sure the boys understood the practices, procedures, and disciplines of the camp and to discourage from accepting an appointment those to whom the camps would not appeal. The fact that C.C.C. rewarded progress and efficiency with promotions in pay and in rank with possibilities for retention in the service is further evidence pointing in the same direction.

One would be inclined to accept the view that many of the boys learned and acquired good work habits and ability to work as a team in getting a job done. On the other hand, it is more questionable whether in many instances the knowledge and skills acquired on the highly specialized government projects were directly applicable in pursuits which the boys might follow after they left the camps. Probably the major contribution from the work experience was an attitude toward hard work and understanding of what was necessary to come up to a standard. Perhaps also there was an awakened appreciation of what one needs to know in order to do an intelligent although simple job. It was part of the policy not only to tell the boys what to do but why it was being done that way. Presumably the United States Forest Service carried into its C.C.C. camps many of the principles of efficient management that have long characterized it and have established its reputation, especially in the field of personnel management.

One suspects that many of the boys will find that they profited most from the educational activities, which were voluntary since they were carried on in the leisure hours. The boys at a camp differed widely with respect to education and schooling, and thus it was impossible to herd them into mass classes. The educational program had to be adjusted to make it applicable to the needs of the boy. If the boy were illiterate he would be encouraged to learn to read and write by the use of material suitable for his age and his interests. If he had a fair education and hoped to get into a good clerical job he might get training in typing, stenography, or bookkeeping. Automobile and truck maintenance and repair might be the subject of study in the evening, in this case often tied up with the day's work. Someone has remarked that the C.C.C. probably trained more good short-order cooks than could ever find such work in their communities, but the cooking in many families would doubtless be materially improved if one member, even a boy, were a reasonably good short-order cook.[9]

Education that may be regarded as teaching youth what to think rather than how to think and how to apply the skills acquired through learning presents a fundamental issue in connection with programs such as the C.C.C. As soon as the plan to have the War Department staff and manage the C.C.C. camps was suggested, opposition arose on the ground that the boys would be militarized, indoctrinated with the philosophies of the professional army officers. It was sometimes said that these boys selected because of their need would be trained to be cannon fodder for the next war, which at that time appeared to many as extremely remote. Assurances had to be given that military training as such would not be included in the program. In general work relief programs specifically designed for preparation for defense and for war were almost universally barred until the gathering storm clouds showed war was almost if not quite inevitable.

Where boys of the ages of the C.C.C. enrollees are gathered together in barracks political, economic, and social discussions are inevitable. For many of the C.C.C. boys the experience partook of the nature of going away to school or college. To give educational values to these discussions, special texts, simply written and tellingly illustrated, were prepared under the auspices of the Office of Education so that the boys could acquire some familiarity with facts and thought in these fields.

A considerable sentiment existed that indoctrination of the youth in the camps should be in sound ways of peace. As one thinks back to the thirties one recalls that the depression had for many shaken the old faiths in democracy, freedom, the Constitution, love of country, and patriotism. Indoctrination with these views conceivably would have been regarded by many in that day as militaristic and not calculated to advance the welfare state. The issue raised by the C.C.C. was whether the American people want the youth of the country indoctrinated

[9] For more detailed information on types of education and numbers participating see S. Doc. 216, pp. 70–71.

by the national government. Hitler and Mussolini both demonstrated what a powerful central government can achieve by almost universal centralized indoctrination of youth. To the retort that the central government in the United States would not indoctrinate the youth in that way, the answer is that other wholesale universal indoctrination may prove equally disastrous, as unfolding historical events disclose fallacies inherent in the indoctrination.

In the United States indoctrination has been perhaps more completely decentralized than any other activity. Complete religious freedom leaves religious indoctrination to the churches and other agencies, provided they can draw the youth within their sphere of influence. Local communities have insisted upon a considerable degree of control over the public schools with no little resistance even to partial dominance by the state. Private schools have been permitted to exist side by side with public schools, so that children could be indoctrinated as their parents thought best. Freedom of speech, freedom of the press, freedom of assembly, freedom of association all operate to prevent centralization and standardization of indoctrination. The American view has been that progress will be furthered more by the conflict of thought among a free people than by indoctrinating the people to make them accept a particular ideology.

A question must be raised as to the wisdom of assembling youth from one general class under an educational enterprise, or partially educational enterprise, conducted by the central government. This question really involves two parts: (1) the segregation or isolation of groups on a class basis, and (2) the entrance of the national government into the sphere of providing mass education for individuals. Take, for example, the discussion of government, economics, and religion that typically arise among youth, particularly unmarried youth, of the C.C.C. ages, 17 to 23; such discussions are greatly enriched if many different points of view and many different backgrounds are represented. Recollection suggests they are likewise greatly enriched if different sections of the country are also represented. If all are from a single class, having gone through a like experience, they tend to be more or less of one mind and to accept as their leader the one most effective in presenting their view. If the group is mixed, views will be divergent and leadership may be divided, as it has been in the past in democratic countries. Other aspects of this problem will be considered in the ensuing discussion of the N.Y.A.

THE NATIONAL YOUTH ADMINISTRATION

The National Youth Administration was an outgrowth of the Federal Emergency Relief Administration, but it became ultimately an entirely separate agency. Its activities were of two main types, and the second type was divided into two distinctive parts. We shall first outline very briefly these several parts and then take up each one separately in some detail.

1. The objective of the first type of N.Y.A. activities was to furnish part-time jobs to youth in school to enable them to earn something so that they could continue their education.

2. The objective of the second type of activities was to give work experience to unemployed but employable youth who had left school, partly to help them meet need and partly to further their education. The two distinctive forms of activity were: (a) To give youth jobs on specially organized projects in the vicinity of their own homes which permitted them to continue to live at home under customary home conditions. (b) To assemble the youth in residence centers which can be roughly described as vocational boarding schools operated by the national government.

THE STUDENT-AID PROGRAM

The basic idea of the student-aid program was to furnish aid to needy youths by giving them jobs on special projects carried on in and by the schools (public or nonprofit) at which they were in attendance, under the broad and general supervision of N.Y.A. officers. Throughout the program the schools were responsible for selecting students, determining their qualifications and need, proposing projects and administering them after approval. N.Y.A., largely through its units established in the several states, was responsible for promulgating general policy and regulations, selecting participating institutions, allocating funds, reviewing selection of students, approving or rejecting projects submitted by schools, keeping statistical and financial records, paying students, and making other necessary disbursements.

Compensation schedules. The salary schedules for N.Y.A. student workers were set up in the original executive order and consisted of an upper limit on amounts which could be earned in any one month. These limits were: for high school students, $6.00; for college students, $20, at first with a provision of not more than an average of $15 for the school year; for graduate students, $40 per month, at first with a provision of not more than an average of $30 for the school year. As these "at first" clauses indicate, the average limitations were dropped as the program progressed, but the maximum limits of $6.00, $20, and $40 were retained.

In February 1941 the average level of monthly earnings per worker was $4.45 for high school students, $13.17 for college students, and $19.61 for graduate students.[10]

Hourly earnings varied. School authorities were expected to set hourly rates for various types of N.Y.A. work which would be roughly comparable to prevailing rates for similar work in the locality. In December 1939 the average hourly rates on high school programs were 25 cents, on college programs 34 cents, and on graduate school programs 50 cents.

A wide variety of work was done by N.Y.A. enrollees at educational institutions in return for the work stipend. The major classes of projects were (1) departmental assistance, (2) construction and maintenance, (3) clerical assistance, and (4) semi-professional assistance. The table presented on page 447 gives the percentage distribution of the N.Y.A. students by type of project for the academic year 1939-40.

[10] *Department of Labor—Federal Security Agency Appropriation Bill for 1942*, Hearings before the House Committee on Appropriations, Pt. 2, 77 Cong. 1 sess., p. 170.

PERCENTAGE DISTRIBUTION OF STUDENTS EMPLOYED ON STUDENT WORK PROGRAMS, BY TYPE OF PROJECT, ACADEMIC YEAR 1939–40[a]

Type of Project	Total	School	College and Graduate
Departmental assistance............	40.2	40.7	39.2
Construction and maintenance.......	25.0	28.9	15.0
Clerical assistance and service........	23.3	21.6	27.4
Semi-professional..................	9.2	6.4	16.1
Miscellaneous.....................	2.3	2.4	2.3
Total.........................	100.0	100.0	100.0

[a] Condensed from table, p. 598, *Department of Labor—Federal Security Agency Appropriation Bill for 1941,* Hearings before the House Committee on Appropriations, Pt. 2, 76 Cong. 3 sess.

The number of students aided under the program was about 417,000 in April 1936 and 444,000 in April 1937. It declined to 336,000 in April 1938 and increased thereafter. In February 1941 it was 460,000. Numerically the most important class has always been the high-school students. Of the 460,446 enrollees in February 1941, the numbers were high school 336,061, college 121,366, and graduate 3,019. At that time nearly 30,000 educational institutions were participating. Of the 29,696 then active, 28,010 were of high school and 1,683 of collegiate grade.[11]

Selection. The law authorizing the selection of students to receive aid specified that recipients must be in need. This requirement was not construed to mean that each recipient must come from a family on relief. The basic criterion was whether the student could continue in school without N.Y.A. assistance. If he could not, he was eligible from the need standpoint. The primary agency for determining need, as for other conditions of eligibility (citizenship, ability to perform useful work on an N.Y.A. project, good character, health, and scholastic ability), was the school itself. Local relief agencies might assist in this determination, by referring students to proper educational authorities or otherwise, but such help was relatively minor. The ordinary student-aid organization and administration of each institution bore the brunt of this task. The N.Y.A. contented

[11] The same, p. 171.

itself with a thorough examination of all papers relating to
each student application; only in cases of apparent error or over-
sight were more direct investigational proceedings taken.[12] The
National Youth Administrator testified that little trouble developed on this score; what little occurred was usually local-
ized, and traceable to particular school officials who failed in
their responsibilities.[13] The practice of allowing the school to
determine need was explained by the director of N.Y.A. as
follows: " . . . Our reason for doing that is that we have tried
to minimize the relief content of this thing as far as young
people are concerned; and at the same time, to safeguard the
truth and verify the facts."[14] The fact that each application
was checked by school authorities and signed by two responsible citizens who knew the applicant, plus the great cost of more
intensive investigations, was cited as defense of the practice.
When anything appeared out of line, "that particular application is carefully investigated through community sources, and
representations are made to the college."[15]

Skepticism is desirable as to the dependability of statements
of fact made by an applicant for a grant, even if signed by two
responsible citizens who know the applicant. Poor indeed is the
individual who has lived in a community for any length of time
who does not have at least two friends or acquaintances willing
to sign for him. Few indeed are the persons who upon being
asked to sign will inquire in detail into the accuracy and inclu-
siveness of the income figures given, or subject the applicant
to a cross-examination. In many an American community a
political precinct captain would regard signing such an appli-

[12] *Department of Labor-Federal Security Agency Appropriation Bill for 1941*, Hearings
before the House Committee on Appropriations, Pt. 2, 76 Cong. 3 sess., p. 592.
[13] The same, p. 594.
[14] The same, p. 593.
[15] The same, p. 594.
In a further supporting statement, it was shown that for the academic year 1938–39,
98.7 per cent of N.Y.A. school students came from families with annual incomes less
than $2,000; that 179 of 338,829 N.Y.A. school students came from families of incomes
over $3,000; that each of these latter cases was being investigated. The average family
income of the N.Y.A. school students was $557. (The same, p. 595–96.) The figures for
the college graduate program were less striking; 80.8 per cent came from families with
incomes below $2,000. The modal class for family income for N.Y.A. college students
was $1,000–$1,249. The same, p. 596.

cation as one of the services which he is glad to render a family.

The last part of this book contains a chapter devoted to the question, "What is need?" Here attention will merely be called to the fact that although Congress provided student aid only for those in need, it did not define need but left definition to administrative officers. Hearsay evidence suggests such questions as: whether a college student is in need if he or she is a member of a social fraternity or sorority the monthly dues of which—not covering either room or board—are almost as much per month as average earnings under N.Y.A. or whether a girl is in need, if unassisted, she cannot afford a fur coat or an adequate wardrobe of party clothes. The position may be defended that students in either high school or college will miss much from the experience if they do not have sufficient funds to participate fully in the extracurricular social activities. The question is whether lack of funds so to participate constitutes need in a legal sense, whether public funds ultimately to be supplied by the taxpayers should provide jobs to enable students to participate in these activities.

One can well understand the point of view that young persons should be spared the humiliation incidental to having the facts as to need investigated by a public welfare agency staffed by trained investigators. On the other hand, one can question the character building value of a system under which several of the sorority members hold N.Y.A. jobs under a program designed for young persons in need. Is the experience good for them? What is the effect of such a demonstration of the use of public funds on other students on the campus who have standards which do not allow them to include expenditures for such social activities as items in a budget of real needs?

In this program, as in several others, there was the conflict between efficiency on the project and the relief of need. One can sympathize with the professor who has at last obtained a grant for a project dear to his heart and desires to get the best available student assistants.[16] He may be excused for not in-

[16] The results of the project may have little real value if the individuals working on it are not selected on the basis of their competence. In many cases, moreover, persons who are doing the supervising as a side issue to their regular job may not have the time

quiring into the facts as to need with the thoroughness of the trained objective investigator. Should a professor attempt to induce one of his able students who is a good typist and a fair stenographer to apply and when she expresses grave doubt as to her need offer suggestions as to how she can prove need and get the necessary endorsements? A student of a professor under such circumstances may be greatly embarrassed, first in declining to help on the project and second in appearing to question the ethics of the devices suggested for proving need. A statistician appreciates that individual instances of this type, although reported by credible witnesses, do not test the program as a whole.

N.Y.A. OUT-OF-SCHOOL WORK PROJECTS

The out-of-school work program of the N.Y.A. represented the most important activity of that organization in terms of amount of money expended for payments, of administrative time and expense, and of range and variety of activities.

The nonresident projects. The nonresident project program, prior to the later defense activities, was patterned closely after the W.P.A. program, with certain variations to adapt it more closely to the presumed needs and problems of unemployed youth. The original executive order (No. 7086) prescribed a full-time program of work and related training, but administrative action reduced the total number of hours of work required and related training expected to much less than that. The basic idea of a part-time work program under which the enrollee works at a prevailing wage scale for a limited security wage prevailed throughout the relief period. From the beginning the element of work was tempered by the objective of training, and as defense activities expanded the objective became more and more vestibule training.

Compensation. The security wage rates were set up much as they were under W.P.A. During the relief stages of the program

---

to give the immediate supervision and direction essential both for obtaining good results and for giving the workers sound training in methods. If the work experience is to be of real value, sound methods must be followed and high work standards maintained.

the wage varied with region urbanization and skill. The range, for example, at one time was from $12 per month for skill B in rural areas in Region III to $21 per month for skill A in urban areas in Region I.

The number of hours which an N.Y.A. project worker had to give in order to earn the security wage was fixed by the N.Y.A. state offices, within the limits of 45 to 70 per month established by national regulation. In January 1940 the average number of hours worked per month was 52.[17] The average rate per hour varied in 1940 from 18 to 41 cents.[18] The average earnings per worker per month during the fiscal year 1940 were $15.32.[19]

Selection. Youths between the ages of 18 and 25 who were citizens, unemployed, in need, of good character, and able to to do the work were eligible. The N.Y.A. itself acted as the selecting agency, although it received referrals from local employment, relief, and welfare agencies. It reserved to itself the right to make its own decisions with respect to what constituted need, although the findings of local relief agencies were relied on in many cases. Unlike W.P.A. it was not restricted to taking only one worker from a family nor did N.Y.A. youth have to come from a family currently receiving relief, although many of them did.

The position of N.Y.A. with respect to selection was stated by its director, Mr. Aubrey Williams, in the following testimony at the House Hearings in 1941:

Frankly, we have tried to get away from relief status and our young people are not just those who come through relief offices, but rather we have set up our own offices and do our own selection. We try to give to the youth the impression he is being given a job; he is not being given relief. He applies for a job with us, and we use the word "employment" rather than "relief," and what the youngster does is called employment, and the place he applies is called an employment office.[20]

---

[17] *Department of Labor-Federal Security Appropriation Bill for 1941,* House Hearings, Pt. 2, pp. 570–73.

[18] The same.

[19] The same, *1942,* Pt. 2, p. 224. A table on employment and earnings on out-of-school projects from 1936 through 1940 is given in the same, *1941,* Pt. 2, p. 569. The average monthly earnings varied from $11.68 in January 1936 to $19.62 in August 1939.

[20] The same, p. 574.

The following description of the youth employed was given at the same hearing:

. . . First of all, two-thirds of them are under 21 years of age and only 5 per cent are over 23 years of age. The average age of the youth working in N.Y.A. is 19 years and 9 months. Four out of ten did not go beyond the eighth grade in their school work; only 29 per cent completed high school, although an additional 30 per cent attended high school for 1 year or more.

Only 1 in 30 was able to go to college and only about 10 per cent of these were able to complete the fourth year. And then this is significant—over one-half of the youth on our projects have had no previous work experience at all. Of the youth who have had previous work experience, 21 per cent were farm laborers; 22 per cent were general laborers; 26 per cent were domestics in private families, hotels, or restaurants; 15 per cent were factory operators or helpers; 8 per cent were clerks in retail stores, and 8 per cent were office workers or professional workers. About 90 per cent of the total either had never worked or had slight work experience in occupations that require little or no skill and which offered few opportunities for developing the skill required for successful competition in the labor market.[21]

Numbers. The figures as to the numbers included in the out-of-school program generally include both those in the residence centers and those living at home. The residence centers, however, never accounted for more than about 11 per cent of the total. In April 1936, four months after the inception of the program, the total was 181,000. It increased to 184,000 in June but declined thereafter. For 1937 the range was from 192,000 in March and April to a low of 123,000 in October. From this point on the numbers increased.[22] When the program was expanded for defense training the numbers were above 400,000.[23]

In considering strength figures for N.Y.A. it must be remembered that turnover was high, so that the number of different

[21] The same, pp. 574–75.
[22] U. S. Social Security Board, *Trends in Public Assistance 1933–1939*, Table 3, pp. 6–7. Bureau of Research and Statistics, Report no. 8. These figures show the number of different employees employed during months referred to.
[23] *Department of Labor-Federal Security Appropriation Bill for 1942*, House Hearings, Pt. 2, p. 186.

youth participating was far higher than the average yearly enrollment indicated. In April 1941, for example, the enrollment was about 406,500.[24] In May of that year Director Williams estimated that over a million youth would participate in the program.[25]

Issues. With respect to this program there are five issues which seem to us to require careful consideration if it is ever proposed to revive it.

1. The unemployed youth who were given jobs and allegedly trained through this program, according to national regulations, worked not less than 45 hours per month nor more than 70. The average number of hours was 52 per month. An eight-hour day with a five-day work week means 160 working hours in a four-week period. Thus on the average in 1941 time worked per youth was only 32.5 per cent of a reasonably short work month. Although in a work relief program one-third work and two-thirds voluntary participation in educational activities may be defended, it is questionable whether any such arrangement is desirable where the objective is training and the development of sound work habits.

2. If the objective is training and the development of essential knowledge and skills, apparently the program should provide for the carefully planned, effective utilization of the two-thirds time left over, and participation should be compulsory. Presumably that time could most effectively be used in schools designed to make up educational deficiencies and to relate instruction to work needs. The educational system in the United States has been controlled by the state and the local governments. The N.Y.A. out-of-school work program was a national program. It would seem as if co-ordination of the N.Y.A. with the state educational system required unification of the two parts which could best be secured under single management.

3. In vocational education a conflict is frequently encountered between training and production. N.Y.A., following the

[24] The same.
[25] The same, p. 940.

W.P.A. pattern, was forced to the production side in this controversy. To illustrate the issue, a construction project requires mixing concrete and delivering it to the point where it is needed. Educationally, a boy may get all such a job has to offer within a day or two. If he is kept on that job for a longer time, the objective becomes production rather than education. In a truly educational job designed to impart knowledge and to develop skills and interests, an educator lays out the work on an educational basis; the youth proceeds from the less difficult to the more difficult through a series of related steps. In production work the various steps are arranged in the order necessitated by production, and the time devoted to them is determined by the amount of work to be done, not by the needs of the youths. If a boy is not equipped for the particular process necessary, he must be treated as an unskilled helper, possibly as a surplus unskilled helper. Yet what he is doing may be called training and work experience, although one can scarcely imagine a private employer in normal times retaining such an employee on the job.

4. Training employees and giving them a valuable work experience requires particularly good foremen with skill in teaching or good vocational teachers. Private employers and regular government agencies tend to retain such foremen. Even permanent, well-established, vocational schools have some difficulty in recruiting persons possessed of the requisite qualifications. The evidence suggests that in many instances N.Y.A. like W.P.A. could not recruit them, and as a result youth whose lack of experience and equipment made good foremen or vocational teachers peculiarly necessary worked under unsatisfactory foremen. Many personnel officers prefer inexperienced but promising youth to those whose experience has been gained in agencies which, to use the common term, permit "sloppy work."

5. So long as production is a major objective, payment of the prevailing wage may be necessary to prevent the fear of competition found among free labor. On the other hand, payment of the prevailing wage to a marginal worker during the learning

period is not necessarily good training, nor does it necessarily produce a sound attitude toward work. If a youth finds he can draw the standard day's pay without doing a standard day's work, he may believe he can always get by on that basis. If the objective is to give the youth a true work experience, it would seem as if he should be started at a very low minimum, with increases for increased productivity and improved quality. A piece-work system of pay or an incentive system, fairly worked out and fairly administered, would be far better as a training device than the relief concepts of a monthly subsistence wage.

From our point of view the N.Y.A. out-of-school work projects appear to have moved from a relief objective to a training objective without sufficient reconsideration of methods. Communities should have a sound, unified program of vocational education effectively linked up with both private and public agencies in the community. If the time comes when youths cannot get regular jobs in either public or private enterprise normally conducted, it would seem desirable for government to relieve their immediate need in so far as that may be necessary through a dole or, if one prefers, "unemployment insurance benefits" in return for which they would be required to attend the prescribed school. It is assumed that the schools in times of extensive unemployment would expand their offerings and make special provisions for small groups or individual workers.

It is definitely assumed that the vocational schools themselves will not go in for production jobs, or organize for any form of mass production. They will concentrate on projects designed to impart knowledge and develop skills. If they eschew large production and concentrate on knowledge and skills, they can give training for either public or private enterprise. To a certain degree particular classes of labor may be opposed to a program that increases the number of youth possessed of their particular knowledge and skills, but that alternative is better than having the youth engaged in competitive production. It is to be hoped that in the postwar world the need for trained workers in particular fields will be the dominant consideration, and separate groups will not seek to prevent a reasonable number of youth from being trained to meet that need.

THE RESIDENCE CENTER PROGRAM

The residence center portion of the N.Y.A. out-of-school program was an outgrowth of small beginnings which assumed increasing proportions when the N.Y.A. sought to become an important defense training organization. On its creation it absorbed (1) some relics of F.E.R.A. attempts to set up resident camps for unemployed girls on a pattern comparable to C.C.C.; (2) some early attempts of students to continue work and education on the campus of a small southern college; and (3) some early experiments at Passamaquoddy and elsewhere which tried out full-time vocational finding programs on which the enrollees were assigned to a number of different jobs while in camp residence to determine the optimum skill aptitude of each participant.

Prior to defense developments, the main objective of the residence centers was to combine improved living conditions for youth workers, many of whom came from underprivileged homes, with training in skills particularly needed by rural young people, notably the domestic arts of cooking, cleaning, washing, housekeeping, and the agricultural skills. Work experience was made available in a variety of shop and clerical tasks. Later, in response to the demand for defense workers, residences were established in industrial areas where there were shortages of young workers.

Residence centers in the regular program were of two types: full time and 15 day alternating. At full-time centers enrollees were at the camps continuously for a period of six months. At alternating camps the enrollees, mainly girls from rural areas, were at camp 15 days and then away for 15 days. After the first six months' period the enrollee was eligible for re-enrollment if in the opinion of the supervisor he would profit from the extended stay. The average period of enrollment was about 9 months. Of the 579 residence camps operated on December 31, 1939, there were 337 being operated as full-time centers.[26]

The stipend for full-time work was on an hourly basis—usually 25 cents for each hour of productive work—with a top limit of $30 from which up to $20 was deducted for maintenance. Thus a total of 120 hours was required to earn a full wage. The average working time was 90 hours and the average earnings around $22.[27] The remainder of the time was occupied in class work and related training.

The typical residence center to care for approximately 200 youths consisted of a director, a youth personnel co-ordinator, a business manager, a shop supervisor, two project clerks, and 12 foremen.[28] The estimated average cost per youth per month for the fiscal year 1942 was $52, of which $30 was the youth's wages and maintenance.[29] Thus the typical residence project cost about $10,400 a month or $125,000 a year with $2,000 a month or $24,000 a year going as cash to enrollees.

We have made no survey to appraise the success of these residence projects. Such a survey would necessitate (1) visits to a large number of camps; (2) visits to the homes and communities from which the youth came; and (3) an attempt to follow the after history of a considerable number of the youth who were enrollees at the camp. To the writer the printed word regarding the camps suggests the United States government Indian boarding school. If there is any analogy, experience would suggest that the camp itself would look better than the real results of its work. A fairly comprehensive study of the Indian boarding schools in 1926–27 led to the conclusion that attendance at public schools, improvement of the public schools, and constructive work with individuals and families in their own homes offered far more promise than institutional treatment.

[26] *Department of Labor-Federal Security Agency Appropriation Bill for 1941*, House Hearings, Pt. 2, p. 633
[27] The same, pp. 630–31.
[28] The same, *1942*, Pt. 2, p. 957.
[29] The same, p. 958.

With respect to both branches of the out-of-school program of the N.Y.A., the basic issue is whether the national government through its own agencies should assume full administrative and financial responsibility for this phase of the educational program or whether the educational system of the states and local governments should be developed to meet the needs, possibly assisted by grants-in-aid from the national government for better vocational education and better guidance and placement by a well-equipped employment service.

As previously noted in the discussion of C.C.C., the writer questions the wisdom of a nationally financed and nationally administered program designed basically and primarily for youth of a particular social or economic class which we may designate the underprivileged, although some of the members are underendowed. It is patent that the future welfare of the country requires that intelligent and determined effort be made to develop these youth to be of service to themselves, their families, and the community. That is not the issue. The issue is whether the public educational system shall be expanded and improved to care for them, or whether they shall be segregated from the mass to become temporarily wards of the nation.

A major difficulty with such segregation is that it draws a sharp line. On one side are those who get their education under a state and local system; on the other those for whom the nation provides. No such sharp line can be drawn with respect to the needs and requirements of young persons. Some youths from families with adequate incomes find no stimulus in the traditional educational pattern and need projects and project education, but they are in no sense underprivileged. One can scarcely visualize parents sending them to a national C.C.C. camp or to a N.Y.A. project. A national institution for underprivileged or retarded youth is not likely to attain prestige; in fact it may be difficult to prevent it from attaching a sort of stigma to its students. A single, well-developed, co-ordinated, public school system would not necessitate the drawing of such sharp lines. It would permit of a considerable degree of movement of individuals within the system and increased opportunity for the youth to find himself. Under a comprehensive co-ordinated system, youths of a particular class would not be segregated in a camp for several months out of contact with youths from other classes.

Another question which should be raised is whether a national agency designed to deal with underprivileged youth can attract as good a grade of personnel as can the public school system which stands high in American esteem. In connection with this question it must be remembered that N.Y.A. grew out of a relief program and evolved in the direction of competition with the established school systems. It never attained that degree of permanence and stability that characterizes the public schools. One could not therefore expect it to be able to draw as well-equipped people. Unfortunately it sometimes seems as if institutions designed for the underprivileged, unfortunate, and retarded, who present peculiar difficulties, are not successful in drawing from the very best. At times one encounters institutional workers of exceptional ability and spirit, but one encounters some who are apparently there because they could not get better jobs.

In the latter part of the present book we shall take up in more detail the problem of co-ordinating welfare, educational, and health activities in the community.

PART II

BRITISH EFFORTS FOR UNIVERSAL
COVERAGE, COMPREHENSIVENESS,
AND CO-ORDINATION

CHAPTER XIV

INTRODUCTION TO PART II

In the preceding part of this book the attempt has been made to describe broadly the major American programs in the field of relief and social security with special emphasis on those features of the program that present issues of public policy. As one studies these separate programs, the fact becomes clear that three issues of public policy exist which are of fundamental importance. They are:

1. The issue of universal coverage. The American programs have so developed that millions of citizens are excluded from the benefits of social security systems despite the fact that directly and indirectly they are now being taxed to maintain them, and they will be more heavily taxed as the systems mature. In some instances, on the other hand, individuals who are not in need and have made only small contributions toward old-age and survivors nsurance are receiving benefits from it, the cost of which will greatly exceed their contributions. Because American governments have legislated piecemeal by categories without consideration of the field as a whole, they have created, sometimes at the behest of pressure groups, specially privileged classes. If it be assumed that social insurance is desirable and necessary, the country faces the problem of extending and broadening it so that possibly with supplemental devices it effects universal coverage.

2. The issue of comprehensiveness. The American programs have developed to give protection in the event of the happening of some of the common major contingencies. If need results from some other one of the common hazards the victim may be dependent on poorly planned, poorly administered, and poorly financed general public assistance. Elaborate and in some instances relatively costly programs have been developed to give protection against one hazard before anything ap-

proaching reasonably adequate protection has been given against another. The United States therefore faces the issue of making its relief and social security system cover all the common major hazards, in other words, making it comprehensive.

3. The issue of co-ordination. Several of our American programs have been independently developed, without reference to other programs to which they are in fact related. One program will offer more to its beneficiaries than another, not because of differences in need of the beneficiaries, but because the programs had different origins and were advocated and supported by different groups. Legislative and administrative responsibility is, moreover, irrationally dispersed. For reasons that have no relationship to either human need or financial or administrative necessity the country has exclusively national programs, exclusively state programs, a state program adopted by national compulsion without national contributions to benefits, and state programs with conditional grants-in-aid from the national government. Thus in addition to the issue of universal coverage and comprehensiveness, the nation faces the issue of co-ordination or integration in the interest of efficiency both in administration and in meeting the needs of its people.

Since the factual analysis of existing programs reveals these issues with inescapable clarity, it is natural to ask whether some other country has not only faced the same issues but made some effort to solve them.

In the fall of 1942 the press of both England and the United States gave wide publicity to *Social Insurance and Allied Services*, a report by Sir William Beveridge on the British programs of relief and social insurance. The British programs, older and more extensive than those in the United States, had like ours grown piecemeal, and also like ours were defective in coverage, comprehensiveness, and co-ordination. These defects had resulted in the appointment in June 1941 of an Interdepartmental Committee on Social Insurance and Allied Services, by the Minister without Portfolio then responsible for the consideration of reconstruction problems. When the fact gathering and investigational work had been completed by the committee, the task of writing the report was assigned to the chairman of the committee, Sir William Beveridge, who was to prepare an individual report based on the officially collected and analyzed data and on conferences with members of the committee and other interested parties.

For the reader who wishes to understand the official status of the *Beveridge Report*, and the subsequent developments with respect to it, we shall attempt a brief explanatory statement.

The Interdepartmental Committee on Social Insurance was made up in the main of permanent civil servants representing government ministries or agencies which were concerned with the programs. Since there were many distinctive programs administratively unco-ordinated, many agencies were represented on the committee, namely, the Home Office, the Ministry of Labour and National Service, the Ministry of Pensions, the Ministry of Health, the Treasury, the Board cf Customs and Excises, the Assistance Board, the Department of Health for Scotland, the Registry of Friendly Societies and Office of the Industrial Insurance Commission, the Reconstruction Secretariat, and the Government Actuary.

According to the practice and tradition of the British civil service, a permanent civil servant does not make public pronouncements nor sign committee reports without authorization of the political minister who is the chief of his organization and personally responsible for all its actions. Since co-ordination of administration and consolidation of administrative agencies were major problems to be treated by the report, the situation was practically impossible. The civil servants could not sign without the approval of their administrative heads, and one can well imagine that it might have been extremely difficult for the civil servants themselves to have agreed on a plan for administrative reorganization. The report, moreover, was to contain substantive recommendations on many issues, some of them highly controversial. The decision was therefore reached that the initial report should be prepared personally by Sir William Beveridge upon his own responsibility.

This procedure meant that no minister in the government was committed to the recommendations which Sir William might make, and the government as a whole was free to take such action as it might see fit with respect to them. The government was, however, responsible for the appointment of the Interdepartmental Committee and for the selection of Sir William to prepare the report. It had therefore placed itself in a position which obviously required it to give the report and the issues involved full consideration, and since public interest and concern were great, it was practically committed in the course of its legislative procedure to take action with respect to them.

Although in the United States the *Beveridge Report* is frequently referred to as the Beveridge plan, it was not a detailed, specific plan. It contained nothing in any way resembling a draft of a proposed bill. With respect to several matters the recommendations were tentative and called for further investigation and consideration. What were set forth with amazing clarity, simplicity, and persuasiveness were the fundamental principles which in Sir William's judgment should be followed in order to give Britain a co-ordinated, comprehensive system providing practically universal coverage.

The report immediately achieved in Britain widespread popular support. Some members of Parliament wanted the government to commit itself to bring in a bill developed in accordance with the recommendations of the report. Although the government was prepared to accept in general the broad principles of the report and to promise ultimate action, it took the position that further consideration was necessary before a bill was presented.

In September 1944 the Minister of Reconstruction "by command of his Majesty" submitted to Parliament a report entitled "Social Insurance," the first part dealing with social insurance and the second with workmen's compensation. This report is not in bill form and does not propose specific, general legislation. It is rather an official declaration by the government of the broad plan which it will ultimately present after the details have been perfected. For the perfection of the details, it proposes the creation, perhaps for a temporary period, of a Minister of Social Insurance, who shall have under him both the administration of insurance and the administration of assistance, although the two administrations will be kept separate.[1] To his jurisdiction will be transferred the existing programs, which will be carried on as in the past until the new system is perfected and detailed plans made for its operation.

This latest report accepts many of the recommendations of Sir William Beveridge in principle, and where a different conclusion is reached, states the reasons. The two documents together afford a good basis for a statement of the way in which another country proposes to solve the issues that we in this country confront with respect to relief and social insurance. They do not enable us to state in detail what Britain has done, but enable us to say with respect to broad principles and many major details "This is what His Majesty's Government proposes to do!"

We also have available one other solution of the problems arrived at by a member of the British Commonwealth of Nations, the Dominion of New Zealand. In 1939 it adopted a system that gives practically universal coverage against all the major hazards with co-ordinated benefits. The system is administered by a single, unified Social Security Department. In this case it is possible to say "This is what New Zealand does."

Obviously Great Britain, New Zealand and the United States differ with respect to many factors in dealing with relief and social security. It does not follow that if Britain proposes to solve a problem in a particular way the United States should, or even could, solve its comparable problem in the same way. The fact that New Zealand has an extremely simple system does not mean that we could get along with something equally simple.

It should be remembered, however, that the designing of a universal, comprehensive, and co-ordinated system necessitates

---

[1] *Social Insurance*, Pt. 1, pars. 30, 152–58, presented by the Minister of Reconstruction to Parliament by command of His Majesty, September 1944.

a re-examination and perhaps a redesigning of the already existing parts which are to be fitted into it. Principles and practices
that seemed logical and desirable when a particular program
was designed for an individual category may appear illogical
and impracticable for universal coverage and co-ordinated
benefits. For this reason, in the chapters which deal with Britain
and New Zealand, we propose to contrast the principles and
practices adopted by those countries with those thus far adopted
in the United States. Some of the principles and many of the
devices have advantages and disadvantages, and choices are a
matter of weighing one against the other. The weights are very
different in a universal, comprehensive, integrated system than
in an independent, special, categorical program.

In reading the two ensuing chapters, it should be kept in mind
that Great Britain was the mother country of both New Zealand
and the United States. To a considerable degree the three countries had a common heritage. The American system of relief, as
has been noted, stemmed from the British poor laws passed in
the reign of Queen Elizabeth. In framing the bill of rights of the
Constitution of the United States, many of the principles were
those established through earlier British experience. The Constitution was interpreted in the light of the common law which
the English speaking colonists brought with them from the
mother country. The three countries have in some respects followed different lines in their evolution, but they can scarcely be
said to have developed entirely alien philosophies. As one examines either the British plan or the New Zealand system, one gets
the impression that we too might have done things their way
with some minor modifications without doing violence to our
basic form of government, political and economic concepts, or
traditions of democracy and individual rights.

CHAPTER XV

THE PROPOSED PROGRAM OF GREAT BRITAIN

In presenting the British proposals for comprehensive, integrated, universal coverage, the origin of which was described in Chapter XIV, we shall deal first with the scheme of classification which the government proposes to use to secure universal coverage. We shall then take up the contingencies to be provided for, together with the amount of benefits to be paid. In other words, we shall treat comprehensiveness and integration together mainly because that appears to be the simplest way to present the facts. After giving the over-all description of the benefits provided, we shall take up each contingency separately so far as necessary to bring out the significant elements in the British plan or significant contrasts between their proposals and our practices. After separate benefits, the proposals with respect to insurance to cover industrial accidents and disease will be summarized. At the end of the chapter we shall present data on the costs of the British plan, together with a statement of the over-all methods of financing.

UNIVERSAL COVERAGE

For purposes of almost universal social insurance, the population of Great Britain is to be divided into six classes as follows: Class I. employees; Class II. the self-employed; Class III. housewives; Class IV. adults of working age who do not earn; Class V. children; Class VI. people over working age.

This classification is not based upon the financial position of the individual. It rests upon the relationship of the individual to the income distributive system. The members of two classes draw from the distributive system directly through their labor either as employees (Class I) or the self-employed (Class II). There are two classes many members of which do not normally draw directly from the distributive system but take indirectly through others, namely, housewives (Class III), and children (Class V). Adults who do not earn (Class IV) are a mixed group. Some of them have income from sources other than earnings and thus draw from the distributive system directly. Some in this class have no income and are dependent on others for an indirect connection with the distributive system. Finally there is the class made up of persons above working age.

These six classes embrace the entire population, exclusive of what we may term transient visitors to the islands. All residents are in one way or another covered. All children, roughly under 16 years of age, are provided for in one of three ways: (1) If they are only children of their parents, and if they are under 16, they are assumed to be provided for by their fathers if their fathers are working. If their fathers are not working because of the happening of a covered contingency, the children are eligible for a child's allowance under the proposals. (2) If they are members of a family which has two or more children under 16 and they are not the oldest of such children, they are to be entitled to a children's allowance whether their parents are working or not. (3) If the child is an orphan or has no person to support him, he is to be eligible for an orphan's allowance.

Housewives are divided into two groups: those who earn and have therefore a direct connection with the distributive system, and those who do not earn directly but are dependent on the earnings of their husbands for support. This grouping is rough and as we shall see later requires detailed refinement, but for the moment we shall confine ourselves to housewives dependent on the earnings of their husbands for support. The proposed system makes provision for them in one of three ways:

1. It assumes that a husband if employed is earning enough to support a wife and one child under 16. Thus normally if a husband is working his nonemployed wife is not eligible for a benefit.

2. If the husband is not working because of the happening of an included contingency, his wife is eligible for a benefit by virtue of the fact that she is the wife of a covered worker.

3. If the husband is not able to support his wife from his earnings, or if for some reason the husband is not insured, the wife is to be provided for under the public assistance part of the program, which uses a means test with legally established standards. In later discussion we shall deal at some length with provisions for widows. Here the essential point is that in the main wives are provided for through their husbands.

Most men are of course in either Class I, employees, or Class II, self employed. The British plan assumes that their earnings are sufficient to enable them to do two things: (1) to support a wife and one child under 16, and (2) when not the victim of any of the contingencies insured against, to pay the contributions that will make them members of the social insurance system in good standing. As we shall discuss later in more detail, workers' contributions are fixed at a point sufficiently low so that the great mass of workers can under all reasonable circumstances pay the required contributions. Provision is made—and this point will require much more elaboration later—whereby if a worker is temporarily unable to pay his contribution for a good reason, such as being unemployed or sick, his non-payment is excused and does not deprive him of his insured status. If he is not able to support such dependents as he may have, and is not able to qualify for insurance, or having been insured has exhausted his benefits, if in need, he and his wife are to be supported through means test public assistance. All his children under 16 years of age would under such circumstances be eligible for children's allowances.

Adults who are not earning (Class IV) are divided into two main groups: (1) those who have sufficient means or access to sufficient means so that they can normally pay regularly the contributions required to make them members in good standing of the insurance system and (2) those who lack such resources or access to them. Those who cannot pay the contributions with the degree of regularity required must be supported by the means test public assistance program.

Two points should perhaps be repeated for emphasis: (1) The British contributions, and the benefits based upon them, are to be kept low so that the maximum number of adults can be members in good standing of the insurance system. (2) Provision for adults who cannot pay or have paid in their behalf the low contributions with sufficient regularity to be insured, or who having been insured have exhausted their benefits must in general be provided for through public assistance. Proposals for training or retraining benefits are made that, as will be discussed later, present in some cases an alternative.

The reader will have noted the sharp distinction this major classification makes between men and women. For the adult man the assumption is that he is married and is responsible for the support of his wife and one child under 16. For the adult woman the assumption is that normally she is a housewife having her contact with the distributive system through her husband and that she is rendering her service to society as a housewife. As a consequence of these assumptions, each of the six major classifications, except that for children, provides for a differentiation on the basis of sex. There is one set of provisions for adult men and another set for adult women. Those for adult women relate mainly but not exclusively to women who for one reason or another have no man upon whom they can depend.

These assumptions with respect to adult men and women obviously do not apply very well to adolescents under 18 years who enter the labor market on completing school and serve for a few years before marriage. According to the British point of view, these youth under 18 have neither the same capacity to pay contributions nor the same requirements as adults, and thus they are distinguished in the proposed basic classifications of employees and self-employed. Prior to attaining the age of 18, they pay lower rates and are entitled in general to smaller benefits.

Thus to secure universal coverage, the British propose division of the total population into six classes on the basis of differences in the connection to the distributive system with subdivisions on the basis of sex and a distinction between adolescents (under 18) and adults (18 or over) where such subdividisons are regarded as necessary. Reasonably regular and consistent payments of contributions are essential for attaining and maintaining an insured status, as will be discussed under the various benefits, and hence the British retain public assistance on a means-test basis for those who have not made the requisite contributions or who have exhausted their benefits under the insurance system.

COMPREHENSIVENESS AND INTEGRATION

The British proposals are comprehensive with respect to the contingencies covered. The arrangements are, however, a little involved, because some benefits are paid largely if not entirely from general tax revenues, whereas others are paid mainly from the insurance fund, which gets some of its money from general taxes. The benefits paid from the insurance fund are, moreover, divided into major benefits and minor benefits. We shall first take up in some detail the benefits to be paid mainly from direct taxes. We shall then outline both the major and the minor benefits under the insurance fund, and follow that with a detailed discussion of the major benefits and of such of the minor ones as have special significance for American readers.

The most important proposed benefit to be provided from the general fund is the family allowance, which Sir William Beveridge called the children's allowance. The Minister on behalf of the government proposes that services in kind, including milk and meals, at primary and secondary schools in receipt of grants from the Ministry of Education or the Scottish Education Department shall be greatly extended. These services are to be free of cost to the parents and will be available to all the children, including the first, of a family attending the subsidized schools. " . . . The cost to public funds will be large. It is estimated that when the service has reached its full development

the cost of supplying meals and milk to children at school will
be of the order of £60 million a year. . . ."[1]

In addition to the free meals a flat rate cash allowance of 5s.
a week will be payable for each child after the first out of general
taxes. When the head of the family is on benefit, 5s. a week will
be paid with respect to the first child also, but this payment will
come from the insurance funds.[2]

The allowance of 5s. a week for each child after the first is
payable week in and week out regardless of the employment,
health, or wealth of the head of the family. It "is not intended
to provide full maintenance for each child. It is rather a general
contribution to the needs of families with children" but "it
is in the national interest for the State to help parents to discharge that responsibility properly."[3]

A contribution of 5s. a week per child to assist the family in
providing for children after the first obviously will not provide
for full orphan children left without means of support. The plan
therefore provides an "orphan's allowance" of 12s. a week payable to all full orphans regardless of their need or in other words
without a means test. Of this 12s. a week, 7s. will come from the
Social Insurance Fund and 5s. direct from general taxes, but
the full amount will be paid in a single payment.[4]

The American reader may want an explanation as to why the
British make the distinction between the Social Insurance
Fund and general taxes with respect to family allowances and
orphan's allowances. The answer is that the British are insurance minded and tend to cling to the insurance concept that all
persons in a given class should have equal protection for
the same premium or contribution. The man with five children to support pays the same insurance contribution as the
man with only one child to support, and therefore his family
should draw no more from the insurance fund than the smaller
family. It would be impracticable and probably socially unde-

---

[1] *Social Insurance*, Pt. I, par. 51, presented by the Minister of Reconstruction to
Parliament by command of His Majesty, September 1944.
[2] The same, par. 52.
[3] The same, par. 50.
[4] The same, par. 60.

sirable to make the head of the large family pay a higher contribution because he has many children to support. The answer is to pay the family allowance and part of the orphan's allowance from general taxes which tends to preserve the individual equities in the insurance system.

It may be pointed out that the single, married, or widowed adult male with no child eligible for a child's allowance pays the same premium or contribution as a married man with a wife and one or more children under 16. This arrangement introduces some inequities into the insurance plan. The British do not propose one contribution rate for single men and childless widowers, another for a married man with no children, and a third for a married man with one or more children. Two factors are probably important here: (1) the marital and family statuses of individuals change from time to time, and it seems preferable to have a constant uniform rate based on a reasonable assumption rather than to have one that is constantly shifting, going up as the family responsibilities increase; (2) contribution collection would be administratively difficult if the rate changed with marital status and situation with respect to children. Hence the contribution rates are fixed on the assumption of equality in marital status and situations with respect to children.

The training allowance is another one which is officially not part of the social insurance plan but is to be paid in the first instance from general taxes. Since the existence of the training allowance will somewhat reduce the expenditures of the Social Insurance Fund for unemployment insurance benefits, the fund will make an annual contribution to the Exchequer or general fund for the cost of training.[5]

An unemployed person, whether formerly an employee, a person working on his own account, a housewife who now needs a job, or a person of working age who has not been gainfully occupied, may receive a training allowance if and when he takes a course of approved training. The allowance will be at a rate higher than the unemployment insurance benefit.

[5] The same, par. 71.

"It will continue for anything up to four weeks after the end of the course, so as to cover any short interval between the course and a new job. People who, after training, are transferred to jobs away from home will receive a settling-in allowance for the first few weeks."[6] This program will be part of the arrangements for promoting employment sponsored by the Ministry of Labour.

If the person receiving a training benefit is at the same time eligible for an unemployment benefit from the Social Insurance Fund, the time he is in receipt of the training allowance will not be deducted from the number of weeks during which he is entitled to unemployment benefits. In other words, the training allowance is distinct from and in a sense an addition to unemployment insurance.

The family allowance, the orphan's allowance, and the training allowance are the three principal proposals to cover situations not covered by the social insurance plan itself. They are, however, integrated with it, and the two taken together will give the comprehensiveness of coverage that the British as a result of their experience deem desirable.

We shall now turn to the four principal benefits proposed under the social insurance system itself, namely, the sickness benefit, the invalidity benefit, the unemployment benefit, and the retirement pension. The table on page 477 shows the cash benefits proposed with respect to persons over 18 years of age (or adults according to the definition used in the plan) who are members of Class 1, employees.

The benefits in the table are increased by 5s. a week if the beneficiary has a single dependent child. If he has more than one such child they are increased by 5s. a week only with respect to the first child since the family regularly receives family allowances with respect to children other than the first.

It will be noted first that the plan covers all major contingencies confronted by a worker, sickness, invalidity, unemployment, and old age. Second in significance is that the benefits under a given category vary, not with what the

[6] The same.

insured earns, but with his family responsibility. Thus the single man or single woman on becoming eligible for unemployment benefits will receive 24s. a week, whereas the married man with a wife not gainfully occupied will receive 40s. A married woman gainfully occupied who has elected to remain under the system and pay her contributions will receive only 20s. if her husband is still in employment. If he likewise is unemployed the two will receive 44s. a week. Basing the amount of benefit for unemployment on family responsibility represents a radically different philosophy from that which prevails in the United States.

SICKNESS, INVALIDITY, AND UNEMPLOYMENT BENEFITS AND RETIREMENT PENSIONS[a]
(Shillings per week)

	Sickness Benefit	Invalidity Benefit	Unemployment Benefit	Retirement Pension
Single man or woman				
Married man with gainfully occupied wife	24	20	24	20
Married man with wife not gainfully occupied	40	35	40	35
Married woman, gainfully occupied	16	16	20	20
Dependent's allowance, where payable	16	15	16	—

[a] *Social Insurance*, Pt. 1, p. 41.

Except for married women gainfully occupied, the benefits for sickness and unemployment, temporary conditions, are higher than those for invalidity and old age, relatively permanent conditions. The assumption is apparently that adjustments can be made to a more or less permanent condition that are far less easily made when a condition is temporary.

These recommendations with respect to benefit levels made by the government represent some departures from those offered by Sir William Beveridge in his report.[7] For the three contingencies, unemployment, disability, and old age, Sir William recommended ultimately for persons 21 years of age or over uniform benefits of 40s. a week for a man with a wife

[7] Sir William Beveridge, *Social Insurance and Allied Services*, 1942, par. 401. Hereafter cited as the *Beveridge Report*.

not gainfully employed and of 24s. a week for a single man or woman or a married man with a gainfully employed wife not on benefit. The government used these recommended rates for unemployment and sickness but reduced them for invalidity and old age.

Sir William's recommendations of 40s. and 24s. were based on the principle that the benefits should be sufficient in and of themselves to enable the recipients to live in accordance with a reasonable minimum standard of subsistence. What constituted the reasonable minimum standard was worked out in terms of necessary goods and services; the goods and services were then priced according to assumptions with respect to the price levels that would prevail in the years immediately following the war; the results gave the standard benefit which should be used almost uniformly throughout the social insurance system. The government did not accept the basic Beveridge principle that benefits should provide a minimum of subsistence. The reasons for rejection were two, one major and the other minor and both had their origin in part in insurance concepts and methods.

The minor objection was that if the principle of minimum of subsistence benefits were adopted, benefits would logically have to be altered from time to time as price levels changed. Minor fluctuations could be ignored, but major changes would require adjustment. Any marked increase in the amount of benefits would materially disturb the balance which had previously been struck between contributions and benefits and would greatly increase the burdens to be paid from general taxes.

The major objection was that the government believed that social insurance must necessarily deal in averages of need and requirement and that contributions toward its costs must be kept down where the bulk of the workers can pay. To quote the report:

Benefits must be paid for, and a high level of benefit must mean a high level of contribution. The Government therefore conclude that the right objective is a rate of benefit which provides a reasonable insurance against want and at the same time takes account of the maximum contribution which the great body of contributors can properly be asked to bear. There still remains the individual's opportunity to achieve for himself in sickness, old age and other conditions of difficulty a standard of comfort and amenity which it is no part of a compulsory scheme of social insurance to provide. And in reserve there must remain a scheme of National Assistance designed to fill the inevitable gaps left by insurance and to supplement it where an examination of individual needs shows that supplement is necessary.[8]

Sir William Beveridge in his report had taken the position that compulsory social insurance should not pay more than is necessary for subsistence. He said:

. . . to give by compulsory insurance more than is needed for subsistence is an unnecessary interference with individual responsibilities. More can be given only by taking more in contributions or taxation. That means departing from the principle of a national minimum, above which citizens shall spend their money freely, and adopting instead the principle of regulating the lives of individuals by law. . . .[9]

He had previously stated: "The State in organising security should not stifle incentive, opportunity, responsibility; in establishing a national minimum, it should leave room and encouragement for voluntary action by each individual to provide more than that minimum for himself and his family."[10]

The differences between Sir William's tentative proposals and the report of the government apparently mean that under the government plan some fully insured families, especially the poorer ones living in higher cost communities, may find it necessary to ask for public assistance to supplement their insurance benefits and submit to a means test. Since some means test assistance is probably necessary under any contributory insurance system, the issue is thus one of more or less.

The British concept that benefits should not exceed a reasonable minimum of subsistence and provision of more than such a minimum should be left to voluntary effort presents a

---

[8] *Social Insurance*, Pt. I, par. 13. See also par. 12.
[9] The *Beveridge Report*, par. 294.
[10] The same, par. 9.

sharp contrast with our old-age and survivors insurance. Under it we relate benefits to earnings not in excess of $3,000 a year and as a result require some persons to contribute materially more than is necessary for a reasonable minimum of subsistence in the communities where they live. We shall consider this contrast further when we present data with respect to the proposed contribution rates, but before we take up contributions we shall present briefly the subsidiary benefits under the British plan.

The minor benefits may be considered briefly under three heads: (1) maternity benefits, (2) widows' benefits, and (3) death grants.

Maternity benefits. In the event of childbirth any woman in an insured class, whether married or unmarried, is entitled to a maternity grant of £4. In addition to this grant (1) a gainfully occupied woman is entitled to a maternity benefit of 36s. a week for 13 weeks provided employment is given up for that period, (2) a woman not eligible for the maternity benefit is eligible for an attendant's allowance of £1 a week for 4 weeks. There are some detailed qualifying conditions with respect to these benefits into which we shall not go.[11]

Widows' benefits. Upon the death of the husband, a widow will be eligible for a benefit of 36s. a week for the first 13 weeks of widowhood. If the widow has a child or children under 16 years of age, she will receive an additional allowance of 5s. a week with respect to the first child. Children other than the first will occasion the receipt of the family allowance of 5s. for each child. The widow will receive this allowance regardless of whether she is above or below 60 years of age and whether her husband had or had not qualified for a retirement pension.

At the end of 13 weeks this initial benefit ceases and may under certain conditions be replaced by another benefit, as follows: (1) If there is a dependent child the widow will receive a guardian's benefit of 24s. a week (with 5s. added for a first or only child). (2) If the widow is over 50 at the time of her husband's death or when her youngest child becomes too old

[11] *Social Insurance*, Pt. 1, pars. 24 and 106–20.

to be eligible for a child's allowance, and provided 10 years have elapsed since the marriage, she is entitled to a pension of 20s. a week. This 20s. a week is the same in amount as the old-age pension. If the widow remarries the pension terminates, and it may be reduced for substantial earnings. If her deceased husband's contribution record under the insurance system was deficient, her benefits will be at a reduced rate.[12]

Widows who at the end of the initial weeks of widowhood are ineligible to benefit under this system appear to be: (1) those who are under 50 years of age and have no dependent child, (2) those who are over 50 years of age but under 60, who have no dependent child and whose marriages at death of their husbands had not covered at least 10 years. Widows of these two groups are expected to go to work to support themselves. If the widows are inexperienced as gainful workers or wish to qualify for a special type of work, they may secure a training allowance which has been previously described.

Attention should be called to the fact that the British system compels the husband to contribute only the relatively low, standard, uniform premium for his social insurance and leaves him free to make such further voluntary provision as he is able and willing to make. The widow and the children get what he has left them over and above the sums payable under the social insurance system. In contrast with the old-age and survivors insurance system of the United States, note the initial provision for the first 13 weeks of widowhood, what may be termed the adjustment period, regardless of age and condition with respect to eligible children. Note also the provision for widows whose marriage has lasted for at least ten years and who are 50 years of age or over on the death of their husband or when their youngest child arrives at the age of 16. The British system is in these respects far less arbitrary than O.A.S.I.

Death grants. British practices with respect to private voluntary insurance have been such that the people there would expect a comprehensive system of social insurance to

[12] The same, pars. 25 and 121-31.

provide a funeral benefit in the case of the death of any member of a covered family. Such grants are provided at the following rates:[13]

Age at Death	Amount of Grant in £
Under 3 years of age	6
Between 3 and 6	10
Between 6 and 18	15
Over 18	20

CONTRIBUTION RATES

The major and minor benefits of the social insurance system, as broadly outlined, are to be supported by contributions to the Social Insurance Fund made by the insured person, employers of the insured person, and the government. There will be deficits resulting from payment of benefits to persons who have not been contributors to the system all their lives, and these deficits will have to be made up by the government from general revenues. We shall reserve that subject for presentation under costs and general financing. Here we shall deal only with the prescribed contribution rates. For adults in Class I (Employees) the data are presented in the table on page 483, reproduced from Social Insurance, Part I.

The term "full actuarial contribution," requires some definition. It represents the sum which would have to be paid into the Social Insurance Fund each week, by or in behalf of an employee who enters Class I on leaving school at age 16, in order to meet the full costs of the benefits to be paid on the insurance basis to members of the fund who entered at that age. Proper allowance has been made for the fact that the rates at ages 16 and 17 are only two thirds of the rate for adults, persons 18 or over.

The contributions shown in column 2 are those which all adult employees will be required to pay regardless of their age at entrance, and those in column 3 are those which employers will have to pay on account of adult employees regardless of their present age or age at entrance.

The fourth column is the balance of the full actuarial contribution which forms a part, but only a part, of what the

[13] The same, par. 26.

RATES OF CONTRIBUTION REQUIRED FOR SOCIAL INSURANCE BENEFITS
FOR AN ADULT IN CLASS I[a]

(In pence per week)

	Full Actuarial Contribution	Contribution from		Balance not Provided for, Forming Part of Exchequer Contribution to Scheme
		Insured Person	Employer	
	(1)	(2)	(3)	(4)
Men:				
Retirement pensions.............	28.8	12.0	12.0	4.8 (⅙th)
Widows' and guardians' benefits....	6.3	2.6	2.7	1.0 (⅙th)
Unemployment benefit............	28.7	9.6	9.6	9.5 (⅓rd)
Sickness and invalidity benefits.....	14.7	6.1	6.1	2.5 (⅙th)
Maternity grant..................	1.2	1.0	—	.2 (⅙th)
Death grant.....................	1.8	1.8	—	—
Cost of administration............	4.2	1.6	1.5	1.1[b]
Total for social insurance benefits...	85.7	34.7	31.9	19.1[c]
Women:				
Retirement pensions.............	26.8	11.2	11.1	4.5 (⅙th)
Unemployment benefit............	19.1	6.3	6.4	6.4 (⅓rd)
Sickness and invalidity benefits....	11.7	4.8	4.9	2.0 (⅙th)
Maternity grant and benefit (including attendant's allowance).......	4.3	2.7	.9	.7 (⅙th)
Death grant.....................	1.1	1.1	—	—
Cost of administration............	4.2	1.6	1.5	1.1[b]
Total for social insurance benefits...	67.2	27.7	24.8	14.7[c]

[a] *Social Insurance*, Pt. 1, p. 46.

[b] Exchequer share taken at one third of the cost of administration for unemployment benefit and one sixth for other benefits.

[c] On average the Exchequer proportion is about 22 per cent of the full contribution.

Exchequer will have to pay. It will have to pay in addition the costs of benefits for past services for which there were no contributions or inadequate contributions and the extra costs for late entrants. Thus the figures in column 4 should not be used as indicating anything like the real cost of the system to the Exchequer, a subject which requires very different figures, which will be presented later.

The total full actuarial cost for the social insurance benefits for men who enter the system on leaving school at 16 is 85.7 pence per week. The three big items in this cost are, in pence per week, retirement pensions 28.8, unemployment benefits 28.7, and sickness and invalidity benefits 14.7, which together account for 72.2 out of the total of 85.7.

For women employees the full actuarial contribution is only 67.2 as contrasted with 85.7 for the men. The women are not insuring either a husband or a child or children whereas, as we have noted, the men are providing through insurance for wives not gainfully employed, widows, and first children.

The division of full actuarial cost between employee, employer, and the government is arbitrary in the sense that it rests entirely on the judgment of the legislature. In the British plan the question of division of cost is considered separately for each major benefit. Thus for unemployment insurance the costs are distributed about equally among the three. For old-age pensions, widows and guardians benefits, and sickness and invalidity benefits, the government bears directly one sixth of the cost and the remainder is divided about equally between the employee and the employer. The employer does not contribute to the maternity grant or the death grant. The whole cost of the death grant is assessed against the employee.

Particularly noteworthy is the inclusion of cost of administration in the full actuarial contribution and its distribution among the three parties, with the government bearing one third of the cost of administering unemployment insurance and one sixth of the cost for the other benefits. For men, administrative costs constitute 4.9 per cent of total full actuarial contributions and for women, just under 6 per cent. Inclusion of administrative costs in the contributions again illustrates the strong tendency of the British to adhere to insurance concepts in designing their Social Insurance Fund. A footnote to the official table places the government contribution "on average" at 22 per cent of full actuarial contribution. Attention is again called to the fact that the government will actually contribute far more than 22 per cent, as will be discussed in detail later.

In addition to contributions for social insurance benefits, the beneficiaries, and for Class I the employers, are compelled to contribute toward the health services. The table on page 485, reproduced from the actuaries' report in the White Paper, shows the contribution rates for men and for women in each of the three classes for which contributions are required.

RATES OF CONTRIBUTION FOR ADULTS IN CLASSES I, II, AND IV[a]
(In pence per week)

	Class I				Class II		Class IV	
	Men		Women		Men	Women	Men	Women
	Insured Person	Employer	Insured Person	Employer				
For social insurance benefits..	34.7	31.9	27.7	24.8	39.3	33.7	29.5	23.7
Towards health service........	8.5	1.5	6.5	1.5	10.0	8.0	10.0	8.0
Total contribution required..	43.2	33.4	34.2	26.3	49.3	41.7	39.5	31.7
Rates of contribution proposed........	s. d. 3 7	s. d. 2 10	s. d. 2 10	s. d. 2 3	s. d. 4 2	s. d. 3 6	s. d. 3 4	s. d. 2 8
	6s. 5d.		5 s. 1d.					

[a] *Social Insurance*, Pt. i, p. 47.

Compulsory contributions to be levied against the insured persons are highest for the self employed (Class II) both for men and for women. The fact that they have to pay more per week results not from provision of better benefits for them but from the fact that they have no employer to share in bearing the cost of their insurance. The combined contributions of employer and employee for Class I exceed those for Class II by about 54 per cent for men and 45 per cent for women. The higher combined contributions for Class I are provided because of differences in benefits and benefit provisions introduced because of differences in the way of life of the three contributing classes. We shall take them up in the ensuing consideration of individual benefits.

CONSIDERATION OF THE SEVERAL BENEFITS

In this section we shall treat first the four major benefits, retirement pensions, unemployment benefits, sickness benefits, and invalidity benefits. We shall then give such additional attention to the subordinate or subsidiary benefits as may appear necessary to round out a general description of the plan.

Retirement pensions. Dependency in old age is of course the major hazard facing all classes of the population. Retirement pensions are therefore provided for all classes covered by the new plan provided they make the necessary contributions to attain an insured status. There are two vital distinctions between the British provisions and those contained under our system of old-age and survivors insurance.

1. Under our system receipt of wages of specified amount in a given quarter is necessary to make that quarter count toward attaining the insured status. Thus if a worker fails to earn the required amount whether because of sickness or unemployment, that quarter will not count. The amount of his earnings, moreover, determines the amount of his benefits. Under the British plan, the worker's nonpayment of contributions resulting from unemployment or sickness may be excused for the period of enforced nonearning and the time thus excused counts for eligibility. The amount of his earnings, moreover, has nothing to do with the amount of his old-age benefit. It is a fixed sum regardless of earnings, and therefore no record of earnings is necessary.

2. Under our system a worker who has not been under the system long enough to qualify gets no benefit. His contributions are forfeited to the fund. The British propose to use an entirely different system which will go a long way toward eliminating forfeitures. Absence of the required number of contributions paid or excused will result not in forfeitures but in a reduction in the amount of benefits. Our citizens who have to forfeit will be dependent under existing law on means test old-age assistance and if not in need will get nothing. Under the British plan, according to the proposals, the British seasonal worker who has averaged only 15 contributions paid or excused per year will get if single a benefit of 5s. a week, and if he has an eligible wife, the two will get 9s. a week. Such a system is administratively simple under a system that uses the flat-rate benefit not connected with earnings. It is easily set forth in a simple schedule showing the benefits for the number of contributions made or excused. The tentative proposal divides contributions made or excused by steps of 5 from 15 to 50 or more.[14]

[14] For the schedule suggested tentatively see *Social Insurance*, Pt. 1, par. 99.

The British situation with respect to qualifying for the retirement pension is necessarily complicated. Four different groups must be provided for:

A. Those who are less than 16 when the new scheme comes into operation.

B. Those who are insured under the present scheme and have reached pensionable age.

C. Those who are insured under the present scheme but have not reached pensionable age.

D. Those who, though over age 16, are not insured under the present scheme but become contributors under the new one.[15]

We have quoted the description of these four groups partly because they show rather simply the intricacies of the problem of revising and extending our existing system. The White Paper gives in detail the proposals for each group.[16] We shall confine our discussion to two groups, (A) those less than 16 on the inauguration of the new plan, and (D) those who though over 16 are not insured under the existing plan but will be contributors under the new one.

The person who enters the new system upon attaining the age of 16 will not qualify for an old-age pension unless he has actually paid 156 weekly contributions. The normal retiring age for men is 65 years; from age 16 to age 65 there are over 2,500 weeks. Thus this basic requirement should not exclude any very large number.

To qualify for the full pension of a pound a week, if single, or £1 15s., if joint, the worker must average 50 contributions paid or excused over his whole working life. The excusal system will greatly mollify the apparent severity of this requirement. As previously noted if the average number of contributions falls below 50, the amount of benefit is reduced. With respect to the average, the report says: "As the yearly average will normally be based on the number of contributions paid or excused from age 16 to 65 (60 for women), divided by the number of contribution years in that period, the divisor (in this group) will be 49 for a man and 44 for a woman."[17]

---

[15] The same, par. 97.

[16] The same, pars. 98–103.

[17] The same, par. 98.

The provisions with respect to persons who are already over 16 when the new system goes into effect and who are not included in any present system are brief enough so that they will be quoted in full.

Those in this group will be required to contribute for 10 years before becoming eligible for retirement pensions. Otherwise, all the conditions which apply to group A will apply to this group except that the average number of contributions paid or excused will be calculated, not over the whole working life, but over the period from the date of the commencement of the new scheme to the date when the contributor reaches pensionable age or completes 10 years insurance, whichever is later.

Persons in this group who are within 10 years of pensionable age when the scheme commences will obviously be in a special position, since they will not be able to fulfil the necessary conditions until some time after reaching pensionable age. For those who remain in employment until the 10 years period has been completed, the contributions paid in respect of that employment will count towards satisfying the contribution conditions for pension. Those who retire before the end of the 10 years will be given an option: they may either continue to pay contributions at the Class IV rate, after reaching pensionable age, in order to qualify for retirement pension; or they may claim a refund with interest of the pension element of their share of contributions which they have paid, and forego any right to pension.[18]

The provisions covering persons who are within 10 years of pensionable age when the scheme commences is another illustration of the British insistence on the principles of insurance. The contributor is given three options: (1) if still employed he can keep on paying until he qualifies; (2) if he retires he can pay contributions at the Class IV rate; or (3) he can take a refund with interest. Like equity, Britain apparently abhors a forfeiture.

To be eligible for a retirement pension under the British plan, a gainfully employed worker must have retired from employment. The British, however, have not designed their system with any idea of encouraging retirement; quite the contrary, it is designed to encourage continuance in employment. Great Britain, like the United States, anticipates an increased number

---

[18] The same, pars. 102, 103.

of persons 60 years of age and over and to an increase in the percentage which such persons form of the total population. If the level of living is to be materially and progressively raised, many will have to remain in productive work after the minimum permissive age for retirement is reached.[19] Thus in the British proposals we find:

1. A flat sum old-age pension sufficiently low to make retirement on it unattractive to persons who have earned reasonably well. To them it offers insurance against want and not insurance of anything approaching the level of income to which they have been accustomed.

2. Provision of an increase in the flat old-age pension of 1s. a week single and 2s. a week joint for each year of work after pensionable age.[20]

In connection with this increase in the pension for work after the permissive age, it should be noted that the worker continues his contributions at the regular rate so long as he works. As a result the fund profits substantially when workers continue beyond the retirement age. Their extra contributions and the savings on the pension payments more than pay for the increased pensions paid for the shortened retirement period.

The joint retirement pensions of the British system present one outstanding contrast with the joint pensions under O.A.S.I. Under our system the wife is not eligible until she attains the age of 65. Under the British system the rule is: "The joint pension of 35s. will be payable on the husband's retirement, provided that his wife is living with him or is wholly or mainly maintained by him, and, if under pensionable age, is not gainfully occupied."[21] Thus under the British plan the wife who has not recently been employed and is past the age when she is readily employable does not have to wait until she has reached 60 or 65 to be eligible for a wife's benefit. The comparatively low, flat benefit of the British system makes

[19] The same, par. 87. The British appreciate the contributions of older workers to wartime productivity.
[20] The same, par. 88.
[21] The same, par. 90.

such a provision more practicable than it would be under our system with its benefits related to past earnings.

Attention should be called to the fact that under the British system with its comprehensive and co-ordinated benefits, the calendar age of the insured is of far less significance than it is under our O.A.S.I. For example, if a fully insured worker under O.A.S.I. is disabled at age 60, he must wait until he attains age 65 before he can draw benefits. Under the British system the person disabled at 60 will be eligible for a sickness benefit for the first three years of his illness at 24s. a week and at the end of three years of continuous sickness to an invalidity benefit of 20s. a week, the same amount as the old-age benefit. The essential difference between the old-age pension and the invalidity benefit under the British plan is that for the invalidity benefit disability must be proved, whereas the retirement pension is paid upon arriving at the retirement age and giving up gainful employment without any proof of incapacity for further work. Thus under the British plan the calendar age affects mainly the assumptions and the need for proof, whereas under our existing plan it may mean the difference between a substantial benefit or only what can be secured from general public assistance if need can be proved. Low benefits providing insurance against want permit such arrangements more easily than a system which relates benefits to earnings.

Unemployment benefits. A striking feature of the *Beveridge Report* was its recommendation that benefits should be paid so long as unemployment continued, subject to the requirement of attendance at a work or training center after a limited period of unemployment.[22] This recommendation did not meet with the approval of the government. The White Paper proposes that unemployment benefits will end after 30 weeks or a somewhat longer period in the case of those with a good employment record. It will be recalled, however, that the government proposals provide for a training allowance paid from the general fund with some contribution from the Social Insurance Fund and that time spent on training allowance is not counted in the 30 weeks of unemployment benefit.

[22] The *Beveridge Report*, pars. 129–31.

The reasons for limiting the employment benefit are thus stated in the White Paper:

... As regards unemployment benefit, they agree that training schemes are of the utmost importance in preventing unemployment and in securing fluidity of labour, and that claimants unreasonably refusing to undergo a course of training should be disqualified from receiving benefit. They are satisfied, however, that a requirement to undergo training after a certain period of unemployment would not constitute an effective safeguard against possible abuse of benefit.[23]

We have previously called attention to the position of the government that the level of contributions must be held down, an action which requires that benefits be held down.[24] In connection with this statement, it is interesting to note that the Government Actuary reports: "The limitation of unemployment benefit to a maximum duration of 30 weeks (apart from added days) [represents as compared with the Beveridge rates]—saving about 7d. [a week] for men and 4½d. for women, but placing a substantial liability on the Exchequer for unemployment assistance."[25]

One naturally is a bit curious with respect to the "added days" for a contributor who has a good record of employment. The White Paper does not present a complete and finished bill. In some instances, as apparently in this one, it announces a policy without working it out in detail. A feature of our American unemployment insurance systems is that the insured who has not drawn any unemployment compensation in 20 years of service may draw no greater benefit in the year he is first unemployed than the employee who has come on the fund time and time again in the preceding 20 years. It will be interesting to see to what extent Britain will go in providing for the man who becomes technologically unemployed after long continued regular employment.

Britain, in the past, used for unemployment insurance an individual benefit year beginning with the filing of a successful claim. The applicant was eligible for a benefit if in the two

[23] *Social Insurance*, Pt. 1, par. 67.
[24] The same, par. 13.
[25] The same, App. 1, p. 48.

years before the claim he had actually paid thirty contributions. For health insurance, on the other hand, the calendar year was the benefit year and the qualifying year was the twelve-month period which ended in the previous July. Under the new co-ordinated plan, both benefits will be paid on the same basis, with the decision in favor of the uniform calendar year as the benefit year and a uniform twelve-month period as the qualifying year.

To be eligible for full benefit, the employee must have 26 contributions actually paid and 50 contributions paid or excused in the last complete contribution year before the beginning of the benefit year.[26] If the employee has not paid the requisite number of contributions to be entitled to full benefit, the amount of benefit will be scaled down according to the number of contributions deficient. Under the existing un-employment system, which is to be replaced, the rule is all or nothing, with a possible forfeiture if the contributions are short of the required number.[27] It will be noted that the new plan is to scale down the amount of benefits and not the period during which they are payable or both benefit rate and duration.

With uniformity of benefits, contribution years, benefit years, and qualifying requirements, the system is administratively so simple that a short waiting period is feasible—three days. Benefits are payable for the fourth and subsequent days. If the unemployment or the sickness has lasted for at least four weeks, benefit for the first three days—the waiting time—will then become payable.[28]

Unemployment benefits are payable only to persons in Class I. They are not applicable to persons working on their own account or to persons of working age not gainfully employed. Such persons who face economic difficulties and decide to seek employment under an employer, as already noted, may

[26] The same, pars. 62–63.
[27] The same, par. 69.
[28] The same, par. 64.

be able to get a training allowance if they take an approved course.

The provisions with respect to the married woman gainfully employed should perhaps be restated here. If she has elected to be excused from contributions, she gets no benefit in event of her own unemployment or sickness. If she has elected to continue contributions after her marriage, she is eligible for either benefit at a reduced rate, provided she earns more than 20s. a week. "In order, however, to confine insurance against sickness and unemployment to those [married women] whose employment is more than casual, married women earning 20s. a week or less will be compulsorily exempt from insurance in Class I or Class II."[29]

The *Beveridge Report* proposed that when an employed woman married she would be paid a marriage grant in lieu of all the rights she had acquired under the social insurance system. If she continued to work for wage or salary as an employee, she could then elect either to pay no contributions and take solely as the wife of her husband or to continue to pay contributions and to be independently insured against sickness and unemployment. If she elected to be a contributor, she would start with a clean slate, as her previous contribution record would be wiped out by the payment of the marriage grant.[30]

The government took the view that wiping out the previous contribution record was disadvantageous to those women who elected to continue as contributors and to earn benefits in their own right. Accordingly it did not adopt the suggestion of the marriage grant but leaves the married woman with such rights as may accrue from her contribution record made prior to marriage. The plan includes some special provisions applicable to married women who continue their contributions which the White Paper says "may seem elaborate, and in some respects restrictive," but space does not permit presenting them.[31] It

[29] The same, par. 108.
[30] The *Beveridge Report*, pars. 340, 345.
[31] For the special conditions see, *Social Insurance*, Pt. I, pars. 112–15.

may be interesting to note that the Government Actuary reports that the omission of the cash grant on marriage of an insured woman and certain other changes with respect to them resulted in a net saving in contributions for women of about a half penny a week over those required for the Beveridge plan.[32]

Sickness benefits. Although the British co-ordinated plan provides for much similarity between unemployment insurance and sickness insurance, there are highly important differences. The outstanding one arises from the fact that sickness insurance is provided both for salary and wage earners (Class I) and self-employed persons (Class II), whereas unemployment insurance is provided for salary and wage earners only. In the judgment of the government, the differences in the conditions surrounding employed workers and persons working on their own account are so great that each class must have its distinctive regulation governing sickness insurance. Following the example of the White Paper, we shall therefore discuss sickness insurance first for wage and salary workers and then for the self-employed.

The salary or wage worker to be eligible for the standard sickness benefit of 40s. a week for married couples or of 24s. a week for single persons must have actually paid 26 contributions and have 50 contributions paid or excused in the last contribution year before the beginning of the benefit year.[33]

If the eligible contributor has actually paid 156 contributions, sickness benefits will be paid for the first 3 years of any continuous period of sickness. For this purpose illnesses separated by less than 3 months will be treated as a continuous period of sickness. If such a contributor has exhausted all the sickness benefits due him, so long as he remains incapable of work, he will receive an invalidity benefit at the same rate as the retirement pension, generally 35s. for a married couple or 20s. for a single person.

If the eligible salary or wage-earning contributor has actually paid 26 contributions but less than the required 156, he will

---

[32] The same, par. 48.
[33] The same, par. 63.

be paid the sickness benefit for only one year and at the end of that year he will not be eligible for an invalidity benefit. An employee who has exhausted his sickness benefit will not be further qualified until he has paid 10 further contributions.[34] As in unemployment insurance a contributor who is not eligible for full benefit will receive a benefit scaled down according to the number of contributions deficient.[35]

Under this plan of sickness and invalidity benefits, the salary or wage worker does not have to work long to be fully insured against total and permanent disability resulting from sickness. If he pays contributions every week for three years, he will have satisfied the requirement of 156 contributions actually paid. It will be noted that the requirement for the last complete contribution year before the benefit year is 50 contributions paid or excused. Sickness or unemployment are reasons for excusing contributions, hence it would seem that men who remain in Class I, the wage and salary workers, could relatively easily establish and maintain the full protection offered by the sickness and invalidity benefits. Women who leave Class I on marriage will lose their protection because, whatever number of paid contributions they may have, they will not continue to have 50 contributions paid or excused in the last complete contribution year before the benefit year. Married women who keep on working but elect not to contribute will likewise lose eligibility. Those who elect to contribute will remain eligible but will receive only 16s. a week for either sickness or invalidity as compared with 24s. for sickness and 20s. for invalidity paid to the employed single women.

The distinctions between the self-employed and the wage or salary workers with respect to sickness and invalidity benefits are introduced almost entirely for reasons concerned with feasibility. The report recognizes that many of the self-employed are well able to take care of themselves, but it says: "Many of the poorer members of this Class will be as much—if not

[34] The same, pars. 65, 68.
[35] The same, par. 69.

more—dependent on good health for their earnings as are
the members of Class I, and accordingly as much in need of
benefit for all periods of sickness, short or long."[36]

The reasons given for not providing sickness benefits for the
self-employed with a waiting period of only three days are
costs and difficulties of effective control. The statement with
respect to costs made in the report is quoted in full:

> The contribution that is required for persons in Class II is high—
> 4s. 2d. for men, 3s. 6d. for women—and, since there is no "employer"
> to bear a share of it as in Class I, it falls wholly on the contributor. If
> sickness benefit were made payable from the onset of illness instead of
> after the first four weeks, as is proposed, the Class II contribution
> would have to be increased by another 3d. a week.[37]

The contributions cited in the quoted paragraph are, it
should be made clear, total costs and not the costs of sickness
and invalidity insurance only. The report does not show the
"full actuarial contribution" for Class II by specific benefits,
and hence we cannot supply the figure for sickness and invalidity insurance.

The emphasis placed on the absence of an employer to share
the costs raises a serious question. Insurance concepts lead
many persons to think of the full actuarial contribution as
practically the same thing as the premium which an individual
would have to pay a voluntary insurance company, although
with less loading for selling and other expenses. The burden
of paying this cost in social insurance for salary and wage
workers may then be split three ways being shared by employee,
employer, and government. What is frequently forgotten is
that the employer's contributions become an inescapable cost
of doing business, virtually a part of the employer's labor
costs. If the employer is to continue a successful business, he
must in the long run get back his production costs from the
consumers of his product. He must pass along his employer's
contributions for the Social Insurance Fund to consumers of his
product or service. Ultimately a large part of the employer's

[36] The same, par. 72.
[37] The same, par. 74.

contributions must be paid by the final consumers. Some of these final consumers are in Classes II to VI of the British plan. They are paying, or helping to pay, the employer's contributions that permit of superior benefits for salary and wage workers in Class I. We shall discuss this subject at greater length in Part III. Here we merely raise the question as to the equity of reducing the benefits for a particular class because for that class there is no employer to share the cost.

The problem of control is difficult. The self-employed contain many who can, and often do, carry on all or part of their work in their own homes. Even though sick, many of them can carry on their businesses and continue to earn their livelihood. Sickness, therefore, does not necessarily mean complete cessation of income. Few would probably disagree with the statement from the report: "It is impossible to assume that medical certification, no matter how efficient, will be able to overcome all the difficulties of administration."[38] Investigations necessary to prevent abuse would be prohibitively costly if made in the case of every illness that lasts into a fourth day.

The solution of these problems of finance and administration arrived at by the government is to have a waiting period of 4 weeks for the self-employed as contrasted with the waiting period of 3 days for the wage and salary workers. This provision is less restrictive than the one proposed by Sir William Beveridge of 13 weeks, but the 4 weeks waiting period proposed by the government applies to each period of sickness, however short the interval separating any 2 periods. Contributions during the 4 weeks waiting period will be excused. Details as to administrative practice with respect to excusal of contributions during the waiting period are not included in the report. Sir William Beveridge, presumably because of the administrative difficulties involved, did not recommend excusal of contributions during the waiting period.[39] In sickness and unemployment insurance for wage and salary workers, the waiting period is 3 days, but if the sickness or unemployment

[38] The same, par. 75.
[39] The same, pars. 76, 77.

lasts at least 4 weeks, benefit for the first 3 days will become payable.[40] Nothing in the report suggests that a similar provision will be included in the provision for sickness insurance for the self-employed.

Although no details will be given here,[41] it is germane to note that some of the plans for sickness insurance in Great Britain were developed on an occupational or categorical basis and now give rise to special problems. Under the new plan the members of some of these older plans clearly belong in Class II, the self-employed, whereas the benefit programs for them were in the initial legislation assimilated with those for wage and salary workers. Such anomalies are apparently inevitable when legislation is passed piecemeal or when existing programs are extended to embrace other small categories with respect to which the facts are somewhat different. The British see things differently when the problem of relief and social security is viewed as a whole.

WORKMEN'S COMPENSATION

When the Interdepartmental Committee on Social Insurance and Allied Services approached its task of reviewing the various British programs, it saw clearly that workmen's compensation was within its field. Sir William Beveridge had to deal with it in his report. Part II of *Social Insurance*, the report of the Ministry of Reconstruction, is devoted to it. The problems presented are extremely detailed. We shall not attempt to do more here than to present a very generalized statement of the issues and the major solutions recommended by the government.

Three of the major hazards that give rise to need are sickness, invalidity, and the premature death of a worker responsible for the support of dependents. So far as the need itself is concerned, it is not particularly important whether the sickness, invalidity, or death that caused it was directly occupationally connected or whether it was due to causes in no way connected with the victim's occupation. The distinction between work-

[40] The same, par. 64.
[41] For the details see the same, pars. 76, 78.

men's compensation and general social insurance involves mainly two issues: (a) Who is liable for the costs? and (b) How large shall benefits be and in what form shall they be paid?

Workmen's compensation grew out of the common law of torts which under certain circumstances made the employer liable to damages for injuries to an employee while engaged in work for the employer. Gradually, by statutory action, the number of defenses which the employer could make against action by an injured employee or his representative were reduced and the responsibility of the employer correspondingly increased. A social insurance point of view tended materially to modify the law and the procedures, and yet many of the old practices carried over. Something in the nature of a judicial procedure remained to determine such issues as whether the accident or disease was of occupational origin and suffered as the result of the employee's service with the employer and the extent and probable duration of the damage with special reference to impairment of future earning capacity. The emphasis was on the employee's earnings and earning capacity without that reference to the question of the number and the type of his dependents that characterizes present-day British thinking with respect to social insurance. Lump-sum payments in settlement of a successful claim might be made and then unwisely used by the recipient, so that he and his dependents were soon in need. Delays and uncertainties in the procedures might lead to the acceptance of a lump-sum settlement that subsequent developments proved did not in fact compensate for the damage.

Sir William Beveridge in his report gave a bill of particulars covering the disadvantages of the British workmen's compensation system.[42] At one point he said, "There should be no hesitation in making provision for the results of industrial accident and disease in future, not by a continuance of the present system of individual employer's liability, but as one branch of a unified Plan for Social Security."[43]

[42] The *Beveridge Report*, pars. 79, 80. See also *Social Insurance*, Pt. 2, pars. 1–13.
[43] The *Beveridge Report*, par. 80.

The government on this particular point was in agreement with Sir William. In the foreword to Part II of the Minister's report, the opening paragraph deals briefly with the defects of the existing plan and then announces revolutionary changes in the Workmen's Compensation system. The last three paragraphs are quoted in full:

Henceforward, the Government, as part of their extension and recasting of the social insurance system, propose that provision for disablement or loss of life from industrial injury shall become a social service, administered as a separate scheme but under the Minister of Social Insurance. Benefits at special rates will be paid from a separate insurance fund, to which the employer, workman and the Exchequer will be contributors. This means a fundamental change in the method of providing against what may be one of the most grievous forms of personal misfortune: it involves also a great simplification of what has become a very complicated and elaborate system.

Under the present system, benefits are related to the estimated loss of earning capacity. Under the Government's plan benefits will be paid at flat rates, with supplements for family responsibilities. In the earlier weeks, while the workman is incapacitated for work, there will be injury allowances at uniform rates. Afterwards, if disablement is prolonged, there will be industrial pensions based, not on loss of earning capacity, but upon the extent to which the workman has suffered disablement by the injury, by comparison with a normal healthy person of the same age and sex. The pension will not be affected by any subsequent earnings of the workman, and (except in some cases of minor disability) will not be replaced by a lump sum payment. There will be pensions for widows, parents and certain other dependents of those who have died as the result of industrial injury.

This system is in many respects like that which is the basis of war pensions schemes. It thus recognizes a certain similarity between the position of the soldier wounded in battle and that of the man injured in the course of his productive work for the community. Neither is liable to have his pension reduced on account of what he may earn after the injury; each is compensated not for loss of earning capacity but for whatever he has lost in health, strength and the power to enjoy life.

Space will not permit us to present in any detail the discussion of principles of workmen's compensation insurance contained in Part II of the White Paper. We commend it, however, to readers who desire to understand the philosophy that underlies the entire new British plan of universal, complete, and coordinated social insurance. We shall confine ourselves to a brief consideration of three major points: (1) the method of financing, (2) the benefits, and (3) provisions for fatal cases.

The method of financing workmen's compensation. In Britain, as in the United States, the existing methods of financing workmen's compensation grew out of the concept of the liability of the individual employer for occupational accidents to his employees. This concept meant that if the employer did not protect himself by insurance, the entire cost of such compensation as was awarded fell on him. If he took insurance, his premiums were generally related to the hazard not only in the industry in which he was engaged but also in his own particular establishment. It was not uncommon for premium rates to be based on the industry with variations from the base rates according to the accident experience of the employer or to the extent to which he introduced safety devices. In Britian, industrial associations in some instances operated the insurance funds for their members and apparently there was less use of general carriers of workmen's compensation than is the case in the United States, and nothing comparable to the "state funds" used in some of our states. Since the liability was on the employer there were no contributions either from the employees or the government.

The government proposes a complete departure from past practice. There will be an Industrial Injury Insurance Fund distinct from the Social Insurance Fund but under the same general overhead administration, tentatively that of the Minister of Social Insurance. For the Industrial Injury Fund an Advisory Committee or Council is proposed to share in the development and administration of the scheme with equal representation of employers and employees. The two sides will also be represented in the local appeal tribunals. The government takes the position that equal contributions by employers and employees are a natural if not a necessary corollary to such arrangements for equal representation, a doctrine entirely foreign to our practice with respect to unemployment insurance.[44]

The proposed distribution of costs is five twelfths by the employer, five twelfths by the employee, and the remaining two twelfths by the Exchequer.

The government specifically rejects all proposals that the contribution rates shall vary by hazard of the industry or the record of individual employers. ". . . Their view is that for further progress in prevention of accidents reliance must be placed on other means, such as the development of the standards set up under the Factories, Mines and other safety enactments, and increasing co-operation between employers and workmen. . . ."[45]

In rejecting proposals for higher rates for hazardous industries, there is one statement that is of general significance with respect to the whole British plan of social insurance. The report says:

. . . Hazardous industries are not hazardous because the employers in them are less active in the prevention of accidents than other employers, or because the workmen in those industries are less careful than other workmen. They are hazardous because of the nature of the employment and the inherent risks. The proposal needs, therefore, strong grounds to justify it, *particularly as the special levy would fall most heavily on certain important industries which have to meet foreign competition.*[46]

Designers of social insurance systems in the United States do not perhaps have to give very much thought to the possible effect of high benefit rates and high contributions on the competitive position of the United States in foreign trade so long at least as protective tariff barriers are maintained. The United States produces largely for its own domestic market. Britain, on the other hand, is largely dependent on foreign markets and the markets of other members of the British Commonwealth of Nations. It is thus acutely aware of the fact that it cannot

---

[44] *Social Insurance*, Pt. 2, pars. 34, 35.
[45] The same, par. 31 (v).
[46] The same, par. 31 (i). Italics supplied.

COMPARISON OF RATE OF INJURY ALLOWANCE AND OF 100% DISABLEMENT PENSION PROPOSED FOR ADULTS UNDER THE GOVERNMENT SCHEME, WITH THE RATES FOR TOTAL INCAPACITY UNDER THE EXISTING ACTS AND UNDER THE BEVERIDGE PLAN[a]

(1)	Government Proposals			Workmen's Compensation Acts			Beveridge Plan	
	Injury Allowance during Incapacity for Work (First 13 weeks)	Injury Allowance after 13 Weeks and Pension Rate for 100% Disablement	Pension, if 100% Disabled and Unemployable	Prewar	With War Increases		Disability Benefit (First 13 weeks)	Industrial Pension (After 13 weeks)
					First 13 Weeks	After 13 Weeks		
	(2)	(3)	(4)	(5)	(6)	(7)	(8)	(9)
	s. d.	s. d.	s. d.	s. d.	s. d.	s. d.	s. d.	s. d.
(a) Single man or woman without dependent	35 0	40 0	50 0	$\frac{1}{5}$ earnings 30 0 max.	35 0 max. (limit of $\frac{2}{3}$rds earnings)	40 0 max. (limit of $\frac{2}{3}$rds earnings)	24 0	$\frac{2}{3}$rds earnings 60s. max. (minimum as in Col. 8)
(b) Single man or woman with adult dependent	43 9	50 0	60 0				40 0	
(c) Married man	43 9	50 0	60 0			50 0 max. (limit of $\frac{2}{3}$rds earnings)	40 0*	
(d) Married man and first child	48 9	57 6	67 6		45 0 max. (limit of $\frac{7}{8}$ths earnings)	55 0 max. (limit of $\frac{7}{8}$ths earnings)	48 0*	$\frac{2}{3}$rds earnings +8s. 68s. max. (minimum as in Col. 8)

* Subject to wife not being gainfully occupied.

[a] *Social Insurance*, Pt. 2, p. 30. The rates in Cols. 3 and 4 may be increased by an allowance up to 20s. where constant attendance on the workman is necessary on account of the injury.

go in for elaborate and costly social insurance benefits unless it can attain and maintain such a high degree of industrial efficiency that it can still successfully compete. With respect to its hazardous industries the government apparently is dubious as to that question, and therefore it spreads the risk over all industry and provides a one-sixth contribution from general taxes.

The benefits. To give a general idea of the benefits for disability resulting from industrial accident or disease, on page 503 there is a table taken from the White Paper which gives the figures for 100 per cent disablement, together with comparisons with rates under the existing plan and with those proposed under the Beveridge plan.

The benefits for industrial cases are higher than those for ordinary sickness and invalidity. The comparison is as follows:

INDUSTRIAL INJURY BENEFITS COMPARED WITH SICKNESS-INVALIDITY BENEFITS

	Proposed Benefits Under				
	Industrial Injury Insurance Fund[a]			Social Insurance Fund[b]	
	First 13 Weeks	After First 13 Weeks		Sickness	Invalidity
		100 Per Cent Disability	100 Per Cent Disability and Un-employable		
	s. d.	s. d.	s. d.	s. d.	s. d.
Single man or woman without dependent....	35 0	40 0	50 0	24 0	20 0
Single man or woman with adult dependent.	43 9	50 0	60 0	40 0	36 0
Married man..........	43 9	50 0	60 0	40 0	35 0
Married man and first child...............	48 9	57 6	67 7	45 0	40 0

a *Social Insurance*, Pt. 2, p. 30.
b The same, Pt. 1, p. 10.

The figures with respect to size of benefits indicate that it is to the advantage of the disabled employee to be able to prove occupational origin of an accident or illness. Moreover, a person is insured against industrial injury the moment he or she goes to

work. The benefit will not depend on a contribution qualification and hence there will not be, as in ordinary sickness or illness, a reduction in the amount of benefit because of a deficiency in contributions.[47]

The distinction between 100 per cent disablement and 100
per cent disabled and unemployable requires some explanation. When an employee suffers a disablement that is likely
to be permanent or prolonged, a medical board will assess
the degree of disablement by comparison with a normal healthy
person of the same age and sex. The amount of pension is to be
determined in accordance with the degree of disablement thus
found. The pension fixed is thereafter payable regardless of
what the pensioner may be able to earn despite his disabilities.
Thus if a pensioner who has been rated as 100 per cent disabled
succeeds in developing an additional means of livelihood, he is
entitled to all he makes over and above the pension whatever
its amount. The government wishes to encourage rather than to
discourage efforts at rehabilitation regardless of the degree of
disability. In those instances in which no rehabilitation at all
is possible and the victim is in fact totally and absolutely unemployable an extra allowance of 10s. a week is provided.

The provision with respect to the married woman who is
wholly or mainly supporting a dependent husband deserves
special mention because of the contrast with provisions under
our old-age and survivors insurance. If such a married woman
is the victim of an occupational accident or disease, her husband
receives a benefit of the amount which would be paid a wife in
the normal case. The first child of such a married woman also
takes under such circumstances.[48]

In event the pensioner who has suffered a 100 per cent disablement needs a constant attendant as the result of the disablement, he may be awarded a special allowance at a weekly rate
not exceeding 20s.[49] Unmarried workmen under 18 years of age
will on suffering an occupational disablement be paid half the

[47] The same, par. 34 (v).
[48] The same, par. 43.
[49] The same, par. 42.

rate for an adult, but when he or she reaches the age of 18 the pension will be raised to the full amount.[50]

Provisions in fatal cases. The pensions and allowances in fatal cases which we outline briefly here are payable if the claimant was wholly or mainly dependent on the workman at the time of the injury and either continues to be so dependent up to the time of death or would but for the injury be so dependent. In event of partial dependency a partial pension or allowance will be made. We shall deal in the order named with widows, children, parents, dependent husbands, and other adults.

A widow is eligible if she was married to the victim previous to the injury and was resident with him at the time of his death. Such widows are divided into two classes much as they are under the general Social Insurance Fund.

The first class consists of widows who at the time of the death have a child or children of the workman under their care, or who are over 50 years of age, or if under 50 years of age are incapable of self-support, or who are over 50 years of age when the youngest child of the workman ceases to be eligible for a child's allowance. They are eligible for a pension of 30s. a week.

The second class consists of widows who at the time of the death (1) are under 50 years of age, (2) have no child of the workman under their care, and (3) are capable of self-support. They are eligible to a pension of 20s. a week.

The pension of a dependent female ceases on her marriage.

For the first dependent child there is a weekly allowance of 7s. 6d. If any child becomes a full orphan by the death of the workman, the allowance is 12s. a week.

A widower who is incapable of self-support will be eligible for a pension of 20s. weekly on the death of his wife through an industrial accident if she was married to him previous to her injury and was resident with him at the time of her death.

A parent incapable of self-support is eligible whether or not a widow's pension is payable as the result of the death. The maximum rate of pension is 20s. for one parent, 30s. for two.

If no widow or parent's pensions are payable, one other adult

[50] The same, par. 44.

member of the family who was residing with him at the time of injury will be eligible for not to exceed 20s. weekly if incapable of self-support.

If no pensions are payable to a widow, a parent, a dependent husband, or an adult member of the family, a woman, whether or not a member of the deceased workman's family, is eligible for a temporary pension of 20s. a week if she was residing with the workman at the time of the injury and if she has the care of his child or children.

Any adult member of the deceased workman's family who is not eligible for any pension under this scheme will be eligible for a temporary allowance of 36s. weekly for 13 weeks.

This summary of the provisions in fatal cases has been given in part because it demonstrates recognition of the different situations which may arise and an attempt to meet each of them in a way which will provide a measure of social security for all who may be rendered dependent thereby without the use of a means test.

THE COSTS OF SOCIAL INSURANCE

We are reproducing on page 508 a table taken from *Memorandum by the Government Actuary on the Finance of the Government's Proposals* which constitutes Appendix I of Part I of the White Paper. It gives the estimated cost of the plan, including national assistance and health service but excluding workmen's compensation for each of the years 1945, 1955, 1965, and 1975. The details of the workmen's compensation system are not so far advanced that precise estimates of cost have been made. The report says: ". . . the Government are advised that it [the cost of benefit] will materially exceed the cost of the proposals in the [Beveridge] Report and is likely to be of the order of £20 millions a year."[51] The administrative costs of the new plan will be lower than under the existing system. "The Government are advised that pending experience of the working of the Scheme it would be wise to allow 15 per cent of the cost of benefits [or £3 a year] for administrative charges."[52]

[51] The same, par. 47 (iii).
[52] The same, par. 47 (iv).

508 · *BRITISH PROPOSALS*

ESTIMATED EXPENDITURE: 1945–1975[a]

(In millions of pounds sterling)

	1945	1955	1965	1975
Social Insurance Benefits:				
Retirement pensions	169	203	272	324
Widows' and guardians' benefits	34	41	40	36
Unemployment benefit	87	87	85	80
Sickness and invalidity benefits	55	66	68	65
Maternity grant and benefits	9	8	8	7
Death grant	4	7	11	14
Cost of administration	16	16	16	16
Total	374	428	500	542
National Assistance:				
Assistance pensions	37	41	39	37
Unemployment assistance	22	22	21	20
Other assistance	6	6	6	6
Cost of administration	4	4	4	4
Total	69	73	70	67
Family Allowances:				
Allowances	57	58	54	50
Cost of administration	2	2	2	2
Total	59	60	56	52
Health Service	148	170	170	170
Total Expenditure	650	731	796	831

[a] *Social Insurance*, Pt. i, p. 49.

The first point to be noted with respect to total expenditure for social insurance, national assistance, family allowances, and health service is the marked and persistent increase in expenditures from decade to decade characteristic of all contributory social insurance systems that do not start under full load. For 1945, which is assumed to be the first year of the new plan, the total cost is 650 million pounds sterling per year. In 30 years the cost is estimated to be 831 millions, an increase of 181 millions or 27.8 per cent. The year 1975, moreover, does not mark the end of the upward movement. It will continue for a number of years thereafter, although at a diminishing rate of growth.

Examination of the figures for individual programs and benefits shows that retirement pensions are responsible—more than responsible in fact—for the marked growth. They begin at the relatively high figure of 169 million pounds sterling in 1945, since Britain starts its new plan with many beneficiaries under old plans. They increase in each decade until in 1975, when they have reached a total of 324 millions. In 30 years they have increased 155 millions or 91.7 per cent. As of 1945, retirement pensions account for 26 per cent of the total estimated expenditures; by 1975 the percentage will increase to about 39 per cent.

Why does the cost of retirement pensions increase so much? This question will be discussed at some length in Part III. Here it will only be pointed out that in Britain there are two principal reasons: (1) the contributory, no-means test system under which they are paid did not start under full load; it gradually moves toward full load as year after year an increasing number of surviving old people become entitled to retirement pensions at full scale. (2) The number of persons of retirement age in the population is increasing annually, as it is also in the United States.

The fact of the aging of the population possibly explains in part the relative stability of the noncontributory "assistance pensions" given on a means test basis. For them the figure is 37 million pounds sterling both in 1945 and 1975, although it is somewhat higher in the intervening decades. If the population remained stable with respect both to members and age distribution, contributory old-age pensions might materially diminish the cost of means test, noncontributory, assistance payments, but growth in the number of aged in the population prevents any radical reduction.

The reader may note the fall in the costs for unemployment benefits, maternity benefits, unemployment assistance benefits, and family allowances. Here one sees the progressive result of the decline in the birth rate, which means fewer children and gradually an actual decrease in the number of persons in the more active ages of life. It is not assumed in the actuarial figures that there will be progressively a decrease in the percentage of unemployment but that there will be a decrease in the actual number of persons of normal working age in the population.

The table just presented shows in some detail what the expenditures will be by programs, but it does not show from whence the money to pay for the programs is to come. Data on the budget as estimated by the Government Actuary are reproduced in the table below.

SOCIAL INSURANCE AND ALLIED SERVICES BUDGET: 1945-1975[a]

(In millions of pounds sterling)

	1945	1955	1965	1975
Estimated Expenditure:				
Social insurance benefits.....................	374	428	500	542
National assistance.........................	69	73	70	67
Family allowances..........................	59	60	56	52
Health service.............................	148	170	170	170
Total expenditure.....................	650	731	796	831
Estimated Income:				
Receipts from contributions of insured persons and employers[b].....................	283	280	275	259
Interest on existing funds...................	15	15	15	15
Balance of expenditure, to be met from Exchequer (or local rates)..........................	352	436	506	557
Total income......................	650	731	796	831

[a] Social Insurance, Pt. 1, p. 53.

[b] In this table, and throughout the memorandum, receipts from contributions relate to the contributions for social insurance benefits and health service and do not include the contributions for industrial injury insurance; the related expenditure and State grant are similarly omitted.

To make the significance of these basic figures a little clearer, it is desirable to show for each of the years 1945, 1955, 1965, and 1975, the percentage of the total costs which will be met from contributions from the insured persons and in the case of Class I, their employers. These figures are given on page 511.

On the initiation of the new plan the contributions of the insured and of employers will pay 43.5 per cent of the actual costs of the system. This percentage falls in each of the succeeding decennial years for which the figures are presented. By 1975, the contributions will pay only 31.2 per cent of the cost. A further projection of the figures beyond 1975 would

ESTIMATED EXPENDITURES FOR SOCIAL INSURANCE AND ALLIED SERVICES[a]

Year	Total[b] (In millions of pounds sterling)	Met by Contributions from Insured Persons and Employers	
		Amount[b] (In millions of pounds sterling)	Per Cent of Total
1945	650	283	43.5
1955	731	280	38.3
1965	796	275	34.5
1975	831	259	31.2

[a] Exclusive of industrial injury insurance.
[b] *Social Insurance,* Pt. 1, p. 53.

presumably show a further decrease in the percentage of costs borne by contributions.

This marked fall in the percentage is the combined result of (1) the marked rise in the cost of benefits and (2) a consistent but far less marked decrease in contributions resulting presumably from a gradual decline in the actual number of persons of working age.

Where is the money to make up the difference to come from? The table shows a uniform item of interest on existing funds of 15 million pounds sterling. The balance comes directly from the Exchequer or from local rates or, in other words, from public treasury balances, current taxes, or public borrowing. Before discussing these figures further, it is desirable to have a clear understanding of the interest item of 15 million pounds sterling a year. With respect to it the Government Actuary says:

In view of the greatly increased burdens placed upon the Exchequer by the enlargement of the benefits of existing insured persons, it would seem equitable that the Exchequer should have the advantage of the existing funds and the Government have decided that they shall be utilised in this manner. I have accordingly assumed that the interest thereon is to be set against expenditure in arriving at the cost of the scheme to the Exchequer.[53]

From this statement it seems not unreasonable to assume that the British practice will not be unlike that of our own national government with respect to the reserves of O.A.S.I., the unem-

[53] The same, Pt. 1, App. 1, p. 54.

ployment insurance systems, and the retirement systems for federal employees and railway workers. In the United States the federal government has the use of receipts, giving its obligations as security to the several trust funds, and assuming the duty to credit the funds with interest on those obligations through the deposit of further obligations and to substitute cash or its equivalent for them whenever necessity for cash arises. When the need for cash or its equivalent arises, the government must secure it from current general balances, current revenues, mainly tax receipts, or further public borrowing.

If the British proceed as we do, the interest item in their social security and allied services budget must be met in the same way from general fund balances, current revenues, or public borrowing. Under such circumstances the interest has to be added to the expenditure to be met from the Exchequer or local rates, to show the burden borne by general funds to support the system. On this basis the general funds would pay about 56.5 per cent of the costs in 1945, and by 1975 the percentage would increase to 68.8 per cent.

These figures relate to the entire costs for social insurance and allied services, exclusive of industrial injury insurance. The social insurance plan and the allied services are as this description has shown integrated into a comprehensive system. Family allowances and national assistance, paid entirely from public funds, are necessary and essential parts of the whole. Some readers may, however, be interested in the figures for the social insurance benefits alone. We shall therefore quote from the Actuary's report partly to give these figures and partly because of the excellence of his explanation of them.

Taking social insurance benefits alone, the Exchequer share will be nearly one-third at the outset, growing to one-half in 1965, with a further increase to about 55 per cent when the scheme has been in force for thirty years. The proportion of the cost met by the Exchequer in the case of social insurance benefits thus very greatly exceeds the proportion of the actuarial contribution allocated to the Exchequer, viz. about 22 per cent taking all benefits together. . . .[54] There are two main reasons for this. First, in addition to this direct subsidy to all

[54] See table on p. 483 and discussion relating to it.

contributors there is a further subsidy due to admitting the existing population of all ages for the ordinary benefits at the same rate of contribution as is charged to new entrants at age 16. Secondly, the liability thus undertaken by the State is not extinguished over a fixed period of years as would be the case if a series of deficiency payments were made to an accumulative fund.

The State will in fact discharge its liabilities, as regards both the proportion of the contributions which it undertakes to meet and the strain of admitting the existing population at the flat rate of contribution, by making good the excess of expenditure over income from contributions as it emerges year by year. The result is a charge on the taxpayer which will increase for a considerable period, as the expenditure on pensions gradually matures, and will last in perpetuity—this burden being attributable mainly to the proportion of the contributions undertaken by the Exchequer and to the substantial increase made in pensions provision and, to a less extent, to the increases in sickness benefits.[55]

After examining these figures as to the cost of the government's proposals for the new British plan one may ask, What would be the cost of such a plan in the United States?

It is not difficult to give a figure as to what such a system would cost in Britain were Britain as populous as the United States while retaining its present population characteristics and distribution. Roughly the cost would be about 3 times as great or 1,950 million pounds sterling for 1945 or 7,800 million dollars taking the pound at $4.00. If the population ratio of 3 to 1 is assumed for 1975 the costs would be for that year 2,493 million pounds sterling or 9,972 million dollars.

Professor Lawrence R. Klein of the Massachusetts Institute of Technology made a study of the costs of the Beveridge plan in which he compared British prices with United States prices for the necessaries included in the Beveridge minimum of subsistence benefits. He reached the conclusion that the pound sterling in Britain had the purchasing power of about $6.00 in the United States. If $6.00 instead of $4.00 be used for converting pounds to dollars, the costs for the government's proposals in a Britain as populous as the United States would be in 1945 11,700 million dollars.

[55] *Social Insurance*, Pt. 1, App. 1, p. 56.

For two major reasons one cannot say that the British plan applied in the United States would cost about 12 billion dollars in 1945 and 15 billions in 1975.

(1) The British systems for contributory old-age pensions are older and more mature than our O.A.S.I. system. Thus their new plan, into which the older schemes are consolidated, starts at a comparatively high point on that rising curve of costs that characterizes the first 60 to 80 years of a contributory, no-means-test system of insurance for old age. The United States, introducing such a system at a later period, would begin at a lower point on that rising curve of costs. If this country should use benefits of no higher costs than those in the British plan, its relative expenditures would lag behind those of Britain.

(2) There are differences between the two countries with respect to the age and occupational distributions of the population and other related matters. For example, among males in the total population, the United States has a higher percentage of employers and others working on their own account—because of our extensive farming population—and a lower percentage of wage and salary workers. It has a somewhat higher percentage of children under 15 years of age. Probably no other country in the world prior to World War II had a higher percentage of youth 15 to 24 years of age still attending school. Factors such as these would affect the social security budget.

CHAPTER XVI

THE NEW ZEALAND SYSTEM

The New Zealand system has been selected for presentation in the present book for two main reasons: (1) it provides for comprehensive, co-ordinated, universal coverage under a system evolved from earlier categorical programs, and (2) it presents an approach to the problem of relief and social security radically different from that thus far used in the United States. The New Zealand law approximates a system designed to give universal, comprehensive protection against want at something approaching minimum cost. In describing this system, we shall start with an over-all description, then take up the specific monetary benefits, and finally present summary statistics with respect to numbers by benefits and costs. We shall not go in detail into the health services which are part of the general system.

We are not considering the question whether New Zealand can as a matter of fact afford this new system. What a nation can afford with respect to relief and social insurance is a relative matter, depending in no small measure on what it does in other fields. The point will be made time and time again that if the nation makes financial commitments beyond its capacity to produce and market needed goods and services without a radical change in wages and prices, inflation may be the politically expedient way out of the dilemma. A radical increase in prices decreases if it does not destroy the real values of the benefits provided under the relief and social security system. If the real values are to be maintained, these benefits have to be increased, and if a new balancing is to be attained, they have to be increased at the expense of some other major categories of public expenditure.

New Zealand is a small dominion with only about 1.6 million inhabitants. It has had a dependent as contrasted with a self-sufficient economy. Its prosperity in the past largely depended on the prices it could secure from its exports, mainly products

515

of its livestock, sold in the world market, with England its principal customer. With the receipts from the sale of agricultural exports, it bought a considerable proportion of the goods which its people consumed. No small part of its public debt was held abroad before the war, mainly in England. Thus its balance of trade, which depended largely on world prices for the products of its agriculture, was the dominant factor in its economy. Since it was so dependent on world markets for a limited number of products, many of the important factors in its economy were very largely beyond the control of its own government. It is entirely possible that its various programs for social and economic advances, of which its social security system is only one, may encounter great difficulties because of the dependence of the economy and the relatively narrow range of its domestic production.[1]

The reader is therefore cautioned that in the subsequent discussion of the social security system we are dealing with it alone, without reference to its relationships to the whole economy of New Zealand. Any commendation of the system or its parts which may be given during the course of the discussion should not be construed as indicating that the system will in our judgment encounter no financial difficulties. Financial difficulties of a social insurance system may arise largely from forces outside the system, and we are not including any of these forces in the discussion of the New Zealand system. In the ensuing discussion, references unless otherwise noted will be to the official pamphlet describing it, entitled *Social Security, Monetary Benefits and War Pensions*.[2] It will be cited hereafter as Pamphlet.

OUTLINE OF THE PLAN

1. The New Zealand system has no tax on employment. Employers as such do not contribute, although companies pay in-

---

[1] The *New Zealand Official Year-Book*, compiled annually in the Census and Statistics Department, is a comprehensive report on the economic and social activities of the dominion government. Among its many chapters is one devoted to social security pensions, superannuation, and the like. Hereafter cited as *Year-Book*.

[2] Prepared by the Social Security Department in 1943 and printed by E. V. Paul, Government Printer, Wellington.

come taxes. The system is financed through a special Social Security Fund into which are paid:

a. Registration fees required of all persons over 16 years of age unless specifically exempted by an order in council. The registration fee is 5 shillings a year for all girls and women, and for boys from 16 to 20; for men 20 years and over it is 5 shillings a quarter.

b. The proceeds of a special earmarked flat income tax or contribution of approximately 5 per cent on all salaries, wages, and other income.[3] No exemptions to this tax are stated, and hence it appears that practically everyone with earnings or income must pay the tax.

c. Money specially appropriated by Parliament to make up the amount by which the earmarked income taxes fall short of the requirements.

2. Since practically all salaries, wages, and other income are taxed, there is no such eligibility requirements as service in covered employment, duration of coverage, or number of contributions paid. The only persons excluded are immigrants who have not lived in the country long enough to attain full rights under the system.

3. All major hazards are covered.

The system provides money benefits for: old age, widows, orphans, families, invalids, miners (the hazardous industry), sickness, war injuries to civilians, unemployment, emergency (a discretionary category that permits provision for those in need who cannot qualify under one of the specific categories). Provisions for medical care are made through universally available health benefits administered by the Health Department.

There are five general classes of health benefits provided for in the act: medical benefits, pharmaceutical benefits, hospital benefits, maternity benefits, and such supplementary benefits as are deemed necessary to insure the effective operation of the aforementioned benefits or otherwise to maintain the public health.[4]

[3] The contribution precisely is "1d. for every sum of 1s. 8d. or part thereof of salaries, wages, and other income, including the income of companies." *Year-Book, 1943*, p. 393.
[4] New Zealand Department of Health, *Health Benefits* (1943), p. 1.

4. Except for the universal health benefits, the system is designed primarily to prevent want. Four features are important in this respect:

a. The monetary benefits are directly related to the number and the type of persons for whom provision must be made. They are not proportionately related to the earnings, or past earnings, of the wage earner.

b. The maximum benefits in all cases appear to be not materially above a reasonably high minimum health and decency standard.[5]

c. Except for the universal superannuation system which is now in operation but will not pay full benefits (84£ 10s. a year)[6] until the fiscal year 1970, all monetary benefits are paid only to persons whose available resources are below amounts specified in the law.

d. The law permits the payment of benefits to persons who have certain other specified resources within limited amounts; but in general the amount of benefit granted is only enough to bring the resources to a maximum prescribed by law with other resources counted.

5. The system furnishes in part an illustration of a modern means test system operated under the following conditions:

a. With special earmarked taxes that according to the latest figures supplied three quarters of the requisite funds. The remaining quarter was supplied by Parliament from general revenues.

b. With the law defining in reasonably precise terms the conditions under which benefits will be granted, the amount of benefits to be paid, and what resources a person may have and in what amount without being ineligible for any benefit, or with being eligible for only a reduced benefit.

c. With requirements that every person 16 years of age or over shall register annually so that the administrators have the necessary data for everyone, whether in need or not.

---

[5] We have not attempted to determine exactly what level of living would be permitted by the benefits provided under the system.

[6] The pamphlet, p. 10.

6. Except for universal superannuation the system started under a fairly close approach to full load in that there was no progressive increase of benefits and that no past payments of contributions were necessary for eligibility. The present generation of taxpayers is paying for those now in need. It is not, except for universal superannuation, making promises for the future to be paid for by the children and the grandchildren. The annual benefit under universal superannuation, when it reaches its maximum in the fiscal year 1970–71, is sufficiently small so that it does not present the financial difficulties inherent in promising big benefits to be paid in the future. It will, moreover, gradually and largely replace the present old-age means test benefit. The increase in cost will thus be solely with respect to old-age protection and will represent the difference between a no-means test benefit and a means test benefit.

With this outline as background, we shall proceed to take up each of the six major features discussed in it in such detail as seems desirable for bringing out the contrasts with the situation in the United States.

FINANCING OF THE SYSTEM

The first point noted in the summary was that employers as such pay no social security taxes. They pay as individuals on their own income for social security, and they pay general taxes[7] that go in part to make up the deficit resulting from the fact that the earmarked special tax is not large enough to carry the full load. Certain implications of this system deserve comment.

The social security income tax offers the employer no special

---

[7] For data regarding the tax system of New Zealand see the *Year-Book 1943*, p. 363. The total tax receipts of the Consolidated Fund in the fiscal year 1939, the last prewar year, were 32.3 million pounds sterling. Of this sum, income taxes and death duties, the two taxes commonly regarded as based on capacity to pay, produced 11.1 millions or 34.4 per cent. Taxes generally regarded as bearing directly on consumers, the customs revenues, the sales tax, and the beer duty combined produced 15.3 millions or 47.4 per cent of the total. Thus in New Zealand in 1939 a very considerable part of the contribution from the Consolidated Fund to the Social Security Fund must have fallen directly on the consumers. Many commodities, including the most important food stuffs, were excluded from the 5 per cent sales tax in effect in 1939 which was paid once, generally when the goods passed to the retailer. Thus persons who buy mainly necessities produced in New Zealand may escape some of the taxes on consumers, used directly for the Consolidated Fund and indirectly for the Social Security Fund.

inducement to cut his pay roll or to substitute machines for men. The size of his pay roll has nothing to do with the amount he has to pay toward social security. How much he will have to pay depends on his income or his profits, rather than on how many men he has hired. If times are bad, he does not have a direct incentive to dismiss people to reduce his tax. If he is losing money instead of making it, he may not have to pay any social security tax.

The rate of the special social security income tax is not graduated progressively in accordance with capacity to pay. It is roughly one shilling to the pound (5 per cent) for all. Even the poor have to pay it. Graduation, however, comes in on the benefit side. The poor person who has to pay the tax receives far more in benefits than he pays in tax, whereas the well-to-do, paying the same rate, may get nothing in benefits beyond medical care and a small individual superannuation payment if he lives to the retirement age.

The merit of the system is that every earner contributes, whether he is an employer, an employee, or a person working on his own account, and whether he is in agriculture, trade, transportation, manufacturing, or mining. If contributions enable the beneficiary to feel that the benefits are something which he or the wage earner upon whom he depends has secured as a right by virtue of payments, then the New Zealand system will permit practically everyone to have that feeling.

The position the general treasury occupies in the financial structure deserves special emphasis. It supplies the sum needed annually to balance the Social Security Fund so that the resources of the fund will meet the claims against it. To a very considerable extent, the volume of the claims will depend on the current situation with respect to employment. Under a means test system such as that in New Zealand, unemployment will not only increase the direct expenditures for unemployment benefits, but it will tend indirectly to increase the costs of several of the other benefits. It is therefore worth while to consider how the New Zealand system will operate with respect to employment.

In a period of full employment the returns from the 5 per cent tax on salaries, wages, and other income will be relatively high, and the demands for unemployment benefits will be relatively low. The drain on the general treasury or the Consolidated Fund will then be at its low point. In the event of a business recession receipts from the social security income tax will fall, demands for unemployment benefits will increase, and the balance to be paid from the general treasury will rise.

In the face of a recession the government and Parliament have the opportunity to adjust their fiscal policy to the situation as they deem best. If the general treasury has a surplus, they can perhaps meet the added drain without special financial action. If the treasury cannot stand it, their alternatives are to increase taxes, to borrow, or to use a combination of the two. If they borrow because of unemployment, short-term borrowing would be appropriate. By the wise use of short-term borrowing, the officials could keep general taxes relatively low in bad times and raise them in good times to pay off the debt incurred for unemployment insurance.

To get the significance of this arrangement, it may be contrasted with the provisions of the state unemployment systems in many of our states. In good times we build a reserve. When a recession comes, the demand for benefits increases, receipts from the pay-roll tax diminish, and the reserves dwindle and may even disappear. If the reserves completely disappear, we face the issue when and how the government shall come to the rescue of those insured who cannot get benefits from a bankrupt fund. In many of the states, moreover, the laws provide that as the funds grow weaker the rate of the pay-roll tax shall be increased. The hard-pressed employer in a substantial recession must either reduce his pay roll or pay a bigger tax, at a moment when everyone wants him to continue to give maximum possible employment.

To diminish the possibility of misunderstanding, it should be repeated that the New Zealand unemployment benefit includes a means test, that its amount depends on the number and type of persons to be provided for, that it does not give more than a reasonable minimum for each person to be cared for, and that it does not give more than enough to bring the individuals up to a minimum after exhaustion of such of their reserves as are not allowed. On the other hand, the system does not limit payments to a specified maximum number of weeks and leaves entirely open the question of what is to be done if the worker exhausts his benefits under the unemployment insurance system. New Zealand insures against want and does not insure to an individual a certain fraction of his earnings for a limited period of time. To commend having the general treasury make up the balance under such a system does not mean one would contend that the general treasury should stand behind a system that bases benefits on past earnings without any means test.

UNIVERSALITY OF COVERAGE

The basic principle of the New Zealand system is to insure everyone against want under a single integrated and comprehensive plan. This purpose is achieved by (1) requiring everyone 16 years of age or over to register and to pay or have paid in his behalf a registration fee; and (2) taxing every person receiving salaries, wages, or other income 5 per cent of that income. It is difficult to conceive of a device that would give more nearly universal coverage.

New Zealand has almost completely eliminated from its system the concepts of private voluntary insurance. There are no such concepts as "currently insured" and "fully insured" and in unemployment insurance of "base year," "benefit year," and "duration of benefits." The framers of the New Zealand act were thinking in terms of insuring the people against want not in terms of insuring a part of income without reference to the number of dependents for whom provision has to be made.

Attention should be called to the absence of distinctions among industries and occupations. Agriculture and domestic service are included on equal terms with manufacturing, mining, transportation, and trade. An individual can move from one to another, seasonally, temporarily or permanently, without any danger of lapses, forfeitures, or loss of rights.

New Zealand has, however, established residence requirements. They are different for the different benefits and will be taken up under each benefit. Here it will only be noted that the Dominion has not seen fit to tax its people to pay old-age benefits to persons who have fairly recently entered the country. This issue is in reality part of the question of immigration restriction and control and does not go to the essentials of the arrangements of the system. A long residence requirement diminishes the cost of the system and may mean that a person over 65 will be in need but will not be eligible for an old-age benefit. By increasing the cost, the residence requirement can be reduced. By introducing lower residence requirements for disability than for old age, the elderly disabled person can be provided for, even if he has not resided in the country a sufficient time to be eligible for an old-age benefit, without the necessity of proving disability. Thus residence requirements are separate and do not go to the heart of the system as do requirements that a person must have served in a covered industry or occupation for a specified length of time.

All major hazards covered. In the summary of the New Zealand system given at the beginning of the chapter, the hazards covered were listed. In this more detailed discussion we shall take up first emergency, as it reflects most clearly the intention of the framers of the act to cover all major hazards. Regarding emergency benefits, the official publication reads:

An emergency benefit may be granted by the Commission on the grounds of hardship to any person who by reason of age, physical or mental disability, domestic circumstances, or any other reason is unable to earn a sufficient livelihood for himself and dependents and is unable to fully qualify for any other monetary benefit under Part II of the Social Security Act, 1938.

The amount of an emergency benefit is at the discretion of the Commission, but is usually as nearly as possible equal to that payable for the type of benefit for which the applicant most nearly qualifies.[8]

OLD-AGE BENEFITS

Old-age benefits, as previously noted, are of two classes, universal superannuation and age benefits.[9]

[8] The pamphlet, p. 24.

[9] In New Zealand, as in the United States and Britain, provision for the old-age pro-

Universal superannuation benefit. The universal superannuation benefit can be treated in brief compass, because of its extreme simplicity. In and after the fiscal year 1970-71, each person who satisfies the residence requirements and has met his obligations under the Social Security Act will, on attaining the age of 65 years, be entitled, regardless of his means, to a flat-rate benefit of £84 10s. a year. From that year on there will be no means test whatever with respect to persons 65 years of age or over. Persons 60 or over but under 65 will still be eligible for old-age benefits, subject to the means test.

Presumably for financial reasons the government did not start no-means test, universal, superannuation benefits immediately at full scale. The system provided for an initial benefit in the fiscal year 1940-41 of £10. The benefit is to be increased by £2 10s. each year until 1970-71 when it reaches the maximum of £84 10s.

With the exception of the residence requirements these two paragraphs give all the essential facts regarding this benefit. The reasons for this simplicity are: (1) the use of the flat-rate uniform benefit, and (2) financing through universal earmarked taxes that eliminate all the elaborate provisions regarding coverage, currently insured, and fully insured.

---

tection of many workers is made through employers' retirement systems, public or private. New Zealand has gone further than the United States or any of its states in governmental ownership and operation. It has, moreover, a largely centralized government. As a result, many workers in New Zealand have substantial protection for their old age under governmental retirement systems in addition to that provided under the general social security system.

The British and the New Zealand systems, with flat and relatively low old-age benefits, permit and even facilitate the continuation and the development of contributory employer retirement systems, public and private. The general system simplifies the problem of making satisfactory provision for low-paid workers under a private or a state or municipal retirement system.

One of the residents of New Zealand with whom the writer discussed the system at some length said that the chief complaint against it arose from persons adequately covered by existing employers' systems operated on a contributory basis. The 5 per cent general income tax gave them no substantial benefits in so far as the means test is used. The universal superannuation benefit, even when it reaches it maximum of £84 10s., will be an inadequate return for an annual payment of 5 per cent of income. The New Zealand system makes clear to persons in the middle- and upper-income brackets that they must supply the purchasing power that is to give protection to persons in the lower brackets.

The universal superannuation benefit is the only point at which New Zealand in supplying benefits other than medical services for individuals departs from the basic principle of preventing want and attempts some deliberate redistribuion of income among the people without reference to need. That statement perhaps requires a little elaboration.

Persons who are in immediate need patently cannot supply that need from their own resources because they do not have the resources. To relieve their want, money has to be taken from those who have to give to those who have not. Except for the universal superannuation benefit, the New Zealand system takes from the taxpayers only so much as is required to relieve need as need is measured under its laws. In one sense this constitutes a redistribution of earnings and income through governmental action, but it is done in applying the old principle of government in English-speaking countries, that relieving want at public expense is a function of the state. A state does not depart from this principle until it takes money from the taxpayers to give to persons who are not in need for the purpose of making sure they shall never be in need. To give effect to this policy of a partial redistribution of wealth through governmental action, the state must take from its financially more successful citizens to give to its financially less successful citizens. Although in New Zealand the financially successful citizens get benefits from universal superannuation, they have to pay more in taxes than they receive in benefits. The social security system is not in and of itself a producer of needed goods and services; it does not make anything; it is a redistribution of the salary, wages, and income of the taxpayers.

The residence qualifications for the universal superannuation benefits and for age benefits are the same. They read as follows:

An applicant who was a resident of New Zealand on 15th March, 1938, is required to have resided continuously in the Dominion for the *ten* years immediately preceding the date of application, subject to an aggregate allowance of *one* year for absence during that period and a further allowance of six months' absence for every year of residence in excess of *ten* years. Where the absence during the *ten* years has exceeded *one* year, however, the applicant must not have been outside

New Zealand at any time during the period of twelve months immediately preceding the date of his application.[10]

An applicant who was *not* a resident of New Zealand on 15th March, 1938, is required to have resided continuously in the Dominion for the *twenty* years immediately preceding the date of application, subject to an aggregate allowance of *two* years for absence during that period and a further allowance of six months' absence for every year of residence in excess of *twenty* years. Where the absence during the *twenty* years has exceeded *two* years, however, the applicant must not have been outside New Zealand at any time during the twelve months immediately preceding the date of his application.[11]

The age benefit. As has been noted, all monetary benefits under the New Zealand system, excepting the universal superannuation benefit, are given on a means test basis. For each benefit a special schedule is used. We shall start our discussion of the age benefit with a detailed description of the provisions which determine whether or not an applicant who has arrived at age 60, the eligible age, is entitled to a benefit, and if he is, the amount of the benefit he may receive.

On page 527 we reproduce from the pamphlet (page 13) a table giving the amount of the age benefits and the conditions with respect to income on which they are payable.

The first point to be noted is that applicants are divided into three classes: (1) single, widowed, divorced, or legally separated persons, (2) married persons (husband or wife not eligible), and (3) married persons (both eligible).

The last column of the table shows that for a single person the total of benefit and allowable income is £136 10s. Thus if a

[10] The pamphlet, p. 10.

[11] The pamphlet, p. 11. In connection with these provisions the following paragraph is of interest:

"Legislation has been passed to enable a reciprocal arrangement to be made between the Dominion of New Zealand and the Commonwealth of Australia to enable age-benefits and invalids' benefits to be paid where the applicant has been resident in both of these countries. For the purposes of this arrangement, residence in Australia may be treated as residence in New Zealand for the purposes of payment of a reciprocal age-benefit or invalid's benefit. The actual rates of benefit cannot be set out in detail, as the more restrictive provisions of the legislation of either country operate.

"Any person who is debarred from receiving an age-benefit or invalid's benefit merely because of residence outside New Zealand and such residence was in the Commonwealth may now qualify. Inquiries should be addressed to the local representative of the Social Security Department." (p. 29.)

single person aged 60 or over has an income of his own of that amount or more, he is ineligible to receive an age benefit. The single person who has no income whatsoever is entitled to the maximum benefit allowable under the law, £84 10s. yearly, as shown in the second column of the table.

AGE BENEFITS

Applicant	Basic Rate		Allowable Income		Total of Benefit and Allowable Income	
	Weekly	Yearly	Weekly	Yearly	Weekly	Yearly
	£ s. d.	£ s. d.	£ s. d.	£ s. d.	£ s. d.	£ s. d.
Single, widowed, divorced, or legally separated persons..	1 12 6	84 10 0	1 0 0	52 0 0	2 12 6	136 10 0
Married persons (husband or wife not eligible)...........	1 12 6	84 10 0	2 12 6	136 10 0	4 5 0	221 0 0
Married persons (both eligible).....	1 12 6 (each)	84 10 0 (each)	1 0 0	52 0 0	4 5 0	221 0 0

A common criticism of a means test system is that it discourages thrift; a person will not save because savings will reduce or remove free benefits. As we shall point out in the course of this discussion, New Zealand has several devices to lessen the force of their objection. The one with which we are here concerned is allowable income, shown in the middle columns of the table. The law permits the single person to have not to exceed £52 of personal income a year without suffering any loss of benefit. Thus for single persons with less than £52 of personal income, the total income in old age is £84 10s. of age benefit *plus the full amount of such personal income as he has.*

For the single person who has a personal income of more than £52 but less than the £136 10s., the amount of benefit is reduced by £1 per annum for every pound of income in excess of the allowable income. To phrase it another way, each single person in the personal income group £52 to £136 10s. is given sufficient benefit to bring his total to the maximum of £136 10s.

The New Zealand system considers two elements in the definition of income: (1) income in the ordinary sense and (2) accumulated property. All income from property whatever its nature is counted as income. Earnings of old people are counted if they remain on benefit. If their earnings are excessive, however, they may surrender their benefits while thus earning and apply for reinstatement immediately the employment ceases. Earnings received while the single person or a married couple are off benefit are not taken into account. Thus the system offers an inducement for old people to work if and when an opportunity is present to earn more than they could get by remaining on benefit. The New Zealand Social Security Office maintains local offices so that individual cases can be handled with dispatch and without putting beneficiaries to any serious inconvenience.

The New Zealand system considers also the accumulated property of the applicant. For each £10 of net accumulated property it deducts £1 from the annual benefit. In determining *net* no account is taken of (1) the home and furniture, (2) any interest in land or mortgages on land, (3) the value of any interest in an annuity or in an unmatured life insurance, and (4) the first £500 of other accumulated property.

Earnings from property, as noted above, are counted as income. If an applicant receives income from accumulated property, that property is not included in the net accumulated property. There is a provision, however, that permits an applicant to elect to have the deduction made on the basis either of the income from the property or the value of the property, whichever may be to his advantage.

In dealing with the accumulated property of a husband or a wife the law assumes that the couple are common owners of the property and for the purposes of the age benefit each upon applying for it is to be assumed to own half of it. For example, a married couple having a total of cash in bank of £1,000 (husband £700, wife £300) would each be deemed to have accumulated property to the value of £500, while the net accumulated property after the deduction of the allowance of £500 would be nil, permitting a maximum benefit being paid in each case.[12]

To return to the two classes of married persons in the table on

12 The pamphlet, p. 13.

page 527, it will be noted that the married couple with one eligible and the married couple with both eligible are entitled to the same total of benefit and allowable income, £221 yearly. Each eligible married person is likewise entitled to the same individual benefit, £84 10s. Thus where both are eligible, the couple together may draw £169 as a maximum benefit, whereas when only one is eligible the couple gets only £84 10s. as a maximum. The allowable income in each case is the difference between the maximum benefit payable and the total of benefits and allowable income. As the table shows, the allowable income is £136 for the couple with one eligible member and £52 for the couple with both eligible. If personal income exceeds the allowable, the amount of benefit is reduced by £1 for each full pound of excess income. In the case of the couple with both members eligible 10s. of the reduction is taken from the man's benefit and 10s. from the woman's benefit.

Each individual upon arriving at age 60 and not possessed of any income or net accumulated property is entitled to the same age benefit, £84 10s., regardless of marital status. Differences arise from differences in marital status and allowable income.

Acceptance of the doctrine that two can live cheaper than one is suggested by the fact that the total of benefit and allowable income for the single, widowed, divorced, and separated, £136 10s., is more than half the allowance for the married couple, £221.

In connection with this use of income and net accumulated property as the means test to determine eligibility and the amount of benefit, attention should be called to the fact that contributions are based on a system of practically universal income taxes and annual or in the case of adult males quarterly registration of workers. The system thus produces most of the data for the application of the means test that has been adopted.

Two discretionary features of the age benefit deserve special comment. Under our system of old-age and survivors insurance, it will be recalled, the wife of a beneficiary does not become eligible for a benefit until she herself has attained the age of 65, regardless of her physical and mental condition. In New Zealand she like her husband automatically becomes eligible upon arriving at the age of 60. If the wife is under 60 and is not qualified to receive a benefit in her own right, the basic rate for the husband may in the discretion of the Commission be increased by an amount not exceeding 10s. 6d. a week or £27 6s. per annum, provided that the total income of the husband and wife, plus any benefit payable, does not exceed £221 per annum. Thus the Commission has discretionary authority to provide from the Social Security Fund for cases in which the wife has not attained the eligible age and is in need.

If a beneficiary of the old-age system has a dependent child under 16 years of age, the Commission may in its discretion increase the benefit by £27 6s. per annum for each such dependent child, with a maximum in any one case of £260 a year.

Under the American system of aid to dependent children, several of the states have insisted that the mother or other relative who is to have the custody of the child must be a person deemed to be a suitable guardian. Under our old-age and survivors insurance system, on the other hand, payments are made regardless of the character and behavior of the beneficiary, his wife, or his widow. A man does not lose his rights if he has failed to support his wife or his children.

New Zealand requires that applicants for old-age benefits shall have fulfilled their obligations to their families. The official pamphlet (page 12) says:

A male applicant must not for a period of six months or more during the period of five years immediately preceding the date of his application have deserted his wife or wilfully failed to have provided her with adequate maintenance or wilfully failed to have maintained any child or children under the age of sixteen years whom he was legally liable to maintain.

In the case of a married woman, she must not during a similar period have deserted her husband or any of her children under the age of sixteen years.

The applicant must be of good moral character and sober habits.

Under the New Zealand system there is no requirement that a child shall contribute to the support of a father or mother whose income or accumulated property is sufficiently low to make that parent eligible for a benefit. In several of our American states, the means test provisions applicable in old-age assistance require children to support their aged parents. The New Zealand system of financing social insurance makes practically all persons with income contribute to the fund from which elderly persons and others with resources below the established levels are supported. Children with income are contributing to the fund, and their parents if eligible for benefit are drawing from that fund. There is no occasion to make the children contribute to the support of their own parents, for they are already paying 5 per cent of their income to the Social Security Fund and in addition may be contributing to the fund through general taxes.

Similarly under the New Zealand plan, the fact that the heirs may inherit accumulated and exempt property from a deceased beneficiary of the fund does not have the same significance as it does in our old-age assistance program. The New Zealand children of parent beneficiaries if they have income, are paying the social security income tax to help support the system. If they secure an income from inherited property, it increases the amount of tax they have to pay. If they themselves become victims of any of the hazards covered by the system, the income from the inherited property will be included in their income used to determine eligibility and the amount of their benefit. Inherited property will likewise be considered in arriving at the value of net accumulated property. If children inherit the exempted home and furniture and use it themselves as a residence and derive no income from it, their payments to the fund are not increased by that part of their inheritance. In several of our American states liens against a house and its furnishings are not enforced where children of small means need the house for their own use. It would seem as if children in New Zealand would profit somewhat by inheriting a house and furnishings if they have need of them.[13]

---

[13] In 1943 in New Zealand a wife paid no succession duty on an inheritance of £5,000 or under and a child on an inheritance of £500 or under. There was also an estate duty on estates of £200 or over. These taxes are progressive. Thus a widow or child on inheriting property may have to pay a tax into the Consolidated Fund from which in part the Social Security Fund is financed. *Year-Book 1943*, p. 369.

In this discussion it has been noted that the New Zealand maximum old-age benefit is £84 10s. a year and that the total of benefit and allowable income is £136 10s. for single beneficiaries and £221 for married couples. We have not attempted the difficult and time-consuming study which would be required to determine the actual purchasing power of these sums. On a purely monetary exchange basis the New Zealand pound was worth in United States dollars about $3.55 in 1939, $3.06 in 1940, and $3.23 in 1941. The average for these three years would be about $3.30. If we use $3.30, the maximum old-age benefit would be about $280 for a single person and $560 for a married couple and the total of benefit and allowable income $450 for a single person and $730 for married couples.

WIDOWS' BENEFITS

The widows' benefits in New Zealand are of entirely different scope than widows' benefits under O.A.S.I. in the United States. The dominion system is based more on the family as a unit than on the individual. The widows' benefits are available for the maintenance of: (a) widows with children under 16 years of age, (b) the children under 16 years of age of such a widow, (c) certain widows without dependent children, (d) wives with children under 16 who have been deserted by their husbands and have taken proceedings under the Destitute Persons Act, 1910, for maintenance, (e) wives of mental patients who are the subject of reception orders or are inmates of mental hospitals as voluntary boarders, (f) the children under 16 years of age of a wife who comes under (d) or (e) above.

The table on page 533 shows the maximum benefit and allowable income for widows' benefits.

Because O.A.S.I. does not give a benefit to widows of covered workers until they have reached the age of 65 unless they have eligible children, we shall first direct our attention to what New Zealand does for such widows. The official pamphlet contains the following provisions.[14]

[14] The pamphlet, pp. 15–16.

Number of Children	Maximum Benefit per Annum			Limit of Income and Benefit per Annum		
	£	s.	d.	£	s.	d.
Widow with one child................	105	6	0	183	6	0
Widow with two children.............	132	12	0	210	12	0
Widow with three children...........	159	18	0	237	18	0
Widow with four children............	187	4	0	265	4	0
Widow with five children............	214	10	0	292	10	0
Widow with six children.............	241	16	0	319	16	0
Widow with seven children or more.......	260	0	0	338	0	0
Widow without children.............	65	0	0	117	0	0

[a] The pamphlet, p. 15.

When the youngest child of a widow in receipt of benefit reaches the disqualifying age of sixteen years the benefit may be continued to the widow, in her own right, at the rate applicable to widows without dependent children, provided a period of fifteen years has elapsed since the date of marriage.

Any widow who has been the mother of children, although she may have never received a benefit in respect of her children, may be granted a benefit at the rate applicable to widows without dependent children, so long as the duration of her marriage was not less than fifteen years or, if less than fifteen years, the total period of the marriage and the subsequent period she had the care and control of at least one of her children under sixteen years was not less than fifteen years.

In the following circumstances widows who have never had children can qualify for benefit:

(a) Every widow who after being married for five years became a a widow after she reached fifty years of age;

(b) Every widow who is not less than fifty years of age and who became a widow after she reached age forty years. In addition, she must have been married for a period of ten years and a period of at least fifteen years must have passed since the date of her marriage.

Attention must be called to the weight which the New Zealand system attaches to the age of the woman when she became a widow and inferentially to the chances that she can earn her own living. It must be repeated that the benefits are so small and the provisions regarding earnings are such that the widows, especially those without children, have a real incentive to earn if they can.

In the preceding section the requirement that men support their wives was noted. The provision with respect to deserted wives who apply for a widow's benefit is significant in connection with enforcing family responsibilities.

As long as a wife referred to in (a) above has made application to the Court for an order under the Destitute Persons Act, 1910, the Commission may pay a benefit during desertion, but any maintenance paid by the husband to the applicant is taken into account by the Commission as a part of the benefit. The Department may take proceedings against the husband in connection with a maintenance order or to enforce the terms of the order.[15]

The definition of a child, the residence requirements for eligibility, and the requirements regarding the character of the widow read:

The term "child" includes a stepchild or a child legally adopted during the lifetime of the husband of the applicant. Any child being maintained by the applicant and who was at any time maintained by the husband of the applicant may also be included.

In the case of widows with children, the benefit is payable in respect of children:

(a) Born in New Zealand;
(b) Born out of New Zealand while the mother was only temporarily absent;
(c) Born out of New Zealand where both the parents have resided in New Zealand for three years immediately preceding the date of the father's death or of his desertion of the mother or of his admission to a mental hospital.

For widows without children the residential qualification requires both the widow and her husband to have been resident in New Zealand for at least three years immediately prior to the husband's death.

The widow must be of good moral character and sober habits, and any amount payable in respect of children must be properly used for their benefit.

Widows' benefits, including any portion payable in respect of children, cease on remarriage.[16]

ORPHANS' BENEFITS

Under the national law in the United States orphans are provided for (a) under the aid to dependent children title of the

[15] The same, p. 15.
[16] The same, p. 16.

Social Security Act provided the orphan is to live with a relative of the degree specified in that act, or (b) under O.A.S.I. provided one parent was currently insured or fully insured. Other orphans are provided for by the state or local authorities under general public assistance. The provisions regarding orphans' benefits in New Zealand are:

An orphan's benefit is payable in respect of any orphan born in New Zealand or whose last surviving parent lived in New Zealand for the three years before his or her death, provided the child is not maintained in a State institution.

Application for benefit may be lodged by any person who has the care and control of the orphan.

Any stepchild or adopted child whose parent and step-parent or whose adoptive parents are both deceased may be granted orphan's benefits.

The rate of orphan's benefit must not exceed 15s. 9d. a week, or £40 19s. per annum, and is reducible £1 for £1 in respect of any income received for the benefit of the orphan. The actual rate of benefit will be fixed by the Social Security Commission, having regard to any income or property of the orphan and any special circumstances.

An orphan's benefit ceases to be payable when the orphan reaches the age of sixteen years.

Payment of benefit will be made to the foster-parent or to any other person who has the care and control of the orphan for the time being.

This class of benefit is payable in monthly instalments and is not payable for any period of absence from New Zealand.[17]

FAMILY BENEFIT

In dealing with families in need, two types of cases cause considerable difficulty.

1. Neither the father nor the mother is the victim of any one of the recognized major hazards. They lack ability to make a living. They do not earn very much as wage workers because they are not worth very much, and they do not produce very much as subsistence farmers or gardeners because they lack knowledge, skill, managerial ability and drive. They have one or more children for whom they make inadequate provision.

2. The father and mother are reasonably industrious, but neither has the capacity to rise above the lowest wage brackets. Were they the parents of only one or two children they could

---

[17] The same, p. 17.

get along, but they are not capable of supporting a large family. No amount which the father and mother could earn in full normal employment will sustain the family on a satisfactory basis.

In the United States little formal provision has been made for families of these two types. They may get some help from relatives, neighbors, the church, organized private philanthropy, or general public assistance. Not infrequently the aid is sporadic, often coming when the family encounters another emergency.

The British government, as we have seen, proposes to meet this type of case through the family allowances paid from the general treasury, without a means test, with respect to each child in the family, excepting the first. The assumption is that a wife and one child can be supported from the father's earnings.

New Zealand meets this problem through its family benefits, which are in fact benefits with respect to children. Perhaps the easiest way to explain this benefit is to start with the official table showing the amount of family benefit payable and the limit of income and benefits.

FAMILY BENEFITS[a]

Number of Children under Sixteen Years in Family	Maximum Benefit (Weekly)			Allowable Income (Weekly)			Limit of Income and Family Benefit (Weekly)		
	£	s.	d.	£	s.	d.	£	s.	d.
1.........	0	7	6	5	5	0	5	12	6
2.........	0	15	0	5	5	0	6	0	0
3.........	1	2	6	5	5	0	6	7	6
4.........	1	10	0	5	5	0	6	15	0
5.........	1	17	6	5	5	0	7	2	6
6.........	2	5	0	5	5	0	7	10	0
7.........	2	12	6	5	5	0	7	17	6
8	3	0	0	5	5	0	8	5	0
9.........	3	7	6	5	5	0	8	12	6
10.........	3	15	0	5	5	0	9	0	0

[a] The pamphlet, p. 17.

The family with one child under 16 and the maximum allowable income of £5 5s. a week, is granted a family benefit with respect to the child of 7s. 6d., bringing the total available to £5 12s. 6d. If the father of the family gets a raise of 3s. a week the family benefit is cut by 3s. and the total available for the family remains the same. If another raise adds 5s. a week more to his income, the family benefit ceases.

If a family has 10 children under 16 years of age and if the income is £5 5s., the family will receive the maximum benefit with respect to the children £3 15s. and will have available £9 a week. As the father's earnings or other resources improve, the benefit is reduced shilling for shilling until it completely disappears when the family income exclusive of the benefit reaches £9.

If the actual income of the family is less than the allowable income £5 5s., the family gets no more than the maximum benefit, and its total resources fall below the figures shown in the last column of the table. Should the family be entirely without income of its own, the maximum children's benefit would be all that was available unless the family qualified under some other category or the Commission exercised its discretionary emergency powers.

The following general provisions are significant.

The term "children" includes stepchildren and children adopted prior to any application for family benefit, but does not include

(a) Any child who has attained the age of sixteen years:

(b) Any child who is not in fact maintained as a member of the family of the applicant:

(c) Any child in respect of whom any other benefit is payable under Part II of the Act.

The Commission may also regard as a member of the applicant's family any child, who, though not a child of the applicant, is being maintained as a member of the family.

A benefit may be continued in respect of any child beyond the age of sixteen years if such child is totally incapacitated from earning a living by reason of some physical or mental defect.

The residential qualification is permanent residence in New Zealand for the twelve months immediately prior to the date of application.

The children in respect of whom any application for family benefit is made must be born in New Zealand or have resided there permanently for the twelve months immediately preceding the date of application.

The applicant is required to be of good moral character and sober habits.

It is an essential condition of the granting of a family benefit that the amount received must be expended on the maintenance or education of the children concerned.[18]

INVALIDS' BENEFIT

In the United States, it may be recalled, the Social Security Act makes a grant to the states which adopt an approved program for aid to the needy blind. The federal civil service system and the railroad retirement system both make some provision for the disabled. If permanent disability results from an industrial accident or from occupational disease, benefits may be paid under workmen's compensation. O.A.S.I. does not include a disability benefit. Under that system a person who is forced to leave covered employment because of disability before he has attained the fully insured status may forfeit his own contributions unless (a) he has attained the status of currently insured and (b) dies before the extended insurance resulting from that status expires. If he has acquired fully insured status, his benefits do not begin until he has attained the retirement age of 65. Most disabled persons in the United States if in need are dependent upon general public assistance unless their disability results from blindness.

By way of comparison a selected portion of the text of the official New Zealand pamphlet may be of interest.

An applicant for invalids' benefit must be not less than sixteen years of age and must not be qualified to receive an age-benefit. He must be permanently incapacitated for work through accident, illness, or congenital defect, or be totally blind, and the incapacity for which benefit is claimed must not be self-inflicted or self-induced.

To qualify for a benefit the applicant must have resided continuously in New Zealand for not less than ten years immediately preceding the date of application. An aggregate allowance of one year for absence is permitted, plus a further allowance of one month for every year of residence in excess of ten years. Where the absence during the ten years has exceeded one year, however, the applicant must not have been outside New Zealand during the period of twelve months immediately preceding the date of application.

Where an application for benefit on account of total blindness is lodged any absence from New Zealand for the purpose of vocational

[18] The same, p. 18.

training or for treatment in respect of the applicant's eyes is not taken into consideration in determining the applicant's residential qualifications.

If the application is in respect of any other class of disablement any absence from New Zealand for the purpose of obtaining any special surgical treatment is not taken into consideration if the Commission is satisfied that there were good and sufficient reasons for leaving New Zealand to obtain such special treatment.

. . . .

The following table shows the rates of benefit and allowable income:

Class of Person	Rate of Benefit		Allowable Income	
	Weekly	Yearly	Weekly	Yearly
	£ s. d.	£ s. d.	£ s. d.	£
Single person under twenty-one years..	1 2 6	58 10 0	1 0 0	52
Married man or widower with dependent children:				
Beneficiary......................	1 12 6	84 10 0	1 10 0	78
Wife (where applicable)............	0 10 6	27 6 0	..	..
For each child...................	0 10 6	27 6 0	..	..
Married woman...................	1 12 6	84 10 0	2 0 0	104
All other persons.................	1 12 6	84 10 0	1 0 0	52

Where the applicant is a married woman and by reason of incapacity necessary nursing or domestic assistance is required to be paid for, the Commission, in its discretion, may increase the rate of any benefit which may have been reduced on account of income or property to an amount not exceeding £84 10s. a year, but so that the total income of the applicant and her husband, including the benefit, does not exceed £5 2s. 6d. a week.

If the benefit is payable in respect of the invalid and his wife and/or family a grant will not be made in excess of a maximum of £5 a week or £260 per annum.

In the assessment of the income of a totally blind person personal earnings up to £3 a week, or £156 per annum, are not taken into account. By way of addition to his benefit his earnings for the year will be subsidized to the extent of 25 per cent so long as the total income, including earnings and benefit, does not exceed £4 12s. 6d. a week, or £240 10s. per annum.

The qualifications in respect of property are the same as those applicable to age-benefits.

. . . .

In the case of any person under twenty-one years of age who is in receipt of an invalid's benefit on account of blindness and who is capable of being trained in any occupation, the Commission may wholly or partly suspend payment of the benefit if the beneficiary refuses, without sufficient cause, to undertake such training when called upon so to do.

Provision is made for medical examination, where necessary, to determine the extent of incapacity.

In the event of any application being declined on the grounds that the applicant is not totally blind or is not permanently incapacitated for work, he has the right of appeal to a Board of three medical practitioners nominated by the Commission. The right of appeal must be exercised within a period of three months after the decision of the Commission has been communicated to the applicant.[19]

MINERS' BENEFITS

The following quotation from the official pamphlet describes the miners' benefits.

To qualify for miners' benefit an applicant must have contracted miners' phthisis while engaged as a miner in New Zealand, and must thereby be permanently and seriously incapacitated for work. Any person who, while engaged as a miner in New Zealand, has contracted any other occupational disease associated with mining, or heart-disease, and is thereby permanently and totally incapacitated for work, may also qualify for a miner's benefit.

The term "miners' phthisis" means pneumoconiosis, and includes tuberculosis of the lungs and any other disease of the respiratory organs commonly associated with or a sequel to pneumoconiosis.

An applicant for miner's benefit is required to have been employed as a miner in New Zealand for at least two and a half years in the aggregate and to have been residing continuously in New Zealand for not less than five years immediately preceding the date of application for benefit. Any absence, not exceeding six months in the aggregate, during the period of five years does not disqualify the applicant.

The applicant must be of good moral character and sober habits and during the period of five years immediately preceding the date of application must not have deserted or wilfully failed to provide for his wife and children.

The rates of miner's benefit are £1 12s. 6d. a week, or £84 10s. per annum, plus 10s. 6d. a week, or £27 6s. per annum, for a wife, and 10s. 6d. a week, or £27 6s. per annum, for each child under sixteen years of age. The maximum benefit payable in any one case is £5 a week, or £260 per annum.

[19] The same, pp. 18–20.

There is no reduction in benefit on account of the value of any property or other assets owned.

. . . .

Provision is made for medical examination where necessary to determine whether the applicant is permanently incapacitated for work, and the extent of such incapacity.

In the event of any application being declined on medical grounds, he has the right of appeal to a Board of three medical practitioners nominated by the Commission. The right of appeal must be exercised within a period of three months after the decision of the Commission has been communicated to the applicant.

On the death of a miner while in receipt of a benefit an amount, to be fixed by the Commission, may be paid towards the funeral expenses. Application for a funeral grant must be lodged within a period of twelve months after the date of death.

The widow of a miner who has died while in receipt of a benefit is entitled to receive during widowhood a benefit of £1 a week, or £52 per annum, without any reduction on account of income or property.[20]

SICKNESS BENEFITS

The New Zealand sickness benefits have, it is believed, no counterpart in the American public welfare system. In many localities, however, individuals or families in need as the result of illness may be given some aid from general public assistance funds. The New Zealand benefits are designed to compensate, at least in part, for loss of earnings resulting from sickness, provided the incapacity has lasted for more than seven days, unless the Commission exercises its discretionary authority. Again it may be simplest to quote from the official pamphlet.

Every person over the age of sixteen years who has resided in New Zealand for not less than twelve months is entitled to receive a sickness benefit if he is temporarily incapacitated for work through sickness or accident and has thereby suffered a loss of salary, wages, or other earnings.

Where a person is engaged in business on his own account and by reason of sickness or accident is obliged to employ a substitute during the period of incapacity, the remuneration paid to the substitute is regarded as loss of earnings.

A married woman is not entitled to receive a sickness benefit unless the Commission is satisfied that her husband is unable to maintain her.

[20] The same, pp. 20–21.

Sickness benefits are payable in accordance with the following scale:

	£	s.	d.
To applicants sixteen to twenty years without dependents.	0	10	6
To all other applicants..............................	1	0	0
In respect of the applicant's wife......................	0	15	0
In respect of each dependent child....................	0	10	6

A Week

Any applicant who is maintaining a home and who is not drawing a benefit in respect of a wife may receive a benefit at the same rate as for a wife in respect of any person who has the care of his home.

The maximum sickness benefit payable in any one case is £4 a week, but no benefit will be paid in excess of the actual amount lost by way of salary, wages, or other earnings.

. . . .

Every application for a sickness benefit is required to be supported by a medical certificate of temporary incapacity for work.

A sickness benefit is not payable for the first seven days of any period of incapacity. The Commission, having regard to any special circumstances, may, however, pay for the whole or part of the first seven days, as it thinks fit.

The Commission has power to reduce the rate of a sickness benefit having regard to any income received or property owned by the applicant.

An applicant who is in receipt of sick pay from a friendly society, or a like payment as the member of any other similar society approved by the Commission, may also receive a sickness benefit in respect of the same incapacity, but in no case must the total income from all sources exceed £5 a week.

A benefit is payable so long as the incapacity from sickness or accident continues, or until the beneficiary becomes entitled to receive some other benefit under the Social Security Act—e.g., invalids' benefit.[21]

The sickness benefit, it will be noted, does not necessarily make good the earnings lost. As in the case of other benefits, a specific amount is allowed with respect to the applicant himself and his wife and each dependent child. He may have lost much more than the amount given in benefits. On the other hand, if he has a large family, he cannot draw more in sickness benefits than he has lost in earnings.

The sickness benefits do not provide for the cost of medical care. Provisions for medical care are made under health services operated by the Department of Health.

[21] The same, pp. 22–23.

UNEMPLOYMENT BENEFITS

In sharp contrast with the provisions for unemployment insurance in our states and our railroad unemployment insurance system the official statement of the New Zealand unemployment benefits can be reproduced in full in less than two pages. It reads:

Every person over sixteen years of age who has resided in New Zealand for not less than twelve months is entitled to receive an unemployment benefit, if he is unemployed, is capable and willing to undertake suitable work, and has taken reasonable steps to secure suitable employment.

A married woman is not entitled to receive an unemployment benefit unless the Commission is satisfied that her husband is unable to maintain her.

Unemployment benefits are payable in accordance with the following scale:

	A Week		
	£	s.	d.
To applicants sixteen to twenty years without dependents.	0	10	6
To all other applicants.	1	0	0
In respect of the applicant's wife.	0	15	0
In respect of each dependent child.	0	10	6

The maximum unemployment benefit payable in any one case is £4 a week.

Any applicant who is maintaining a home and who is not drawing a benefit in respect of a wife may receive a benefit at the same rate as for a wife in respect of any person who has the care of his home.

The term "child" means a child under sixteen years of age, and includes a stepchild or a child legally adopted prior to the date of application for benefit. The Commission in its discretion, may regard as eligible for benefit any child who is not in fact the child of the applicant, but who is maintained by him and is dependent on him.

An unemployment benefit is not payable for the first seven days of any period of unemployment. The Commission, having regard to any special circumstances, may, however, pay for the whole or part of the first seven days, as it thinks fit.

The Commission has power to reduce the rate of an unemployment benefit having regard to any income received or property owned by the applicant, his wife, and dependent children. In no case is the total amount received from all sources, including benefit, to exceed £4 a week.

An unemployment beneficiary who becomes temporarily incapacitated for work through sickness or accident may be granted a sickness benefit in lieu of unemployment benefit, but may not receive both.

The Commission has power to postpone the commencement of an unemployment benefit for a period not exceeding six weeks if the applicant:

(a) Has become voluntarily unemployed without good and sufficient reason;

(b) Has lost his employment through misconduct as a worker;

(c) Has failed without good and sufficient reason to accept an offer of suitable employment;

(d) Has received from seasonal employment earnings sufficient for the maintenance of himself and family, notwithstanding a period of temporary unemployment.

The benefit is payable so long as the beneficiary is unemployed or unless he becomes eligible to receive another class of benefit—e.g., an age-benefit.

An unemployment benefit is payable by weekly instalments, but is not payable for any period the recipient is absent from New Zealand.[22]

Certain aspects of this system deserve comment. The unemployment benefit continues so long as the beneficiary is unemployed or unless he becomes eligible to receive another class of benefit. There is no limit on the duration of the benefit, such as twenty weeks. From the standpoint of practical politics in a democracy there is probably no question as to the solvency of the New Zealand unemployment insurance fund, for under the New Zealand system Parliament is expected to make up the difference between the special fund receipts and the total costs. As pointed out earlier in the present chapter, it can if necessary borrow for that purpose in a depression to avoid raising taxes and then increase taxes when employment is high.

The advantages of this system for men and women who become technologically unemployed in the later years of their working life can scarcely be over-stated. If the provisions they have made voluntarily prove inadequate, they can go on unemployment benefit and remain there until eligible for an old-age benefit, although the benefits are so low that they have a real incentive to get other work if they can. A man who has worked steadily for many years does not exhaust his right in

[22] The same, pp. 23–24.

some twenty weeks of unemployment. If he gets another job, temporary or seasonal, he does not have to work in it a specified length of time or until he has earned a specified amount before he is again eligible for unemployment insurance.

The amount of unemployment benefit depends on the number of persons dependent on the unemployed worker, but no family whatever its size, can draw more than £4 a week. The Commission need not pay the full benefit if the family has other income, and "in no case is the total amount received from all sources, including benefit, to exceed £4 a week." Nothing more clearly demonstrates than these provisions the fact that New Zealand insures against want and is not insuring either income or maintenance of the social and economic status attained by the insured. The employees are put on notice that if they want greater protection than this system affords, they must provide for it personally through voluntary action.

During the depression in the United States, one of the most serious problems was presented by youths who had finished their schooling and were eager to secure employment. Many of them could not find regular jobs. Under our system of unemployment insurance, they are not insured because to be insured they must get a job in a covered occupation, and remain in it long enough to attain eligibility. Under the New Zealand law these youth are eligible if they are over 16 years of age, if they are unemployed, if they are capable and willing to undertake suitable work, and if they have taken reasonable steps to secure suitable employment. To be sure, the youths 16 to 20 years old do not get very much in benefits, but they have something to put into the pool that will help pay the family bill.

The provisions regarding the married woman who works are simple. The assumption is that her husband is able to maintain her, and therefore she herself receives no unemployment benefit. But it is a rebuttable presumption. The Commission can allow her an unemployment benefit if it "is satisfied that her husband is unable to maintain her." If both she and her husband are unemployed, she may be allowed a benefit of

15 shillings a week as the wife of her husband, which is three fourths of the benefit she could be allowed as an unemployed individual. Her children, it is assumed, are provided for by their father, but again the Commission apparently has discretionary authority to provide for the children if as a matter of fact they are dependent on her. When she works she pays the same income tax on her earnings that all others pay. New Zealand treats the tax as a tax, and does not regard it as a contribution in the nature of an insurance premium.

WAR BENEFITS

New Zealand has tended to integrate war pensions with its social security system, but "war pensions and other similar pensions and allowances are paid out of the Consolidated Fund from general taxation." The war pension legislation is administered by the Secretary for War Pensions, who is an officer of the Social Security Department. The power to grant such pensions and allowances is vested in a War Pensions Board of four members, one of whom is a registered medical practitioner and another a representative of the members of the forces appointed on nomination of the Retirement Services Association Incorporated. No attempt will be made to go into detail with respect to war pensions. In general, the law prescribes the extent to which war pensions and other allowances are to be regarded as income under the social security system. The position appears to be that the security system is designed to insure against want, and that a person is not in want if he or she is in receipt of a war pension or allowance sufficient for maintenance. In some instances, however, a part of the pension or allowance is disregarded so that the beneficiary derives some slight advantage from it. The New Zealand taxpayers, however, are not required to pay for full war pensions and for full social security benefits for the same individual.

FINANCE AND COSTS

A table on page 547 taken from the *New Zealand Official Year-Book for 1943* gives the figures regarding the sources of

SOURCES OF SOCIAL SECURITY REVENUE IN NEW ZEALAND, FISCAL YEARS 1939–40, 1940–41, AND 1941–42[a]

(All money figures in thousands of pounds sterling)

Source of Revenue	1939–40		1940–41		1941–42	
	Amount	Percentage Distribution	Amount	Percentage Distribution	Amount	Percentage Distribution
TOTAL REVENUE	11,367	100.0	13,968	100.0	14,688	100.0
Registration fees	635	5.6	604	4.3	605	4.1
Charge on salaries and wages	5,541	48.8	6,174	44.2	6,489	44.2
Charge on company income	658	5.8	1,107	7.9	1,283	8.7
Charge on other income	2,662	23.4	2,828	20.3	2,661	18.1
Penalties and fines	33	0.3	28	0.2	26	0.2
Transfer of Consolidated Fund surplus (Finance Act, 1939)	809	7.1	—	—	—	—
Grants from Consolidated Fund (Social Security Act)	1,000	8.8	3,200	22.9	3,600	24.5
Other receipts	28	0.2	26	0.2	24	0.2

[a] Basic data from the *New Zealand Official Year-Book, 1943*, p. 393.

social security revenue in the fiscal years ending in 1940, 1941, and 1942. The percentage distribution by sources has been added.

Grants from the Consolidated Fund, the general treasury, made up in the fiscal year 1941–42 not quite one quarter (24.5 per cent) of the total revenues. Charges on company income produced 8.7 per cent of the total. Charges on salaries and wages and on other income together constituted 63.3 per cent of the total, or a little less than two thirds. The registration fees produced 4.1 per cent.

Another table based on figures from the *Official Year-Book*, presented on page 549, gives for the fiscal years ending March 31, 1940 and 1942 the number of the several monetary benefits in force as of March 31, the payments for each benefit during the year, and the annual value of certain of the monetary benefits as of March 31, 1942. Average figures per monetary benefit in force on March 31, 1942 and the percentage distribution of total payments by benefits have been added.

In the fiscal year 1939–40 the monetary benefits made up not quite 90 per cent of the total payments. The relative importance of the monetary benefits dropped in the ensuing years as the medical service cost increased. In the fiscal year 1941–42 the monetary benefits formed only 81.4 per cent of the total and the medical service benefits 18.6 per cent. The increase in the cost of the medical services resulted in part from the fact that it took time to get the health program in operation. It also resulted in part from a natural tendency for persons to make a far greater use of free services than of services for which they must pay. The *New York Times* of October 7, 1945 reported that the Minister of Health of New Zealand had stated in the House of Representatives that because of abuses the government is seriously considering whether free physician services will be continued. It admits widespread racketeering which followed the institution of a system under which a New Zealander may consult a physician as frequently as he likes, and the doctor can collect a fee for each visit. The costs are running far higher than the govern-

NUMBER OF BENEFITS IN FORCE AND AMOUNT OF BENEFIT PAYMENTS, FISCAL YEARS ENDING MARCH 31, 1940 AND 1942[a]

(All money figures in thousands of pounds sterling, except those for per benefit in force)

Class of Benefit or Pension	Number in Force on March 31		Annual Value March 31, 1942		Payments during Year ending March 31			
	1940	1942	Per Benefit in Force	Total	1940 Amount	1940 Percentage Distribution	1942 Amount	1942 Percentage Distribution
TOTAL	135	189		10,454	10,394	100.0	13,139	100.0
MONETARY	135	189		10,454	9,337	89.8	10,703	81.4
Universal superannuation	—	41	12.5	513	—	—	446	3.4
Age	93	99	74.0	7,337	6,518	62.7	7,191	54.7
Widows	10	11	78.9	849	786	7.6	845	6.4
Orphans	[b]	[c]	50.8	19	15	0.1	18	0.1
Family	11	18	34.5	632	253	2.4	539	4.1
Invalids	12	12	84.5	1,023	942	9.1	1,011	7.7
Miners	1	1	90.5	80	93	0.9	83	0.6
Maori War	1[d]	[e]	78.0	[f]	1	[g]	[h]	[g]
Unemployment	4	4			434	4.2	139	1.1
Sickness	3	4			209	2.0	304	2.3
Emergency	1	2			87	0.8	127	1.0
MEDICAL					1,057	10.2	2,436	18.6
Medical					607	5.9	206	1.6
Hospital					166	1.6	1,191	9.1
Mental hospital							181	1.4
Maternity					284	2.7	559	4.2
Pharmaceutical							280	2.1
Supplementary							28	0.2

a Basic data from the *New Zealand Official Year-Book, 1943*, p. 405.
b Actual figure £330.
f Actual figure £312.
c Actual figure £372.
g Less than .05 of 1 per cent.
d Actual figure £12.
h Actual figure £440.
e Actual figure £4.

ment had anticipated when it instituted the system, and they constitute a serious drain on the Social Security Fund. Placing physicians on salary is one of the possibilities under consideration.

The old-age provisions are, as is generally the case in a social security system, the most expensive benefit. Age and superannuation benefits combined in 1941–42 accounted for 58.1 per cent of all payments from the fund. The costs of universal superannuation will continue to increase substantially each year until 1971 when the maximum benefit is payable to all residents 65 years of age or over. The increase thereafter will result mainly from the gradual aging of the population.

The effect of the war is clearly apparent in the figures for unemployment benefits. Actual payments dropped from 434 thousand pounds sterling in 1939–40 to 139 thousands in 1941–42. In 1941–42 unemployment insurance accounted for 1.1 per cent of the total payments from the fund as contrasted with 4.2 per cent in 1939–40. The average payment per benefit in force is higher for unemployment than for any other category.

The New Zealand Legation has supplied the latest available figures for the system. They place the total expenditures at about 16 million pounds sterling. Of this amount 12 millions came from the social security taxes and 4 millions from the Consolidated Fund. Three quarters thus came from social security taxes and one quarter from general taxes. A rough calculation indicates that the New Zealand system at present is costing in the neighborhood of 6.7 per cent of the salary, wages, and other income of the people of New Zealand.

Because the amount of the universal superannuation benefit will increase each year from now until 1970, the percentage of salaries, wages, and other income required for the system will increase materially. We have not attempted any actuarial calculations to measure by how much.

The increase in cost for the aged will represent under the New Zealand law the difference in cost between a no-means test system and a means test system. Gradually and progressively the no-means test universal superannuation payments will practically absorb and replace the means test age benefits.

A person cannot draw both. A recipient of a means test age benefit at a rate not greater than the statutory rate for the universal superannuation benefit may on application have the no-means test benefit substituted for his means test benefit. By 1970–71 everyone on reaching the retirement age will be eligible for a no-means test benefit equaling the maximum possible benefit under the means test system. Thus there will be practically complete extinction of the age benefit for persons 65 years of age or over.

A considerable increase must also be anticipated in the cost of unemployment benefits. New Zealand benefits continue for the duration of unemployment. The system has not been in effect long enough to give any significant figures as to average, annual unemployment. Two factors are present, however, that would make it seem inevitable that costs for unemployment benefits will increase. (1) The experience since the passage of the act has practically all been during the man-power stringency resulting from the war. Full employment means high revenues and low payments; it cannot be anticipated that such a high degree of employment can be attained after the war, and therefore payments for unemployment benefits will probably increase. (2) Over the years, the number of technologically unemployed and those on the borderline between employables and unemployables may tend to accumulate on the pension rolls.

As one studies the monetary benefits provided in New Zealand, it seems as if broadly speaking the system represents about the least expensive one that could be devised to give universal coverage and to insure against all hazards. It achieves its low cost by three principal devices (1) it uses for its monetary benefit a modernized and carefully worked out means test so that except for universal superannuation it pays no monetary benefits to persons who already have sufficient income of their own to provide for themselves and their dependents according to a health and decency standard; (2) it limits its maximum benefits to something approaching a minimum of subsistence; and (3) it bases its benefits upon the number and type of persons who must be provided for through the benefit. It is in sharp contrast to our W.P.A. system, which paid the single unskilled worker with no dependents just as much as the married unskilled worker with many dependents and paid skilled workers more than unskilled workers regardless of the persons to be provided for through the wages.

If universal coverage against all hazards were retained, New Zealand could reduce the costs of its monetary benefits apparently in three main ways: (1) It could abolish universal superannuation which would not save much currently but would result in material savings in later years. (2) It could adopt more restrictive rules with respect to allowable income and allowable property or, in other words, it could make its means test more severe and incidentally less acceptable. (3) It could lower its maximum benefit provisions.

The New Zealand law, moreover, as has been repeatedly pointed out in describing the system, vests a considerable measure of discretionary authority in the Commission. The delegation of this discretionary authority appears to us as a highly desirable and perhaps a necessary feature of the system. It is to be anticipated that it will gradually result in subordinate rules and regulations and decided cases that establish precedents so that discretion will not be arbitrarily exercised. We have, however, made no study of the use of this discretionary power. We do not know whether the Commission has been severe, moderate, or liberal. It is impossible to say, therefore, whether savings could be effected by more restrictive use of discretionary authority. Anyone who has studied the actual administration of a public welfare agency applying a means test under laws, rules, and regulations, knows that administrative policy, attitudes, and methods affect costs. That element is present in New Zealand, but it would take a difficult first-hand study to attempt to determine what if any savings could be effected through more strict administration.

It appears safe to conclude, however, that so far as monetary benefits are concerned, New Zealand represents complete protection against want at an approach to lowest possible cost.

PART III

MAJOR ISSUES TODAY

CHAPTER XVII

INTRODUCTION TO PART III

In the preceding parts of this book the major programs in the United States, the proposed plan for Britain, and the New Zealand system have been broadly described with special emphasis on the important issues that are illustrated by them. The present part is to be concerned with the major issues. Occasionally, illustrations will be drawn from the earlier parts, but no detailed descriptions will be repeated. It will, however, be necessary from time to time to introduce fairly detailed discussions of certain social, economic, and governmental factors that have to be considered in connection with the major issues. These matters have not been taken up in the earlier chapters with respect to the United States because in this country the problems of completeness of coverage, comprehensiveness of benefits, integration of benefits, and integration of administration have not as yet been squarely faced. When they are faced, certain social, economic, and governmental issues stand out with clarity and are not lost in the fog which prevails when the nation and the states legislate more or less independently by categories.

The problem of the selection and the arrangement of the major issues has presented no little difficulty. The chief trouble arises from the fact that few of the issues are independent; most of them are interrelated. For example, decisions with respect to the size of benefits to be granted and the conditions under which they are to be given would be relatively simple did they not involve issues with respect to the cost and who is to bear the cost. In the following pages we present first the social factors, second the financial factors, and third the governmental factors. These lines cannot, however, be sharply drawn and some cross referencing and even repetition will be necessary. The reader is cautioned, however, that because of the interrelationships, it is necessary to read practically the entire part in order to understand all the ramifications of any one issue. Because of the physical characteristics of the printed page this part of the book may be likened to a series of maps whereas what the reader who wishes to form his own conclusions on the issues really needs is a globe that would facilitate study of interrelationships.

The major issues that have been selected for chapters in this part are grouped as follows:

A. The predominantly social issues
   1. What are the objectives of relief and social insurance?
   2. What is need?
   3. What are the defects and the merits of a means test?
   4. Who should be covered by the social security system?
   5. Against what hazards should protection be afforded?
   6. In general, how large should benefits be?
   7. What special factors have to be considered in connection with
      a. Old age
      b. Disability
      c. Sickness
      d. Unemployment
      e. Death
   8. What special factors have to be considered with respect to dependents?
      a. Children
      b. Wives or widows
      c. Deserted or divorced women
B. The fundamentally financial issues
   9. Upon what broad factors does the cost of a social security system depend?
   10. What estimates are possible regarding the costs of social insurance?
   11. What methods should be used in financing social security and relief? Special attention will be devoted to:
      a. Contributions by employers
      b. Contributions by employees
      c. Earmarked special taxes
      d. General taxes
      e. Borrowing
      Under each of these headings questions regarding equities will be raised.
   12. Are reserves necessary in social security financing? A distinc-

tion will be drawn between financing old age and financing unemployment insurance and other benefits.

13. Obligations for the future

C. The fundamentally governmental and political issues

14. Do social insurance and relief have to be integrated and coordinated?

15. Should the national government or the state government determine policy? A distinction will be drawn between:
    a. Broad over-all policy
    b. Detailed policy

16. Should the national government or the state government finance relief and social security? Distinctions will be drawn among:
    a. Complete federal financing
    b. Complete state financing
    c. Grants-in-aid by the national government to the states

17. Should the national government or the state be primarily responsible for administration?

18. Should individual or family social service be administered in connection with relief and social security?

19. What should be the relationships between social security and relief to:
    a. The employment services
    b. The educational services
    c. The health services
    d. The agricultural services

20. What are the political factors involved in the choices?

CHAPTER XVIII

THE OBJECTIVES OF RELIEF AND
SOCIAL INSURANCE

In considering the development of a universal, comprehensive, and co-ordinated system of social security, the first question that must be faced is, What are the objectives to be attained? Examination of existing programs and the literature in the field discloses no well-defined consensus regarding objectives either among proponents of social security systems or among legislators. On the contrary, there are divergent and often conflicting points of view. At the outset of this chapter an effort will be made to enumerate, without detailed discussion, what appear to be the major objectives advanced by various groups. Then each of these objectives will be examined in some detail.

The major objectives advanced are: (1) to prevent any person in the country from having to exist in need or want; (2) to guarantee to each person or family in the country an income sufficient to provide a living in accordance with a standard deemed suitable by the legislature; (3) to keep the economic system functioning at something approaching a maximum level of production by redistributing part of the purchasing power through the social security system, (4) to use the social security system as a device to equalize the distribution of income.

THE PREVENTION OF WANT

The next chapter is to be devoted to a consideration of what constitutes need, a subject with respect to which there is wide divergence of opinion. In this chapter the term will be used broadly since the present purpose is to bring out the distinctions among the several major objectives just enumerated.

As was pointed out in the historical introduction to Part I, it has always been an accepted doctrine in the United States that relief of want from public funds is a necessary and proper function of government. Thus advocates of social security for the purpose of relieving want have not proposed a new and revolutionary principle. What they seek is an efficient, well-developed system, properly financed, to make sure that no person will be forced to live in need provided he is willing to accept aid from the public treasury in accordance with such terms and conditions as may be prescribed by the legislature.

The fact that the principle of relieving need at public expense has been so long established and so generally accepted explains why leaders of no political party have openly opposed that principle. The arguments that have taken place have been with respect to systems and methods, how far to go and how to go, what standards should be used, what levels of government should finance, what levels of government should administer.

It is true that probably at all times some people, presumably very few in number, have believed in the doctrine of the survival of the fittest and that it is not economically or socially desirable to support at public expense those who cannot maintain themselves and their dependents and contribute to the economic and social welfare of society. No attempt will here be made to consider the religious, ethical, and moral aspects of such a doctrine. It may be dismissed with the statement that it is entirely foreign to the ethical concepts of the great mass of the American people, so foreign that advocates of sterilization of the unfit have made little headway in the several states. It is, however, desirable that the economic arguments against application of this theory should be briefly reviewed.

The high degree of economic development in the United States which has afforded the best material level of living ever enjoyed by any people in recorded history has been due to three major factors: (1) the great natural resources with which the country was endowed, (2) a form of government which afforded maximum opportunity to develop and apply individual talents, and (3) a genius for organization and for the development and application of power machines and scientific methods.

This economic development has resulted in (1) a high degree of specialization and a minute subdivision of labor, (2) a highly

integrated system which makes the functioning of one sector
of the economy largely dependent upon the proper functioning
of other sectors, (3) a rapid change in production resulting
from the introduction of new enterprises and new techniques,
and (4) a diminishing opportunity for persons who can bring
to their task mere physical strength and who lack the skills
required by present machine technology.

As a result of these developments the nation has had, and
may have at any time again, large numbers of persons who are
in need through no fault of their own. Although a few of them
undoubtedly are mentally and physically unfit in the Spartan
sense, the great mass of them are reasonably fit. To appreciate
the situation one only has to compare the years of the thirties,
when prophets of gloom declared that thousands of workers
would never again get worth-while jobs, with the early forties,
which have been characterized by a shortage of man power.

Under such an economic system, it is essential that provision
be made to relieve want at public expense so long as it exists and
at the same time, in so far as possible, to remove the causes
that produced want. Such action is necessary in the long-
run, economic interests of the nation, although in certain
instances it may be dictated by ethical and moral concepts
rather than economic materialism. To illustrate the point
certain particular classes who may be in need will be considered.

1. *Children.* Modern technology has, as previously noted,
reduced the demand for mere brawn and has increased the
necessity for education and development of the capacity to
acquire special skills. To meet this demand, the nation has
long been committed to public education. It has extended the
school system into the higher levels necessary for technological
operation and advance, and it has broadened and extended its
training in the lower schools, particularly the secondary schools.
To a very considerable extent, activities to develop and
maintain the health of children and to teach healthful ways of
living are centered in the educational system. It follows, therefore, that it is not in the national interest for children to be so

greatly in need that they cannot take advantage of the opportunities which the school system affords.

The economic interest of the nation in the development of the children who may be in need is not dependent upon what caused the need. School officials and social agencies endeavoring to do what is in the best interests of the child may be concerned with causes. But the question whether the need of the child should be met, in the public interest, does not turn on the cause. Cause should affect methods and procedure, but no cause should preclude public action. Among the important causes are: (a) the death, disability, desertion, or incarceration of the father; (b) the unemployment or underemployment of the father or other responsible relative; (c) physical, mental, or moral defects of the father which prevent him from so supporting his children that they can take advantage of the opportunities afforded by the state to children in general; (d) inability of the father, with such help as the mother can give, to support the number of children for whom they are responsible.

2. *Women responsible for the care of children.* The maintenance of a suitable home for a child is a basic requirement, normally met by the child's mother. The woman customarily is supported by the father of the child, possibly with some assistance from the mother herself. For the reasons cited in the preceding paragraph, the woman may be deprived of the support of a male primary breadwinner and be forced to be at once homemaker and principal or sole wage earner. If she lacks the opportunity or the capacity successfully to perform the two duties, which are often inherently inconsistent, it is in the social and economic interest that provision for the future of the child shall have priority. That may mean that public funds have to be used to support the woman while she is caring for the child or to supplement such sums as she can earn in ways that do not preclude giving proper care to the child. This aid, it may be said, is given basically in the interest of the child.

3. *Unemployable widows, divorced, and separated women.* Women who have devoted many years to household duties and

the care of children may be deprived of the support of the husband through death, disability, or desertion. They may be unemployable under practically any condition of the labor market, or unemployable only under conditions existing at the moment in the labor market. Deprived of their previous means of support, they may be in actual want. In case of divorce or separation there may be a cause of action or even a judgment or a decree against the husband, but it does not relieve need unless the husband actually pays.

4. *Members of the labor force, unemployed or underemployed.* A great majority of persons in the labor force are responsible for their own support if not also for the support, in whole or in part, of dependents. For reasons frequently beyond their control, they may be unemployed or so seriously underemployed that they cannot supply their own needs or the needs of those who may be dependent upon them. Because of conditions prevailing in their locality or in the country as a whole, they cannot secure work immediately. In a severe depression, many of them may be average or better than average workers. Many of them have followed occupations that are generally classified as unskilled or semi-skilled; they have rarely had large earnings; and even in good times there has not been much of a margin between earnings and necessary expenses. Thus unemployment and underemployment occasion want.

5. *Disabled workers.* Because of disease or accident a worker may be either temporarily or permanently so far disabled that he cannot, at least for the time being, support himself or those dependent upon him. He may be in no way responsible for the accident or disease that has deprived him of earning capacity. If he has no resources of his own and no one to support him, he is in need of aid from some outside source.

6. *The aged.* In the later years of life one may be more or less disabled either from a specific disease or from a general slowing down of the physical and mental functions. This familiar phenomenon is so well recognized that many employers will not hire an elderly worker except in periods of great labor scarcity.

When an enterprise encounters a recession in demand and has to cut force, there is naturally a tendency to make reductions on the basis of efficiency. This practice is particularly hard on elderly workers, not possessed of relatively scarce skills and experience and engaged in tasks that call for physical strength or agility. They are frequently at a great disadvantage as compared with younger workers who are physically more able and often better prepared by education for learning new tasks or new ways of doing things. These older persons are not necessarily unemployable in the absolute sense but only unemployable in the current labor market situation. If they have exhausted their savings, they are in need.

With respect to these elderly workers the fact should be stressed that often unemployability is a question of the state of the labor market. The man who in the decade of the thirties appeared permanently unemployable because of age may have rendered invaluable service to the nation in the past few years. Probably few would have said in the thirties that money paid to relieve the need of such workers was economically in the nature of a standby wage and that the worker again would be called to active, productive service.

The facts regarding these six groups of persons seem to us to demonstrate beyond argument that members of these groups, if in need, must be relieved if necessary at public expense. Thus relief of persons in need regardless of the cause of the need appears to be the first and primary objective of a sound system of relief and social security.

The requirements of such a system would be satisfied under the following conditions:

1. The fact of need is established by the application of established standards through an adequate investigation.

2. A person found to be in need according to these standards is given a sufficient amount of assistance at public expense to relieve his need.

3. The system is so administered and so financed that the necessary relief is given promptly and certainly.

GUARANTEED INCOME

The objection to the system just outlined, advanced by many proponents of the social insurances, is that it necessitates the application of tests and standards of need and gives only so much as may be necessary to bring the recipient to a specified minimum. To overcome this objection, they would provide in the great majority of cases that upon the happening of certain specified contingencies a person shall receive as of right without any tests as to need a regular payment of money sufficient to keep that person from being in want. Whatever his resources or the resources of his family, they would be in addition to the sum he receives from the state. Further, to reduce the psychological humiliation that may arise from receipt of public funds, it is customarily provided that the beneficiary during his working years shall contribute toward the social insurance fund from which the benefits are paid.

In a subsequent chapter individual contributions to the insurance fund will be considered at length. Here it will only be pointed out that in a contributory social insurance system relatively few persons pay in the costs of their own benefits. Part of the cost, perhaps a very substantial part, is paid by taxes levied either on employers, as such, or upon general taxpayers.

The essential feature of such a system is that benefits are paid regardless of need and that the state uses its sovereign power to tax to take money from one individual to give to another. In the early days of such a system, when persons who have been in the system only a few years are retired on substantial benefits, it frequently happens that persons without great capacity to pay are taxed to supply benefits for persons who are not in need at all.

Obviously the cost of benefits paid to all without any means test is greater than the cost of benefits paid only to those in need. Equally obvious is the fact that it costs more to provide each person with a minimum of subsistence regardless of his need than to give to a person in need only such sums as may be necessary in addition to what he already has to bring his total resources to a minimum of subsistence. In other words, the no-means test system increases both the number of beneficiaries and the average amount paid to each beneficiary.

So far as we can see the major objective of such a no-means test system is to relieve recipients of the embarrassment and humiliation of the means test and to give every person something in return for the contribution or taxes which he individually is compelled to pay. Since the cost is arbitrarily divided by the legislature among the individual, often the employer, and the general taxpayers, it is not difficult to so design a system that almost everyone will receive a larger benefit than he himself has paid for by his own contributions, and the cost of preventing humiliation is paid through taxes on employers or general taxes.

In favor of such a system, one of the objectives often cited is to keep the economic system functioning at something approaching a maximum level of production by redistributing at least a part of purchasing power through the social security system.

REDISTRIBUTION OF PURCHASING POWER

Money to pay social security benefits must come either from taxation or from public borrowing. Each of these sources will be considered in turn.

Taxation for social security benefits involves taking purchasing power from one individual to give to another. It does not create new purchasing power; it merely transfers it.

Whether such a transfer is or is not advantageous to the economy as a whole appears to us to depend basically upon the conditions existing at the time the transfer is made. If stagnation exists and there is a large accumulation of idle savings in financial institutions, the economy may be stimulated by taking these idle savings away from the owners and giving them to persons who will spend them immediately for consumers' goods. Such action will stimulate the demand for consumers' goods and result perhaps in increasing employment. If, on the other hand, the taking prevents the taxpayer from actually spending his money himself it does not necessarily increase purchasing power and employment.

If the taxation prevents the original owner from spending his money for producers' goods or durable goods, the taking may operate against stimulating employment and the general economic interest. For example, during the depression the construction and durable goods industries were hard hit, and their stagnation was responsible for much unemployment. It would have been greatly in the general economic interest if savings had poured into the construction industries, especially the housing field. More stimulation of employment would have resulted from such a flow than could have resulted from the transfer of purchasing power to persons who would use the money for nondurable consumers' goods. There is reason to believe that such a transfer may perhaps affect prices rather than immediate production and employment, and that its effect on employment and production may be very considerably delayed.

The truth seems to be that the basic problem of maintaining a large volume of production of needed goods and services and a high level of employment is one of preserving or restoring a reasonable balance among the several sectors of the economy. To restore or maintain balance means that purchasing power should flow in one direction at one time and in another direction at another. If such be the case, it does not follow that a permanent system of social security designed to make purchasing power flow in a more or less constant volume in established channels will necessarily benefit the economy. Under circumstances which call for development of capital goods and investment in durable consumers' goods, it may even impair it.

The immediate purchasing power of the economy may be actually increased by public borrowing so carried on that purchasing power is not taken from individuals. If the government then distributes that purchasing power to individuals who will use it immediately, the economy will be at least temporarily stimulated. As World War II has so abundantly demonstrated, if such public borrowing is carried on after a high level of employment has been reached, drastic measures of wage control, price control, and rationing have to be introduced to prevent the vicious spiral of wages and prices. An elaborate and expensive system of social security may force the government to indulge in inflationary borrowing at a time when such borrowing would be contrary to the general interest, and it may increase the demand for consumers' goods at a time when the government is seeking to control the demand.

At this point it should be repeated that the vicious spiral of wages and prices may impair or destroy the value of fixed money benefits provided under social security systems. These benefits are paid in the main to persons who are unable to work, and therefore they derive no benefit from such upward movement of wages as may take place as the result of the inflation, but they bear the brunt of any upturn of prices. If they are entirely dependent on their social security benefits, and if these benefits at the old price levels were not more than would provide a reasonable minimum of subsistence, a 50 per cent increase in prices would mean their benefits would purchase only two thirds of the minimum requirements.

It seems impossible to accept the argument that an elaborate social security system for the redistribution of purchasing power will always work in the general interest, promote a high level of employment, and maximum production of needed goods and services. Real social security, as distinguished from an elaborate social security system, calls for an economy in balance at a level which will insure large production and a high level of employment. In a dynamic industrial society successive legislatures will have to face the problems of adjusting to current conditions. It hardly seems as if future legislatures will necessarily be helped in this difficult task by the commitments for redistribution of purchasing power made by past legislatures whose forecasts as to future conditions may prove disastrously wide of the mark.

The position of a social security system as such appears to be distinctly secondary and defensive. The real hope appears to be in positive, constructive actions to promote the full functioning of the economy with a high degree of efficiency. Given those conditions, adequate provision for persons in need can be made without great difficulty if the public conscience of the day so directs. The question may be raised as to whether it is not at least as safe to place reliance upon the American public conscience as upon an elaborate system that is based on money and prices.

EQUALIZATION OF INCOME

A tenet of communism is "From each according to his ability: To each according to his need." This tenet finds acceptance among some groups in the United States; and it can to some extent be given effect through social security systems. The device is to use the progressive income tax and other progressive taxes to take property away from persons who have in abundance and to distribute the proceeds among those who are less privileged, less fortunate, less effective, and perhaps less industrious.

In the past half century there has been increased acceptance of the doctrine that the necessary costs of government should be distributed among the people in accordance with their capacity to pay. The new element introduced by some social security systems is that it is a proper function of the state to take property from one citizen, not to carry on a needed public service but to give money, purchasing power, or property to someone else.

As has already been noted in the section of this chapter that deals with the relief of want, it is not a new function of government to take from those who have to give to those who are actually in need. The new element consists in taking to give persons who are not in need at all according to any of the old concepts as to what constitutes need. The new element is seen in the various benefit formulae which discriminate against employees in the upper-income brackets and in favor of those in the lower brackets. The state is using its sovereign power to tax to equalize income and property.

The Bill of Rights in the Constitution (Amendment V) provided that private property should not be taken for public use without just compensation and that no person should be deprived of life, liberty, or property without due process of law. These constitutional guarantees are stripped of all substance when the state assumes as one of its functions promoting the general welfare by taking property from one citizen to give to another. Such a taking by the state through the exercise of the sovereign power to tax avoids the safeguards thrown around the institution of private property by the Constitution. The degree to which individual ownership is to be respected then lies very largely within the discretion of a majority of the elected legislature.

Among the leading exponents of social insurance and a governmentally planned and controlled economy, Sir William Beveridge is distinguished for the frankness of many of his statements as to what the proposals involve. Many others either have not carried their analyses as far as he has or for strategic reasons have avoided full discussion.[1] Sir William finds it necessary to omit from his list of the essential liberties the liberty of a private citizen to own means of production and to employ other citizens in operating them. He says: "Whether private ownership of means of production to be operated by others is a good economic device or not, it must be judged as a device. It is not an essential citizen liberty in Britain, because it is not and never has been enjoyed by more than a very small proportion of the British people."[2]

The American economic system, unlike the British if Sir William's statement be accepted, is characterized by a wide dispersal of ownership of productive property. The American agricultural system has been largely built on the basis of individual farm ownership, and thousands of persons own productive enterprises in whole or in part or have financial interests in them. Through life insurance companies and other financial institutions millions more have a direct interest in the productive enterprises of the nation.

[1] For a report that avoids clear analysis of the issues of social security and relief, see National Resources Planning Board, *Security, Work, and Relief Policies* (1942).
[2] Sir William H. Beveridge, *Full Employment in a Free Society* (1945), par. 17, p. 23.

Thus there is in the United States a very real issue as to how far the people wish to go in having the government redistribute wealth through the device of a compulsory social insurance system. It seems perfectly clear that government in the United States, whether national, state, or local, must go far enough to prevent want. How much further it should go is a question that demands very thorough consideration, especially when systems are introduced that cost almost nothing at the outset but will become heavy burdens for successive generations.

In this chapter the terms need and want have been used without any effort at analysis. The following chapter will be concerned with the question, What is need?

CHAPTER XIX

THE NATURE OF NEED

The present chapter is to analyze in some detail the question, "What is need or want?"—a question which is perhaps as basic as any which has to be considered in connection with relief and social security. It is not our purpose to attempt to give answers to the detailed questions, but merely to present them as constituting a major element which has to be considered in arriving at decisions. Before the scope of the chapter is outlined, one basic matter should be clearly set forth.

NEED NOT CONSIDERED IN TERMS OF MONEY

No attempt will be made to discuss need in terms of money. Obviously money is only a medium of exchange and a common denominator that enables us to add together values or prices of unlike things. Our needs are not satisfied directly by money but by the things which money will buy. If discussion is attempted in terms of money, several difficulties are encountered, some of which deserve enumeration.

1. Money figures depend on prices. If the price level changes greatly through either inflation or deflation, the money figures change, although the basic minimum requirements for food, clothing, and shelter may remain almost constant.

2. In the United States conditions vary widely. At one extreme are industrial workers in urban centers who secure almost all the needed goods and services through the payment of money. At the other extreme are the families that still live to a substantial degree under a subsistence economy. Food, clothing, housing, and fuel are largely the direct product of their own labor or of barter or exchange of labor with their neighbors. The amount of money which passes through their hands in the course of a year may be extremely small. To get money figures for them, it is necessary to attach values or prices to things

which are not sold for money. The results will depend almost entirely upon the assumptions made with respect to prices.

3. To get comparisons between different localities on a money basis, it is necessary not only to make assumptions regarding prices and values but also frequently to assume a standard level of living. A statistician can determine, with some difficulty perhaps, what a specified standard would cost in New York City and what it would cost in the rural areas of the deep South. But things are necessary in New York City that are not necessary in the South. The standard, therefore, may give an artificial result. If no standard is used, the money figures reflect different levels of living and do not necessarily throw much light on whether the people with low money incomes are or are not in need. Unfortunately the variations are so great that persons with low money incomes in some localities may be comfortably fixed, whereas persons with very much higher money incomes in other localities are in need.

Statistics regarding money income, therefore, do not help much in determining whether persons are or are not in need. To get at the real condition one must consider what the individual needs in goods and services and what he has. This chapter will therefore consider first in general terms what the needs are and in connection with each need resources meeting it. The discussion will be followed by a consideration of the question whether an individual or a family is in need of assistance from public funds if relatives exist who could maintain the persons in need if required to do so.

THE MAJOR REQUIREMENTS

Needs may be considered under six major headings: (1) food, (2) shelter, (3) clothing, (4) medical care, (5) recreation, and (6) other. Although shelter is second only to food in importance, discussion of it will be reserved to the last because it presents so complicated a problem.

Food. In dealing with the question of food requirements, we can come closer to scientific answers than we can in dealing with any other item on the list. Scientific studies have been conducted to determine the requirements of individuals of different ages, doing different kinds of work, for the several food elements, such as protein, carbohydrates, and fats; and in recent years vitamins and minerals have received marked attention. Various articles of food have been studied to determine what food elements they contain and in what amount, and the availability of these elements for use by the normal body. Great progress has been made in the study of deficiency diseases and in the variations among individuals in metabolism and in the extent to which they are allergic to special articles of diet. Thus it is possible for a committee of well-equipped scientists to say with a considerable approach to accuracy what the food requirements are for a normal person of a given sex and age engaged in certain specified types of work. They will also be able to give in general terms the requirements of persons who vary in a fairly common way from the average. In unusual cases study of the individual will permit of the development of a fairly exact statement of the requirements for that individual.

The food requirements of the individual rarely necessitate the use of any one particular article of diet. They can be satisfied by many alternative articles or combinations of articles. Thus in many communities it is possible for competent dieticians, with consideration of local conditions, to work out relatively low-cost diets which will be satisfactory from the nutritional standpoint. In developing such diets, they give consideration to the cost of preparation both in money and in time. Thus they can arrive at an approximation of what a family would need as a minimum to be assured of satisfactory nutrition.

From the standpoint of the individual, a satisfactory low-cost diet may be unsatisfactory for three principal reasons: (1) it does not appeal to the individual's food tastes or habits; (2) it may be lacking in variety; and (3) it may require more time and trouble in preparation than the individual will care to expend. The individual left to follow his own tastes and practices would spend far more for food, although as a result of the additional expenditure he might get no greater nutritional value. In fact in some instances he might get lower nutritional value in spite of the extra expenditure.

Thus an issue arises as to whether an individual or a family is in need for food if resources are available to purchase a scientifically adequate low-cost diet. Is the desire for a more expensive diet a need that calls for payment of benefits from public funds?

Clothing. Clothing presents a far more difficult problem than food for there is far less in the way of scientific determination as to what is necessary. It is worn (1) to protect from the elements and (2) to maintain an appearance satisfactory to one's self or one's associates.

So far as protection from the elements is concerned, scientific investigations will produce some significant results if due differentiations are made for climatic conditions and the extent to which exposure to the elements is essential to suitable activities. The results for school children during the school year would not be much alike for Duluth, Minnesota and Miami, Florida. The cost of protective clothing is in part a factor of climate since the warmer garments made of wool are more expensive than the lighter garments made of cotton; foot protection from snow, ice, and cold is more expensive than protection from mere rain and dampness.

The question with respect to clothing which occasions so much difficulty in relief administration is what account is to be taken of the elements of personal appearance and fashion in determining the clothing necessary in a particular case. A position frequently taken is that the person should be so clothed as to conform with the reasonable minimum standard prevailing in the community for other persons engaged in like activities. For example, a child attending school should be so clothed that he is not conspicuous because of poor clothing. A man or woman out of work and seeking a job in an occupation formerly followed, or for which qualified, should not be so poorly clothed that appearance will be a distinct handicap. On the other hand, where personal contacts are not materially involved, as in the case of elderly retired persons living at home, the question of style and appearance is less important. If clothing is adequate for protection and physical comfort, no great harm is done if some of it is outmoded.

Psychologically the question of clothing is particularly important for school children and young people not long out of school. To them personal appearance may be a matter of first importance, and their desire may be not merely to conform to a reasonable minimum standard but to equal or to excel the best dressed person in their immediate universe. Lack of resources to do so may prevent them from putting their best effort into their activities. The home environment may be such that this unfortunate point of view is not corrected. Essentials may be sacrificed for the purpose of maintaining a good front. In such a case should public funds be used to enable the youth to maintain what the youth, and perhaps the parents, regard as a superior appearance?

In small communities an important situation may develop if members of families in receipt of public funds are obviously more expensively or more modishly dressed than members of families getting along by their own efforts. The old virtues of thrift, self reliance, and independence may be pretty hard to develop if to the youth relief and social security appear the easy way.

How far is it necessary for a person to be reasonably stylish in appearance as well as protected against the elements and suitably covered? The answer appears to turn on the nature of the requirements of the activities in which he is engaged which depend in no small part on the standards of the neighborhood or community in which he dwells.

One cannot say, therefore, that there is anything approaching a standard requirement for clothes applicable throughout the United States. Even the primary requirement of protection from the elements varies widely with climate. In a given community the requirements will differ according to sex, age, and activities and possibly also according to the standards set by the groups with which one ordinarily associates.

Medical care. The high degree of variation among individuals with respect to the need for medical care is a matter of common knowledge. Some persons are endowed by nature with a sound body that functions with a close approach to perfection. "I have never had a sick day in my life" or "I never have to consult a doctor," may be in some instances literally true. On the other hand are persons who have some congenital weaknesses or unbalanced functioning which necessitates almost continuous medical care. Persons otherwise strong and well may have defective eyesight requiring frequent visits to the oculist. Some have teeth that a dentist has difficulty in preserving. One encounters occasionally an individual or a family which seems cursed with bad luck. Members of the family seem to fall victims to every communicable disease that visits the community, and every now and then one of them has an accident. Preventive measures can materially reduce the number who fall victims to contagious disease, and safety work may cut down the accidents, but today most of us know families in which the costs of medical care are high.

Because of these wide variations between individuals and families, it is fairly obvious that an average requirement for medical care is a statistical abstraction. To give as relief the average amount required for medical care to each person would leave many still in need while supplying others with money which they could divert to different purposes.

Practical provisions for necessary medical care can be made in any one of several ways:

1. The state can give free medical care, using either (a) practitioners carried on the pay roll of the state, (b) practitioners engaged primarily in private practice, paying them by fees.

2. The state may pay into a special fund a premium for each individual or family found to be in need. The proceeds of such fund are used to pay the practitioners, presumably on some fee basis, for those needing medical care.

3. The state may operate a general health insurance system under which all covered workers pay premiums or taxes. General revenues may or may not be used. The proceeds of such funds are used to pay practitioners, either employed by the state or engaged in private practice.

Any one of these systems eliminates the cost of medical care as an item in the individual or family budget. All that remains is at most the contribution tax or premium for medical care.

So far as family finances are concerned, the need of the family resulting from illness is thus determined by the extent to which sickness, accident, or other disability deprives the individual of earnings or the family of the earnings or services of a member.

In the absence of some such provision for medical care, an individual or a family may be in need almost entirely because of the costs of medical care and the loss of earnings resulting from illness. Many a county or urban welfare agency has at present the function of arranging for medical care for persons who would not otherwise be in need. They can ordinarily get along without any public assistance. It is the emergency that creates temporary need. In this connection emphasis should be placed on two points: (1) many families in need from this cause will not ask for public assistance, and (2) many practitioners render a large amount of service to such families for little or no actual compensation. They make no charges, or a nominal charge, or render a bill for the customary fee without expectation that any substantial part of the fee will ever be paid. In some jurisdictions hospital fees must be paid and provision for their payment has to be made at once. The practitioner either goes without full compensation or waits for his money.

Recreation. In some cases expenditures for recreation present difficult problems. Although they may not constitute a heavy item in the average budget of low-income families, exceptional families may give a high priority to expenditures of this nature, so high a priority that funds are not available for more essential purposes. The three categories of recreational expenditure that occasion the most difficulty are those for (1) alcoholic beverages, (2) gambling, and (3) ownership, maintenance, and operation of automobiles for purely recreational purposes. Excessive use of alcoholic beverages causes the most trouble because it frequently reduces the earning capacity of the principal breadwinner and disrupts orderly, family life. Payment of public funds to support families whose resources are spent in part for objectives that are disapproved by local public opinion occasions, moreover, no little ill feeling. Great care has to be exercised lest members of families who are violating community standards of right living may appear to enjoy at public expense things which prudent, thrifty, temperate, hard-working citizens cannot afford and possibly do not desire.

When a considerable proportion of available resources goes for things which community standards classify as vices, and when the difficulties of a family are occasioned by the lack of judgment, managerial ability, and reasonable standards on the part of one or both responsible parents, mere payment of money to the family will not meet the situation. A later chapter will be devoted to a more detailed discussion of this subject. Here it will only be pointed out that certain recreational expenditures of low-income families cannot be classified as necessaries so far as any generally applicable standard is concerned.

A very different question is whether a family is in need if it lacks the resources to participate moderately in the recreational activities that are approved by conservative community standards. To illustrate the type of recreational activities involved, we shall deal first with children and then with adults.

In many communities the public schools have extracurricular activities the cost of which are borne in considerable part by the families of the children. Participation is not generally compulsory, and a child does not have to take part in everything. On the other hand, complete exclusion from all activities of this kind constitutes a real limitation on the child's opportunity for adjustment and may set up socially undesirable psychological reactions. In many communities, too, organizations such as the Scouts, the Future Farmers of America, and young people's societies connected with the churches play an important part in the normal social life. If the available family resources are insufficient to permit of participation in these activities, should they be supplemented from public funds? Some communities are sufficiently large to permit operation of special recreational facilities for youth from such families, generally supported by private voluntary contributions, but other communities are too small to warrant such activities. Because of the relationship of these activities to the efforts to prevent and control juvenile delinquency, it would seem as if absence of family resources to permit participation might well be considered as a form of need to justify modest provision.

With respect to adults the major question likewise is whether in case of need provision should be made to permit a reasonable amount of participation in the accepted community activities. Participation in church activities, membership in local organizations for men or for women, membership in trade unions, illustrate the type of recreation involved. In connection with them, it should be remembered that membership and participation in such activities frequently had their origin in a period before the family was the victim of the hazard that caused the need. Although fellow members might be pleased to have the old member continue without payment of dues or making contributions that cost money, it seems certain that psychologically such an arrangement does not work out. The question therefore has to be faced whether a modest allowance for expenditures of this type should be permitted in a budget designed to meet minimum needs.

Shelter. Shelter presents by all means the most difficult problem in attempting to analyze what constitutes need. The difficulty arises in no small part from lack of flexibility. Most dwellings are relatively permanent and expensive structures; the number of new dwellings added in any one year constitutes a small proportion of the total in existence, and hence to a very great extent the immediate problem has to be considered in each locality upon the basis of what the situation is there at the moment. What the situation ought to be, what the housing program should be, lies beyond the scope of the present volume. It belongs not in the field of relief and social security as defensive measures but in the broader, more constructive field of increasing the supply of needed things and services through efficient economic direction and operation.

In the present section dealing with need for shelter the subjects to be considered will be (1) differences due to climate, (2)

differences among communities of different sizes, (3) effect of
supply and demand, (4) modern labor-saving devices and con-
veniences, (5) home ownership.

A dwelling should provide the family with protection from
the elements, suitable sanitary facilities, adequate light and
ventilation, and sufficient space and privacy for decent living.
The factor of protection from the elements obviously varies
widely as, for example, between Duluth and Miami. A commonplace in private residence construction is that the three most
expensive parts of the house are the foundation, the roof, and
the heating plant. In the warmer sections of the United States,
expensive heating plants may be entirely eliminated, substantial but relatively inexpensive piers may be used for founda-
tions, and roofs may be safely used which would not carry the
weight of a heavy northern snow. If insulation is used in the
south, it is to keep the heat out in summer rather than to hold
it in during the cold, winter months. Even if all other things
were equal, adequate shelter would cost materially more in the
cold sections of the country than in the warmer sections.

The greater the degree of population congestion the greater
the necessity for extensive and expensive municipal services for
the preservation of health and safety. Among the urban essentials are sewer and water systems, paved streets and street
cleaning, public lighting, garbage collection and removal,
police and fire protection, an adequate health service to prevent
the spread of contagious diseases, and in many instances parks
and playgrounds. All these municipal activities involve heavy
operating costs, and most of them heavy capital investments.
Since these costs have to be met largely through taxes on real
estate, it generally follows that in cities land costs are high,
rents are high, and the wages of workers engaged in municipal
services and building construction and maintenance are relatively high. Factors too numerous to list combine to prevent
the occupants of the dwelling—frequently an apartment—from
themselves doing the necessary maintenance and repair work
much less remodeling and extension. Especially in the larger
cities, transportation facilities have to be provided, and many

business and residential buildings are equipped with elevators, expensive to install, maintain, and operate.

Rural communities and small towns can provide satisfactory shelter at much less cost. Many of the municipal services can be entirely dispensed with or supplied in very rudimentary form. Absence of land congestion permits the safe use of much less expensive sanitary facilities. Low capital investments in municipal service facilities and absence of congestion means low land cost and relatively low taxes. Conditions are frequently such that members of the family can themselves do most of the work connected with maintenance and repair, if they cannot do a considerable amount of actual construction. Because of the relationship between wages and the cost of living, wages for persons skilled in construction of the simple type of residence required are comparatively low, especially since many such workers have different occupational activities which together yield them a satisfactory living. A house, for example, may be built during what is the slack season on the farm. The nature of the economy often means no long trips between home and work place. Thus eminently satisfactory shelter may be available for a mere fraction of what comparable shelter would cost in a metropolitan area.

Since housing is relatively permanent, it does not respond quickly to changes in demand. Changes in the economic activities of a community may take place that create either a surplus or a shortage of houses. Rents are quickly responsive to such changes. There may be wide differences in rents for comparable accommodations between two different communities or at different periods in the same community. The newcomer to a crowded community may find it necessary to pay a far higher rent than his fellow workers who have the advantage of arrangements made in an earlier period. Circumstances may force him to pay more rent and to occupy better quarters than he would have taken if he had a wider choice or if he could have selected a house as he would food or clothing. Thus one cannot say what a family should pay for rent except on the basis of averages which may be entirely inapplicable in the face of the existing housing situation in the community where the family lives. What amount is necessary for rent thus frequently depends on local conditions at the moment.

Two of the most significant developments in residence construction have been the great increase in labor-saving devices in the home and the amount of plumbing and plumbing fixtures. These developments have largely increased first cost and often the costs of operation, maintenance, and depreciation. Interest costs and taxes have necessarily gone up. Frequently maintenance and repair of the new appliances are beyond the range of skills of the ordinary handy man, and since their consistent functioning is frequently essential to home operation, prompt service must be secured and paid for.

The manufacture and distribution of these appliances have unquestionably resulted in a large volume of direct and indirect employment. The employment is related to residence construction, a segment of the economy which was greatly depressed during the thirties. In view of these facts the position is sometimes taken that such modern appliances should be regarded as necessaries and that if individuals do not have the personal resources to obtain them, money should be made available through public funds. Thus electricity, running hot and cold water, toilet facilities, mechanical refrigeration, and where necessary automatic heat would be included among the essentials of life to be provided through relief and social security payments if not otherwise available.

A substantial number of persons of moderate means have foregone possession of some of these appliances on the score of additional costs. They would rather do the work required by the older methods than incur the fixed charges. It would be somewhat ironical if such people should be taxed to provide the needy with labor-saving devices that the thrifty felt they themselves could not afford. From the standpoint of family support and maintenance, additional commitments for a labor-saving device are economically advantageous only if the time saved can be profitably utilized for some other purpose. The question must be raised whether public funds should be used to relieve persons of work unless the time thus saved can be effectively employed for the advancement of the individual or the family.[1]

Home ownership raises issues with respect to what constitutes need. Private ownership of property, especially of the family home, has been distinctly in the American tradition. With the question whether home ownership is or is not desirable, either financially or psychologically, the present book is not concerned. The fact is that thousands of American families either own their homes outright or have equities in them. It should be remembered, moreover, that through the Federal Housing Administration the national government has encouraged home purchase on the installment plan and has tended to increase the length of the period within which the loan is to be paid.

Home ownership is a complication when need is considered. In the case of elderly people, one may encounter a furnished home owned outright and yet no available funds to pay taxes and the necessary costs of operation and maintenance. If the home is mortgaged, interest may be past due and foreclosure threatened. The death, disability, or serious unemployment of the principal wage earner may find a family with an equity in the home as a major asset and with no resources to meet debt charges and taxes. The family may be threatened with eviction and with the loss of equities which often comes with a forced sale.

Two different situations may be distinguished here, although there are many gradations. In one situation the family has made a prudent investment and the fair rental value of the property is not materially in excess of what the family would have to pay for suitable rented quarters under the new conditions that confront it. In other words the amount required for rent in a budget

---

[1] What has been said does not apply to government guarantees of private loans to facilitate such things as the acquisition of useful appliances and home modernization and for stimulation of the sector of the economy engaged in such activities. Under that system the person obtaining the improvements generally pays for them and gets them as a reward for effort. With respect to such activities, the question is whether they encourage families to make unwise commitments of their credit.

of necessaries would not be very different from what would be required for taxes, interest, and essential maintenance, not including payments on the principal. In the other situation the family is purchasing or now owns a house, the rental value of which is materially in excess of what would be a reasonable rent for them to pay under the new circumstances in which they are placed. Public funds could not with propriety be used to pay taxes, interest, necessary maintenance, and operating costs on such a home with any degree of fairness to other taxpayers.

Where public assistance is effectively administered, a family is frequently permitted to occupy a wholly or partially-owned home the rental value of which is reasonable under the circumstances. Taxes, interest, operating costs, and perhaps even essential maintenance are allowed in determining what are the necessaries for shelter in the family budget. The law may or may not require that a lien be taken on the property or the equity in it for the sums paid on behalf of the family. This question will be considered further in the discussion of the responsibility of relatives for the support of persons in need.

If the fair rental value of the home is materially in excess of what can be classified as necessary, a question arises as to whether the family is in need if it owns the house outright or has a substantial equity in it. If the sale of the property would yield enough to maintain the family in suitable quarters for a considerable period, the position may be taken that the family should reduce or even exhaust this resource before receiving relief from the public treasury. In some cases aid may be extended temporarily on a lien basis until the house can be disposed of at a fair price.

Home ownership is thus another element in the problem of shelter that can be dealt with satisfactorily only upon the basis of knowledge of the facts in a particular case. Rules and conclusions based on the average will not work well in practice because individual cases may deviate so widely from the average.

Similar situations may be confronted where the primary wage earner or some other member of the family is carrying a substantial amount of life insurance. Continuation of the insurance in force generally calls for the regular payments of premiums. On the other hand, the policy may have a substantial cash-surrender value. Cashed in, it might maintain the family for some weeks or even months without resort to the public treasury.

Two different points of view may be taken with respect to such insurance. The first is that the family is not in need if it can for even a short period get along on the cash which can be obtained by surrendering the policy. The other is that it is in the interest both of the family and of the public treasury to appraise the situation and take action with consideration of the probable future. What are the chances that the insured will again earn and be able to continue his policy in force? What are the facts with respect to his expectation of life? To take a possible case, let it be assumed that the need arises from the disability of the insured and the prognosis of the physicians is unfavorable. Under such circumstances it is clearly in the interest of the public treasury that the policy be maintained in full force if there are dependents for whom provision will have to be made. The insurance, in other words, is from the standpoint of the public treasury worth far more than is its cash surrender value.

Many life insurance contracts contain provisions under which adjustments can be made to meet the new situation. It is always possible, moreover, for the law to authorize the public agency, unless the policy is nonassignable, to continue payment of the premiums and to take a lien on the policy itself or on the policy and other property, either for the amount advanced as premiums or for all money expenses in assistance to the family. Use of the lien procedure may justify continuing even a fairly substantial policy in full force during a considerable period, if satisfactory arrangements cannot be worked out with the insurance company or with local banks.

The facts with respect to insurance and home ownership both suggest the importance of distinguishing between temporary need and need which according to indications will be of considerable duration. It would seem that in dealing with temporary need, the treatment of property in the form of houses, including farm homes, and life insurance through a loan procedure may be more in the interest of both the family and the public than requiring the immediate conversion of the assets into cash. It should be noted in this connection that unemployment insurance benefits and disability insurance benefits are based on averages and are not adjusted to the needs in particular cases.

At the time a family gets into financial difficulties it may have outstanding obligations for things being purchased on the installment plan. Furniture, household appliances, and automobiles are the three principal classes. Is a family in need of aid from the public treasury if these installment purchases and the effort to make the payments are among the principal causes of the immediate difficulty if it could get along on a modest scale were it not for these commitments? Three points need emphasis in connection with such situations: (1) at the time the contract was made the worker may have been in good health and fully employed; his mistake was in not making suitable allowance for the possibility of unemployment, disability, or death; (2) the equity which the family has in the article being purchased may be substantial, but it will realize little on the equity should the article be repossessed under the contract; and (3) it may be in the long-run, social interest that the family have the advantages of the furniture or other appliances being purchased. Here again the distinction between temporary and prolonged need is important as is also the distinction between a prudent expenditure and dissipation of family resources.

Since the automobile has occasioned more controversy than other durable goods purchased it will be considered in detail. Is a family in need because it lacks the funds to maintain and operate a car and, unless ownership is complete, to continue payment on it. There are two parts to this question. The major one is to what extent is the automobile contributing to the economic efficiency of the family, and the subsidiary one is whether the value of the car is greatly out of proportion to the prospective resources of the family.

As World War II has abundantly demonstrated, the American people have distributed themselves and their activities upon the basis of private automobile transportation. Suburban residential communities have developed that are not served by any public transportation facilities.[2] They have offered relatively low-cost land and frequently low charges for municipal services because the degree of congestion did not necessitate highly organized and developed services. So far as the automobile was used for necessary transportation to and from work or to and from adequate public transportation facilities, the expenditure for it could be put in the category with rent. In some instances plants furnishing employment were so located that many of the workers were obliged to come to work in privately owned automobiles. Housing was not available within walking distance of the plants nor along the line of public transportation systems. Private automobile transportation had been assumed in the developments that had taken place.

Under circumstances such as these, ownership of a car by a family the breadwinner of which is temporarily unemployed or disabled is not necessarily evidence of absence of need. To force the family to sell the car and live on the proceeds while they lasted would be like forcing the sale of machinery temporarily idle because of a recession in demand. The family will need that car again, and it may be presently necessary to enable the worker to seek a new job or to get to jobs that offer part-time employment. To a person situated as he is the car may be a tool necessary for his employment.

It does not follow, however, that the costs of using that car for recreational purposes is a necessary expense to be covered by relief or social security payments. Much less does it mean that the recreational use of the car should be greatly increased by the family because the worker is not using it in going to and from work and because he has idle time on his hands. The wartime distinction between pleasure driving and necessary driving has to be made in determining whether the car is essential and if so what use of the car is necessary.

[2] In some instances public transportation facilities which had been developed prior to the general use of the automobile had been abandoned because they were rendered obsolete by the automobile.

Occasionally a case arises in which a family in need owns or more probably is purchasing a far more expensive car than can be justified on the basis of the current situation. Hindsight may prove beyond argument that its purchase was unwise in the first instance. One can easily understand the bad effect on public relations, especially in a relatively small community, if the owner of such a car is receiving relief from the public treasury, or if a work relief recipient drives to work in it. The situation is particularly bad if the owner of the car has a reputation in the community for irresponsibility and lack of ordinary sense. To conservative residents that car may exemplify the reasons for the family's need. Behind the intensity of the feeling frequently encountered with respect to cars may lie the fact that many thrifty workers have an unfulfilled desire to own such a car, which they have repressed because they could not afford it "with taxes what they are." Here again arises the question whether a government should make relief standards approximately as high as the standard which is attained by fully employed workers in the lower-wage brackets.

RESPONSIBILITY OF RELATIVES

One issue of great significance is whether a person in need should receive public funds if he has relatives who could or should support him. Discussion of this subject will be confined to two questions: (1) the responsibility of grown children for the support of their parents and, (2) the responsibility of a father who has deserted his family for the support of the children whether or not he is divorced from the mother.

With respect to support of parents, situations may be broadly classified somewhat as follows:

1. The parents are not in need, according to any reasonable definition, and hence their financial relationship with their children is not a matter of public concern.

2. The parents would be in need according to a reasonable definition were it not for the voluntary action of children contributing to their support. (a) The resources of the children are such that the amount remaining for their use after the con-

tribution is sufficient to meet their needs according to a satisfactory standard. (b) The resources of the children are too small to permit of contributions without socially undesirable sacrifices on the part of a child or possibly of several children.

3. The parents are in need according to the legal definition of need, but no child is voluntarily contributing in sufficient sums to make payment from public funds unnecessary. (a) There is a child (or more than one child) possessed of such resources that adequate contributions could be made without undue hardship. (b) There is no child who could contribute in any substantial way without socially undesirable hardship.

The first point to be noted is that children who are voluntarily supporting their parents in whole or in part are taxed to help take care of parents whose children are not contributing to their support. If the contributing child is the sole support of a dependent parent, he may take a deduction from the national income tax, but if he is one of several contributors or if the parent has resources which only require supplementation, he can take no deduction. Thus the child who observes the scriptural injunctions is at a financial disadvantage, for he pays taxes for relief, yet his own voluntary action may make his parent ineligible for the receipt of public funds.

The second point to be noted is that a child may have so little capacity to pay that a contribution, voluntary or compulsory, is socially undesirable. It may prevent the child from making suitable provision for his own child, or it may be a factor in preventing him from marrying or having children. A daughter may stay single to support or help support a parent, or if married may work outside the home to get the needed money. The elderly parent may be a member of a child's household under circumstances that create problems, financial, physical, and mental. Basic emotional difficulties may arise. A parent might prefer extreme want to any action to force a child to pay. Payment to a parent of one spouse may create serious difficulties with the other. For reasons such as these, experienced family case workers frequently take the position that the law should not make the child responsible for the support of a parent. Their position would be that, if the parent lacks sufficient resources of his own, he should be eligible for public assistance regardless of the means or capacity to pay of a child.

If it be accepted that the child should not be held responsible for contributing to the support of a parent, then it would seem to follow that all the resources of the parent should be regarded as available for his support in so far as necessary. Practically, that means that assets such as real estate and life insurance contracts shall be utilized in the interest of the parent if needed and that the adult child gets as an inheritance only what was not so required. The lien against the parent's property for the cost of aid extended is the simple way of enforcing such a policy. It necessitates legal provisions to prevent gifts from parents to children for the sake of establishing eligibility and avoiding the lien law. Presumably such laws should make the child responsible for the support of parents to the extent of any gifts or transfers made without adequate consideration after the child had ceased to be a dependent.

At this point attention should be called to the provisions of the New Zealand system as described on pages 515 to 552. New Zealand requires all persons to contribute 5 per cent of their income to the social insurance fund. From this fund all need is relieved, including that of elderly persons. Thus all children with capacity to pay are contributing to a fund from which the needs of their own parents will be met should their parents be in need. Under such circumstances there is little reason to use liens or to interfere with inheritances. The child has paid if he has income. If he inherits property which produces an income for him, that income will be subjected to the social security tax. A person with capacity to pay cannot leave support of his parents to someone else unless the cost of the relief exceeds the proceeds of his 5 per cent contribution. If he wishes, he can do more for his parents than is thus required, but such action is voluntary.

To indicate the importance of the question of the responsibility for the support of his children of the father who is estranged from his family a table is reproduced on page 591 taken from a report of the Social Security Board entitled *Families Receiving Aid to Dependent Children*, October 1942, page 27.

Reason for Lack of Support or Care by the Father	Per Cent of Total Families
All reasons.............................	**100.0**
Not in the home..........................	**78.8**
Dead..................................	37.2
Estranged from family[3].................	35.8
Incapacitated.........................	2.7
Absent for other reasons.................	3.1
In the home............................	**21.2**
Incapacitated.........................	19.4
Other reasons..........................	1.8

It will be noted that estrangement from the family, which includes divorce, desertion, separation, and the father not married to the mother, includes 35.8 per cent of the families and is almost as important as death of the father (37.2 per cent) as a reason for lack of paternal support. It materially exceeds incapacity which accounts for 22.1 per cent (2.7 not in the home and 19.4 in the home).

These figures demonstrate clearly that a social insurance system which provides only for death and disability leaves without protection a substantial number of children. If it be assumed that children under 16 years of age require the major time of the mother, then a substantial number of mothers are likewise left without protection.

Under existing laws these estranged husbands are generally liable for the support of their children. They can be brought in court for nonsupport, ordered to pay, and committed for nonpayment. Such evidence with which we are acquainted would suggest, however, that such a source of income is extremely uncertain. The responsible father may be unable to pay, unwilling to pay, or both, and not infrequently he has incurred new responsibilities for another wife and perhaps additional children. As was noted in the discussion of O.A.S.I. and as is true under most retirement systems, the deserted wife and children cannot gain possession of the contributions paid by the father for his

[3] Includes divorce, desertion, separation, and the father not married to the mother.

own old-age protection. From a social point of view it can be said that the problem of making suitable and adequate provision for the children in broken homes is more complex and difficult than any other in the whole field.

The New Zealand solution deserves mention at this point. If the deserted family has inadequate income, and if the mother has taken appropriate court action, she and the children are thereupon entitled to the same benefit they would receive were the father dead, with the proviso, however, that if contributions are received from the father, the benefits paid from the fund will be reduced by a like sum. In other words, the mother and the children are assured of the amount allowed by the law whether it comes from the father or from the fund. It will be recalled, moreover, that under the New Zealand law the rights of the father under the system are contingent upon meeting his responsibilities in so far as he is able. Apparently New Zealand, like the United States, has experienced difficulty in cases where the father for one reason or another leaves the mother to care for herself and the children. It would be interesting to know how well the New Zealand system is working out in actual practice. Theoretically it appears sound to determine need on the basis of the number in the family to be provided for and to treat the estranged father's contribution not as a certain source of income but merely as an offset to payments from the fund. Need is met, regular and certain receipt of what is regarded as a suitable minimum is assured, and the state assumes the risk of whether the father can or cannot pay or be forced to pay.[4]

---

[4] From the writer's point of view the broad conclusion regarding need is that the number of variables is so great, especially in a country like the United States, that it is impracticable to attempt to express need in terms of money income, uniform for the nation as a whole. Even within a state or a community, there may be wide differences among individual families. In cases where the need is temporary and the chances of rehabilitation are great, it may be desirable to follow principles and practices that would not be suitable where the need is more permanent and the chances of rehabilitation comparatively slight. Legislation based on averages will not provide suitably for the manifold departures from average.

CHAPTER XX

THE MEANS TEST

A relief or social security system designed exclusively for relieving need with a minimum collection and distribution of funds procured through taxation or compulsory contributions will use a means test. The present chapter will deal with the defects and the merits of a means test.

DEFECTS OF THE MEANS TEST

The means test is to many persons anathema. Almost anything, except total neglect of need, is better than a means test. The explanation of this antipathy lies at least in part in the fact that the means test was an essential element in a system cursed with many other defects. To it are attributed faults that on analysis appear to have resulted from other features of law or practice. In considering defects those that are putative will be taken up as well as those that are inherent.

Inherent in the use of the means test is ascertaining the facts to establish need or eligibility in the individual case. The person or a member of a family must supply the basic facts, for no government so far as we know keeps for all its citizens detailed records of all the essential facts. When facts are supplied by an individual to be used in determining whether or not he is to receive a grant or a benefit from public funds, it is essential that they be verified. Verification of facts regarding the resources and the activities of individuals or families means that public officials are inquiring into, even probing into, personal affairs. There was a time when such government inquiries were rarely made on a large scale except in connection with relief administration; but under modern conditions with wide use of income taxes, inheritance taxes, and other taxes based on capacity to pay, the state frequently inquires into matters that used to be regarded as private and personal, and the government may check these reports by methods that strike the subject as inquisitorial.

When the facts have been established, some governmental agency must apply the law and the regulations to them to determine whether the person is or is not eligible for benefits. This process is, as a matter of fact, necessary in many forms of social insurance where in general no means test is used, notably under some of the benefits for widows, children, and parents under old-age and survivors insurance, but there is an essential difference in degree. Under a means test system the agency must not only determine eligibility or need as it is defined in law or regulations, but also the degree of need, since under such systems the beneficiaries generally get no more than is necessary to bring them up to a certain standard.

A means test law commonly, although not necessarily, requires the governmental agency to pass upon factors such as the sobriety and morality of the individual or the suitability of a mother, father, or other relative to have the care and custody of a child. Although a trace of this sort of determination may be involved in disqualifications for unemployment insurance benefits, it is likely to be more important in means test, social security legislation. Again it should be emphasized, however, that a government could, if it saw fit, provide as it has done by inference say in O.A.S.I. that benefits shall be paid without any reference to character or behavior of beneficiaries.

Under the typical means test relief administration in the United States prior to the passage of the Social Security Act, a high degree of discretion was vested in administrative officers, generally local administrators. In many places granting of relief was in fact almost purely discretionary, or, if one prefers, arbitrary. But as administration in many of the states under the three assistance categories of the Social Security Act and in New Zealand under its act has demonstrated, unlimited discretion is not inherent in such administration. The law and the rules and regulations under the law may narrow discretion to a point where legally it scarcely exists, and provisions may be made for appeals at least to a higher administrative authority if not to the courts of law. Some discretion still exists in connection with ascertaining the facts, but experience suggests that such discretion is at least as likely to be exercised in favor of the applicant as against him. The code governing means test provision against want can be developed to the point where those concerned with its application have almost no legislative or discretionary power.

The means test in many northern states, was identified with settlement or residence laws. Persons naturally associated the two. Obviously there is no necessary connection. If the law has residence requirements, administrators must go into the question of residence in all the detail required by the law, but if there are no such requirements, the administrators naturally omit such questions. But a question of residence is not a question of means.

The old poor laws were in many instances apparently deliberately designed to humiliate the recipient. Applicants might be required to take the pauper's oath. In several states they were disenfranchised. Administrators not infrequently were discourteous and harsh with the poor or undoubtedly lectured them on the virtues of work, thrift, frugality, sobriety, and morality. Certainly such must have been the practice in New England. As has been repeatedly pointed out, many persons who are in need under modern social-economic conditions should be spared humiliation so far as possible. A means test can be administered with consideration and understanding. It necessarily involves, however, an official determination of the fact that the individual or the family is in need and that the normal link with the system of money distribution has broken. If prevention of that degree of humiliation is essential, then a more costly no-means test system is indicated.

A major defect of several means test systems—and this defect is present in the Social Security Act assistance categories—is that no device has been adopted so that sufficient appropriations are made to relieve all cases of genuine need. A practice common in some states has been to deny old-age assistance to persons who are in want simply because all available funds have been allotted, even if some persons whose need is much more questionable than that of the applicant are getting benefits from those funds. In some states inadequate appropriations have resulted in giving benefits in certain cases that are insufficient to meet need. Inherently defects of this type are not due to the means test. The New Zealand system affords an example of a means test plan that is to a very considerable extent specially and independently financed, although a parliamentary appropriation from general funds is necessary to make up the balance:

A casual examination of the figures for the no-means test old-age and survivors insurance might suggest that this no-means test system is free from dependence upon appropriations. This system, as has been explained at length elsewhere, will in its early days not only pay all maturing benefits from its own revenues but will develop a substantial surplus. As its true load develops with the passing years it may, however, develop deficits which will call for appropriations from general funds. If changes in the price level occur which make the lower benefits under this system inadequate to meet need, the meeting of need will depend on appropriations. Improper or unsuitable financing would not under such circumstances be attributable to the means test.

THE MERITS OF THE MEANS TEST

To turn now to the merits of the means test, some of them lie directly in the field of finance. Under a well-designed system, such as that in New Zealand, practically all persons in need according to the legal definitions are immediately given such assistance as is necessary to relieve that need. The taxpayers, or if one prefers the contribution payers, of today take care of all the need existing today. The means test is the device used to determine (1) the existence of need as defined by law and (2) the amount of benefit necessary to relieve that need.

Under a means test system no more money is taken from the taxpayers or contributors than is necessary to relieve need as defined by law. There is practically no taking of money by the exercise of the sovereign power of the state to give to persons who are not in need. A no-means test social insurance system avoids the inquisitorial character of the means test system by

collecting more money than is necessary to relieve need and distributing it among people, some of whom are not and never have
been in need. Such a system inevitably necessitates higher taxes
and higher contributions, although these higher taxes and contributions may not be paid currently but may be passed along
to future generations.

Administration of a means test system makes representatives
of the state determine the facts in each case. If the facts disclose
that need results from a remediable cause, qualified employees
of the state can seek to have remedial action taken. Several different situations may be encountered. (1) The persons in need
may not themselves know the causes, the remedial actions possible, and the necessary procedures; their basic need may be for
information and guidance. (2) Whether they know the action
called for or not, they may lack the initiative and the executive
capacity to do what is required; their basic need may be for
someone to exert friendly pressure. (3) An element of anti-social
behavior may be present in the case; it may be an offense in the
eyes of the law; it may be only a failure to co-operate with the
state in efforts the state is making in the interest of all its people of a given age or of some other particular category. Under
a means test system the state can say in effect through its representatives: "The state will relieve your need but you, in co-
operation with the state, must seek to remedy the conditions
that are causing or contributing to the cause of your need." The
need of the individual or the family is used as an incentive to
have the causes of that need removed.

Social insurance without a means test frees the individual or
the family from such pressure. It deprives the state of that device for securing co-operation and leaves it dependent on other
methods. In this connection it should again be emphasized that
beneficiaries of social insurance in very few cases have paid contributions that actually cover the costs of insurance on an
actuarial basis. A considerable part of their benefits come from
general taxes, and much of the remainder may come from premiums paid by others. General taxes may be meeting not only
part of the costs of the no-means test benefits but also the costs

involved in seeking to get the beneficiary to co-operate wit..
the state in its activities designed for the protection and advancement of all in a category. The state more or less has to
subject some individuals to pressure; the question is what devices shall be used to exert pressure.

The means test therefore involves the ascertainment of facts
that are highly personal, decisions as to eligibility or ineligibil-
ity, often the determination as to the amount of benefit, perhaps the use of the pressure of need to secure co-operation with
the state, and official recognition of the fact that the individual
or the family is in need. These features appear to be inherent
in its use. Other objections often cited as adhering to it really
relate directly to other features of a plan. Its use permits relieving need with a minimum collection and redistribution of
taxes or other compulsory contributions.

CHAPTER XXI

COVERAGE

In the present chapter we are to deal with the question, "Who should be covered by a system of relief and social security?" We shall start with an attempt at a very general answer and then take up qualifications. In giving a broad answer we shall assume that there is substantial agreement that the basic fundamental objective of social insurance and relief is to prevent anybody from being or remaining in want. The existence of want requires the state to take appropriate action to see that want is relieved. If that general assumption is accepted, the broad answer to the question is simple. Every man, woman, and child resident in the country should be covered without any exceptions.

That answer does not mean, however, that every man, woman, and child should be relieved from want in precisely the same way, that there should be no differentiation with respect to the causes of want, or that the social security system itself should be all embracing. In the next chapter the question of what causes of need should be covered by the social security system will be taken up in detail. Here we need only point out that certain classes of the population require treatment, custodial care, or restraint in specialized public institutions. Institutional care prevents them from being in want. If they happen to have dependents who do not require institutional care, these dependents lie within the sphere of the social security system.

From the broad assumption another conclusion seems to follow. Relief of actual want occupies a position of very high priority in its claims on the funds of the state. Ahead of it one would place necessary operating costs of government, preservation of law and order, national defense, essential health protection and governmental activities essential for the continued production of necessary goods and services. The theory underlying this statement is that the safety of all cannot be jeopardized for the relief of the few. In the United States, however, governments, national, state, and local, have in the past spent so much for governmental activities that are of lower priority than the relief of want that there appears to be little danger that such relief would jeopardize the basic essentials.

The fact should be squarely faced that our existing social security and relief programs do violence to this basic principle of giving relief of want an extremely high priority. Let us cite certain concrete examples.

Many persons are in want who are not protected by old-age and survivors insurance, unemployment insurance, or the three relief categories of the Social Security Act. They are in theory to be provided for under the general public assistance laws or other laws of the several states. In fact, however, they are not provided for at all because the states have not raised the necessary funds or passed the necessary laws or set up the necessary administrative machinery. Yet at the same time the national government is levying a tax on employers to support O.A.S.I., which provides benefits for persons some of whom will not be in need at all or will not be in need to the extent of the full amount of their benefits. Surpluses from these taxes are built up in the national treasury, although the actual money has been used for other purposes. These taxes on employers are largely passed on to consumers so that the people are paying for future old-age protection while some present-day want remains unrelieved. Through federal action the states are influenced to make provision for the three relief categories of the Social Security Act, whereas other citizens may be in far greater want than some, perhaps many, of the old-age beneficiaries.

The classic illustration in American relief history was W.P.A.[1] To the unemployed employable who was in need

---

[1] Some more vivid illustrations, not so well known and not involving so much money, are to be found in resettlement projects and subsistence homesteads. Thousands of dollars were invested in projects designed to aid a small group of specially selected families in particular neighborhoods. Elsewhere in the same state or in neighboring states were individuals or families almost entirely dependent for food on the distribution of surplus commodities. It is extremely difficult to understand why our governments in the emergency failed to recognize that their first obligation in the field of social security and relief was to prevent want and that other things they did in this field were of secondary or even lower importance.

and succeeded in getting a place on a W.P.A. project, the national government, aided by some sponsors' contributions from state or local governments, paid a security wage. This wage was not related to either the degree of need of the individual nor to the number or need of persons dependent upon him. Some got much more than was required. To the unemployed employable who could not be assigned to a project, to his dependents, and to the unemployable not provided for under a Social Security Act category, the national government gave nothing. Several states practically confined their own appropriations to programs into which federal money went and did practically nothing for others in need. To the relatively fortunate went in many cases more than was necessary while other needy remained in want. The localities got roads, parks, playgrounds, histories, guide books, indexes of county records, and other things for some of which the priority was extremely low, while some of their residents remained in desperate want. Basic priorities got lost to view in the haste and confusion of the legislation and administration.

Attention should be called in this chapter to the fact that the existing systems of social insurance are limited in the extent to which they actually extend protection. The details have been given in earlier chapters and will not here be repeated, but to summarize:

1. O.A.S.I. covers only salary and wage earners in included occupations and establishments. Certain classes of establishments or occupations are excluded, including among others agriculture and domestic service. Persons working on their own account are likewise excluded. Thousands who are paying contributions under O.A.S.I. are not protected by it because they have not been under it long enough to be either currently insured or fully insured. They lose coverage if they leave gainful employment or move into uncovered work before they are permanently fully insured or if they outlive the extended insurance available for the currently insured.

2. Unemployment insurance likewise is not all inclusive with respect to industries and occupations. Not all workers on whose account taxes are paid are actually insured. The number of

weeks during which benefits are paid is limited. The persons who
have the longest periods of unemployment are the ones most
likely to be in real want, and they are the ones for whom systematic provision has not been made.

Perhaps the most noteworthy omission of all is that victims
of disability, either temporary or permanent, occurring before
age 65 are left to general public assistance unless they receive
payments under workmen's compensation laws.

Thus in the United States today our systems of relief and
social security do not give assured universal coverage against
want. Some classes are assured more than that degree of coverage, others far less.

CHAPTER XXII

HAZARDS TO BE RECOGNIZED

In earlier chapters the evolution of relief and social security has been briefly traced. It will be recalled that in the early days all persons in need were largely included together regardless of the cause of their need, the care they required, and the possibilities of restoration. The treatment of all was, from the standpoint of present day scientific knowledge, unenlightened and often harsh. Because of the attitudes of administrators, legislators, and the public at large, progress was made by isolating from the mass special categories members of which were to receive special care and special treatment. Public opinion could be changed with respect to a category, whereas it could not be changed with respect to the undifferentiated mass. To make a categorical system work under these circumstances, it was necessary to set up conditions of eligibility for the special category, because members of it were to receive what was in fact preferred and more advantageous treatment in view of their condition. As previously noted, to get the category freed from old prejudices and old standards of administration, the common practice was to have the new categorical systems administered by agencies other than those operating under the poor laws.

When the idea took hold that some of the concepts of private voluntary insurance should be applied in the solution of problems resulting from need, legislators commonly proceeded by categories. Independent systems were developed for selected categories. Thus today we have in the United States experiments in providing some of the concepts of insurance to old-age protection for most but not all of the salaried and wage workers and to partial unemployment protection for most of these same workers. Need resulting from other hazards is in the main cared for, if it is cared for at all, through other and older devices.

The fact that existing systems are incomplete and unco-ordinated gives rise to the question, Against what hazards should protection be afforded? To show the nature of the issue we shall resort to illustrations.

In a large industrial city there are several families comparable with respect to their degree of need and to their composition. As dependents each family includes three children under 16 years of age and their mother. The age of the children is such that the mother has a full-time job in keeping house and in caring for the children. The differences among the families arise from differences in the hazards that have deprived the dependents of the support of the father. These hazards may be classified as follows:

1. The father is dead
    a. From a disease not connected with his employment.
    b. From an accident connected with his employment.
    c. From a disease resulting from occupational causes.
    d. From an industrial accident.

2. The father is sick or disabled, either temporarily or permanently. The subclassifications shown under (1) above are also applicable here.

3. The father is an unemployed employable, willing and able to work but unable under existing economic conditions to find a suitable job.

4. The father has deserted his family and is not contributing to the support of his dependents.

5. The father is an alcoholic or has other habits that prevent him from supporting his dependents.

6. The father has committed an offense and is being punished by imprisonment.

So far as the basic minimum needs of the wife and the children in these families are concerned, there is no substantial difference. The differences arise from the hazards that permanently or temporarily deprived them of paternal support.

As one reads the list of hazards the words deserving and undeserving may come to mind. Two points, however, must be noted in this connection: (1) the husband who is dead may have been no more deserving than the one whose conduct on the face of the record is obviously reprehensible, and the same may be true of the husband who is ill or disabled; and (2) there is no necessary relationship between the hazard that deprived the family of support and the character, behavior, ability, and capacity for sound development of the children. The basic fundamental needs of the mother and children are not dependent on the cause responsible for their situation.

The differences in causes relate solely and exclusively to the fathers. If relief of need is the social objective, then this classification by cause is significant, if it is significant at all, only with respect to the size and nature of benefits and any action to be taken with respect to the father. If the father is living and is unemployed or disabled, provision must be made for him in the family budget. If he has deserted his family or if he is in an institution being housed, clothed, and fed by the state, no provision for him is necessary. What is to be done about the fathers in the cases of failure to meet responsibility is another matter which will not here be considered.

Two systems that cover or propose to cover all hazards have been examined earlier in the present book, the proposed British plan and the New Zealand system. The no-means test contributory insurance system of the British plan covers all major hazards for all persons who can make such contributions as are required of them; all children under 16 are provided for; others are taken care of through a means test, public assistance program. The means test New Zealand system established qualifications and standards for all major hazards; persons in need who cannot meet the established qualifications or who are in need for causes not specifically mentioned in the act may be taken care of by the administrative agency by virtue of discretionary power specifically delegated to it in the law. Both these plans practically provide coverage for all against all major hazards.

To us it seems inescapable that if the object of the social security system is to prevent want then want must be relieved regardless of the cause which occasioned it. In other words, provision must be made within the system for all persons who are in need. Every hazard must be provided for in one way or another. The issue is how they shall be provided for systematically and not whether some shall be included and others excluded. To exclude need resulting from a given cause would be to fail to make provision for those in need from that cause. The real issues are those treated in other chapters.

CHAPTER XXIII

SIZE OF BENEFITS IN GENERAL

In the preceding chapter the conclusion was reached that the social security system should provide benefits for all persons who are in need regardless of the specific cause of their need. The chapter following this one will deal with the special factors that have to be considered with respect to old age, disability, sickness, unemployment, and death. Specific questions regarding the size of benefit to be granted arise in connection with each of them. There are, however, certain questions with respect to the size of benefits that are common to them all, which will be presented in the present chapter.

RELATION OF BENEFITS TO EARNINGS

Ignoring details and variants, one may say there are two major schools of thought with respect to the size of benefits in general. The first school maintains that the social security system should go no further than to insure to every resident a minimum level of living in accordance with a standard established by the government. The government may provide this level, as Sir William Beveridge proposed, by seeing that each individual is provided for personally or through a parent or guardian with enough to live according to that level regardless of what other resources he or she may have; or, as under the New Zealand means test system, it may if necessary supplement his available resources with sufficient funds to bring them to the established levels. Under either of these systems, if the individual desires more, he must get it through his own efforts or the effort of his family.

The second school apparently takes the position that the level of living to which an individual or family is accustomed depends largely upon the salary or wages of the individual or the wage earner of the family. If the individual or the family suffers from economic reverses, the amount of benefit supplied by governmental action should bear some relationship to his earnings. This school recognizes that the low-income families have to spend a higher percentage of their income for necessities than do moderate- to high-income families. The program advanced by this group therefore gives a subsistence benefit to the low-income group and a larger amount to the higher-income groups. A uniform, definite, percentage relationship between benefit and earnings is not maintained; the low-bracket group gets a larger percentage; but there is a relationship.

The first group regards the prevention of want as its major objective. The size of the benefit is determined upon as part and parcel of the determination of what is need. In view of what has been said in earlier chapters, it is unnecessary to discuss this point of view further. We shall instead confine ourselves to a consideration of the arguments in favor of a relationship between earnings and benefits, with some benefits materially exceeding a reasonable minimum of subsistence.

In retirement systems for public and private employees there is a general demand for a relationship between salaries or wages and benefits. This demand has been discussed at some length in the chapters on the retirement systems of federal employees and railroad workers. The demand for a relationship between benefits and earnings is particularly insistent if the retirement system is contributory and contributions are a percentage of salary or wages or of salary and wages up to a specified maximum. The individual who pays the larger amount not unnaturally feels that he is entitled to a larger benefit. As one reads the original provisions regarding old-age insurance in the Social Security Act, it appears that the framers of the act had been greatly influenced by retirement system philosophy; as if they planned to have a universal retirement system under which would come almost all salary and wage workers. Because of this application of retirement system philosophies to general old-age insurance, it is pertinent to note similarities and differences.

Membership in a retirement system was generally made compulsory not only for all new employees but for all old employees who elected to remain in the service. If an employee or an applicant for employment did not like the retirement system, his alternative was to get a job with a concern which had no retirement system or one more to his liking. The national system is likewise compulsory, but if an employee does not like it or regards it as doing grave injustice to persons of his grade, there is very little he can do about it. Every employer to whom he could possibly sell his services may be under the same system.

On the establishment of a retirement system, the present employees cannot be assessed for any great part of the cost of paying benefits with respect to services rendered prior to its adoption. If the employer has low-bracket employees, the percentage of their pay withheld as contributions may not, even in the case of new entrants, be sufficient to pay the same proportion of the cost of their benefits that the higher-bracket employees are paying. The employer must therefore contribute (1) most of the cost of benefits allowed for past services, and (2) a higher proportion of the cost of the benefits for the low-paid workers than he is paying for his high-bracket workers.

The universal national O.A.S.I. retirement system faced this same problem, inherent in making benefits relate to salary and wages if adequate benefits are to be paid lower-bracket employees and if sufficient benefits are to be granted workers who retire in the early years of the system. The employers or the general taxpayers must contribute heavily. There was, however, a fundamental difference between the universal system and the individual employer systems.

Under an individual employer system the employer's money went to his own employees. If he paid well and had few low-paid employees, relatively large contributions for low-paid employees was not a significant matter. Under the universal national system, the taxes paid by the employer with high salary and wage standards with high regularity of employment go to pay the benefits for employees of employers who pay low wages or furnish irregular or intermittent employment. The employer who is conducting his business in a high cost-of-living, urban center is helping pay the benefits given to low-paid workers in low cost-of-living areas. Neither he nor his own employees will in the long run derive any substantial benefit from his contributions. If his employees are paid enough to subject them to substantial federal taxes, they may in the long run be better off without the system than with it. Thus such a system involves a redistribution of earnings not inherent in anything approaching the same degree in employer retirement funds. The higher the benefit schedules the greater the degree of such redistribution.

RELATION OF BENEFITS TO COST OF LIVING

A national system confronts another difficulty arising from variations in the cost of living and the level of living in different sections of the country. These variations have already been discussed at some length in the chapter on need, and that discussion will not here be summarized. The significant point here is that the United States has these wide variations; whether they are due to differences in cost or differences in levels is not for the moment material. Politically it is inexpedient for the national government under a nationally operated system to use a different benefit formula for different sections of the country or for different areas within a state. A universal national benefit formula is almost inevitable in a nationalized system.

The national old-age insurance system establishes a relationship between the amount of benefit and wages or salaries. Wages and salaries have a relationship to cost of living and levels of living. Thus there is an indirect relationship between old-age insurance benefits and the cost and level of living. Indeed the relationship of benefits to wages and salaries may have been adopted in part to secure this indirect relationship.

How satisfactory is this method of establishing a relationship to the cost and level of living from an economic and social point of view? The economic and social implications can be most easily brought out by another question, "How satisfactory from a social and economic standpoint is an income of $2,400 a year for a family consisting of a man and wife and three children under 18 years of age?" The father of such a family offered work at $2,400 a year would ask where the job was and what it would cost him to live in that community. Such a family income is one thing in New York City or Washington, D. C. and quite a different thing in the rural South or even in rural New England. In the two cities named, practically the whole sum would have to go for the necessaries of a minimum health and decency level of living with little margin for saving. Prior to World War II in many rural areas a satisfactory house could be purchased for between $2,000 and $3,600 or rented for $15 to $30 a month. With a little effort the family could supply many of their needs for food without expenditure of cash. With prudent management such an income would permit of substantial savings. Consistent earnings of such an income with good management would make the man in his later years on a modest scale a capitalist.

Under the O.A.S.I. formula, average annual earnings of $200 a month for 35 years would yield a man retiring after attaining the age of 65 a benefit of $47.25 a month. If he had an eligible wife, also 65 years of age or over, she could draw $23.62, giving the couple a total of $70.87. For a couple in a rural community who have lived prudently and have managed their savings with reasonable skill, a benefit of $70.87 a month added to their other resources would mean a living well above a minimum health and decency standard. It is questionable whether at any time since the outbreak of World War I $47.25 a month for a single person or $70.87 for a married couple would have produced anything approaching a minimum health and decency standard in Washington.

For the man who has earned an average of $50 a month for 35 years the O.A.S.I. formula would yield $27 a month for a man 65 years of age or over and $13.50 for his wife if eligible, a total of $40.50. In a rural community with a low cost and level of living $40.50 would mean no great change. In a metropolitan center such as New York City or in Washington, average earnings of as little as $50 a month would suggest that the man had not as a matter of fact been supporting himself, his wife, and his children on so small a sum. Investigation would probably reveal either that he had other earnings not included under the system or that he had other sources of income. In high-cost-of-living cities two or more wage earners in a family are necessary if the principal breadwinner cannot average materially better than $50 a month. It will be recalled, however, that where husband and wife have both worked in covered employments and paid social security taxes, the wife cannot draw both the benefit which she has earned through her own labor and the benefit to which she would have been entitled through her husband had she never worked in covered employment. She can take whichever is the larger, but she cannot take both.

The O.A.S.I. benefits are based on average monthly earnings for the entire period of covered employment. The use of average earnings throughout service leads to some striking differences between (1) employees who reach their maximum earnings fairly soon after beginning work and hold them fairly consistently throughout, (2) employees who start low but work up gradually and fairly consistently throughout service, and (3) employees who start at close to their maximum, hold fairly consistently during the years of their physical strength and vigor, and drop after that vigor is lost. Highly skilled labor typifies the first group; professional workers, and successful clerical and sales people, the second; and unskilled manual laborers the third. Relating the amount of benefits to average earnings throughout the working years makes retirement particularly difficult for the most successful people, who have advanced gradually but consistently during the years. It makes a wide gulf between their benefits based on average earnings and the salary or wages they were earning when they reached the retirement age. On the other hand it encourages prompt retirement for persons whose earnings are declining rapidly.

The use of a national formula for relating benefits to earnings and thus remotely and without any considerable degree of precision to cost of living and levels of living is a highly unsatisfactory method for a nation such as the United States with its wide variations in costs and levels of living.

Wide variations in costs and levels of living likewise preclude the adoption by the United States of uniform money standards such as are used for the means test New Zealand system. They would at best be right on the average, but they would be grossly harsh in the great industrial cities, particularly in the North, and they would be unnecessarily liberal in rural areas, particularly in the South. Should the political pressure of the industrial centers bring the national standards to a satisfactory level for workers in those areas, benefits in the rural areas would often equal and perhaps in many instances exceed prevailing wages. Action taken to raise prevailing wages to exceed benefits by a sufficient margin to make work preferable to retirement would greatly increase the cost of commodities produced in those areas and the prices which would have to be charged for them.[1]

Wide variations in costs and levels of living likewise preclude the successful use in the United States of a flat minimum of subsistence benefit throughout the nation, such as was proposed for Britain by Sir William Beveridge. Sir William[2] himself recognized that even in as compact and homogeneous a country as Great Britain the flat benefits might have to be supplemented by extra allowances for rent in London and other high-rent districts. In a few agricultural areas in Britain, too, the uniform national minimum benefit as proposed by Sir William might have exceeded the prevailing wage. Those agricultural enterprises, desired for purposes of national defense, would probably have to be subsidized by the state if they were to pay a prevailing wage as high as the standard uniform flat rate benefit. It is generally admitted that the social security schemes will not work satisfactorily if persons on benefit get more money than the active workers who are producing the

[1] Query: If subsidies are to be used in adjusting wages and earnings to make a social security benefit plan work, would it be better to subsidize the municipal services which make rents and the cost of living so high in urban industrial communities and relieve real estate of some of the burden of the resulting taxation? Then the cost of living in these centers could be reduced. If rural industry is subsidized where shelter is relatively cheap, the subsidies may go largely for things not essential to maintain a reasonable level of living. The big cities are the places where essential costs are high.

[2] It will be recalled that the British government did not accept Sir William's proposals on this point but made some reduction in the standard. See p. 477.

goods and services to maintain the beneficiaries. For too many persons there is no incentive to work if they can get more being idle.

If benefits are to be related to the cost of living and prevailing level of living in the various parts of the United States three devices deserve consideration.

1. A very difficult one: To attempt to define national standards in terms of essentials for food, clothing, shelter, recreation, medical care, and the like, and to base the amount of the benefit in money on what these items cost in the particular area.

2. To classify communities or areas on the basis of costs of living and levels of living in those areas and to have for each class of community or area a benefit scale.

3. To have the national government abandon all efforts to operate and set uniform monetary benefits in any part of the social security system but instead to rely entirely upon the grant-in-aid system or the tax-control system now used for unemployment insurance. Under such a system the national government would set certain minimum standards with which all states would have to comply. These standards would be appropriate for the lowest cost or lowest level of living states and would be adjusted from time to time to correct for changes in prices and other factors. States which deemed those minimum levels unsatisfactory to meet their situation would raise their level above that required under federal law.

Both the first and second devices, if used by the national government, involve a monetary although not necessarily an actual discrimination between sections of the country. Politically, in our judgment, such discrimination is highly inexpedient. Pressures develop under this kind of a system in a democracy. Voters in an area will demand that action be taken that will raise the benefits in their area. It is extremely difficult for elected officials to resist these pressures. Top ranking administrators, politically appointed, may be only a little less sensitive to this pressure, for they know they will go out on a change of administration.

Use of the state legislatures and the state administrators appears to be the feasible solution if benefits under a social security system are to be based on need or are to be related directly to levels and cost of living. This subject will be further considered in subsequent chapters.

RELATION OF BENEFITS TO COSTS OF THE SYSTEM

Although the cost of social security systems is to be considered in detail in later chapters, it seems necessary to present here a broad statement of cost as it affects the general question of the proper or desirable level of benefits.

If need is to be relieved, it can be done at the lowest cost by (1) paying benefits only to those who are in need and (2) making the benefits only as large as is necessary to relieve need. Under such a system the cost will depend on the exact standards used to measure need. If these standards are strictly or conservatively fixed and administered at a point no higher than is necessary to relieve need, the country has practically the lowest cost system that can be devised. Every action taken to increase benefits above this level increases costs. The use of the means test has already been discussed. Here we are concerned only with levels of benefits.

Some readers will at once ask, "Should people be required to get along on what will be a bare minimum of subsistence in a country which can afford far more?" Few persons no matter how conservative want large numbers living at a minimum of subsistence. The more conservative will ask, however, "How far should the sovereign power of the state be used to take property from one group to give to another after need has been relieved?" After need has been relieved, should not persons be dependent on their own activities and upon their own thrift and savings? After need has been relieved, should not public funds be used for developing and perfecting public services and opportunities available for all who can profit by them rather than in giving publicly collected funds to individuals? These opposing points of view raise again the issues discussed at length in the chapter on need.

The larger the benefits the larger the amount of money which must be collected and distributed by the government. The more money taken by the government from the taxpayers, directly or indirectly, the less margin the individual has to use as he sees fit. It is possible to develop a social security system to a point where many individuals will find all their margin absorbed by social security contributions and other taxes. They will have little with which they can do as they please. They will have little for voluntary insurance or savings, but it may be said they will have little reason to save, for the state has provided for them through social security. Compulsory saving through social security has been substituted for voluntary saving. No longer can a person spend what he should have saved and run the risk of ending up with only a minimum of subsistence and that given him by the state after a means test. It is probably fair to say that the higher the benefits under a social security system the less personal freedom with respect to property remains to the individual.

Brief reference should again be made to the dangers inherent in a system that does not immediately assume the full load but will have a progressively heavier burden in each ensuing year for some eighty years. The larger the benefits promised under such a system the greater this danger. Unfortunately it is easy to promise large benefits if the promise involves no immediate costs. Large money benefits payable in the fairly distant future will, moreover, only be large real benefits if purchasing power is maintained. If promises can only be fulfilled by government depreciation of the currency, the promises do more harm than good.

CHAPTER XXIV

FACTORS AFFECTING SPECIFIC BENEFITS

In the preceding chapter broad factors were considered regarding the general level of benefits for the system as a whole. The present chapter will deal with special factors regarding benefits in the case of (1) old age, (2) disability, (3) sickness, (4) unemployment, and (5) death.

OLD-AGE BENEFITS

The first question which should be answered with respect to an old-age benefit in a social security system is "What is its purpose?" The major purpose, beyond argument, is to provide at least a subsistence level of living for persons who because of their age are no longer able to earn a living for themselves and, in the case of married women, can no longer be supported by their husbands.

In the case of individual employer or industry retirement funds, a definitely recognized objective was to enable the employer, without committing a grave injustice, to retire an employee when his effectiveness began to wane because of advancing age, and to be in a position to replace the old worker with a younger one, presumably more efficient. That replacement, moreover, opened up opportunities for the younger employees to advance to the higher positions and, as the phrase ran, "resulted in promotions all down the line." To secure these results without embarrassment or hard feeling, most retirement systems provided a compulsory retirement age, although many systems permitted continuance beyond the compulsory age, usually in the discretion of the employer. Thus a major objective was to permit an organization to maintain its efficiency and still not do a grave injustice to the individual. To prevent injustices to workers who had attained the more responsible, more highly paid positions, substantial retirement allowances were paid to them. Not infrequently average salary in the last

617

five years or average salary in the five best consecutive years was the basis.

Should a governmentally operated social security, old-age system adopt such an objective in addition to the objective of promising persons at least a minimum of security in their old age? The objective of government, it would seem, should be, in so far as possible, to maintain conditions under which all persons willing and able to work can secure employment. The interests of the country as a whole are apparently best served when the largest proportion of its citizens are engaged in activities that are immediately or prospectively productive. The elderly person still rendering useful service is more of a social and economic asset than the one who has laid aside his work and become dependent on his own accumulations or upon the work of others.

Is such a point of view inconsiderate of the interests of elderly people? Elderly workers can be divided into two broad classes: (1) those who are so far disabled, whether from a specific cause or from a general slowing down, that they cannot support themselves, and (2) those who although well along in years are still able to render effective service. Provision obviously must be made for those in the first group who have no other available resources. It is the second group with which we are here concerned.

Elderly people who are still able to render effective service differ widely in their interests and desires. At one extreme are those whose desire is to remain at work so long as health permits. As a rule they have had a deep interest in and enthusiasm for their work. At the other extreme are those who stress their desire to retire while they are still young enough to enjoy retirement. Work is something done to secure a living. If a living were available without work, they would prefer to devote their time to other activities, free from the discipline and compulsions that are involved in group enterprises.

With respect to the elderly people who desire to remain at work, the question is whether a social security system adopted by a government should contain anything like the compulsory retirement provisions of an individual employer or individual industry retirement system. These provisions are part of the system of personnel administration in that particular organization. Has the government a like reason for including such clauses?

With respect to those who wish to retire while they are still young enough to enjoy it, are there valid distinctions among (1) those who retire on their personal accumulations either earned and saved or inherited; (2) those who have worked in establishments where formal or informal negotiations between employer and employee have resulted in provisions permitting retirement at an early age, without disability, on a benefit, sufficiently substantial so that securing another job is not imperative; and (3) those who retire under a state social security system so designed that the high costs of early retirements are borne in the main by taxes on employers,—presumably passed along to consumers—and by general taxes?

Upon one's answers to these questions will turn in no small measure one's opinion as to the size of the old-age benefits which should be provided and the age at which one should be entitled to retire solely and exclusively by proving attained age.

In arriving at a decision on these questions some persons will want information as to relative costs. For their convenience on page 620 we shall include two tables bearing on that subject. The first will be based on the population of the United States, showing numbers at or over 55, 60, 65, 70, and 75, respectively, with the costs of furnishing each individual at or above the specified age a benefit of $100 and $400 a year. The second will deal with white men at each of those ages and will give (1) their average remaining lifetime, (2) the present value of a life annuity of $100 for about that expectancy, and (3) the present value of a life annuity of $400 for about that expectancy. For the present values of the annuities, 3 per cent interest is assumed.

On examining these tables the reader may note that to pay an annuity of $400 a year to each person in the population 70 years of age or over would cost about 2.1 billion dollars a year. Decreasing the age limit to 60 years would increase the cost to about 5.5 billions or by about 3.4 billion dollars. The present value of the annuity for the white man 70 years of age would be roughly $3,116 whereas that for the one 60 years of age would be roughly $4,776.

POPULATION ABOVE CERTAIN SPECIFIED AGES, 1940

Specified Age	Population (In thousands)	Cost in Millions of a Pension per Annum of	
		$100 Each	$400 Each
75 years or over...........	2,643	$264	$1,056
70 years or over...........	5,213	521	2,084
65 years or over...........	9,019	902	3,608
60 years or over...........	13,748	1,375	5,500
55 years or over...........	19,592	1,959	7,836

AVERAGE FUTURE LIFETIME AND ANNUITY VALUES, WHITE MALES OF SPECIFIED AGES

Specified Age	White Males of Specified Age		
	Average Future Lifetime[a]	Approximate Present Value of Annuity for Average Future Lifetime	
		Years	$100	$400
75 years...........	7.1	7	$623	$2,492
70 years...........	9.3	9	779	3,116
65 years...........	11.9	12	995	3,980
60 years...........	14.9	15	1,194	4,776
55 years...........	18.2	18	1,375	5,500

[a] Bureau of the Census, *United States Abridged Life Tables, 1930–39* (Preliminary).

Figures for the annuity of $100 a year have been included in these tables for the convenience of anyone who desires to figure annuities of other amounts. An annuity of $900 would, for example, cost 9 times as much as an annuity of $100. At age 65 an annuity of $900 a year for a white male would have a present value of $8,955, whereas a like annuity for the white man of 70 would have a present value of $7,011.

Reduction of the age at retirement greatly adds to the cost of the system at any given rate of benefit. As rates of benefit are raised for any age, moreover, the inducement offered to persons to retire on benefit is greater. A low rate of benefit, such as the uniform minimum of subsistence of the Beveridge plan, offers a minimum inducement to retire. It will be recalled, moreover, that the Beveridge plan offers some inducements for persons to remain active after attaining the retirement age, by promising higher benefits to those who retire later. That plan, however, does not increase the benefit by the full saving in costs resulting from late retirements, and hence the fund profits from them.

Where the minimum age for eligibility for old-age benefits should be placed will depend in no small measure on whether benefits have been provided for disability occurring before the retirement age and the relationship between the old-age benefit and the disability benefit.

The Beveridge plan, it will be recalled, pays the same standard benefit, a liberal minimum, whether the worker is disabled before he reaches the retirement age or whether he retires on reaching that age. So far as the worker is concerned, he gets no more for age retirement if he withdraws voluntarily on attaining the minimum required age than if he is retired earlier because of disability. From his point of view the difference is, if he desires to retire at an earlier age than the one fixed for the old-age pension, he must prove disability or unemployment, and he may be called upon from time to time thereafter to prove the continuance of the disability or unemployment. After he has attained the minimum age for old-age pension, he does not have to prove either disability or unemployment in the first instances, nor may he be called upon thereafter to demonstrate the continued existence of either the disability or the unemployment.

Under the Beveridge plan the minimum retirement age is simply the point at which the law will assume disability or unemployability by the mere proof of age. When that age has been attained, the worker is free to decide for himself whether he will keep on working so long as he is able or whether he will retire and enjoy leisure. The Beveridge plan gives him no more than the standard uniform minimum no matter what his earnings have been. The life of leisure, therefore, cannot hold forth much attraction to an individual unless he has means to supplement the old-age pension under the social security system.

The present situation in the United States is radically different, basically because no special provision has been made for disability occurring before attainment of the retirement age, except in certain employer or industrial retirement systems or in cases of occupational accidents or diseases covered by workmen's compensation. For many persons attainment of the age line established for old-age assistance or for old-age and survivors insurance represents the first protection from the uncertainties of general public assistance.

Where the age line is drawn is thus far more vital in the United States than it is under the Beveridge plan. The individual below it who is disabled may have little or nothing for himself and those dependent upon him, whereas the covered employee who is above it may be reasonably well provided for either through his benefits, through his own resources, or through the two in combination. This discrimination results apparently from three principal factors: (1) our concentration on categories has prevented us from seeing that want however caused is the heart of our problem; (2) powerful political pressure groups have developed to further provisions for the aged and the unemployed; and (3) categories require the establishment of rules of eligibility, and rules of eligibility are almost invariably based on standards applicable to that particular category.

Chronological age is a poor indicator of the mental and physical condition of the individual and his elasticity and adjustability. Reference has already been made to persons whose value remains high long after they have passed their 65th birthday. Here we are basically concerned with persons whose powers are seriously diminished long before they have attained that age. Some of us have known men and women who although still in their fifties acted, and even appeared, really old. Performance of their accustomed routine duties deteriorated, and it was quite out of the question to give them new assignments requiring the acquisition of new knowledge, new skills, and new interests.

As one begins at say 70 years of age and goes down the age classes the chances that the employee will have family responsibilities increase. Children over 16 years of age but still in educational institutions are encountered first and then children under 16.

The high costs of old-age pensions available at ages under 65 years make them a doubtful wisdom. A basic issue in the United States is whether the sovereign power of government should be used to give no-means test pensions of more than a reasonable minimum of subsistence to persons 65 years of age or over before any provision has been made for many disabled before they have attained 65.

Attention should at this point be called to the extent to which the old-age concept has entered the provisions for wives and surviving widows in the national old-age and survivors insurance. To be eligible for benefit the wife of the retired worker and the widow with no child under 16 years of age must have attained the age of 65. No consideration has been given to her physical or mental condition, to her training and experience for getting a job, and supporting herself. If she is mentally or physically unfit, or if economic conditions preclude successful employment, she must depend on the uncertain general public assistance if her husband's primary benefit under O.A.S.I. and the family's resources are insufficient for her support.

DISABILITY BENEFITS

In individual employer and industrial retirement systems, three related questions are commonly encountered with respect to disability provisions:

1. Should any provisions with respect to disability protection be included?

2. If disability provisions are included, how long should an employee have to serve before being actually insured?

3. How large should disability benefits be?

We shall take up these questions in the order given, to get the contrasts between the retirement point of view and social security.

Employers frequently draw a sharp distinction between (1) disability resulting from an accident or disease directly connected with service rendered for them, and (2) disability resulting from other causes. We shall for the present confine our discussion to the second group, nonservice connected accidents and diseases.

Employers frequently take the position that they are in no sense responsible for the accident or the disease that is not connected with the service rendered them. Provision for such disability is the responsibility of the individual. To give a specific illustration, on a holiday week end an employee driving his own car on a pleasure trip has an automobile accident that permanently and totally disables him. Although the company may voluntarily deal generously with him with respect to sick leave for a few weeks, it takes the position that it is under no financial or moral obligation to give him a benefit for the balance of his life. That responsibility rests first on him, then on his relatives, and finally on the state. Similarly a young girl recently employed in the office develops tuberculosis and has to go to a sanatorium for long treatment. The final outcome is at the outset uncertain. Again the company says, "The financial responsibility rests on the individual, the relatives, and the state." The costs of such accidents and diseases are in no sense a cost of production of the goods made or the services rendered by the company. They are general social costs.

When an employer establishes a compulsory, contributory, old-age retirement system, the employees generally abhor the forfeiture which results if an employee who has been contributing for some years becomes totally disabled and can never qualify for a benefit. As a very minimum they insist that in event of disability, or death in the active service, all an employee's contributions toward old age, with interest, shall be returned to him or to his dependents. Employers very commonly have seen the justice of this position. Many of them have appreciated that the conditions of employment which they offer employees will be more attractive if something more than a mere return of contributions with interest is included in their retirement systems.

They must, however, protect themselves from the possibly heavy costs of generalized disability insurance. Protection against these heavy costs is generally achieved in three ways:

1. A fairly rigid medical examination is given all new employees before they are actually employed. Bad risks are rejected.

2. Employees are required to serve a specified number of years before they are insured against disability. A requirement of five years of service for eligibility would be commonly regarded as generous.

3. The amount of the benefit is commonly related not to the need of the employee but to such factors as years of service, amount of contributions, and salary or wages earned. Frequently the size of the benefit does not approach social adequacy until the employee is nearing the retirement age. In well-designed retirement systems, the disability benefit in the later years of working life for the employee of long service gradually merges into the old-age benefit and is not much smaller than that benefit. Thus the disability benefit is an adjunct to the old-age benefit.

From the point of view of social security and relief of want, it would seem that provision by the state for need resulting from disability should be on an entirely different basis.

1. The employer for valid reasons declines to hire the poor risk. He must protect the fund made up of his own and his employees' contributions, and in certain instances he must protect the health and safety of his employees.

2. The applicant for employment who is a poor risk cannot secure, at least for any reasonable premium, either life insurance or disability insurance. In fact the experience of voluntary insurance with health insurance other than accident has been such that even a person who is a good health risk has

difficulty in securing it. Voluntary insurance purely for old-age protection is readily available because one has to live to draw it, but the risks of disability are so uncertain that society as a whole has to underwrite them if they are to be underwritten.

3. The amount of benefit necessary to relieve want is not directly and positively connected with the age at which disability occurs. The requirements in the case of the male worker follow a pattern something like this. While he is single, they are relatively low. When he marries and has young children, they are high for he must provide both for the children and for the services the mother must give them. It is in this period that the demands for necessaries are at their peak. As the children advance in years, the demands for absolute necessaries may grow less, although the father may be spending more in his efforts to fit his children to render more valuable services to the economy and to achieve a greater degree of economic security. As he grows older, moreover, if he has been diligent, thrifty, and reasonably successful, he has accumulated some resources which can be utilized in event of disability occurring in his later years, when he and perhaps his wife are the principal ones dependent on his resources.

To the writer nothing in this whole field is more difficult to understand than a philosophy that provides no-means test old-age protection before action has been taken to insure the minimum essentials to those persons disabled in the early years of life. The effect is heightened by the fact that O.A.S.I. actually involves a forfeiture if a person who has been contributing for years is disabled before he is fully insured or if at the time he became disabled, he was currently insured but subsequently lived beyond the extended term of that insurance. Even were he fully insured at the time of disability, he would have to wait for a benefit until he had attained the age of 65. Should he die before age 65, his wife would in her turn have to attain the age of 65 to be eligible as his survivor unless she had children under 16.

Designers of employer or industry retirement systems are, it seems to us, right in taking the position that the primary responsibility for provision for ordinary disability rests (1) on the individual, (2) on the relatives, and (3) on the state. It would therefore seem to us that a first obligation of the state is to make systematic provision to relieve need among the disabled, especially the younger ones, who have had little or no opportunity to make provisions for themselves through their own savings.

The fact of need resulting from disability should be the only criteria necessary for establishing eligibility. Any requirement of contributions or coverage by a contributory system for any specified number of years places mechanisms above the real objectives mechanisms are designed to serve. The amount of benefit should be at least such a sum as added to the available resources of the disabled will give him and those dependent on him a suitable minimum.

The number of eligibles in this category is probably too small and the individuals are too scattered to make them an effective political pressure group. Apparently one of the severest tests that lies ahead for democracy is whether it can determine priorities on the basis of need and social justice in the public interest rather than on the basis of the power of pressure groups.

What has been said thus far relates to disabilities not resulting from service-connected accidents and diseases. In considering them some classification as to cause is desirable. They may result from:

1. Something inherent in the job or process that has not yet yielded to scientific progress. If society is to have the product or the service, disability is part of the price.

2. The particular employer or the industry has failed to install the necessary safety devices or is using an old or a cheaper process when a new or safer one is available.

3. An employer or an industry is making a product or is rendering a service which is inherently dangerous when an alternative product or service is available.

4. Employees, with or without pressure from their employers, operate equipment that is in bad condition.

5. An employee regularly or on occasion fails to use the safety devices or to follow the safety rules. Employers or fore-

men may know of these violations and ignore them because violations speed production, or the employer or foreman may seek to the best of his ability to enforce full compliance with all safety requirements.

6. An employee may be permitted to work when he is not in full normal control of all his faculties.

The fact will be recalled that the victim of the industrial accident in a substantial number of cases is not the person guilty of the fault. He may be injured by the negligence of his employer or of a fellow employee.

So far as need is concerned the fact that the accident or disease resulted from industrial causes makes no difference. It is no greater or no less than if the disabling accident or disease was not service connected. But concepts of public policy and of legal rights and responsibilities may be very different. Again we shall resort to examples, assuming in each case that the totally disabled breadwinner was the sole support of a wife and two young children.

A was disabled while driving his own automobile. The accident was entirely his fault. Had he not been so severely injured, he would have been prosecuted for reckless driving. He has no cause of action against another.

B, likewise injured while driving for pleasure, was injured through the fault of another. We shall subdivide this case into two, B1 and B2. Both have a cause of action against the other driver. B1 can collect because the other driver is insured or has means. B2 gets a judgment, but he cannot collect on it because the driver of the other car is not insured and has no property.

C was injured in the performance of his duties through no fault of his own. The insurance carrier under the workmen's compensation law is prepared to make a settlement which will provide substantially more than a minimum of subsistence.

D was injured in the performance of his duties, but the evidence is conclusive that he was grossly and deliberately negligent. Except when under immediate supervision, he would not use the safety devices supplied and maintained in excellent condition by his employer. The use of these devices was mandatory under the shop rules, and the foremen did their best to enforce them. He had done the work for several years without the safety devices before they were invented, never had had an accident, and believed a good experienced man like himself did not need them. The insurance carrier and the employer had taken the position that the industrial commission and perhaps the courts should determine the extent of liability under the law.

We shall not go further here than to present the issue. The need of the wife and children for a minimum of support from public funds if necessary is clear. Whether more should be given under certain circumstances is another matter, a complex one which requires far more study than we have given it.

SICKNESS

Need may result from sickness or accident that temporarily disables a wage earner of the family or the housewife or house manager. It may result in a need for medical care, which constitutes a separate problem which we shall not discuss here. It may also result in a marked fall in family income through temporary loss of wages of workers, or through the necessity of hiring extra help to do what the housewife ordinarily does, or through a combination of the two. When the housewife is ill, some other member of the family may stay home from school or work to help out, washing may be sent to the laundry, meals may be eaten out, and the whole economy of the household may be upset.

The pregnancy of the mother may be the disturbing factor. Despite her condition she may be under compulsion to continue to do all the work she customarily does. The doctor's orders may call for greatly reduced activities both before and after the birth of the child and for special diets throughout both periods. All may be part of a public health program designed to reduce both infant and maternal mortality.

The question may be raised as to how far temporary disability resulting from sickness or accident is in and of itself a cause of need. It is unquestionably true that families already in need or barely above the level of need are generally unable to meet the extra burdens of temporary disability. Families higher in the scale have in the past met them from savings or credit or a combination of the two. Many a family of comfortable means has seen its reserves dwindle and its debt increase because of temporary disability of one or more members, although it is probably true that the costs of medical care are often as important a factor as loss of earnings or the costs of extra service in the home.

Three types of families may be distinguished with respect to temporary or even partial disability:

1. Those who almost entirely escape any serious costs and have only small bills for dental care or care of the eyes.

2. Those who go for years without any serious costs and then for a relatively brief period encounter extremely heavy costs.

3. Those for whom relatively high costs are normal, either because of the presence of chronic difficulties, or because some members seem fated to contract every illness that is going the rounds or to have accidents.

For families normally above the level of real need, the issue seems to be whether the costs of temporary or partial disability should be spread by an insurance system; whether the families which escape should help pay the costs for families whose temporary or partial disability seems to be almost ever present; and whether families in their good years should pay for the right to be cared for in their bad years at low cost.

Such a situation does not yield very well to competitive voluntary insurance because of the element of selection of risks. A company which selects carefully and excludes all suffering from chronic difficulties and all having a poor past history can sell insurance cheaper than one which does not select. The voluntary insurance company in a competitive situation could assume responsibility for the known and obviously poor risks for the same premium it is charging the preferred risks. Under a competitive voluntary system, a classification according to the degree of risk, resembling for example that in accident insurance, would be necessary.

If collectivism of insurance is to be introduced there appear to be certain choices:

1. For the state to make health and accident insurance mandatory for all, admitting all regardless of the degree of risk and forcing the excellent risks to help pay the costs for the poor risks.

2. For the state to require that all be insured either under approved and regulated private companies or under a state system operated primarily to provide insurance for those risks which are so bad private companies will not take them. The premium rates charged by the state system would be comparable to the rates charged by the private companies. Excess losses resulting from handling the poor risks would have to be paid from public funds.

3. For the state greatly to liberalize the provisions under which the costs of medical care can be deducted from income and other taxes. The state would then pay a high percentage of the cost of medical care indirectly through a loss of receipts from taxation and not directly by a formal insurance system. Its rules and regulations governing the amount of allowable deductions would then be the instrument of control. Conceivably, for example, the rules might permit of a deduction of actual expenditures for a hospital bed but not exceeding a certain amount per day. The person who elected to occupy a de luxe room in an exclusive hospital would have to pay for all the costs above the maximum allowable deduction. Similarly there would be a schedule of operations with a maximum allowable deduction for each one. The taxpayer could deduct his actual expenditures up to that maximum. If he elected to employ a surgeon who charged more than the maximum, he would have to pay the difference from his own pocket.

Under such a system, allowable deductions would be cumulative. The family, for example, which in any year spent more for allowed medical care than the amount of its income or other tax for that year would carry over the balance of its deductions to the succeeding year or even to succeeding years. The state would say in effect, "Necessary medical care, as it has been defined by law, has destroyed your capacity to pay by that extent." Patient and physician would still have the old relationship except that the practitioners might find it difficult to charge more than the maximum allowable fee. From time to time the state would make investigations as to the truth of the reports on deductions, as it has to make other investigations of deductions.

Such a system would not provide for persons whose income and resources are so low that they pay far more for sickness and medical care than they ever pay in income taxes. For them the state itself would in many instances have to pay the costs of medical care because the persons are in actual need. With respect to these cases the state would exercise a greater degree of control over the medical and related professions than it would in cases where an individual or the family is not in need.

Money payments to a family to enable it to pay for medical care, to hire additional help, or to purchase medicines or special articles of diet present one difficulty; the family may not apply the money for the purpose for which it was given. In many instances where money is to be used for a specific purpose, it has been found necessary for someone outside the family to supervise the expenditure. These devices are sometimes used: (1) the person who renders the service presents the bills to the agency supplying the money, and the agency pays them; (2) the individual or family pays for the services from its own funds and presents vouchers to the agency for reimbursement; or (3) the family gives the practitioner an order on the agency. Under the Farm Security Administration, in some instances families had to deposit all checks issued to them in a controlled account; no check could be drawn on that account until countersigned by a government representative. Payment of money to a family will not guarantee its use for a particular purpose.

From the standpoint of seeing that public funds are used to effect the purposes for which supplied, much is to be said in favor of rendering service as service instead of giving money with which service is to be purchased. It may be questioned whether the argument against giving relief in kind, applicable in the case of general family expenses, is equally applicable when the state wishes the family to take action with respect to health that seems to the family unnecessary.[1]

UNEMPLOYMENT

No branch of social security systems presents more or more vital issues than unemployment insurance or unemployment compensation. We shall take these issues up under three main heads: (1) Who shall be covered? (2) For how long shall they be covered? (3) How large shall benefits be?

Who shall be covered? Once again in attempting to see what specific issues are involved in this question, we shall present typical but hypothetical cases.

John, 18 years of age, has finished high school. He is the oldest child in a family which has three other children, only one of whom is of legal working age. She is in high school. The family is just able to get along at or about the minimum of subsistence because the father is underemployed. John is willing, even eager, to work and capable of working. He has had no real working experience. His education has given him no highly specialized training. Because of general economic and local conditions, he has not been able to get a regular, steady job. The best he has been able to do is to get occasional work as an extra man, in a store or a filling station. Should John be covered by an unemployment compensation system?

William is 27 years of age, is married and has one child 18 months old. At the time of marriage he was a junior partner in a real estate concern which was doing fairly well in developing small communities for persons of modest means. A change in

---

[1] In one case a benefactor felt that the greatest assistance he could render the family in which he was interested was radically to curtail the mortgage on the house. Interest payments would thereby be greatly curtailed and money made available for other purposes. He gave the family a check for curtailment. A family conclave decided that a new automobile, well up in the middle price range, stood much higher on the priority list and most of the money was so applied. Some time later the mortgage on the house was foreclosed.

economic conditions prevented further sales and developments and wiped out the firm's reserves. William is willing and able to work, but he is unable to find a regular job.

Henry is 35 and has a wife and three children. For many years he worked as an agricultural laborer and was supplied with a house and some food by his employer. He left that job to become a member of a construction gang building a new section of a state highway. That job lasted three months. The state decided not to go on with the next section, and the contractor had no other projects in the area. Henry went back to the rural area to see if he could get his old job back, but his employer had another family in the tenant house. The only thing Henry could find in that area was odd jobs, and they would be few and far between until harvest time. As he cannot find a job, should he be eligible for unemployment compensation?

Thomas is 35 and has a wife and three children. On finishing high school he went into the office of the knitting mill as a bookkeeper and advanced to the job of head bookkeeper. The owners of the mill decided to abandon it. Thomas drew such unemployment compensation as he had coming to him and then went to the home of his wife's mother where he thought he would make a living running the old farm. A year of that convinced him that he lacked the training, experience, and capital necessary for farming. He is now back in an urban industrial community looking for a regular job, preferably on books, but he will take anything. Should he be eligible for compensation?

Old Mr. Smith is a perennial job seeker. For years he earned good wages on the railroad as a telegrapher, but he lost that job when a new automatic control system was installed. Since then he has never been able to establish himself with another employer. One reason is that he is more than a bit difficult. The jobs he could get did not pay as well as the old one. He did not learn easily, and it irritated him to be supervised by younger persons and to have them calling attention to his mistakes and his bad spoilage record. Since unemployment compensation came in, he has never succeeded in attaining eligibility for benefits because he has not worked long enough in the base period. He and his wife made out by using their savings and selling their possessions. Now he has to work again to live. He is willing and physically able to work, although mentally he still presents something of a problem to anyone who will hire him.

Under the New Zealand system of unemployment insurance, all of these men would be eligible for unemployment insurance because they were willing and able to work, and neither in receipt of sufficient income nor possessed of sufficient property to give them the minimum standard of living without work. In most if not all states of the United States none of them would be eligible; young John because he has never as yet held a job for any length of time, William because he worked on his own account and was not an employee, Henry because he was an agricultural laborer, Thomas because in the base period he was a farmer, and old Mr. Smith because he did not work long enough in a covered occupation to be eligible. New Zealand takes the position that the basic criteria is need. The states of the United States take the position that the person must have worked long enough or have earned enough in a covered position in the base period to be insured.

How long shall benefits be paid? New Zealand takes the position that the criteria is need, as evidenced by lack of either income or property in the amounts specified by law. Unemployment benefits will be paid so long as the man is unemployed, employable, and in need. Under the no-means test British Beveridge plan the criteria was to be unemployment. Benefits were to last as long as unemployment lasted, but after a specified length of time the unemployed person would have to present himself for retraining. In fact the farmer or the man who had been working on his own account and decided he could not make a go of it would get not an unemployment benefit but a retraining benefit identical in amount. The United States proceeds on a concept born of private insurance. During a specified base period or premium period, the worker must have worked in a covered occupation and must have earned at least a specified amount, thereupon he is insured in case he becomes unemployed in the benefit year or the insurance year. The amount and duration of his benefit will depend largely on his earnings in the base or premium period, but the number of weeks he may receive benefits is directly or indirectly limited by law. In hundreds of cases, each succeeding week of unemployment will witness an increase in the family's degree of need, but at the end of the period prescribed by law the insured will have exhausted his benefits. When benefits are exhausted, resources gone, and real need is faced, the United States system says, "We have not gone that far yet."

In the United States, it will be recalled, except in a few states, unemployment insurance premiums are paid in the first instance by taxes on pay roll paid exclusively by the employer. Except in a few states the employees pay nothing. In the long run employers must pass the pay-roll taxes on to the consumers. Thus the state to a very considerable degree makes the employers its tax collectors to raise funds for unemployment compensation. If the state levied direct taxes on the general public to raise funds for this purpose, would it ever conceivably have devised any such formula for their distribution?

How large shall benefits be? New Zealand says that benefits shall be such sums as are necessary to bring the income of the family to a prescribed minimum level. In figuring needs the composition of the family is the major factor. A single man gets so much. A married man gets the same amount on his own account, but he gets an additional allowance for his wife and for each dependent child. Thus basically need is the criteria.

The Beveridge plan differs from the New Zealand plan in that something approaching a reasonable cost of subsistence has been worked out for men, women, and children of specified ages. When a man is unemployed, he gets the standard allowance for himself and for each person dependent upon him. The essential difference between the New Zealand system and the Beveridge plan is that in New Zealand the resources of the family are taken into consideration and only so much is given as is necessary to bring them to the legally determined standard, whereas under the Beveridge plan the benefits are paid regardless of resources. If the wealthy president of a big corporation should be dismissed by the board of directors and should not immediately secure another job, he would be eligible for the same benefit as the lowest-paid worker in the corporation if the lowest-paid worker were unemployed, provided both had families of the same composition. If the low-paid worker were single and the corporation president married and possessed of a child under 16, the president would get the larger benefit, so that he would have in his possession at least the standard minimum for himself, his wife, and his child.

In the United States, with few exceptions, the number of dependents has nothing whatever to do with the size of the unemployment compensation benefit, and no consideration is given to the resources of the unemployed or his family. The lowest-paid worker with a wife and five children will get materially less than the well-paid single woman with no dependents who worked in the office, provided each of them worked sufficiently long during the base year to be entitled to maximum benefits. If, as is frequently the case, employment in the office is far more stable than employment of unskilled or semi-skilled workers in the plant, the single woman will not only draw a larger benefit than the married man with a big family, but she will draw it for a greater number of weeks. Her employer has paid more actual dollars on her account than he has paid on account of the unskilled laborer, and therefore he has bought her more insurance.

The employer, however, has not bought the higher-bracket single woman in the office as much insurance per dollar of tax as he has bought the unskilled family man in the plant. The benefit formulas generally recognize need to a limited degree by giving in proportion to premium paid more to the low-bracket than to the high-bracket employees. Since that is true, let us compare two unskilled workers in the plant. A is a man with a wife and five children. B is responsible for no one but himself. He may be anywhere between two extremes, the man who never makes an unnecessary expenditure but saves all he can, and the man whose wages are gone by Monday morning and who borrows from his fellow employees to tide him over till pay day. With like wages and service in the base period, these two get the same unemployment benefit. As between the high- and low-bracket employee our American systems give some consideration to need, but as between two employees of the same bracket no such consideration is given.

The New Zealand system and the Beveridge plan are designed respectively to relieve or to prevent need from unemployment almost regardless of the nature of unemployment. The American systems make provision for unemployment of relatively short duration but make no provision for unemployment extending beyond the maximum number of weeks permitted under the law. In other words, our system is favorable to seasonal workers, men who lose a considerable number of days of employment in a normal year, men who move from one employer to another and lose time between moves. It is unfavorable to the technologically unemployed, the workers unemployed for a long period as the result of a depression, and the marginal or submarginal workers who only in periods of full employment earn enough in the base period to enable them to qualify for benefits in the benefit period.

With respect to the marginal or submarginal workers whose need is likely to be greatest, insurance concepts in some states may play strange tricks. For example, a submarginal worker may be fortunate enough to get the first good job he has had for months early in the fixed twelve-month period established as the base or premium year. He works at it for six consecutive months and is therefore insured against unemployment. Upon losing his job at the end of six months, however, he is entitled to no immediate benefit: He must wait at least six months for the opening of his benefit year. To be eligible for an immediate benefit, he should have had a job in the preceding base year when nobody in a covered establishment desired him for a sufficient length of time to enable him to qualify. Insurance concepts appear at times to take priority over social objectives.

A prudent, thrifty person in considering a hazard that may strike him weighs self insurance against collective insurance. The question which he asks himself is, "Shall I figure on meeting such a hazard by drawing on my own reserves or my credit, or shall I pay some insurance carrier a premium for carrying the risk for me?" In arriving at a decision, he considers the size of the benefit the insurance carrier would pay him in event of the happening of the contingency and his chances of building a reserve of similar amount by saving or using his credit.

Under the American system of unemployment insurance, the maximum unemployment compensation a covered worker may draw in any benefit period rarely exceeds $500 a year even for the most highly paid worker, and of course for many workers it is in several states materially less than that. Except for the lowest-paid workers, the marginal or the submarginal workers, and workers with large numbers of dependents, it would not be hard for the worker in the course of a few years of good employment to build a personal reserve equal to or exceeding the amount of his unemployment benefit for a single benefit year. To the well-paid, thrifty workers who are steadily employed, the unemployment benefits although helpful do not give a protection they could not provide for themselves.

The risks against which the worker cannot except in rare instances insure himself are prolonged unemployment, particularly technological unemployment, or that resulting from a long-drawn-out recession. Such a depression exhausts his reserves. The American system does not help such a worker very much, for he may draw nothing under it for many years, and then exhaust his rights in the first twenty or less weeks following the waiting period, and thereafter be on his own resources. Some evidence suggests, moreover, that the availability of benefits for short periods of unemployment or underemployment become in effect additional income for seasonal workers and persons usually intermittently employed. The benefits remove the necessity of spreading the seasonal or the intermittent earnings over the entire year. In some trades or crafts high wages for seasonal or intermittent work have been justified on the ground that these earnings must maintain the man and his family for the entire year. Today unemployment compensation adds to income for the year. It may be true in isolated cases that the American system provides vacations with pay rather than insurance against want.

The point may well be made in this connection that the employee, except in a few states, is not paying for his own unemployment compensation. The employer is paying for it. Thus the thrifty employee does not have to weigh the advantages of self insurance against carrier insurance, because the employer is paying the premiums. The validity of that argument depends on the extent to which employers are able to pass the unemployment compensation taxes along to consumers. Although the worker may be paying no direct tax for his unemployment insurance, he may be paying a very substantial part of its costs and the administrative costs in the prices he has to pay for necessary goods and services for which much of his income goes. So long as he does not know that the tax is concealed in the price, he does not have to face the question whether the system represents a wise use of his own funds, or whether he and his dependents would have greater real security, a security they could not insure by their own efforts, under a New Zealand plan or a Beveridge plan.

The issue may be stated in another way. Taxes for unemployment insurance have, according to the latest available figures, built up a reserve as of July 31, 1945, amounting to 6.8 billion dollars. In event of serious and prolonged unemployment, which use of that reserve would be socially the more desirable: to distribute it among those who are unemployed in accordance with their need and the need of their dependents, as under the New Zealand plan; to give to each unemployed person and each of his dependents a fixed amount, enough to get along on regardless of their needs, as under the Beveridge plan; or to pay each unemployed worker the amount to which he is entitled for the specified number of weeks regardless of his need or the number of his dependents? Before one attempts to answer that question in his own mind, he should consider the matter of financing social security, which will be taken up in later chapters.

DEATH

Under a system designed exclusively for relief or prevention of want, a death benefit is not of particular significance unless the deceased was responsible for the support of dependents. There is of course the question of the costs of a suitable funeral in those cases where the resources of the deceased who dies without dependents will not provide one, but from the standpoint of public finance, it is not very consequential. From the social and economic standpoint, a funeral benefit becomes significant when dependents survive the deceased, and funeral expenses become an emergency item in a family budget.

The real question with respect to a death benefit is whether the dependents shall take in their own right as persons who are in need and have their benefit based on that need, or whether they shall take by virtue of the fact that the deceased was insured. In the first case the state makes what it deems suitable provision; in the second the amount of benefit depends on whether or not the deceased was insured and the amount of insurance.

The question of provision for dependents is so important with respect to all benefits that the following chapter will be devoted to it.

CHAPTER XXV
DEPENDENTS

The application of the methods of voluntary insurance to the provision of social security is greatly complicated by the existence of the family. If every person in the country were responsible only for himself, it would be unnecessary to discuss what is to be done with respect to persons who have been dependent for their support upon a socially insured individual deceased, disabled, or unemployed. The dependents with whom the present chapter is to be concerned are children, women, and parents. The dependent women are principally widows, wives of husbands who are unable to support them, and women estranged from their husbands whether they are divorced, legally separated, or just separated. With women who are self-supporting or supported by a husband, this chapter is not directly concerned.

Before proceeding to a consideration of these several classes of dependents, attention should be directed to the fact that there is wide variation among workers with respect to their status as to dependents. At the one extreme is the individual who is responsible for only himself. It would be difficult to describe the other extreme, for a primary breadwinner may be responsible for a wife, children, parents, brothers, sisters, nephews, nieces, and grandchildren whether related by blood or marriage.

In private voluntary insurance the situation is simplified because the responsible breadwinner alone may be insured, and he himself determines who his beneficiaries are to be. Moreover, he generally has the right to change beneficiaries from time to time as family responsibilities change, and he can allow a policy to lapse or take its cash surrender value. If he so desires, he may have a policy made payable to his estate and direct the distribution of the proceeds by his will.

It is possible to devise a compulsory system of old-age insurance that would protect the insured individual only. If he should die before drawing any annuity his payments would go into the fund. Such plans, however, are not generally acceptable because insured persons with responsibility for dependents want the money they have paid as premiums used for those dependents in the event of death or disability and would rather pay more premium for that protection.

It is likewise possible to design a compulsory old-age insurance system that in the event of death of the insured before retiring upon annuity pays the value of the annuity thus far purchased to his designated beneficiary or to his estate. The main objections to such a system are: (1) the cost is relatively high because the fund derives no profit from the death of a member before retirement; (2) the benefits to survivors, particularly if the insured dies early in his working life, are comparatively small; and (3) if the insured has no dependents, the money may go to individuals who have no real claim upon him and no real need for the money. As a matter of fact, such an individual in the absence of compulsion might have elected to pay less in annual premium and to take an annuity with no payments to anybody in event of his death before retirement.[1]

When a government adopts a compulsory old-age insurance system, it is necessarily compelled to give large weight to administrative practicability and simplicity. It may not be feasible for it to allow the individual that freedom of choice that is inherent in private voluntary insurance with respect to amount of premium, choice of beneficiaries, and optional methods of settlement. The government may feel itself more or less compelled to legislate on the basis of norms, averages, or typical cases, although such action may not meet the needs of individuals who vary widely from the pattern adopted as standard by the government.

In the ensuing consideration of dependents, it should be remembered that the extent of injury done persons whose cases depart widely from the average depends largely upon the percentage of the income of the insured which the government

---

[1] See the descriptions of the railroad retirement system and of the general system for federal employees in Pt. 1, for illustrations of the application of this general principle.

forces him to put into social insurance that does not fit his own personal needs or those of his dependents. The British Government in its white paper on social insurance, for example, takes the position that the enforced contributions and the resulting benefits should both be kept so small that all the covered workers can pay them without great hardship and have the maximum possible amount left to use as they see fit and to make additional provision for the contingencies of life in accordance with their own needs and desires.[2] As a government advances beyond such minimum provisions and increases the compulsory takings from employees, employers, and general taxpayers, it greatly increases the chance that serious injustices will be done to persons who do not conform to the pattern the government used when it legislated. It is from this point of view that questions regarding the several classes of dependents will be considered.

CHILDREN

Under this heading are included not only the children born to a wage earner and his wife but also those children who are dependent on the family for support. Among them may be stepchildren, nephews, nieces, grandchildren, and other children not of the blood, whether legally adopted or not. From the standpoint of relieving or preventing want, the essential fact is obviously the existence of a dependent child.

Indeed the position may well be taken that the first obligation of the state in the field of public relief and social security is to provide for children—legitimate or illegitimate—who are not in receipt of adequate support or care. The cause that deprived the child of suitable support or care puts the state *in loco parentis*. A state, as well as a family, is open to censure if it is using available funds in the interest of favored members who are not actually in need, before it has made sure that all dependent upon it have the essentials of life.

A major question that requires thorough examination in studying relief and social security legislation is, "At what age

[2] See p. 478 for a more complete statement of the government point of view.

shall dependency of a normal child be deemed to end"? The most liberal answer thus far given in the United States appears to be that used in the Social Security Act with respect to O.A.S.I., which fixed the limit at 18 years.[3] The aid to dependent children title of that act fixes the age at 16, or 18 if the child is regularly attending school.

Such answers may appear reasonable under systems that do not pay greater benefits than are necessary to relieve or prevent need. They become increasingly questionable as the state uses its sovereign power to tax to provide benefits materially in excess of what is required to relieve or prevent need and embarks on a policy of redistribution of income. Such a policy means that the state forces individuals or families to pay, directly or indirectly, more for social security than would be required to effect the primary purpose. As the state restricts to an increasing degree the freedom of the family to use its income as it sees fit and to an increasing degree distributes the money thus collected by governmental formulas, it becomes more and more important for families to examine with care the provisions that may affect their children and grandchildren.

The major issue that may concern many families is what effect elaborate and costly systems of social insurance may have upon the higher education of children after they have attained the age of 18 years. If the primary breadwinner survives and continues to earn, he can see his children through the higher educational institutions, although possibly with greater difficulty because of high social security and other taxes. The real issue will arise if the primary worker dies before the children have finished their education. Despite his compulsory contributions paid through the years, the children cannot receive a benefit after they are 18 years of age regardless of their ambitions and their competence.

The practical issue, as we see it, is not whether under certain circumstances the compulsory social insurance system should pay benefits to selected children during the long period between

[3] Sec. 202(c) (1).

graduation from high school and successful completion of professional training, but whether contributions and benefits under the social insurance system should not be kept down close to the irreducible minimum to leave a maximum degree of personal freedom to individuals and families.

Three points with respect to this issue call for special emphasis:

1. Persons engaged in occupations that demand scientific, technical, or professional education of college grade or beyond, now constitute a relatively small proportion of the total number in the labor force. Although they are essential to the operation of our social and economic system, and the need for them will probably continue to increase as it has in the past, one can scarcely look forward to a time when all youth will require such training. There are wide differences among youth with respect to capacities, interests, and ambitions, and many have no desire to prepare for high-type technical work. As is well known, the financial rewards of highly trained workers are frequently materially less than those of persons who left school considerably earlier and have been successful in activities that do not demand higher education. Thus there appears to be no necessity for provision for universal benefits for children until they have completed college training.

2. If the social security system pays large benefits and compels substantial contributions, it will increase the difficulties of those families with low or modest incomes that seek to educate their children for callings that require several years of education beyond high school. No state of the American Union has ever adopted with respect to its white population[4] the philosophy, not uncommon in European countries, that the social and economic status of the parents should largely determine the

---

[4] With respect to the non-white population the view has prevailed in some areas that the children were not capable of profiting from more than rudimentary education. Private funds were used both for Negroes and for Indians to supply them with greater educational opportunity, to demonstrate their capacity to advance, and to train leaders of the race for the race. One could scarcely find a better illustration of funds and effort supplied by a minority against the beliefs or the inertia of a controlling political majority.

type of education to be made available to the child. On the contrary, the prevailing American philosophy has been that superior educational opportunities shall be open to all classes. The newcomers to the United States have generally appreciated this distinctively American opportunity. The census of occupations in the United States has for decades shown large numbers of children of immigrants in occupations that require higher education. This means that the immigrant family gave a high priority in family management to enabling the children to take advantage of educational opportunities. It would be, from our point of view, extremely unfortunate if a high-cost, elaborate social security system should hamper these families in giving priorities to those activities which they regard as in the interest of their children and succeeding generations of the family.

3. If the high costs of elaborate social insurance are largely placed upon those with capacity to pay, the action may dry up the sources of revenue that have supported private educational institutions in the United States. The nation will thereafter be increasingly dependent on public educational institutions financed by and subject to control by political majorities. The great contributions of the private educational institutions have arisen in no small part from the fact that minorities with vision have been able to blaze new paths and demonstrate the desirability and practicability of new ways and new things. In a country which has complete separation of church and state, the private educational institutions have permitted the introduction of religious elements into education. Complete religious freedom could hardly be preserved if education should become virtually a state monopoly.

The fact should be recalled that religious, moral, and ethical interests and concerns of minorities have in the past been an important factor in the provision of higher education. Thus persons with a financial margin, individually or collectively, have helped to support the educational institutions themselves and to make provision for the introduction or improvement of education in particular fields, and they have enabled many youth of limited means to attend those institutions. Scholarships have been endowed but perhaps fully as important are the cases in which persons have helped particular children—relatives, friends, the promising youth in the school or the church, the youth who is ambitious to go to the institution favored by the benefactor, or youth of a race regarded by the donor as underprivileged. The motives underlying this action may be minority or personal, but they are part of the complex that results from the rights to life, liberty, and the pursuit of happiness. The exercise of such motives will be greatly thwarted if the state through its power to tax cuts down the margin that permits of independent private and minority action.

Thus youth who wish to continue their education after they have attained their eighteenth birthday present one of the issues which have to be considered in connection with proposals for high-cost social insurance.

WOMEN

From the standpoint of social security, it is almost impossible to talk or legislate with respect to women in general or women on the average. The social and economic variations are so wide that no one situation is representative or typical. Among the significant variables are:

1. The age of the woman.

2. Her marital condition.

3. Her physical and mental capacity.

4. The resources which are available for her support if she does not seek gainful employment.

5. The number, age, and physical condition of children, and perhaps of other relatives, for whom she has responsibilities as a homemaker.

6. The resources which are available for the support of children, and perhaps of other relatives, if she herself does not engage in gainful employment.

7. The extent to which she can delegate to others such duties as she may have with respect to homemaking or satisfactorily combine them with gainful employment.

8. Her own personal preferences or sense of relative values.

She may desire a career, prefer gainful employment to home-making, or seek for herself or family a level of living that is not attainable unless she herself earns. "Level of living," as here used would include the woman who works to give a child or other relative an education which he could not otherwise obtain.

It is perhaps obvious that these eight major variables are not mutually independent. From the standpoint of a statistician cross classifications embodying many of them would be necessary to show the true problem of providing satisfying social insurance for women.

Two points in connection with classifications based on these variables require emphasis.

1. As life progresses, a woman generally moves from one class or subclass to another. There is nothing fixed or static about her status. In many instances the economic position of the woman depends in a large measure on the economic position of her husband. The death of a husband or divorce or separation may mean a radical change. Remarriage may likewise mean a radical change.

2. With respect to some of the classes, it may fairly be said numerically that class is not very important, or, women do not stay in that class very long. Some experts trying to write into law insurance concepts and precisely defined categories apparently take the position that the number in a class is so small that it can be ignored. However, the extent of need in a small class may be far greater per individual than it is in a numerically larger class. If prevention of want is the basic objective, great attention will be given to the small classes to make sure that none has gone entirely unprotected while elaborate provision has been made for other more numerous classes. Again, legislators must be particularly on guard if numerous classes are effectively organized in political pressure groups, whereas the small classes are too small and the individual members too widely scattered to be politically effective.

Provision for certain of the classes of women outlined above call for special comment. Widows under 65 with no dependent child under 18 years of age will be considered first. The American system of old-age and survivors insurance assumes either that she is willing and able to work and can get a job or if not she will be provided for if in need through general public assistance. Her deceased husband may have been compelled by the state to put his money into that kind of insurance despite the fact that he knew his wife was physically unable to work or lacked qualifications which would make her employable under ordinary conditions in the labor market in the locality of the home. Had he been free from government compulsion he would not put money into that kind of insurance. It may be pointed out that primarily he was providing for his own old age and that provision for his wife in event of his death was only subsidiary and incidental. Such a position is, however, that of the state and not necessarily that of the individual. The individual with knowledge of the facts in his particular case might give provision for his widow a high priority over provision for his own and his wife's old age. In some cases the husband may be reasonably certain that neither he nor his wife will attain the age of 65.

Women, other than wives, who are homemakers and are supported by some other primary worker constitute another class deserving special comment. They assume the duties and responsibilities of the homemaker often with increased duties because some member of the family is sick or disabled. This sickness or disability may be the factor that makes their presence necessary. Generally property laws do not give them the legal rights which they would have were they married to the male breadwinner. If such a woman is devoting full time to maintaining a home for a parent, the property laws give no right superior to the rights of other children. Introduction of insurance concepts into social security systems may make it inexpedient or impracticable to provide benefits for such women arising from the insurance of the parent. The elderly insured person under O.A.S.I. does not do anything for the daughter who has made a home for him since the death of his wife even though the mother has been dead for years. The widower under O.A.S.I. does not do anything for the relative who cared for his children upon the death of his wife. Upon his death the relative must take care of herself or seek general public assistance.

Women who are working in occupations covered by O.A.S.I. to earn money to put their children or other relatives through college or professional school, to supplement the earnings of a husband in supporting the children, or to support a husband unable to support himself are another group that requires special mention. O.A.S.I. does not meet their needs for the following reasons:

1. In the event of their death no child over 18 can be paid a benefit as the result of their O.A.S.I. insurance even if the child is still in university or professional school.

2. In event of their death their children under 18 cannot be paid a benefit as the result of their O.A.S.I. insurance unless "no parent other than such individual was contributing to the support of such child and such child was not living with its father or adopting father."[5]

3. If both the father and the mother die fully or currently insured, the children under 18 take as a rule from the father. The rebuttable presumption of the law is that the father was responsible for and was as a matter of fact supporting the children. The mother's contributions not infrequently will be forfeited to the fund.

4. A husband, whatever his mental or physical condition, cannot take by virtue of his wife's insurance under O.A.S.I. The state assumes that husbands support wives and does not allow for conditions that may reverse the normal situation.

Mention should also be made of women whose husbands are not employed in occupations covered under O.A.S.I. and who are not themselves employed in such occupations. Wives of farmers and agricultural workers are omitted from coverage, although their domestic duties are commonly relatively heavy, and as a class they have more children than urban women. Domestic service, a leading occupation for women, is excluded. Teaching, the principal professional occupation for women, is

[5] Social Security Act, Title II, sec. 202(c) (4).

also excluded, but if a woman school teacher comes under a
modern retirement system operated on a sound financial basis,
she is ordinarily far better off than she would be under O.A.S.I.

The broken home is a major problem. The distinction between the divorced or separated woman and other women is,
however, of major significance in social security legislation
mainly under two circumstances:

1. That she has children who require her services as a homemaker, usually, although not necessarily, under 18 years of age.

2. That the divorce or desertion took place after many years
of married life, and at the time of divorce or desertion the woman is either absolutely or practically unemployable.

The insurance concept that dependents take by virtue of the
insurance of the covered worker makes it difficult to deal satisfactorily with such cases. Under our O.A.S.I. system, the divorced or deserted wife cannot be treated as a widow nor her
children as children of a widow. The husband and father is still
living and if working in a covered occupation is adding to his
own protection for his old age. He may remarry and have additional children. The divorced wife and her children attain no
rights as the result of the man's insurance under O.A.S.I. unless
or until he dies or attains the age of 65 and retires and then only
if he has been contributing to their support or has been ordered
by a court to so contribute.

Under the existing social security law, the court which has
jurisdiction over the issues between husband and wife and
has the duty of safeguarding the interest of the child, has no
authority over the equities of the family in the O.A.S.I. system. The court, for example, could not rule that the equities be used immediately in the interest of the child, that the
claims of the children for the necessaries of life take precedence
over the man's provision for his own old age. If private property, including private voluntary insurance, is involved in the
case, the court can issue orders which, in the case of existing
property, the parties must carry out. The court acts in the
light of the facts in the particular case and not on the basis of
statistical norms or averages such as are used in social insurance
systems.

Attention should again be called to the simplicity and directness of the New Zealand system in handling such cases. If the
divorced or separated woman and her children have sufficient
resources so that they are not in need according to the legal
definition in New Zealand, no payments are made from the
social security fund. Property settlements and payments regularly made by the husband may preclude any necessity for expenditures from the fund. On the other hand, if the resources
fall below the limits prescribed by law, payments are made on
the basis of the number of dependents to be supported. The
woman can count on that amount of income as certain; she will
get it either from her husband or from the fund; in other words,
if the husband fails to pay, the fund will. New Zealand puts its
emphasis not on insurance concepts, but on individual persons
who are in need. Such emphasis overcomes many of the difficulties with respect to provision for dependents.

PARENTS

Consideration of parents may be best begun by attempting
a general classification of them according to their status with
respect to dependency and resources available for their own
support. The term parents will be used throughout, although
there may be only a single surviving parent in the family. Since
social security is a family matter there may be four surviving
parents, two of the husband and two of the wife; and the situation may be even more complicated if divorce and remarriage
have taken place introducing additional step-parents. The man
and wife may have:

1. All surviving parents possessed of sufficient resources for
their own support.

2. Parents not possessed of sufficient resources for support
but able to get along with small contributions from: (a) several
children living in different households with no one child actually
contributing a substantial sum; (b) one child making up the
budget deficiency of the parents with or without minor contributions from other children in other households.

3. Parents with little or no resources and entirely or almost
entirely dependent on children for support: (a) with several

children living in different households contributing, but with
no one child contributing a major amount; (b) with one child
paying practically the entire required sum with or without
minor contributions from children in other households.

4. Parents with inadequate resources and no child contributing in any substantial amount: (a) there are children who could
contribute but are not doing so; (b) there are no children who
could contribute.

The situation would not be very difficult if the social security
system regarded the parents as individuals and handled them
entirely on the basis of their own needs and resources. Complications arise from the introduction of employee contributions
for old-age insurance and related insurance concepts. In the
absence of government compulsion and control, a breadwinner
possessed of private voluntary insurance or other resources
could, within certain legal limits, direct the distribution of his
property. If, for example, he has been one of several children
aiding in the support of parents he could make some provision
for those parents, although leaving most of what he had to his
wife and children. His decision would be based on his own
judgment in the light of the family situations, which judgment
might be bad, fair, or excellent.

Fitting social security insurance benefit payments to the facts
in the case or permitting the insured to so fix them is perhaps a
little too complicated for governmental administration, and
therefore the legislators substitute their judgment for that of the
insured.[6] In the case of O.A.S.I. the legislature has decided that
existence of a widow or an unmarried surviving child under 18
precludes payment of a benefit to a parent regardless of the
status of that parent with respect to dependence upon the insured. A forfeiture of everything the insured has contributed to
the fund over and above the lump-sum death benefit is, according to legislative decision, preferable to any payment to a parent

[6] The making of adjustments and the exercise of options necessarily adds materially
to administrative costs. A private voluntary insurance company must by the nature
of its business provide these services, and include their cost in its loading. Only a
government possessed of powers to compel can make administrative convenience a determining factor.

unless such parent (aged 65 or over) was wholly dependent upon and supported by the insured at the time of the death of the insured. Thus even when no wife and no child under 18 survives, the social security fund will pay nothing toward the support of a parent who was in fact maintained in part by the insured and may be in need without such support. If the insured leaves a widow with no child under 18 years of age, until she has reached 65 she receives no social security payment from which she can make a contribution to the support of the wholly or partially dependent parent. If the parent is sufficiently in need to qualify for old-age assistance, the solution of the family problem may be for the parent to get a means test benefit under that system and try to take care of the widow until she attains the age of 65.

As the New Zealand system shows, it is possible to have a social security system that deals basically with individuals and avoids the complications inherent in adopting a contributory insurance philosophy. If the contributory insurance philosophy is more important than the systematic, prompt, and effective relief of need, the fact that arbitrary decisions have to be made by the legislature on the basis of averages or norms would suggest holding contributions and benefits to the lowest possible levels and leaving to individuals maximum freedom to meet the requirements of their own families.

CHAPTER XXVI

THE MAJOR FACTORS AFFECTING COST

The preceding chapters of Part III have been devoted primarily to a consideration of what we have termed predominantly social issues. We turn now to the financial issues. Among the questions to be considered are: What estimates are possible regarding the costs of social insurance? What methods should be used in financing social security and relief? Are reserves necessary in social security financing? and What are the obligations of the future? Before starting the specific chapters, it seems desirable to present a summary of the broad social factors that determine the cost of social security and relief. It will be in the nature of a brief review of the preceding chapters considered from the standpoint of costs.

The basic element in determining costs is the standard used for defining need. The higher this standard is placed the larger will be the costs. Two factors operate to make this fact inescapable. The first is that the higher the standard is placed, the larger benefits will have to be; the second, the higher the standard, the greater will be the number of persons who will have to be given funds to raise them to the standard.

A second major factor is whether a means test is used, and if it is to what extent. If like standards of need are assumed, the least costly system is the one which employs a means test for all benefits and gives benefits only to the extent necessary to bring the individual or the family to the standard level. Cost increases as the means test is abandoned or relaxed for successive categories. Abandonment of the means test necessitates payments to persons not in need, and in some cases to persons who have never known need.

Costs are greatly increased if the system minimizes the objective of relieving or preventing need and moves in the direction of insuring the beneficiary a substantial fraction of the earnings to which he has been accustomed. It then partakes more of the nature of a well-rounded, universal, retirement system, such as many employers have established for their employees. It becomes basically income insurance, and the higher the percentage of income insured the greater the costs.

The degree of completeness of coverage affects costs. An old-age pension system without a means test will cost materially less if agricultural workers and domestic servants are excluded. An unemployment or underemployment insurance system will cost less if confined to wage and salary workers than if extended to persons who have been working on their own account.

The degree of comprehensiveness in covering hazards materially affects cost. A system designed primarily to provide for old age will cost much less than one which provides something approaching equal liberality for disability occurring prior to the retirement age or for children deprived of a supporting parent before the retirement age. Universal children's allowances add substantially to costs.

The specific conditions governing benefits for each category may greatly increase costs. The outstanding illustration is the age at which retirement is permitted without proof of disability or unemployability. Another is the number of weeks of unemployment for which compensation will be paid. The longer the duration the higher is the cost. In connection with practically every benefit, costs are affected by what may appear at first glance rather minute details.

If at any point in the system a means test is introduced, decisions with respect to (1) responsibility of relatives and (2) ownership of property, particularly income-producing property or property that can be readily converted into cash, will materially affect costs. Assumptions embodied in law such as the one that a child with both parents working is supported by the father should be included here. The law may infer means from the existence of certain facts.

The aggregate cost of a system thus results from an involved complex of factors. In the following chapter we shall attempt to give some figures indicative of costs for certain benefits or for certain systems.

CHAPTER XXVII

COSTS OF SOCIAL SECURITY AND RELIEF

The ultimate success of a social security system will depend to a large degree upon cost. As has previously been discussed at length, a social security system is in the main a defensive program which occupies a subordinate position in maintaining and developing the productivity of the nation, upon which rests true social security. If excessive cost should reduce productivity and lessen employment, the system will do more harm than good. As the cost of a system increases, moreover, the danger becomes greater that the costs will have to be met through inflationary processes that tend to prevent the system from attaining the desired objectives. The question of costs is not, therefore, one to be left to a blind faith in the future. The interests of true social security are not served by the individual who suggests to the American people that when the danger of excessive costs is mentioned they should ostrich-like bury their heads.

Social security systems may be developed in either of two ways or through a combination of them.

1. The more common way, as exemplified in the American old-age and survivors insurance system, is at the outset to include only those employees in the active service, and to pay benefits only as those covered employees gradually, class by class, reach the retirement age. Under this system, costs will increase annually until the system reaches maturity or full load, which will be sometime after the year 2000.

2. The less common way, to a considerable degree exemplified by the New Zealand system, is to begin at once to pay benefits to all members of the population who qualify for them. A system entirely designed upon this principle would start under approximately full load. The cost today would not be radically different from the cost in 2000 except for the gradual changes which may take place in the composition of the population and adjustments that have to be made because of price changes and other economic factors.

The question of costs can therefore be approached in either one of two ways.

1. The costs of existing systems, or proposed systems, that start with little or no load, can by actuarial methods be estimated for the future. Such estimates require making assumptions with respect to the future movement of the several variables in the system that determine its cost. If ultimate cost is to be estimated, the assumptions must be carried some 70 or 80 years beyond the origin of the system if the amount of benefit increases with increased length of service.

2. It may be assumed that on the date of the latest available population census the country had a universal, comprehensive, and co-ordinated social security system. Then by the use of the census data one can arrive at estimates as to what such a system would have cost in that census year had it then been in effect. This method likewise necessitates making assumptions as to how many persons in the population classes involved would meet the eligibility requirements and, if choices are involved, as in old-age retirement, elect to take benefits.

Both methods call for assumptions. The results depend in no small measure upon the assumptions. The actuaries in the Social Security Board, for example, have recently estimated the cost of O.A.S.I. benefits under the present system in the year 2000. The benefit cost according to their lower assumptions is about 3.2 billion dollars and according to their higher ones 6.1 billions. Neither set of assumptions is regarded by the actuaries as extreme. The figures are presumably presented to show the range within which the true figure is likely to fall, namely, between 3.2 billions and 6.1 billions, provided the Congress makes no changes in the law and actual economic developments stay within the range of the two sets of assumptions.[1]

In the present chapter therefore no attempt whatever will be made to give precise estimates of cost. The most one can hope to do is to establish roughly a very broad range within which the cost will probably fall, provided the legislatures make

[1] Dorrance C. Bronson, *Old-Age and Survivors Insurance 1943–44 Cost Studies,* Social Security Board, Actuarial Study No. 19, No. 19(a), and No. 19(b), p. 10.

no radical changes in the laws, and provided further that economic changes keep within the bounds of the high and the low assumptions. With respect to changes in the law, it should be repeated that governmental social insurance, unlike private voluntary insurance, is not contractual; the legislatures at most create a legislative right, the terms of which, in the absence of constitutional provisions, can be changed by any succeeding legislature.

The present chapter will be divided into two parts. In the first we shall present such data as are available regarding the estimated cost of certain programs, including the proposed British plan and the New Zealand system. Since the existing programs in the United States do not give universal, comprehensive coverage, figures regarding them do not produce a grand total cost for a universal, comprehensive system. In the second part we shall first summarize the results of our own efforts to arrive at some idea of what a universal, comprehensive, and co-ordinated system would have cost had one been in effect in the census year 1940. We shall then attempt to indicate the major effects that reasonable predictable changes in the composition of the population would have on the 1940 estimates with reference primarily to old-age benefits. At the end of the chapter we shall give some estimates derived from the same census and related data as to the range of cost of a comprehensive means-test system.

In presenting the available data on estimated cost of existing systems, we shall neither summarize nor subject to criticism the numerous assumptions upon which the estimates are made. We shall merely give in each instance references to the reports from which the figures are taken so that the reader can study them if he so desires.[2]

---

[2] The actuaries of the Social Security Board in estimating the future costs of O.A.S.I. had to make assumptions with respect to nine variables: mortality, marital and parental status, wages (assumed wages for a work year), wages (assumed per number of work quarters per year), employment assumption to age 65 (covered and excluded combined), covered employment assumptions, covered pay rolls (in billions), total population age 20+ (in thousands), and insured and retired proportion of population (derived percentages). Separate computations of course had to be made for men and women.

The methods and assumptions used in our own estimates based on census data will be given in detail in the Appendix. Only the major results and discussion will be given here.[3]

ESTIMATED FUTURE COSTS OF VARIOUS SYSTEMS

The reader will recall that New Zealand has, and the British government proposes, a universal, comprehensive, co-ordinated system. Before considering the fragmentary programs in the United States, it may be helpful to repeat in summary the cost data for these two parts of the British Empire, not because the conditions in the several countries would be the same, but because the data give a rough idea of the general magnitude of the cost of such systems.

The New Zealand system. The New Zealand system, which makes wide use of a means test, in the latest year for which figures are available cost about 16 million pounds sterling. The population of the United States is roughly 80 times that of New Zealand. Thus if New Zealand were as populous as the United States and other conditions remained the same, the cost of its system would have been 1,280 millions. If the value of the New Zealand pound is taken as $3.30, the cost of the system for a New Zealand as large as the United States would have been about 4.2 billion dollars. It will be recalled that the New Zealand plan includes a modest no-means test superannuation benefit that will not come into full effect until the fiscal year 1970–71. It will substantially increase the ultimate cost of the New Zealand system. New Zealand also has an aging population. The current costs are, moreover, those of a year of reasonably good employment. Thus ultimate costs will probably be materially higher than the 4.2 billion dollar figure.

The government's plan for Britain. The estimated costs of the government's plan for Britain are given in a table on page 662.

---

[3] The writer should say that he originally combined the method and the results in a single chapter, which turned out to be long, dry, and hard. It did, however, have one great advantage: method was considered first, it was then applied; and the results flowed from the application of the method. The reader could form his own judgment as to the method and upon that judgment appraise the results. Under the present arrangement the reader who wants to appraise the results will have to study the appendix.

The first column of the table gives the estimated cost of the proposed British plan in the year 1975. We have added two columns to the British figures. In the second column the British

ESTIMATED EXPENDITURES BRITISH PLAN, 1975

	In Millions of Pounds Sterlingª	Converted to Millions of Dollars and Adjusted for Population Differences	
		$4.00 to the Pound	$6.00 to the Pound
Social insurance benefits:			
Retirement pensions............	324	3,888	5,832
Widows' and guardians' benefits...	36	432	648
Unemployment benefit..........	80	960	1,440
Sickness and invalidity benefits....	65	780	1,170
Maternity grant and benefits.....	7	84	126
Death grant..................	14	168	252
Cost of administration..........	16	192	288
Total......................	542	6,504	9,756
National assistance:			
Assistance pensions.............	37	444	666
Unemployment assistance.......	20	240	360
Other assistance...............	6	72	108
Cost of administration..........	4	48	72
Total......................	67	804	1,206
Family allowances:			
Allowances...................	50	600	900
Cost of administration..........	2	24	36
Total......................	52	624	936
Health service.................	170	2,040	3,060
Total expenditure............	831	9,972	14,958

ª *Social Insurance*, Presented by the Minister of Reconstruction to Parliament by command of His Majesty, September 1944, Pt. 1, p. 49.

figures are multiplied by 12, by 3 for the difference in population and by 4 for the conversion from pounds to dollars. In the third column the British figures are multiplied by 18, by 3 for the difference in population and by 6 for conversion into dollars of purchasing power in the British pound.[4]

[4] The figure of $6.00 for conversion is taken from Professor Lawrence R. Klein's study published in the *Quarterly Journal of Economics*, Vol. 58, 1944.

These figures suggest that in 1975 the cost of the British plan in a Britain as large as the United States would be about 10 billion dollars a year, without any correction with respect to purchasing power. Allowance for differences in purchasing power would raise the figure to almost 15 billion dollars a year. It will be recalled, moreover, that 1975 by no means represents full load for the British plan. The ultimate annual cost will be substantially higher.

The costs of the social insurance benefits alone are estimated to be 542 million pounds sterling in 1975. This figure would give 6.5 billion dollars as the comparable amount if the pound is taken at $4.00 and a little less than 10 billion dollars if the pound is taken at $6.00. Again, it must be repeated that 1975 does not represent the top figure.

Old-age and survivors insurance. For the American system of old-age and survivors insurance two sets of figures are available. The first, including a high and a low, are taken from a recent report from the Office of the Actuary of the Social Security Board. This report carries the figures up to the year 2000 and assumes a level wage scale.[5] The second are from a study made under the direction of Professor Harley L. Lutz of Princeton by the Tax Foundation. They stop at the year 1980. We produce these figures by years in the table on page 664.

For 1980 the estimates of the Social Security Board place the benefit cost of O.A.S.I. between 2.6 billion dollars and a little less than 4 billions.[6] The Tax Foundation study places the benefit cost in 1980 at about 3.3 billion dollars.[7] In the 20 years between 1980 and 2000 benefit costs will materially increase. The actuaries of the Social Security Board place the benefit costs for the year 2000 between 3.2 billion dollars and 6.1 billion dollars. These costs are for the existing old-age and survivors system which does not include the workers on the steam rail-

---

[5] The report also contains figures assuming an increasing wage scale that are somewhat higher than those here used. See Bronson, *Old-Age and Survivors Insurance 1943–44 Cost Studies,* Table E, p. 29.

[6] The same, Table IV, p. 15.

[7] The Tax Foundation, *Social Security: Its Present and Future Fiscal Aspects,* June 1944, p. 23.

roads who are under the railroad retirement system, employees of the federal, state, and local governments or of educational or benevolent institutions, nor the thousands of gainfully employed in other occupations which are excluded from O.A.S.I. The most important excluded classes are persons working on their own account—including farmers, professional workers, and business men—and agricultural laborers and domestic servants.

BENEFIT COSTS OF OLD-AGE AND SURVIVORS INSURANCE
(In millions of dollars)

Year	As Estimated by		
	The Social Security Board[a]		The Tax Foundation[b]
	Low Assumptions	High Assumptions	
1945	233	325	236.4
1950	587	774	924.8
1955	893	1,171	1,242.6
1960	1,235	1,666	1,636.0
1965			2,035.8
1970	1,863	2,670	2,428.9
1975			2,852.1
1980	2,625	3,958	3,305.6
2000	3,232	6,066	

[a] Dorrance C. Bronson, *Old-Age and Survivors Insurance 1943–44 Cost Studies*, p. 14.
[b] The Tax Foundation, *Social Security: Its Present and Future Fiscal Aspects*, June 1944, p. 23.

In December 1943, according to the estimates of the Social Security Board,[8] the total labor force in the United States 14 years of age and over was 62.3 millions, of whom 10.3 millions were in the armed forces. The number of employed workers who were covered by old-age and survivors insurance was 30.2 millions. Covered as here used means taxed to support the system and not necessarily currently insured or fully insured. Thus, employed persons under O.A.S.I. constituted somewhat less than half of the labor force including those in the armed forces and less than three fifths of the civilian workers.

The number of variables is too great to permit of a statement

[8] *Social Security Yearbook 1943*, p. 5.

that if all gainful workers in the United States were brought under O.A.S.I., the benefit costs would increase proportionately. A proportional increase would make the costs in the year 2000 range from 6 billion dollars to 12 billions if the figure of one half now excluded is used, and from 5 billions to 10 billions if two fifths is taken as the proportion now excluded. Emphasis should be placed on the fact that these figures for O.A.S.I. relate exclusively to benefit costs. They do not include administrative costs.

The amendments to the Social Security Act adopted in 1939 provided that the federal old-age and survivors trust fund should reimburse the Treasury for expenses in administering O.A.S.I. The expenses include those of the Social Security Board in administering the system and of the Treasury Department in collecting the taxes on employment. The figures in thousands for these reimbursements by fiscal years are as follows:[9]

1941	$26,840
1942	26,766
1943	27,492
1944	32,607
1945	26,950

The average administrative costs for the years 1941 to 1945 according to these figures has been a little more than 28 million dollars a year. A substantial increase in administrative costs is to be anticipated, as the number of beneficiaries increases. The estimated number of beneficiaries and of lump-sum death payments according to the low and the high assumptions of the actuaries of the Social Security Board are given in the table on page 666.

The number of monthly payments which have to be made will increase about tenfold between 1945 and 2000 according to the low assumptions and more than fourteenfold according to the high assumptions. This increase in work load will result in a substantial increase in administrative costs over the years. There will also be some increase, although comparatively slight,

[9] Compiled from *Daily Statement of the United States Treasury* for June 30, 1941, June 30, 1942, June 30, 1943, June 30, 1944, and June 30, 1945.

in the costs of collection of the pay-roll tax. The system started, however, with full administrative load with respect to tax collections, hence the major increases in administrative costs will come from the growth in number of beneficiaries.

ESTIMATED NUMBER OF BENEFICIARIES, O.A.S.I., 1945–2000[a]
(In thousands of persons)

Calendar Year	Low Assumptions		High Assumptions	
	Monthly Beneficiaries	Lump-Sum Deaths	Monthly Beneficiaries	Lump-Sum Deaths
1945.	1,295	170	1,451	179
1950.	2,782	218	3,260	227
1955.	4,026	270	4,683	268
1960.	5,270	323	6,390	314
1970.	7,712	430	9,592	428
1980.	10,501	542	13,876	569
2000.	12,714	623	20,734	773

[a] Dorrance C. Bronosn, *Old-Age and Survivors Insurance 1943–44 Cost Studies*, p. 12.

The railroad retirement system. When the railroad retirement system was under consideration by Congress in 1937, the Board submitted to the committees estimates of receipts and expenditures by years from 1937 to 1975 inclusive. The expenditures, according to these estimates, increased from about 11 million dollars in 1937 to about 231 million dollars in 1975, the latest year shown. It was suggested at the time that the tax on pay rolls, which was to begin at 5.5 per cent in 1937 and increase to 7.5 per cent in 1949—shared equally by the employer and the employee—would make the fund operate on an actuarial reserve basis so that the benefits as they became due could be paid from the accumulated reserves and the interest earned on them.

The data submitted to Congress were entirely inadequate to demonstrate that the tax would actually support the system. Being somewhat skeptical regarding the figures submitted, we projected them beyond 1975, assuming contrary to fact that the expenditures would remain constant after 1975 at the 1975 level. It was obvious that for many years after that date benefit payments would continue to increase, although at a reduced rate of acceleration. We did not attempt to allow for this increase but used the assumption of leveled cost that overestimated the strength of the fund. According to this calculation, the fund increased each year up to and including 1961. It turned downward in 1962 and began that decline at an accelerated rate, which is characteristic of an old-age retirement system that pays higher benefits than the contributions or taxes will support. By 1991 the fund was completely exhausted. The estimated annual receipts of 162 million dollars were short of benefit requirements in that year by 69 million dollars a year.

The *Report of the Railroad Retirement Board for 1943* contains as an appendix the "Second Actuarial Valuation of the Railroad Retirement Act." Because of the difficulties in forecasting future economic conditions, the actuaries used three different assumptions, a high, a low, and one which might be called a probable. The probable assumption would call for contributions or taxes amounting to 10.4 per cent of pay roll. The low would be 8.1 per cent and the high 14.5 per cent.[10] These percentages are level premiums.

The actuarial report does not project benefit costs beyond the year 1955. For that year it gives two estimates, a low of 190.3 million dollars and a high of 227.9 millions.[11]

Summary of Tax Foundation estimates, 1945–60. Of interest in regard to the general magnitude of expenditures for social security and relief is a summary table from the report of the Tax Foundation which is reproduced on page 668. It includes the items of old-age and survivors insurance, unemployment compensation, public assistance and general relief, and public health, and gives the estimates by five-year periods from 1945 to and including 1960.

The Tax Foundation estimates that the aggregate payments for these programs will increase from a little less than 1.3 billion dollars in 1945 to slightly more than 4 billions in 1960. If in this table we should substitute the cost of O.A.S.I. benefits in 1980, as estimated by the Tax Foundation for 1960, we would get a figure of about 5.7 billions.

[10] Pp. 118, 119.
[11] *Report of the Railroad Retirement Board for 1943*, p. 114.

A SUMMARY OF ALL PAYMENTS FOR SOCIAL SECURITY AND PUBLIC HEALTH AND
WELFARE, 1945–60, BY FIVE-YEAR INTERVALS[a]

(In millions of dollars)

	1945	1950	1955	1960
Old-Age and Survivors Insurance.	236	925	1,243	1,636
Unemployment Compensation.	90	874	881	889
Total.	326	1,798	2,124	2,525
Public Assistance and General Relief.	770	1,173	1,217	1,284
Public Health.	192	212	232	251
Total.	962	1,385	1,449	1,535
Grand Total[b].	1,288	3,183	3,573	4,060

[a] The Tax Foundation, *Social Security: Its Present and Future Fiscal Aspects*, p. 58.
[b] Totals are the sum of figures rounded to thousands and may not agree with the
sum of figures here given.

ESTIMATES OF COST OF A UNIVERSAL, COMPREHENSIVE
SYSTEM BASED ON 1940 CENSUS DATA

As is repeated from time to time in this book, the three outstanding characteristics of existing American programs for relief and social security are:

1. Absence of universal coverage. Many are left without provision except as they may be cared for by general public assistance, which in a number of localities is extremely uncertain.

2. Lack of comprehensiveness. For example, disability not
resulting from advanced age is not specifically covered for the
great majority of the people.

3. Benefits are not co-ordinated. The existing systems make
certain classes especially privileged, whereas they leave others
to the uncertainties of general public assistance.

As study of the several programs brought these three cardinal
defects more and more to a sharp focus, we became more and
more interested in what a universal, comprehensive, and co-
ordinated system would cost in the United States. The simplest
way to answer the question appeared to us to be to assume that
such a system had been in effect in 1940 and, by use of the data
contained in the 1940 census and of certain estimates, to derive
figures which indicate the range of costs.

The assumed system used for this purpose included ten major items, as follows:

1. A no-means test old-age benefit to which all were eligible upon attaining the age of 65 but not payable to an individual who elected to continue earning a substantial sum or to the wife of such an individual.

2. A means test allowance payable on behalf of children under 18 years of age provided they could not be supported by the father or mother according to a legally established minimum standard.

3. A no-means test benefit to single women and to widowed, divorced, or separated women 50 to 64 years of age not in the labor force whether they had or had not children under 18 years of age.

4. A no-means test benefit to widowed, divorced, or separated women 15 to 49 years of age, provided they had the care of and responsibility for a child or children under 18 years of age.

5. A no-means test benefit for women under 50 years of age unable to work as home makers or in gainful employment.

6. A no-means test benefit for men under 65 years of age unable to work.

7. A no-means test benefit for medical care.

8. A no-means test maternity benefit.

9. A no-means test funeral benefit.

10. A no-means test unemployment benefit.

The amount of benefit under each of these ten major items is a question of public policy. In our cost calculations we made no attempt to say exactly what the amount of benefit would be. Instead we used three different figures, (1) a low which was so small that relatively few persons would say that if such a benefit is to be provided, the amount given should be less; (2) a high which many may regard as not high enough; and (3) an intermediate figure. In other words, our objective was to arrive at a rough range of cost.

The census figures often do not supply data which would enable one to say with any degree of precision how many in a given population class would prove eligible to take a benefit.

For example, we know the number of persons 65 years of age or over reported at the 1940 census, but we do not know how many of them would elect to retire at a given level of benefit. Experience suggests that the higher the benefit the more the inducement to withdraw from active work. To give another example, it is very difficult to say how many children there were in 1940 whose parents could not provide them with adequate support.

To arrive at the desired goal of a very rough estimate of the possible range of cost between a low and a high, we combined our low estimate of the number who would receive benefit with our low benefit, and our high estimate of the number who would receive benefit with our high benefit. An intermediate figure is generally arrived at by combining an intermediate benefit with an intermediate number of beneficiaries. It is hardly necessary to say that some of the assumptions are based on inadequate and unsatisfactory data, but we have described the basis used in the appendix.

With this broad explanation of method and with the caution that the figures are at best very rough estimates, we present the summary figures in a table on pages 671–72.

According to these figures the cost of a universal, comprehensive, social security system with no-means tests, except for children's benefits, would in the census year 1940 have ranged between 7.6 and 16.8 billion dollars. It can, we believe, be said with a reasonable degree of assurance that to get a figure substantially below the 7.6 billion minimum figure it would be necessary either (1) to eliminate certain of the contingencies covered or (2) to make a far wider use of the means test.

Universal insurance for medical care, old-age protection, and unemployment insurance are the big items in these cost figures. The three combined account for about 5.7 of the 7.6 billion minimum and for about 12.1 of the 16.8 billion maximum. The reader will recall, however, that we assumed a means test for children's allowances. Had no-means test children's allowances been used, this item would have been of major importance. We shall discuss the three major benefits in summary in the present

Estimates of What Comprehensive Social Insurance Would Have Cost in 1940
According to Different Assumptions
(In millions of dollars)

Contingency and Conditions	Estimated Cost		
	Low Benefits	Moderate Benefits	High Benefits
1. No-means test old-age benefit payable on or after age 65:			
Average benefit $25 per month, assuming 67 per cent retired..........................	1,825		
Average benefit $30 per month, assuming 78 per cent retired..........................		2,535	
Average benefit $40 per month, assuming 87 per cent retired..........................			3,749
2. Means test child allowances for children under 18:			
Average benefit $10 a month paid to 5 per cent of children............................	240		
Average benefit $15 a month paid to 10 per cent of children..........................		720	
Average benefit $20 a month paid to 20 per cent of children..........................			1,920
3. No-means test benefit to single, widowed, divorced, or separated women not in labor market 50 to 64 years of age, with or without children under 18:			
Average benefit $20 a month, low estimate as to number separated...................	432		
Average benefit $25 a month, middle estimate as to number separated.................		555	
Average benefit $30 a month, higher estimate as to number separated.................			684
4. No-means test benefit to widowed, divorced, or separated women 15 to 49 years of age, with children under 18 years of age:			
Average benefit of $20 a month, low estimate of number separated and number with children under 18......................	305		
Average benefit of $25 a month, middle estimate of number separated and number with children under 18......................		457	
Average benefit of $30 a month, higher estimate of number separated and number with children under 18......................			640
5. No-means test benefit for males under 65 unable to work:			
Average benefit of $25 a month.............	558		
Average benefit of $30 a month.............		669	
Average benefit of $40 a month.............			892
6. No-means test benefit for females under 50 years of age unable to work:			
Average benefit of $25 a month.............	187		
Average benefit of $30 a month.............		224	
Average benefit of $40 a month.............			299
7. No-means test medical care:			
Present levels ($23.58 per capita annually)....	3,105		

ESTIMATES OF WHAT COMPREHENSIVE SOCIAL INSURANCE WOULD HAVE COST IN 1940
ACCORDING TO DIFFERENT ASSUMPTIONS—*continued*
(In millions of dollars)

Contingency and Conditions	Estimated cost		
	Low Benefits	Moderate Benefits	High Benefits
Levels of families with income of $3,000 to $5,000 ($28.52 per capita annually).......		3,756	
Adequate ($36 per capita annually).........			4,741
8. No-means test maternity benefit:			
Benefit of $25 for the period...............	59		
Benefit of $37.50 for the period.............		89	
Benefit of $50 for the period...............			118
9. No-means test funeral benefit:			
Adults $80; 10 to 19 years $60; 3 to 9 $40; under 3 $24...........................	105		
Midway between 1 and 3................		131	
Adults $120; 10 to 19 years $90; 3 to 9 $60; and under 3 $36......................			157
10. No-means test unemployment premiums:			
Average weekly benefit $9.62 to provide for equivalent of annual average of 1.5 millions unemployed and on benefit throughout year	750		
Average weekly benefit of $17.31 to provide for equivalent of annual average of 2 millions unemployed and on benefit throughout year.		1,800	
Average weekly benefit of $23.08 to provide for equivalent of annual average of 3 millions unemployed and on benefit throughout year.			3,600
Total...................................	7,566	10,936	16,800

chapter. The discussion of the other benefits will be found in
the appendix.

Medical care. Because of the high cost of no-means test medical care, a few words of explanation should be given with respect
to that item. Our figures on per capita costs are taken from the
studies made by the Committee on the Costs of Medical Care in
1928–30. Our low figure represents a pooling of the risks; no
more would be spent in the aggregate than the amount represented by multiplying the population in 1940 by the average
per capita expenditure for medical care in these years. If it be
assumed that the per capita actual expenditures in 1940 were
approximately the same as in 1928–30, the cost, 3.1 billion dollars, would represent merely spreading the cost through a
publicly operated insurance system. The intermediate or moderate cost would mean providing for all, through an insurance

system, the level of care purchased in the years named by families with an income of from $3,000 to $5,000. The cost of such care, 3.8 billion dollars, would thus represent an additional aggregate expenditure of about 700 million dollars. The high figure, about 4.7 billion dollars, represents the provision for all of what the Committee on the Costs of Medical Care regarded as adequate. It would mean an increase of current expenditures of about 1.6 billion dollars a year.

Unemployment compensation. The figures with respect to unemployment insurance are not based on unemployment in the year 1940, but on a series of assumptions explained at some length in the appendix. In a comprehensive social security system, it is to be expected that persons who are continuously unemployed for long periods of time because of technological changes or prolonged depressions will not be dropped from the benefit roll at the expiration of a fixed number of weeks, as at present, or if they are, some will be provided with a training benefit, and others will be given public assistance. We have set up in our table no separate item either for public assistance to the long unemployed or for a training benefit. So far as this rough estimate is concerned, all benefit payments resulting from unemployment are included in the unemployment figure, except in so far as (1) some children's allowances might be paid primarily because of unemployment of the father or mother; (2) some old-age benefits because the elderly person could no longer get work; and (3) some disability benefits because the disabled person could not get work in a period of slack employment.

The low estimate assumes a fairly high level of employment and low-average, weekly benefits ($9.62 a week). If it be assumed that the labor force in 1940 was about 50 millions, unemployment of 1.5 millions at any moment throughout the year would be 3 per cent. It would represent in the main frictional unemployment, and only in years of highly satisfactory employment can a much smaller number of unemployed be expected. In years of high employment, it may be expected that many frictionally unemployed will be re-employed before the waiting period expires, and hence costs will be kept down.

The intermediate figure, as given in the table, represents a substantially higher average benefit ($17.31 a week) to 2 million unemployed at any time throughout the year or 4 per cent of a labor force of 50 millions. The same amount of money, 1.8 billion dollars, would, as the tables in the appendix show, provide for a much larger volume of unemployment at a lower, average benefit. At an average benefit rate of $13.46 a week, for example, it would provide for almost 2.6 millions and at an average benefit rate of $9.62 a week, for 3.6 millions. This latter number of unemployed would constitute 7.2 per cent of a labor force of 50 millions. There is some opinion to the effect that an unemployment compensation system should not attempt to provide for an annual average of more than about 8 per cent unemployment, and that unemployment above this figure should be taken care of through other methods. It should be repeated that in this computation no other methods are included except as previously noted.

Our high figure of 3.6 billion dollars a year may appear to many as excessive and unreasonable as an average annual cost. The two factors which produced it, selected for presentation in the table, were an average benefit rate of $23.08 a week and an equivalent number of unemployed throughout the year of 3 millions or 6 per cent of a labor force of 50 millions.

The same annual cost would provide for any one of the following combinations of the two factors, average rate of benefit and equivalent number unemployed throughout the year.

Equivalent Number Unemployed Throughout Year (In millions)	Per Cent of Labor Force of 50 Millions	Weekly Benefit Rate
4.0	8.0	$17.31
5.14	10.3	13.46
7.2	14.4	9.62

Because of the size of this high estimate, it may be well to enumerate the reasons that led us to include it.

1. This figure includes practically all payment for need resulting from unemployment.

2. A fairly strong argument can be made for an unemployment compensation system that operates as a standby wage. The theoretical advantages of an annual wage as contrasted with an hourly, daily, or weekly wage are widely recognized, but its practicability in many industries is open to serious question. Conceivably a well-developed unemployment compensation system could be designed to effect the objectives of an annual wage in industries for which it is impracticable.

3. To provide full employment, planned economy advocates are recommending a high degree of government control and management, a degree that in some cases approaches that developed in Nazi Germany. The Beveridge plan for Britain, which has aroused wide interest in the United States, involves, for example, government action to provide jobs through public works, control of production and consumption, fixing of prices, control of credit and investment, regulation of foreign trade, control of the persons seeking employment, particularly of youth about to enter employment, the regulation—self-regulation—of the labor unions and other organizations of workers, and abolition of the right of private ownership of productive property and the hiring of workers to operate it. Such a system would be extremely inflexible because of the difficulty to make adjustments in an economy in which at all times there is practically full employment. In such an economy an all-powerful state will have to make adjustments.[12] An alternative which will preserve a far higher degree of personal freedom and flexibility is to provide workers temporarily unemployed with reasonable standby wages.[13]

[12] William H. Beveridge, *Full Employment in a Free Society* (1945).

[13] Money may be likened to a liquid the flow of which is, on a purely comparative basis, relatively easy to control. Its rate of flow can be regulated. Public works, private construction, production of durable consumers goods, production of agricultural commodities are on the other hand solids—solids that are in many cases in such big units that they will not flow. Governments cannot turn them on and off at will. Many once started have to be finished. Started in a period of threatened unemployment, they may have to be continued in a period of full employment and labor shortage; hence the necessity in the planned economy for regulation of wages, prices, and production of consumers goods to prevent inflation. It may therefore be questioned whether a reasonable standby wage provided through unemployment compensation may not

Old-age pensions. The costs for old-age pensions as included in the table on page 671 range from the low of about 1.8 billion dollars to the high of 3.7 billions. It cannot be too strongly emphasized that these costs are based on the number of persons 65 years of age at the census of 1940 and are not indicative of what the cost will be in 2000. It is necessary therefore to consider at some length the future costs.

Future costs of old-age pensions. The number of persons 65 years of age or over in the United States is increasing every year, and hence the aggregate cost of paying an old-age benefit of a specific amount will increase each year. The discussion of the effect of these increases will be based on estimates of the future population of the United States as prepared by Warren S. Thompson and P. K. Whelpton.[14] Upon the basis of these figures we have prepared some figures on the cost of old-age benefits in later years.

In estimating the future population of the United States, scientists like Thompson and Whelpton must necessarily use several different sets of assumptions with respect to three major variables: (1) the fertility rate, (2) the mortality rate, and (3) the immigration rate. There will be a fourth, the losses resulting from World War II, but obviously Thompson and Whelpton could do no more than recognize that fact in the absence of reliable data on what the losses would be. Each set of assumptions will give a different figure for the population as a whole. For the purpose of this chapter on costs, we shall in the main use only one of the Thompson-Whelpton sets of assumptions, the one which seems to us the most probable; it assumes medium fertility and medium mortality with immigration. We are summarizing the results in the expectation that persons who want more will consult the appendix and the Thompson-Whelpton study. All figures will be rounded to the nearest million.

---

in the long run be far less costly to the economy. It might have greater efficiency in meeting the needs of the people. It would represent far less of an encroachment by the state on the inalienable rights of man that are the foundation of a free society.

[14] *Estimates of Future Population of the United States 1940–2000*, Scripps Foundation for Research in Population Problems (National Research Planning Board, August 1943).

In the table below we give in rounded numbers the cost in millions of dollars of a no-means test old-age benefit of $100 a year for persons 65 years of age or over by a five-year period from 1945 to 1950 and ten-year periods from 1950 to 2000. Figures are given for three different assumed retirement rates: 100 per cent, 75 per cent and 50 per cent.

FUTURE COSTS OF AN OLD-AGE PENSION OF $100 A YEAR 1945 TO 2000
(In millions of dollars)

Year	Cost for Persons 65 Years of Age and Over Assuming—		
	100 Per Cent Benefited	75 Per Cent Benefited	50 Per Cent Benefited
1945	1,000	750	500
1950	1,100	825	550
1960	1,300	975	650
1970	1,600	1,200	800
1980	1,900	1,425	950
1990	2,100	1,575	1,050
2000	2,200	1,650	1,100

The essential point to be noted is that because of the growth in the number of old people in the population the cost of old-age pensions will be, other things assumed equal, more than twice as great in 2000 as in 1945. For example, to pay half of the persons 65 years of age or over a pension of $100 a year would cost 500 million dollars in 1945 and 1,100 millions in 2000. A pension of $300 a year paid to half the elderly people would thus cost 1.5 billions in 1945 and 3.3 billions in 2000.

In connection with these figures it should be noted that they are based on the assumption of "medium mortality" between 1945 and 2000. Should there be substantial, progressive decreases in the mortality rate in that period there will be even greater increases in the costs of old-age pensions, unless improved health of elderly people and good employment opportunities reduce the rate of retirement.

The increased number of elderly people is not the only factor to be considered in connection with the cost of old-age pensions. The number of persons 65 years of age or over per 1,000 persons in the active working years of life may increase under such circumstances. The cost of providing for the retired will have to be borne by a relatively smaller sector of the population.

The table below shows the per capita contribution in dollars which would have to be made by persons 20 to 64 years of age to pay a pension of $100 to persons 65 years of age or over. In this table we have used three different retirement rates, 100 per cent, 75 per cent, and 50 per cent.

PER CAPITA PAYMENTS BY PERSONS 20 TO 64 YEARS OF AGE TO PROVIDE PENSIONS FOR
PERSONS 65 YEARS AND OVER, 1945–2000

(In dollars)

ASSUMPTION 1. HIGH FERTILITY, MEDIUM MORTALITY, WITH IMMIGRATION

Year	Contribution to Pay Benefit of $100 a Year		
	100 Per Cent Benefited	75 Per Cent Benefited	50 Per Cent Benefited
1945.............	12	9	6
1950.............	13	10	6
1960.............	15	12	8
1970.............	16	12	8
1980.............	18	14	9
1990.............	19	14	10
2000.............	18	14	9

ASSUMPTION 2. MEDIUM FERTILITY, MEDIUM MORTALITY, WITH IMMIGRATION

Year	100 Per Cent	75 Per Cent	50 Per Cent
1945.............	12	9	6
1950.............	13	10	6
1960.............	14	11	7
1970.............	16	12	8
1980.............	19	14	10
1990.............	21	16	10
2000.............	22	16	11

ASSUMPTION 3. LOW FERTILITY, MEDIUM MORTALITY, WITH IMMIGRATION

Year	100 Per Cent	75 Per Cent	50 Per Cent
1945.............	12	9	6
1950.............	13	10	6
1960.............	15	12	8
1970.............	16	12	8
1980.............	20	15	10
1990.............	22	17	11
2000.............	24	18	12

The number of persons 20 to 64 years of age in the later years of the period 1945 to 2000 will be materially affected by the birth rate that prevails between 1945 and 1979. In this table, therefore, figures are given using the Thompson-Whelpton population figures for high fertility, medium fertility, and low fertility. Since the estimates are forecasts of the fairly distant future, we give the figures only to the nearest dollar.

Before the figures in the table are discussed in detail, it should be pointed out that the cost of providing benefits for relief and social security will be borne in the first instance primarily by the members of the population who have a direct immediate connection with the circulation of income. It would therefore be more effective to show the cost of an old-age pension of $100 a year per person gainfully employed in the years from 1945 to 2000. Such figures would, however, require assumptions as to the percentage gainfully employed which will prevail among men and among women in the years which lie ahead. Will women to an increasing degree work for compensation? Will an increasing number of young men and women continue their educational preparation beyond the age of 20? Will anticipated increases in productive capacity result in a higher percentage not gainfully employed at all or will workers have shorter hours and more leisure?

We decided against making elaborate series of assumptions with respect to these questions. We used simply the per capita contributions based on the total population 20 to 64 years of age. The figures thus include women not gainfully employed, youth still attending educational institutions, and persons unable to work. It must be remembered, however, that some of the cost will be borne by persons who became gainfully employed before the age of 20, and some who continue to work after attaining age 65.

In this connection a table is presented on page 680 which shows by age groups and sex the percentage of the population 14 years of age or over in the labor force at the census of 1940. In examining these figures it should be remembered that a universal, comprehensive, social security system will tend to reduce the percentages in the labor force, since persons who have difficulty in getting jobs because of age or other compensated difficulties will tend to go on benefit.

PERCENTAGE OF THE POPULATION 14 YEARS OF AGE AND OVER IN THE LABOR FORCE
BY SEX AND AGE 1940[a]

Age	Total	Male	Female
TOTAL 14 YEARS AND OVER..	52.2	79.0	25.4
14 and 15 years...........	5.2	8.0	2.2
16 and 17 years...........	21.0	29.0	12.9
18 and 19 years...........	52.7	65.6	40.0
20 to 24 years............	66.2	88.0	45.1
25 to 34 years............	63.6	95.2	32.9
35 to 44 years............	60.8	94.7	26.9
45 to 54 years............	58.0	92.1	22.1
55 to 64 years............	50.9	83.8	16.4
65 to 74 years............	29.0	50.8	7.5
75 years and over........	9.5	17.8	2.1

[a] Census of 1940, *The Labor Force*, Vol. III, Pt. 1, p. 6.

With these limitations in mind we turn to the table on page 678 that shows the estimated cost in dollars per individual 20 to 64 years of age of an old-age pension of $100 a year for persons 65 years of age or over. Discussion will be confined to the figures that are based on the assumption that 75 per cent of persons 65 years of age or over will retire on benefit.

If the United States experiences high fertility, the per capita cost in the year 2000 of an old-age pension of $100 a year paid to 75 per cent of the people 65 or over would, if borne entirely by the individuals 20 to 64, be $14. If the United States should experience low fertility the per capita cost would be $18.

These figures, it will be noted, are for a pension of $100 a year. A pension of $25 a month or $300 a year would cost per person 20 to 64 years $42 if fertility proves high and $54 if it proves low. A pension of $500 a year—a little better than $40 a month—would cost with a high fertility $70 per capita and with a low $90.

It may be worth while to look at these figures from the standpoint of a hypothetical family. We shall assume that the family contains two adults between 20 to 64 years and that it has an income of $2,400 a year. We shall further assume that the tax system is such that a family with an income of $2,400 bears the entire per capita cost; that it is not relieved of any of the cost because of its low income, nor is it charged with any of the cost for providing pensions for very low-income families because of its high income. Under such assumptions it would pay $84 a year or 3.5 per cent of its income for a $300 pension if fertility proves high, and $108 or 4.5 per cent of its income if fertility proves low. For a $500 pension it would pay $140 or 5.8 per cent of income if fertility is high, and $180 or 7.5 per cent of income if fertility is low.

High fertility, it will be noted, reduces the per capita cost of old-age pensions for persons in the age period 20 to 64 years, but it increases the amount which these persons must spend for children.

Future costs for children. To illustrate the possible situations with respect to children we again utilize the Thompson-Whelpton figures, selecting the three assumptions that use medium mortality and immigration and vary only with respect to fertility. In the following table we show the estimated number of children under 15 years of age, and the percentage ratio of such children to the estimated population 20 to 64 years of age.

The percentage ratio of children under 15 years of age to the population 20 to 64 years of age can be read as the number of

NUMBER OF CHILDREN UNDER 15 YEARS OF AGE WITH RATIO TO POPULATION 20 TO 64, 1945 TO 2000

Year	Assumption 1. High Fertility, Medium Mortality, with Immigration		Assumption 2. Medium Fertility, Medium Mortality, with Immigration		Assumption 3. Low Fertility, Medium Mortality, with Immigration	
	Number (In millions)[a]	Per Cent of Population 20 to 64	Number (In millions)[b]	Per Cent of Population 20 to 64	Number (In millions)[c]	Per Cent of Population 20 to 64
1945	34	41	34	41	34	41
1950	36	42	36	41	35	41
1960	38	42	35	38	32	35
1970	39	40	34	35	29	30
1980	42	40	34	34	27	27
1990	44	40	32	32	23	25
2000	46	40	31	31	21	23

[a] Warren S. Thompson and P. K. Whelpton, *Estimates of Future Population of the United States 1940–2000*, prepared for the Committee on Population Problems of the National Resources Planning Board (1943), p. 53.
[b] The same, p. 74.
[c] The same, p. 98.

dollars per capita persons 20 to 64 years of age would have to contribute to give each child under 15 years of age an allowance of $100. For example, according to the assumption of high fertility, the number of children under 15 years of age in the year 2000 would be 46 millions and there would be 40 for each 100 of the estimated 115 million persons 20 to 64 years of age. An allowance of $100 for each child would cost in the aggregate 4.6 billion dollars. If each of the 115 million adults 20 to 64 contributed $40 the total resulting contribution would be the required 4.6 billions.

Thus the per capita cost to persons 20 to 64 of an allowance of $100 to each child under 15 years of age would be in the year 2000 about $40 should high fertility be realized, $31 if fertility should be medium, and $23 if it were low. Low fertility would therefore place on the persons of working age a relatively heavy burden for old-age pensions and a relatively light burden for the support of children. High fertility would do the reverse.

A question which should be noted in connection with these figures is whether high old-age benefits with their inevitable high costs to persons of working age would have an influence on the fertility rate. Thompson and Whelpton express the opinion that the decline in the birth rate which has been taking place in the United States has resulted more from social and economic forces than from biological causes. In other words, families could as a rule have had more children if they had deemed it wise to have them. If families in the future are called upon materially to increase the provision they must make for persons 65 years of age or over, will that fact reduce the number of children born?

Cost figures adjusted for increased numbers of elderly persons. Because of the increase in the number of persons 65 years of age and over which will take place between 1945 and 2000, estimates of the cost of a universal, comprehensive, social security system based on the 1940 census are too low to reflect future costs. The Thompson-Whelpton estimates indicate that the number of persons 65 years of age will a little more than double in the 55 years. If the cost of old-age pensions in the 1940 estimates are doubled, but no change is made in the other nine items, the range of cost of the assumed social security system would be from a low of about 9.4 billion dollars to a high of about 20.5 billions. Two points should be repeated: (1) in our judgment a figure substantially below 9 billion dollars a year could be secured only by doing one or both of the following things: (a) omitting certain of the contingencies from the system or (b) making fairly general use of the means test, giving only so much in benefits as may be necessary to bring those found in need to the suitable minimum standard established by law. (2) The high figure does not represent the cost of extremely liberal benefits paid on a no-means test basis. If extremely liberal benefits are promised now, the cost in the year 2000 may materially exceed the high estimate of over 20 billion dollars a year.

ESTIMATED COSTS OF A MEANS-TEST SYSTEM

From time to time in the preceding discussions of cost, the point has been made that costs can be reduced by the introduction of a means test. Such a reduction results from two major factors: (1) a decrease in the number who receive benefits, and (2) since available assets are taken into consideration in determining the amount to be granted as a benefit, a decrease in the average amount which has to be paid to bring those below the legally established level to that level. Some readers may desire more concrete figures as to the range of costs of a comprehensive means-test system.

To meet such a request, some rough figures will be presented, based on the same basic data from the census of 1940 and other sources that were used in estimating the cost of a comprehensive no-means test system, as given on pages 671 to 672. Again the attempt will be merely to establish a possible range of costs, from a low to a high with an intermediate figure.

Four points should be made before these rough estimates are presented:

1. The cost of a means-test system will depend in part on the standard adopted by the legislature to be used in determining need and hence eligibility. The higher the standard, the more

persons will be eligible, and the more money will be required to bring those who are below that standard up to it. Since in existing national legislation no uniform standards have been adopted either in terms of money or real levels of living, it is necessary to assume a series of standards in making estimates.

2. The cost of a means-test system will vary somewhat with prevailing economic conditions, or more particularly with the availability of employment. In periods of labor shortage elderly persons, those partially disabled, marginal workers, widowed, divorced, or separated women, and youths of working age can get jobs and support themselves. Employment for adults, moreover, reduces the need for assistance to dependent children. It decreases the number who will need assistance with respect to medical care, maternity, and funeral expenses. The ratio of needy to the total number in a population class is not therefore fixed and stable; it is a variable. It will move up and down with employment conditions, being high in bad times and substantially lower in good times.[15]

3. The degree of variability will be influenced by the size of the benefits. It can apparently be generalized with a fair degree of assurance, that the higher the benefits the less the movement from the benefit rolls to employment. If an elderly person, a partially disabled person, or a widowed, divorced, or separated woman is getting along with reasonable comfort on a grant from public funds, there may be little inducement to seek more through effort and the discipline of work. Sheer inertia is a factor.

4. The ratio of eligibles to the total number of a class will under a means-test system vary with the duration of any economic recession. A worker can often provide for himself and those dependent upon him through short periods of unemployment or temporary disability. As the period lengthens, his available cash resources are exhausted to such a point that he

---

[15] If a means-test system establishes a legislative right to assistance for those in need and is well administered, the degree of variation will be increased. Beneficiaries will tend to go off the rolls in substantial numbers when they can earn more through work if they are sure they can get back on if their jobs peter out. A modern means-test system would be designed to facilitate such movements.

becomes eligible for assistance. In a no-means test unemployment insurance system under which benefits are payable only for a limited number of weeks, the drain on the insurance fund ceases as the insured exhaust their benefit rights. Under a means-test system the rights are not exhausted with the lapse of the weeks, but tend to increase as more and more persons use up their available resources and have to depend on social security funds.

For these four major reasons it is quite impossible to do more than to present a range within which the cost of a comprehensive means-test system would probably fall. The rough estimate here presented places that range between 1.8 billion dollars and 7.6 billions a year. The intermediate figure is about 3.7 billions.

The figures from which these totals are derived are shown in the table on pages 686–87, which provides for the same ten classes that were used in the similar computations for the no-means test system.[16] Each of these classes will be briefly discussed.

Old-age assistance. The low for old-age assistance assumes an average benefit of $25 a month paid to 25 per cent of the persons 65 years of age or over in 1940. Roughly the low represents about what was being done under old-age assistance in 1942. The high assumes that the average payment, in addition to the resources already possessed by the eligibles, will be $40 a month and that half the people 65 years of age will be eligible. Roughly it represents the general adoption of the liberal policies of those few states that have had the old-age pension philosophy.

Aid to dependent children. It may be recalled that in the figures for the no-means test system, an exception was made with respect to children's allowances. They were put on a means-test basis. The same figures are used here. The low figure, 240 millions, is based on $10 a month to 5 per cent of all children under 18 and the high figure, 1.92 billions, on an average of $20 a month to 20 per cent of the children. Most children under 18 years of age have parents of working age and for this reason the high percentage in need was not carried above 20. It hardly seems reasonable to assume that except in the event of a long depres-

16 See pp. 671–72.

sion the number of children in need, to the extent of an average benefit of $20 a month, would exceed 20 per cent.

ESTIMATES AS TO COSTS OF A COMPREHENSIVE MEANS-TEST SYSTEM
(In millions of dollars)

Benefit	Low	Inter-mediate	High
1. Old-age Assistance:			
Average benefit $25 a month, 25 per cent on benefit..	677		
Average benefit $30 a month, 33 per cent on benefit..		1,082	
Average benefit $40 a month, 50 per cent on benefit..			2,165
2. Aid to Dependent Children:			
Average benefit $10 a month paid to 5 per cent of children...................................	240		
Average benefit $15 a month paid to 10 per cent of children...................................		720	
Average benefit $20 a month paid to 20 per cent of children...................................			1,920
3. Assistance to widowed, divorced, or separated women not in the labor market 50 to 64 years of age, with or without children under 18 years of age (high estimate as to number used for all three):			
Average benefit $25 a month, 20 per cent on benefit.	114		
Average benefit $30 a month, 33 per cent on benefit.		229	
Average benefit $40 a month, 50 per cent on benefit.			457
4. Widowed, divorced, or separated women 15 to 49 years of age with children under 18 years of age (high estimate as to number used for all three):			
Average benefit $25 a month, 20 per cent on benefit.	107		
Average benefit $30 a month, 33 per cent on benefit.		213	
Average benefit $40 a month, 50 per cent on benefit.			426
5. Males under 65 years of age, unable to work:			
Average benefit $25 a month, 33.3 per cent on benefit.	186		
Average benefit $30 a month, 50 per cent on benefit..		335	
Average benefit $40 a month, 66.6 per cent on benefit.			595
6. Females under 50 years of age, unable to work:			
Average benefit $25 a month, 33.3 per cent on benefit.	62		
Average benefit $30 a month, 50 per cent on benefit..		112	
Average benefit $40 a month, 66.6 per cent on benefit.			199
7. Medical Care:			
10 per cent population provided for at present levels.	311		
20 per cent population provided for at present levels.		621	
30 per cent population provided for at present levels..			932
8. Maternity Benefits:			
Average benefit $25 for period, 10 per cent of births..	6		
Average benefit $37.50 for period, 20 per cent of births		18	
Average benefit $50 for period, 30 per cent of births..			35
9. Funeral Benefits:			
Adults $80, 10 to 19 years $60, 3 to 9 $40, under 3 $24 for 10 per cent of deaths......................	10		
Midway between 1 and 3 with respect to benefits for 20 per cent of deaths........................		26	
Adults $120, 10 to 19 years $60, 3 to 9 $60, under 3 $36 for 30 per cent of deaths...................			47

ESTIMATES AS TO COSTS OF A COMPREHENSIVE MEANS-TEST SYSTEM—*continued*
(In millions of dollars)

Benefit	Low	Inter-mediate	High
10. Unemployment Assistance:			
Average weekly benefit $9.62 to provide for equivalent of annual average of 1.5 million unemployed, 10 per cent of whom would be eligible under means test.	75		
Average weekly benefit $17.31 to provide for equivalent of annual average of 2 million unemployed, 20 per cent of whom would be eligible under means test		360	
Average weekly benefit $17.31 to provide for equivalent of annual average of 3 million unemployed, 30 per cent of whom would be eligible under means test.			810
Total.	1,788	3,716	7,586

Single, widowed, divorced, or separated women not in the labor market 50 to 64 years of age. The high estimate of costs here used for women in this group is directly comparable with the high figure for the aged, 50 per cent eligible and an average benefit of $40 a month. Except in prolonged bad times, it seems doubtful that so high a figure would be reached. A considerable proportion of the women in this group should be employable in good times and earn enough to maintain themselves, possibly with some slight assistance. The low figure used, 114 millions, assumes an average benefit of $25 a month with 20 per cent eligible.

Widowed, divorced, or separated women 15 to 49 with children. Here again the high figure is directly comparable with the high figure for the aged, an average benefit of $40 a month and 50 per cent eligible. This figure may be too high since these women are of working age, the widows may have received some property from their husbands, and the divorced or separated women may be in receipt of contributions from the father of the children. The low figure, 107 millions, assumes an average benefit of $25 a month with 20 per cent eligible.

Males under 65 and females under 50 unable to work. For these two classes the high figure provides an average benefit of $40 a month and assumes two thirds of the estimated number in the class to be eligible. The low figure assumes an average benefit of $25 with one third eligible. The intermediate figure uses an average benefit of $30 and 50 per cent eligible. In connection with these estimates it should be noted that the assumed disability rates[17] are relatively low prior to age 40 and that they increase fairly rapidly from age 40 to age 65. It may be assumed that a considerable number of men disabled, say after 45, have accumulated enough to be beyond need of immediate public assistance. In the case of married women, a considerable number can be cared for by their husbands without recourse to public funds. After age 65 has been reached these disabled persons would be included in the estimates for the cost of old-age assistance. Provision for children of disabled fathers is included under aid to dependent children.

Medical care. The estimates for medical care are all based on the average expenditure per family as reported by the Committee on the Costs of Medical Care.[18] The assumed percentages eligible are 30 high, 20 intermediate, and 10 low. Under a means-test system, it is to be assumed that the growth of nongovernmental, and from the standpoint of government, noncompulsory group health and hospital plans will continue, with a large measure of support from the medical and allied professions. The growth of these independent nongovernmental systems would tend to reduce the number of persons who will need public assistance in meeting the costs of medical care.

Maternity and funeral benefits. For these two benefits the assumptions as to percentages eligible are the same as for medical care: high 30, intermediate 20, and low 10. The amount of benefit is different for each of the three assumptions, as is set forth in the table on page 686.

Unemployment assistance. In the computation of the costs of a comprehensive no-means test system, the estimates with respect to unemployment were based not on unemployment in 1940 but an assumed average annual number unemployed through the year. The same method is used here with further

---

[17] For the rates see App., p. 888 for women and p. 889 for men.
[18] See p. 890.

assumptions as to the number of unemployed who would be eligible under a means test. For the low estimate 10 per cent eligible is used, for the intermediate period 20 per cent, and for the high 30 per cent. The high figure assumes that the average number of unemployed in need and on benefit will be 900,000.

As is explained in the appendix this figure does not mean there will be 900,000 individuals continuously in receipt of unemployment benefits. The number of individuals personally benefited will be far greater than that number, since individuals will come on the benefit rolls, remain there for a few weeks or months and then go off. Some will under a system based on need remain on the rolls for many months.

The average annual number of 900,000 does not mean that there always will be 900,000 on benefit. In good times the number will be smaller, in bad times perhaps materially higher. The high estimate is based on the assumption that over the years the average number will be 900,000.

Both in the high estimate and the intermediate estimate the assumption is that the average benefit will be $17.31 a week or $900 a year. A means-test unemployment insurance system, it should be repeated, would be based on need and not on past earnings, as under existing American practice. Benefits would therefore be based on the number of persons who were in need as the result of unemployment of the individual. The single man or woman with no dependents when unemployed would get materially less than the married man with a wife dependent on his earnings. The married man with a dependent wife and several dependent children would under a means-test system draw substantially more from social security funds than the married man with a dependent wife and no children. Hence the benefit here partakes something of the nature of a family allowance as distinguished from an individual allowance.

Provision has been made previously for aid to dependent children, and it is assumed that children of the unemployed and underemployed will in ordinary times be provided for under that category, but in periods of prolonged unemployment there may be additional demands. For these reasons the rather high average benefit of $17.31 a week or $900 a year is used for the purpose of establishing roughly a range of costs.

COMPARISON BETWEEN MEANS TEST AND NO-MEANS TEST COST

The rough estimates derived from the same basic data permit of some comparison between possible costs of comprehensive systems, one using a means test and the other not. The figures are (in billions):

	Low	Intermediate	High
No-means test.	7.6	10.9	16.8
Means test.	1.8	3.7	7.6

From these figures, it seems reasonably safe to generalize that probably substantially more than half the money for a no-means test system is used to pay benefits to persons who are not in need. The state takes this extra money from the citizens through its exercise of the taxing power and redistributes it according to a governmentally determined formula. The great majority under such a system get back part of the money the state has required them to contribute, but some get back far less than they have paid in contributions or in direct or indirect taxes. This subject will be considered in detail in subsequent chapters.

CHAPTER XXVIII

METHODS OF FINANCING

Relief and social security systems are devices which operate to redistribute part of the earnings of the people in accordance with a governmentally designed plan. They are not themselves directly productive of wealth; they have no source of income of their own; they must secure their income through taxes, or compulsory contributions, collected by the government through the exercise of its sovereign power. In the present chapter we shall be concerned, therefore, basically with methods of taxation and with borrowing, which means taxation deferred. As in most discussions of taxation, attention will have to be given to the incidence of taxation and to individual equities. Since social security systems are devices to redistribute income to achieve certain governmental purposes, it is particularly necessary to consider incidence and equities because of the possibility that the methods of financing selected may operate against the basic objectives sought.

As was shown in the earlier parts of this book, revenues for relief and social security ordinarily do not come from a single tax but rather from a battery of taxes. Sometimes, as in unemployment insurance in the United States, the revenues come almost exclusively from a single tax—in this case a tax on employers—but for the relief and social security system as a whole, the revenues come from many taxes or from borrowing. For purposes of exposition it is necessary to take them up one at a time. We shall follow this general classification: (1) contributions from employers; (2) contributions from employees; (3) earmarked special taxes; (4) general taxes; (5) borrowing.

CONTRIBUTIONS FROM EMPLOYERS

In American social security practice special taxes levied against employers as contributions are a percentage of pay rolls. That part of the wage or salary of an individual employee

691

which exceeds a specified maximum—$250 or $300 a month—
is ordinarily exempt. With respect to these taxes three issues
seem of particular importance: (1) Who actually pays the tax?
(2) What effect do these taxes have on employment? (3) Do
they promote fair competition among employers?

Who pays the tax? Some people assume that if a law imposes
a pay-roll tax upon employers, the tax falls on profits and it
has no effect upon either the prices charged the consumers or
the wages obtained by the employees. The tax, however, adds
to the cost of the labor factor in production. It does not bear on
the other factors. It thus changes the previously existing
relationships. Changes necessitate widespread readjustments,
which to a very substantial degree may shift the burden of the
tax either forward to the consumers or backward to labor
through reduced wages, although under some circumstances a
part may "stick" to the employer.

The number of factors which influence the direction and the
degree of the shifting is large. Their weight, moreover, does not
remain constant. It changes with changes in the general economic situation, in conditions affecting a particular industry,
in the degree of mechanization of establishments, and in the
relative strength of labor, capital, and consumers. Even a
change in style or in the buying habits of the people may affect
the incidence of the tax.

A percentage pay-roll tax bearing about equally upon the
pay roll of all industries and establishments[1] becomes an
inescapable part of labor costs, and thus, so far as producers
are concerned, it has the same effect as an increase in the
covered wages of a like percentage. Since the relationship
between wages and capital does not remain static but undergoes
frequent changes, it is no more significant to say that industry

---

[1] It is true that employers of less than eight are exempt from the federal unemployment insurance tax and some states have followed the federal law in drafting
their respective acts. Thus the small establishments are given a competitive advantage,
but one they cannot push very far. They cannot expand beyond seven employees
without becoming liable to the tax. Their exemption perhaps permits them to make
somewhat better profits so long as the establishment remains under eight workers and
they may expand through increased mechanization.

becomes adjusted to the tax than that industry becomes adjusted to the wage scale prevailing at any particular moment. Since the tax is related to wages on a percentage basis, it moves with them and is involved in every readjustment to meet changed conditions. It is therefore impossible to make final and conclusive statements regarding the incidence of the pay-roll tax on employers. We shall therefore here consider in summary form some of the major situations.

In many communities the rates charged by privately owned public utilities are fixed by regulatory agencies. In the regulatory process it is a common practice to allow what is regarded as a reasonable rate of return on capital. Where such is the practice, an increase in the cost of production warrants either an increase in rates or, what amounts to much the same thing, less of a reduction in rates than otherwise would have taken place. Since the demand for the services of the utility are frequently relatively inelastic, and the industries are monopolistic in character, it may be assumed that the pay-roll taxes can in a large measure be passed along to consumers.

Manufacturers of durable goods, such as automobiles and household appliances, generally fix their prices in advance upon assumptions as to each factor they deem significant. One factor is labor costs. In this advance price fixing, which is subject to the intense competition that prevails in this field, they are free to attempt to meet increased labor costs either by increasing the price to be charged or by diminishing what they spend on the article to be sold at substantially the old price. A dominant characteristic of these industries is that the manufacturer must make heavy outlays for machines and tooling before the first unit comes off the assembly line. These capital costs of production are spread over the units sold. If the manufacturer sells the number of units he assumed he would when the price was fixed, he realizes the expected profits over and above cost of production. If he sells more, he makes large profits. If he sells less, he has little profit and perhaps an actual loss. When sales equal or exceed the assumed number, the tax is apparently passed along to consumers. When sales are smaller, the tax may rest for awhile on the manufacturer. If he should reduce prices and continue to produce, he would continue to bear the tax, unless he reduced wages or other non-fixed costs. If wages are reduced, the tax falls on the workers. If the manufacturer meets the situation by curtailing production, his pay roll and his pay-roll tax are both reduced. Employment is then diminished.

In other highly competitive industries in which the product itself, its costs of production, and its price are less subject to administrative control by management, the situations are diverse. If the product is one which the consumers regard as essential and buy in substantially the same volume whatever the price fluctuations, it seems reasonable to assume that pay-roll taxes may be largely passed along to the consumer.[2] On the other hand, if an increase in price tends rapidly to curtail the demand for the product or to cause consumers to turn to alternative products, the makers with the highest costs of production have to forego profit, attempt to lower wages, or, if worse comes to worst, go out of production. Going out of production curtails both wages and tax. Lowering wages shifts the tax to the workers. Producers with relatively low costs of production can much more readily absorb the tax, although they may attempt to lower wage rates or curtail production to a point at which the reduced supply will move at a price that is satisfactory to them in the light of existing conditions. Under these circumstances some of the tax may stick to the employer, some may pass back to labor, and some may go on to those consumers who continue to buy the goods at an increased price.

Part of the complexity of the incidence of a pay-roll tax on employers results from the fact that consumers often have a choice among several products which will satisfy the same general need. If the price of one goes up, they will switch to another. In such a situation the producer who would lose his market by

[2] A favorably situated producer with low costs of production may absorb the tax and attempt to take away business from a high-cost producer who cannot afford in the long run to pay the tax out of gross profits or capital. But low-cost producers may take such action at any time. The pay-roll tax is of importance only as it weakens the competitive position of producers who have high costs of production resulting from a high labor cost.

raising prices must take a smaller profit or reduce his cost of production, which may involve a downward revision of wages.

From the point of view of the present book, the most vital complication in this matter of incidence is the fact that competitors differ in the extent to which labor costs, including the tax, affect their costs of production. Within a given industry one producer may have relatively high labor costs and relatively low capital costs, whereas a competitor may have relatively high capital costs and very low labor costs. An industry with relatively high labor costs may be in competition with one with relatively low labor costs because it is so highly mechanized. The tax on pay rolls tends to strengthen the competitive position of the establishment or the industry with relatively low labor costs. It may absorb its small pay-roll tax or pass it forward to the consumer through a small price increase. The competitor with the high labor costs must absorb a heavy tax or else decrease his cost of production lest he lose his market to competitors. Cost of production may be decreased by mechanization or by paying lower wages.

The position may be taken that labor ultimately pays most of the pay-roll tax on employers either through an increase in prices where the tax can be passed forward to consumers or through a decrease in wages where the employer has to adjust wages downward to retain his market. It should not be assumed however, that so far as elaborate social insurance systems are concerned it is immaterial whether prices rise or wages fall. Beneficiaries of a social security system are consumers, mainly dependent on the money income fixed by the social security law. If prices remain stable, their real income in necessary goods and services remains constant. An upward spiral of wages and prices reduces the necessary goods and services the pensioner can obtain with his budget payment. Thus in so far as increases in labor costs result in price increases, they reduce the real utility of a social insurance[3] system that pays fixed money

---

[3] The government may increase the benefits to offset the increase in prices. If such legislation is to be socially effective, the benefits of persons already retired and actually living on these benefits must be increased. Such increases destroy any actuarial balance that may have existed in the past between contributions and benefit payments.

benefits. In social security financing, a tax which does not affect cost of production is therefore preferable to one which does so.

What is the effect on employment? So much need arises from unemployment and underemployment that the influence of a pay-roll tax on employment deserves special attention. From the standpoint of management what an employee costs per hour or per unit of output is a total consisting of his pay-roll earnings plus the tax which has to be paid with respect to those earnings. Since management in a covered industry cannot hire an employee without paying the tax, it is immaterial from a business standpoint whether the money goes to the worker as wages or to the government as a contribution to a social insurance fund.

In periods of reasonably good employment, good demand for products, and fair profits, the cost of salaries and wages plus tax presumably does not greatly worry employers. The only issue then is more or less profit. At such a time labor may have the upper hand, since a strike would hold up production and possibly diminish profits.

The real difficulty with such a tax comes when the demand for goods is poor, prices are falling, and the employer is thinking much more about holding down losses than he is about profits. The questions before management then are, Can we earn enough by continued operation to pay operating costs and leave something over to help pay fixed charges, or are we likely to spend more in operating costs than we can get for our product or our services? How long can we continue to run with an actual operating loss that must be paid out of capital?

No attempt will here be made to enumerate the various factors that may influence the decisions of management, or the

---

They create a new liability with respect to benefits for past services, a liability which must be financed by using reserves accumulated to meet other liabilities, by further taxation, or by borrowing. In the case of unemployment insurance, the increase in benefits may be of relatively slight significance because they are payable for a limited number of weeks. The increases will operate to reduce the unemployment reserves more rapidly. In the case of old-age insurance, such increases are of great significance because they may be effective for the remaining lifetime of all persons on the pension rolls. The liability thus created may be of very substantial proportions.

wide differences in the weight these factors have in different industries or establishments. The essential fact is that shutting down completely or running on reduced schedule is one obvious device for meeting an operating loss real or anticipated. Such action will reduce labor costs, both wages and taxes. The tax itself does not create the incentive to cut employment, it merely adds to it.

Management, moreover, is under almost constant incentive to reduce production costs. To some that is equivalent to saying management is always seeking larger profits. If we add to the objective larger profits the prevention of larger losses, that statement is a fair though partial answer. Management has other objectives. Reduction in production costs may be a necessary prelude to a reduction in price, and a reduction of price may make the product available to thousands who cannot now afford it. Management may be manufacturing a product that is in competition with an entirely different product—the mechanical refrigerator in competition with the ice refrigerator. Unless cost of production is reduced, the new device will be available only to the well-to-do. In a highly competitive field, management may know that a competitor who has achieved more efficient production will absorb much of the business unless it too can cut production costs. Under such circumstances management may know that savings in production costs must all be passed along to the consumer, but that course is necessary if its position in the industry is to be maintained or possibly if management is to achieve high profits resulting from a tremendous volume sold on a very small profit margin per unit.

In the United States to perhaps a greater extent than elsewhere, the level of living has been raised because of genius in making machines and power substitute for men and women. The immediate effect may be unemployment or underemployment, but the long-run effect is to permit a higher level of living, especially when the labor released from one industry finds employment in another, or when the resulting reduction in price opens up new markets. The new demand resulting from mechanization may create far more demand for labor than the introduction of the new system temporarily destroyed.

High wages such as prevail in the United States create a positive incentive to the introduction of labor-saving devices. A pay-roll tax on the employer merely adds to that incentive. The device that cuts the pay-roll cuts the tax. The higher the percentage tax on pay roll the greater the incentive to substitute machines for men.

Does the tax make for fair competition? The pay-roll tax paid by the employer does not tend to promote fair competition, nor is it related to capacity to pay. It bears most heavily on those competitors who have a relatively high labor cost per unit of output. Since the maintenance of a large volume of employment at a reasonable wage is generally regarded as essential to the health of the economy, it appears desirable briefly to enumerate some of the more significant conditions which give a relatively high labor cost per unit of output.

1. The amount of capital used, per employee, in the form of power, machinery, and automatic controls may be low, so that it takes a relatively high volume of labor to produce the goods.

2. The establishment may be located in an area where wages and the costs and levels of living are comparatively high. The pay-roll tax adds to the handicap of the establishment in competition with those located in lower-cost areas.

3. Management may be relatively inefficient or the conventions with respect to the utilization of scientific procedures and methods of pay based on incentives may obstruct the development of efficiency comparable to that of competitors.

4. Management may be endeavoring to maintain a high degree of stability of employment and to get away from the practice of relating the number of employees to the demand or prospective demand for the product. The practice of hiring when the demand appeared good and firing when it appeared bad operated toward stabilizing hours of labor paid for per unit of output, for the employer did not have to meet so much of a pay roll in periods of slack demand.

At times suggestions have been made that establishments which attain a strong competitive position through the introduction of labor-saving devices should contribute to unemployment insurance more heavily than their rivals who are still giving a relatively large volume of employment. A discussion of the intrinsic merits of such a proposal lies beyond the scope of the present undertaking. It should, however, be pointed out that the present system of pay-roll taxes operates on a reverse philosophy. It adds to the cost of labor and thereby increases the competitive advantage of the establishment that introduces labor-saving devices. Under such a system, the establishment that cuts pay rolls can often make its competitors pay the costs of the unemployment which it causes.

Under the American system of old-age and survivors insurance, moreover, the establishment located in a high-cost area is providing through its pay-roll tax funds to pay benefits to its competitors in low-cost areas. This fact results from the O.A.S.I. benefit formula which gives 40 per cent of the first $50 of average monthly earnings and only 10 per cent of the balance of covered earnings from $50 to $250.

This formula also operates against the employer who pays better than the lowest rate at which he could hire and endeavors to keep his employees working in periods of recession. His taxes help pay the old-age benefits for the persons whose earnings have been low because of either low wages or intermittent employment or because of the two combined.

In those states which have a uniform tax on all covered employees and a pooled fund, or in other words have no individual employer funds or experience rating, the pay-roll tax operates to give the advantage to those competitors who are able to reduce their labor costs per unit of product.

All the evidence of which we know leads to the conclusion that the pay-roll tax operates in general to increase the competitive advantage of establishments that can reduce their labor costs in relation to their output and penalizes the establishments that have relatively high labor costs.

By way of summary regarding pay-roll taxes levied on employers it may be said:

1. They constitute an easy and convenient way to raise money.

2. They are probably in the main passed along to consumers or back to labor and do not in the long run come out of the profits or capital of the employer.

3. They are not based on the capacity of the employer to pay.

4. They rest in the first instance on employment and hence offer inducements to employers to substitute mechanical devices for men to avoid the tax.

5. Used in connection with the benefit formula of O.A.S.I., they do not promote fair competition but tend to intensify the advantage of competitors in low-cost areas or those who pay low wages and drop employees quickly when business is slack.

How serious the defects of the pay-roll tax may be depends naturally on the degree to which the tax is used. A very small tax, although productive in the aggregate, may strike the employers as scarcely more than an administrative nuisance. When, however, these taxes get up to 3 or more per cent of the pay roll on all salaries or wages not in excess of $250 a month, they become a serious item in production costs for all employers for whom labor is an important item in costs.

CONTRIBUTIONS FROM EMPLOYEES

Contributions from employees have certain marked advantages and certain important disadvantages. We shall take up the advantages, which can be presented rather briefly, first and then go into the disadvantages which involve no small amount of technical detail.

Advantages of employee contributions. The first big point in favor of employees' contributions is that they are highly productive and as a rule are paid without any serious objection. So far as the masses of employees under O.A.S.I. are concerned, they will get in benefits far more than their own contributions will ever pay for, and thus the taxes are for them a profitable investment. Payment of these taxes gives most of them a contingent right to share in the proceeds of taxes levied against employers and possibly some of the proceeds of general taxes. An intelligent person is not likely to protest a tax that is in fact a small payment for a special privilege. In the distant years high-bracket employees will discover that they personally would be better off without the system; but for some years to come the older, high-bracket employees too will get far more in benefits when they retire than their contributions could purchase in any other way.

Contributions permit the employee to accept his benefits as something bought and paid for. To increase this feeling, the term social insurance is used, and contributions are likened to premiums in voluntary insurance. The system is made to appear contractual in nature. Although it is not contractual in law, it does create a contingent right which can only be taken away by a subsequent legislative act. The employee can say and feel that by virtue of his contributions he has a right to the benefits.

Payment of contributions by the employees over a period of years greatly lessens the chance that in later years, when costs for old-age benefits become extremely high, the Congress will abandon the system. If benefits are pure gratuities with no contributions, a Congress might well say, "Nobody has any right to a pure gratuity." It would be quite a different thing for a Congress to say to an individual who has contributed for years, "You have no rights," especially when that individual is one of millions in the same position. Legally the United States government could abandon the system in the years to come, but the political chances that it will do so are materially diminished by contributions from the employees.

Employee contributions can perhaps be made a brake to curb a demand for an increase in benefits. Much has been made of this point in the literature of individual and industry retirement funds. If the employees want more benefits, they will have to pay larger contributions. Often they have been more than willing to do so. There is, however, in this respect a vital distinction between a private retirement system and a social insurance system, and another between a civil service retirement system and a social insurance system. The private retirement system has no pipe line to the public treasury; increased benefits must be paid for either by the employers or the employees; tax receipts cannot be used for this purpose. In the past, government employees have constituted a small fraction of the working population; people outside the government were likely to oppose increased benefits for the government employees unless the government employees increased their contributions to the fund. A general social insurance system has a direct pipe line to the public treasury already laid, although at the outset not in use. A large proportion of the population will personally profit, or appear to profit, from an increase in benefits. Thus one is inclined to question in general social insurance the validity of the argument that employee contributions will be actually used as a brake to check a demand for an increase in benefits.

Objections to employee contributions. From this writer's point of view, the major objection to employee contributions is that they introduce into the system the concepts of coverage, currently insured, and fully insured. They borrow from private voluntary insurance the idea that a person must pay premiums to be insured and use it in a system designed for a public purpose, in which a considerable part of the expense falls on taxpayers in general through the shifting to consumers of taxes on employers or possibly later through general taxes. Payment of a contribution gives an employee a right to share in the distribution of funds collected from others by compulsory taxation. That right is denied to persons who have not paid such a contribution—to citizens who have not been in a position that gives them the privilege of sharing in the bargain insurance the government offers.

One might dismiss this objection if the bargain insurance were available exclusively to the persons most in need but the facts are quite otherwise. Our old-age and survivors insurance system resembles private insurance in this respect; to be eligible for its benefits, one must have not only been in a covered employment, but he must have been in it long enough and paid premiums enough to be eligible. The system as at present constituted leaves out some of the classes that need protection most, the domestic servants and the agricultural laborers.

Almost as bad, it has introduced forfeitures, something which over the years the law has to a considerable degree eliminated from many forms of private voluntary life insurance, and which many employers or industries have materially reduced in their retirement systems. To refresh the memory:

A man or a woman works in an occupation covered by O.A.S.I. and each year makes the compulsory contribution but leaves that covered occupation before becoming currently insured. Contributions are forfeited to the fund, unless later the individual returns to coverage. The reasons for leaving are significant. What are some of the possible reasons?

1. The employee died. There are significant subdivisions: (a) leaving dependents, (b) leaving no dependents.

2. The employee was disabled. The same subdivisions are pertinent.

3. The employee was marginal so that he or she was only employed in rush periods.

4. The woman employee resigned on marriage or, more significant from a social point of view, when her baby arrived, and she had to change from an employed worker to a woman giving all her time to homemaking.

5. The employee lost his or her job in a covered occupation and because of general economic conditions could not get another in a covered occupation, but had to return to an uncovered job in domestic service or agricultural labor.

Under any of those circumstances the employee who has not attained a currently insured status[4] forfeits his contributions unless later he returns to a covered position. If the employee withdraws after attaining the currently insured status, his rights terminate if he survives beyond the extended insurance

[4] For the detailed discussion of acquiring the insured status, see pp. 108–12.

period. Only those who withdraw permanently fully insured are free from forfeitures.

Thus insurance concepts have been carried over into a socialized system resulting in forfeitures and lapses if the covered employee does not pay his contributions for a sufficient period of time.

The O.A.S.I. system does not carry over from private voluntary insurance the concepts of individual financial equities. Since social insurance, especially if it pays high benefits without a means test, is in a sense a competitor of voluntary insurance, we shall go into the matter of individual equities in some detail.

Competitive forces in private voluntary insurance so operate that as a rule every member of a class pays the same premium rate for the same degree of protection. Competition tends to result in classification according to one or both of two factors: (1) the degree of risk from a hazard and (2) the costs of administering the insurance. We shall deal first with administrative costs, and then with the more technical subject of the degree of risk from a hazard.

A premium for private voluntary insurance carries a loading for the costs of doing business. Included in the loading for costs are the various taxes that private insurance companies have to pay to governments, national, state, and local, in connection with the conduct of the company. Thus when the insured pays his insurance premium, he is paying a contribution toward the taxes levied against the company with which he is insured. Whether the company is a mutual or a stock company, it must in the long run make the insured pay the taxes levied against the company and against its agencies. Only a government insurance system can escape the necessity of paying taxes toward the support of national, state, and local governments.

After insurance has been written, the chief costs that are variables are concerned with (1) collections, (2) record making, and (3) keeping the insurance in force or preventing lapses. The costs of collections and records will depend basically on two factors: how frequently collections are made, and the methods used for collection. For example, it costs far less to collect an annual premium than it does to collect four quarterly premiums when the same system of mail billing is used. Quarterly premiums collected by mail billing are vastly cheaper than weekly or monthly premiums collected by the personal visits of collecting agents, although these personal visits may be the cheapest method for collecting large numbers of very small payments generally available to private insurance companies.[5]

Under competitive conditions the person who pays for his life insurance or his automobile liability insurance by a single annual premium is charged less than his friend and associate who pays quarterly. He costs the company less for clerical work, postage, and printing. When one company gives an inducement to pay annually, other companies must follow suit. Thus within any class based on hazards, one is likely to find subclasses based on differences in costs of doing business.

Far more significant, however, are the effects of competition in promoting classification according to the degree of risk. Perhaps this effect can most easily be illustrated by accident insurance. Insurance companies find that certain occupations are materially less hazardous than others. Thus a company, either mutual or stock, that confines its business exclusively to persons in safe occupations can sell insurance much cheaper than companies which have been taking all classes of risk. Companies offering low rates to preferred risks would get all the business of preferred risks if the other companies did not offer equally favorable rates to preferred risks. When a company gives low rates to preferred risks, it can no longer use an average rate for the residue, because it has taken preferred risks out of the average. It must classify all down the line with premium rates varying according to the degree of hazard. Each class confronting the same degree of hazard pays the same rate.

Voluntary insurance under a competitive system must work that way. A man in a nonhazardous occupation is not likely

[5] Material savings are possible when by agreement among employees, employer, and a private insurance company the employer deducts the premiums from the pay roll and makes the payment for all the insured with a single check.

voluntarily to insure against accident if he must pay for the costs of insuring people in hazardous occupations. Perhaps more to the point, a single man without dependents would scarcely voluntarily insure his life in a system that paid benefits exclusively to widows and children of members. The married man who has been carrying voluntary insurance of that kind would be very likely to drop it if his wife should die and all his children had passed the eligible age.

If men and women are to pay premiums for insurance without reference to the hazard class to which they belong, compulsion becomes necessary. Compulsion may be brought to bear in either one of two ways: by employers, industries, or associations or by the government.

Employers, industries, or associations may say, as many of them have done, "As long as you work for us or as long as you are a member of our association, you must be a member of our system and pay the contributions." Competition, however, still remains. The person who does not like the system is free to get a job somewhere else or to resign his membership in an association. In employer or industry systems, moreover, the terms of the system become elements for adjustment closely associated with other questions of compensation. Although the effectiveness of competition may have been impaired, enough generally has remained so that financial equities are seriously considered and members are given a fairly wide range of options with respect to benefits.

Government can introduce compulsion so that the citizen virtually has no escape short of leaving the country. Payment of the premium or contribution becomes a tax. The government in its wisdom can go as far as it likes in disregarding individual financial equities and in distributing the proceeds of the compulsory contributions. The further it departs from individual financial equities, the less contributions resemble voluntary insurance premiums, and the more they resemble ordinary taxes earmarked for a special purpose.

We shall now consider in some detail the departures from the individual financial equities presented by the social security programs we have been studying. This discussion may throw some light on the question, "Are contributions by employees to be properly regarded as taxes to support the system or as insurance premiums to cover hazards?" We shall deal first with working women because the distinctions with respect to them are most striking.

Under the proposed British plan sharp distinctions are made between men and women both with respect to contributions and benefits. The British plan, as compared with our O.A.S.I. for example, goes a long way in preserving individual equities. Its two major features in this respect are:

1. Women pay a materially smaller contribution than men of like age, because the assumptions with respect to them are different. It is assumed that the typical woman worker is single and without dependents and is therefore insuring only herself, whereas it is assumed that the typical man is married and is responsible for the support of a wife and one child.

2. When a woman marries, the system recognizes that a radical change has taken place in her situation. She is henceforth covered by insurance by virtue of the fact she is now a wife and hence covered by her husband's insurance. If she decides to keep on working for salary or wages, she can get a certificate of exemption so that she no longer pays any contribution from her wages but depends on the protection she has by virtue of being a wife. She can, except under certain circumstances, elect to pay the contribution if the extra benefits thereby gained seem to her to be worth the price, but she is not compelled to do so. She can avoid the tax.

Under the American system men and women pay the same percentage tax or contribution with respect to their earnings up to $250 a month. But it must be noted that:

1. If the woman on marriage or upon the arrival of a child withdraws from a covered occupation without having served long enough to be either fully or currently insured, she forfeits her contributions to the fund unless she later returns and works long enough to be currently or fully insured.

2. If the married woman continues to work she must con-

tinue to pay full contributions, although she may not be acquiring for herself or her dependents the benefits acquired by men by their payments. She cannot provide a benefit for her husband, even if he is dependent upon her, although a man gets a benefit for his wife. She provides a benefit for her children under 18 only if they are not living with or being supported by her husband. The presumption is that children are dependent on the father. The old-age benefit she earns for herself is not in addition to the old-age benefit she might receive because of her husband's insurance. If her benefit exceeds her share of her husband's primary benefit, she gets only her benefit. If her share of her husband's benefit exceeds her own benefit, she gets the share of her husband's benefit.

3. The widow with no dependent children and the single woman, even when passed the child bearing age, must pay the same premium as all other employees.

So far as women are concerned, the contributions are taxes rather than insurance premiums.

The O.A.S.I. system requires the well-paid employees to contribute more per dollar of prospective benefit than the lower-paid worker. Under the British plan the contribution is the same for the low paid and the more highly paid and the benefits are the same. Such discrimination as there is in the British plan arises from the progressive nature of the general tax system. No discrimination exists in contributions. The O.A.S.I. gives those who retire after relatively short service a marked advantage over those who retire after long service.

The single man in the O.A.S.I. pays the same percentage contribution as the married man with a wife and numerous eligible children. Under the British plan the single man pays as much as a married man with a wife and one child. The cost of benefits for children after the first is met from general taxes. All things considered it seems much more accurate to think of contributions under O.A.S.I. as earmarked special taxes based on earnings than as insurance premiums.

One more objection to employees' contributions of a different nature needs emphasis. If, as under O.A.S.I., insurance is based on number of contributions paid, and the amount of benefit depends on average monthly wages earned in covered employments, records of earnings must be kept for each individual employee. Millions of dollars must be spent for bookkeeping by the government and millions more must be spent by employers for submitting the proper records. It seems obvious that public funds could be more advantageously spent for education, health, or relief of destitution, and that the employees engaged in the elaborate record keeping could devote their energies to something socially and economically more worth while.

EARMARKED SPECIAL TAXES

The New Zealand system, described in Part III, is supported in the main by a universal income tax, paid by all persons with income, without substantial exemptions. The proceeds go into the Social Security Fund. This special tax is a tax pure and simple, with no suggestion of a premium for voluntary insurance.

Its chief merit, from our point of view, is that it completely eliminates the question of coverage, forfeitures, and lapses. Everyone is covered, except some newcomers to the country with respect to old-age pensions. There are no forfeitures or lapses.

Payment of the special earmarked tax should, it would seem, give just as much feeling that the individual, or the person responsible for support of a dependent, has helped pay the costs as does a contribution under O.A.S.I. Under O.A.S.I. only the better-paid persons in the later years of the system can feel assured that their own contributions have paid the costs and that they are not benefiting from public funds collected directly or indirectly from the general taxpayers. Why a contributory system more than an earmarked special tax system should create an illusion of self provision is difficult to understand unless one assumes a low order of ability to grasp simple figures.

A special earmarked tax bearing on all persons with income would seem better adapted than contributions to serve as a brake on a demand for high benefits. Under the New Zealand plan, it is immediately obvious to everyone that if higher benefits are to be paid, they must be paid for either by an increase in the earmarked income tax or by general taxes. Part of this difference, perhaps most of it, arises, however, from the fact that the New Zealand system was so designed that it picked up at the outset a large part of its ultimate load and, as compared with our O.A.S.I., left a relatively small part of the burden to be assumed by the children and the children's children. Thus the people of New Zealand have a far clearer idea of costs than have the people of the United States.

An earmarked sales tax or transaction tax offers another method of financing social security systems either in whole or in part. It has a particular merit for rural areas where money incomes are small as compared with industrial areas, but where the relative capacity to pay is greater than the money income indicates.

Some persons are strongly opposed to the levying of any tax—income, sales, or pay-roll contribution—against any person with a very low income. Three points are highly significant in this connection.

1. The people with very low income are given more through social security or relief than they pay in taxes for social security. The tax is levied not so much for the purpose of raising revenue as for the purpose of creating in the minds of the recipients a feeling that they have paid something toward their benefits, that they take as of right. Under the New Zealand plan with all hazards covered, a family may in any one year receive far more in benefits than it pays in years as earmarked social security income taxes. In the United States, with our emphasis on old age, a family may be taxed in its period of greatest need to provide security in an old age which may be far in the future; but from our point of view that is an argument for a wiser system of hazards covered than against levying any tax on the low brackets.

2. Unless taxes are levied on all, some classes will be legally exempted from taxation. Then political forces will be in operation to raise the level of exemption or to raise the benefits for those exempted.

3. Social security benefit payments are to be distinguished from most other governmental payments. As a general rule government payments are for services rendered to all without discrimination or to all of a class without discrimination. Social security payments are money turned over by the government to an individual or a family with a degree of discrimination among individuals or families not present to such an extent in any other major activity of government. One might say that the very poor should not be required to contribute directly for schools, public health work, police, or general administration of government, but that line of reasoning is not necessarily applicable where the special service is giving them money for their personal support.

From the legislative and administrative standpoint, there is one great argument in favor of the universal income tax for social security with no exemptions; it furnishes the data for a real understanding and measurement of the problem of relief and social security. Under prevailing income-tax practice the poorest people, about whom information is most needed for the purposes of relief and social security, are exempt from filing reports as to their income. Thus the country lacks accurate data regarding those people who constitute the major public welfare problem of the state.

Income-tax practice furnishes a precedent for having different forms for different income classes. It would appear entirely feasible to design a form for the low-income individuals and families which would call for somewhat greater detail regarding responsibility for dependents and major expenditures than is required from persons whose income is above a reasonable minimum.

With such an income-tax blank in use, it would appear to be entirely feasible for the tax authority to turn over to the public welfare department either the original or a copy of all reports which on their face suggest need and eligibility for public assistance. From part of the blank showing income and its source, it would in all probability be possible immediately to identify those already in receipt of assistance in some form. These income reports could be checked against the existing records for the cases and made part of those records. Cases which on the face of the record showed need could be investigated by the welfare department to determine whether the facts were as stated. Particular attention would be given to those cases in which children are concerned.

The advantages of such a system would be:

1. Legislatures could be supplied with reasonably accurate data regarding the extent and degree of need.

2. The income reports for persons already in receipt of social security benefits or relief would permit of something approaching an annual audit. Conceivably some cases would be found in which changes in income or in responsibilities would require reconsideration of the case.

3. The reports would reveal some cases in which ignorance, pride, or other cause is making the family, especially the children, get along at a level that is against the public interest.

The income tax report, well drafted, could in a large measure take the place, for chronic cases, of the relief application blank. Each year the poor family or the poor individual worker would be doing just what all other heads of families or individual workers are doing, making out on the form appropriate to his income, the income-tax report. If an income tax without exemptions were used, everyone who made a report would have to pay some tax, in the case of the poorest families nothing more than a token tax.[6] For the poor families, however, the report would become the basis for consideration by the welfare department to determine whether assistance was indicated. If such a form were used in connection with a universal income tax, a means test could be used without the degree of objection that has arisen when the poor have had to file a special application and submit to special investigation. The poor would know that all families must report and that all must submit to investigation.

GENERAL TAXES

At present in the United States the national grants for the public assistance categories of the Social Security Act come

---

[6] For persons with income below a certain figure, the tax would be little more than a registration fee.

from general taxes or borrowing on the general credit. Within a decade or two general taxes may have to bear a considerable and a growing burden for O.A.S.I., since the combined revenue from employers' and employees' contributions will not produce the funds needed to pay the promised benefits unless Congress permits increases in tax rates for this program.

Under the British plan, it may be recalled, the burden on the general treasury tends to increase year by year, mainly because of old-age pensions. By 1975 the actuaries estimate that more than two thirds of the costs of the proposed plan will be borne by the general funds, and that percentage will increase in subsequent years. Because of the complicated nature of our O.A.S.I. system, actuarial computations for the future cannot be made with accuracy. They must rest on assumptions—or if one prefers forecasts or guesses—not only as to the movement of the average level of wages in the United States for the next 80 years but also as to the actual distribution of wages. Such assumptions are in and of themselves extremely hazardous, and they ignore an unpredictable political factor of major importance. An increase in wage levels under the O.A.S.I. system means a decrease in the potential load on general taxes. Such a decrease may be the result if the increase is in real wages, if prices do not advance, and if the purchasing power of the dollar remains fairly constant. On the other hand, if prices rise and the purchasing power of the dollar diminishes, then if O.A.S.I. is to achieve its purposes, the benefit schedule will have to be increased. The political demand for an increase will be powerful. In the main an increase in benefits will have to be paid for from general funds.

If the reverse assumption is made that the level of wages falls, prices fall, and the purchasing power of money increases, then the burden of general funds will tend to increase. The explanation of this phenomenon lies in the benefit formula. Benefits on low wages cost more per dollar than benefits on high wages. Employees' and employers' contributions on low wages fall far short of paying the costs. Thus if the wage levels fall and large numbers are in the low brackets, general taxes will have to make up the difference. One conclusion seems safe; if the

Congress holds the O.A.S.I. contribution rates to 1 per cent for the employees and 1 per cent for the employers, the future burden on general taxes will be extremely heavy.

The chief issue with respect to general taxes which will be discussed here is the choice between (1) progressive taxes based on capacity to pay and (2) other taxes not so based. This issue will be broadly discussed, for a detailed consideration of taxation in general scarcely lies within the scope of the present undertaking.

Many of us can recall the time when practically no taxes in the United States were based on capacity to pay, and the principle of progressive taxation according to capacity was not in use. We have seen in our lifetime the introduction of progressive taxation with respect to income and inheritances. We have seen the arguments of economists and others in favor of progressive taxation become the orthodox principle accepted as a matter of economic faith. The poor are not to be subject to direct taxation, the well-to-do are to bear the costs of government, and they are to pay these costs in so far as possible by taxes which cannot be so passed along that ultimately they will fall on the poor.

Unfortunately we have likewise witnessed a tremendous growth in the expenditure side of governmental budgets. The people have demanded more and better governmental services, all of which call for increased public expenditures and ultimately for higher taxation. This movement, which had been going on for years, was given new impetus by the depression and then by World War II. As a result of World War II the sum required to pay interest on the public debt will be almost as much as the aggregate amount the national government collected in taxes in its best prewar years.

The fact appears inescapable that if the rich and the well-to-do are to pay the costs of government in the future, our concepts of rich and well-to-do will have to be radically revised. Many persons who had what appeared to be modest or moderate incomes will have to be regarded as rich or well-to-do.

Extremely high taxes on inheritances will destroy the big estates; inheritance taxes will not meet so much of the costs. Very high taxes on income will prevent the accumulation of large estates in the future. As these sources tend to give out, the government will have to turn in increasing degree to the middle class, including the lower middle class. During the war, exemptions were lowered and rates raised. For many years to come the prospects are that the level which indicates some capacity to pay will have to be kept low, and persons who are above that level will have to pay taxes at a substantial rate.

What does that mean with respect to relief and social security? Let us take O.A.S.I. for an example.

Persons whose incomes are so low that they are exempt from direct taxation will, if covered by O.A.S.I., continue to get their old-age benefits in return for their own contributions. They may have to pay a little more indirectly as employers' contributions are passed along to consumers, but their position will remain about as it has been.

Persons whose incomes make them subject to income and other direct taxes will, if covered by O.A.S.I., pay for their old-age benefits through (1) contributions levied against their pay, (2) direct income taxes, (3) employers' taxes shifted to consumers.

O.A.S.I. is in part, as we have seen, a device to redistribute income in accordance with a governmental formula. The further down the income scale the government has to go in levying an income tax, the more people have to contribute funds for redistribution and the fewer who will profit from the redistribution. Even before the great increase in governmental expenditures resulting from World War II, the upper-bracket employees covered by O.A.S.I. were going to pay more for their benefits in contributions and in taxes than they would have had to pay for them under voluntary insurance. As the level of income-tax exemptions is lowered and the rate raised, the greater is the number of workers who will be paying for more than they are getting. They are becoming the well-to-do, part of whose surplus is being redistributed by the government formula.

This situation is apparently inescapable although its degree can be reduced by a modification of the substantive features of the system, such as reduction of the benefit rates to a reasonable subsistence level as under the British plan or the introduction of the means test as under the New Zealand plan.

Taxes not based on capacity to pay and taxes that can be shifted to consumers will not be very effective as devices to redistribute income. It would, for example, be relatively simple to use a national retail sales tax or transaction tax to make up the deficit that will develop and grow in O.A.S.I. unless the tax rates for this system are raised. The effect will be obvious. Poor people with children to support will be paying both old-age contributions and sales taxes to support the old; in return they will be promised support in their old age. A sales tax will raise the money, but before it is used one must face the question, Which is socially the more important, provision for the young, for the old, or balanced, integrated provision for all in need?

Taxes on special commodities may be regarded as one source of revenue to make up deficits. None of the three big commodity taxes offers much promise. The poor people in the United States in the past have often paid direct taxes for automobiles and gasoline, and many of the taxes of this type are shifted to them. Many a poor family pays more taxes on alcoholic beverages than does a wealthier family of temperate habits. The poor man often spends a far higher percentage of his income for tobacco than does the well-to-do man.

BORROWING

The national government can finance a deficit for social security and relief by borrowing. In discussing borrowing, a sharp distinction must be made between unemployment insurance and old-age insurance.

Unemployment results from economic factors that follow no natural law. The country has good years, fair years, bad years.

Although in bad years prophets of gloom predict that full employment will never come again, history has always proved their prophecies false. So far as history means anything in this field, it is that bad years will be followed by good and perhaps vice versa. A government may, therefore, in theory at least, borrow to pay unemployment benefits in bad years and pay off its loans in good years; it may lay up a reserve in good years and pay it out in bad; or it can combine the two methods. In other words, a government does not have to have its unemployment insurance budget in constant balance. It can perhaps best achieve its purpose if over a number of years, including good and bad, the unemployment insurance budget has been in substantial balance. One does not need to be greatly disturbed in very bad times if some borrowing is done to replenish an unemployment insurance fund, if in good times the fund tends to accumulate a substantial balance. A real cause for alarm would come if borrowing should reach such proportions that repayment within any reasonable time appears quite out of the question, and the nation has made a substantial addition to its outstanding debt that obviously cannot be retired in good times.

Borrowing for old-age benefits presents an entirely different situation if the nation, as in O.A.S.I., starts a system without any immediate pension load and begins to pay pensions with the first class to become eligible after the system is established. Under such a system, each year the obligation for old-age pensions will be higher than it was in the preceding year for a matter of some 80 years, and then it will tend to level off in the maximum. Year in and year out after that, the sum required will be about the same. Never in a general old-age pension system can one expect a fall in the demand for pensions to permit paying off earlier borrowings to meet pension claims. Whenever a nation borrows to pay old-age pensions, it has incurred debt that is permanent, unless it is paid off by levying taxes to pay it. An old-age insurance system such as O.A.S.I., it may be emphasized, is assumed to operate in perpetuity. On that score it is to be distinguished from a war veterans pension system un-

der which the load rises for several years after a war, and then
tapers off as death gradually thins the ranks of the veterans.
In a general old-age pension system, new entrants are always
keeping the system full; in a growing population, in fact, the
total number under the system rises a little each year.

Borrowing versus taxation to pay brings us to the question
of the desirability of building reserves to be available to meet
the mounting demands for old-age pensions. This technical subject will require discussion at some length and is therefore presented by itself in the following chapter.

CHAPTER XXIX

ARE RESERVES NECESSARY IN SOCIAL INSURANCE?

To many persons the word insurance means a reserve. Long experience with life insurance has taught state legislatures that actuarial reserves are essential for the financial security of the policy holders, and they have required them. As a matter of fact, many persons know the actuarial reserve under its more common designation legal reserve. Is there any necessity for legal reserves in social insurance? The question is of great significance only with respect to old-age annuities. We shall therefore discuss reserves in connection with old age first and then take up their place in unemployment, health, and disability.

RESERVES IN OLD-AGE INSURANCE

Let it be assumed first that the government has decided that every old person in the country is immediately to have a pension of, say, $30 a month regardless of means. The legislators take the position that whatever arrangements they may make for financing the system, the aged of today must be supplied by the workers of today with food, clothing, services, and shelter. The legislature makes no distinction between present-day workers who will hereafter pay taxes earmarked for old-age insurance, and retired workers who in their working years never paid an old-age tax because the legislators of their day never imposed one. The retired persons paid the taxes their legislatures imposed, direct and indirect; many of them supported their parents in old age when support from earnings was mainly a moral and social obligation and not enforced by law, and they worked and supported their children. Government thus draws no dividing line between present workers and retired workers.

Under such a system there is no necessity whatever for a reserve. The financial security of the aged is legally assured by the legislature. The money to pay the benefits is collected each

719

year and is paid out in benefits within the year. So long as no changes are made in benefits, the amount paid in one year is substantially the same as in the next year, although there may be a progressive increase each year due to population growth or improved expectancy of life.[1] The calculations are simple arithmetic; the number of people in each of the several classes provided for by the law is multiplied by the benefits for that class, and the products for the several classes are totaled to give the sum to be appropriated. Actuarial science, the forecasting of the distant future on the basis of the past by use of experience and interest tables, has no place.

Reserves and contributions. The complicated questions of reserves arise when in effect the government says: "This system we are providing is social insurance, and as in private insurance no one shall benefit under it unless he has paid premiums for the number of years we specify or unless his employer has paid them on his account. In all other cases, we shall depart so far as we see fit from the principles that have been found sound in private insurance, because this is social insurance, something different. But on this point we are adamant. No benefits are to be paid to a worker or his surviving dependents unless he has been covered for the period of time we designate. We may give him benefits that he has not himself paid for at the expense of the employers, the general taxpayers, or other covered workers, but to be eligible he must himself have paid contributions for the required period."

Such a decision means that for the minimum payment period necessary to establish eligibility, all are paying in and none are drawing out. Then one by one insured workers move from the pay roll to the retirement roll drawing pensions for the balance of their lives. Each year witnesses an increase in the number retired and in the aggregate pension payments even if the system provides uniform flat pensions for all. It takes actuarial science to tell with even an approach to accuracy what such a system will cost 10, 20, or 30 years from now, and how nearly the con-

---

[1] The small progressive increase each year would result in a very great increase if, for example, 1945 is compared with 2000.

tributions will pay for the costs. Experience tables have to be used to determine both how many will survive to draw benefits, and how long they will survive to draw them, and how many will contribute or cause contributions, for how long, and how much. Generally survivors' benefits and some death benefits are provided, and the actuarial problem becomes about as intricate as any that actuaries are called upon to solve. However much one may dislike the gloomy reports of actuaries and question their predictions of the future on the basis of the best and most applicable experience of the past, the fact remains that only competent and experienced actuaries can give accurate estimates as to what such a system will cost in the future.

In considering whether an actuarial reserve is or is not desirable under a system which starts only with active workers and gradually pays pensions to them as they reach or pass the retirement age, two points should be made as clearly as possible.

1. The cost of the system depends on the number who draw benefits and the amount of the benefits they draw. Reserve or no reserve, the actual cost will be the same. In private insurance actuarial reserves earn interest; and interest affects the amount the insured has to pay in premiums. In other words, interest affects the source of the money to pay benefits, but not the amount the insurance company must pay. The question of interest in social insurance, to be discussed later, is not a question of cost but of who pays the cost.

2. The person covered by social insurance is not dependent on the maintenance of a legal reserve for his financial security. His security basically is the promise of the legislature to use the sovereign power of the state to tax, which is perhaps greater security than any legal reserve can give. True, no legislature in a democratic country can bind a subsequent legislature. A subsequent legislature can repeal the whole system, or revamp it, cutting benefits and raising contributions. Many retirement systems for public employees met that fate. But social insurance, although it may not cover all citizens and may create a specially privileged class, nevertheless does cover so many that a legislature cannot wield the axe with political impunity. A

government may be applauded for cutting benefits for its own employees whose jobs may appear to some to be "a racket," but it is politically a very different thing radically to cut benefits or increase contributions when, as was the case of old-age and survivors insurance in 1940, over 35 million persons were covered, probably more than 80 per cent of whom were of voting age.

The only strong argument in favor of an actuarial reserve in social insurance is that it may serve as a brake to prevent the legislature of today from promising benefits that will put too great a burden on the children and the grandchildren who will have to pay them in the future. Under an actuarial reserve plan, premiums sufficient to meet the costs are on an annual level basis. The covered workers, their employers, and the government begin to pay in the first year with respect to an employee the same amount that they will have to pay in every other year until the retirement age is reached. The premium, the contribution, or the tax is a sort of average amount figured in such a way that by the time the employee retires all the money necessary to pay his benefits is in the reserve. Stop all future entrants from becoming members of the system, collect no more premiums from present employees with respect to future service, and practically all liabilities for past services rendered under the system can be paid from the accumulated reserve.

Under the pure cash disbursement plan, or as it is sometimes misleadingly called "the pay-as-you-go plan," only enough is collected in any year to pay the benefits coming due in that year. Since costs increase each year for some 80 years, the amount that has to be collected likewise increases each year for 80 years. The money paid in by active workers is almost immediately paid out to retired workers. No considerable reserve is accumulated. Hence if the system should be closed to new entrants and to present employees for services rendered after the closing, money would have to be raised in some way to continue payments to those already retired and to give the benefits promised to present employees with respect to services rendered before the system was closed. The cash disbursement system thus accumulates a debt; the actuarial reserve system accumulates a reserve. The size of the debt and the size of the reserve are approximately the same, because the aggregate costs of the benefits are the same.

Under the cash disbursement system the present generation says in effect, "We promise you the benefits; we charge the cost of them to the contributors and the general taxpayers who are paying the bills when finally you reach the retirement age." Under the actuarial reserve system the present generation says, "We promise you the benefits and we begin at once to pay in our share of the cost so that when you reach retirement age the money to pay your benefits will be in the reserve." The actuarial reserve is, as was noted, like legal reserve life insurance, whereas the cash disbursement system is like assessment life insurance but with this essential difference: the government can compel the children and the grandchildren to stay in the system and pay the high contributions required to maintain it, whereas in voluntary assessment insurance no such force can be used.

Since the actuarial reserve system compels the generation that makes the promises to begin at once to pay its share of the cost of the promises, it serves as a brake. It is, therefore, unpopular because it means high taxes now, which taxpayers do not like, and because it means conservatism in promising benefits, which prospective beneficiaries and advocates of liberality do not like. The cash disbursement system increases the possibility of promising high benefits, charging a very small part of the true cost to the present employees, and leaving a large part of it to be paid in the future through general taxes.

Interest on reserves. The factor of interest on the actuarial reserve is not the same in public old-age insurance as it is in private life insurance or in private annuities purchased by annual premiums. In private insurance the legal reserves are invested in income-bearing securities or other properties with the result that the company has an actual income from investments, income which does not come from the policy holders unless they have borrowed from the company. In public old-age insurance the reserves ordinarily are invested in government bonds when the outstanding public debt is sufficient to absorb them. Money to cover the interest on government bonds must be collected from the taxpayers. Money to pay this interest on the actuarial reserve would be approximately the same as money to pay the accrued interest on the debt that accumulates under the cash disbursement system, and it would come largely from the same taxpayers under either system. The actuarial reserve reduces the cost of insurance and annuities to the policy holders in private insurance, but it does not decrease the cost of social old-age insurance where people are at the same time policy holders and taxpayers. Both the premiums and the interest must ultimately come from the taxpayers.

Does a reserve help future generations? Can the taxpayers of the future derive any benefit from an actuarial reserve? The answer to that question turns on public finance in general, especially upon the handling of the public debt.

At the end of World War II financing, the national debt will be over 275 billion dollars. First, let it be assumed that the old-age insurance system is operating on a cash disbursement basis, and that no taxes are being levied to retire any part of the public debt. Each year the taxpayers will have to pay the interest on the outstanding public debt and an increasing amount for old-age insurance.

Now let it be assumed that the old-age insurance system is operated on an actuarial reserve basis. The payments are used to transfer national debt from its present holders to the reserve fund. Taxpayers will still have to pay interest on the public debt, but this interest will go either to the reserve fund to be used in absorbing more of the public debt or to beneficiaries of the retirement system. Payment of interest on the bonds held by the old-age reserve would go toward reducing the amount which had to be collected from the taxpayers for old-age benefits. The children and the grandchildren might still be paying several billions a year interest on the inherited public debt, but they would not be paying as much for old-age insurance, because their interest payments would be used for old-age insurance.

Would not the results be the same if taxes were collected to pay off the debt directly without any paper actuarial reserve? The answer is probably "yes." The same amount of payment would have the same effect whether it were used to pay off the funded debt or to prevent increasing the unfunded debt resulting from the growth of the hidden liabilities of an old-age insurance system operated on a cash disbursement basis. The only practical question is whether taxes for old-age insurance could be levied and collected with less opposition than general taxes to pay off debt. It seems probable that special taxes earmarked for social security are more acceptable to the persons who are beneficiaries of the system than are taxes for general purposes.

One danger that lies ahead for the cash disbursement plan is that added to the other heavy obligations the national government has incurred it may increase the danger that the government will have to resort to inflation as a way out. A form of taxation that bears on purchasing power whether for social security or debt reduction, is one device that lessens the chance of inflation.

Reserves and governmental extravagances. Would the revenues coming in for an old-age insurance reserve be conducive to governmental extravagance? Opinion may differ widely on this subject. The opinion of the writer has been that a reserve means current taxation, and that taxation, on a basis so wide that every one feels it, is one of the greatest deterrents of governmental extravagance. More conducive to extravagance is ignoring the hidden debt that results from old-age insurance, operated on a cash disbursement basis. When a government can easily and quickly dispose of bonds to the banks, money is so readily available that it scarcely seems a reserve would be an added inducement to extravagance.

RESERVES IN UNEMPLOYMENT INSURANCE

In unemployment insurance there is no such thing as a true actuarial reserve. Since unemployment is the result of economic as distinct from natural forces, the future cannot be foretold with any substantial degree of reliability by a study of the past. Both in 1914 and 1939 a world war completely reversed the economic situation and resulted in a man-power shortage. Unforeseen international complications have in the past resulted in severe economic depressions. No study of the past will permit of accurate forecasting of when radical changes in trends will take place, or the seriousness or the duration of a recession. The actuaries, therefore, cannot tell how much premium should be charged for unemployment compensation, for they cannot tell how many will be unemployed or for how long.

As was pointed out in some detail in Chapter VIII, it can be fairly said that Congress arrived at a conclusion that, on the average, a 3 per cent tax on pay rolls, excluding pay of more than $250 a month, would make a reasonable provision for unemployment compensation, with the understanding that excessive unemployment would have to be cared for in other ways. In the absence of sufficient data and clearly established principles, Congress left to the individual states such important questions as the amount and duration of benefit, minimum and maximum benefits, provisions for underemployment, and whether rates of contribution should be uniform for all covered employers, or whether rates should be varied on the basis of the experience of the individual employer or industry. Obviously nothing in this arrangement suggests an actuarial reserve.

The present practice is for the individual state to levy the tax required by its law (which may be varied from 2.7 per cent in states which have adopted merit ratings or employers' reserves), pay lawful claims as they mature, and let the balance accumulate as a reserve to meet future claims. The law, it will be recalled, requires the state to bank its unemployment funds with the United States Treasury, where they are "invested" in obligations of the government of the United States.

Since 1942 the national economy has had a shortage of man power and as a result claims against the funds have been mainly for frictional or seasonal unemployment. With low unemployment and underemployment, the reserves have grown to larger proportions than almost anyone would have anticipated when the national act was originally passed. As of July 31, 1945 the amount of the reserves was about 6.8 billion dollars.[2]

A discussion of whether these reserves will prove sufficient to meet the claims that may arise against them in the postwar reconversion lies beyond the scope of the present book. In theory, it should be recalled, the American system of unemployment insurance is not designed to take care of all unemployment or underemployment. It is expected to take care of only a part of it. It has always been recognized that some individuals would exhaust their benefit rights before getting a new job, and that in a period of prolonged depression the number of such individuals might run into the millions. The real issue here is the relative merit of the American plan of benefits for a limited duration regardless of need, and the New Zealand plan of benefits of unlimited duration given only on the basis of need. If the American plan is retained, the issue becomes the co-ordination of unemployment compensation with general public assistance or other devices for providing for persons who have exhausted their rights under the compensation system.

The question which is here germane is, "What is the value of the unemployment reserves to the national economy?" As has been noted, the reserves are invested in the obligations to pay of the national government. The actual money transmitted by the states to the national government has been spent by it for other objectives. Thus when and if the states make demands on the national government for a part or the whole of their reserves, the national government will have to decide how it will get the funds to meet the call. It can meet it from available cash balances, from tax receipts, from new borrowing, or from currency manipulation. Borrowing may be deflationary to absorb purchasing power of individuals or inflationary borrowing from banks. It may be assumed that in a recession inflationary action of one kind or another would be preferred to either taxation or deflationary borrowing.

From the point of view of general finance, the most signifi-

[2] *Emergency Unemployment Compensation*, S. Rept. 565, 79 Cong. 1 sess., p. 16.

cant fact regarding unemployment reserves, such as are used in the United States today, appears to be that they may absorb purchasing power in substantial amounts in good times, through the tax on employers, and release it in bad times through the inflationary processes used by the national government to obtain the necessary cash. In good times the receipts from the tax on employers may be applied so far as they will go (1) to transfer government obligations from holders outside the Treasury to the trust fund, (2) to lessen the extent to which the government borrows from individuals or financial institutions, or (3) to maintain a high level of governmental expenditures without immediately increasing general taxes.

The decisions with respect to how the trust receipts shall be used are actually made under our American practice by the national government, when it determines its objectives for expenditure and the amounts to be appropriated for the several objectives. It can use the money wisely for the economic and social advancement of the nation, or it can dissipate the funds. So far as the economy is concerned, the question is not so much what the government does with respect to a particular trust account invested in its promises to pay as what it does in the aggregate.

In so far as the objective of an unemployment reserve is to absorb purchasing power in times of full employment and to release it in periods of poor employment, the question should be raised as to whether the New Zealand system may not be superior to the American one. New Zealand levies year in and year out an income tax of fixed rate (5 per cent) practically without exemptions. The returns will be high in good years and low in bad years. The balance needed for social security payments each year are made up from the general fund, which means that the general fund will make relatively high payments in bad times and relatively low payments in good times. The requirements for the social security fund thus come up for consideration each time the legislature considers the full budget, and a deficit in the fund receives consideration as part of the national financial situation.

Under the American plan the social security trust funds are not tied into the general budget in such a way that they are considered annually in connection with the other factors that affect national finance. As was noted in the previous chapter American unemployment insurance is financed by a tax on pay roll or employment, which is not directly related either to capacity to pay or purchasing power. Its value as an automatic absorber of purchasing power in periods of a heavy demand for goods and services is further reduced in those states which lower the tax rates when reserves are getting high, and raise them when the demand is falling. Under the American system the question as to what is to be done in the event that large numbers of workers have exhausted their rights or that a state fund is at least temporarily bankrupt is left open. It is generally admitted that unemployment compensation is merely a cushion covering part of unemployment and that unemployment insurance giving complete protection cannot be operated successfully on an actuarial reserve basis.

RESERVES FOR MEDICAL CARE

If the United States should include systematic insurance for medical care in a universal, comprehensive, and co-ordinated system of social security, the question of reserves for that type of protection will arise. No question of reserves would arise if all years were alike with respect to the accident and sickness rates. Each year a sufficient amount would be collected to pay the costs of that year. Reserves are only necessary to allow for deviations from the average year. The premium must be so fixed that surpluses in good years will be sufficient to offset the deficits in bad years. Since in this case the factors at work are to a substantial extent natural, actuarial methods are applicable to a considerable degree, although a common experience is that introduction of insurance, spreading the cost among all and reducing the burden on the individual, increases the extent to which the insured service is utilized. The results of this tendency generally become apparent soon after the introduction of the system and may necessitate upward revision of the initial premium rates. Once the rates have been adjusted to the new situation created by insurance, reserves are only necessary to maintain the fund so that income and outgo are substantially in balance when moving averages, say for five or ten years, are employed in the financial control of the system.

RESERVES FOR DISABILITY INSURANCE

Reserves for disability insurance resemble rather closely reserves for old-age insurance. The three outstanding differences are (1) the number of disabled persons, say from 18 to 65 years, does not begin to equal the number of persons 65 years of age or over who are eligible for age benefits, (2) a considerable number of disabled persons may recover from their disability at least enough to resume active work, and (3) malingering plays a far greater part in disability insurance than it does in an old-age system. Many disabled persons survive for years after the onset of disability; in fact the disability may be such that it does not materially affect their expectation of life. Since disability may take place at a relatively early age, the number of years during which disability payments are made may be relatively high. As a result of these facts the aggregate benefit costs for disability insurance increase materially every year for many years under any system that starts only with active workers. Thus the arguments for and against reserves in disability insurance are much the same as those previously given for old-age insurance.

CHAPTER XXX

OBLIGATIONS FOR THE FUTURE

A social security system based on principles of insurance by its very nature projects itself forward over an indefinite future. As indicated in a preceding chapter, it will be 80 years before the schedule of disbursements under the present American old-age insurance system reaches its maximum. It was estimated that by the year 2000 total annual disbursements for a comprehensive no-means test system covering the entire population would range from 10 to 20 billion dollars.

The present O.A.S.I. system does not provide for the accumulation of any real, tangible, income-producing reserves. Nor is it practicable in any comprehensive government system to accumulate the reserves from which ultimate payments might be made. Accordingly, a universal insurance system inevitably establishes a schedule of obligations covering a long period of years without accumulating investments out of which the obligations can be met. In a sense security is being bought on credit, with the problem of paying for it deferred to the future.

Neither the government nor the public has squarely faced the implications involved in this piling up of obligations for the distant future. The establishment of bookkeeping reserves has created an illusion that something tangible is being accumulated, whereas in fact current receipts are being used for current expenses of government. Disbursements made in the future will thus have to be met out of revenues raised in the future. The nation's ability to meet the social security load over the years will depend upon the financial capacity of the government in ensuing decades. Financial capacity in turn will depend chiefly upon (1) the growth of productive capacity and national income; and (2) competing claims for such income.

It is impossible for anyone to forecast with accuracy whether obligations of the magnitude involved in the social security sys-

731

tem can readily be met 40, 60, or 80 years hence. If, as some have argued, this nation has passed out of the period of growth and into the stage of economic maturity, the prospect of a growth in national income that will keep pace with the rising schedule of the social security requirements would not appear good. If, on the other hand, as others believe, the nation is only at the threshold of a new and highly productive technological age, the magnitude of the obligations created would not appear disturbing. The realization of the technological potentialities, however, depends upon the ability to manage successfully the complex economic and governmental system of today both in the domestic and the international fields. Although no one can read the future with certainty, it is possible to point out a number of factors in the domestic economy which will have an important bearing upon the ability to sustain the social security system.

First, the maintenance of the system will depend upon the continued ability and willingness of workers to shoulder the financial costs involved. Up to the present, it has been widely assumed that a substantial proportion of the large ultimate costs involved will come out of taxes paid by the wealthy classes. But through the progressive income tax rates and the heavy levies on inheritances, the distribution of wealth and income is being rapidly altered. At the same time constant pressure is exerted toward raising wages and reducing the margins of profit. If the goal of progressively broader and more equal distribution of income is realized, it follows inevitably that in the future a steadily increasing proportion of the tax load will have to be borne by the middle- and lower-income groups. This fact has not been appreciated either by the public or the legislative bodies. It appears still to be assumed that so far as the masses are concerned the social security program will impose small burdens.

It is easy for the government to promise the people liberal benefits in the future; it is another thing for the people in the future to meet the ultimate obligations out of current income. The cumulative costs of the program will inevitably appear as a hardship to all except those who are unable to pay their proportionate share of the costs. Eventually the question may well be raised by persons engaged in current production: Are we not making undue present sacrifices in standards of living in order to provide for future old age and other contingencies?

Second, the nation's capacity and willingness to meet social security obligations will depend upon the magnitude and insistency of other competing claims against the national income. Modern governments are expected to support or contribute to a wide range of economic and social activities deemed to be in the public interest. Demands and pressures for government appropriations appear, moreover, to rise at a geometric ratio. So long as available revenues are not superabundant, choices have to be made between the more urgent and important and the less urgent and important.

One part of expenditures for relief and social security is obviously among the most important and urgent, namely, that which goes to relieve want. Such expenditures occupy a position of extremely high priority, perhaps of first priority.

The second part of the expenditures for social security is, however, in a different category. These expenditures go to persons who are not in actual need, according to a reasonably strict definition of need, and are given to insure them at least a minimum income without the humiliation or embarrassment of a means test. There is a real issue as to whether such expenditures have a high priority in comparison with those made for other government services.

For the purposes of the present discussion governmental expenditures may be arranged in eight groups according to purpose:

1. General government, which includes legislative, judicial, and executive general expenditures.

2. Current national defense, which excludes veterans' benefits.

3. Protection and regulation, embracing law enforcement, public safety, and the regulation of commerce and industry.

4. Payments resulting from past commitments or obliga-

tions, made up primarily of interest on the public debt and veterans' benefits.

5. Promotion of economic development, including transportation, commerce and industry, labor interests, agriculture, and other natural resources.

6. Promotion of social welfare which in addition to social security and relief contains education, public health and sanitation, recreation, and housing.

7. Governmental business enterprises.

8. Miscellaneous.

With respect to the first four groups—general government, current national defense, protection and regulation, and payments resulting from past commitments—there is no point in discussing priorities as compared with social security benefits higher than are necessary to prevent want. One may deeply regret that the succeeding generation will have to assume so high an obligation for interest on the public debt, and that the country was forced to fight a war so great that for years to come heavy payments will be made for veterans' pensions. One may hope that developments in the field of international relations may within not too many years warrant a large reduction in expenditures for current national defense. It would, however, be extremely rash to predict tremendous reductions in the expenditures for such objectives within the next few decades or to assume a situation in which payments for high social security benefits would have a priority over any of them.

Expenditures for the promotion of economic development, if wisely and efficiently made, may well appear to have a distinct priority over payments for high social security benefits. They increase the productivity of the nation; they are directly or indirectly largely self-liquidating; and in many cases they will furnish employment. A high level of employment materially lessens need and reduces the necessity for the old, the handicapped, or the partially disabled to depend on social security benefits.

By common consent, education and public health and sanitation rank high among the objects of government support not only because of their cultural and social values but also because they contribute directly to the efficiency of the individual and to the productivity of the nation. If choices have to be made between expenditures for social security beyond the point of relieving actual need and those for education, public health and sanitation, many would certainly choose the latter.

We are not here interested in trying to gauge the relative importance of the various economic, social, and cultural needs which compete for government support. We are concerned primarily with pointing out that a comprehensive social security system which seeks something in the nature of a first mortgage against the nation's future financial resources is endangering its own perpetuity. In any case, to go far beyond the prevention of want at a time when it is impossible to measure the nation's future revenue-producing capacities against urgent competing needs does not appear to be prudent management.

In concluding this discussion, it is important to repeat that the success of a social security system depends upon the attainment of a reasonably stable level of prices, or better, a declining level of prices. If prices should rise over the years, the purchasing power of the money benefits received would obviously decline. A great inflation of prices would virtually wreck the system.

A great rise in the general level of prices may result either from unsound fiscal policies or from forces operating on money costs of production. An increase in wage rates, out of line with improvements in productive efficiency, necessitates rising prices. And, as is well known, once an upward movement of prices—for whatever reason—gets under way there shortly develops the well-known vicious spiral in which wages, prices, and again wages and prices chase one another upward.

Given a strong inflationary movement, a conflict in interest develops between active workers in the prime of life and older persons living on social security benefits or other fixed money incomes. In such a conflict the active workers are sure to win. A way out for them appears to lie in seeking increased money wages to offset the rising cost of living; but the pensioners have no such redress. The consequence of the struggle is that advancing wages and the subsequent rising spiral may undermine the entire system.

It is not here contended that such an outcome is inevitable, but the possibilities of inflation are such as to warrant caution in the creation of future obligations beyond the requirements for the alleviation of real want. To go beyond that may render impossible the attainment of the primary goal.

CHAPTER XXXI

CO-ORDINATION IN SOCIAL SECURITY AND RELIEF

The present chapter and the two which follow are to be concerned primarily with the problem of the co-ordination of social security and relief. It may be well to start the chapter by repeating the significant sentence which Sir William Beveridge used to describe the conditions prevailing in Britain after years of experience in dealing with social security and relief.

. . . Social insurance and the allied services, as they exist today, are conducted by a complex of disconnected administrative organs, proceeding on different principles, doing invaluable service but at a cost in money and trouble and anomalous treatment of identical problems for which there is no justification. . . . [1]

COMPLEXITIES AND ANOMALIES

The complexity of the British system and the anomalies in treatment are as nothing compared with the situation that prevails in the United States under our federal form of government. The salient facts regarding administration which have been set forth in detail in Part I of this book are here briefly reviewed.

1. The national government finances and administers without any state participation whatever (a) the system of old-age and survivors insurance, (b) the railroad retirement system, (c) the railroad unemployment insurance system, (d) benefits for veterans. The states may also give benefits to veterans.

2. Each state administers its own unemployment compensation system, under the persuasive force of a federal tax act, which requires the states to meet certain standards prescribed in that act. The national government is currently contributing nothing for the unemployment insurance benefits, but it does contribute to the costs of administration.

3. Each state administers its own system of old-age assistance in harmony with a grant-in-aid act passed by the national

[1] *The Beveridge Report*, p. 6.

government. The national government pays one half of the cost of each benefit not in excess of $40 a month and contributes to administrative costs.

4. Most of the states operate a similar grant-in-aid system for aid to dependent children and aid to the needy blind.

5. The states, or the local governments, or the two combined operate general public assistance programs, sometimes with further division into special categories. The federal government makes no contributions either to benefits or to costs of administration.

6. The states sometimes with grants-in-aid from the national government operate the services which are closely allied with relief and social security, notably public health, education, including vocational education, and developmental work for agricultural communities. During the war the employment service was operated by the national government, but under existing permanent law the individual states operate the system under grant-in-aid legislation.

The anomalies are too numerous and too detailed for complete summarization. The outstanding ones are:

1. Unless the Congress permits increases in tax rates to go into effect, the national government will ultimately contribute from general taxes a considerable part of the costs of the no-means test O.A.S.I., yet thousands of citizens are excluded from that system, and thousands of others who have been under it for a short time will not derive any benefit from it.

2. The national no-means test railroad retirement act is far more favorable for railroad workers than is O.A.S.I. for general workers.

3. Although the national government pays half of the cost of the means test old-age assistance benefits granted by the states not exceeding $40 a month, it has established no definition of need and has adopted no device to require the states to make even minimum appropriations. Whether an old person gets anything, and if so how much, depends on state law, state administration, and state appropriations. The same situation

prevails with respect to aid to dependent children and aid to the needy blind.

4. The state unemployment compensation systems provide for unemployment that does not exceed the maximum allowed under the law of the particular state. It makes no provision for unemployment extending beyond that duration, leaving that to general public assistance.

5. General public assistance reveals extremely wide variations both in standards and in appropriations so that cases of the greatest degree of need may go uncared for.

6. National grants-in-aid for certain categories and national assumption of responsibilities for others have tended in some states toward a large measure of neglect of those entirely dependent on state or local aid. Thus under the present arrangements, we have persons in really great need receiving no assistance from public funds, while at the same time persons not in need are receiving benefits under O.A.S.I. that are paid for through contributions of others. Unless Congress permits the increase in specific taxes, these O.A.S.I. benefits will result in substantial deficits that ultimately will have to be met by general taxation.

If the United States is to have a comprehensive, co-ordinated, and integrated program, the whole subject of relief and social security will have to be reworked with respect to (1) policy, (2) finance, and (3) administration. Although the three are interrelated, they will be taken up in successive chapters in the order indicated. This chapter will be concerned with questions as to which level of government should determine policy.

THE NATIONAL GOVERNMENT AND POLICIES

Comprehensive, co-ordinated policy requires action by the national government. In the absence of national policy determination, each state is left free to go its own way. Unfair competition among the states may develop, and some citizens of the United States may be left in real need because of failure of a state to act.

The national government is free to act in either of two ways: (1) it may assume complete control as it has done in O.A.S.I. and the two railroad systems; or (2) it can use state-federal co-operation as in the relief categories of the Social Security Act and in general unemployment compensation. To get comprehensiveness and co-ordination, it must use one or the other of these two methods with respect to the whole and all its parts. Which of the two methods is preferable?

Dangers of unified central power. Vesting complete and undivided control over policy in all its detail in the national government would represent a radical departure from the principles on which our national government was founded. It would give us in effect a single, almost all-powerful, central government instead of a federal government. Although the states might remain as vestigial organs, so little power would be left to them that they would have little significance.

No attempt will be made to discuss the constitutional issues involved in such a proposal. Under existing circumstances one hesitates even to assume what is actually the constitutional law. The position here taken is that if such complete centralization is deemed desirable by the people of the United States, it can be effected either by stretching or by amending the Constitution. We shall therefore confine the discussion to questions of desirability.

The framers of the national and of the state constitutions feared power in the hands of government. To lessen the dangers of the abuse of power by government, they divided it. A major division was between the national government and the governments of the several states, with residual powers vested in the people. To centralize power in the national government would represent an almost complete reversal of the old position.

Until very recent years the national government had few direct and immediate contacts with the mass of individual citizens, except in time of war. The legislation of the national government was mainly concerned with broad social and economic problems. Direct personal contacts between the citizen and his government took place at the local or the state level. Under the new centralized system, every citizen covered by social security law—under a comprehensive system that would be practically everyone—would have a direct contact with the national government.

The political implications of such a relationship between all individuals and a central state must be squarely faced. An essential element of social security and relief is the use of the sovereign power of the state to redistribute income. Persons in the lower-income brackets get far more in benefits than they ever pay for; they get it because the state takes the money to pay them from the people in the upper brackets. Distribution of income has been such that one can say roughly that voting power is more or less in inverse ratio to income. The persons in the lower brackets who stand to profit from the redistribution might have power to control the central government and exercise this power to further what appeared to them to be their own immediate self-interest. Inevitably political leaders would arise who would seek to gain control of the central government by enlisting the support of those voters through promises of more and better benefits. Party competition would consist of seeing which one could outpromise the other. On a national scale we might easily duplicate the relationships which in some of our large cities have prevailed between the organization and voters in the congested districts. Wielders of the vast powers could make or break individuals, corporations, communities, or areas. Thus the possibilities for corruption on a far-reaching scale would be present.

American success with the merit system and nonpartisan administration has not been such as would justify a prediction that we could actually secure it under an all-powerful national government. It would be far safer to assume that the important administrative officers, particularly those vested with substantial administrative discretion, would be first and foremost party men. Thus during a Democratic administration the controlling administrative positions in Republican states like Maine and Vermont would be filled by Democrats and during a Republican regime the controlling administrative positions in the solid

South would be filled by Republicans. The local residents constituting a political majority in their state would have no control over the national administrators unless their party was in
control of the national government at Washington.

Even if a Hatch Act were so administered as to prevent the
workers for the central government from active participation
in politics, it could scarcely extend to members of their families.
A man can have his politics in his wife's name.

An all-powerful central government would deprive the country of what may be termed a government of appeal, something
the country has had under the federal system. If a state or a
group of states under the federal system has taken an action
which is deemed unfair or improper by the other states, an appeal to Congress has always been available, and generally it
has been possible to secure a correction.

There seems to be a political psychology about this sort of
appeal that deserves note. When a state has so acted as to result in putting an issue before Congress, there does not appear
to be great emphasis on whether the state is Democratic or
Republican, whether the state administration will be sustained
or reversed. The tendency is rather toward developing a rule
or a principle that will be fair to all the states, perhaps because
the senators and representatives appreciate that their respective states will be governed by the same rules. The federal
legislators seem to be able to view the problem with a considerable degree of judicial detachment. It often appears to be quite
otherwise where the acts complained of have been committed by
national administrators representing the party in control of the
executive branch of the government. Then the unwritten rules
seem to require the party leaders in Congress to take sides
for and against, to make the matter a party issue regardless of
the merits of the case. If results are to be secured, it seems almost essential that some members of the party in control of the
administration shall play an active if not a leading part in
presenting the charges, and then a coalition of the party out
of administrative control and critics of the administration in the
other party achieve the reform.

The position of the President in the two situations is radically different. Under a state system Congress presents to him a bill that had its origin in dissatisfaction with the action of some state. It is not an obvious and direct reflection upon him or upon an officer for whom he is directly responsible. It is commonly couched in general terms. The public press ordinarily has not connected the President personally with the issue. He is in a position to consider the bill on its merits. The President may become personally involved when the bill relates to the central government and represents criticism of his administration or the action of one of his lieutenants or disagreement with his policies. Such a situation has dramatic possibilities that the press is quick to seize. It is so difficult and embarrassing that efforts may be made first to kill the bill in committee, second to line up enough party votes to kill the measure, and if neither is possible, to work out a compromise preferably one that will not involve formal legislation. Sometimes all these devices are combined. It will be remembered, moreover, that if the president vetoes the bill, it takes a two-thirds vote of each of the two houses to pass it over his veto.

Centralization of power in the national government would, moreover, vastly increase the volume of work to be done both by Congress and the administration. They would have to go into a great mass of minute detail. It would seem as if the detail would be so overwhelming that more and more Congress would have to resort to the device of delegating legislative and judicial powers to administrative agencies, thus vastly increasing the amount of government by bureaucrats.

The United States is so large, and so much of the market for its goods is domestic, that interstate and interregional competition is often keen and sometimes intense. An important function of the federal government has been to regulate that competition and to check the states if the competition is unfair or against the national interest. A unitary central government could by itself largely determine the fate of a section. Even under O.A.S.I. as it at present operates, the taxes levied against the better paying employers in the big industrial states will be used in substantial part to pay for benefits to the employees of low-paying employers in other states and sections. It seems safe to assume that it would not take long for the representatives of the already developed metropolitan areas to discover that they must stand together to prevent national action inimicable to their interests. The smaller, less populous states might wake up to find themselves a neglected minority and understand why the framers of the national Constitution preferred a federal form of government with a large measure of home rule for the states.

The difficulties of governing a country with the area, population, and diversity of conditions in the United States from a central government at Washington are almost overwhelming. Consider, for example, the variations in the costs and levels of living, a matter already discussed at some length in a previous chapter. Living in a northern metropolitan center is vastly more expensive than living in the rural South. Part of the difference results from differences in the cost of necessaries and part in differences in community standards. Community standards may be materially lower than is economically and socially desirable; on the other hand, in some areas they may be materially higher than is in any reasonable sense necessary. In fact many of us can think of areas in cities or suburbs where we would find the level of living uncomfortably high; as far as we are concerned lower and simpler standards yield more enduring satisfactions.

If a central government at Washington is to legislate for relief and social security, it must determine questions of standards. It must choose between two general courses: (1) to provide uniform benefits over the entire nation or (2) to vary benefits in accordance with differences in the cost and level of living.

If, as pointed out in an earlier chapter, the central government provides uniform money benefits on a nationwide scale, social and economic anomalies will be plentiful. A resident of New York City will be in want on a benefit which will yield a fair degree of comfort in any one of many rural areas. If the central government meets the not unreasonable demands for relatively high benefits in the populous and politically powerful metropolitan districts, particularly in the northern states, it will have to give unnecessarily high benefits in the rural areas. In fact, the benefits may be out of all proportion to the prevailing wage scale and thus offer too great an inducement to retire on benefits.

The alternative of varying benefits according to the cost and level of living presents serious political difficulties. No representative of a congressional district can have much sense of security of tenure if his constituents know that residents of other districts are getting bigger benefits than they are. He can feel reasonably certain that in the next primary or election he will face an opponent who attributes low benefits in the district to the ineffectiveness of the incumbent. Frequently, particularly just before an important primary or election, the administrative officers responsible for the scientific determination of the facts upon which benefits are based will receive visits from congressmen or party committeemen who will explain, generally in no uncertain terms, that if the party is to win in the next election adjustments upward must be made. For reasons valid in a democracy, the scientific technicians are subordinate to politically selected officers vested not only with a considerable measure of administrative discretion but also with extensive power over personnel—power to assign duties, to make out efficiency reports, to increase or decrease pay, and even to dismiss. To quote one irate senator who was laying down the law to a junior administrative officer, "It is a wise young man who knows on which side his bread is buttered."

Costs and levels of living are not determined by one single, dominant factor readily determined and checked by anyone; they result from determination of a great mass of detailed facts, so numerous and so detailed that they cannot be checked without enormous and costly effort. They are generally made, moreover, not by a complete enumeration but by a sampling technique. Under these circumstances, the politically minded administrator is not far wrong in assuming that a co-operative statistician can produce the results the politician desires in a set of tables which on their face cannot be distinguished from similar tables prepared with integrity and scientific objectivity. They frequently know, moreover, that nobody can check the work without access to the files and records of the agency, and generally the accuracy of the records would have to be tested by a field audit.

Thus even if a central government should start with benefits adjusted according to costs and levels of living, the trend would be toward uniformity. When one considers the voting power now concentrated in the great metropolitan areas, it would seem not unreasonable to predict that the trend would be toward uniformity at a relatively high level—for the rural areas of the country an unnecessarily high level.

NATIONALLY DETERMINED MINIMUM STANDARDS

From our point of view, the far more promising course is for the national government to confine itself to the establishment of low minimum standards with which all states must comply, and then leave it to the state legislatures to determine to what extent they wish to go above the national standards. If co-ordination of benefits is to be secured, all forms of relief would of course be handled in the same general way.

As has been pointed out in Part I, the national government has two devices for inducing the states to comply with the minimum standards prescribed by the national government: (1) the grant-in-aid basis exemplified in the three assistance categories of the Social Security Act and (2) the newer device of the national tax with offsets for payment of a state tax for like purposes, as exemplified in the general unemployment compensation system.

The reasons for the preference for the co-operative state-federal system over the centralized national system are:

1. It leaves the national government in the position of determining broad social and economic policies, as embodied in minimum standards, and relieves it from a mass of details so minute that they must be handled by an appointed, administrative, quasi-legislative and quasi-judicial agency and not by

an elected legislature. Most of the detail is left to state legislatures responsible to the electorate of the state.

2. Politically the system is much less dangerous for it minimizes the extent to which relief and social security benefits may be used as devices to obtain or retain control of the national government. Since it prevents an enormous increase in the power of the central government, it lessens the importance of control of the national government. The question may be raised as to whether control of the national government is not already too important for the preservation of reasonable individual freedom.

3. It leaves the national government in the position of a government of appeal, able to pass upon the administration of the several states, without being called upon to approve or to censure the action of the President of the United States and his subordinates.

4. It means that the administrative agencies in each state are subject to the control of the government of that state and hence of the people of that state. They are not subject to the control of an administration that may have been opposed by a majority of the voters of the state.

5. The large number of government employees necessary for the administration of a comprehensive social security system cannot be effectively marshaled behind any one political party. In this connection, it should be noted that the national government can require the states to use a merit system, and it can supervise its enforcement. In the national government the President controls the administration of the merit system under the Constitution of the United States. As experience has demonstrated, moreover, Congress may at any time provide that positions be excluded from the operation of the Civil Service Act and the Classification Act. There is considerable evidence to suggest that the co-operative grant-in-aid system with its dual control is more favorable to a sound application of the merit system than is exclusive control either in the national government or the state governments.

6. Within the limits permitted by the national law, the states can adjust the system to meet state and local conditions. The co-operative system does not entirely prevent state experimentation that has been a distinctive feature of the federal system of the United States.

7. An individual state is free to go as far as it wishes above the minimum provided in the national law. After it has complied with the minimum requirements, it is free from national control. States with large municipalities with the resulting high costs and high money wages can provide relatively high benefits without being compelled to contribute substantial sums to pay high benefits to beneficiaries in other states who may not need them. The minimum requirements of the national act can be made to prevent unfair competition among states and regions without substituting for natural competition complete control by an all-powerful central government.

CHAPTER XXXII

DISTRIBUTION OF COSTS AMONG LEVELS OF GOVERNMENT

When the United States squarely faces the problem of welding its various categorical programs for relief and social security into a co-ordinated system which will give comprehensive coverage to all its citizens upon a reasonable basis, it will confront the issue as to how the costs are to be distributed among the several levels of government under our federal system. The descriptions of existing programs as given in Part I demonstrate that the present method of distribution rests not on any carefully worked-out plan but on happenstance. To review the facts briefly they show:

1. Old-age and survivors insurance, railroad retirement, and railroad unemployment compensation entirely supported by national taxation.

2. Old-age assistance, aid to dependent children, and aid to the needy blind supported jointly by the national and the state governments, often with local governments participating in the state's share.

3. General public assistance supported usually by state and local funds.

4. Unemployment insurance supported in the main by state taxes, levied in response to the pressure of a national tax act. All the national government actually contributes according to basic law is a small sum toward administrative costs.

During the depression, the national government supported and administered W.P.A., N.Y.A., and C.C.C., paying by far the largest part of costs.

We shall not here review the historical factors that explain why the financial burdens were distributed as they were. In the present chapter we shall attempt first to outline the basic elements in relief and social security financing and administration that make important the question of distribution of costs among the levels of government, and then take up the several methods of solving the problem of distribution that appear to be available. The three major interrelated factors which will be considered in the first part of the chapter may be summarized as (1) available resources, (2) effectiveness in taxation, and (3) establishment and maintenance of standards. In the second part of the chapter the several methods which will be dealt with are (1) allocation of function to a particular level of government, (2) centrally administered, locally shared taxes, (3) the national tax with offsets for state taxes for like purposes, and (4) the grant-in-aid method. The grant-in-aid method, which seems to us the most desirable, will require discussion in considerable detail.

BASIC ELEMENTS IN THE PROBLEM

Students of public finance often divide many of the functions of government into two broad groups: (1) the betterment functions, which advance the social and economic interests of individuals who can be required directly or indirectly to pay the costs of carrying on those functions, and (2) the welfare functions, which do things for individuals that are deemed necessary as a matter of public policy regardless of the capacity of the individual directly or indirectly to pay the costs.

Relief and means test social insurance are the extreme illustrations of the welfare functions of government. Persons who are in actual need cannot at the time of their need pay any part of the cost of the financial aid which is extended to them. Prior to the origin of their need, they may have contributed to the support of others who were in need; after they have survived the period of need, they may again so contribute. The state cannot and does not make past or future contributions a condition precedent to the granting of relief in its lowest terms. No other major function of government more completely exemplifies the welfare group.

Capacity of a community to pay for relief and social security, considered by itself without reference to the other necessary functions of government, depends on three primary factors:

(1) How many persons in the community are in need? (2) What standards are used in determining eligibility and the amount of benefit? and (3) What are the resources of the community from which the benefits may be paid? The essential factors in the equation are the very simple ones of ordinary transactions: Number of units involved x average price per unit = amount to be paid, now or later.

Practically the amount available for financing relief and social security is the difference between (1) all the resources available for the support of governmental functions and (2) the amount that is necessarily spent for other functions of government. The amount available for relief can thus be increased in either or both of two ways: by increasing the amount of the public revenues mainly through increased taxation, and by decreasing the amount spent for other functions of government. Each of these two methods requires examination with respect to local and state governments.

The amount of money a local government can raise is mainly dependent on two factors: the resources within the jurisdiction of the local government and the extent to which those resources can be effectively tapped by forms of taxation available for use by the local government. Local governments may thus be strictly limited by lack of resources within the jurisdiction, by inability effectively to tax the existing resources, or by a combination of the two.

Within a state it is not unusual to find that most of the local governments are using essentially the same taxes, although the rate for them may vary from locality to locality. The per capita returns from these taxes are often far higher for some communities than for others, because the communities with the higher per capita returns have more resources than the others that are being reached by the taxes. Not infrequently one finds the rate of certain taxes higher in the communities with the low per capita return from that tax than in the communities with good per capita returns. Generally a low per capita return indicates that the county or other locality is relatively poor, although in a few cases it may mean that certain resources can-

not be effectively tapped by taxes available to the local government. In many states there is a wide range between the rich
counties and the poor counties or the rich cities and the poor
cities. The fact of the differences is often indisputable, though
differences in per capita revenue from local taxes may not
measure it with precision.

States have the same limiting factors as local governments:
(1) the resources within the state and (2) the extent to which
those resources can be effectively tapped by the state. The
state has a great advantage over the local government, however,
in that it can, if it sees fit, use forms of taxation that are better
adapted to modern economic conditions and, unlike the local
government, it does not have to depend almost exclusively on the
general property tax. To a limited extent it can use such taxes
as the income, the inheritance, or the sales tax, without forcing
too much in taxable resources to migrate beyond its reach.

Where most of the local governments within a state use the
same tax system, it is possible to use the tax data for both state
and local taxes to arrive at some reasonably satisfactory conclusions as to the relative resources of different counties or municipalities, although allowances may have to be made for differences in assessment of property for tax purposes. The several
states, however, have radically different tax systems, so that
it is far less feasible to arrive at satisfactory conclusions as to
the relative resources of the several states by comparison of tax
revenues raised by local, state, and federal taxes. Differences
may be due to one or more of several factors, among the most
important of which are actual resources, the tax system, the
functions and activities undertaken by government, and the
standards at which activities undertaken are carried on.

To overcome the difficulties that arise from variations in the
tax systems and their administration, Dr. Mabel Newcomer,
Professor of Economics at Vassar College, devised a uniform,
standard tax system which she applied to all the states, using
the best available data to show the basis to which the uniform
rates in the standard tax system would apply. From this system,
the gasoline and motor vehicle taxes and other specific better-

ment taxes were excluded. The taxes which she used for the standard were (1) personal income, (2) real estate, (3) business income, (4) corporation organization, (5) stock transfer, and (6) severance. These taxes were selected in the main because they reflect capacity to pay.[1]

Professor Newcomer first applied her method to the data relating to the year 1930. Later it was applied to the data for the year 1935 in connection with the work of the President's Advisory Committee on Education.[2] In a table on pages 754–55 we reproduce the figures for the two years by states. We have added to the table per capita income figures for the year 1942, as another indicator of capacity to pay. The states are arranged in accordance with the per capita income payments in 1942. The rank of the states by Professor Newcomer's method are also shown.

The first point to be noted in this table is the wide difference between the top state and the bottom state with respect to these indicators of resources. With respect to per capita income payments the top state in 1942 was Nevada with $1,352 and the bottom state Mississippi with $407. For each dollar of per capita income in Nevada, there was in Mississippi a per capita income of 30 cents. According to Professor Newcomer's method, Delaware stood at the top of the list in 1935, with a per capita yield from the uniform tax system of $55; Mississippi was at the bottom with $6.00. For each dollar the tax system would yield in Delaware, Mississippi would get only a little less than 11 cents.

Although the range between the top state and the bottom state is the most significant indicator of variation, it may be interesting to make comparisons with the average for continental United States. In 1935 Professor Newcomer's standard tax would have produced per capita for the United States $21, for Delaware $55, and for Mississippi $6.00. In 1942 the per

---

[1] Mabel Newcomer, *An Index of the Taxpaying Ability of State and Local Governments* (1935). Also Paul R. Mort, *Federal Support for Public Education* (1936).

[2] Paul R. Mort, Eugene S. Lawler and Associates, *Principles and Methods of Distributing Federal Aid for Education* (1939), Staff Study Number 5, Prepared for the Advisory Committee on Education.

State	Per Capita Income Payments 1942[a]	Estimated Yield of Professor Newcomer's Standard Tax System					
		1935			1930[d]		
		Total[b] (In millions)	Per Capita[c]	Rank of State by Per Capita	Total (In millions)	Per Capita	Rank of State by Per Capita
ALL STATES.......	$ 852	$2,692.7	$21		$4,861.5	$ 40	
1. Nevada.......	1,352	4.1	41	4	12.8	141	2
2. New Jersey...	1,304	134.1	33	5	233.8	58	5
3. Connecticut...	1,296	50.0	30	6	88.3	55	6
4. Delaware.....	1,186	13.9	55	1	92.7	390	1
5. California.....	1,167	177.0	29	7	299.2	53	7
6. Washington...	1,166	27.0	17	30	63.2	40	16
7. District of Columbia.....	1,164	26.8	44	2	32.0	66	4
8. New York....	1,106	575.4	43	3	990.0	79	3
9. Maryland.....	1,077	38.9	22	13	58.7	36	23
10. Oregon.......	1,046	23.5	23	11	39.1	41	14
11. Massachusetts.	1,024	122.7	28	8	209.4	49	9
12. Rhode Island..	1,016	18.4	27	9	30.9	45	11
13. Illinois.......	979	155.6	20	17	354.0	46	10
14. Michigan....	960	92.7	19	21	196.2	41	15
15. Ohio.........	957	146.3	22	14	263.7	40	18
16. Pennsylvania..	894	206.6	21	16	381.2	40	19
17. Wyoming.....	883	6.4	27	10	11.4	50	8
18. Montana.....	860	12.7	23	12	22.7	42	13
19. Utah.........	850	9.3	18	26	17.4	34	29
20. Arizona.......	832	5.8	13	38	16.0	37	20
21. Indiana.......	827	52.1	16	34	101.3	31	31
22. Iowa.........	823	48.1	19	19	104.4	42	12
23. Kansas.......	814	36.5	19	18	68.4	36	22
24. Maine........	786	12.7	15	35	24.6	31	32
25. Wisconsin.....	786	51.9	17	29	104.9	36	25
26. Colorado......	785	18.9	18	27	37.9	37	21
27. Nebraska.....	774	29.1	21	15	55.6	40	17
28. Missouri......	762	73.1	19	20	126.0	35	28
29. Minnesota....	761	50.3	19	23	92.0	36	24
30. Idaho........	758	9.0	19	22	15.8	35	26

[a] *Social Security Yearbook 1942*, p. 90.

[b] Paul R. Mort, Eugene S. Lawler and Associates, *Principles and Methods of Distributing Federal Aid for Education*, Staff Study Number 5, Prepared for the Advisory Committee on Education (1939), Table 10, p. 50.

[c] Based on U. S. Census estimate of population, July 1, 1935.

[d] Mabel Newcomer, *An Index of the Taxpaying Ability of State and Local Governments* (1935), pp. 54, 59.

INDICES OF REVENUE-RAISING CAPACITY BY STATES—*Continued*

State	Per Capita Income Payments 1942[a]	Estimated Yield of Professor Newcomer's Standard Tax System					
		1935			1930[d]		
		Total[b] (In millions)	Per Capita[c]	Rank of State by Per Capita	Total (In millions)	Per Capita	Rank of State by Per Capita
31. South Dakota.	725	11.1	16	31	24.3	35	27
32. North Dakota.	721	10.6	16	33	19.4	28	34
33. New Hampshire	719	8.9	19	24	14.7	32	30
34. Vermont......	698	5.2	15	37	10.1	28	36
35. Virginia......	697	38.1	15	36	51.9	21	40
36. Texas........	677	97.1	16	32	137.2	24	38
37. Florida.......	655	28.7	18	25	41.7	28	35
38. West Virginia.	598	30.9	17	28	50.5	29	33
39. Oklahoma.....	598	30.8	13	39	57.5	24	37
40. New Mexico...	558	5.0	11	42	9.1	22	39
41. Louisiana.....	534	20.9	9	44	30.4	14	44
42. North Carolina	523	37.7	11	40	52.0	16	42
43. Arkansas.....	514	13.8	7	46	24.2	13	45
44. Georgia.......	498	23.5	8	45	35.0	12	46
45. Tennessee.....	492	31.0	11	41	51.3	20	41
46. Alabama......	480	18.1	7	48	29.0	11	47
47. Kentucky.....	477	26.4	10	43	41.2	16	43
48. South Carolina	459	12.9	7	47	18.0	10	48
49. Mississippi....	407	12.4	6	49	20.0	10	49

capita income payments were for the United States $852, for Nevada $1,352, and for Mississippi $407.

The second point to be noted from the table is that Mississippi, the low state according to both the indicators used, is merely the lowest among several low southern states. States with a per capita income below $500 in 1942 were Georgia $498, Tennessee $492, Alabama $480, Kentucky $477, South Carolina $459, and Mississippi $407. In 1935 there were 5 states that would have had a per capita yield of less than $10 from the standard tax, Louisiana $9.00, Georgia $8.00, Arkansas, South Carolina, and Alabama $7.00, and Mississippi $6.00.

We do not present any of these indicators as measuring capacity to pay. As previously pointed out, that must be determined by contrasting what must be bought with what it will cost with the resources available to pay the costs.

State and local governments in the United States have in the past spent a large part of their available resources for the welfare functions of government, for those services which must be rendered for individuals regardless of their capacity to pay. A table reproduced on page 757 shows the expenditures of state and of local governments in the calendar year 1940 by functions.

The social welfare functions of government as shown by the table accounted in 1940 for 57.6 per cent of the aggregate cash expenditures of state governments in the United States. Public assistance with 29.9 per cent and education with 24.7 together accounted for 54.6 per cent. Transportation, mainly highway construction and maintenance, a betterment function, was the third large item, making up 25.5 per cent. These three functions combined accounted for 80.1 per cent of the cash expenditures of state governments in 1940.

These total figures for state expenditures include those made from federal grants to the states. The third column of the table shows that in 1940 the states disbursed 684 million dollars which they received as grants from the national government. Of these grants 43.9 per cent went for public assistance, 29.1 per cent for highways, and 3.9 per cent for education. In addition to the 43.9 per cent for public assistance, there were grants for social security administration amounting to 8.5 per cent of all grant money spent.

Local governments in 1940 made cash expenditures of approximately $7,044 millions of which $5,633 came from their own funds and $1,411 from grants from the state and indirectly through the state from the federal government.

Education was the chief item of expenditure by local governments, accounting for 28.0 per cent of expenditures from its own funds and 32.5 per cent of its total expenditures. Public assistance was the second item in total expenditures with 14.2 per cent. More than half the total expenditures of local governments went for the social welfare functions, including public health and sanitation and recreation.

CASH EXPENDITURES IN 1940 BY STATE AND LOCAL GOVERNMENTS[a]

(Dollar items in millions)

Function	By State Governments						By Local Governments					
	From Own Funds		From Grants		Total		From Own Funds		From Grants		Total	
	Amount	Per Cent	Amount	Per Cent	Amount	Per Cent	Amount	Per Cent	Amount	Per Cent	Amount	Per Cent
ALL PURPOSES	$3,314	100.0	$684	100.0	$3,998	100.0	$5,633	100.0	$1,411	100.0	$7,044	100.0
VETERANS' BENEFITS	16	0.5			16	0.4						
REGULATION AND PROTECTION	219	6.6			219	5.5	638	11.3	8	0.6	646	9.2
Law enforcement and public safety	154	4.6			154	3.9	611	10.8	8	0.6	619	8.8
Regulation of commerce and industry	65	2.0			65	1.6	27	0.5			27	0.4
PROMOTION OF ECONOMIC DEVELOPMENT	902	27.2	233	34.1	1,135	28.4	751	13.3	221	15.7	972	13.8
Transportation	822	24.8	199	29.1	1,021	25.5	682	12.1	220	15.6	902	12.8
Commerce and industry	4	0.1			4	0.1						
Labor interests	3	0.1	3	0.4	6	0.2						
Agriculture	53	1.6	25	3.7	78	2.0	43	0.8			43	0.6
Other natural resources	20	0.6	6	0.9	26	0.6	26	0.4	1	0.1	27	0.4
PROMOTION OF SOCIAL WELFARE	1,898	57.3	407	59.5	2,305	57.6	2,694	47.8	1,135	80.4	3,829	54.4
Education	963	29.0	27	3.9	990	24.7	1,577	28.0	709	50.2	2,286	32.5
Public health and sanitation	28	0.8	22	3.2	50	1.3	368	6.5	3	0.2	371	5.3
Recreation	12	0.4			12	0.3	170	3.0	b		170	2.4
Public assistance	895	27.0	300	43.9	1,195	29.9	579	10.3	422	29.9	1,001	14.2
Social security administration			58	8.5	58	1.4			1	0.1	1	c
Housing												
INTEREST ON PUBLIC DEBT	121	3.7			121	3.0	490	8.7	d		490	7.0
GENERAL GOVERNMENT	168	5.0			168	4.2	601	10.7			601	8.5
MISCELLANEOUS	43	1.3	44	6.4	87	2.2	414	7.4	47	3.3	461	6.5
Retired government employees	36	1.1			36	0.9	105	1.9	2	0.1	107	1.5
Undistributed grants	-5	-0.2	44	6.4	39	1.0	-42	-0.7	45	3.2	3	c
Other	12	0.4			12	0.3	351	6.2			351	5.0
GOVERNMENT BUSINESS ENTERPRISES (NET)	-53	-1.6			-53	-1.3	45	0.8			45	0.6

a Compiled from Lewis H. Kimmel, Postwar Fiscal Requirements (1945).
b Grants received amounted to $299,000.
c Less than .05 of 1 per cent.
d Grants received amounted to $59,000.

These figures demonstrate that it has already been found necessary in many states to make grants to the local governments to enable them to carry on the welfare functions.

With respect to relief and social security and to a lesser extent with respect to education, the cost of the function will depend in part on the cost and the customary level of living in the particular community. This subject has been discussed at some length in the earlier chapter on what is need. Here we shall only repeat that the evidence is fairly conclusive that in a given state with both rural areas and urban centers the cost of living is generally lower in the rural areas than in the cities, mainly but not exclusively because of higher rents in the cities, because of the necessity of more municipal services, and hence higher land and construction costs. Among the several states there are differences due primarily to degree of urbanization, climate, and costs of transporting and handling food and fuel. These differences are due to actual differences in costs of living and in theory are to be sharply distinguished from differences in the level of living. In practice, however, distinctions between levels and costs have not been generally made. It is certain that a given level of living will cost more in some communities than in others, in some sections of the country than in others, but we do not know how much more. In the absence of reliable data, there is wide difference of opinion as to how important this element is in judging capacity to pay for necessary services.

In providing for relief and social security, we have relatively little data to determine the actual load, a situation very different from that with respect to education. Population and school statistics give the educators the basic data as to numbers for whom education is to be provided. All children are to be given opportunity regardless of their financial need. The educators have only to develop educational standards and costs. Their figures as to load, moreover, do not fluctuate widely from year to year. For relief and social security there are no basic figures as to load, for the service is not required by all the people but only by those who are in need. The number in need, moreover, is not uniform from year to year but fluctuates widely with changes in economic conditions. The fluctuations in a community with a normally healthy economy may be very unlike those in a community whose major industries are chronically depressed, and from which workers of the most productive ages tend to migrate in search of better opportunity. The truth appears to be that qualitatively we know that there are wide variations among the states with respect to (1) the resources that can be reached by taxation, (2) the relative number in need of relief, and (3) the average amount of relief required per case, and that these figures fluctuate widely but not uniformly with changes in economic conditions. Quantitatively we know very little because of the absence of standards applied with any approach to uniformity.

POSSIBLE METHODS

Upon the basis of qualitative information, we can fairly reach a conclusion that because of variations in capacity to pay some action is necessary. Four possible lines of action will be considered in turn: (1) the assumption of full financial and administrative responsibility for various functions of government by specific levels of government; (2) the collection of revenues by the central government and the distribution of all or part of the proceeds to state or local governments; (3) the levying of taxes by the federal government with an offset against the federal tax for state residents who have paid a like tax to the state of their residence; and (4) federal grants-in-aid.

Nationalization of relief and social security. In the United States the national government appears to be the only government which could by itself assume full and undivided responsibility for financing universal, comprehensive, and co-ordinated relief and social security. The reasons for this conclusion are:

1. All the resources of the nation are within reach of the taxing power of the national government.

2. The national government can effectively use taxes designed to reach nearly all taxpaying capacity of the country.

3. The national government has power to borrow and to regulate and control the currency, a power which enables it to en-

gage in deficit financing to a degree impossible for any state or local government. Both in relief and social insurance, times may come when neither taxes nor accumulated surpluses or special fund reserves will meet the needs, and large resort to borrowing may prove necessary.

4. There are unquestionably a few states which lack the resources to finance the welfare functions of government, especially education and relief and social security at a minimum level that would be acceptable to the rest of the nation.

Complete assumption by the national government of the functions of relief and social security would enormously simplify financial administration. It is necessary therefore to consider the arguments that may be raised against such a procedure.

Assumption of full responsibility for relief and social security might be advocated on the ground of a principle which may be stated as "the highest level of government which is called upon to support a function of government should assume full financial responsibility for it and administer it." Before any such simple and in some ways appealing principle is accepted, it is desirable to see where it might lead.

It is extremely doubtful whether complete assumption of the relief load would free the financial resources of the poorest states to such an extent that they could by themselves support that other important and costly welfare function, education, at a minimum level satisfactory to the national interest. Application of the principle would call for making education a national function. Indeed if education were nationalized, there might be little financial reason for nationalizing relief and social security, since freeing the states from the burden of educational costs would enable them to furnish relief where necessary according to a reasonable standard. From our point of view, the principle does not serve as a controlling factor, and decisions must be reached on the basis of matters not purely financial.

The political implications of relief and social security will be considered first. This subject was considered in the preceding chapter, but it is so important with respect to financing that it warrants some repetition. Inevitably and inherently relief and social security involve a redistribution of income effected by the government through use of its sovereign power. Income or wealth must be taken from individuals who have to give to individuals who have not. The recipients do not get a governmental service available to all, or all of a class, but money to meet their own personal needs, to be expended by them for consumption. It is entirely possible that under a nationally financed and administered social security system the national government might be controlled by regional blocks and pressure blocks that would work for and secure bigger benefits paid under more liberal conditions. Such a movement could easily weaken the strong states and the strong elements in the communities, without increasing the productive capacity of the nation upon which the social security of all ultimately depends.

The executive branch of the national government is always in the hands of a single political party. Under the American system there is no minority chosen representation in the executive branch; and the executive branch is not directly answerable to the representative Congress. The policy-making administrative officers in charge of nationalized social security and relief would all be selected by the representatives of a single political party. Although the local examiners and clerks in contact with the people might be selected under a merit system honestly administered, they would be controlled and directed by politically selected policy-making officials. Nothing in American history to date suggests that partisan political action could be effectively kept out of such an arrangement.

The national administrators in a state or a locality would not be subject to the voters of that state or community. When the Democratic party is in power, officers appointed by its representatives would administer relief and social security in states which had gone Republican in the last election and had elected a majority of Republicans to represent them in Congress. Should the Republicans return to power in the national government, the Democratic states of the South would have relief and social security administered by federal employees over whom they had no control. The device of the division of powers be-

tween the states and the nation, which was adopted in part to
protect the rights and interests of minorities, would be gone.
Majorities in many states would be subject to rule by a party
which was a minority in that state despite its control of the
national government.

National financing and administration would in some states
and communities remove the restraining influence which comes
from state and local participation in paying for relief. Both
relief recipients and local businessmen might well take the
position, "The national program is a fine thing; it brings federal
money into the community; we all prosper because of it." A
small minority in those communities would be the only ones who
would be paying direct federal taxes in sufficient amounts to appreciate the costs. Under such circumstances, local pressures on
administrators might be very strong for lax investigations and
for maximum allowances, and upon members of Congress to
vote for larger benefits and less strict eligibility requirements.

Dangers of demoralization, pauperization, and corruption of
the electorate appear so great that from our point of view
nationalization of the function of relief and social security has
to be rejected as a device.

Shared taxes. The device of having the national government
levy a tax and then turn back to the state some or all the
federal revenues collected in that state overcomes that part of
the difficulty that arises solely from inability of the state to
develop an effective tax system. If all the difficulties of the
existing situation arose from this one score, the system of sharing taxes would have much to commend it. The difficulty is,
however, that there are a few states that do not have the
resources to support adequate welfare services, notably education and relief and social security. The amount of taxes collected
within their borders by the federal government and turned back
to them would not support these services at a satisfactory level.
The problem of equalization would still remain.

A federal tax with offsets. The device of levying a uniform
federal tax and permitting taxpayers to offset payment of a
state tax for a like purpose is open to the same objection. It

will not meet the situation in the poorest states, although it would be a great help to many states. Both this device and the redistribution of federally collected taxes to the states deserve consideration as parts of a financial system, but they will not meet the needs of equalization by the federal government in the welfare functions of government.

The grant-in-aid. To those who see in complete federal financing and administration of the welfare functions of government a great threat to democracy and personal and local freedom and initiative, the one practicable solution is the federal grant-in-aid, with intelligent and reasonable provision for equalization. It will require discussion in some detail. We shall take up four major questions with respect to it: (1) the need for national standards, (2) the preservation of local initiative, (3) the methods of securing responsibility and accountability, and (4) the financial problems involved in the distribution of federal funds.

The major objective of the national government in making a grant-in-aid to the states for relief and social security would seem to be to insure that no person in the country shall be in want without being eligible for such benefit as may be necessary to relieve that want, paid without question as to the availability of appropriated funds. We are speaking here of a minimum benefit necessary to prevent want and not of a benefit sufficient to enable the beneficiary to live according to some higher level.

The national government in its grant-in-aid law would have to establish the minimum level below which no person could fall without becoming eligible as a legislative right to sufficient relief or social security benefit to bring him to that minimum level. Because of the differences in cost of living among urban and rural communities and among different sections of the country, this standard would have to be based fundamentally on real things, such as housing, food, and clothing. Given the things necessary for a reasonable minimum, they can be converted into money terms on the basis of prices. The national government cannot know what it is doing until it has far better data on costs of living according to minimum physical standards than are at present available.

Minimum physical standards arrived at by competent specialists working under the direction of a congressional committee, commission, or other agency could of course be written into law. Congress itself could embody in the same law the money figures that result from the pricing of these physical standards, using a schedule to cover the variations among different communities in the costs of the standard schedule. It could include only the physical standards and leave to the federal administrative agency the pricing of the standard in different communities. Another possibility would be to include in the law only the money schedules that resulted from the initial application of the physical standards to different parts of the country, but if this were done, it would be necessary for Congress from time to time to have the physical standards revised and repriced and to amend the money schedules in the act according to the new results. After a sound system has been once designed and installed, much of the data needed for revision would come from the administrative records.

As in most grant-in-aid systems, the standards established by the national law would be minimum standards. The states should be free to go as much above the national minimum standards as their legislatures see fit. In Great Britain and in New Zealand, as was pointed out in Part II, the compulsory social security system provides relatively low minimum benefits, and the people are put on notice that if they want more they must provide it by voluntary action. Under a grant-in-aid system the national government could take a similar position with respect to the states. It could say in effect, "The nation will use that element of almost compulsory persuasion that is inherent in grants-in-aid only in so far as it is necessary to make the states provide in co-operation with the national government a low minimum benefit; if the people of a state want more, they must provide it by state action at state expense."

Highly urbanized industrial states with adequate resources to support larger benefits and more liberal eligibility conditions would not be forced to do so by the national government. The question of whether they should do so would be left to the voters of those states. They would have to weigh their higher living costs and the resulting need for better benefits against the higher taxes necessary to support those benefits.

The differences among the individual states with respect to such vital factors as climate, industries, urbanization, density and characteristics of the population, and even cultures are so wide that much latitude for adjustment to state conditions is in our judgment essential. The people of the state should have no small measure of power and responsibility for maintaining their own efficiency and social well-being. No passion for national uniformity can eliminate the wide variations among the states with respect to natural resources and the works of man that have largely taken their pattern from the natural resources. The national government has a responsibility for laying down rules of fair competition and for establishing minimum standards where they are essential in the national interest, but if initiative, resourcefulness, and ambition are to be preserved, the people of a state or a community must be free to go as far as they can through fair competition to increase their own productive and social efficiency and to raise themselves well above any reasonable national minimum standard.

When the national government makes a grant-in-aid to a state for the purpose of establishing a minimum standard and helping to maintain it, the national government must see that the state meets that minimum. The grant is not given to the state to use in any way it sees fit. It is given conditionally. To be entitled to it the state must meet the conditions. The national government has to hold the states to those minimum responsibilities placed upon them by the national law, even though it leaves them entirely free after they have satisfied the minimum requirements.

The problem of holding states to their responsibilities and more especially of preventing them from taking advantage of the national treasury is greater with respect to the relief function than to any other major function of government. Little in the way of physical plant and equipment is involved in relief administration. The bulk of the work is concerned with passing upon individual cases, to make sure that the persons are in fact eligible under the law and that benefits granted do not exceed the amounts authorized by law. The national treasury may be raided by declaring persons eligible when they are not and by paying benefits larger in amount or for longer periods than the law authorizes. The purpose of the law, on the other hand, may be partially defeated if the state refuses to declare eligible a person who is in fact eligible or to pay the full amount to which the eligible person is entitled under the law.

Thus the national government in administering a federal grant-in-aid system for relief and social security must establish and enforce standards of administration. Among them we shall mention requirements for:

1. Effective organization.

2. An honestly administered merit system with strict prohibitions of political activities.

3. A sound, uniform system of financial accounting and reporting including appropriate auditing.

4. Full complete statistical reports which will permit of thorough analysis and comparisons of the several states and communities to disclose inconsistencies and anomalies that require investigation.

5. Co-operative supervision of the work of the states by competent, trained, federal workers with the understanding that the power and authority of the federal government cease when a state complies with minimum requirements and do not extend to activities which are over or above the national requirements.

6. From time to time, if and when deemed necessary by the national government, a recheck of the investigations made by the state agency in cases to which the national government is contributing. Such rechecks may be made upon complaint of citizens that the state is paying excessive benefits or paying benefits to persons not eligible.

7. A right of appeal, at least to the highest welfare administrative agency of the state, if not to an appropriate state court,

for any resident of the state who deems himself eligible but has been denied the benefits to which he regards himself as entitled under the law.

Congress might consider a provision to give to a resident of a co-operating state whose final appeal to a state agency has been denied a right to a hearing by appropriate officers of the national agency supervising the grant-in-aid system. If the federal examiners found the appellant had a good case, the national agency could be authorized to request the state agency to pay to him the amount which the national government would have contributed had the state approved the application. The national government presumably would not be authorized to request the state to pay its share if the final appeals agency of the state had declared the applicant ineligible under the state law. It is assumed that such appeals to the national agency would be rarely taken, and when they were would be held in the state of residence by an examiner or board of examiners presumably from the regional office of the national agency.[3]

A conditional grant-in-aid constitutionally is an offer from the national government to pay the state certain moneys, provided the state accepts the conditions set forth in the offer. Unless the state accepts the offer, it cannot get the federal money for its residents and hence presumably most if not all the states would accept such a condition.

The real constitutional issue would be whether a mandatory provision either for the payment of the nation's share alone or of the state's share in addition constituted actual federal administration of a state function. It is of course constitutional for the national government to refuse to pay its share of a benefit improperly allowed by a state, but in that case the federal government does not force the state to pay. It would be entirely different to require a state to pay upon the order of the national government.

[3] A constitutional issue has been raised by a member of the writer's advisory committee. Would it be constitutional for the national government (1) not merely to request but actually to require a co-operating state to pay the national share after the final agency in the state has denied eligibility under the state law or (2) to require the state agency under like circumstances to pay also the share of the state.

For this reason we would not recommend going further than authorizing the national agency to give a hearing to an appellant from state action and, if the facts warrant, formally to request the state agency to pay the national share. The state agency would naturally be somewhat embarrassed by receipt of such a request after a formal federal hearing. Probably in most cases it would pay both the national share and the state share, but it would not be legally compelled to do so. This provision has been suggested for consideration because of a belief that the appeals mechanisms can be developed into an effective measure for the control of administration in the field.

Devices such as the seven just enumerated are essential both to protect the national treasury and to insure to the individual the legislative right which the national government attempts to give him through the grant-in-aid system. We come now to the difficult question of the basis upon which the federal funds should be allocated among the states.

From our point of view, the justification for the choice of a grant-in-aid financed system rests basically upon the variations in the capacity to pay among the several states. As we have seen, this variation arises from (1) differences in resources that can be reached through taxation, (2) differences in the relief and social security load, and (3) differences in capacity to maintain the other welfare functions of government in which the nation as a whole has a significant interest.

If it were not for these differences in capacity to pay, and if the difficulties arose exclusively from methods of taxation, the problems could be solved through the use of either of the two other devices, the sharing of federally collected taxes with the states, or the federal tax with offsets for like state taxes. These two relatively simple and largely automatic devices do not serve as equalizers, although they would greatly improve the effectiveness of raising revenue for state and local governments. The situation, however, calls for some equalization with respect to the welfare functions of government.

With respect to the three public assistance categories of the Social Security Act as described in Part I, the nation is at present using the grant-in-aid system, with the national government giving 50 per cent of the cost of such benefits as are paid by the states, subject to a national limit on the amount that it will match in any one case. The national government has not established a national standard or a national minimum. Within limits the state determines what it will take from the national treasury. States with adequate capacity to pay take relatively more than states with small capacity, because their eligibility requirements are more liberal and their benefits are higher. The poor states take less, at least partly because they cannot afford to take more.

This system served neither to establish a national minimum standard nor to equalize the burden. It merely operated to force the states to provide the three specific kinds of public assistance and relieved them of part of the cost. The poor states were forced to put money into public assistance which in the absence of the federal law might have gone for education.

Now let us consider what the effect would be if the percentage furnished by the federal government were substantially increased. To be concrete let it be assumed that the national government paid 90 per cent of the old-age benefit up to $40 a month and the state and local governments only 10 per cent. The poorer states with inadequate capacity to pay might with no increase in expenditures increase benefits and liberalize eligibility requirements and perhaps pay an entirely acceptable minimum allowance. The well-to-do states that now pay substantial benefits might increase them to the allowable maximum and still achieve a real saving of their own resources. The bulk of the cost would have been shifted to the national treasury. The result would not be equalization but a mere shifting of the burden from one level of government to another. A state contribution of as little as 10 per cent, moreover, would not in many states be much of an incentive to reasonably strict administration. The tendency to loose administration and the strength of the argument for outright administration by the national government would be greatly enhanced.

The conclusion seems inescapable that no fixed percentage

system will solve the problem of equalization satisfactorily. The proper approach to secure equalization would appear to be somewhat as follows:

1. On the basis of the available statistical evidence, to select for intensive and objective scientific study a limited number of states, not less than 3 nor more than 5 which appear to have the least capacity to pay.

2. For each of the selected states to determine with reasonable accuracy: (a) The resources of the state and local government that could be subjected to taxation. (b) The amount that could be realized from these resources through taxes that would not be so high as to be destructive. (c) The amount which people would need to have in the various sections of the selected states to live in accordance with a minimum acceptable standard. The items on a suitable standard would be priced according to prevailing prices in the community. (d) The number of persons in the community who are in need according to the standard. (e) The amount of money which would be required to bring those persons to the established standard, with due consideration of their existing resources. (f) To what extent this required sum could be paid from state and local resources with due regard to the requirements of other functions of government, especially education, public health, and the other welfare functions.

3. Analyze and compare the results for the states specifically studied to determine whether there are marked and significant differences among them. If there are, select the states which clearly belong in the groups with the lowest capacity to pay.

4. Upon the basis of the data for these lowest states, construct a schedule of needed relief as if a system were being designed exclusively to relieve want and suffering in those states, without reference to the question of what level of government should pay the bill.

Upon the basis of such statistical evidence, we should expect to find that the poorest states in the union could not at the same time support all the welfare functions of government—education, relief and social security, and public health, according to a satisfactory minimum standard. If such should prove to be the case, a question of policy would arise, which may be stated as follows: Should the amount of the resources of the state which are available for the welfare functions of government be concentrated on some one function such as education, for example, or should they be distributed among the functions according to a reasonable plan? One reasonable plan would be based on something approaching the past distribution.

This question is of importance because federal grants-in-aid for purposes of equalization are under consideration for education, public health, relief, and social security. Obviously what is done with respect to any one will affect what would have to be done with respect to the others. Heavy grants for education, for example, might release some funds for relief and social security. We shall here assume for purposes of illustration that the funds available for the welfare functions in the poor states are distributed among those functions approximately on the basis of past experience and that the studies show that the state and local governments could supply only 10 per cent of the relief and social security costs.[4]

The national government could then make the schedule of benefits which it had prepared for the poorest states the minimum standard for every state in the union. Through the persuasion of the grant-in-aid system, it would require each state to pay all persons eligible according to the national standard benefits according to that minimum standard, and provide further that the national government would reimburse each state for such minimum benefits to the extent of 90 per cent of the cost. So far as the national government was concerned, each person in need according to the national standard would get the same allowance—the sum necessary to give a reasonable benefit in the poorest states with the lowest costs of living.

Obviously these minimum benefits supplied to the extent of say 90 per cent by the national government would be inade-

---

[4] Attention should be called to the fact that 10 per cent is merely used as an illustration. The actual percentage would be determined on the basis of thorough study of the states selected because of their apparent low capacity to pay.

quate for the states with higher living costs and higher capacity to pay. Their citizens would urge bigger benefits and perhaps more liberal eligibility provisions. The national government would leave them free to grant at their own expense whatever higher benefits they might see,[5] but it would always pay to citizens of that state who are in need according to federal standards the amount of money it would pay to citizens of other states under like circumstances.

[5] The states in the lower range according to capacity to pay would be materially helped because the national government would pay 90 per cent of the minimum benefit instead of 50 per cent as under the present public assistance categories of the Social Security Act. Payment of 90 per cent of the minimum benefit might release some state funds which could be used for increasing benefits above the federal minimum. The states in the upper range of capacity to pay would probably have to pay in the aggregate substantially more than the present 50 per cent of the cost of their present benefits under the public assistance categories of the Social Security Act. They might find, however, that the net cost to their taxpayers would not increase, for less of their money might be taken from them to pay the federal contribution toward high benefits in reasonably well-to-do states that have adopted the pension philosophy. The pension philosophy states would be the ones most severely hurt by such an arrangement, since they would have to pay for that philosophy largely from their own taxes.

CHAPTER XXXIII

DIVISION OF ADMINISTRATION

Chapter XXXI was devoted to a consideration of the question of the division of power to determine policy between the national government and the state governments. Chapter XXXII took up the question of the division of financial responsibility. The present chapter is to deal with the division of administration. The chapter will be divided into two parts. The first will be concerned mainly with a generalized discussion of the nature and extent of administrative discretion in a program of relief and social security. The second will deal in considerable detail with the form of organization which would seem desirable if the nation had a single, universal, comprehensive, and co-ordinated system operated co-operatively by the nation, the states, and the local governments under a federal grant-in-aid system.

ADMINISTRATIVE DISCRETION

The importance of administration depends in no small measure upon the extent to which discretionary power is vested in administrative officers. Sometimes governmental administration is so purely ministerial that administrators have scant power to exercise discretion. Upon the happening of certain simple, easily ascertained, and patent facts, administrative action is mandatory. If an administrative officer fails to do what the law orders him to do, he may as a rule be taken before a court where the judge may order him to do what the law requires, under pain of punishment for contempt of court.

Administration may begin to lose this purely ministerial aspect when the facts to be determined are no longer simple, easily ascertained, and patent. The law may, as is frequently the case in social insurance legislation, give the individual a clearly defined right upon the fulfillment of certain conditions, but the determination as to whether those conditions have actually been fulfilled may require detailed investigation to get the necessary facts. In some cases the task also involves an application of rules and regulations to the facts as ascertained. The administrator begins to have a not inconsiderable degree of freedom, resulting from his powers to direct and control the investigations, to determine what is and what is not a fact or a relevant fact, to interpret the complex of facts and possibly to interpret the law and rules in applying them to the facts. The individual with a claim is beginning to encounter administrative discretion, to appreciate how much depends on the government representatives with whom he has to deal.

A claimant versed in the law knows that his relationships with the government depend in no small measure on whether he has (1) a constitutional right, (2) a legislative right, or (3) whether he is a mere suppliant for a governmental grant or favor. If he has a constitutional right, he can take the administrative officer into court, for at least in theory the courts will protect his constitutional rights against encroachments from the legislature, the executive, or the bureaucrats. If his right is legislative only, he has in general only such lines of action and appeal as the legislature has granted to him. If he is a mere suppliant asking the government to grant him such aid as the law has made permissible but not mandatory, he may have no redress at all. He will then appreciate that legally he is entirely in the hands of the administrative officer, although, if he is versed in practical politics, he may know the place and value of influence.

In dealing with the administration of relief and social security, we are not much concerned with constitutional rights, for few if any jurisdictions give a constitutional right to relief or social security. Social security and relief laws, moreover, rarely make the relationship between the government and the beneficiary contractual, so that the beneficiary can take advantage of the constitutional provisions which prevent states from impairing the obligation of contracts. At best the rights are contingent, legislative rights. Often as in the three assistance categories of the Social Security Act and in general public assistance laws of the states, they partake more of the nature of pure gratuities, although in some states the legislatures have given suppliants an appeal to the courts. The Social Security Act, moreover, requires the states to provide an appeal to an administrative appeal body. Thus administration of social security and relief is vitally important to beneficiaries and suppliants because both legally and practically they are so largely dependent on the exercise of discretion by administrative officers.

Administrative legislation. In several branches of social security and relief administration, moreover, administrative officers are exercising legislative powers delegated to them by the elected legislature. In the public assistance categories, and in some parts of unemployment compensation, the elected legislatures have found it impracticable to legislate in minute detail. They have, therefore, laid down broad guiding principles which administrators make detailed and specific in either or both of two ways: (1) by adopting detailed rules and regulations or (2) by interpreting the statute or even their own rules and regulations in the decision of the individual case. With a good deal of assurance it can be said the greater degree of legislative power delegated to administrative officers, the greater importance of administration to beneficiaries, taxpayers, and the public.

The means test and administrative discretion. It can be safely generalized that the less the means test is used, the more benefits are matters of absolute legislative right upon the fulfillment of conditions, the more administration approaches the ministerial, and the less room is left for administrative discretion. If the elected legislature itself legislates in detail, administration may become mainly a matter of fact finding.

Under a no-means test system with detailed legislation adopted by the elected legislature, the importance of administration will depend largely on the nature of the fact-finding job. Under O.A.S.I., for example, a person is entitled to a primary old-age benefit as a matter of legislative right (1) if he is fully insured, (2) if he has attained the age of 65 years, and (3) if he is not employed, or if employed, he is not earning enough money to make him ineligible. With the elaborate punch card records developed to prove full insurance and establish the amount of benefits, determination of rights for a primary benefit are largely ministerial in the bulk of the cases. The fact finding for survivors' benefits, particularly parents insurance benefits, lump-sum death benefits, and to some extent even widow's and children's death benefits, are much more complicated, involving questions of who was supporting whom, whether persons were or were not married, whether the court had ordered support, and so on.

Unemployment compensation in the United States involves no means test and benefits are matters of legislative, contingent right but the states generally provide for disqualifications. A beneficiary may forfeit his rights if he was discharged for misconduct, if he refuses to accept suitable employment, if his unemployment is due to a strike in which he himself or the group with which he is affiliated is participating. In several states, moreover, within limits established by the legislature, the penalties for a disqualifying act are discretionary. Administrators may have a discretion similar to that exercised by a judge in fixing penalty for a misdemeanor.

Whenever benefits for disability are provided, even under a no-means test system, the fact finding is extremely difficult. Is the applicant actually physically or mentally disabled? Is he malingering? Is the disability temporary or permanent? What is its degree? Was it service connected? Was it the result of misconduct or gross negligence on his part? Anyone who has ever sat through or followed any considerable number of disability cases is likely to find little short of amazing the divergencies in the expert testimony. Administrative officers, after investigation, make the decisions as to what are to be officially regarded as the facts. It may not be proper to speak of this power as discretionary; it is perhaps better termed quasi-judicial, but whatever it is called, it makes administration highly important.

Under a means test system the fact findings are, as a rule, more complicated because questions of means, responsibility of relatives, and so on, have to be answered. It is entirely possible that a legislative right to a benefit may be established under a means test system so that the only difference between means test and no-means test administratively is in the fact finding. Under the traditional means test system, however, the entire handling of the case was discretionary. In general it is safe to say that the power of administrators is greater under a means test system than under a no-means test system, but the difference is more in degree than in kind.

Biases in the exercise of administrative discretion. Whenever one encounters discretionary, quasi-legislative, and quasi-judicial powers in the hands of administrative officers, the question of possible biases requires examination. What appear to be the major ones in the administration of relief and social security will be considered.

Unquestionably the student of relief administration would place first the old bias of local officials granting purely discretionary relief from local revenues. It sprang perhaps from two main causes: (1) the attitude that the poverty and misfortunes of the poor were their own fault, and (2) the fact that such relief as might be given had to be paid for entirely by loyal taxpayers. These biases of administrators and legislators were in no small part responsible for the hatred that developed against the means test. In many parts of the United States, especially in rural areas, there was little separation of the legislative and the administrative functions in local government. The county commissioners or county supervisors who appropriated the money for relief and were held responsible by the voters for the tax rate were the ones who passed out the funds.

The second bias is political. In some jurisdictions relief grants have unquestionably been given for the purpose of influencing votes.[1] Perhaps less reprehensible is the practice of reminding

---

[1] *Taps for Private Tussie,* by Jesse Stuart, is a fascinating fictional presentation of the operations. The writer of fiction, incidentally, has a great advantage over those of us who occasionally make governmental surveys in that he cannot easily be sued for libel for "all names and places are fictitious and any resemblances to any person or persons living or dead are purely coincidental." The surveyor may secure a large body of evidence from trustworthy sources that seem to him to prove beyond any reasonable doubt that public funds have been improperly diverted to political purposes but he cannot prove it in a court. Not infrequently the facts come from a public officer who was in a position to know them, yet this public officer cannot be quoted. If he is quoted, his administrative indiscretion in talking to a surveyor may cost him his job. If called to the witness stand he is in an extremely difficult position and may be excused either

recipients of relief or other grants that they are indebted to the party in power for the grant and to suggest to them that the opposition party would, if elected, remove them from relief. A relief administrator trying to do a good, honest job may be seriously embarrassed by a communication, generally not reduced to writing, from one of the political leaders to the effect that to his own knowledge the applicant is eligible, and he wants the grant made without delay.

The third bias may be called temperamental. Relief and social security examiners should be possessed of what is commonly termed the judicial temperament. In a government of laws and not of men, they should accept as completely governing their actions the intent of the legislators as expressed in the laws, the rules and regulations, and the decisions under them. Their duty is diligently and resourcefully, without fear or favor, to secure all the essential facts to permit of the honest application of the policies determined upon under legislative authority.

In some fields of governmental action, however, notably in the field of public welfare, examiners and other employees may be possessed of zeal for reform. Many of them would not have been drawn into that field had they not possessed it. Exercised in its appropriate place it is entitled to high respect. Unfortunately, in some cases it leads examiners and others to take the view that their job is to do what is right and desirable according to their own lights—law, regulations, and decisions to the contrary notwithstanding. Two concrete illustrations may be worth while.

The law makes eligible only persons not possessed of a certain amount of resources. It establishes a maximum limit for a grant and provides that available resources shall be deducted from that maximum. All the examiners agree that the limits are too low. Examiner A, despite her beliefs, honestly gathers the facts and

for a loss of memory or for a denial. Thus it is common practice among surveyors to assure government officers and others interviewed that they will not be quoted and any information they may give will be regarded as strictly confidential. It is frequently possible to verify a considerable part of the statements from the financial accounts. They show the payments were actually made, but they do not prove the objective was political, although the dates of payments may be correlated with the dates of primaries or elections.

applies them and disqualifies many whom she thinks should have aid and gives to others far less than she thinks they should have. Examiner B, on the other hand, looks for no hidden resources, undervalues all the obvious resources she cannot ignore, and thus qualifies many whom Examiner A would be forced to exclude and gives to all she finds eligible more than they should have. She does not subscribe to the administrative doctrine that no money shall be drawn from the public treasury except in accordance with law.

Similarly, the law and regulations contain provisions making adult children, without reference to their means and responsibilities, liable to contribute to the support of their parents. Examiner A on all possible occasions speaks against this policy, but in her investigations she gets all the facts with a thoroughness that could not be excelled by one who believed in it. Examiner B, on the other hand, only turns up a relative who might be required to contribute when the existence of such a relative is a matter of common knowledge.

Public attitude toward these biases in administration depends in no small measure upon where the money comes from. Local financing tends toward strict interpretation. National financing tends to make the local citizens, especially in poor communities, extremely tolerant. Examiner B may be the local ideal of an administrative officer because she helps so many to share in the federal bounty.

If the objective is sound, honest, effective administration, within the law, the chief administrative problem is how to overcome or neutralize these biases. As pointed out, one device is so to finance the programs that part of the burden falls on local taxpayers in a sufficient amount to make them conscious of the cost. Other devices include the form of organization, the procedures, and the methods of personnel administration.

ADMINISTRATIVE ORGANIZATION AND PROCEDURE

From our point of view, the most desirable form of organization involves co-operation among the three levels of government, national, state, and local.

To prevent unfair competition among the states, and to insure that no person in the United States is forced to live below a minimum standard fixed by the national government, it is assumed that the national government has adopted compelling and, with respect to its minima, controlling legislation practically binding upon the states. It is further assumed that to effect this purpose the national government has used one or both of the following methods: (1) the national tax with offsets for payment of state taxes for like purposes, or (2) the more traditional grants-in-aid to the states.

National organization. The national government must have an agency devoted to the administration of relief and social security. If co-ordination and comprehensiveness are to be secured, one national organization must have jurisdiction over all aspects of relief and social security administration, and it must be so placed in the governmental structure that it can co-operate effectively with national agencies concerned with education, public health, and rural extension work.

The principal duties of this organization would be:

1. To advise the President and Congress with respect to needed national legislation for the perfection and development of the system and with respect to national appropriations.

2. To perform such legislative duties in the preparation of detailed rules and regulations as may be delegated to it by Congress.

3. To collect and compile such statistics and conduct such research as may be necessary and desirable to obtain accurate data as to what conditions actually are and how they may be improved.

4. To exercise sufficient supervision over the state agencies to make sure they are complying with the minimum standards required under the national law.

5. To develop and maintain a staff of special consultants to work co-operatively with the states in perfecting and developing the state systems. In general these consultants would have no authority to order or command a state agency to take any

action. The assumption is that if a state agency is complying with the minimum requirements of the national law the national agency has no power to order or direct it to do more. The state may, however, find it highly advantageous to get the advice and co-operation of federal consultants conversant with particular fields.

6. To assist in the development of interstate compacts and devices to provide for persons who move from one state to another.

7. Actually to operate any system or systems that may be found necessary to provide for persons who are engaged in interstate commerce or given to interstate migration to a degree that makes national administration desirable. The general objective, however, would be unified administration within a state so that every person would deal with one responsible agency.

How would the duties of this agency differ from those of the present Social Security Board? It is assumed that a new national law would provide for complete and comprehensive coverage, and hence the agency would deal with all causes of need and with all classes of the population. It is further assumed that when O.A.S.I. is re-examined in the light of the new financial situation resulting from World War II and the desirability of protecting all from want, O.A.S.I. will be radically revised, partly to minimize the dangers of inflation and partly in the interests of simplicity and the elimination of voluminous clerical work both in the government service and in private offices. If the assumption regarding O.A.S.I. is correct, the Social Security Board would be materially reduced in size, and it would have few mass routine operating functions.

Since the national agency will have to draft rules and regulations and determine whether or not the individual states are complying with the terms of the national law, it seems clear to us that the board form of organization should be preserved. It would seem highly desirable that members be appointed for reasonably long terms, properly staggered. Although it is unquestionably true that a requirement that not more than a specified number of members of the board shall belong to the same political party does not offer a safeguard against packing a board and controlling its actions, it is doubtful that it does any harm. The law may also specify some high, general qualifications which should be possessed by members of the board. It will be remembered, however, that such provisions are primarily advice to the President, who determines whether or not the persons he nominates meet those qualifications. Their inclusion may, however, strengthen the hand of senators in opposing a poor nomination.

State board general organization. Each state would have a single board with jurisdiction over all cases involving relief or social security benefits, regardless of the cause which necessitated payment. The duties of this board would be:

1. Under such conditions as the law of the state provides to conduct all detailed transactions with the national government, generally through the national board.

2. To advise the governor and the legislature with respect to needed state legislation for the development and perfection of a complete and comprehensive system for the state and with respect to appropriations.

3. To perform such sublegislative duties in the preparation of rules and regulations as the elected legislature may delegate to it, and to develop a complete, detailed relief and social security code for the state.

4. To serve as a final administrative appeal board to decide all cases or all important or legally significant cases brought up from lower administrative authorities, or to have under it and subject to its exclusive jurisdiction a final appeal unit whose decisions would in no way be controlled by the executive officer of the board.

5. To select and to exercise broad and general supervision over a chief executive officer who would be immediately responsible for the detailed execution of the policies of the board, and who would at the request of the board aid it in its sublegislative tasks and in making recommendations to the governor

and the legislature for changes in law and appropriations.

Neither the board itself nor a member of the board under this plan has any detailed administrative duties. Its duties would be quasi-legislative, quasi-judicial, and supervisory, much like a board of directors of a company. It would be concerned primarily with matters of policy and with making sure that the policies were being carried out by the executive officer of the board and the staff under him. It would hear appeals or keep in close touch with its independent appeal agency for two reasons: (1) because appeals often throw great light on how the system is actually working both substantively and administratively, and (2) because the code for which the board is immediately responsible will in part grow through the decisions in appealed cases.

Relationship of board to the legislature and the governor. In theory it would be desirable if the elected legislature could adopt for the state a social security code so detailed that substantive rules and regulations would be unnecessary and so clear that few cases would require an interpretation of the law. Such a course is, however, impracticable in a field in which there are so many combinations and permutations of fact. It is almost essential for the legislature to delegate some of its legislative power to be exercised by the board under such supervision as the legislature can conveniently exercise. This supervision includes having a report from the board each time it requires an appropriation and each time it asks the legislature to amend or extend the basic law. The legislature may at any session investigate the board or any of its work or its employees, and if it sees fit, it can abolish or reconstitute the board, revolutionize the law, or both. Unless the people through legal procedures write provisions regarding the board into the state constitution, the board remains subject to a large measure of control by the elected legislature, although the governor's veto power may offer some restrictions.

Rules and regulations that have been developed over the years and have not encountered any adverse legislative action become a tacitly accepted part of the code. The legislature may decide that it is wise to protect the administratively developed details of the code from radical and hasty revision by a new board or by executive pressure of a new governor. Neither a new governor nor a new board can change so much as a word of the basic law without action by the elected legislature, but unless the legislature takes some action to prevent such a course, a new governor or a new board can completely change the rules and regulations and the interpretative cases decided under them.

To minimize the chances that such action may be taken without at the same time depriving the board of a reasonable amount of freedom in amending or reinterpreting, the legislature can restrict the governor's power over the board. It can provide that each member of the board shall serve for a term longer than that of the governor, and that the terms shall be so staggered that an incoming governor does not actually appoint a majority of the board during his first term in office or not until close to the end of his first term. It may also place some restrictions upon the power of the governor to remove a member.

Occasionally one encounters a person who feels that the legislature should not so curb a governor who comes with a fresh mandate from the people. It is a fresh mandate even if the governor won by an extremely narrow margin. Because of the limitations of our mechanisms for choosing party candidates, it sometimes happens that even a newly elected governor does not command the respect and confidence of the majority of the people of the state. Our system of fixed terms of office, moreover, results occasionally in the retention of a governor in power after he has lost a substantial part of his support. The doctrine of the division of powers has of course handicapped some good governors; on the other hand, it has minimized the damage that can be done by a poor governor.

In the absence of constitutional provisions, laws which minimize the power of the governor to control the legislative and judicial actions of the board do not free the board from responsibility to the voters.[2] If the governor and a majority of the legislature believe that the board needs complete revamping, the legislature can pass and the governor sign an act abolishing the old board and creating a new one, which permits the governor to appoint an entirely new set of board members. In some jurisdictions in fields other than welfare, this device has been used for partisan political reasons, to obtain for the new administration the patronage not only on the board itself but in the subordinate positions and in the contracts and purchasing. The point here is that the governor cannot take action of that kind by himself; he must get his authority from the legislature, and the legislature may be unwilling to permit a governor to wreck a board which has established a reputation for sound nonpartisan administration. Legislators as well as governors are answerable to public opinion.

The courts. In the opinion of the writer, a comprehensive, coordinated system of relief and social security should go as far as is practicable in creating a legislative right to a true minimum of subsistence benefit in case of want. How far substantially higher benefits should be made a matter of right is another question; but agreement is so general that nobody should be permitted to starve that it seems the benefit to prevent starvation could well be made a legislative right.

If a legislative right is created, then it is entirely practicable to give the appropriate courts jurisdiction over appeals from the final action of the administrative board or its last appeal unit. Such an appeal to the courts on a matter of law presents no practical difficulties. It is also simple to have the courts pass on charges of arbitrary action by the board or on exceeding or abusing its powers. The real difficulties arise on questions as to whether there is to be a new and independent fact finding by the courts and whether the court is to substitute its discretion for that of administrative officers.

---

[2] Constitutional provisions could be adopted to protect the board from political action, but unless they provide for the election of board members, they may operate to remove the board from popular control.

With respect to a new and independent fact finding, the sums at stake may differ widely depending on the nature of the benefit. Under existing unemployment compensation systems the largest sum involved with respect to a single individual is not much more than $500. The present value of an old-age annuity, on the other hand, may be several thousand dollars. Although the individual benefits in unemployment compensation may be only a small sum, the aggregate amount involved in a decision regarding the nature and causes of a labor dispute may reach very substantial totals because of the number of individual cases determined by the basic decision.

One can have great sympathy with the argument that the regular courts should not be overburdened with the costly, detailed fact findings in a host of cases concerned with small sums. It is very easy in the field of social security and relief to get into a position where administrative costs plus court costs will exceed the amount of the benefits, and one does not like to see money which ought to go for relieving want consumed by governmental machinery.

On the other hand, governmental agencies that are concerned with giving away public money or distributing the proceeds of insurance premiums are peculiarly in need of supervision and review, particularly if prospective beneficiaries are represented in the administration or have great political influence. When the composition of a board clearly indicates a large measure of class control, it is more than a little disturbing to find provisions to the effect that findings of fact shall be final and shall not be subject to review by any other agency, or even that the findings of fact if supported by evidence or substantial evidence shall be final. Such provisions may deprive parties with a real interest of their day in court, unless an administrative board is to be regarded as a court.

This whole subject as to the degree to which the findings of fact by administrative boards and commissions shall be final seems to deserve much more comprehensive investigation. In the field of welfare and relief, it might be wise to adopt legislation permitting parties in interest after a final administrative decision has been rendered to petition the court to hold a trial *de novo* of a case with such review of the fact findings and such fresh fact findings as may be deemed necessary by the courts. Parties in interest under such a plan should be broadly defined, so that with proper safeguards taxpayers' petitions for a court trial could be heard. It is not assumed that any considerable number of petitions would be filed, or that after a preliminary hearing or investigation by the court more than a very few would be granted. It is believed, however, that the possibility of such a petition would have a wholesome effect on an administrative agency, and it would be advantageous if occasionally the fact-finding work of administrators were checked by an independent fact finding of a court.

The effect would probably be wholesome whichever way the court found. In relief and social security administration, one often encounters a widespread belief that the administrative agency is biased, or that considerable numbers of beneficiaries are taking advantage of loopholes in the law. If occasionally such matters were taken into court and the action of the board found fully justified by the facts, some of the feeling against the administrators would at least partially subside. If, on the other hand, the board were reversed, evils would be corrected. A court case might easily demonstrate the existence of loopholes in the law to which administrative bodies give no publicity and may not admit. An administrative agency frequently has a clientele which it hesitates to offend, although the action of the clientele may be questionable.

Thus far we have discussed the state board that would serve as a board of directors for the social security and relief administration and be responsible for the necessary quasi-legislative and quasi-judicial functions. The board, it is suggested, should select an executive director who would be responsible under it for the detailed administration. Before discussing the organization of the central state office under the director, we shall take up the local offices of the organization or the primary operating units. We shall assume that (1) the local government makes a substantial contribution toward the costs of relief and social security and (2) it shares in the administration. In dealing with the local officers we shall begin with the basic primary officer.

The primary examiner or case investigator. The examiners or case investigators are generally the primary class of employees in a local relief and social security office. Under our assumptions, the law and the rules and regulations have given to the people legislative rights to certain benefits in the event of the happening of certain contingencies. The duty of the examiners or case investigators is to determine whether those things have happened in a particular case that make the individual or the family entitled to a benefit. They are basically fact finders.

The nature of the fact finding or examining varies with the type of contingency dealt with, as has been previously discussed. Certain common factors, however, deserve special emphasis.

1. The person or family who claims eligibility is at the time of the claim generally a resident of the jurisdictional area of the local office.

2. The client is ordinarily desirous of prompt action. In some instances the need for prompt action may be so great that emergency aid may have to be given prior to complete investigation.

3. In a great majority of cases the facts required are available locally. The client himself is present and can give the required answers to questions. Except in the case of transients and recent comers to the community, most of the other sources of necessary information are in the immediate locality.

Except in a very small state these three factors dictate local or district offices to facilitate prompt and accurate information, even if there is not the co-operation between state and local governments that we are assuming.

Occasionally one encounters the view that examiners and case investigators are unnecessary; that it is sufficient to have persons claiming eligibility fill out an application blank giving the essential facts. Although perhaps the great majority of persons are honest, there are enough who are not to warrant the rule that all essential facts in a claim against public funds shall be verified. Occasionally, moreover, some applicants will be found (1) who do not understand the meaning of the question, (2) who are honestly mistaken as to the facts, or (3) who misinterpret a law, rule, or regulation. On its face the application shows eligibility, and the applicant believes himself eligible, but verification of the facts brings to light the mistake. Means tests are as a rule much too complicated to be answered readily and easily by an applicant. An examiner has to get at the essential facts by piecing together many detailed items. Local examiners or case investigators are essential for fact finding, even if the relief and social security laws do not provide constructive social service in efforts to rehabilitate individuals and families and thus to reduce the drain on tax-collected funds.

The findings of primary examiners or case investigators must be subjected to review in the interest of the clients, the government, and the taxpayers. If power to make the final decision were vested in the primary examiner, innumerable abuses would be possible—personal or political favoritism, religious or cultural biases, race prejudices, or an over-liberal or over-harsh philosophy.

The local executives. The primary examiners in a locality are, except in a very small community, generally subordinate to a local executive or supervisor. The supervisor is responsible for seeing that the primary examiners perform their duties, assigns cases to them, and in general keeps the work moving. He is also a reviewing officer. To be an effective reviewer, the executive or supervisor must be thoroughly conversant with the locality and must be available to the parties in interest or able to get to them or to other persons possessed of the facts quickly. Mrs. A, for example, did not get along at all well with the case investigator and is convinced that the investigator is prejudiced against her. She should be able without difficulty to see the executive or supervisor to present her case. In another instance the supervisor is reviewing the primary invesigator's report on a family. The family and its friends are making no complaint with respect to the primary investigator. On the face of the record the supervisor finds no question whatever as to eligibility; but the recorded facts do not quite square with the supervisor's impressions regarding the persons involved or the environment. Perhaps also the supervisor knows the soft spots in the make up of that investigator. The supervisor, therefore, undertakes an independent investigation. If the independent verification checks the questionable items, the supervisor may approve the case; if not, the whole matter may be reinvestigated.

Executive supervisors and primary examiners in a well-conducted agency are salaried workers, not only trained on the job but generally possessed at the time of their appointment of special qualifications in education and experience. They are professionals, often having special skills and a wide range of special knowledge. Not infrequently the position is taken that the executives or the supervisors, because of their special skills and knowledge, should make the final determinations in each case.

From the point of view of the writer it is highly questionable whether legal power to make the final decision should be vested in the top local executive. With special knowledge, skills, and education, and with intimate close contact with distress and in some instances sordidness, often goes a particular point of view and philosophy. Similar things develop in most other professions. For example, much as one may admire professional soldiers, it is commonly recognized that they necessarily look at many things from a military point of view. Social workers likewise tend to look at things from a social worker's point of view. It is a point of view that deserves careful consideration by all concerned, but in many instances, it is in need of correctives to get a balancing of values, just as the point of view of the military men, the educators, or even the public health men may need balancing.

The local board. This necessity for balancing and the need for the maximum verification of the facts in all cases leads us to prefer the form of local organization that gives a local lay board a strong position in the local organization. In a state-local coöperative system, it is entirely feasible to adopt devices whereby the persons appointed to the local lay boards are acceptable to both the state administrative agency and to the local government. Members can be appointed for fairly long, staggered terms so that under ordinary circumstances the boards develop a large measure of continuity of policy.

With respect to final approval of cases, either one of two courses is apparently reasonably satisfactory, (1) the local board may have the legal power to approve, subject however to reversal by the state agency, or (2) the local board may have power to reject, to remand for further investigation, or to recommend to the state for final approval. Under either method nothing goes through initially without the real or constructive approval of the local lay board, although that board can under a proper appeals procedure be reversed by the state board.

The phrase "real or constructive approval" of the local lay board requires some explanation. In practice under such a form of organization, the professional executive and the board members learn to work together. The executive learns not only the general policy of the board as a whole but the point of view of individual board members, and often the interrelations among the board members. The board members tend to appraise the strengths and weaknesses of the executive; they learn, each from his own point of view, what to watch for. Most executives will appreciate the necessity of gaining and maintaining the confidence of the board in the executive's integrity and the great dangers inherent in any resort to factual trickery or manipulation to get a case by the board. The board members would generally almost unanimously condemn trickery, but most of them expect from the professional worker argument and persuasion on the basis of the facts. The result often is that a very high percentage of the cases are actually approved by the board on the statement of the executive that they are within the approved policy of the board and are "on all fours" with cases already approved. A board member may glance down the lists or through the papers and ask a few questions concerning persons about whom he knows something or concerning neighborhoods. If the answers regarding the cases the board members know about are satisfactory, they are willing to assume the others are all right.

The intelligent, efficient executive will bring up for detailed discussion individual cases which (1) involve issues of policy, (2) differences of opinion among board members, or (3) public relationships in the community. These cases, perhaps few in number, are the ones to which the board really gives its time.

Often the executive officer prior to the formal board meeting has discussed a particular case at some length with an individual board member. For example, in an aid to dependent children case there is a real question as to whether the mother is a suitable person to have the child. Sentiment against the mother is strong among the neighbors, but the executive officer and the examiners believe she ought to be given a chance. Prior to the meeting of the board to pass on the case, the executive secretary has discussed it first with the board member who came from the neighborhood and second with a board member who has a very strict moral code which he observes himself and applies to others. At the board meeting the strict moralist expresses his doubt as to whether the experiment can possibly succeed but agrees that it should be tried for a reasonable length of time; the member from the neighborhood says that he thinks after he has explained the action to a few leaders in the neighborhood, approval of the action of the board will be fairly general.

In this illustration it may be contended that the results would have been the same had there been no board and had the executive officer proceeded as professional judgment dictated. The difference lies in public relations of the executive officer to the community and in the attitude of the neighbors to the mother.

Let it be assumed that the executive officer's arguments and persuasive powers failed, and that the two board members took the position that the child should be placed in a foster home. The executive officer still has the opportunity to attempt to gain a majority vote in the board. If he fails, he is somewhat in the position of a lawyer who has been unable to get a jury to accept his view regarding the character of the defendant; and he likewise knows that his chances of success with the experiment in the face of community attitudes would not have been very good.

The lay board serves in a way as a combination judge and jury, for within its powers it determines the law, and interprets and applies the law to the facts. Since the tendency in selecting board members is to choose persons who have some influence in their neighborhoods and have an interest in welfare work, the board is likely to be more sympathetic to the professional point of view than a jury drawn by lot would be. Frequently, moreover, the question of representation of areas, interests, and professions is taken into consideration in selecting the board members. Incidentally, an executive officer may get a considerable amount of professional advice and assistance from members of the board who are engaged in related fields.

Special categories. Thus far we have discussed examiners and case investigators without reference to any particular category of relief or social security. In small local areas, the volume of work is so small that the organization uses only general examiners. They handle all sorts of cases. As the volume of work increases, specialization by categories may be introduced.

In densely populated areas, one may find a separate unit consisting of a supervisor and several primary examiners for each different category. The number of examiners in each unit will depend on the volume of work in that unit. A county fairly large in respect to both population and area may be divided into districts with a general examiner in each district. Attached to the central office and under the executive officer may be several examiners, each specializing in a particular category or group of related categories. They may handle all cases that arise in their particular fields anywhere in the county, or they may work with and advise the district general examiner when that officer has cases in their particular fields.

Obviously the factor of administrative costs enters into decisions as to the exact form of organization to be used. A few local governments may have so small an aggregate volume of work that only one employee, the executive officer, is used to do all the work, sometimes even without clerical assistance for record making, filing, and correspondence. The salary of such a position may have to be relatively low because the volume of work and the resources do not justify more. A general worker with a small case load and an intimate knowledge of the community may do an excellent job. On the other hand, the lone worker may be scarcely better than passable in handling the most common type of cases and highly inefficient in the rarer and more involved ones. Where distances are not too great and public sentiment will approve, some consolidations may be worked out, at least with respect to the professional staff.

Relationship between state staff and local agencies. We have now considered the state board and its executive officer as the top overhead and the local board with its executive officer and its corps of examiners and clerical assistants as the operating unit in direct contact with the clients and the people of the locality. We are, therefore, in a position to consider the detailed organization of the staff of the state board whose duties are to see that the local boards meet state standards, that on the one hand the localities are not raiding the state treasury, and on the other they are not so niggardly with respect to local funds that national and state objectives are not being attained.

The first thing the state agency has to develop is the method for keeping in touch with what the local units are doing. As we have seen, a local board, after investigation by its examiners and a report by its executive officer, either recommends that a benefit be granted by the state or authorizes a benefit subject to a reversal by the state agency. Thus papers are regularly flowing into the state office which must be immediately examined by state employees. Under the one legal system, the question is whether the state shall approve the benefit recommended by the local board. Under the other, the issue is whether there is any reason why the state should reverse the action of the county board or reverse it temporarily pending further investigation. Thus the state office has at least one examining unit and possibly in larger states one for each category or group of related categories.

Approved grants or benefits result in state expenditures from state funds. Thus the state must keep accounts and audit expenditures. Two major financial procedures are possible. Under the first the state agency issues its checks to the beneficiaries for whom benefits have been approved. Under the second, the local board does the disbursing to the beneficiaries, and the state makes lump-sum payments to the local agency or the local government to cover the state's share of the costs. A compromise plan is for the state to prepare the benefit checks and send them to the local board to be verified and issued.

State disbursement of benefits permits a large use of mechanical equipment for accounting, check writing, addressing, and mailing. In many cases once the addressograph plate for check writing or mailing or the master accounting machine card has been prepared and verified, all subsequent operations are speedy, accurate, and inexpensive, provided no changes have taken place with respect to beneficiaries and amounts. It is changes in beneficiaries and amounts, taking place between one pay period and the next, which sometimes makes the economy and efficiency of centralized disbursing more apparent than real. If large numbers of accounts have to be altered each pay period, and the local agency has either to send in pay-roll revisions each month prior to running the checks or return many checks for revision, the savings may largely disappear and delays may be serious.

A disturbing fact about centralized disbursing is that it tends to relieve local agencies, which have the direct personal contacts with beneficiaries, of the responsibility and control that come from local disbursement. In a local office a beneficiary is known at least to one examiner and often to others. The place and the neighborhood where he lives are known generally not only to the examiners but to the clerks who are keeping the accounts and preparing the checks. Thus at each pay period there may be a partial review of the facts in each case, and the person who signs the checks or the register or pay roll for the period has a direct responsibility. Mechanical disbursement from a central office eliminates this personal review and may make responsibility much less direct. In mechanized centralized pay-roll disbursing in the national government, cases have arisen in which frauds have been perpetrated which in our opinion would have been far less likely had an agency disbursing officer been liable for disbursements.

The records and accounts flowing to the state office from the local offices furnish the basis for statistics and reports. The state office under a grant-in-aid system must supply such reports and statistics as are required by the national board. It also needs them for its own reports to the governor, the legislature, and the public. A good state agency, moreover, has a strong research division which uses statistics as an effective device for the control of local agencies. This use of statistics for control deserves some elaboration.

Only occasionally, and then generally as a result of an error, will an able local agency submit to a state agency papers which do not in every detail support the action taken or recommended by the local agency. Papers on their face are commonly perfect and will generally pass any paper audit or review. If they contain errors, the errors are of fact. The facts recorded in the papers are not precisely accurate. The investigations may not have been carried far enough to develop evidence that would negative eligibility or reduce the amount of the grant; or a law or a regulation may have been given an interpretation contrary to the policy of the legislature or the state board. Even the most painstaking auditor or state examiner cannot discover the truth from the face of the record, for the case may look like the good ones coming from that local agency or other local agencies.

If, however, a local agency has a bias either in the direction of over liberality or over strictness that trend will be revealed in the statistics if they are properly analyzed by a competent research unit. A competent research agency will develop a large body of quantitative and qualitative data regarding each local jurisdiction in the state, covering population classified by age, income, industries, living conditions, living costs, and so forth. It can make comparisons among local agencies on several bases, and possibly it can classify local agencies into comparable groups or rank them according to significant indexes. When that work has been done, and statistics for cases from the local offices are studied, the research unit can ask such questions as, "Why is it that locality A has so many more cases or so many more cases per capita or per family than any other comparable agency or gives so much higher average benefits?" Or, at the other extreme, "Why is it that locality A, despite all the adverse general factors, has comparatively a low ratio of cases or low average benefits?" Neither the research division nor the auditors can answer these questions from the records. The research division can merely pass the questions to the executive officer of the state board or other appropriate state officer to be answered through investigation or supervision.

Any state, except a very small one, may well be divided into state administrative districts, each district containing a number of local agencies. In each such district the state agency may have a state district representative or supervisor who serves as a professional liaison officer between the state agency and the local agencies within the district.

The duties, responsibilities, and powers of these district supervisors or representatives are frequently called co-operative supervisory, a term which calls for some explanation. In the field of education and much later in that of welfare, the effort has been made to preserve a large measure of local control and support, but at the same time to have the state require compliance by local governments with minimum standards established by the state. To get the necessary state legislation through, to make state participation acceptable, and in some instances to give the poorer communities equalization funds, the state governments have customarily made grants-in-aid. The division of responsibility and authority which resulted in this effort to reconcile traditional home rule and local powers with a considerable measure of state control gave rise to co-operative supervision. It is an administrative device used when state administrative officers appreciate two facts: (1) that it is highly questionable whether a drastic use of state power would be sustained by public sentiment even if the law ostensibly gives that power; an attempt to use drastic power might easily result in legislation curtailing it; (2) that state objectives can be best achieved through educational processes, through a gradual modification where necessary of the local attitudes and local sentiments. Both in education and in public welfare, local co-operation is essential in effecting environmental and community changes; thus the maintenance of proper public relations is essential.

The state district representative must be a diplomat. On the one hand he must interpret the law, regulations, and policy of the state administration to all persons connected with the local agency directly or indirectly, including board members, staff, local legislators, and interested public, and in so far as possible convince them of the wisdom of the state policies. On the other hand, he must advise the executive officer of the state agency or his assistant to whom he directly reports as to the attitude and the point of view of the local units in the district. A good rule of the state agency may be too far in advance of local sentiment to be acceptable, or a rule believed by the state to be good may not be working out well in practice. The state agency needs to know such facts so that it can chart its own course.

In theory at least the district supervisor or representative has no authority to give any orders to the local board or to the executive officer and the staff. He may advise, and the advice of one whose official duties call for a report and probably a recommendation to the state office, carries great weight. If the district supervisor is not satisfied with local action, the local people are often more likely to try to find an acceptable compromise than to fight, and the state agency likewise is likely to prefer a reasonable compromise to a battle.

Under a merit system with a good classification, the state district supervisor and the local executive officer generally belong to about the same profession, they talk the same language and have a great deal of the same philosophy. A wise executive officer may discuss difficult cases with the state representative.

What action would the state representative take in such a situation? If the executive follows the advice of the state representative, he is not likely to have any difficulty with the state office. If the case is difficult because of local sentiment, either as represented on the board or in the community at large, the state representative can legitimately undertake to harmonize that sentiment with the state point of view, perhaps under the guise of seeking to determine first hand, local public opinion. A local board may be more willing to accept the advice of its own executive officer if the board members know that the state representative is in agreement with that advice. The state office, on the other hand, may be a little more ready to accept its own representative's report on public sentiment and on defects and weaknesses of its rules and regulations than the report of the local executive officer.

Under conditions such as these, it is apparently sound practice to keep the state administrative districts small enough so that the state district representative can know well the executive officer and the leading members of the staff, and at least be acquainted with board members and the principal members of the local government.

If reports from the research division show that a local government is getting out of line in either direction, the district representative may be the first one called upon to investigate and report. It may happen that the statistics merely demonstrate the existence of a bias the district representative already suspected but could not quite prove. Armed with the statistics, and operating under state orders calling for a report, the district officer may without creating much friction bring the local agency into line.

District local representatives or supervisors are, as a rule, good, all-round workers but not necessarily specialists in any one field. A state agency may have in the central office a small staff of advisers, each specializing in a particular branch of the work either in categories or in processes, such as accounting, statistics, or office management. They may from time to time on their own motion, subject to approval at the state office, make the rounds of all the local agencies or of such as seem to require a visit. They may be called in by the district representative or the local executive secretary or the two jointly.

A distinction should probably be made here between the state specialists on business practice and procedure and those on a particular category. Although local boards may think some of the business practices and procedures are unnecessarily complicated and involve too much red tape, they are likely to recognize that the state has to require uniformity. It is therefore feasible for the state to delegate to these specialists some authority to give orders and possibly temporarily to take charge of the procedural work of a local agency while a revised system is being installed or while clerical employees are being trained. Category specialists, on the other hand, may be dealing with conflicts regarding policy between the state and the locality, and here again the category specialists may be diplomatic advisers, conducting relationships with the local agencies in much the same way as was described in connection with the state district supervisor.

Co-operative organization and procedure of this type is at the opposite extreme from administrative absolutism. The state executive director knows that his success depends not on the exercise of the power to give commands which must be obeyed but on his ability to influence others to follow his leadership. He may be likened to the spark plug in an automobile engine. He is not effective if the gap between himself and his board, his staff, the government in general, and the people is too wide, nor is he effective in developing and improving the system if there is no gap at all.

The relative advantages of co-operative leadership as compared with administrative absolutism depends in no small measure upon the extent to which constructive service to individuals and families is to be included in the administration of relief and social security. To this subject the next chapter is devoted.

CHAPTER XXXIV

SOCIAL SERVICE AND SOCIAL SECURITY

The essence of social security and relief is that the government exercises its sovereign power to tax and distributes the proceeds as it deems best to promote the general welfare. With respect to the manner of distribution, two extremes of thought may be recognized. One holds that social security payments should be made as of right with no governmental effort to use the payments as a means of influencing or controlling the behavior or actions of the beneficiary. The beneficiary, according to this point of view, should have practically as great freedom in using the proceeds of his grant as he would have in using his own earnings or the proceeds of a private voluntary insurance policy, the premiums for which he has paid by his own efforts.

At the other extreme are persons who regard as the ideal, support of one's self and one's dependents through one's own efforts without dependence upon the state. If it becomes necessary for the state to contribute by taxing others, it is incumbent on the state to do what it can toward re-establishing the economic independence of the beneficiary and those dependent upon him, and it is incumbent on the beneficiary and his dependents to co-operate with the representatives of the state in return for the public funds spent in their behalf.

At the very outset of this discussion, we should distinguish between activities of the state undertaken for all members of a general class and activities undertaken with respect to a particular individual or family. Two illustrations may help make the distinction clear: (1) the state operates a first-class public school system which is open to all. A boy comes from a family so constituted that he is not getting the advantages of the opportunities the state has made available to all normal boys of his age. The truant officer can and does compel attendance, but far more intensive work with the boy and his family is required if the opportunities presented by the public school are to be realized. (2) The state has made available public health clinics for the treatment and cure of certain diseases, and anyone can take advantage of them. Family X needs the services of that clinic, but the members are not co-operative. Even if they are forced to submit to examination by the clinic, they will not carry out the directions of the doctors and nurses and make the changes in the manner of living necessary for a cure. If the public health service is to be made effective, work must be done to make the individuals co-operate.

The issue with which we are concerned is thus: Shall relief and social security benefits, paid for at least in large part by taxes imposed on others, be used as a device to require beneficiaries to accept efforts to rehabilitate them? and Shall the state furnish personal and family services designed to achieve these objectives as part and parcel of its social security and relief administration? In the discussion of this issue we shall assume that the necessary group services for all of a general class are available and confine ourselves entirely to personal and family services designed to adjust the individual or the family to the community in which he lives, in accordance with an acceptable minimum standard.

TYPICAL CLASSES OF CASES

It may be well to begin the detailed discussion with a review of some of the more important classes involved in relief and social security administration.

In a severe depression there are some, even a substantial number, who are in need through no fault of their own. Their only requirement is sufficient purchasing power to get along. If that purchasing power is supplied, they need no special service to adjust them to the community in which they live. The standards of the family and the individual are at or above a satisfactory minimum. Competent social workers would in all probability agree that such individuals and families require no rehabilitative services involving standards, and that constructive service should be confined largely if not entirely to efforts to secure suitable employment for members of the family who are employable. If in fact this class were the only one involved, there would scarcely be an issue.

As recovery follows a deep recession, administrators find that persons of this general description are among the first to leave the relief or unemployment insurance rolls. They are quickly reabsorbed into private industry or normally conducted public enterprises. It then becomes apparent that no small part of the administrative task is concerned with individuals or families who are materially below average, normal, or typical. Consideration of the major issue requires examination of the question, In what respect are the individuals below average, normal, or typical? The lines between certain major classes are not sharp and fast and sometimes members of families are in two or more categories.

Some families are atypical solely because death, disability, divorce, desertion, or unemployment has deprived them of the normal support of the father. The mother is competent to carry on her duties in accordance with an acceptable minimum standard, but she cannot do so and at the same time earn a living. To restore that family to a satisfactory approach to normal, it is only necessary to supply minimum means of support with due regard to the composition of the family. In dealing with families such as these control and supervision are generally unnecessary.

In some families whose immediate need arises from the absence of the earnings of the father, the mother may be far from competent and dependable. Divorce, desertion, even the imprisonment of the father may be explained in part by serious deficiencies in the mother. Competent investigators may be unanimous in their opinion that the best interests of the dependent children cannot be served by giving money to the mother. The alternatives are (1) taking the children away from the mother and placing them with relatives or in a foster home, and (2) having a competent case worker supervise the family so that if possible it will conform to a suitable minimum standard. Cases of this type clearly present the issue of whether the money grant to the mother and children is to be conditional on accepting supervision, or whether it is to be unconditional with the state depending on other devices to secure observance of reasonable standards.

Families may vary from the typical or average basically with respect to the mere number of dependent children. The facts may practically prove that the father and mother could have managed without substantial difficulty had there been fewer children. Under such circumstances an uncontrolled money grant might be all that is needed. Investigation may, however, reveal that the father is not a very satisfactory worker and is irregularly employed even at best. A trained investigator may feel reasonably certain that a straight money grant without supervision would reduce rather than increase his incentives. On the other hand, a rational family plan that meets immediate difficulties and offers him a possible way of increasing his own earnings might increase his self-respect and self-confidence and improve his value as an employee. Investigation might also show the mother ineffective in meeting her responsibilities. The mere size of them may have discouraged her, or she may be the type of woman who would not have been successful even with a very small family.

Then there are the numerous cases in which individuals are materially below average in native intelligence and ability. Even in communities where adequate educational opportunities were available, they have not taken advantage of them, because they did not have the requisite capacity. In communities where educational opportunities are poor, we may blame the government and forget that some of the underendowed people would be only little better off had the schools been far more adequate. Despite limited opportunity many young persons from such a community have achieved real success, because of their native ability, ambition, and good family environment.

Underlying all these cases is the fact that fathers and mothers perform a vitally important duty in rearing a family. The father is far more than the breadwinner who supplies the money; the mother far more than the manipulator of things purchased with money. They create an environment within the home, they influence the environment of a neighborhood, and they may greatly influence the attitude of their children toward life in that environment and toward the opportunities that may be available. Children may be handicapped more by the mental and spiritual poverty of their parents than by their lack of worldly goods and income. Every now and then a court case reveals the great damage done where mental and spiritual poverty prevails in the presence of abundant purchasing power. American history reveals many cases in which men and women born and nurtured in the simplest surroundings with a minimum of purchasing power have become leaders in their chosen fields. A good home environment, it may be reasonably contended, is far more important than the amount of purchasing power available.

THE NEED FOR FAMILY CASE WORK

To us it seems undeniable that in a substantial number of cases families and individuals require more than money or the things that money will buy. They may need guidance from persons possessed of more knowledge than they have; pressure from outside to help them overcome their own inertia; inspiration from persons with visions of possibilities to awake determined ambition. Children may be effectively insulated from the driving forces that mean success by the limitations of their parents and the environment in which their parents maintained them. In a few cases they may be not only insulated from constructive forces but left widely exposed to destructive forces.

It is not enough that the state supply the necessary opportunities open to all of a class. Someone must see that the individual knows of the opportunity, appreciates its value, and finds means of overcoming the obstacles that lie in the way of taking advantage of it. That task involves work with individuals, not one short inspirational talk but prolonged, intelligent effort such as an enlightened, resourceful, and persevering parent would make with his children.

Should the state impose the services of such a worker upon an individual or a family simply because that individual or family is receiving money collected by the state from the tax-payers? Should it use the need of the individual or the family as a means of forcing the person or persons involved, at least to pre-tend to follow the program suggested by the worker?

The state secures the money for relief and social security by an encroachment on the freedom of the people to do as they see fit with the proceeds of their own activities. Compulsion nega-tives free will and voluntary action. It is open to question whether the freedom of the individual to use his own property as he desires should be restricted by the state for the purpose of continuing benefit payments to individuals who might through constructive service be made self-sustaining, but whose idea of freedom is such that they want no representative of the state interfering with their lives. Should the state curtail the freedom of those who have earned it by their talents and efforts to give freedom from state interference to those dependent on the state for their support?

SERVICE THE CASE WORKER MAY RENDER

Constructive social service, moreover, is not necessarily re-garded as improper state interference with personal liberty by many individuals and families who need it. The child who did not want to be discharged from court probation because things had gone better than ever before under the guidance of the probation officer is by no means unique. The able social worker can gain the confidence, respect, and even the affection of the members of the family and help them work out of their difficulties. He brings to their aid a power of diagnosis and a knowledge of resources, opportunities, and procedures that few families possess.

Local boards, made up of citizens who have major occupa-tions of their own which necessarily consume much of their time, rarely can give the hours required by an active case calling for constructive, individualized service. Rarely today does any one of them have the detailed knowledge of subject matter, laws, and procedure that is now necessary for constructive work, although each may have a part of it. The professional knowledge of the well-trained social worker is in fact to a large extent made up of parts from each of several professional fields, particularly those parts that permit of understanding situations and knowing what lines to follow.

As was clearly stated at the outset of this chapter, there are many cases in which no such constructive case work is necessary or even desirable. Examiners, as described in the preceding chapter, can determine the facts that establish eligibility. These facts, the report of the examiners, and the knowledge possessed by the local board and its staff will make it at once obvious that little if anything more is necessary than payment of benefits. In some cases, however, it will be equally obvious that service is essential in the interests of both the family and the community.

The amount of time and service that will be required by individual cases is highly variable. In many the volume of intensive work at the outset when a catastrophy has just happened is heavy, because a good many things have to be straightened out. When that first work is over, the case may become largely inactive so that an occasional visit is adequate. In some cases the worker must be prepared to be called upon for advice and assistance in every emergency because members of the family do not know what to do, have no confidence in their own judgment, or cannot agree among themselves.

THE POINT OF VIEW OF CASE WORKERS

Although the need for well-trained, effective case workers seems fairly obvious, the existence of serious doubts regarding them must be frankly recognized. They are sometimes ticketed with such terms as "sentimentalists," "uplifters," "do gooders," or "sob sisters." Some of them may be actively identified with radical, even ultra radical, groups. To promote understanding of them, certain observations regarding their work should be set forth.

1. Probably to a greater extent than any other large group, they see first hand the distress that results from poverty, lack of opportunity, exploitation, ignorance, and crime.

2. The objectives of their work are to relieve the distress, to rehabilitate the individual, to improve the environment, and to eliminate causes. Like public health physicians, they are likely to have much more confidence in prevention than in cure. Their professional ethics require them to do their best on a case even when they know the chances for success are small.

3. In work for the rehabilitation of individuals, psychology practically requires that the workers find the good in their client and attempt to build on that good. It is practically essential for a case worker to have a deep conviction that there is much good in the worst of us.

4. The necessity for finding the good tends to make case workers attorneys for the defense. The client's shortcoming must be so explained that there can be no verdict of total depravity. To factors not incriminatory—imperfections in government and in the social and economic system, exploitation, and so on—must be attached a weight greater than would ever be admitted by a prosecuting attorney or found by an impartial judge or jury. It must be remembered, however, that the case worker frequently has more first-hand knowledge of extenuating circumstances than anyone else possesses.

5. If the client is to be helped, he must feel that the case worker has some faith in him, and it is doubtful whether he can have that feeling if the worker actually has no such faith. His explanations, if supported by evidence, must at least be temporarily accepted as well as his repentances and his promises. Employers, foremen, or personnel officers may say, "I heard all that last time; I gave you one more chance; you are through." It is only fair to note that many case workers pick up where the personnel man lets go. The case worker cannot so readily say, "You are through," for such a declaration may mean separation of child from parent or commitment to an institution—custodial, correctional, or penal. That action represents another failure, which raises a doubt either as to the skill and ability of the case worker or as to the soundness of the basic premises on which the work rests.

6. Case workers looking at the social and economic system

from the bottom, and perhaps to no small extent through the eyes of their clients, note vast sums of money being spent for things which seem to them far less important than the relief and prevention of the distress that is always before them. It is almost inevitable that they should feel that the world might easily be made much better. Many of them have never occupied positions that give them a different view of the whole or a chance to understand the responsibilities of those who must pay the money to support relief, social security, or private philanthropy.

The degree to which individual social workers possess these characteristics differs widely. There are some to whom few would attach the words radical or militant, yet the group as a whole would doubtless be placed by most persons as left of center. This fairly common appraisal has led in certain instances to the suggestion that some or all welfare examiners should be drawn from the ranks of credit examiners, secret investigators, or detectives. A few words should perhaps be said regarding this type of examiner.

EXAMINERS OF THE DETECTIVE TYPE

In many kinds of private and public work, it is necessary to know whether there is anything against a person who is to be employed or with whom business is to be done. The government of the United States, for example, proposes to employ a person in the Civil Service or to commission him in the armed forces. The information secured from the person himself and those to whom he refers or names in his record is all satisfactory. Then a special investigator is asked in essence, "Is there anything against this man?" A store receives an application for credit which appears good on its face and seems satisfactory on a check of references. Again comes the question, "Is there anything wrong with this man?" An insurance agent takes an application for life insurance from a client he considers reliable, the local agency regards him as acceptable, he passes his physical examination, the policy is issued subject to cancellation within a specified period. To protect itself and its other policy holders, the insurance company asks a special investigation agency to determine whether there is anything wrong with the client.

The job of these investigators is to turn up something wrong if something wrong can be found. The task frequently necessitates the assumption by the investigator that a man is guilty until proved innocent. Effort must be made to prove misstatements of fact and to locate persons who will give adverse evidence. Police and court records may be searched and any domestic difficulties gone into thoroughly. Today in the government service work of this character is expedited by fingerprinting. If during the course of the investigation, the examiner questions the applicant, the tendency is to confront him with such adverse evidence as has been turned up and to try to make him admit at least that the worst possible interpretation is the correct interpretation, or preferably that the full truth is even more damaging.

Investigators of this type often turn up enough evidence of fraud, misrepresentation, and bad behavior patterns to force administrators to admit that work of this character is essential if the interests of the innocent are to be protected. Insurance, either public or private, offers great temptation to the weak. Having paid a premium, the insured feels he is entitled to get something for his money.

Some evidence suggests that benefits which are paid from public funds are particularly tempting. A philosophy may develop that: "If the government is giving money away, we ought to get in on it." Although this temptation may be greater in means test systems than in no-means test systems, it exists in both. It is the bugbear in the administration of disability insurance, and it is probably an extremely important factor in unemployment insurance, where both employer and employee can take advantage of the system either separately or in collusion.

With regret we are forced to conclude that the use of investigators with such an approach is often necessary and that probably most social workers are ill-equipped either by temperament or training successfully to perform such duties.

It is equally clear, however, that investigators experienced in ferreting out the bad are in general not equipped by temperament, training, and experience to render constructive rehabilitative service. The relationship that exists between prosecuting investigator and applicant is almost the extreme opposite from the relationship which must exist between the constructive social worker and the client if the chances of success are to be reasonably high.

The conclusion seems to us to be inescapable that if the prosecuting type of investigators and examiners is to be used: (1) the work should be done mainly in connection with the initial application with possibly an occasional rechecking from time to time in cases remaining long on the rolls, and (2) they should have no direct personal contact with applicants unless such contacts are specifically authorized by or under the authority of the local executive officer or the appropriate state officer. It is assumed that the direct contacts would not be authorized unless the facts secured by the prosecuting investigator without such direct contacts establish a prima-facie case of misrepresentation. Direct contacts under such circumstances might have wholesome results if it becomes generally known through the community that serious misrepresentation is likely to result in unpleasantness. It is further assumed that the administrative officers in dealing with families will give predominant consideration to the interests and needs of children. In some cases the constructive services of a case worker are needed because one parent or both parents have low ethical standards, and the children are being trained to follow in the parents' footsteps. The very facts regarding the parents discovered by the detective may demonstrate the need of constructive case work with the children.

BUSINESS INVESTIGATORS

Without any reflection upon social workers, moreover, it may be said that some of them have little aptitude or training for appraising the value of property or verifying reports as to income from sources other than salary or wages. They may not be familiar with significant details in insurance policies regarding such matters as surrender values, extended insurance, conversion privileges, and so on. A large local agency may, therefore, find it advantageous to have on its staff an investigator and adviser who is an expert in matters of this kind, especially if a means test is used for certain parts of the system.[1] The state agency may have specialists in this field who may be sent to small local agencies when their services are needed. Although such specialists may at times bring to light evidence which disqualifies an applicant, they are frequently of very great service both to the family and the case worker in helping work out a financial program. Death, disability, and prolonged unemployment frequently force a family to face a problem of financial management for which it has no training or experience. There may be debts and claims—current or outlawed, thoroughly established or highly dubious—back taxes, mortgages due, and possibly on the other side money owed the worker, claims for workmen's compensation or rights under an insurance policy. If a person skilled and experienced can be quickly called into the case, he may prevent any considerable loss of assets and materially reduce dependence upon public funds.

The family financial program should be completely integrated with the rest of the program. The skilled case worker, the skilled financial man, and the members of the family who are old enough to understand financial matters should co-operate in evolving the plan. How well a family or an individual can make out depends not alone on the amount of money available but also on the skill and judgment with which it is used. At times demagogues attempt completely to separate human rights and property rights and allege that property rights have been made superior to human rights. For the vast majority of people the two are closely interrelated, and all but the most ignorant families appreciate the fact. If the family wants to get ahead, to realize opportunities, and to achieve a considerable measure of independence, it must learn to make the most of what it has and to earn more through work in legitimate fields. If this position is sound the state does not fulfill its obligation to

---

[1] Sometimes a member of the local board renders excellent service as an adviser in such matters.

dependents in need by giving them relief or by paying the benefits due under social insurance. To those who have capacity to learn and to grow, it owes assistance in developing the skills necessary for successful management, and nowhere can the skills be better developed than in the actual conduct of family affairs under the conditions in which the family finds itself. The true social case worker is not a lady bountiful giving away other people's money to persons in need, but a skilled teacher and demonstrator helping a family or an individual to attain independence and efficiency.

CHAPTER XXXV

RELATIONSHIPS WITH OTHER AGENCIES

The preceding chapter ended with the statement that the true social worker is a skilled teacher and demonstrator helping an individual or a family to attain independence and efficiency. In the present chapter, we are to be concerned primarily with the relationships that should exist between a public welfare agency working constructively with individuals and families and other public agencies concerned with furthering their interests. The public agencies with which we shall deal are (1) the employment office, (2) the schools, (3) the health agencies and, in rural communities (4) the agricultural development agencies.

THE EMPLOYMENT SERVICE

The basic foundation for the social security of an adult individual is ability to do a good job in a necessary calling. Give him a job that he can do well at a reasonable wage and the problem of his social security is largely solved. It is recognized that such a solution does not provide for dependent children too young to work or for the disabled, including those disabled from advanced age. But, as has been previously pointed out, in each succeeding generation the dependent children and the disabled must be provided for by the active workers of that generation. Thus developing individual efficiency and maintaining production of needed goods and services are far more basic than legislation with respect to money benefits to be paid on the happening of any contingency.

In considering the relationships between the public welfare department and the employment service, we may start with the principal worker who must support himself and possibly some dependents. If the head of the family is entirely unemployed, he must register at the employment office in his community and be available to accept a suitable opening when and if it is offered to him. Under the New Zealand plan, he is entitled to a benefit if he is in need according to New Zealand standards; under our state plans, he is entitled to a benefit if he has attained an insured status and has not already exhausted his benefit rights.

If continued unemployment follows as a result of a general economic recession or a temporary depression in the particular industry for which the worker is fitted by training and experience, there is relatively little the public welfare department can do about employment, although it may have an important part to play if work relief projects are organized, in seeing that persons who are really in need get the jobs.

If the unemployment is caused in whole or in part by the limitations of the individual, or if the employment situation calls upon him to make radical readjustments, the case workers from the welfare department may have an essential role. Employers, whether public or private, who strive for efficiency in production rarely want to be bothered with the inefficient or unreliable employee if more efficient, more reliable employees are available. Although some of them have personnel departments that help good employees in overcoming personal and family difficulties of one kind or another, they generally do not assume responsibility for inferior workers who are commonly the ones resulting in maximum costs of production, spoilage, and mistakes. If such employees are to be up-graded, some public agency with an educational developmental objective must bear the principal load. Upgrading unfortunately is not simply a matter of vocational education, it involves mental attitudes, personal behavior, and often domestic relations. Here then is a substantial area in which the employment service and the welfare service have a common interest.

The alternatives appear to be either to have the employment service equipped to do a very considerable amount of individual case work or to have the welfare agency do it in co-operation with the employment service. Overlapping, duplication, and possibly conflicts may develop if two different agencies are dealing with a single family. From our point of view, it seems preferable to have the welfare department responsible for all the personal work with individuals and families, but it must co-operate closely with the employment service.

In some cases the evidence may be almost conclusive that the individual can scarcely hope again to secure full employment in his customary occupation in the neighborhood where he lives, and no other local employment offers reasonable expectation of earnings such as he has enjoyed in the past. The solution may be to migrate. The employment service is the logical agency to furnish data regarding employment opportunities, but the case workers of the welfare agency are far better equipped than the employment service to help in solving the personal and family problems that arise in connection with migration. For many persons the problems are new and baffling and require a break-ing of old ties that may be extremely distressing. It is not sur-prising that many families cling to their old homes and neigh-borhoods after all real opportunity there has vanished. Neither is it surprising that families are ultimately broken because a man goes away to get a job in a distant community leaving his wife and children behind. It takes a good deal of intelligent and managerial ability moreover to make wise decisions with respect to what to do about any real property owned and about household furniture and equipment.

The employment service and the welfare department clearly should be in close co-operation in communities to which large numbers of workers are drawn. The industries there may offer jobs at wages higher than the migrants have ever before earned, but the conditions under which the families are to live are be-yond their past experience. It is entirely possible that the new employment possibilities that appear so attractive from the wage standpoint will result in new slums unless there is good social planning and engineering. Much of the migration has been, and will probably continue to be, from a rural environ-ment in which money plays only a small part to a complex ur-ban industrial environment in which money is necessary in almost every transaction. The problem of helping people to adjust to the new environment is largely one in specialized adult education. It lies largely in the field of social work, both family case work and group work, with close co-operation with the public educational system.

In dealing with individual families in distress, the family case worker often encounters the question of supplementary or secondary breadwinners. For example, the primary worker periodically goes on a spree. His employment status and his earnings grow progressively worse, and it is clear to the case worker that in the near future the family will need income from some other source. The mother or the adolescent children will have to take up the burden. Two alternatives are open, one is to let the situation drift and when the time comes have the mother and the children get such jobs as they can. The other course is to begin at once preparation for the crisis which appears inevitable. With respect to the children, the case worker wants to know their capacity and their vocational aptitudes and interests, and further what their opportunities would be for employment in jobs which would offer them real opportunity. The reefs which the worker particularly hopes to avoid are the "blind alley jobs" and the constant shifting from one job to another in the attempt to find something that awakes interest.

The employment service, through its junior placement service, should be the logical place to which the case worker should send the children for vocational aptitude tests and for a report as to where their vocational interests lie. Persons who know the duties and responsibilities of jobs, the qualifications required for the performance of the duties, the opportunities for employment and the chances for advancement are best qualified to develop aptitude tests and through interviews with the youth to determine where their interests lie. Neither the social case worker nor the public school teacher can be expected to have all-round knowledge in these special fields. The knowledge, skills, and techniques lie in the province of the employment service, which should co-operate with both the welfare department and the public school system.

Reports from the employment service and from the schools, and interviews with teachers may show that native ability, aptitudes, achievements, and interest are such that one or more of the children ought not to become a full-time worker at an early age but should get the education required for entrance into professional, scientific, or technical work. The case worker will then try to develop a program which makes continuance at school possible. In some instances one or both parents may oppose such a program, being unwilling to forego the child's earnings or feeling that the child wants to be better than his parents. The child also may feel that he ought to give up his interests and ambitions and begin at the earliest possible moment to earn as much as he can. As a rule, however, the case worker will give great weight to the long-run interests of the child, which are likely to be the long-run interests of society as a whole.

THE SCHOOLS

In indicating the relationships between the employment service and the welfare department, we have incidentally touched upon the relationship of each of them to the schools. One of the essential objectives of the schools is to fit the child to make a living for himself and those dependent on him either by work outside the home or by services rendered in the home. The schools need close contact with the employment service so that they can determine from the experience of their graduates how well they are achieving this objective and from time to time modify their curricula or their methods to secure better results. They particularly need such contacts with respect to those who leave school at the earliest possible age without having secured the minimum of education that is needed for success. Vocational education of less than college grade ought to be planned and administered by educators in close cooperation with the employment service.

The function of the public welfare department is to do all that is possible to make sure that children under its jurisdiction take full advantage of the opportunities presented by the public schools, and that the public schools do as much as possible for children who for one reason or another come under the jurisdiction of the welfare department.

Several types of cases require brief mention here.

First are the children within the compulsory school age who are unquestionably a responsibility of the school but who fail to attend or to make satisfactory progress because of home conditions or lack of co-operation between home and school. There was a time—and in some jurisdictions it is probably still true— when such children year after year failed of promotion and reached the end of the compulsory period without having attained the minimum elementary education necessary for successful work. The substantial public funds spent for their education were largely wasted for one of the major objectives was not obtained.

Second are the children who are beyond the compulsory school age, who may be regarded as no longer a responsibility of the schools, but who are getting nowhere. They may move from temporary job to temporary job not making good in any of them. Some of these children are known to the police and to the courts. They may be the victims of inadequate homes and bad environment. They may damage otherwise satisfactory homes and themselves contribute to making bad environment for others. Some of them will be problems for the community for the balance of their lives, in some cases simply because of their inadequacy and in others because, unable to get along by legitimate activities, they resort to the illegitimate.

As in many physical diseases, the chances for effecting a cure and preventing serious developments are better the earlier the case is taken in hand by competent practitioners. The knowledge and skills required are basically those of the social case worker, with some special emphasis on child welfare and relationship with schools. In some jurisdictions these workers are connected with the school system and are called visiting teachers. Employment by the school system probably has one marked advantage over employment by the welfare department. Occasionally the child who needs the services of a visiting teacher comes from a family with which the welfare department has had no occasion to deal, and it may be more pleasant for that family to receive a visiting teacher from the school than a case worker from welfare. On the other hand, in many communities the families that are known to welfare are the same families whose children require the services of the visiting teacher.

The typical visiting teacher gives a relatively large amount of time to each family; in other words, she has a small case load made up for the most part of active cases. Her work is to be sharply distinguished from that of employees of the welfare department who are primarily social investigators or examiners mainly concerned with fact finding. They give relatively little time to individual cases and hence can carry a large load. They may have no active cases to which they give intensive service.

If the local welfare agency has only social fact-finders on its staff, and public policy is against developing intensive case work there, it may be advisable to let the public school system be responsible for case work among families whose children need it. If, on the other hand, public policy favors intensive case work with all individuals and families where rehabilitation and development seem possible, it would seem desirable to consolidate all these activities in the welfare department. Consolidation prevents overlapping and duplication in dealing with families, and for smaller communities it does not divide the load into small segments that may give high cost per case. The local case workers of the welfare department in the small community may also have the aid and assistance of the various specialists attached to the state department. If the work is scattered among several agencies, the tendency may be to have one more or less independent worker in each agency. Since the load is light and the responsibility when measured by the number of cases does not appear heavy, only small salaries are paid. Much better results may be secured by putting all the cases together under one agency and paying adequate salaries to such employees as are necessary to carry that load.

The question of administrative costs in local agencies deserves a brief statement. If an agency is merely doing social investigating and examining, it should have low administrative costs per case and a low ratio of administrative costs per dollar of benefit, grant, or pension. If, on the other hand, it is giving intensive service to individuals or families which need it, it will have much higher administrative costs per case and a high ratio of administrative costs to benefits. Indeed if case service is successful, in many cases the expenditures for service will exceed the expenditures for relief because the individuals and the families are getting back to financial independence, although they may still be dependent on the case worker in matters requiring judgment and perhaps for the impetus to continue the effort.

Administrative cost figures in relief and social security are by themselves almost meaningless. They must be analyzed with reference to the quantity and quality of the work being done. High administrative costs per case may represent gross waste and extravagance—political loading of the staff—or excellent work of the highest grade, a far wiser use of public funds than spreading them round among the Tussies.[1]

THE HEALTH SERVICE

Medical service and public health work are from the point of view of our problem divisible into two parts:

1. Rendering to the individual the professional medical service which his case demands.

2. Persuading the individual or members of his family of the wisdom of availing themselves of the medical service, solving their personal problems which stand in the way of taking advantage of the medical service, and helping or encouraging the individual or the family to follow the instructions of the medical people.

In the rural economy and in small towns, the family doctor frequently performed both of these functions with some assistance from friends and neighbors. As medical science and agencies for medical care have advanced, the field has been divided; the demands upon the medical personnel have so increased that they must devote the greater part of their time to their medical duties. The personal work with individuals has increasingly been delegated to persons specially trained for it, visiting nurses,

---

[1] See *Taps for Private Tussie* by Jesse Stuart.

hospital social service workers, medical case workers, and general social workers. The knowledge, the skills, and the techniques required for the two types of work are different, although generally each group possesses something in common with the other; but the main reason for the division is the amount of time required for the nonmedical service to families and individuals.

This same overlapping of the two fields of medical care and social service is manifest in the operation of institutions for medical care, notably hospitals for the insane, institutions for the feeble minded, tuberculosis sanitoria, convalescent homes and homes for the incurable. In some states such institutions will be under the department of welfare, in others under the department of health. During a survey of a state government we have never found either the public health doctor or the specialist in welfare administration contending as a matter of principle that this particular class of activities belongs to him.[2] Both recognize that the field is common ground and that co-operation is essential wherever primary administrative responsibility is placed.

So far as individual case work with families is concerned, it seems to us the weight of the evidence is in favor of placing the responsibility in the welfare department provided it has well-qualified case workers. These case workers are in touch with all families in need of relief, and they can make contacts with the health agencies when needed care is indicated. The health agencies on the other hand are in contact with families only when medical care is required. If primary responsibility is in the welfare department, the public health nurse or the visiting nurse

---

[2] There is commonly opposition to a consolidated department of health and welfare, because such consolidation would mean that the doctors would be subordinate to a welfare man if a welfare man were selected as head of the department and vice versa. This same issue may arise with respect to the head of a hospital or sanatorium, but it is by no means so acute. If the medical men have full and undivided responsibility for the medical work in an institution, they may prefer having a lay superintendent responsible for all the housekeeping and social service work. Their concern is whether the housekeeping and social work are well done rather than whether they are done under the department of welfare or the department of health. Poor work by either department often results in transfer of such agencies to that state department which is not responsible for them at the moment. Then poor work will mean a second transfer, returning them to their original position.

devotes herself to the health aspects, and the family case workers do the work incidental to family adjustments which may be spread over a period considerably longer than that of the illness.

AGRICULTURAL AGENCIES

Farm families, whether owners, tenants, or share croppers present a distinctive problem because family life is often so completely integrated with farm production. Father, mother, and children have a part to play in making a living. So far as family income is concerned, the task is less finding jobs for the workers than helping them to be more efficient in the jobs they already have. There is no such separation between working conditions and family or personal life as one commonly finds in urban or nonfarm families.

The situation seems to us to indicate that a single agency should be primarily responsible for all work with farm families that require constructive rehabilitation service. The case workers in this agency ought to combine the knowledge and skills of the family case worker with knowledge and skills in farm management. The major question is therefore whether the responsibility should rest basically with the welfare department with assistance from the agricultural agencies or vice versa.

As one reads the voluminous record regarding the rural rehabilitation work of the Farm Security Administration, one gets the impression that in many cases farm management largely eclipsed constructive work with individuals and families. It should be noted, however, that the hearings dealt especially with rural resettlement projects and collective farming rather than with individual purchases of one man farms or with the rehabilitation of families on their own land. With respect to the large projects, there were many cases in which the individuals were apparently objects of experimentation.

The Farm Security Administration was moreover a national agency which operated in practically complete independence of the established national-state co-operative system which includes the state agricultural colleges, the county agents, the home demonstration agents and often local farm bureaus. The

Farm Bureau Federation and the Grange were as a matter of fact the leading critics of the resettlement and the collective projects of F.S.A. Both, however, approved the program for aiding persons to become successful owners of single family farms and undifferentiated members of the local farm community and commended the work of committees of local farmers who assisted clients in the selection of farms to purchase. Representatives of both agencies saw the difficulty of raising a family to an independent status if the family were permitted or induced to borrow more than it could pay from the proceeds of the farm, especially if the loans were made for durable consumers' goods which produced no direct income.

The Farm Security Administration seems to us to demonstrate the necessity for integrating these efforts with other agricultural programs in the state and county, which are in turn integrated to no small extent with the educational program. It seems highly undesirable to have a national program operating separate and apart from the others and at times in opposition to them. The alternatives appear to be a nationalization of almost all the programs or preserving a large measure of state and local control with respect to all.

We shall not here attempt any recommendations as to whether the public welfare or the agricultural development unit should be the agency with primary responsibility for rehabilitation of farm families in need of relief and rehabilitation. The point we would emphasize is that the type of service such families need requires a combination of the knowledge and skills of both social service and agricultural development service.

If one of the major objectives of the program of relief and social security is preventive and curative and wherever possible to help the needy become independent and self-supporting, then the welfare agency must work in close co-operation with the employment service, the schools, the health services, and in rural communities with agricultural development agencies. These agencies must work together in the locality where the family concerned actually resides. Such co-operation is difficult unless all four agencies are subject to much the same governmental control. This governmental control should, in our judgment, include a substantial measure of local responsibility and authority. The processes are in a considerable measure educational and require response and acceptance from the local community. It seems doubtful whether satisfactory results can be secured if a distant central government attempts to impose its will, if that will runs counter to the views and wishes of a substantial body of local citizens. Co-operation is essential to success, and if co-operation is to be attained, the local citizens must have a substantial voice in management.

CHAPTER XXXVI

THE MERIT SYSTEM IN ADMINISTRATION
OF RELIEF AND SOCIAL SECURITY

From time to time in the preceding chapters the dangers of political manipulation of social security and relief have been stressed. One of the devices for lessening these dangers is to require administration under the merit system.

Experience, according to our opinion, justifies the conclusion that the efficacy of the merit system depends far more on the integrity and ability of the responsible administrators than upon the precise provisions of the merit system act. History of the merit system reveals poor results under an act hailed on its passage as a model and good results under an old act regarded by many technicians as almost completely outmoded. Although an act that will win the approval of competent technicians unquestionably will facilitate good administration, it cannot guarantee it; it cannot prevent perversion if all key points in the administrative structure are occupied by persons intent on circumventing it.

In some of the states, the state constitution requires the use of the merit system. Where such is the case, the courts have jurisdiction to review the actions of both administrators and legislators and to set aside such actions as are contrary to the state constitution. The national government and most of the states have no such constitutional provisions, and therefore the legislators and the administrators have a free hand.

The terms of the national constitution are such that it is generally held that Congress cannot compel the President to use the merit system. It can authorize him to do so; it can give him all the administrative machinery for doing so and supply the necessary funds, but he has the power to ignore the permissive legislation either in general or in particular cases. The rules and regulations under which the national civil service system works are in the main the rules and regulations which the President makes with the advice of a Civil Service Commission which he appoints. The members of the Commission hold office at his pleasure. At times Congress may adopt acts prohibiting the political activity of government employees, the levying of campaign contributions, and so on, but the enforcement of these acts depends on the action of administrative officers responsible to the President. Such real force as they have depends more on public opinion than on anything else. Even a President may hesitate to ignore or circumvent them because such a course might result in adverse political reaction not only from the opposition but also within his own party.

Many a member of Congress is opposed to a full, logical, and effective application of the merit system. This opposition explains the fact that not infrequently laws creating a new agency or providing a new function for the national government have excluded the new service from the operation of the Civil Service Act of 1883 and the Classification Act of 1923 both as amended. Whatever the current explanation may be—the positions are temporary, civil service will not work, administrators must have freedom—the real reason generally is a desire for patronage.

When a single party controls the presidency and both houses of Congress, the desire for patronage may be strong. If the party has just come into power rewards are needed for the faithful; when an old administration faces an election, patronage may be deemed necessary to hold the lines. As one reads the history of civil service reform, numerous cases will be found in which staunch believers in the merit system have been torn between their belief and their advocacy of certain substantive policies to which one of the parties subscribes. Shortcomings of the merit system are forgiven or even condoned because of the nobility of the larger purposes. It is fairly easy to adopt a philosophy that the end justifies the means, or to say a certain amount of the spoils system is inevitable in politics; both sides do the same thing.

The same forces that operate in the national government are also in effect in the state and the municipal governments. The merit system in the United States has never gained the position of a sacred tradition that neither party can violate with impunity. Where the system is most strongly intrenched, the wise politicians will not make a direct frontal attack but rather will use an encircling movement which ultimately gives them control of the agency administering the system.

Observation suggests that co-operation between the nation and the states, possibly with local governments participating, creates the best media for developing a sound merit system. If the Democratic Party is in control of the national government, its representatives will not want Republicans in control of a state government perverting the merit system to advance their cause at the polls. The members of the dominant party at Washington are likely to appreciate that they cannot legislate solely for states controlled by the opposition, they must legislate for all. Factionalism within the major parties may also help. A United States Senator or Representative may not look with favor on the efforts of a governor, a mayor, or a boss to develop a strong machine by the use of patronage because that machine may want his job at the next election. Within a given state normally controlled by a single party, there may be a state group and a federal group each trying to dominate, each trying to use patronage against the other.

Under such circumstances the merit system may be a good practical compromise. The national government then tends to become a monitor to see that the states observe the system. It writes requirements for a state merit system into its grant-in-aid or tax offset laws, and it will have reason to enforce these laws against states controlled by the minority. In some cases it may be equally anxious to enforce them in states controlled by the party dominant at Washington.

Such laws bring much needed reinforcements to the civil service reformers and others with a concern for clean government. In the absence of such laws, legislators who believe in the merit system frequently in voting have to weigh immediate party advantage against more or less abstract virtue. The civil service reformers have often found only a few upon whom they can rely at all times. The device of making the merit system a condition for federal grants-in-aid or for offsets against federal taxes creates a situation where there are party advantages and disadvantages in many situations, so that abstract virtue has more chance.[1]

After merit system laws are passed and enforced, the technicians have a chance to do the constructive work required to bring well-qualified people into the civil service. It is doubtful whether at any previous time in the nation's history more rapid advance has been made in the introduction of sound techniques than that which occurred after the Social Security Act was amended in 1939 to the effect that state plans to be acceptable to the national board must provide "methods relating to the establishment and maintenance of personnel standards on a merit basis." It was little short of amazing that several states where conditions approached a public scandal should in a few months become the field for great technical advances. It is also doubtful whether any group of administrative personnel has ever made greater contributions to merit system techniques than has the professional group concerned with welfare administration.

[1] In the past it has often seemed as if the "outs" were the great champions of the merit system. If the merit system is to be effective the "ins" must support it.

CHAPTER XXXVII

CONCLUSIONS FROM EXPERIENCE

In Part I of this book the principal American programs relating to relief and social security were broadly described with detail mainly in respect to those parts of the programs that appeared to present issues of real significance. Part II gave for comparative purposes similar descriptions of the proposed plan for Great Britain and of the system adopted by New Zealand. These two plans were selected first because those countries had faced the problem of welding the separate programs that had evolved through the years into a single, universal, comprehensive, and co-ordinated system, and second because they illustrated radically different approaches to many of the problems that arise in framing a sound system of relief and social security. Comparison between the action taken by those countries and what the United States has done thus far seemed to clarify and illustrate the issues which must be considered in an effort to appraise what has been done in the United States and to formulate the policies to govern future action.

Analysis of the material in Parts I and II permitted the presentation in Part III of a series of issues grouped under three headings: social considerations, cost problems, and administrative problems. To each of these issues, which are mutually interrelated, a separate chapter has been devoted. The task in this concluding chapter is to attempt to draw the lessons from the experience that has thus been analyzed and presented.

Conclusions in so detailed and intricate a field as relief and social security can only be drawn in the light of basic fundamental assumptions regarding the rights and liberties of the individual and the relationship of the individual to the state. An assumption of a totalitarian state would lead to conclusions radically different from those which will result if it be assumed that the freedom of the individual and the restriction of the power of the state are to be retained. In the ensuing chapter the assumption will be that the basic principles of the American way of life with respect to these fundamentals are to be preserved, and that the power of the state is to be kept constitutionally circumscribed in the interest of the individual and groups of individuals constituting political minorities.

These fundamental assumptions upon which the conclusions are based fall into two groups: the first deals with the rights of individuals as they have prevailed in the United States, and the second with the position of a social security system in an economy that preserves those rights. The two groups will be considered in turn.

THE RIGHTS OF THE INDIVIDUAL

In the United States the rights of the individual are not infrequently summarized by quoting the familiar passage from the Declaration of Independence: "We hold these truths to be self evident, that all men are created equal, that they are endowed by their Creator with certain inalienable Rights, that among these are Life, Liberty and the pursuit of Happiness."

The pursuit of happiness is necessarily an individual venture. The individual must determine for himself what are the satisfactions of life. Liberty means freedom to pursue these individual objectives so long as that pursuit does not encroach upon the like right of others.

From this basic statement of the rights of the individual in the United States, certain more specific assumptions may be derived that will serve as guiding principles in arriving at conclusions with respect to relief and social security. In connection with their presentation, it should be clearly stated that frequently they affect mainly the degree to which certain things should be done, notably the extent to which the state shall redistribute income through the social security system. The specific assumptions are:

1. In so far as possible, government should permit the individual to go his own way in the pursuit of happiness. It should

interfere with his freedom only in so far as such interference is necessary to protect the rights of others or to secure the funds necessary to support essential activities of government. Restrictions on the liberties of the individual are no less restrictions if they are imposed by a majority proceeding by democratic processes. A transitory majority in a democratic government from the standpoint of a minority may be as tyrannical as any despot, unless the rights of individuals are adequately safeguarded by the Constitution, and the government proceeds with complete respect for that fundamental law.

2. Liberty to pursue happiness requires opportunity to achieve, or attempt to achieve, personal economic independence, free from control by the state so long as the individual proceeds within the law. If this opportunity is to be preserved for the individual, the right of private ownership of productive property, recognized by the Constitution of the United States from the beginning, must be preserved. The personal liberty of the individual will not be great if the state owns or controls the productive property, and the individual must live by working for the state, or an employer controlled by the state, or subsist on such consumer purchasing power as the state has permitted him to save for his own free use.

3. The owner of property must be free to utilize that property as he deems best, provided he stays within the law. The right extends to the use of property either for production or for consumption. A producer has a right to produce for a minority. From the standpoint of the majority, as represented in democratically elected legislatures, such activities of a minority may not be socially useful or far less socially useful than other things the majority would prefer, but if the activity is not socially dangerous, the minority should be free to make their own decisions as to what they want to do, and for what they wish to spend their labor and its products.[1]

4. The pursuit of happiness requires that many avenues to

---

[1] The Constitution, of course, recognizes that the state may have to take the property of an individual for a public purpose but it provides in Amendment V: "No person shall be . . . deprived of life, liberty, or property, without due process of law: nor shall private property be taken for public use, without just compensation."

leadership in the several activities of life shall be kept open and that the state shall not acquire complete control. History suggests that individuals with vision and creative ability have frequently been right in situations where majorities and entrenched public officials have been fundamentally wrong. With freedom of speech and freedom of property the individual has been able to devote himself to the pursuit of his vision, to enlist the support, usually at the outset of a very small minority, and to demonstrate its economic or social soundness. Little in past history suggests that such leadership germinates freely in government, that the man with inspiration can quickly command a majority following, get elected to public office or, if in the classified civil service, convince his official superiors that his idea has merit. If new industries, new services, and new philosophies are to develop, men and women must be free to venture both with their talents and their own resources and to enlist the talents and resources of others who volunteer to join them in the venture. The roads to leadership must be open to them. The state must not take from them the means to venture, in an effort to give them in exchange a high measure of social security.

5. If the avenues to adventure and to ultimate leadership are to be kept open, the state must not itself determine what reward an individual shall receive for the product of his labors nor what he shall do with his income. Under the American system, the individual has been free to determine how his money shall be spent. If someone developed a new enterprise, a new service, or a new philosophy, his reward depended in no small part upon what priority people gave to it in determining their own expenditures or their own action. In the case of new products or new services, it frequently happened that a minority of consumers, the well-to-do with an available margin, gave the new invention or the new service the necessary initial demand and paid the high prices required in the experimental period. A new device thus established has frequently become widely popular and has resulted in a great productive enterprise and great opportunities for employment. This freedom

of consumers to determine priorities by the way they spend their income is a method of proportional voting as to how the activities of the country shall be directed. It is far simpler and far more effective than any scheme of proportional representation that political scientists have conceived to give minority representation in politically chosen legislatures. It is the antithesis of the concept, "From each according to his ability and to each according to his need" and leaves the people free to determine the awards in accordance with their own effective demands. They determine what they want, and the reward of individuals depends upon the degree of popular approval as measured by the way individuals elect to spend their money.[2]

THE PLACE OF SOCIAL SECURITY AND RELIEF

The five assumptions just given deal with the rights of the individual to life, liberty, and the pursuit of happiness. There are two assumptions with respect to the place of social security in the economic and social systems that underlie the detailed conclusions in the present chapter. They are:

1. Social security and relief are not in and of themselves directly productive; they are primarily defensive devices. The constructive devices for preventing want and raising the level of living lie in maintaining and developing the productive capacity of the nation. The individual or group of individuals

[2] From the point of view of experts or of governmental majorities, the people, or considerable numbers of them, may want the wrong things. To use one of Sir William Beveridge's illustrations (*Full Employment in a Free Society*, p. 185): "In a free market economy under pressure of salesmanship the negroes of the Southern States of America have, to a large extent, obtained automobiles and radios and have not obtained good housing, sanitation and medical service." On the basis of American experience one would say that education and not state compulsion is the proper method to induce individuals to want the things that are good for them. American experience with prohibition does not commend the method of determination by transitory political majorities. It should be observed, too, that many people work for the sake of acquiring the things they personally desire. It does not follow that they will work hard to acquire things for which they feel no need, despite the fact that experts and the political majorities think they ought to want and to have them. The pursuit of happiness requires that the individual shall have the opportunity to work for what he personally wishes to attain. The American experience suggests that in influencing demand the gradual education of individuals is preferable to state compulsion both in political theory and in actual practice.

who introduce a new industry or greatly expand the needed output of an old industry do more toward increasing employment and the level of living than do those who merely provide unemployment insurance or reduce the output of needed goods and services for the sake of making employment go round. An assumption specifically rejected in these conclusions is that the United States lacks the capacity and the resourcefulness to increase its levels of production and of living, and that it must surrender to the thought that thousands of persons must in the future be supported from the public treasury by social security payments.

2. For normal persons able and willing to work, a useful job is generally preferable to any kind of benefit. Even if such a benefit has been earned and paid for by the beneficiary through his own labors, it apparently brings less happiness than a worthwhile job, because so commonly it means the end of the productive trail. Those who attain happiness after retirement are apparently those who have attained a new leisure to devote to activities for which they formerly did not have the time or from which the financial return was too small or too uncertain to meet their needs. Retirement, also, frequently means that the venture in pursuit of happiness is largely concluded and that with resignation one must accept the retirement allowance. On the basis of these assumptions, conclusions will be drawn with respect to the issues discussed in Part III.

THE OBJECTIVES OF RELIEF AND SOCIAL INSURANCE

The basic objective of relief and social insurance is to relieve need. Relief of need necessitates some redistribution of income. A social insurance system should, however, go no further in redistributing wealth than is necessary to achieve this primary objective.

In a free society that strives to preserve opportunity and liberty for the individual, it is hard to justify the use of the sovereign power of the state to take the earnings and the property of one citizen to give to another if the one to whom it is given is not in need according to a fairly strict definition.

In the use of the taxing power of the state, a sharp distinction should be drawn between (1) compulsory contributions to render a necessary public service and (2) compulsory contributions to take resources from one citizen to give to another. Use of the power of the state for redistribution of wealth according to a governmentally determined formula in all probability will mean, in a democracy, progressive encroachment by a majority upon the minority, and the growth of two philosophies: (a) that the state owes everyone a good living regardless of the contribution the individual makes to society, and (b) that the able, thrifty, and hard working must support the state and those who would live on grants from the state.

Does this statement imply a conclusion against having the state operate compulsory insurance systems that involve that degree of collectivism necessary to make the principles and mechanisms of insurance applicable? An idea appears to be prevalent in some quarters that social insurance is much like private voluntary insurance except that it is operated by the state, and it is compulsory. It seems wise, therefore, at this point to summarize certain major distinctions between private voluntary insurance and compulsory social insurance as it has been introduced, since these distinctions are vital to these conclusions. Other more detailed consideration of the distinctions will be made later in the present chapter in the discussion of financing.

1. Shall insurance be purchased? In private voluntary insurance, a person does not ordinarily purchase a policy unless (a) he is exposed to the hazard against which he is insuring, and (b) he or someone dependent upon him or to whom he is under obligation should be protected against the risk. In social insurance the government frequently forces the individual to insure though he is little exposed to the hazard insured against and has no beneficiary who would be eligible to take in the event of the happening of certain of the contingencies covered. Thus O.A.S.I. forces all to insure and charges all the covered workers the same premium, despite the wide variations among them with respect to eligible prospective beneficiaries.

2. What premiums shall be charged? In private voluntary insurance, competitive forces lead to classification of policyholders according to the degree of risk and to the establishment of premium rates fixed in accordance with that degree of risk. As a result all the insured in a given class pay substantially the same premium for the same protection. There is no greater degree of collectivism or of redistribution of wealth than is necessary to apply the principle of insurance. In social insurance, compulsion is substituted for voluntary action and for competition. The government, using its sovereign power to tax, is under no obligation to relate the amount of premium to the degree of risk and to the amount of protection given. It can, as it does in O.A.S.I., charge the employee in the upper brackets far more in relation to the cost of benefits promised than it charges the employees in the lower brackets. It introduces a degree of redistribution of wealth which goes far beyond that minimum necessary to give application to the principles of insurance.

3. Who supplies the money for benefits? In private voluntary insurance, the policyholders supply the money to pay benefits.[3] Some of it may go into a reserve which earns interest, but the interest is earned by the policyholders' money. In social insurance a very substantial part of the money to pay benefits is supplied other than by premiums paid by the insured. It may come in part, as in O.A.S.I. from a tax on the employer, with a possibility that a very substantial burden will ultimately fall on the general taxpayer. Under the proposed British plan a high percentage will come from the general treasury. Thus, social insurance gets a substantial part of its revenues from taxes levied against persons or agencies not directly benefited by the system. This device of financing through taxation permits (a) the payment of benefits greatly in excess of what the contributions of the insured would have purchased, and

---

[3] In stock companies the money to pay benefits may come in some instances from the investments of the stockholders in the company; but obviously a stock company cannot long continue unless it gets the money to pay benefits from the premiums of policyholders.

(b) the redistribution of wealth according to a governmentally determined formula.

4. Are reserves necessary? In private voluntary insurance all the money to pay benefits must be put up by the insured. It must be so handled that when a benefit is payable the carrier has on hand the money to pay the benefits. Thus the safety of the insured depends on the maintenance of adequate reserves determined on a sound actuarial basis. In social insurance there is generally no attempt to make the insured pay all the costs. Part is to be made up by taxation of persons or agencies not directly benefited. Politically, if not legally, the government is liable for making good any deficit. The subject of reserves in relation to finance will be treated in more detail later in this chapter. Here it is sufficient to point out that the solvency of voluntary insurance rests on adequate premiums and adequate reserves, whereas the solvency of government systems rests on the sovereign power of the state to tax.

These differences between private voluntary insurance and social insurance show that, in devising social insurance systems, the government is not bound by the principles and practices that control private insurance. It can depart from them in such degree as it sees fit, for it has the power of compulsion; it can levy far less than actual cost against the insured, and it can force other taxpayers to make up the difference. Both in its benefit formula and its methods of distributing costs, it can go as far as it sees fit in effecting a redistribution of wealth. Thus the fact that a system is labeled social insurance does not mean it involves no more collectivism than is essential to give effect to the principles and methods of insurance. It may be designed in part to take money from some to give to others without reference to the degree of need. It is this deliberate use of the taxing power to effect a redistribution of wealth regardless of need that appears to do violence to the principle that the government should not interfere further than is necessary with the freedom of the individual to use his earnings and his property as he sees fit within the limits of the law.

THE NATURE OF NEED

A person should not be defined as being in need if he himself or a relative normally responsible for him has sufficient resources to support him in accordance with a very strictly defined minimum standard of health and decency. This standard should be somewhat higher than a minimum of subsistence, but not greatly higher. In the case of children and adults who may later become fully self-supporting members of the economy, it should be high enough to enable them to continue educational and other preparation for effective future service. Extra allowances in such situations should, however, be conditional upon the effective use of time and effort. Well-designed public educational and other services, with scholarships or other grants given under rules and regulations in the light of the facts in a particular case, are vastly superior to money allowances based on averages and turned over to the individuals to use as they see fit.

The amount of money that is necessary to maintain the strictly defined minimum health and decency standard should be determined on the basis of actual facts regarding the cost and levels of living prevailing in the community in which the persons in need are living. The variations in the costs and levels of living in the United States are too great to warrant the establishment of a single monetary standard applicable to the nation as a whole. Even in some states a differentiation in standards appears necessary to allow for the differences between great urban centers and rural communities.

Relief and social security are not suitable devices to raise the level of living in states which have low levels of living. The necessity for raising the level of living in such areas calls for increasing the efficiency and earning capacity of the people either where they are or by encouraging migration to other sections where they will have greater opportunity. In this connection another distinction must be made. It is one thing for the national government to take funds from the wealthier states to help develop educational facilities and opportunities in the poorer states, because educational facilities are essential to developing the efficiency of the people. It is another matter to take income from the people in the wealthier states, with their higher living costs and standards, to give it to individuals in the poorer states to enable them to enjoy benefits higher than they have been able to earn by their own efforts. Improvement in productive capacity belongs primarily in the constructive field and not in the defensive field of relief and social security.

A rigidly established minimum health and decency standard would put a floor under the individual below which he could not fall without becoming eligible for assistance from the public treasury. On the other hand, he would definitely be placed on notice that if he desires to live at a higher standard or to have those dependent on him live at a higher level, it is incumbent on him to make provision by his own efforts. Insurance to give more than this minimum would have to be voluntary insurance. Included as voluntary insurance are the retirement systems developed by employers, public or private, as essential parts of their compensation systems. If forfeitures under such systems are prohibited by law, these systems will be an important element in the provisions for voluntary protection against risks.

THE MEANS TEST

Unless the state is to pay benefits to persons regardless of their need, a means test is an essential part of a relief and social security system. Under modern conditions, however, a means test may easily be stripped of the features which made it so objectionable when used in connection with the old poor laws. Today a very substantial proportion of the workers of the country are required to make annual reports on their income to the national government and in many cases also to the state government. A modern means-test system could have as its basic document the income reports. Persons with low incomes would not be free from the obligation to make a report. Instead, persons with incomes below specified figures could be required to make a report on a special form which would call for the essential facts not only regarding income but also regarding family responsibilities. If these reports revealed a level of living below the minimum standard, the allegation would be verified by suitable investigation, and if established as fact, the individual and those dependent upon him would be eligible for public assistance.

Part of the hostility toward the means test arose from other things not necessarily connected with it. Among them were (1) discretionary grants, (2) absence of precise rules and regulations, (3) absence of legislative rights, (4) inadequate appropriations, and (5) harsh and unsympathetic administration. None of these features is a necessary and inescapable feature of a means test.

A conclusion in favor of a modern means test calls for a clear statement of certain broad principles that apparently should govern in devising such a test. Immediate need results basically from the cash position of the individual or the family. An individual or a family is in need of assistance when cash cannot be obtained to provide the necessaries of life. From both an administrative and a humanitarian standpoint, it is undesirable that an individual or a family should be required completely to exhaust all available resources before becoming eligible for public assistance. In many cases it is highly advantageous to have the services of the public welfare agency, if not the money grants themselves, available before all resources are exhausted and heavy debts incurred. Thus the legislation for a modern means test should make the individual or the family eligible for assistance when and if the resources fall below a sum, or a schedule of sums, set forth in the law. What sums should be allowable should be determined upon the basis of sound research.

The objective of the state in dealing with persons in need should be restoration of individuals to economic and social independence in so far as such restoration is possible. A modern means-test system should be designed to further such restoration. If restoration is the objective, the means test should not require that the individual or the family dispose of all property, owned in whole or in part, before becoming eligible. Property owned may be an important element in that restoration. Its value as a factor in rehabilitation may greatly exceed the amount of money which it would bring at a forced sale. Proceeds of a forced sale are likely to be materially less than what would have to be spent to replace the property when and if the family or the individual is again moving toward economic and social independence. The means-test law, therefore, should permit the ownership of certain classes of property within limits and the possession of specified amounts of income, without destroying eligibility for sufficient benefits to make up the budget deficit.

The question of loans and liens is involved in designing a means-test system. Three fairly typical situations will be cited to illustrate the nature of the issue:

1. An elderly couple own their house and its furnishings, but they do not have income enough to pay taxes and to make minimum essential repairs. Should the welfare agency pay the taxes and the cost of essential repairs, permit the couple to continue to live in the house, and take a lien on it for the money thus advanced?

2. A primary breadwinner responsible for a wife and minor children is disabled. He has been carrying a life insurance policy for their benefit which has a cash surrender value. Should he be required to take the cash surrender value and use it for current maintenance, or should the agency have authority to advance the money to keep the policy in force, taking a lien on it for the sum thus advanced? If the man dies, the amount of the policy, less the advance will be available for his dependents. If he recovers he will have either to repay the advance or have it remain as a lien against the policy. The lien would be recorded with the insurance company and would take priority over other claims.

3. A family in need because of unemployment or disability still owes money on necessary articles, reasonably suitable to its ordinary economic status, which were being purchased under an installment contract. The equity in the goods is substantial. Should the agency have authority to advance the money

necessary to prevent their being repossessed by the seller, taking a lien on the property for the amount so advanced?

If the objective of a means-test system is to alleviate the suffering that comes from want and, in so far as possible to rehabilitate, a fairly wide use should be made of advances from public funds secured by liens. An advantage which a well-designed means-test system has over an insurance system paying fixed money benefits is that it permits adjustment to the great diversity of individual situations. If a loan transaction will further the immediate interests of the beneficiary and apparently also the long-run interests of the public, a loan suited to the particular case is preferable to a fixed money payment which may not meet the actual situation.

Liens on the property of old-age beneficiaries have a priority over the rights of such of their children or other heirs as are no longer dependent upon them for support. A common practice under a modern means-test system is not to enforce a lien against a home so long as there are eligible dependents who need it for shelter. Another common practice is to notify the children or other prospective heirs who are not living with or dependent upon the old people that a lien will be taken on the house for either all or part of the sums to be advanced. The children or heirs then have the opportunity to supply the money required to support the old people or to permit the liens to go against the property.

A means-test system necessitates establishing definite rules regarding the responsibility of children for the support of parents who are in need. In New Zealand, as has been noted, all children who are earning pay 5 per cent of their earnings to the social security fund, from which benefits will be paid to their parents should the parents be in need according to the legal definitions of need. Under such a means-test system, there is no further legal liability on children to support their parents.

Another device which has merit is to determine the responsibility of children upon the basis of their capacity to pay as measured by the income tax. If the child has no income in excess of personal exemptions for himself and immediate dependents, there is no liability to contribute for the support of parents. If the child has income subject to taxation, liability is determined by the amount of that income above exemptions.

The question should be raised as to whether the amount of public money required for the support of elderly parents could not be reduced by liberalizing the income tax laws with respect to deductions for contributions toward their support. The income tax laws might be so drafted as to encourage children to make an annual contribution. Contributions from each of several children, although not large in individual amount, might make a total big enough to remove the necessity for assistance from the public treasury. From an emotional standpoint, such contributions would appear preferable to grants from public funds. As the income tax laws now stand, children who contribute a minor part of the cost of maintaining an elderly parent cannot deduct that payment from their income tax, but they are being taxed for old-age assistance payments for others.

COVERAGE

Coverage should be universal. There are persons whose conduct has been so anti-social that they are held in penal or correctional institutions. Since they are presumably receiving support while in custody, they themselves would not be eligible for assistance. Those dependent on them would be eligible if they were in need according to the established standard. There are also persons who are lazy, shiftless, and irresponsible, and others whose habits are at least partially the cause of their difficulties. Neither they nor their dependents would be ineligible, but in return for their benefits they would be required to accept guidance and counsel from qualified public officials whose objective would be rehabilitation. The children of such families would be the concern of these officers.

HAZARDS TO BE COVERED

The essential question is whether an individual or a family has access to sufficient resources for maintenance according to a low and strictly defined minimum standard of health and decency. What particular hazard caused the need is not the issue upon which eligibility for public assistance should turn. Causes may be of vital importance with respect to what should be done to remedy the situation. The remedy may be either in general constructive economic and social legislative action or in constructive case work with the individual, the family, or the neighborhood. It is impossible to accept the view, however, that an innocent dependent should be given aid if deprived of normal support from one cause and denied it if the loss was due to another. It is even more difficult to believe that a dependent not in need should receive a no-means test benefit because his father was covered by a certain form of social insurance paid for in part by funds other than his own, while a similar child actually in need is not systematically provided for at all. Such discrimination is introduced by legislation, often on grounds of administrative convenience or because of the power of pressure groups. Under some circumstances, which will not be discussed here, the victims of certain hazards may be entitled to a somewhat larger benefit than the victims of some other hazard. That does not mean, however, that the victims of these other hazards should be excluded from eligibility. The general conclusion is that the basic system should provide benefits for all cases of need regardless of the hazard that caused the need.

THE SIZE OF THE BENEFITS

The general rule should be that the amount given as a benefit should not exceed the amount required to bring the recipient to the minimum health and decency standard. The New Zealand system where it uses the means test has much to commend it. It fixes two levels, (1) a maximum benefit and (2) a maximum allowable income of personal resources plus benefits. Under this system an individual with nothing gets the maximum benefit. If his actual income equals or exceeds the maximum of allowable benefit plus income, he gets nothing. If in need, he gets full benefit up to the point where benefit and available private resources equal the allowable maximum; above that point benefits are reduced as available private income increases until they disappear entirely at the point where private resources alone reach the allowable maximum. Under such a system the incentive to work and save is preserved to a very substantial degree, and the person who saves gets advantage from his efforts.

DEPENDENTS

Need is obviously directly related to the number and type of dependents. The single man or the single woman with no dependents presents a very different problem than the married man upon whom rests the direct responsibility for providing for a wife and three children. Any device is to be viewed with skepticism that attempts to deal with such situations on the basis of statistical averages or assumptions as to averages. The individual case is the only thing which can be dealt with intelligently. Who must be fed, clothed, and provided with shelter according to a strict minimum standard of health and decency? Obviously people. When the taxpayers of the country are called upon to contribute the cost, they should not complain too much if payments are made according to demonstrated need of real individuals. They may have cause to complain if a person not in need and with no dependents gets a large benefit under a compulsory social insurance system because he earned well during his working life, whereas a person actually in need and with several dependents gets very little either because he did not earn very much, or because he was not sufficiently fortunate to belong to a class that was insured, or to remain in such a class long enough to become fully insured.

COSTS

Conclusions are necessarily materially influenced by the question of costs. No attempt has been made in the present book to give precise estimates as to what the cost of a universal, comprehensive, and co-ordinated social security system operated without use of a means test would be. By the use of data from the 1940 *Census of Population*, calculations have been made as to what the range of costs would have been had such a system been in effect in 1940. However, a means test was used with respect to children's allowances. As is customary in this type of work, different assumptions were used, one giving a possible low, one a medium, and the third a high. The range resulting was an annual benefit expenditure of from 7.6 billion dollars to 16.8 billion dollars. Because of the aging of the population, which is taking place, consideration was given as to its effect on costs. An allowance only for changes in the cost of old-age benefits gave a range from 9.4 billion dollars to 20.5 billion dollars for the year 2000. Figures for the proposed no-means test British system, corrected solely for differences in size of the total population, gave a figure of about 10 billion dollars for 1975 and, corrected for differences both in size and cost of living, a figure of 15 billions. Actuarial data with respect to the future cost of the present system of old-age and sur-vivors insurance that applies to only about half of the gain-fully employed workers gave a range of between 3 billion dollars and 6 billion dollars for the year 2000.

One cannot read the literature on social insurance systems without appreciating that their social and economic utility may be almost completely destroyed by changes in the level of prices and wages. An upward movement of prices and wages does not prevent promised benefits from being paid; it does prevent the beneficiaries from getting the necessary food, clothing, shelter, and care by spending the money they receive from the social insurance system. If the government commits itself to pay high cost social security benefits in the future, it will almost unquestionably pay the promised number of dollars. Political forces will not permit it to do otherwise. It cannot permit a universal fund to go bankrupt. The only politically feasible solution to meet serious financial difficulties if they arise is, therefore, to inflate.

METHODS OF FINANCING

Relief and social security should be financed out of ear-marked special taxes, with a universal flat income tax with no exemptions the preferred, although not necessarily the exclusive, tax.

The tax on employers based on pay rolls should be abolished for three main reasons: (1) it is a tax on employment, (2) it has no necessary relationship to capacity to pay, and (3) it may tend to be shifted to consumers in the form of higher prices than would be charged were there no such tax. The tax system should encourage rather than discourage expanding employment.

This recommendation does not mean that an individual, firm or corporation would entirely escape taxation for relief and social security on the ground that the individual, firm, or corporation is an employer. It would mean that the individual, firm, or corporation would pay on the basis of income. The employers with the same capacity would pay the same amount regardless of the part that labor costs played in their business expenses. The employer with high labor costs and low capital costs would pay no more than the employer with low labor costs and high capital costs.

Wage and salaried workers would still have deductions made from their pay envelopes to pay the costs of social security and relief. There would, however, be several significant differences from the present deductions for old-age and survivors insurance or for the general income tax.

1. The tax would apply to the entire income and not only to the first $250 a month as in O.A.S.I.

2. There would be no deductions for dependents as in the case of the general income tax. A low-paid worker might at the very time he was paying the tax be in receipt of assistance under the social security system because his resources were inadequate to support his family in accordance with the legally established minimum.

3. Although these taxes might be called social security contributions, they would be taxes pure and simple. They would have no relationship to insurance premiums for the amount of tax would bear no relationship to the amount of benefit or the degree of hazard. This tax would be a welfare tax and would not

attempt in any way to disguise the facts that social security and relief are in essence welfare functions and that people who have must be called upon to pay the cost of benefits for those who have not.

Workers other than those who work for salaries and wages would pay the income tax at the same rate as salary and wage workers. All classes of workers now excluded from taxation for old-age and survivors insurance would pay.

Persons with income from savings, investments, and so on would pay, even the widow or the orphan who at the very time the tax was collected might be receiving benefits under the social security system.

The major reasons for recommending this form of taxation may be briefly summarized:

1. Every citizen should be periodically reminded of the fact that social security benefits involve heavy expenditures of tax-collected funds. The financial policy should be to couple all proposals to increase benefits with a proposal to increase the rate of the earmarked special tax by an amount sufficient to pay the additional costs. The desirability of making the people aware of costs leads to the recommendation of the special earmarked income tax with no exemptions. It is of course true that with respect to persons of low-income, the actual receipts will perhaps not equal the cost of collection and these taxpayers may currently receive more in benefits than they pay in taxes. Exemptions would, however, prevent these taxpayers from being aware of costs and would probably give rise to a movement to increase the exemptions progressively.

2. Many students of social security maintain that the payment of contributions by the prospective beneficiaries is psychologically desirable. It makes the beneficiary feel that he has paid at least part of the cost and therefore takes as of right, and it perhaps lessens the chance that the legislature will regard the payments as pure gratuities. This point of view again leads to a preference for an earmarked income tax with no exemptions.

3. The objective of social security and relief is to banish want in the sense in which want has been defined. A system designed to achieve this purpose must be universal, comprehensive, and co-ordinated. The simplest and most direct way to achieve this purpose appears to be to tax all persons with income, at a flat rate so fixed that on the average it will produce a sum sufficient to bring all persons who are in want up to the very strictly defined minimum standard of health and decency. No other system of taxation will give more complete coverage.

This proposed system of taxation, it will be noted, completely eliminates the concepts borrowed from private voluntary insurance, although anyone who so desires may call the special income tax payments social security contributions. Earlier in the present chapter, the distinctions between private voluntary insurance and social insurance were discussed. It was there pointed out that it would be necessary to return to that subject and treat it in more detail with respect to finance.

The objections to the introduction of the concepts of private voluntary insurance into social security fall into two groups, the first relates to the unfortunate effect on the system itself and the second to the possibly disastrous future effect on public finance in general. The two groups will be treated in turn.

There are two major bad effects within the system itself:

1. Under private insurance the right to a benefit is contingent upon the payment of the necessary premium. The system can operate in no other way because the premiums supply the money from which benefits are paid. Carried over into a social security system, this principle means that to be entitled to a benefit the insured must have paid the required premiums for a specified length of time. The length of time is arbitrarily determined by the government, since the system does not necessarily depend on premiums for all its benefit payments. The poorest people in the country, the ones who are most in need, are the ones who cannot pay the premiums with the regularity required under the system, and hence they are the ones who are either not covered or who do not remain covered long enough to attain the insured status. Under the

old-age and survivors insurance system, there will be many who will forfeit such premiums as they have paid because they have not paid a sufficient number to acquire an insured status. Among them will be the women who work for a few years before marriage, the marginal worker who cannot get steady employment except in a time of labor shortage, and the man or woman who is permanently disabled before attaining the insured status.

2. Under private voluntary insurance, every insured person gets protection for his premiums and, broadly speaking, all persons in the same class get equal protection per dollar of premium. To create a resemblance to private voluntary insurance, the social insurance system must appear to give every participant who attains an insured status some benefit or some protection for his premium. It is, however, generally designed to effect a redistribution of income that goes beyond the mere pooling of risks that is inherent in insurance. For social purposes the system provides substantially more per dollar of premium to the low-paid workers than to the better-paid workers. If, as under the proposed British plan, all pay the same for the same benefit then the redistribution is affected through the general taxes.

The fact is inescapable that the people with income must be taxed to supply the social security benefits for those who have insufficient means to supply their own. If this fact be recognized, together with the fact that benefits should be paid to all who are below a reasonable minimum standard, it is unnecessary to camouflage the situation by attempting to make social insurance resemble private voluntary insurance.

Perhaps the major danger of applying the concepts of private voluntary insurance to social security lies in the nature of the problem of financing old-age benefits. This danger is so important that the nature of the financial problem should be restated in this concluding chapter.

1. A person cannot be insured unless he has paid the necessary premiums.

2. Since the payment of premiums is a prerequisite, an insurance system must at the outset be made up exclusively of

persons who are in active service or, in other words, are earning money from which the premiums can be paid.

3. In an old-age retirement system, the persons who are in the active service and can pay premiums, if arranged by age, form a pyramid. At the apex of the period are those—relatively few in number—who are approaching the retirement age. At the base are those—relatively large in number—who have many years to serve, say 40 to 45, before they will be eligible for old-age benefits. This distribution results from fundamental forces including the mortality rate, the disability rate, and the rate of growth of the population.

4. The number of pensioners in such a system starts at zero and increases every year thereafter for many years. Successive classes of active workers pass to the pension rolls, there to join the survivors of classes which had passed to the pension rolls in earlier years. Not until some 80 years has passed is the system under full pension load or, in other words, until there is something approaching a permanent balance between the number of active members of the system and the number of retired members who are drawing the maximum benefits possible under the system.

5. Since the system starts with no load at all, and since there are no pensioners at all to balance the premium paying members, payments into the fund in the early years vastly exceed all current requirements for cash to pay benefits. The cash surpluses are so great that persons who are not familiar with the financial nature of such systems believe that reductions of premiums or increases in benefits are entirely warranted by these surpluses.

The tendency for great apparent surpluses to develop in the early years of either a life insurance or an old-age annuity system wrecked many early ventures in this field. In some instances both the insurers and the policyholders were entirely innocent, merely ignorant of the nature of the natural forces with which they were dealing. In some cases the development was sinister. The promoters could entice uninformed people to buy policies by promising high benefits at low cost, take as a profit a substantial part of the apparent cash surpluses that inevitably develop in the early years, even in an unsound system, and then leave the policyholders with a bankrupt company unable to pay the promised benefits.

To protect the policyholders, to prevent benevolent but uninformed people from starting unsound systems, and to circumvent the fraudulent, the states adopted laws to regulate private voluntary insurance. Under these laws the insurance companies had to develop and maintain adequate reserves on a sound actuarial basis; the reserves could only be invested in approved securities or properties; and the states regularly examined the financial position of the companies to make sure they were financially sound. If a company was not financially sound, steps had to be taken to make it so or it was liquidated.

Obviously a private voluntary insurance company could not develop and maintain the required legal or actuarial reserves without charging a sufficient premium for the insurance sold. Gone were the days when the benevolent but uninformed or the unscrupulous could promise large benefits for premiums which would not pay their cost.

The fact must be frankly faced that a government may itself establish an old-age retirement system with a premium and benefit structure which would be illegal if used by a private voluntary insurance company. The present national old-age and survivors insurance system would be promptly liquidated as unsound if the standards governing private voluntary insurance were applied to it. But it must be remembered that governmental social insurance is something entirely different from private voluntary insurance and is not to be judged by the same standards. There is no essential reason why any of the forms or practices of private voluntary insurance should be carried over into social insurance, although the word insurance has pleasing and acceptable suggestions.

LEVEL PREMIUMS AND ACTUARIAL RESERVES

In actuarially sound retirement systems used by private employers or by governments and in the purchase of individual, deferred annuities from private voluntary insurance companies, the common practice is for the prospective beneficiary to pay a definite amount each pay day in a retirement system or quarterly, semi-annually, or annually under a private contract. The amount paid is either a fixed number of dollars under a private contract or a fixed percentage of salary or wages under a retirement system. The amount of the premium is so calculated actuarially that placed in a reserve and invested at compound interest it will, when the beneficiary reaches the retirement age, provide an annuity of approximately the amount deemed expedient and practicable by the framers of the system or by the purchaser of the deferred annuity from the private company. This statement is perhaps considerably oversimplified and is subject to numerous qualifications. With these technicalities it is not here necessary to deal. The essential point is that the costs of the old-age pension are met by regular periodic payments or on an installment plan and that the money, as part of a reserve, is invested at interest until the insurance company or carrier has to begin paying benefits to the retired worker.

The question which is of concern here is whether these twin devices of approximately level payments and an actuarial reserve, characteristic of sound private finance, are essential to a social insurance system.

It has already been noted that they are not necessary for the protection of the insured in a national social insurance system, since his safety is at least as well protected by the promise to pay given by the government to a politically powerful block of citizens. His safety lies in the power of the government to tax, to borrow, or even to print money. Neither actuarially adequate premiums nor actuarial reserves are essential. Are they desirable?

The strongest argument in favor of actuarially adequate, reasonably level premiums for social security is that they bring home to all concerned the actual cost of the promised benefits. Thus they lessen the chance that present-day legislatures will attempt to commit future generations to excessive payments.

With respect to the maintenance of an actuarial reserve, the position of a government in operating a social security system providing wide coverage is entirely unlike that of a private voluntary insurance company in insuring a relatively small number of policyholders.

A private insurance company invests its reserves in approved securities or makes loans on first mortgages. The nature of the transactions are such that individuals or corporations who thus borrow from the private insurance company reserves are under contractual obligation to pay the agreed upon interest and in general to repay the principal. The laws regulating investment of reserve funds are such that the reserve funds may only be loaned (1) to productive enterprises which will probably be able to earn the money to pay the necessary interest and to repay the principal or (2) to governments, national, state, or local, which can pay interest and principal through exercising their power to tax. Thus, in the main, the reserves of a private insurance company are invested in obligations to pay given by substantial agencies and often there is added security in the nature of a mortgage lien on physical properties.

In a private insurance company, moreover, there is relatively little overlapping between (1) the individuals and organizations that are under obligation to pay the insurance company interest and principal on reserve funds, and (2) the policyholders who may ultimately have matured claims against the company. Under this arrangement one class, the policyholders, have through the insurance carrier valid legal claims against another class, the substantial enterprises and governments that have borrowed from the insurance reserves.

The American practice with respect to the reserves of the old-age and survivors insurance system, the railroad retirement and unemployment systems, and the general unemployment compensation system is radically different. The national government has been spending the money as it has been received from these social security taxes and contributions for governmental expenses. In return for these funds, it has placed government obligations to pay in the portfolios of the social security reserves. As interest has become due on these obligations, the government has paid the interest by depositing in the portfolio additional government obligations.

What are these obligations of the government that are held in the reserves? They are obligations to pay in the future. When the time comes that the interest on the reserves or the principal of the reserve itself is required to pay maturing claims, the government in office at that time will have to determine how it will raise the money to pay its obligations held by the reserve. Its possibilities will be to tax the working generation of that day to raise the necessary money, to borrow, or to reduce the value of the currency. A governmental promise to pay in the future is not a device to lessen the burden on future generations, it is a device that transfers burdens from the present to the future.

If one really wants to know what burden is being passed on to future generations, one will add to the government obligations held outside the Treasury by the general public the government obligations held by the social security reserves in the Treasury. This total represents the public debt for which the future generations are responsible. In this summary chapter the question of transfers of government obligations from the general holders to the reserve funds or vice versa will not be considered. Such transfers affect the immediate cash position of the government, but they do not affect the true total public debt with which succeeding generations will be concerned.

In social insurance, moreover, there is no such separation between the persons who owe the money borrowed from the reserve, and the people who are entitled to benefits as characterizes private insurance. The greater the degree of coverage in a social security system the more the two groups become merged. The people owe the money which is to be used to pay the people the promised benefits.

Despite all the confusing and expensive elaboration of contributions and reserves, the future generations will still confront the problem, "How are we to raise the money?" It is impossible for anyone to forecast with accuracy whether obligations of the magnitude involved in the social security system can readily be met 40, 60, or 80 years hence. It is possible, however, to point out a number of factors in the domestic economy which will have an important bearing upon the ability to sustain the social insurance system.

First, the maintenance of the system will depend upon the continued ability and willingness of workers to shoulder the financial costs involved. Up to the present, it has been widely assumed that a substantial proportion of the large ultimate costs involved will come out of taxes paid by the wealthy classes. If the goal of progressively broader and more equal distribution of income is realized, it follows inevitably that in the future a steadily increasing proportion of the tax load will have to be borne by the middle- and lower-income groups.

Second, the nation's capacity and willingness to meet social security obligations will depend upon the magnitude and insistency of other competing claims against the national income. So long as available revenues are not superabundant, choices have to be made between the more urgent and important and the less urgent and important.

One part of expenditures for relief and social security is obviously among the most important and urgent, namely, that which goes to relieve want. Such expenditures occupy a position of extremely high priority, perhaps of first priority.

The second part of the expenditures for social security is, however, in a different category. These expenditures go to persons who are not in actual need according to a reasonably strict definition of need and are given to insure them at least a minimum income without the humiliation or embarrassment of a means test. There is a real issue as to whether such expenditures have a high priority in comparison with those made for other government services.

Certain governmental expenditures, namely those for general government, current national defense, protection and regulation, interest on the public debt, and veterans' benefits, must be met. Expenditures for the promotion of economic development, if wisely made, increase the productivity of the nation and in many cases furnish employment. A high level of employment materially lessens need and reduces the necessity for the old, the handicapped, or the partially dependent to depend on social security benefits. Expenditures for education, public health, and sanitation contribute directly to the efficiency of the individual and to the productivity of the nation.

To repeat, in concluding the consideration of costs and finances, the success of a social insurance system depends upon the attainment of a reasonably stable level of prices, or better, a declining level of prices. If prices should rise over the years, the purchasing power of the money benefits received would obviously decline. A great inflation of prices would virtually wreck the system.

It is not here contended that such an outcome is inevitable, but the possibilities of inflation are such as to warrant caution in the creation of future obligations beyond the requirements for the alleviation of real want. To go beyond that may render impossible the attainment of the primary goal. Each generation of active workers will have to support the dependents of that generation. It would therefore seem wise to substitute a simple system under which the workers of today would support the dependents of today from current funds.

CO-ORDINATION IN SOCIAL SECURITY AND RELIEF

In the United States at present, responsibility for planning, financing, and administering relief and social security is divided, purely by happenstance, among the three levels of government, national, state, and local. It is inconceivable that a universal, comprehensive, and co-ordinated system could be developed with responsibility and authority thus divided. There are apparently two practical solutions, namely:

1. To transfer to the national government full and undivided responsibility and authority over relief and social security.

2. To operate relief and social security entirely upon a federal-state co-operative basis through federal grants to the states. Under such a system the national government would establish certain minimum standards with which the several states would

have to comply to secure federal aid. The states would themselves administer the system, under the minimum necessary federal supervision to secure compliance with national requirements. They would be free at their own expense to go as much above the federal minimum standards as they might see fit.

Nationalization of the functions of relief and social security appears undesirable in the United States for eight major reasons:

1. Relief and social security necessitate the taking of money from one group and giving it to another, not in the form of a generalized public service believed to be in the public interest, but as money which the recipients are practically free to do with as they will. Inherent in these functions is the danger of political corruption in its worst form, the corruption of the electorate itself.

2. Among the several states of the union, there are wide variations with respect to such factors as natural resources, wealth, capacity to pay taxes, the cost of living, and the customary levels of living. Certain states are retarded, not necessarily because of lack of natural resources or opportunity to produce the goods and services essential to the maintenance of a satisfactory level of living. The solution of their difficulties lies in increasing their productivity both through better utilization of their natural resources and better education and training of those of their people who are retarded. This objective is not to be attained by giving these people relief and social security benefits beyond the point necessary to prevent want. They may need federal assistance for a time for education and publc health and the conversion of their economy to activities that will be more in balance with present-day requirements. The retarded people in such areas should be afforded an opportunity to work their way out of their present difficulties. They should not be encouraged to use their voting power to secure relief payments and social security benefits at the expense of other sections of the country.

3. Because of differences in the cost and levels of living, there are substantial differences among the states with respect to the

number of dollars required as relief or social security benefits to give a satisfactory minimum standard. If the national government has exclusive jurisdiction over relief and social security, citizens living in the great centers of population in the northern areas of the country will naturally demand that relief and social security benefits be high enough to afford them protection. If the national government pays high benefits in these areas, the representatives of other areas will want like benefits for their areas. Few elected representatives from the low-benefit areas could survive if they failed to work and vote to eliminate discrimination. Political forces would operate toward uniform national rates at the level necessary for the high cost-of-living areas.

4. Since the states with relatively little capacity to pay would be contributing little toward the costs, they would be little influenced by the resulting taxes. Someone else would be paying the bills.

5. Under the American form of government a single political party is always in control of the executive branch of the national government. The policy determining officers, who direct and control the supposedly nonpolitical permanent civil servants, are appointed by the President or by other officers subordinate to him. It is almost inconceivable that the political party in control of the executive branch of the government would abstain from using the obvious power to influence voters that is inherent in the functions of social security and relief.

6. Social security and relief administration extend to every place in the United States where people live. National administration would mean that federal employees would be in contact with all the people in the country. It would be almost inevitable that they or their superiors would be working for the success of the party in control of the executive branch of the government.

7. The administration of social security and relief call for the existence of a government of review and appeal which is superior to and has authority over the particular government that is carrying on these functions. If relief and social security are

nationalized, there will be no government to which an appeal can be taken.

8. The question of what the nation can afford for relief and social security is a relative matter and depends on what it will spend for other functions, such as education and public health. If relief and social security are nationalized, there will develop strong new arguments for nationalizing education and health so that all can be co-ordinated and developed in accordance with a big central plan, centrally controlled.

For these reasons nationalization of relief and social security appears highly unwise. Instead, it seems much more promising to have the national government through grant-in-aid legislation influence the states to provide universal, comprehensive, and co-ordinated protection according to a very low minimum standard. This standard could well be based on the amount required in those states which have the lowest costs and levels of living. The standard should be designed not to raise the level of living possible through benefits above that which persons in those states can achieve if fully employed at the prevailing wages for employees in the lowest wage classes in that locality. The position is not taken that it is not highly desirable that the low wages prevailing in these states and localities should be raised. The position is that relief and social security benefits paid to persons in need should not, as a rule, be higher than the wages which they could earn through employment in occupations for which they are fitted in the communities where they dwell. Raising wages and the levels of living calls for constructive social and economic action and is not to be achieved by making relief and social security benefits more attractive and more advantageous than wages earned through labor.

It should be clearly stated that the minimum standard required by the national government would presumably be inadequate and unsatisfactory in states which had higher costs of living and higher wage levels. These states, however, have the resources and the tax-paying capacity to provide higher levels of relief and social security benefits if the voters of those states desire to provide them for their citizens. The national government would say, in effect, to the states: "The national government will pay to you in behalf of each resident of your state who is in need according to national definitions exactly the same amount in dollars that it will pay on behalf of any resident of any other state who is likewise in need. If your state regards the amount thus made available for the relief of need as inadequate, it may go as far as it likes in supplementing the grant at its own expense. The national government will not force the state to pay more, nor will it tax the residents of the state more for relief and social security than is necessary to pay the uniform minimum benefit throughout the nation."

Examination of the available data with respect to the capacity of the states to pay suggests that the national grant-in-aid legislation should provide a measure of equalization. To provide equalization, the national government would supply a very substantial part of the minimum benefit. The poorest states would be required to pay a small percentage, only enough to discourage them from padding the relief and social security rolls. Other states would be required to pay from their own funds exactly the same percentage of the fixed federal grant. If they chose to pay higher benefits, they would pay them entirely from state or local funds or from the two combined.

In some states there is wide variation between the rural areas and the large cities with respect to wage levels and costs of living, and possibly also with respect to ability to support the necessary welfare functions of government. The situations do not conform to a single standard pattern. There is no single standard device to apply in every state. Every state would have a fairly wide range of possible choices. Each state legislature should answer for itself the question of what it will do, what device it will use. Each resident of the state who is in need will be entitled to the minimum grant toward which the national government would contribute. Whether more should be given and how it should be given would be for the states to decide, since they would be paying for the extra benefits with state or local funds or the two combined.

DIVISION OF ADMINISTRATION

Under a conditional grant-in-aid system, direct responsibility for and control of administration would be vested in the state. The people of the individual state, through the administrative officers and legislators elected by them, would have authority over the administration. There would be no such thing as domination by the party in power at Washington, unless that party also had been elected to power in the particular states.

So long as the state complied with the conditions prescribed by the national government and came up to the prescribed minimum standard, the national government would have no control beyond the power to audit and examine to determine the fact of such compliance. Since the national government would be contributing part of the cost of benefits on the basis of state determination of eligibility, it is both desirable and necessary that the national government should audit and be in a position, if necessary, to say that a benefit has been improperly paid.

Although the administrative representatives of the national government would have no power greater than has been indicated, they would have influence. It is assumed that they would be professionally and technically competent and possessed of wide knowledge of the practices and procedures of other states. The governor, the administrators of the welfare agency, and the legislators of the state would properly be influenced by the suggestions and recommendations of representatives of the national government. But the power to decide would remain completely in the hands of the state. If the duly constituted authorities of the state should be opposed to the recommendations of the federal agency they should have unquestioned legal authority to say "No."

Does this statement mean that the state and its officers could defy the national government despite the fact that the national government was contributing substantially toward the cost of the system? The state would not be defying the national government; it would be defying at most the executive branch on the ground that the national officials were attempting to go beyond the authority vested in them by Congress. If the action of the state seemed to the national administrative officers inimicable to the national interest, their remedy would lie in reporting the facts to Congress with recommendations for such changes in the conditional grant-in-aid law as they believed necessary to correct the situation. Then Congress would determine whether the law should be changed, and if it changed the law, the state officials would have either to comply or forfeit the grant. The national government would thus have the power, but it could only exercise it through the legislative process, which would give the senators and representatives from the state full opportunity to present their case and to vote on the issues.

In this concluding chapter, suggestions regarding organization and procedure within the states will not be considered at length. Three major points will be summarized.

1. The administration of relief and social security generally requires the state agency to perform the legislative function of perfecting rules and regulations within the broad principles laid down by the legislature and also the judicial function of passing upon appeals from citizens who are dissatisfied with the initial administrative action. For both such legislative and judicial functions a board is preferred to a single executive. The governor of the state, moreover, should not be able, without fresh authority from the legislature, to repeal or amend the social welfare code that has developed over the years by boards acting under the authority of the legislature, whether the governor acts directly or through his power to remove and appoint board members. Long and overlapping terms for board members who exercise the legislative and judicial functions and suitable restrictions to prevent the governor from acting without the current approval of the legislature are therefore recommended.

A preference is to be noted in favor of the arrangement whereby the board appoints and removes its chief executive officer who is responsible for direct administrative action. Appointment of the executive officer by the governor is not necessarily objectionable, provided (a) the board exercises the legis-

lative and judicial powers, (b) decisions of the board are binding upon the executive officer, and (c) the principles established
by its decisions have to be followed in all like cases.

The major reason for stressing these points is that the legislation should go as far as possible in eliminating political influence of one kind or another from relief and social security
administration. The potential dangers of improper use of power
are peculiarly great when individuals may be given public
funds.

2. Substantial participation by local governments is desirable both in financing and administering social security and relief
in all cases in which a means test is used or where a considerable
body of personal facts has to be collected to determine eligibility. If the local governments have no financial responsibility, a
tendency may develop to put as many as possible on the benefit
rolls, especially in communities where relatively few residents
pay direct state and national taxes.

3. The national government should require the state government to comply with sound minimum standards of public
administration.

SOCIAL SERVICES AND SOCIAL SECURITY

Persons who are in need may be divided roughly into two
broad classes:

1. Those who are reasonably competent to manage their own
affairs and care for and guide the children who may be dependent upon them.

2. Those whose need results in part from their inability
to manage their own affairs with a passable degree of success,
and who cannot care for and guide the children dependent on
them in accordance with acceptable minimum standards.

Payment of money benefits under a sound social security system will in a large measure overcome the difficulty of the first
group, those who can manage their own affairs. It is not contended that they should have just as much freedom in handling
the money that comes to them from the public treasury as
they have in handling the resources that they have earned by

their own efforts. The receipt of funds collected through taxation gives the state a right to supervise that it may not have in other cases, but this right should be sparingly exercised, since the objective of the state should be to develop and sustain the personal independence and self-sufficiency of its citizens, and therefore it will avoid wherever possible governmental interference.

Benefits resulting from private voluntary insurance are to be distinguished from benefits coming from social insurance which involves a substantial measure of deliberate redistribution of wealth. Beneficiaries who profit from the deliberate redistribution of wealth have not, as a matter of fact, paid for their social security benefits through their own premium payments or through the premiums paid on their individual account by their employers. These two premiums combined would not produce the amount of benefits they will take from the system. Their benefits have been paid for in part by the taxes levied against others to provide for them. Both the collectivism inherent in insurance and the social action of the state in redistributing wealth are necessary to produce benefits of the size they will be paid. Such beneficiaries of social insurance are not in precisely the same class with persons whose insurance benefits are paid as the result of private voluntary insurance. Despite this distinction, it is not in general desirable to have the state exercise that right to regulate and direct which ordinarily is associated with disbursement of public funds.

Conclusions are quite different with respect to those persons whose need results in part from their inability to manage their own affairs, especially if they have children who need care and guidance. The people of the country have a great stake in these children. Probably few would object to the taxes they may have to pay to provide them with the necessaries of life and with opportunities up to a reasonable minimum standard. But most persons would like some assurance that the money thus paid is wisely spent in the interests of the health, education, and normal development of the children. It is disturbing enough if the money is imprudently spent on things that are relatively harmless; many people are more than disturbed when it is spent to maintain a way of life that is injurious to the children and that jeopardizes their chances of becoming well adjusted, self-supporting members of the community.

In such cases, the recipients of the benefits should be subject to the supervision of competent, professionally trained, public employees, and payments should be contingent upon suitable use and application of the public funds provided. The accepted principles of social case work dictate that wherever possible children be left with their parents or—if there are no parents or no parents competent to care for them—then with suitable relatives, and that every effort be made to develop a satisfactory family life. Despite fictional stories and moving pictures, in actual practice professionally trained social case workers go very close to the limit in following this principle. It seems reasonable to conclude that payment of public funds for persons whose need results from their personal limitations should be sufficiently contingent to make it necessary for the recipients to comply with minimum standards.

To prevent misunderstanding, the fact should be emphasized that a sound and adequate appeals procedure is recommended. A person or a family believing that the public employees in immediate charge of the case are dealing unfairly or making unreasonable demands should have opportunity to appeal to a higher authority, which has full power to order and enforce changes if the conduct of the examiners and case workers is not in accordance with the law, the regulations, and sound professional standards for dealing with people who need guidance and supervision.

RELATIONSHIP WITH OTHER AGENCIES

The conclusions that are here set forth represent obviously the acceptance of welfare concepts rather than wage and money insurance concepts. They are based on the idea that the state should go only far enough to establish a floor below which none would be permitted to fall without becoming eligible to such assistance from the public treasury as may be necessary.

One reason for this conclusion is the conviction that at least as important as money in many cases is constructive developmental service. The task is, in so far as possible, to rehabilitate and to lead to self-support, confidence, and respect. This task demands that the welfare agencies of government work in the closest possible co-operative relationship with such public agencies as the employment offices, the schools, the public health services, in rural communities the farm agencies, and even in some cases with the courts and the law enforcement officers. Co-operation is also necessary with private citizens and voluntary community organizations, notably the churches, the medical organizations, the parent-teachers associations, and organizations providing suitable recreation. Rehabilitation and adjustment to environment have to be achieved in the community where the individual lives. This adjustment cannot be effected merely by giving money from the public treasury. Such grants do not necessarily change the attitude of the neighbors toward the recipient; they may, as a matter of fact, impair them. Grants do not necessarily give self-respect, for self-respect often depends in part upon meriting and receiving the respect of neighbors.

The United States is far too large and too diverse to permit the successful direction of local affairs from Washington. Democracy requires the preservation of a very large measure of local self-government. The activities of government that touch the individual, the family, and the community must be co-ordinated and largely controlled at the local level. A national government and a state government can do much in the way of prescribing minimum standards, aiding in finance, and supplying technical and professional standards, but success depends on the co-operation and the spirit of the people in the community. They must have real responsibility and authority. If responsibility and authority are taken from them, many communities will be divided into hostile camps, the one made up of those who look to a faraway government for gifts and grants, and the other comprising persons hostile to the programs and policies of the national government and antagonistic toward the persons who have become its wards.

THE MERIT SYSTEM AND HIGH STANDARDS OF ADMINISTRATION

The welfare function of government, which necessitates the taking of money from one group to give to another, demands, perhaps more than any other, the maximum possible protection from political abuses and the consistent maintenance of high standards of competence in actual administration.

Experience suggests that the best possible device for securing sound personnel administration is through the grant-in-aid plan. Under this plan the national government is preserved as an agency to establish standards, to supervise administration and to review. It is freed from the dangers that arise when it has a vast army of national civil servants so dispersed that every city and every rural county seat has its quota of federal employees in immediate contact with recipients of federal money. Merit system laws are far too weak to stand such a strain. Their value depends on the integrity and intelligence with which they are administered. The chances for success are far greater if the national government compels the states to adopt and use such laws and supervises their administration and enforcement of them, than it is if the national government itself has an army of employees controlled and directed by politically appointed policy-making officers at Washington.

In summary, the United States has, at present, a chaotic, unsystematic, and improperly financed system of social security and relief that leaves many large segments of the population unprotected from want. It is essential to establish a universal, comprehensive, co-ordinated system of social security and relief that will protect all persons in need. In advocating such a system we are not unmindful of the major financial and administrative difficulties involved.

Expenditures for relief and social security must be made from current income. It is impracticable to meet them through any system of reserves. Insurance reserves of the national government consist only of its own obligations to pay in the future. Consequently the reserve system does not and cannot actually lessen the burden on future generations.

Social security is only one among many competing claims on the limited revenue of government. The people through their government must therefore weigh the merits of various competing claims on public resources. Expenditures for social security and relief are primarily remedial or defensive in nature; they are essentially different from expenditures for constructive programs that promote increased efficiency in the production of needed goods and services. Payment for relief and social security cannot be given a priority over all other forms of expenditure. In establishing standards of payments for relief and social security it is necessary to keep in mind the limited funds available, competing claims upon the government, and the remedial nature of relief and social security payments.

The United States is a vast country with dissimilar economic and social conditions; consequently different sections have different problems to meet. This country has a federal form of government which makes it possible to meet different situations in various ways in the several parts of the country. While the federal government ought to insure a minimum standard of benefit payments for relief and social security, an absolutely uniform system of social security and relief would not be desirable because of the differences in the planes of living and in the costs of living in the various sections of the nation. In developing and administering the program, the active co-operation of the national government with the several states is required.

APPENDIX

THE USE OF CENSUS DATA IN ESTIMATING COSTS

I. THE OLD-AGE PENSION

The cost of an old-age pension will depend basically upon four factors: (1) the age at which retirement is permitted; (2) the number of persons at or above the retirement age; (3) the percentage of the persons above the retirement age who will elect to retire; and (4) the amount of the pension allowed. The amount of pension allowed and the percentage of persons who will elect to retire are related in that the higher the benefits the greater the inducement to retire.

The table below shows the number of persons reported in the 1940 census at or above five different age levels from 75 and over down to and including 55 and over. The costs of pensions of five different amounts per annum are shown for each age at retirement upon the assumption of 100 per cent retirement.

AGGREGATE ANNUAL COST OF SPECIFIED PENSIONS
ESTIMATED FOR VARIOUS RETIREMENT AGES
(Cost items in millions of dollars)

Retirement Age	Number 1940 (In thousands)	Cost of an Annual Pension of				
		$100	$300	$500	$700	$900
75 years or over.	2,643	264	793	1,322	1,850	2,379
70 years or over.	5,213	521	1,564	2,607	3,649	4,692
65 years or over.	9,019	902	2,706	4,510	6,313	8,117
60 years or over.	13,748	1,375	4,124	6,874	9,624	12,373
55 years or over.	19,592	1,959	5,878	9,796	13,714	17,633

From this table it will be noted, that on the assumption of complete retirement a pension of $300 a year would in 1940 have cost 2.7 billion dollars with retirement at 65 years of age, 4.1 billions at age 60, and almost 6.0 billions with age 55. A retirement age of 60 would add roughly 50 per cent to cost as compared with age 65; and one at age 55 would substantially more than double the cost.

In discussing the cost of provision for old age we decided not to go below age 65. This decision meant that in a universal, comprehensive system provision through other benefits would have to be made for persons under 65 who were incapable of self-support, and for widowed, divorced, or separated women whose family responsibilities precluded

871

substantial gainful employment. They are accordingly provided for by benefits which necessitate establishment of eligibility proof of other facts in addition to calendar age.

The next question we had to face was how many would retire. The three assumptions made and the method used are shown in the table below.

ASSUMED RATES OF RETIREMENT

Specified Age	Population of Specified Age, 1940	Assumption 1		Assumption 2		Assumption 3	
		Percentage on Pension	Thousands of Pensioners	Percentage on Pension	Thousands of Pensioners	Percentage on Pension	Thousands of Pensioners
65 years or over	9,019	87[a]	7,811	78[a]	7,042	67[a]	6,082
75 years or over	2,643	100	2,643	95	2,511	90	2,379
70 to 74 years..	2,570	90	2,313	80	2,056	70	1,799
65 to 69 years..	3,807	75	2,855	65	2,475	50	1,904

[a] Calculated on basis of assumptions for each specified age period.

These estimates are made upon judgment. We started with the lowest one and built up from it.

It seemed reasonably safe to assume that a man 65 years of age or over who was not in the labor force in 1940 would in all probability elect to take a pension under a no-means test system even if he had means enough to support himself. The census data showed that in 1940 males in the labor force formed 50.8 per cent of the men 65 to 74 years of age and 17.8 per cent of the men 75 and over.

It seemed entirely reasonable to assume that a substantial number of men 65 years of age or over who were reported as in the labor force would not continue in it were no-means test old-age pensions available. Some farmers and a substantial number of farm laborers would withdraw from work if withdrawal meant a cash payment each month. Men whose efficiency was substantially impaired would no longer feel under obligation to stick to a job or to hunt a new one if they should be dropped.

At age 65 and over there are many widows who have never been in the labor force at all or who have not been in it for years. These widows added to the men over 65 years of age who were not in the labor force and their wives seemed to us to warrant an assumption that 50 per cent of the population between 65 to 70 would take advantage of a no-means test, old-age system even if the benefits were fairly low. It may be recalled that in the states which have a pension philosophy, such as Oklahoma, Texas, and Colorado, in the neighborhood of 50 per cent of the persons 65 years of age and over had by December 1942 obtained benefits under the means test old-age assistance program. Elimination of the means test, bringing eligibility to persons regardless of their resources, would in our judgment materially increase numbers throughout the country. We therefore assumed a rate of retirement at 50 per cent for those 65 to 69 years of age, 70 per cent for persons 70 to 74 years of age, and 90 per cent for those 75 years of age and over. The number of men over 75 who are still working and have wives must be relatively small and the number of women 75 or over who are still in the labor force was only 2.1 per cent in 1940.

The assumptions produced a rate of retirement for persons 65 years of age or over of 67 per cent as the lowest of the three given in the table. The reader may note that in Chapter XXVII we occasionally use as our low an assumption of a straight 50 per cent. It has the advantage of arithmetical simplicity, but in our judgment it is extremely doubtful whether a no-means test system would have such a low retirement rate unless benefits were extremely small or opportunities for gainful employment at substantial earnings were good.

Our second assumption produces a weighted average retirement rate for persons 65 years of age or over of 78 per cent. A figure in this neighborhood could, it seems to us, be reasonably expected if benefits were fairly high and conditions with respect to permitted earnings after 65 were liberal. It would seem highly probable that in rural areas, where money wages and housing costs are relatively low, and where an elderly couple can supplement their pensions by subsistence farming activities, the retirement on pensions might prove attractive. The figures for old-age assistance permit an interpretation that retirement on a money pension is more attractive in rural areas and small towns than it would be in high-cost, high-wage, metropolitan centers. If pressure should develop from economic conditions, public opinion, or the desire of employers to encourage or even to force retirement at approximately age 65, an estimate of 75 or 78 per cent retired would not appear to us unreasonably high.

Our high figure gives a weighted average retirement rate of 87 per cent. Such a figure would result from high benefits, very liberal provisions with respect to earnings after retirement and with respect to eligibility of a wife whose husband still earned, and a considerable degree of pressure from one source or another to encourage or force retirement. In this connection it should perhaps be noted that individual employer retirement systems both public and private have rarely if ever attempted to restrict a retired employee from earning after he has retired. Many persons retired on pension from an individual employer retirement fund continue gainful employment. Thus retirement rates for such funds are inapplicable to a universal, governmental, old-age retirement system.

II. CHILDREN'S ALLOWANCES

Under the existing programs in the United States direct provision for children is made in three principal ways:

1. Children who are in need and who are to live with a relative within the degree specified by the Social Security Act may receive an aid to dependent children benefit under that grant-in-aid program.

2. Children who are in need but are not eligible or regarded as eligible under the aid to dependent children program may be given assistance by the state, the local government, or the two combined under general public assistance.

3. Children of a father who retires at age 65 as fully insured, persons under old-age and survivors insurance, and children of a father who on his death was currently insured under O.A.S.I. receive a benefit as of right regardless of need. Under certain circumstances children of a mother who was fully or currently insured under O.A.S.I. may take as of right regardless of need.

Obviously the existing programs do not afford much of a basis for figuring the cost of a comprehensive system for insuring the social security of children. In the United States emphasis has been placed on security for persons 65 years of age and over and persons of that age only rarely have direct personal responsibility for the support and care of children under 18 years of age. It is necessary for us in approaching the question of costs for providing for children to proceed very largely on the basis of assumptions.

The basic data regarding the number of children under 18 years of age as given in the 1940 census are presented in the table below.

Children under 18 years of age, it will be noted, numbered approx-

NUMBER AND PERCENTAGE OF CHILDREN IN THE POPULATION, 1940

Specified Age	Number (In thousands)	Percentage of	
		Total Population	Population 20–64
UNDER 18 YEARS OF AGE..	**40,288**	*30.6*	*52.1*
16 and 17 years.......	4,892	*3.7*	*6.3*
15 years..............	2,423	*1.8*	*3.1*
Under 15 years of age..	32,973	*25.0*	*42.6*
10 to 14 years.......	11,746	*8.9*	*15.2*
5 to 9 years.........	10,685	*8.1*	*13.8*
Under 5 years of age.	10,542	*8.0*	*13.6*

imately 40.3 millions in 1940. They constituted 30.6 per cent of the total population in that year and 52.1 per cent of the population 20 to 64 years of age. Thus an allowance of $100 a year paid in behalf of each child under 18 years of age would have cost in 1940 over 4 billion dollars and, had it been financed entirely from contributions by persons 20 to 64 years, would have necessitated a payment of $52.10 per capita of this group.

A question may properly be raised as to whether children over 15 years of age but under 18 years should be universally eligible to a child's allowance even if one should be provided. It is therefore significant to give the figures for children under 15 years of age. They numbered about 33 millions in 1940 and made up 25.0 per cent of the total population and 42.6 per cent of the population 20 to 64 years of age. Thus an allowance of $100 a year to each such child would have cost almost 3.3 billion dollars in 1940, and if financed from contributions from individuals 20 to 64 years, would have required an average per capita contribution of about $42.60.

Neither the proposed British comprehensive system nor the New Zealand system provides for a universal children's allowance. New Zealand uses a means test, so it only pays allowances to children in need according to the legally established definition. The proposed British plan assumes that a gainfully employed father can support a wife and one child from his earnings or other income. It proposes to pay the regular no-means test children's allowances only to second and subsequent children, unless the father is unemployed, disabled, or deceased. The British system proposes larger allowances for orphans than for children with one or both parents living. A benefit is to be paid to the widowed mother who has one or more children, and the child of a widow derives part of its support from the allowance to the mother.

The national income tax law and state income tax laws provide for exemptions on the basis of children, and hence some indirect contribution is allowed for their support. In view of these facts we decided against including in our rough estimates of cost an item for no-means test children's allowances. Instead we have assumed that children's allowances will only be paid when the evidence shows that an insufficient sum is available to care for the child in accordance with a standard established by law. If a family is possessed of sufficient resources to care for a child, a benefit would not be paid on the sole ground that the child's father had retired at age 65 as a fully insured member of O.A.S.I. or that he had died a currently insured member of O.A.S.I. If the family had insufficient resources to provide for the child, a grant would be made regardless of the cause of the deficiency of family income.

We have not made the detailed studies which would be necessary to arrive at anything approaching a precise estimate as to what such a system would cost on the basis of a graded series of assumptions regarding the conditions upon which the benefits should be granted. Instead we prepared only some crude figures to indicate roughly the range of costs. They are presented in the table below and are based on the approximately 40 million children under 18.

ESTIMATED COSTS OF ALLOWANCES FOR CHILDREN

Assumed Percentage of Children in Need	Number of Needy Children at Assumed Percentage (In millions)	Cost (in millions) of an Annual Benefit of				
		$60	$120	$180	$240	$360
2.5 per cent...	1	$ 60	$ 120	$ 180	$ 240	$ 360
5 per cent.....	2	120	240	360	480	720
10 per cent.....	4	240	480	720	960	1,440
20 per cent.....	8	480	960	1,440	1,920	2,880
30 per cent.....	12	720	1,440	2,160	2,880	4,320

The lowest percentage of need used in this table is 2.5. In December 1942 children in receipt of aid to dependent children formed 2.1 per cent of the children under 18 years of age as reported at the census of 1940.[1] The children under this program were both in need and living with a relative within the prescribed degree. There were other children in need who could not qualify under this program. We therefore have used 2.5 as the lowest figure. In our opinion, however, the figure is lower than would be experienced under a comprehensive system, and therefore in the summary table in Chapter XXVII we have used a low of 5 per cent.

For the high figure we have used 30 per cent, influenced perhaps by the frequently quoted statement that a third of the population of the United States is ill clad, ill housed, and ill fed. If the United States should again experience a deep and prolonged depression, with millions of people in the age groups 20 to 64 years of age unemployed for considerable periods of time, it is conceivable that the number of children in need, according to a reasonable definition, might approach 30 per cent. In our opinion 30 per cent is much too high a figure to represent any probable annual average in the United States. Accordingly in the summary table presented in Chapter XXVII we have used 20 per cent which we believe would prove high as an annual average.

Annual average is stressed because the number of children under 18 years of age who are in need will vary with employment conditions.

[1] *Social Security Yearbook, 1942*, p. 77.

If the nation, in perfecting and developing its system of social security, should stress the prevention of want and the welfare concepts, it will pay benefits with relation to the number of dependent children. It will not pay benefits according to an insurance plan based on the past earnings of the worker with no reference whatever to the number of children who are dependent on that worker for their support.

In the table on page 876 figures are given for five different rates of benefits ranging from $60 a year to $360 a year. Two different policies, with various combinations of them, are possible. Both involve establishing the fact that the child is in need or at least is so circumstanced that eligibility is established in accordance with legal standards. Under the first policy the amount given is only sufficient to bring total resources, including the benefit, to the prescribed legal standard. Under the second, each child who is eligible gets the same amount of benefit, which is added to whatever resources he may have, provided those resources are not high enough to preclude eligibility.

If the benefit is only enough to bring the income available for the child to the prescribed standard, the average per capita allowance may fall as the percentage of children covered increases or as the standard used is made more liberal. The last increment of children added to the benefit rolls may require less than the first increment to bring them to the standard. Thus under such a system one might use the $240 average benefit if only 5 per cent of the children were involved and the $120 figure if 20 per cent received benefits.

If flat sum benefit payments are made to all in need without reference to the degree of need, the cost will depend solely on the number on benefit and the amount of the benefit. Thus a benefit of $20 a month or $240 a year would cost 960 million dollars if 10 per cent were eligible and 1.9 billions if 20 per cent were eligible. Under the other system with benefits adjusted to the degree of need, 10 per cent in need might require an average of $20 each or a total of 960 million dollars, whereas 20 per cent might require only an average of $15 each per month or a total of a little over 1.4 billions.

In the summary table in Chapter XXVII we have used a low benefit rate with a low percentage eligible and a high benefit rate with a high percentage eligible. Our objective there was to establish the limits of reasonable variation in an effort to estimate costs. We were not attempting to do more than that or to show what a children's allowance system that we might regard as desirable would cost.

III. WOMEN'S BENEFITS

If one takes as the criteria for evaluation, the concept of universal, comprehensive, and co-ordinated coverage, the provisions of our existing programs with respect to women are open to serious and fundamental questions. A comparison between our present provisions and those embodied in the New Zealand system and the proposed British plan suggests that in the United States this subject has largely escaped real analysis and presentation.

In the earlier section of this appendix dealing with old age, we allowed for no-means test pensions for women aged 65 years and over if unemployed and not the wife of a fully employed man. In the present section we shall be concerned with three other major classes of women.

1. Widowed, divorced, or separated women 50 to 64 years of age who are not in the labor force. In many cases they had not been in it for some years at the time they lost the support of the husband. Whether they have or have not the responsibility for a child under 18 years of age is not here treated, although such responsibility would increase the argument in favor of a benefit for them. Included with them would be those single women of like age who are not in the labor force and may have spent many years as housekeepers for a parent, or other relative and are cut off from connection with the income stream when the supporting relative dies or makes other domestic arrangements. Women in this group may not be able to obtain gainful employment.

2. Widowed, divorced, or separated women 15 to 49 years of age (a) who have direct and immediate responsibility for one child or more requiring their care, (b) who cannot obtain gainful employment which does not conflict with the obligations to the child or children, and (c) who cannot make satisfactory family arrangements whereby the child or the children will receive the needed attention from other qualified members of the family.

3. Women under 50 years of age who are unable to work either in a gainful occupation or as a homemaker. If they are married women living with the husband, the husband may be at extra expense both for their care and for procuring substitute services for the family. Age 50 is used as the upper limit because of the assumption that if the woman is above that age she can be provided for in group 1. If these women have a child under 18 they are eligible under group 2 above, although they may not be able to give the child the necessary service.

Data are not available to permit anything approaching a precise statement as to the number of women in these three groups. The only practicable course appeared to be to use the available census data and to make some assumptions with respect to factors not measured by the census. The customary device for trying to arrive at a probable range generally has to be employed, namely using both a low and a high assumption neither of which seems out of reason.

Three difficulties deserve special mention:

1. The census classifies women by age and by marital condition,

single, married, widowed, and divorced. Among the women who report themselves as married are some who are as a matter of fact divorced but prefer to be known as married and others who are separated from their husbands. The husbands may or may not be supporting them or contributing to their support. From the census reports it is possible to determine how many married women were not living in the same household with the husband, but these data do not answer the question whether the husband is supporting the wife and such children as they may have. The same problem arises with respect to divorced women. Some may receive sufficient alimony to support them and their children. For women at ages 15 to 49, the question of whether a husband is or is not providing support is of significance from the standpoint of our present task only in so far as the women have children under 18 years of age who are dependent on them.

2. The census has not presented figures cross-classifying women by age, marital condition, gainful employment, and status with respect to care and responsibility for a child or children under 18 years of age. It is therefore necessary to make certain assumptions on the basis of such data as are available and to estimate the range within which the correct figures would probably fall.

3. The census does not collect data with respect to the physical and mental capacity of women for either gainful employment or for keeping house and caring for children. The fact that a woman is actually gainfully employed may be regarded as fairly well establishing at least a minimum degree of capacity, and the fact that she is in the labor force although at the time of the census unemployed, creates a presumption of capacity. With respect to women not in the labor force there is little to go on. Single, widowed, and divorced women not in the labor force may not be gainfully employed or seeking employment because they have sufficient resources in one way or another to get along. On the other hand, some may not be able to work. Married women not in the labor force are in the main physically and mentally equipped for their duties, but there are some who are not. How many is the question which will require use of assumptions.

A table on page 880 presents a summary of the available basic data for 1940 with respect to women 15 to 64 years, classified according to age in quinquennial groups. It shows (a) marital condition, (b) for married women whether they were or were not living in the same household with the husband, (c) how many women were heads of households, and (d) how many were reported as in the labor force.

Women 50 to 64 not in labor force and without husband. Our first effort will be directed toward estimating the number of women 50 to 64 years of age who (1) are not in the labor force and (2) do not have a husband from whom they may receive support.

WOMEN 15 TO 64 YEARS OF AGE, 1940
(Number in thousands)

Age	Total	Marital Condition[a]				Married with Husband[b]		Heads of House-hold[c]	In Labor Force[d]
		Single	Married	Widowed	Divorced	Present in Household	Not Present in Household		
15 to 64 years.........	44,749	12,322	28,504	3,134	789	27,039	1,465	3,760	12,573
15 to 19 years......	6,153	5,424	714	6	9	653	61	15	1,377[e]
20 to 24 years......	5,895	2,781	3,026	33	56	2,850	176	98	2,659
25 to 29 years......	5,046	1,288	4,185	72	101	3,977	208	190	1,987
30 to 34 years......	5,172	762	4,156	128	126	3,956	200	281	1,574
35 to 39 years......	4,800	536	3,912	220	132	3,715	197	399	1,346
40 to 44 years......	4,369	415	3,519	318	117	3,345	174	479	1,119
45 to 49 years......	4,046	349	3,168	433	96	3,013	155	552	937
50 to 54 years......	3,504	305	2,569	559	71	2,441	128	592	729
55 to 59 years......	2,833	246	1,902	635	49	1,806	96	579	508
60 to 64 years......	2,331	216	1,353	730	32	1,283	70	575	337

[a] Census of 1940, *Population*, Vol. IV, Pt. 1, p. 16.
[b] The same, p. 25.
[c] The same, p. 28.
[d] The same, p. 7.
[e] Includes girls of 14.

The number of women 50 to 64 years of age who are single, widowed, or divorced is available from the census. To the total for these three classes, should be added the number of married women who are separated from their husbands and are not supported by them. Estimates of this number are based on the number who are not living in the same household with their husbands. For our low estimate, we assume that four absent husbands out of five are continuing to meet their responsibilities, and therefore we add only one fifth of the women not living with their husbands to our known total of women 50 to 64 without husbands. For our high estimate, we assume that only two absent husbands out of five continued to meet their responsibilities, and hence we add 60 per cent of the married women not living in the same households with their husbands.

By the method just described, an estimate is made of the total number of single, widowed, divorced, or separated women aged 50 to 64 years. From this total number must be subtracted those who are in the labor force and are assumed to be self-supporting. Among the women of these ages who are reported by the census of 1940 as in the labor force, are some who are married women living in the same household with their husbands. Census tabulations do not show how many. They do show, however, that of all women 45 years of age or over in the labor force 29.2 per cent were married women living in the same household with their husbands. That figures means that 70.8 per cent of women 45 years of age or over in the labor force were single, widowed, divorced, or married women not living in the same household with their husbands. For the purposes of the present estimate, it is assumed that this 70.8 per cent applies equally in the three quinquennial age groups between 50 and 64. From the total single, widowed, divorced, or separated, we shall therefore subtract 70.8 per cent of the women of the respective ages in the labor force.

The figures used in this method of estimating are presented in the table on page 882.

According to this method of estimating there were in 1940 between 754,000 and 782,000 women 60 to 64 years of age who were not in the labor force, and either had no husband or if still married were not supported by the husband. If an average annual benefit of $20 a month or $240 a year were paid to these women, the cost would be between 181 million dollars and 188 millions a year.

The total number of women 50 to 64 years of age in 1940 who were not in the labor force and either had no husband or if still married were not supported by the husband is estimated to have been from 1.8 millions to 1.9 millions. An average benefit of $240 a year for them would thus have cost between 432 million and 456 million dollars.

With respect to the women 50 to 64 years of age who are not in the labor force and either have no husband or if married are separated from the husband, we have assumed that the question of whether they had or had not the care of a child under 18 years of age would be immaterial. In other words that if they were unemployed and could not get suitable employment, they would be entitled to a small benefit.

ESTIMATED NUMBER OF WOMEN AGED 50 TO 64 YEARS
WITHOUT A HUSBAND AND NOT IN LABOR FORCE

	Number (in thousands) of Women at the 1940 Census Aged		
	60 to 64	55 to 59	50 to 54
Single...	216	246	305
Widowed...	730	635	559
Divorced..	32	49	71
Total without a husband.......................	978	930	935
20 per cent of those married but without a husband present in household..............................	14	19	26
Total with 20 per cent included................	992	949	961
Less 70.8 per cent of the women in the labor force.....	238	360	516
Estimated number without a husband and not in the labor force..................................	754	589	445
Total without a husband.......................	978	930	935
60 per cent of those married but without a husband present in household..............................	42	58	77
Total with 60 per cent included................	1,020	988	1,012
Less 70.8 per cent of the women in the labor force.....	238	360	516
Estimated number without a husband and not in labor force..................................	782	628	496

Women under 50 years of age without a husband and with care of a child under 18 years of age. With respect to women under 50 years of age, the assumption is that if widowed, divorced, or separated and physically able to work, they will not receive a benefit unless they have the care of and responsibility for one child or more under 18 years of age. If they have no responsibility for such a child and are physically fit, they will be expected to enter the labor market and get gainful employment. Should no work be available, they would have to qualify for unemployment or training benefits under the unemployment compensation system. The question regarding the widowed, divorced, or separated women under 50 years of age is therefore how many have the care of and responsibility for children under 18 years of age.

In the table below are presented two estimates as to the number of women 15 to 49 years of age once married but now without a husband or, in the case of women married at the date of the census, without a husband contributing to their support. The two estimates are based on different assumptions as to the number of women married at the time of the census but not living in the same household with the husband who are not supported by their husbands. The aggregate number, in thousands, under one estimate is 2,081 and the other 2,550.

Estimates of the Number of Women[a] Aged 15 to 49 Not Supported by a Husband
(Number in thousands)

Age	Widowed	Divorced	Of Those Married but Not in Household with Husband		Total Once Married but Now Without a Husband	
			20 per cent	60 per cent	20 per cent	60 per cent
15 to 49 years....	1,210	637	234	703	2,081	2,550
15 to 19 years..	6	9	12	37	27	52
20 to 24 years..	33	56	35	106	124	195
25 to 29 years..	72	101	42	125	215	298
30 to 34 years..	128	126	40	120	294	374
35 to 39 years..	220	132	39	118	391	470
40 to 44 years..	318	117	35	104	470	539
45 to 49 years..	433	96	31	93	560	622

[a] Census of 1940, *Population*.

How many of the approximately 2 million once married women without a husband, or married women without a husband supporting them, have children under 18 years of age? The census, through a sampling method, gives the percentage of women ever married who by 1940 never had had any children. These percentages are given in the table on page 884 and they serve as the basis for two estimates, a higher and a lower as to the number who have children under 18 years of age living with them. These percentages with children under 18 are estimates, although there are some data against which they will be checked in the footnote on page 885. The percentages are lower than the percentage who had borne children, because (1) some of the children born to them have died, (2) some are not living with their mothers, and (3) in the case of the older women, some have reached the age of 18. It should be clearly understood that a woman belongs in our category so long as she has one child under 18 years of age still living with her and receiving her care.

ESTIMATES OF THE PERCENTAGE OF WOMEN 15 TO 49 YEARS OF AGE WHO HAVE
BEEN MARRIED WITH CHILDREN UNDER 18 YEARS OF AGE

Age	Women Who Have Been Married			
	Percentage Childless[a]	Percentage Who Have 1 or More Children[a]	Assumed Percentage with Children under 18 Years of Age	
			Higher Estimate	Lower Estimate
15 to 19 years.....	49.1	50.9	45	40
20 to 24 years.....	36.6	63.4	55	50
25 to 29 years.....	27.7	72.3	65	58
30 to 34 years.....	21.5	78.5	70	60
35 to 39 years.....	18.2	81.8	75	65
40 to 44 years.....	16.0	84.0	75	65
45 to 49 years.....	15.4	84.6	70	60

[a] Census of 1940, *Population: Differential Fertility 1940 and 1910*, p. 13.

By applying the assumed percentages given in this table to the numbers in the preceding table we get the four different answers, presented below.

ESTIMATES OF NUMBER OF WOMEN WHO HAVE BEEN WITHOUT SUPPORTING
HUSBAND WITH CHILDREN UNDER 18 YEARS OF AGE
(Number in thousands)

Age	Low Estimate			High Estimate		
	Number	With Children under 18		Number	With Children under 18	
		Higher Estimate	Lower Estimate		Higher Estimate	Lower Estimate
15 to 49 years......	**2,081**	**1,464**	**1,270**	**2,550**	**1,777**	**1,545**
15 to 19 years....	27	12	11	52	23	21
20 to 24 years....	124	68	62	195	107	98
25 to 29 years....	215	140	125	298	194	173
30 to 34 years....	294	206	176	374	262	224
35 to 39 years....	391	293	254	470	353	306
40 to 44 years....	470	353	306	539	404	350
45 to 49 years....	560	392	336	622	434	373
15 to 44 years......	1,521	1,072	934	1,928	1,343	1,172
Percentage with children under 18....		70.5	61.4		69.7	60.8

According to this method we estimate the number of widowed, divorced, or separated women aged 15 to 49 years of age with children under 18 living with them as ranging between roughly 1.3 millions and 1.8 millions.[2]

If each of these women were given a no-means test benefit of $30 a month to enable them to devote their time to the child or children under 18 years of age, the cost could be between 468 and 648 million dollars a year.

What would be the difference between such benefits and the widow's current insurance benefit, as provided under O.A.S.I.?

1. They would be paid to all widows with a child or children under 18 years of age regardless of whether the husband was or was not either fully or currently insured under O.A.S.I.

2. They would be paid to divorced women who have the care of a child under 18 years of age. O.A.S.I. does not provide a benefit for a divorced woman if her husband is still living.

3. They would be paid to married women whose husbands have left

---

[2] The Census Bureau has a report on "Types of Families" which presents data with respect to the number of families which contain children under 18 years of age, but the data it gives were not well suited for our immediate purpose. They do, however, permit some method of checking the estimates we have used as to the percentage of widowed, divorced, or separated women who have children under 18 years of age.

For families with a male head and with the wife present in the household, the report gives the number with children under 18 together with an age classification according to the age of the father. The comparison between these figures and the high estimate used by us is as follows:

Age of mother in our estimate Age of father in the Census data	Our High	The Census Figure
Under 25 years of age	53.0	53.5
25 to 29 years	65.0	65.7
30 to 34 years	70.0	74.7
35 to 44 years	75.0	77.0

In our opinion it is extremely doubtful whether our high should be raised to the high for fathers. Many of the fathers have wives younger than they are and they are living in the same household with their wives. Such families are more likely to have children under 18 years of age than the widowed, divorced, or separated women of comparable age.

For families with a female head, widowed, divorced, or separated, there is no detailed classification by age and presence of children under 18 years of age. The figures show, however, that the percentage with such children for these classes of women under 45 years of age combined is 64.5. Our estimates give a range from 60.8 to 70.5 for women under 45 years of age. The census figures, by classes, are for divorced women 55.1, for widows 68.3, and for married women with husband absent 65.3. We use as our low a smaller figure than these data suggest, because it seems probable that these once married women who have become heads of families are more likely to have children than those who are living with relatives or boarding.

One could of course go into these figures in far greater detail and refinement than we have attempted here. Our object has been merely to get a general idea of costs and not to present precise figures.

them with a child or children under 18 years of age and are not contributing substantially to their support. We should repeat here that our figures as to the number not supported by absent husbands are based on arbitrary assumptions.

Obviously these estimates of a cost of 468 to 648 million dollars could be materially decreased by introducing means tests into the situation. For example:

1. The money which a divorced woman received from her husband could be treated as an asset, and if it exceeded a certain amount, could be deducted from the benefit.

2. The money which a widowed woman received from her husband's estate could be similarly deducted.

3. If any of these women with children under 18 years of age worked and had earnings above a given amount, earnings could be deducted from benefits.

4. Other income from whatever source could be deducted.

If, however, a means test system is introduced for widowed, divorced, and separated mothers who are responsible for children under 18 years of age and are not eligible for benefits under O.A.S.I., it is questionable whether no-means test benefits should be provided for women under O.A.S.I. In this connection, it should be noted that we are here dealing with widowed, divorced, and separated women aged from 15 to 49 years. Current widows' benefits for widows of these ages under O.A.S.I. will be paid for largely by (1) employers' contributions for the most part passed along to consumers in a hidden tax and possibly (2) contributions from general tax funds.

Another census report entitled *Employment and Family Characteristics of Women* permits the presentation of more precise data, secured by the Census Bureau by its scientific sampling technique, for the number of women between the ages of 18 to 64 who have children under 10 years of age. These data, with an age classification, are summarized in the table on page 887.

According to the figures in this table, the number of women 18 to 44 years of age widowed, divorced, or married but not living in the same household with the husband, who had children under 10 years of age in 1940 was only 660,000. A subsistence benefit of $30 a month to these women would cost annually 238 million dollars a year. It will be noted, moreover, that all women married but not living with their husbands are included in these figures, and many of them are presumably supported by their husbands. Material reductions in costs could thus be attained in a no-means test system by reducing the age of the child below which the mother's care is deemed necessary.

Women 20 to 49 years of age unable to work. In the discussion of benefits for widowed, divorced, or separated women in the age groups 20 to

WOMEN WITH CHILDREN UNDER 10 YEARS OF AGE CLASSIFIED BY MARITAL STATUS

Age	Married Women with Husband in Household				Women Widowed, Divorced, or Married but with Husband Absent			
	Number (In thousands)[a]	Without Children under 10		Per Cent with Children under 10	Number (In thousands)[a]	Without Children under 10		Per Cent with Children under 10
		Number (In thousands)[a]	Per Cent			Number (In thousands)[a]	Per Cent	
18 to 64 years	26,642	16,003	60.1	39.9	5,423	4,680	86.3	13.7
18 to 44 years	18,197	8,277	45.5	54.5	2,372	1,712	72.2	27.8
18 to 24 years	3,341	1,479	44.3	55.7	336	196	58.3	41.7
25 to 29 years	3,950	1,332	33.7	66.3	392	229	58.4	41.6
30 to 34 years	3,934	1,437	36.5	63.5	463	318	68.7	31.3
35 to 39 years	3,675	1,837	50.0	50.0	564	441	78.2	21.8
40 to 44 years	3,297	2,192	66.5	33.5	617	528	85.6	14.4
45 to 64 years	8,445	7,725	91.5	8.5	3,052	2,968	97.2	2.8

[a] Census of 1940, Population: Employment and Family Characteristics of Women, p. 9.

49 years no special allowance was made for those who because of physical or mental condition are unable to work either in or outside the home. Among married women with husbands supporting them or endeavoring to support them are some who are almost entirely incapacitated. For two main reasons estimating in this field is particularly difficult: (1) marriage is something of a selective process so that the proportion disabled from congenital causes or early diseases and accidents is probably materially higher among the single than among those ever married; and (2) a legislature might take the position that a disability benefit would be paid to disabled women without a supporting husband, whereas no benefit would be paid to a disabled woman with a supporting husband. Unfortunately we know of no general data which would furnish a basis for guessing at disability rates for women classified by age, marital condition, and support by a husband.

The best course to pursue in seeking rough estimates seems to us to be to give figures for all women in the age groups 20 to 49, and to use disability rates derived from those used for men as set forth in the following section. The rates used for the women are substantially lower than those used for men mainly on the assumption that the disease and accident rates for women are materially lower than those for men. These estimates are presented in the table below.

ESTIMATED NUMBER OF WOMEN[a] AGED 20 TO 49 YEARS UNABLE TO WORK

Age	Number (In thousands)	Estimated as Unable to Work	
		Per Cent	Number (In thousands)
TOTAL 20 TO 49 YEARS.....	29,928	2.0	623
20 to 24 years.............	5,895	1.5	88
25 to 29 years.............	5,646	1.7	96
30 to 34 years.............	5,172	2.0	103
35 to 39 years.............	4,800	2.2	106
40 to 44 years.............	4,369	2.5	109
45 to 49 years.............	4,046	3.0	121

[a] Census of 1940, *Population*.

This method of estimating gives 623,000 as the number of women 20 to 49 years of age who are unable to work. If a subsistence benefit of $30 a month were paid to each of them without a means test, the cost would be about 224 million dollars a year. Some of them are married women supported by their husbands. Under a no-means test system a legislature would have to decide whether the fact of marriage should or should not make the woman ineligible. If the married woman should be declared ineligible whereas the unmarried were eligible, there would be the anomalous situation of a woman with means not presently married receiving a benefit, whereas the married woman with a husband who had small earnings would be ineligible.

IV. MEN'S BENEFITS

Males 20 to 64 unable to work. There are in the population males who are unable to work even if jobs are plentiful. If they are 65 years of age or over they would be provided for through an old-age pension if universal old-age pensions were available without a means test, and therefore they have already been considered. Here we are concerned with males in the age groups 20 to 64.

The table below gives by five-year age groups (1) the total number of males 20 to 64 years of age in the population, (2) the number not in the labor force, (3) the percentage not in the labor force, (4) a rough estimate as to the percentage of the total not in the labor force because they are unable to work, and (5) an estimate based on that percentage as to the number unable to work.

ESTIMATED NUMBER OF MEN AGED 20 TO 64 NOT IN LABOR FORCE AND UNABLE TO WORK

Age	Total Number of Men (In thousands)[a]	Not in Labor Force		Estimated as Unable to Work	
		Number (In thousands)[a]	Per Cent of Total[a]	Per Cent of Total	Number (In thousands)
TOTAL 20 TO 64 YEARS..	38,749	3,181	8.2	4.7	1,859
20 to 24 years.........	5,692	681	12.0	2.0	114
25 to 29 years.........	5,451	281	5.1	2.5	136
30 to 34 years.........	5,070	225	4.4	3.0	152
35 to 39 years.........	4,746	225	4.7	3.0	142
40 to 44 years.........	4,419	261	5.9	4.0	177
45 to 49 years.........	4,209	299	7.1	5.0	210
50 to 54 years.........	3,753	334	8.9	6.0	225
55 to 59 years.........	3,011	368	12.2	9.0	271
60 to 64 years.........	2,398	507	21.1	18.0	432

[a] Compiled from Census of 1940, *Population*, Vol. IV, *Characteristics by Age*, p. 7.

This estimate gives as the number unable to work about 1.9 millions or 4.8 per cent out of a total of about 38.7 millions. Our estimates for those unable to work starts at 2 per cent for the age group 20 to 24 years and rises slowly to 4 per cent at 40 to 44 years. It rises more rapidly from then to 59 years and goes up sharply from 60 to 64 years. In the later years, it follows fairly closely the movement of the percentage not in the labor force. The high percentage not in the labor force in years 20 to 24 and the relatively high one for the period 25 to 29 are of course due to the large numbers of youth still in school. The low point in the percentage not in the labor force (4.4) is reached in the age period 30 to 34 years. We assume that, of these 4.4 per cent, 3 per cent are the result of incapacity for work.

If this estimate of 1.9 million men 20 to 64 years of age incapacitated for earning a living is anywhere near correct a no-means test benefit of $30 a month per man would cost about 684 million dollars a year. If the estimate of 1.9 is one third too high, the number of men unable to make a living would be 1.3 millions and the cost about 468 million dollars a year.

The past history of disability insurance, however, suggests the possibility that the estimate of 1.9 millions is too low. It is based entirely on men not in the labor force in 1940. There were, without doubt, on the census day men in the labor force working or seeking work who were more or less disabled. If the social security system provided a disability benefit, some of them, possibly a very substantial number, would prefer the certainty of a fixed benefit to the uncertainties and difficulties of employment. The higher the disability benefit granted, the greater would be the incentive to retire. The rules regarding allowable earnings would also have a significant bearing on costs. If a significant amount of earnings were permitted without destroying or impairing eligibility for a disability benefit, large numbers suffering some physical or mental impairment would doubtless apply. Because of these tendencies in disability insurance, it seems highly probable that the estimates used understate rather than overstate what disability benefits would cost.

V. MEDICAL CARE

Proposals are frequently made that the cost of medical care be covered by social insurance. It therefore seems desirable that we should include some figures as to costs. In making rough estimates, we shall apply to the population figures the per capita cost figures given by the Committee on the Costs of Medical Care as procured by its extensive studies in 1928–31.

Proposals of three different degrees will be used.

1. The amount spent for medical care should not be greatly increased, but the distribution of the cost should be changed. All persons with reasonable ability to pay should contribute about the average annual cost. Thus persons who escape the need for medical care in any year would help pay for those who required much care in that year. Those in need of much care would get it by contributing the average. Persons unable to pay the average would pay less or nothing which means that persons of superior capacity to pay would be taxed.

Persons of means would thus pay the average cost for themselves plus that part of the cost for the poor which is assessed against them.

2. The amount now spent for medical care would be increased so that all persons in the country would have available to them the degree of medical care that has been purchased on the average by families of comfortable means—$3,000 to $5,000 a year. In other words, all with less than comfortable means would with respect to the item of medical care be brought to the level of that group. Persons in the lower middle brackets would on the average pay more than they had previously paid and receive a higher level of service. Persons in the $3,000 to $5,000 bracket would pay larger amounts for about the same service, for they would bear a substantial part of the costs for improved service to those who cannot pay the average cost of such service.

3. Even the average payments of the $3,000 to $5,000 group have been inadequate to provide the amount of medical care deemed desirable by the Committee on the Costs of Medical Care. Many persons who could well afford the ideal service have not elected to use their money in that way. They should have, for example, regular medical examinations, more immunization, more dental work. The compulsory social security system might be designed to make available to all something approaching adequate medical care with special emphasis on preventive and corrective treatments and upon dental care, which is one of the items frequently neglected.

From the reports of the Committee on the Costs of Medical Care, we can get the approximate per capita cost at each of these three levels. These figures, it should be noted, include only the costs incurred by the individual or the family. They do not include the costs of medical care which is supplied by official agencies through the use of tax funds or by philanthropic agencies.

The actual average per capita cost in the period 1928–31 was placed at $23.58.[3] The average charge per person per annum in families with incomes from $3,000 to $5,000 was $28.52.[4] The per capita cost of adequate medical care exclusive of dentistry was placed at $25.30.[5] The cost of adequate dentistry was placed at $10.70.[6] Thus the total for adequate medical care was $36.00.

The total population of the United States in 1940 was 131.7 millions. Calculated on the three assumptions shown below, this would mean annual costs in millions of dollars in 1940 as follows:

[3] I. S. Falk, C. Rufus Rorem, Martha D. Ring, *The Costs of Medical Care* (1933), pp. 83, 96.
[4] The same, p. 93.
[5] The same, p. 151.
[6] The same, p. 153.

1. Even distribution of the average per capita cost
   in 1929–30 ($23.58)........................... $3,105
2. All getting the service purchased by the average
   family with an income between $3,000 and
   $5,000 in 1929–30 ($28.52).................... 3,756
3. All getting adequate medical care ($36.00).... 4,741

The first cost, 3,105 million dollars, represents roughly what medical care cost in 1940 if there had been no substantial changes since 1928–31 when the studies of expenditures were made by the Committee on the Costs of Medical Care. Through compulsory insurance, to raise the level to that of the $3,000 to $5,000 income family would therefore involve an increase of 651 million dollars a year. To provide adequate medical care would involve an increase of about 1.6 billion dollars over and above what the country is estimated to have been spending for this purpose, and an increase of about 985 million dollars over what would have been spent for this purpose had the per capita expenditure for all been equal to the per capita expenditure of members of families with incomes of $3,000 to $5,000.

Time lost through disability. The figures just given for the cost of medical care do not include payments to families to compensate them for loss of income which may result from disability of a worker because of accident or illness or to enable them to hire help during the illness of the homemaker. Medical care insurance would mean that medical care would be paid for by families on an insurance basis and would appear in the family budget only in the form of a premium or tax, either specific or included with other taxes. The money to pay for medical care would presumably not be given to the family at all but would go directly to the individuals or agencies rendering the service. The family budget would be affected by illness only through loss of earnings of the head of the family or by sums the family may find it necessary to pay for extra domestic, as distinct from medical care, service.

The average number of days work lost on account of illness of men and women workers in a year is generally so low that a waiting period of even as little as one week would eliminate most of the cases, and a waiting period of two weeks would take most of the rest. The great majority of male workers are, moreover, in the age groups 15 to 50 years, sometimes referred to as the ages of good health, when a fairly high percentage suffer no illness at all in the course of a year.[7] No comprehensive data with which we are familiar classify male workers who are ill by the duration of the illness. We shall therefore make no

[7] The same, p. 44.

estimate as to the cost of reimbursing families for the loss of services of a head of the family from a temporary totally disabling illness which lasts more than two weeks.[8]

VI. MATERNITY BENEFITS

Payments to families to enable the employment of extra help for the homemaker for several weeks both before and after the birth of a child are entirely distinct from payments to reimburse for lack of earnings. In some cases women are almost totally incapacitated during this period. The arrival of a baby, and its proper care during the first few months of its life, moreover, enormously increase the amount of work that has to be done in the home. The position is therefore frequently taken that a comprehensive no-means test social insurance system should provide an allowance for each woman during the later weeks of pregnancy and the first weeks of the baby's life to enable her to procure additional assistance. No-means test in this instance signifies that the payment will be made regardless of whether the mother has relatives or friends who will assist her, adequate domestic help already employed, or adequate means to hire whatever additional help may be needed. It will also be paid regardless of the type of experience through which the mother passes, whether she recovers quickly and is a highly efficient worker and manager or recovers slowly and is inefficient and a poor manager.

The number of births in the United States furnishes a readily available figure upon which to base an estimate of cost. Between 1933, the first year of nominally complete registration, and the present it has never fallen below 2 millions. In 1940 it was 2.36 millions.

A benefit of $25 for the period would cost 59 million dollars, and one of $50 about 118 million dollars a year.[9]

[8] A large part of the cost of medical care goes for treatments of short illnesses that disable for only a few days or for correction of defects that do not prevent the patient from continuing his regular occupational duties.

[9] The cost and the availability of domestic help varies so widely from place to place and even in the same community from time to time that there would seem to be a question as to which would be preferable, cash payments to the individual families or an organized mothers' helper service staffed with women specially trained for their duties. Such a service would doubtless necessarily have a considerable number of women on call who would be able and willing to leave their own homes for a few days or for a few hours each day to help in the family needing extra service. Department stores have found it practicable to get part-time assistance from women who are not anxious to be regularly employed full time. The availability of such a service would in many communities be of far more help to the mother than a payment of money which leaves to her the problem of locating and securing efficient and dependable help. It would seem that a service could be better adjusted to individual situations and local variations than a uniform lump-sum payment.

VII. FUNERAL BENEFITS

The proposed plan for Britain and the Beveridge plan, it will be recalled, provide a specific funeral benefit. Our O.A.S.I. provides a lump-sum death benefit payable if an individual died fully or currently insured leaving no surviving widow, child, or parent who would on filing application in the month in which such individual died, be entitled to a benefit for such month. Thus for the fully or currently insured who dies without a beneficiary eligible to take immediately, what is equivalent to a funeral benefit is provided, amounting to six times the primary benefit. For persons who die while covered but before attaining an insured status, no funeral expenses are paid, and the contributions made by them or on their behalf revert to the fund. It is customary in many sections of the country for the local government to pay the funeral expenses of those who died without resources, often with interment in a special cemetery, perhaps on the poor farm or near the poor house, a practice that gave rise to the term "a pauper's grave."

Statistics regarding the number of deaths in the United States furnish one of the two items in the cost of a funeral benefit. For the cost of a funeral for the different age classes we shall use (1) the cost as given in the Beveridge report and (2) that cost plus 50 per cent.

COST OF A FUNERAL BENEFIT

Age	Number of Deaths: 1940 (In thousands)	Beveridge Rate[a]		150 Per Cent of Beveridge Rate	
		Allowance	Aggregate (In thousands)	Allowance	Aggregate (In thousands)
ALL AGES.................	1,417		$104,796		$157,194
Adults 20 years of age or over[b]	1,237	$80	98,960	$120	148,440
10 to 19 years..............	33	60	1,980	90	2,970
3 to 9 years...............	19	40	760	60	1,140
Under 3 years.............	129	24	3,096	36	4,644

[a] Sir William Beveridge, *Social Insurance and Allied Services* (1942), p. 151. Beveridge does not include persons of age 20 with the adults. Conversion rate used is $4.00 to the pound.

[b] Includes 1.7 thousand age not stated.

It may be worth noting that a fully or currently insured worker who had earned an average of $50 a month would have a primary benefit of over $20 a month and therefore if a lump-sum benefit were payable on his death, it would be more than $120, the higher figure we have used here for a funeral for an adult. Lump-sum death benefits under

O.A.S.I. will not cost anything like the $105 to $157 millions here indicated, since O.A.S.I. pays one only if there is no beneficiary immediately eligible to take. If there is such a beneficiary, that beneficiary presumably pays the funeral expenses.

VIII. UNEMPLOYMENT INSURANCE

The cost of unemployment insurance is a matter of guess work. The hazard insured against is an economic not a natural factor and is therefore largely unpredictable. To arrive at a cost, one must guess at what will be the average annual number of unemployed eligible for benefits over a period of years and at the average benefit which will be paid during the period. If the guesses are too low, the unemployment insurance fund will be bankrupt in periods of excessive unemployment and the unemployed will have to be provided for in other ways. If the guesses are too high, the surplus in the fund will grow.

To give a rough idea of the approximate costs of unemployment, we shall present a series of purely arithmetical tables using certain assumed numbers entitled to unemployment benefits and certain assumed average benefit rates.

The cost of unemployment benefits depends on three major factors:
1. How many persons draw benefits
2. For how many weeks they draw them
3. How large the benefits are.

Under certain economic conditions, such as a brief but severe economic upset, it is possible for the nation to have very large numbers on unemployment benefits. The recovery may, however, be so prompt that few individuals receive benefits for any very considerable length of time. As a result the cost of benefits for that unemployment is not great relatively and constitutes no severe drain on the unemployment reserves. Prolonged unemployment for a very much smaller number of persons on benefit at any time during the year may, as a matter of fact, prove almost as costly as that resulting from a severe economic squall that passes quickly. In order to give figures in brief compass, it is therefore desirable first to be able to translate figures for number on benefit at any time during the year into the equivalent number on benefit throughout the year by using average numbers of weeks on benefit.

The method we shall use can perhaps be best illustrated by taking the actual figures for unemployment insurance as given by the Social Security Board for 1942[10] and applying the method to them, as follows:

---

[10] *Social Security Year Book, 1942*, p. 162.

Unemployment Insurance in 1942[11]

I. Estimated number of persons on benefit in year[11].............   2,765,700
II. Amount of all benefit payments in year[11].................... $345,514,909
    For total unemployment[11]............................ $327,661,636
    For partial unemployment[11].......................... $ 10,709,245
III. Number of weeks compensated[11]...........................   25,882,527
IV. Average number of weeks of compensation per person on benefit
    (III ÷ I)..   9.358
V. Average benefit per week of compensation (II ÷ III).......... $13.35
VI. Equivalent number on benefit for entire year................   497,720

$$\text{(I or Number on benefit in year} \times \frac{9.358 \text{ (or IV above)}}{52 \text{ (or weeks in year)}})$$

VII. Average benefit per unemployed throughout year (II ÷ VI).... $694.20

It may come somewhat as a surprise that in a year of peak employment and serious shortages of man power 2.8 million people drew unemployment benefits. They drew them, however, on the average for only 9.4 weeks. If unemployment had been spread evenly throughout the year, on each working day of the year there would have been about 500,000 on benefit. The 2.8 millions who drew benefits in 1942 were equivalent to only 500,000 on benefit throughout the year.

In the purely arithmetical table on page 897, numerous different assumed numbers of persons on benefit at some time during the year are translated into equivalent numbers on benefit throughout the entire year for different average numbers of weeks on benefit.

Since this table is purely arithmetical the figures in it can be read to apply to some other situations of significance in connection with unemployment. It need not be used exclusively with respect to number on benefit at some time in the year and the resulting equivalent number on benefit throughout the year at assumed duration of benefits. For example:

1. If it be assumed (a) that there is no waiting period in the law and payments of benefits begin on the first day of unemployment, and (b) that benefits are paid so long as unemployment continues, then the figure can be read as relating to all unemployment. To put it another way, the word unemployed can be substituted in the table headings for the words on benefit.

2. If the law provides for a waiting period of two weeks, with respect to which no benefits are ever paid, one can add two to the average number of weeks on benefit as shown in the box heading of the table in stating the duration of unemployment. In such a state, an average of eight weeks on benefit means approximately an average of ten weeks of unemployment. If the table is so used, the provisions of state law with respect to duration of benefits should be kept in mind. Under existing state laws, it is possible to have a substantial number

[11] The same.

of unemployed who have exhausted their benefit rights. Thus the aggregate number of unemployed in the state will not bear a fixed relationship to the number of unemployed in receipt of benefits. The table can only be used to show total unemployment if it be assumed that benefits are paid for unemployment so long as it lasts.

UNEMPLOYMENT INSURANCE LOAD IN MAN-BENEFIT YEARS
Calculated on Assumptions as to (1) Number on Benefit and
(2) Average Number of Weeks on Benefit
(Figures in thousands)

Assumed Number of Different[a] Persons on Benefit During Year	Equivalent Number on Benefit for One Year, if Average Number of Weeks on Benefit Is:								
	1	6	8	10	12	15	18	20	26
2,600....	50	300	400	500	600	750	900	1,000	1,300
3,900....	75	450	600	750	900	1,125	1,350	1,500	1,950
5,200....	100	600	800	1,000	1,200	1,500	1,800	2,000	2,600
6,500....	125	750	1,000	1,250	1,500	1,875	2,250	2,500	3,250
7,800....	150	900	1,200	1,500	1,800	2,250	2,700	3,000	3,900
9,100....	175	1,050	1,400	1,750	2,100	2,625	3,150	3,500	4,550
10,400....	200	1,200	1,600	2,000	2,400	3,000	3,600	4,000	5,200
11,700....	225	1,350	1,800	2,250	2,700	3,375	4,050	4,500	5,850
13,000....	250	1,500	2,000	2,500	3,000	3,750	4,500	5,000	6,500
15,600....	300	1,800	2,400	3,000	3,600	4,500	5,400	6,000	7,800
18,200....	350	2,100	2,800	3,500	4,200	5,250	6,300	7,000	9,100
20,800....	400	2,400	3,200	4,000	4,800	6,000	7,200	8,000	10,400

[a] In some instances the same person may be on benefit two or more times during the year and be counted two or more times.

If it be assumed that an average number of unemployed throughout the year of 1 million represents something approaching reasonably full employment, we would have full employment with 2.6 million unemployed at some time during the year if the average unemployment was 20 weeks. The number unemployed at some time during the year could rise to about 9 millions provided average weeks of unemployment fell to six.

A figure of 2 million unemployed throughout the year would result if 5.2 millions were unemployed at some time during the year, provided the average duration of unemployment was 20 weeks. If the average duration of unemployment was only six weeks, the number unemployed at any time during the year could rise as high as 17 millions.

Psychologically, there are very great differences between different amounts of unemployment that have the same benefit cost. Prolonged unemployment amounting on the average to 20 weeks for 2.6 million people might scarcely create a ripple in the public press, but if some catastrophy should happen so that some 6.5 millions should more or less simultaneously be unemployed for a period averaging 8 weeks, something approaching a panic might result. Unfortunately the duration of the unemployment is not known in advance. Because of the employment history from 1929 to 1939 the nation will long have a terrific fear of prolonged mass unemployment. Three conclusions can perhaps be drawn from these facts:

1. The existence of unemployment insurance may materially help in reducing the national fear.

2. Prompt steps should be taken to restore normal employment so as to hold down average duration.

3. Prolonged unemployment for the few may cost almost as much as brief unemployment for a very substantial number and probably involves more suffering, although it may have less psychological effect.

In the following table the equivalent numbers on benefits throughout the year are translated into sums of money by assuming different average weekly benefit rates.

In 1942 the contributions collected for unemployment compensa-

COSTS OF UNEMPLOYMENT BENEFITS FOR DIFFERENT DEGREES OF UNEMPLOYMENT
AND FOR DIFFERENT BENEFIT RATES
(Cost figures are in millions of dollars)

Equivalent Number Unemployed and on Benefit throughout the Year (In thousands)	Cost if the Average Weekly Benefit Is					
	$9.62	$13.46	$17.31	$19.23	$23.08	$25.00
500.........	250	350	450	500	600	650
800.........	400	560	720	800	960	1,040
1,000.........	500	700	900	1,000	1,200	1,300
1,500.........	750	1,050	1,350	1,500	1,800	1,950
2,000.........	1,000	1,400	1,800	2,000	2,400	2,600
2,500.........	1,250	1,750	2,250	2,500	3,000	3,250
3,000.........	1,500	2,100	2,700	3,000	3,600	3,900
4,000.........	2,000	2,800	3,600	4,000	4,800	5,200
5,000.........	2,500	3,500	4,500	5,000	6,000	6,500
6,000.........	3,000	4,200	5,400	6,000	7,200	7,800
7,000.........	3,500	4,900	6,300	7,000	8,400	9,100
8,000.........	4,000	5,600	7,200	8,000	9,600	10,400
9,000.........	4,500	6,300	8,100	9,000	10,800	11,700
10,000.........	5,000	7,000	9,000	10,000	12,000	13,000

ª The annual equivalent benefits are respectively: $500, $700, $900, $1,000, $1,200, and $1,300.

tion amounted to $1,139,331.[12] It may therefore be interesting to examine this table and the one preceding it to see what an annual contribution of about 1 billion dollars would provide.

In the first column of the table just presented, that relating to an average benefit of $9.62 a week or $500 a year, we find the figure of 1 billion dollars as providing for 2 million persons unemployed continuously throughout the year. Referring back to the table on page 897 we find that 2 millions continuously unemployed equals approximately any one of the following:

> 17.0 millions unemployed for 6 weeks
> 13.0 millions unemployed for 8 weeks
> 10.4 millions unemployed for 10 weeks
> 9.0 millions unemployed for 12 weeks
> 7.0 millions unemployed for 15 weeks
> 5.2 millions unemployed for 20 weeks
> 4.0 millions unemployed for 26 weeks

If we take the column showing average benefits of $17.31 a week or $900 a year, we do not find our precise figure, but $900 into 1 billion dollars gives us 1.1 million. By referring back to the earlier table we find that 1.1 million continuously unemployed equals roughly any one of the following:

> 9.1+ millions unemployed for 6 weeks
> 6.5+ millions unemployed for 8 weeks
> 5.2+ millions unemployed for 10 weeks
> 3.9− millions unemployed for 15 weeks
> 2.6+ millions unemployed for 20 weeks

If average benefits are raised so that they come to $25 a week on the average, we find the figure of 1,040 million dollars for 800,000 full-time beneficiaries a year. That number of full-time beneficiaries equals about 7 million unemployed for 6 weeks, 5.2 millions for 8 weeks, 4 millions for 10 weeks, and 2.9 millions for something better than 15 weeks.

If the annual cost of unemployment insurance is not to exceed 1 billion dollars a year, these figures suggest that:

1. Average benefits should be kept down in the neighborhood of $10 to $12 per week.

2. Waiting periods without any compensation should be fairly long.

3. The reserves in good periods should be allowed to accumulate without any reduction in tax rates or increases in the rate of benefits. Such adjustments as are made on account of growing reserves should be in the direction of increasing the maximum duration of benefits.

4. The governments, either national or state, should have definite

---

[12] The same, p. 171.

plans as to the course to be pursued in case of a severe prolonged depression, which will, as the figures in the second table indicate, rapidly exhaust even very substantial reserves. In this connection, it must be repeated that a severe and prolonged depression will result in a serious decrease in the current tax returns based on pay rolls.

5. Much serious thought should be given to the proper handling of unemployment insurance reserves. As things stand at the moment some 6 billion dollars is invested in obligations of the national government and, as has been pointed out previously, these obligations in part or in total will have to be converted into cash whenever current contributions fail to provide enough to pay maturing benefits. Despite the unemployment compensation system, the nation is at present in the position in which it will have to borrow to meet the costs in any year in which current costs exceed free cash belonging to the system.

The truth appears to be that our elaborate system of unemployment compensation has given the insured worker a contingent legislative right to a benefit, the real security for which is the I.O.U. of the national government. The national government cannot choose its time for redeeming those promises; it must redeem them when severe and prolonged unemployment presents the demand. If the public debt were at a low figure, the possibility of a sudden and inopportune demand for several billion dollars for settling unemployment insurance claims would not be a serious matter. But when the debt is already of huge proportions, additions to it may be serious. For this reason, we deem it highly important to hold down the size of weekly unemployment benefits, and if reserves seem to be becoming unduly large, to lengthen the benefit period rather than to raise the rate of benefit.

A high benefit for a short period, as the tables show, may cost the same as a low benefit for a long period, and therefore the national government may have to borrow no more for one than the other. But after benefits have been exhausted, a very considerable number of the unemployed will have to be provided for through public funds, which will doubtless mean more government borrowing on top of all that has gone before. Again attention should be called to the fact that if borrowing results in inflation that permanently raises the price level, the value of the old-age insurance system is jeopardized.

INDEX

INDEX